INTERNATIONAL SURROGACY ARRANGEMENTS

This book addresses the pressing challenges presented by the proliferation of international surrogacy arrangements. The book is divided into three parts. Part One contains National Reports on domestic approaches to surrogacy from Argentina, Australia, Belgium, Brazil, China, the Czech Republic, France, Germany, Greece, Guatemala, Hungary, India, Ireland, Israel, Japan, Mexico, The Netherlands, New Zealand, Russia, South Africa, Spain, Ukraine, the United Kingdom, the United States of America and Venezuela. The reports are written by domestic specialists, each demonstrating the difficult and urgent problems arising in many States as a result of international surrogacy arrangements. These National Reports not only provide the backdrop to the authors' proposed model regulation appearing in Part Three, but serve as a key resource for scrutinising the most worrying incompatibilities in national laws on surrogacy. Part Two of the book contains two contributions that provide international perspectives on cross-border surrogacy such as the 'human rights' perspective. Part Three contains a General Report, which consists of an analysis of the National Reports appearing in Part One, together with a proposed model of regulation of international surrogacy arrangements at the international level written by the co-editors, Paul Beaumont and Katarina Trimmings.

Volume 12 in the series Studies in Private International Law

Studies in Private International Law

International Surrogacy Arrangements

Legal Regulation at the International Level

Edited by

Katarina Trimmings

and

Paul Beaumont

·HART·
PUBLISHING
OXFORD AND PORTLAND, OREGON
2013

Published in the United Kingdom by Hart Publishing Ltd
16C Worcester Place, Oxford, OX1 2JW
Telephone: +44 (0)1865 517530
Fax: +44 (0)1865 510710
E-mail: mail@hartpub.co.uk
Website: http://www.hartpub.co.uk

Published in North America (US and Canada) by
Hart Publishing
c/o International Specialized Book Services
920 NE 58th Avenue, Suite 300
Portland, OR 97213-3786
USA
Tel: +1 503 287 3093 or toll-free: (1) 800 944 6190
Fax: +1 503 280 8832
E-mail: orders@isbs.com
Website: http://www.isbs.com

British Library Cataloguing in Publication Data
Data Available

ISBN: 978-1-84946-280-8

Typeset by Compuscript Ltd, Shannon
Printed and bound in Great Britain by
TJ International Ltd, Padstow, Cornwall

SERIES EDITOR'S PREFACE

This book grew out of pioneering research undertaken by Dr Katarina Trimmings and Professor Paul Beaumont from 2010 to 2012, funded by a grant of over £112,000 by the Nuffield Foundation. The aim of the project was to examine private international law problems that arise in cases of cross-border surrogacy arrangements and to propose a global model of regulation of such arrangements. To facilitate the research, a workshop was organised in Aberdeen from 30 August to 1 September 2011, funded by the Nuffield Foundation, University of Aberdeen, Royal Society of Edinburgh and the Clark Foundation. The Workshop was attended by specialists from 22 jurisdictions who shared information on the domestic and private international law approaches to surrogacy in their respective jurisdictions and was the genesis for the National Reports that are published in this book (Part I), as well as two papers providing an international perspective, respectively considering the lessons to be learnt from the 1993 Hague Intercountry Adoption Convention and a human rights perspective on regulation in this field (Part II). Part III of the book contains a General Report written by Dr Trimmings and Professor Beaumont, which consists of an analysis of the National Reports appearing in Part I, together with a proposed model of regulation of international surrogacy arrangements at the international level. The project also included an empirical survey of cross-border surrogacy arrangements which sought to map current patterns and the magnitude of the problems in international surrogacy. The study produced somewhat limited results, primarily owing to the unwillingness of private intermediaries to share information for research purposes. The findings of the survey are set out in the General Report. This book provides a wealth of information and perspectives for reform and will make an excellent addition to the *Studies in Private International* Law series.

Professor Jonathan Harris
King's College, London
2 April 2013

SUMMARY CONTENTS

PART TWO: CROSS-BORDER SURROGACY: INTERNATIONAL
PERSPECTIVES

CONTENTS

LIST OF CONTRIBUTORS

Claire Achmad Barrister and Solicitor of the High Court of New Zealand; PhD Candidate at the Faculty of Law, Leiden University, The Netherlands (on the topic of international commercial surrogacy from a child rights, perspective); and Senior Adviser to the Chief Human Rights Commissioner and the Executive Director of the New Zealand Human Rights Commission.

Marcelo de Alcantara Associate Professor of Law at Ochanomizu University, Japan.

Nadia de Araujo Professor of Private International Law, PUC-Rio, Brazil.

Hannah Baker Senior Legal Officer, the Hague Conference on Private International Law.

Paul Beaumont Professor of European Union and Private International Law at the University of Aberdeen; and Director of the Centre for Private International Law at the University of Aberdeen, UK.

Ian Curry-Sumner Freelance Lecturer and Researcher with Voorts Legal Services.

Gennadiy Druzenko Director for Central and Eastern Europe, Williams WorldWide Group llc, Ukraine.

Yasmine Ergas Associate Director of the Institute for the Study of Human Rights; a Director of the Program on Gender and the Human Rights of Women; and an Adjunct Professor of International and Public Affairs at Columbia University, New York, USA.

Susanne L Gössl LLM (Tulane), Legal Stagiaire at the Hanseatic High Court of Hamburg, and PhD candidate at the University of Cologne, Germany.

Maebh Harding Senior Lecturer in Family Law at the University of Portsmouth, UK.

Zhengxin Huo Associate Professor of Law, School of International Law, at China University of Political Science and Law (CUPL); Deputy Director of the Institute of Private International Law of CUPL.

Mary Keyes Professor at Griffith University, Australia.

Olga Khazova Professor at the Institute of State and Law, Russian Academy of Sciences, Moscow.

Eleonora Lamm Postdoctoral Researcher at the *National Council* for Scientific and Technical Research (*Consejo Nacional de Investigaciones Científicas y técnicas*), Argentina.

Letícia de Campos Velho Martel Professor of Constitutional Law, PUC-Rio, Brazil.

Patricia Orejudo Prieto de los Mozos Tenured Lecturer of Private International Law at the Universidad Complutense de Madrid, Spain.

Csongor István Nagy Associate Professor of Law, Head of the Private International Law Department, University of Szeged, Hungary.

Monika Pauknerová Professor at the Faculty of Law, Charles University, Prague, Czech Republic.

Konstantinos Rokas PhD candidate in Private International Law at the University Paris I—Panthéon/Sorbonne, and an Attorney-at-Law at the Athens Bar Association.

Christa Roodt Lecturer at the University of Aberdeen, Scotland.

Louis Perreau-Saussine Professor at the University of Paris-Dauphine, France.

Nicolas Sauvage Independent Consultant and a Former Legal Officer at the Hague Conference on Private International Law.

Sharon Shakargy Research Fellow at the Aharon Barak Center for Interdisciplinary Legal Research and at the Law Faculty, Hebrew University of Jerusalem, Israel.

Melodie Slabbert Professor and the Director of the School of Law at the University of South Africa.

Usha R Smerdon Vice President of a non-profit organisation Ethica, Kansas City, Missouri 64113, USA.

Steven Snyder, Esq Chair of the American Bar Association Family Law Section Assisted Reproductive Technology Committee.

Jaime Tecú Guatemalan expert on human rights of children and adolescents.

Katarina Trimmings Lecturer at the University of Aberdeen, Scotland.

Daniela Vargas Professor of Private International Law, PUC-Rio, Brazil.

Gerd Verschelden Director of the Institute for Family Law, Professor in the Department of Civil Law, Faculty of Law, Ghent University, Belgium.

Jinske Verhellen Postdoctoral Researcher, Department of Procedural Law, Arbitration and Private International Law, Faculty of Law, Ghent University, Belgium.

Machteld Vonk is a Lecturer and Researcher in family law and child law at the Department of Child Law of the Leiden University Law School, The Netherlands.

Michael Wells-Greco Solicitor of the Senior Courts of England and Wales, Partner, Lecturer in International Family Law and Private International Law at Maastricht University.

Introduction

KATARINA TRIMMINGS AND PAUL BEAUMONT

This book grew out of research undertaken by Katarina Trimmings and Paul Beaumont from 2010 to 2012, funded by a grant of over £112,000 by the Nuffield Foundation. The research focused on the growing social phenomenon of international surrogacy and how it could be regulated at the global level. To facilitate the research a workshop was organised in Aberdeen from 30 August to 1 September 2011, funded by the Nuffield Foundation, University of Aberdeen, Royal Society of Edinburgh and the Clark Foundation. This workshop was the genesis for the National Reports and two papers providing an international perspective that are published in this book. Part Three of the book contains the General Report which gives a comparative law overview of the range of domestic approaches to surrogacy. It then highlights the legal problems caused by cross-border surrogacy. The empirical research into cross-border surrogacy that was attempted as part of the two-year research project produced disappointingly meagre results. This was in particular due to the unwillingness of private intermediaries to share information for research purposes. The findings are set out in the General Report even though they are of very limited value. Lastly, an attempt is made to set out a framework for a future Convention that could be constructed in The Hague to regulate international surrogacy arrangements.

We should like to acknowledge the help of William Duncan, the former Deputy Secretary General of the Hague Conference on Private International Law, for lending us his support in our search for funding for the project; of Hannah Baker, Senior Legal Officer at the Hague Conference on Private International Law and Nicolas Sauvage, former Legal Officer at the Hague Conference on Private International Law, for hosting Katarina Trimmings during her research visit at the Hague Conference; of Vishwam Jindal of the National Law University, Delhi, India, for his assistance in obtaining some valuable resources on surrogacy in India; of the anonymous external reviewers for the National Reports contained in Part One of the book; of Jean Stevenson of the Law School of the University of Aberdeen, for her invaluable administrative assistance; and of the anonymous surrogacy agencies and legal practitioners that participated in the empirical part of the study.

Part One

National Reports on Surrogacy

1

Argentina

ELEONORA LAMM[*]

I. Legal Framework

In Argentina there is no domestic law on surrogacy nor a general law that regulates assisted reproductive technology (ART),[1] although in Argentina ART is a common, frequent[2] and advanced practice, and there are many bills before the National Congress.[3] Most of these bills on ART prohibit surrogacy.

Despite the lack of law, to date there are five bills specifically on surrogacy. Four bills cover implementation at national level, while the fourth is limited to the territory of the Province of Santa Fe (as to which, see section I.B. below).

A. National Bills on Surrogacy

While three of the four bills for implementation at national level are in favour of surrogacy, the fourth one expressly prohibits it.

[*] I am deeply thankful to Dr Adriana Dreizin de Klor, since without her kind help it would have been very difficult for me to write this report.

[1] In the last few years, three Argentinean provinces have enacted local regulations regarding ART, although these laws exclusively regulate aspects related to the coverage of these techniques by the local health system. These provinces are: Buenos Aires (Law 14208, enacted 2 December 2010, *Boletín Oficial* (*Official Gazette*) 04/01/11 and its Regulatory Decree No 2980), Rio Negro (Law 4557, enacted 23 July 2010, *Boletín Oficial* 09/08/2010) and Cordoba (Law 9695, enacted 4 November 2009, *Boletín Oficial* 222).

[2] For more information on the frequency and importance of this practice in Argentina, see The Latin America Network of Assisted Reproduction (RED) at <www.redlara.com/aa_ingles/default. asp>. The RED is a scientific and educational institution, which brings together more than 90% of the centres engaged in ART in Latin America. The RED was established in 1995, with 50 centres, and today boasts a total of 141 centres; it produces the Latin American Register of Assisted Reproduction (RLA), which annually catalogues all the results concerning ART reported by these centers. The RLA is the main source of information regarding ART procedures performed in the region. It accounts for more than 90% of regional ART procedures. Available at <www.redlara.com/aa_ingles/REGISTRO.ASP>.

[3] To date there are 15 bills on this topic. For more information on these bills see <www.diputados .gov.ar>.

The first bill to permit surrogacy was submitted in August 2011.[4] This bill regulates the creation of a Public Agency on Surrogacy that will register all the approved 'surrogacy instruments' and all births which are a consequence of this practice.

The intending parent(s) and the surrogate mother should sign the 'surrogacy instrument', which should be approved by the National Agency on Surrogacy. If this document is approved, the intending parent(s) would be the legal parent(s) following the implantation of the surrogate mother.

The surrogate mother may be economically compensated and none of the parties may withdraw their consent.

According to the bill, the surrogate mother should be older than 18 and younger than 35 years. She cannot provide her eggs. She must have full capacity, be physically and mentally healthy, and she must be registered with the Registry of the National Agency on Surrogacy. No woman can participate more than twice in a surrogacy procedure. Also, the surrogate mother must have been a resident of Argentina for at least five years.

Regarding the intending parent(s), he or she or they may be married, unmarried, heterosexual or homosexual, couples or single persons. The intending parent(s) must be unable to procreate and be older than 18 years and younger than 50 years. (If they are a couple, at least one of them must be younger than 50 years). The intending parent(s) must have been residents of Argentina for at least three years.

According to the explanatory note, the residence requirement demanded from the surrogate mother and the intending parent(s) would make reproductive tourism to Argentina difficult.[5]

The second bill to permit surrogacy was submitted on October 2011.[6] For the purposes of this bill, surrogacy is an agreement between a woman and a couple through which the woman agrees to be implanted with an embryo comprising the couple's genetic material, to carry out the pregnancy and delivery, and to give up the baby who may be born for the couple's adoption. The surrogacy agreement must be altruistic.

As with the previous bill mentioned above, this bill also regulates the creation of a Public Agency on Surrogacy and states that the agreement between the surrogate mother and the couple must be formalised under a 'surrogacy instrument'. The differences between this bill and the first one are as follows:

(a) The consent given for the surrogacy agreement may be withdrawn by any of the parties at any moment before the finalisation of the procedure to establish the filiation (ie the relationship of a child to a parent) of the child to be born.

---

[4] File N 4098-D-2011. Parlamentary procedure: 112 (17/08/2011).
[5] It followed the criteria of the Greek Law (3089/2002) and Israelian Law (5746-1996).
[6] File N 5201-D-2011. Parlamentary procedure: 159 (25/10/2011).

If the consent is withdrawn by the intending parents, the bill specifies that revocation by one of them does not relieve them of their responsibility to the other party. If the consent is withdrawn by both members of the couple, the bill clarifies that it means only the relinquishment of their right to adopt the child born as a consequence of the surrogacy agreement. Support obligations assumed by the intending parents towards the surrogate mother for the period of pregnancy, childbirth and post partum are irrevocable, and if a child is born the couple must economically assist him or her until his or her majority.

If the surrogate mother withdraws her consent, it will mean giving up the right to payment of expenses.

(b) The child born as a consequence of the surrogacy agreement is considered the child of the surrogate mother until the judge approves (within the 20 days following the birth of the child) the adoption by the intending couple.

(c) The intending parents must be a heterosexual couple, married or not, who must have been resident in Argentina for at least five years before signing the surrogacy agreement.

The third bill to permit surrogacy was submitted in November 2011.[7] The important (and distinctive) aspects of this bill are that the intending parents must be a married heterosexual couple and they must provide their genetic material (sperm and eggs), and that it allows commercial surrogacy agreements.

With regard to the procedure, this would be under a contract which should be submitted to the registering authorities jointly with the birth certificate for the registration of the child born as a consequence of the surrogacy agreement. In those cases it will be presumed that the baby is the legal child of the intending mother's husband.

Lastly, a bill that expressly prohibits surrogacy was submitted on March 2007.[8] This bill proposes the incorporation of Article 63 *bis* into the Civil Code (CCiv). This article would state that the surrogacy contract is null and void.

B. The Bill for the Province of Santa Fe

The procedure in the Province of Santa Fe would comprise an agreement (contract) supervised by lawyers. Commercial surrogacy agreements would be allowed. The contract should be signed by all parties and it should be submitted to the National Register for the registration of the child born as a consequence of the surrogacy agreement.

---

[7] File N 5441-D-2011. Parlamentary procedure: 169 (08/11/2011).
[8] File N 0138-D-2007. Parlamentary procedure: 002 (02/03/2007).

All parties must be older than 18 years and must have been residents of Santa Fe for at least two years before signing the surrogacy agreement, and one of the intending parents must provide his or her genetic material (sperm or eggs).

II. The Reality in Argentina Before the Lack of Legal Regulation

As there is currently no law on surrogacy in Argentina, the principle could be stated as being that it is not allowed but it is not forbidden. This principle needs some clarification though.

Although surrogacy is not forbidden, according to Article 242 CCiv,[9] the mother of a child is the one who gives birth to the child. So, even if the surrogate mother and the intending parents agree something different, the surrogate mother would be considered as the legal mother.

Regarding paternity, according to the Civil Code, if the woman who gives birth is married, the child will be registered in the name of her husband as father. It is presumed that the mother's husband is the father of the child (Article 243 CCiv).

Thus, according to the Civil Code, the legal parent of the child will be the surrogate mother (and her husband), not the intending parents.

Today, one of the procedures that is used so that the intending parents may become the legal parents of the child is 'partner adoption', ie 'the spouse adoption' (known in Argentina as 'integrative adoption'). According to that, the surrogate mother gets pregnant using sperm of the intending father (or she is impregnated with an embryo comprising the intending parents' genetic material).[10] After the birth, the intending father recognises the baby as his child if the surrogate mother is single; if she is married, the child is presumed to be the child of the surrogate's husband. Subsequently, the surrogate mother's husband should contest the paternal filiation (based on the lack of biological link, ie that he is not the biological father) so that the intending and genetic father is able to recognise the child as his (Articles 250 and 259 CCiv[11]).

In both cases, after the recognition by the intending father, the intending mother may adopt the baby using 'integrative adoption' (the spouse adoption),

---

[9] Art 242 CCiv: Maternity will be established, even without explicit recognition, by the proof of birth and the identity of the baby.

[10] The surrogate mother can also be impregnated with an embryo comprising the intending father's sperm and a donor's egg.

[11] Although these articles give the right to contest paternity only to the mother's husband, many judgments have recognised this right in favour of the biological father too. See, among others, Corte Suprema de Justicia de Mendoza—Sala I—12/05/2005. 'L.C.F. por la menor A.M.G. c/ A.C.A.G.P.A.C. p/ Filiación s/ Inc. Casación' Filiación. Impugnación de la paternidad del marido de la madre. Art 259 CCiv. Legitimación del padre biológico.

which implies a relatively easy process.[12] To sum up, the process involves: recognition by the intending—and genetic[13]—father, followed by transfer of sole parental responsibility from the surrogate mother to the intending father, followed by the spouse adoption.

The problem that arises in this situation is that this mechanism not only would imply an 'infringement' of the adoption rules, but also that if the intending mother is also the genetic mother—cases of gestational surrogacy—we would be asking her both to adopt her own biological child and to do that via a simple adoption.[14] In contrast, the intending (biological) father is not required to adopt the child.[15]

Another option that occurs in practice, if the intending parents have not provided their gametes[16] or if the surrogate mother is married, is that once the baby is born, both the surrogate mother and her husband deliver the child to the intending parents who, after some time—in order to establish some bonds with the child—ask to adopt him or her. This behaviour is forbidden under the Argentine law because it does not allow adoption in favour of certain persons. Article 318 of the Civil Code[17] expressly prohibits the direct delivery of children.[18] Furthermore, if the intending parents are the genetic parents (gestational surrogacy), they would be requesting the adoption of their own biological child.

In all these situations, as there is no law concerning surrogacy, and Article 242 states that the woman who gives birth to the child is considered the legal mother, the surrogate mother can always decide to keep the baby. In that case, the intending parents would have no action and no right or claim.

---

[12] According to Art 316 CCiv, it is not required to comply with the requirement of pre-adoptive custody. However, it is a simple adoption, so it creates no family relationship between the adoptee and the biological family of the adopter (Art 329 CCiv).

[13] If the man who recognises the baby as his child is not the genetic father, this behaviour constitutes a crime penalised by Art 139 of the Penal Code.

[14] As explained above, when it is about the adoption of the spouse's child, the CCiv allows only simple adoption.

[15] New York courts have granted petitions for maternity without requiring her to go through adoption proceeding in cases of gestational surrogacy (see *Doe v New York City Bd of Health*, 5 Misc 3d 424; *Arredondo v Nodelman*, 163 Misc 2d 757; see also *Matter of Doe*, 7 Misc 3d 352). Also see the recent judgement of the Supreme Court of the State of New York, Appellate Division: Second Judicial Department in the case *TV (Anonymous) v New York State Department of Health* (2011 NY 06229, decided on 9 August 2011, Appellate Division, Second Department). The Court of Appeals found that the Supreme Court does have the authority to issue a maternal order of filiation, that discrimination between demands for maternal and paternal order of filiations after birth is not justified, and that the validity of the surrogate contract is immaterial to the question of the order of filiation, since the court is not being asked to enforce the contract.

[16] Thus the intending parent cannot recognise the child.

[17] Art 318 CCiv expressly prohibits the direct delivery of children through public or administrative act.

[18] However, there have been some jurisprudential cases that admitted this kind of adoption in the interests of the child. It is considered that in those cases it is centered on the bond generated between the child and the parties to the marriage.

Despite that, the origin of the genetic material is not irrelevant and could have some importance. According to a case solved by the *Cámara de Apelaciones Civil, Comercial y Laboral de Gualeguaychú* (Civil, Commercial and Labour Chamber of Appeal of Gualeguaychú) in April 2010,[19] if the intending mother is also the genetic mother, she may contest the maternity of the surrogate mother. But it is relevant to say that these situations must be discussed in court. This case was about a woman (the genetic and intending mother) who provided her eggs for the in vitro fertilisation of another woman, and after the birth of the child she contested the legal maternity (Article 242 CCiv) of the woman who gave birth to the baby (gestational mother). The Chamber of Appeal based its decision on the importance of the genetic link. It isnecessary to emphasise, however, that this case was not an 'open' case on surrogacy (nothing was said about the surrogacy agreement). Thus, the Chamber of Appeal did not pronounce on the legality of surrogacy agreements. Nevertheless, it is still important, because with this background, the Argentinean courts would be implicitly accepting gestational surrogacy, if the intending mother provides her eggs.

Lastly, another mechanism that is used in Argentina, but with less frequency, to avoid the civil law and to determine parentage in favour of the intending parents, is to do it illegally and falsify the birth certificate in order to certify the intending mother as the one who gave birth to the child. In Argentina, this is a crime penalised by Articles 139ff[20] of the Penal Code.

III. Positions Among Scholars

The lack of legal framework has generated different positions among scholars. Most of the Argentinean authors[21] consider that surrogacy contracts are null and

---

[19] CApel Civ, Com y Lab Gualeguaychú, 14/04/2010, *B, MA c FC, CR*, La Ley on line, AR/JUR/75333/2010.

[20] See above, n 13.

[21] Among others, E Zannoni, *Derecho civil. Derecho de familia*, 3nd edn (Buenos Aires, Astrea, 1998) 533; GA Bossert and E Zannoni, *Régimen legal de filiación y patria potestad* (Buenos Aires, Astrea, 1985) 237; JC Rivera, *Instituciones de derecho civil*, 4th edn (Buenos Aires, LexisNexis—Abeledo Perrot, 2007) 414; GA Borda, *Tratado de derecho civil. Familia*, 10th edn (Buenos Aires, La Ley, 2008) 28, 29; MJ Méndez Costa and DH D'antonio, *Derecho de familia* (Buenos Aires, Rubinzal-Culzoni, 2001) 71; A Wagmaister, 'Maternidad subrogada' (1990) 3 *Revista de Derecho de Familia* 20; A Wagmaister and L Levy, 'La intención de ser padres y los mejores intereses de los hijos. Trascendencia jurídica' (1995) I *Jurisprudencia Argentina* 440; DB Iñigo, A Wagmaister and L Levy, 'Algunas reflexiones sobre reproducción humana asistida (esquema comparativo de tres legislaciones vigentes)' (1991) *La Ley* 1135; PF Hooft, *Bioética y derechos humanos* (Buenos Aires, Depalma, 1999) 45; JN Lafferriere and UC Basset, 'Dos madres, padre anónimo, presunción de maternidad en parejas de hecho no comprobadas, un niño con identidad paterna pretorianamente silenciada' (2011) *LL Revista de Derecho de Familia y de las Personas* 1; EA Sambrizzi, 'El pretendido derecho a tener un hijo y la maternidad subrogada' (2010) *La Ley* 1; EA Sambrizzi, 'Maternidad subrogada. Reforma proyectada' (2011) *La Ley* 1; SM Berger, 'Maternidad Subrogada: un contrato de objeto iícito' (2010) *La Ley* 1.

void because their object would be illicit and against public policy, according to Article 953 CCiv, which states that

> the object of juridical acts must be things which are in commerce or things which have not been forbidden for some special reason to be the object of a juridical act, or facts which are not impossible, illegal, contrary to good morals or prohibited by laws. Juridical acts that do not conform to this provision are null as if they had no object.

Others argue that in the absence of an express prohibition, the practice would be allowed. This position adopts a broad conception of surrogacy[22] and promotes its regulation. It is considered that:

(a) the lack of legal regulation creates problems that could be avoided if there were a legal regulation that contemplates and resolves them;

(b) the lack of legal regulation 'forces' the couple or person desirous of having a child to resort to the black market,[23] and it expands the possible abuses and injustices;[24]

(c) related to the previous reason, the lack of legal regulation promotes reproductive tourism. The reality is that despite the lack of law, people resort to surrogacy in countries where it is allowed, so the legal system should provide an answer when the intending parents want to register their children who are born as a result of a surrogacy agreement entered into abroad;[25]

(d) legal restrictions (or the current legal restrictions that arise from the lack of law) would be discriminatory for three main reasons:

    (i) because they would apply primarily to low economic class couples looking to have a child through surrogacy. Couples with financial resources always have the opportunity to go to countries where surrogacy is permitted, while other poor or middle-class couples do not have this option,

    (ii) because in Argentina, despite the lack of legal regulation of ART, egg donation is allowed and is being done in practice. It is considered that if Argentina provides a solution for women who cannot have children

---

[22] Among others, MV Famá, 'Maternidad subrogada. Exégesis del derecho vigente y aportes para una futura regulación' (2011) *La Ley* 1; A Kemelmajer De Carlucci, M Herrera and E Lamm, 'Filiación y homoparentalidad. Luces y sombras de un debate incómodo y actual' (2010) *La Ley*, 20/09/2010; M Herrera, 'Filiación, adopción y distintas estructuras familiares en los albores del siglo XXI' in E Ferreira Basto and MB Dias (eds), *A família além dos mitos* (Belo Horizonte, Del Rey, 2008) 186; E Lamm, 'La autonomía de la voluntad en las nuevas formas de reproducción. La maternidad subrogada. La importancia de la voluntad como criterio decisivo de la filiación y la necesidad de su regulación legal' (2011) 50 *Revista de Derecho de Familia* 107; A Dreyzin de Klor and C Harrington, 'La subrogación materna en su despliegue internacional: ¿más preguntas que respuestas?' (2011) *Revista de Derecho de Familia* 301–29.

[23] When I say 'black market' I mean those countries in which, although they have no law on surrogacy, it is a developed and frequent practice.

[24] Lamm, above n 22.

[25] N Lloveras and MB Mignon, 'La ley 26618 de Matrimonio Igualitario Argentino: la filiación y el Registro Civil' (2011) 8 *SJA* 1.

of their own because of their lack of ovaries, it should also allow surrogacy to also help women who cannot gestate, for example because of their lack of a uterus. It is important to stress that according to doctors' testimonies, there are many surrogacy petitions nowadays founded on medical reasons,[26]

(iii) because surrogacy is the only option that a gay male couple has to have a child genetically related to at least one of them. Thus, according to the principles of liberty, equality and non-discrimination, that becomes an argument in favour of legalisation and regulation of these agreements,[27] especially after Law 26618[28] which legalised gay marriage in Argentina;

(e) regulation becomes the solution that best satisfies the interests of the child.[29] The child is born into a family that truly wants him or her, and would not have existed without the surrogacy agreement. The best interests of the child present *a priori* and *a posteriori*. *A priori*, this interest demands a legal framework that protects the child who is born, provides legal certainty and guarantees a filiation that is according with his or her reality. On the other hand, a child is born as a consequence of this practice, and subsequently his or her best interests require that the person(s) who really wanted to assume the role of parents can do so. In other words, that the intending parents can also be the legal parents;[30]

(f) lastly, it is argued that surrogacy, as a potential tool for people who want to have a child and are unable to do so, is protected in the Argentine legal system under the 'personal rights' enshrined in the Treaties and Conventions contemplated under Article 75, paragraph 22 of the National Constitution. It is understood that the rights to privacy and freedom and personal rights constitute part of the 'right to procreate', and the right to procreate should comprehend the liberty to choose the means to exercise that right.

---

[26] In a symposium entitled 'Ethical and Legal Aspects of Assisted Reproduction Techniques', held on 29 and 30 April 2011 in the City of Buenos Aires and sponsored by the Argentine Society of Andrology (SAA), Argentine Society for Reproductive Medicine (SAMER) and the Latin American Network of Assisted Reproduction (Red LARA), 80 doctors participated who discussed various aspects of ART: 53% of them agreed with surrogacy when the intending mother has no uterus but can still provide her eggs (the intending parent(s) must provide their genetic material), or in case of serious risk of death of the intending mother in cases of pregnancy. As for gay male couples, 60% of participants said they disagreed, 20% agreed and 20% did not know or did not answer.

[27] Lamm, above n 22.

[28] Law 26618, sanctioned on 15 June 2010, enacted on 21 July 2010, and published in the Argentine *Official Gazette* on 22 July 2010.

[29] See SV Shiffrin, 'Wrongful life, procreative responsibility, and the significance of harm' (1999) 5 *Legal Theory* 117. He says: 'There is no evidence in the literature to suggest that in the vast majority of such arrangements there is any detrimental effect on the child or the other parties involved.'

[30] Lamm, above n 22.

IV. Project for the Amendment and Unification of the Civil and Commercial Codes

On 23 February 2011 the President of Argentina, Fernandez De Kirchner, by Decree 191/2011,[31] created a Commission to undertake a project to amend, update and unify the Civil and Commercial Codes.

This Commission is composed of three of the most important jurists in Argentina: ministers of the *Corte Suprema de Justicia de la Nación Argentina* (CSJN) (Argentine National Supreme Court), doctors Ricardo Luis Lorenzetti and Elena Highton de Nolasco, and the former minister of the *Suprema Corte de Justicia de Mendoza* (Supreme Court of Justice of Mendoza), Professor Aída Kemelmajer de Carlucci. The Commission's remit is to draft a unified Civil and Commercial Code and submit it to the treatment of the National Congress within 365 calendar days from the date of its constitution.[32]

In order to reflect the highest possible degree of consensus, the Commission decided to invite the most important Argentinean scholars to collaborate on the draft. Thus, it has created 32 subcommittees, composed of three or four scholars each. The writer of this report, Eleonora Lamm, was appointed to the Subcommittee on Bioethics, which, together with the Subcommittee on Family Law, was responsible for writing the articles on surrogacy. After much study, meetings and discussions, the proposed articles are as follows:

A. Domestic Surrogacy Rule

The free and informed consent of all parties to the surrogacy process must conform to the provisions of this code and the special law.

The filiation is established between the child born and the intending parent(s) by the proof of birth, the identity of the intending parent(s) and the consent duly approved by a judicial authority.

The judicial authority must approve the consent only if, in addition to the requirements provided by the special law, it is proved that: (a) it is in the best interests of the child to be born, (b) the surrogate mother has full capacity and good physical and psychological health, (c) at least one of the intending parent(s) has provided his/her gamete, (d) the intending parent(s) are unable to conceive or carry a pregnancy to term, (e) the surrogate mother has not provided her own gametes, (f) the surrogate mother has not received any financial benefit, (g) the surrogate mother has not acted as

---

[31] *Boletín Oficial* (Argentine *Official Gazette*) 28/02/11.

[32] Thus, the analysed text is a provisional one which may be modified up until the end of the term; once it is approved by the Commission, it has to be submitted to the treatment of the National Congress.

a surrogate mother more than two (2) times, (h) the surrogate mother has given birth to at least one child of her own.

Doctors cannot proceed with the implantation of the surrogate mother without judicial authorisation.

If the surrogacy agreement is not judicially validated as provided for in this article, the parent–child relationship is determined as provided for natural filiation (blood filiation).

i. Analysis of the Article

a. System

The system is similar to the one regulated under Greek law.[33] It protects against legal uncertainties and changes of mind of the surrogate. It establishes that the intending parents must apply for a judicial authorisation before the implantation of the surrogate mother and that doctors cannot carry out any surrogacy procedure[34] (the implantation of embryo into the surrogate) without this judicial decision. Once such implantation occurs the parties cannot withdraw their consent. Any conflict shall be resolved through the courts.

The effect of a judicial order validating the surrogacy arrangement shall be the automatic termination of the parental rights of the surrogate mother (and her husband) and a vesting of those rights solely in the intending parent(s).

b. Determination of Filiation

If the requirements stipulated by law are satisfied, a court will issue an order validating the agreement and declaring that the intending parent(s) will be the parents of any child born as a consequence of the surrogacy agreement. The intending parents are therefore the legal parents of the child as soon as the child is born.

This judicially-approved agreement, along with the birth certificate and the identity of the intending parent(s), should be submitted to the appropriate civil registry for registration of the birth.

If the court does not validate the agreement (and despite this the parties carry on with the surrogacy process), or the parties do not apply for the judicial

---

[33] Law 3089/2002, Art 1458: 'The transfer of fertilised ova to another woman and pregnancy by her is allowed by a court authorisation issued before the transfer, given that there is a written and, without any financial benefit, agreement between the involved parties, meaning the persons wishing to have a child and the surrogate mother and, where the latter is married, her spouse as well. The court authorisation is issued following an application by the woman who wants to have a child, provided that evidence is adduced not only as to the fact that she is medically unable to conceive but also as to the fact that the surrogate mother is in good health condition and able to conceive.'

[34] A surrogacy agreement does not apply to the birth of a child conceived by means of sexual intercourse.

authorisation to carry out a surrogacy process, the bill provides that the legal mother is the woman who gave birth to the child.

c. Intending Parent(s)

The intending parent(s) can be married or unmarried couples, heterosexual and homosexual.[35] Also, a single person may be an intending parent.[36]

d. Requirements for the Judicial Authorisation

Prior to implantation of an embryo into a surrogate, the parties to the surrogacy agreement shall jointly petition the court for judicial authorisation of the surrogacy arrangement. An order validating the surrogacy agreement shall be issued only if the court makes the following findings:

(a) *The surrogacy agreement is in the best interests of the child to be born.* This means, among many other things, that the intending parent(s) has or have been evaluated.

Evaluations and counselling must have been completed, and the intending parent(s) must have been determined by the persons performing the evaluations or counselling to be qualified to enter into the surrogacy arrangement.

The best interests of the child comprise the main issue to be taken into account for the purposes of authorising a surrogacy agreement. The judge could always deny authorisation if he or she considered that in the particular case it was not in the best interests of the child to be born.

(b) *The surrogate mother has full capacity and good physical and psychological health.* The surrogate mother shall be in good health without recurrent conditions that may affect pregnancy.

(c) *At least one of the intending parent(s) has provided his or her gamete.* At least one of the intended parents must be genetically related to the child to be born of the gestational agreement. It is considered that surrogacy is presented as a remedy for those who, for whatever reason, are unable to conceive or to carry a pregnancy to term, but do not want to forgo having a child genetically their own. Otherwise, the couple or person could adopt.[37]

---

[35] It is important to emphasise that Law 26618, which legalised gay marriage in Argentina, grants the same rights to heterosexual and homosexual marriages, including the right to adopt.

[36] It is also important to note that according to the Argentinean Civil Code, single parents can adopt (Art 312 CCiv).

[37] It is important to say that today, with the options of full or part biological offspring available to infertile/subfertile populations, adoption tends to be seen as a last resort, or as a second best choice. One study of adoptive parents, who subsequently conceived naturally, reported that they were significantly more likely to say that if they could do it again, they would not adopt: M Berry, 'Adoptive parents' perceptions of, and comfort with, open adoption' (1993) 77(3) *Child Welfare* 231. Miall found that "a paradox was evident in her study sample: although adoptive mothers were generally

(d) *The intending parent(s) are unable to conceive or to carry a pregnancy to term.* This requirement prevents those women who are medically able to have children, delegating the barriers and discomforts of pregnancy to other women for their own comfort. This is known as social surrogacy.

   For biological reasons, this requirement also comprehends gay male couples, ie for biological/natural reasons gay male couples cannot conceive or carry a pregnancy to term, thus they would also comply with this requirement.

(e) *The surrogate mother has not provided her own gametes.* It must be a gestational surrogacy.[38] It is considered that is easier for the surrogate mother who is not genetically related to the child to hand over him or her and to relinquish her parental rights.

(f) *The surrogate mother has not received any financial benefit.* The surrogate mother cannot receive payment, which does not mean that she cannot be compensated for the expenses (including medical, legal or other professional expenses).

(g) *The surrogate mother has not acted as a surrogate mother more than two times.* This requirement aims at preventing abuses and that women become 'machines that produce other people's children'.

(h) *The surrogate mother has given birth to at least one child of her own.* No woman may be a surrogate unless she has a documented history of at least one pregnancy and viable delivery. This requirement ensures that the surrogate mother comprehends the seriousness of her commitment because she has suffered the rigours of a pregnancy and a birth. Also, it alleviates the concern that might arise from depriving a mother of her first child, and allows a check to be made that the surrogate mother is able to conceive and give birth without problems for the mother or the child.

B. Rules for Private International Law

With regard to private international law (PIL) the proposed article is as follows:

All filiation constituted in accordance with foreign law will be recognised in Argentina in accordance with the principles of public policy of our country, especially those that make it a priority to consider the best interests of the child.

The principles that regulate the use of assisted reproductive techniques are public policy principles and must be verified by the competent authority if its intervention is required for the recognition of the status and/or registration of persons born through these techniques. In case of doubt the decision must be the one that best benefits the interests of the child.

---

very positive about adoption, a biological child will always be seen as best, perhaps more consonant": C Miall, 'Reproductive technology versus the stigma of involuntary childlessness' (1989) 70(1) *Social Care Work* 43.

[38] According to the trends (eg Greece, Israel, etc).

i. Analysis of the Article

The filiation must be in accordance with the foreign law, but must also conform in substance with the Argentine law. In all cases, the barrier of public policy must be applied, with the best interests of the child as a guiding principle.

The article establishes the general conditions to be fulfilled for access to the registry, ensuring continuity of the legal relationship established abroad.

The aim of the article is to protect the best interests of the child to be born under the agreement, as well as the interests of the surrogate mother and the intending parents. Also, the article seeks to avoid people travelling to foreign countries that permit surrogacy agreements without meeting the conditions set by the Argentinean law, and enables filiation established in those countries to be registered in Argentina.

However, if the surrogacy agreement does not conform to the Argentinean law, the public policy will be always defined by the best interests of the child. In this sense, for example, the project would only admit altruistic surrogacy agreements, thus the public policy grounds might be invoked in the case of a commercial surrogacy agreement. But even in those cases, it might be possible to recognise the surrogacy agreement if this is considered to be the best decision in the interests of the child. This is reinforced by the provisions of the second paragraph of the rule, which stipulates that in case of 'doubt', the decision must be the one that best benefits the interests of the child.

V. Jurisprudence

Regardless of the case decided by the Civil and Commercial Chamber of Appeal mentioned in section II. above, the Argentinean courts have not had the opportunity to pronounce on the legality of surrogacy agreements, nor yet on the determination of filiation in these cases. However, Argentina may have a precedent very soon because there is a case pending before the Argentinean courts.[39]

The case concerns a gay married couple who decided to 'rent a womb' in India. They entered into a surrogacy agreement in India. The problem is that in India, the birth certificates of children born through surrogacy contain the name of the father—the genetic father who provided the sperm—and as the name of the mother the words 'surrogate mother or mother without a State'. The certificate does not recognise the child's Indian citizenship, so if the child is not granted Argentinean citizenship, he or she acquires the status of 'stateless'.

---

[39] *Grinblat, Alejandro y otros c/ Estado Nacional s/ amparo* (Expediente No 48453/2011) Juzgado Nacional de Primera Instancia en lo Contencioso Administrativo Federal No 7 of the City of Buenos Aires.

On 28 June 2011, the head of the Consular Section of the Embassy of Argentina in India, based in New Delhi, communicated to the couple the resolution of the General Director of Legal Affairs regarding births achieved through the practice of surrogacy. It said that it was not possible to proceed with the registration of a birth certificate which does not show the name of the mother, since this did not conform to Article 36, paragraph c) of Law 26413,[40] which requires that such registration must contain the name of both parents (father and mother[41]), except in the case of a child born out of wedlock (child of single mother) where there will be no mention of the father.[42] Consequently, the only possible way forward was to ask for a specific judicial authorisation (ie a judicial decision issued by a competent court in Argentina) to order the registration of the child born in India, to give to him or her Argentinean nationality by option, ignoring the name and nationality of the mother.

Thus on 15 December 2011, the couple submitted a writ of *amparo* so that the Foreign Ministry (through the Embassy of Argentina in the Republic of India, New Delhi Consular Representation) will give them the documentation (birth certificate, passport and national identity) that recognises the legal parenthood of the couple (based on the procreational will) and that the child will require at birth in order to be able to leave India.

The case is pending at the *Juzgado en lo Contencioso Administrativo Federal No 7* and its resolution may set an important precedent.

VI. Private International Law

Argentine Private International Law (PIL) is characterised by many complexities. This may be perceived primarily from two interrelated perspectives: substance and methodology. On the one hand, it involves significant normative dispersion because rules are scattered throughout different normative bodies, such as the Civil Code, the Commercial Code (CCom), the National Civil and Commercial Procedural Code (*Código de Procedimiento Nacional en lo Civil y Comercial* (CPCCN)), and provincial procedural codes. Special laws relating to diverse areas should be added to the abovementioned texts. These special laws aim to provide private law remedies. On occasion, they include rules applicable to private law relations with foreign elements. On other occasions, they repeal existing rules, without replacing the rules that originally dealt with foreign traffic.[43]

---

[40] Law 26413. Registro del Estado Civil y Capacidad de las Personas (Registry of Civil Status and Capacity of Persons). *Boletín Oficial* 6-10-08.

[41] In case of children of same-sex marriages the inscription must contain the name and surname of the mother and her spouse. Art 36 inc C Law 26413 modified by Law 26618.

[42] The main reason is the previous existence of the surrogacy agreement.

[43] Eg Commercial Companies Law (No 19550), Bankruptcy Law (No 24522), Adoption Law (No 24779), Intellectual Property Law (No 11723, modified by Law 25036), Law of Name of Natural

On the other hand, the discipline shows a clear lack of provisions to regulate some international private situations. This is caused by the lack of regulation of relationships that have developed since the 1950s, a fact that entails a large number of regulatory gaps.[44] Court decisions reflect developments that try to solve these problems in particular cases.[45] Thus, court decisions have even acted as precedents for the development of new PIL rules and of constitutional provisions related to PIL.[46]

Argentine PIL is composed of rules containing autonomous, conventional, institutional and transnational dimensions. The first 'autonomous' dimension relates to legislation from Congress applicable to particular legal situations with foreign elements that exceed the scope of international treaties.

The conventional dimension includes rules developed in international codification fora and, in general, all PIL treaties ratified by Argentina.

Argentina is party to numerous multilateral and bilateral treaties, which are applicable after ratification by Argentine domestic law.[47] The provisions of those treaties are considered part of Argentine law.[48] One of the most important treaties is the Convention of General Rules of Private International Law of 1979 (CNG). Article 1 provides:

> Choice of the applicable rule of law governing facts connected with foreign law shall be subject to the provisions of this Convention and other bilateral or multilateral conventions that have been signed or may be signed in the future by the States Parties.

In the absence of an international rule, the States Parties shall apply the conflict rules of their domestic law.

Also, the CNG establishes that foreign law shall be applied by judges and authorities as by judges of the State whose law is applicable. Parties may plead and

---

Persons (No 18248) and Law on Immunity of Jurisdiction of Foreign States before Argentine Courts (No 24488). See A Dreyzin de Klor, 'Private International Law in Argentina' in R Blanpain, M Colucci and B Verschraegen (eds), *IEL Private International Law* (Alphen aan den Rijn, Kluwer Law International BV, 2011).

[44] Eg in the field of law applicable to complex situations that derive from *ART* or the multiple human relationships (commercial and civil) that are triggered by developments in technology and communications. Dreyzin de Klor, above n 43.

[45] Jurisprudence is not regarded as a formal source of PIL. In other words, judicial precedents are formally not a source of legal rules. However, jurisprudence is a material source for the interpretation of laws and treaties. Nevertheless, important judgments rendered mainly by the CSJN are carefully studied and generally followed. Judge-made law plays a very relevant role in PIL because statutory law is far from comprehensive.

[46] CSJN, 27/11/86, 'Sejean' is a leading case for litigation regarding divorce. See CSJN, 27/11/86, *S, JB v Z de S, AM, LL,* 1986-E, 648.

[47] Treaties in force affect Argentine PIL in many ways. On the one hand, it is important to emphasise that international treaties have supremacy over domestic laws. On the other hand, conventions update and modernise domestic PIL. Hence, due to the abovementioned supremacy, solutions in given cases better suit current times. Dreyzin de Klor, above n 43.

[48] Constitucion Nacional (CN), Art 31: 'This Constitution, the laws of the Nation enacted by Congress in pursuance thereof, and treaties with foreign powers, are the supreme law of the Nation; and the authorities of each province are bound thereby, notwithstanding any provision to the contrary included in the provincial laws or constitutions, except for the province of Buenos Aires, the treaties ratified after the Pact of 11 November 1859.'

prove the existence and content of the foreign law invoked (Article 2). Therefore, the CNG advances significantly over domestic PIL; the latter, on the contrary, considers that the application of foreign laws will be permissible only upon request of the interested party. That party must also prove the existence and validity of these laws.[49]

The 'institutional dimension' refers to PIL rules drafted within the scope of MERCOSUR.

The final dimension is *lex mercatoria,* or the transnational dimension, a typically international source.[50]

The current rules on international jurisdiction and international judicial assistance are included in the CPCCN and in the provincial procedural codes.

The Civil Code provides most autonomous rules of PIL. Private International law rules are set up in the first title of the preliminary titles of the Civil Code. The main connecting factor for capacity is the domicile rule, with no specific rule for family relations or other situations related to that.

The Civil Code originally did not include PIL provisions regarding filiation. Consequently, the gap was solved by the Treaty of Montevideo on International Civil Law (TDCIM) 1889 and 1940. The TDCIM of 1940 has the same (and few) provisions as the TDCIM of 1889, and covers an area that is gaining an important dynamic. Notwithstanding, a gap still exists in international jurisdiction[51] and applicable law, and there is a loophole regarding the relationship of filiation through ART.[52] In particular, there is no specific rule in Argentinean PIL for international surrogacy cases in Argentina.[53]

A. International Surrogacy Cases in Argentina: Analysis of the Problem[54]

It is necessary to distinguish two situations (one could be more complicated or generate more difficulties than the other):

(a) If the intending parents are domiciled abroad and the child is born abroad, in this case the applicable law on the surrogacy agreement is not

---

[49] See Art 13 CCiv.

[50] Dreyzin de Klor, above n 43.

[51] CNCiv, Sala I, 21/11/2002, *SBI v C, V y otro s/ impugnación de maternidad,* ED 201–154.

[52] Dreyzin de Klor, above n 43.

[53] The *Proyecto de Código de Derecho Internacional Privado* (Project for a Code of International Private Law) 2003 has no specific rule on surrogacy either.

[54] According to recent news, consultations about the possibility of surrogacy in foreign countries increased five times in the last few years. See, eg, L Reina, 'Se quintuplicaron las consultas de argentinos en los Estados Unidos' *La Nacion* (Buenos Aires, 20 August 2011), <www.lanacion.com.ar/1399381-crece-el-interes-por-el-alquiler-de-vientres>. Surrogacy is becoming quite 'popular', and generally there is news related to surrogacy in the newspapers every week. See, eg, V Dema, 'Cómo es el trámite para el alquiler de vientres en el país', *La Nación* (Buenos Aires, 25 August 2011), <www.lanacion.com.ar/1399339-el-nexo-entre-los-padres-y-las-madres-sustitutas>.

Argentinean law but local law,[55] and surrogacy may be legal. Nonetheless, if the intending parent(s) go to Argentina and ask for its recognition of the arrangement, Argentinean authorities could still deny it based on public policy grounds.

(b) If the intending parents are permanent residents of Argentina and the surrogacy agreement was entered into in a foreign jurisdiction and the child was born abroad, when the intending parents ask for the recognition of the surrogacy agreement—or its consequences/effects[56]—once they are back in Argentina or at the Argentinean consulate in that country, problems may arise.

i. Formal Aspects

Formal aspects are governed by the laws of the place where the agreement was entered into.[57] If the agreement was made according to foreign law and fulfilled that law's formalities, it would also be valid in Argentina.

ii. Substantive Aspects—Content

With regard to content, in Argentina there are two different positions. The first one considers that the Argentinean authorities should recognise the surrogacy agreement celebrated abroad and its consequences/effects, and it would not be admissible to invoke fraud of law or violation of public policy. According to this position, fraud of law cannot be invoked because there would be no manipulation or malicious alteration of the connection point, therefore fraud of law would be inappropriate.[58] Regarding public policy,[59] it is considered that to establish that

---

[55] Art 21 TDCIM of 1940: 'Issues related to legitimacy of filiations, other than those regarding validity or nullity of marriage, are governed by the law of the domicile of the spouses at the time of birth of the child.'

[56] Eg birth certificate granted in the foreign State recognising the intending parents as legal parents, or a foreign judgment recognising the intending parents as legal parents.

[57] Art 12 CCiv: 'The formal validity of contracts and all public instruments are governed by the law of the place where they were entered into.' Art 950 states the same rule for juridical acts.

[58] AL Calvo Caravaca and J Carrascosa González, 'Gestación por sustitución y Derecho Internacional Privado: Consideraciones en torno a la Resolución de la Dirección General de los Registros y del Notariado de 18 de Febrero De 2009' (2009) *Cuadernos De Derecho Transnacional* 316.

[59] No definition of *ordre public* is provided in the Argentine autonomous PIL; not even the doctrine of scholars provides one. Values related to that notion change according to time and place. The content of *ordre public* is generally accepted as being determined by the national conception of basic principles underlying constitutional rights and legal norms. The Civil Code includes *ordre public* within a general clause. The latter indicates that foreign laws will not apply when their application contradicts the spirit of the legislation of the Code (Art 14, para 2). However, together with that generic clause, the concept of *ordre public* has survived in several provisions in specific areas of law, eg, in the Argentine provisions that govern capacity and incapacity, the object of juridical acts and vices of substance (Art 949). Another example, amongst others, is found in immoral contracts, the recognition of which in Argentina would contradict local laws and the interests of either the State or its inhabitants (Art 1206). See Dreyzin de Klor, above n 43. There are many Argentine court decisions regarding *ordre public*. Nevertheless, that exception is applied in Argentine courts only when facing specific and manifest contraventions

surrogacy violates public policy grounds would be contrary to the *favour filii* principle,[60] to the best interests of the child and to the right to identity. It is also considered that the recognition and registration of the birth and parentage established abroad as a result of a surrogacy agreement must be accepted in Argentina on the principle of *favor filiationis*, as a rule of international law aimed at applying the law that promotes the recognition of filiation. This principle is also based on the Argentine constitutional system that protects the right to identity.[61] To sum up, the public policy grounds could not be invoked because of the prevalence of the principles of *favor filii*, *favor filiationis*, the best interests of the child and the right to identity. It is considered that the welfare of any child would be gravely compromised by a refusal to recognise the intending parents' legal parentage.

On the other hand, the second position argues that the recognition in Argentina of a surrogacy agreement or the consequences of a surrogacy agreement entered into abroad would violate the public policy ground. According to this position, the lack of any rule that expressly permits surrogacy in Argentina, as well as the lack of PIL rules, makes it possible for Argentinean authorities not to recognise a surrogacy agreement or the consequences of a surrogacy agreement celebrated abroad because it is or they are contrary to public policy, especially the principle of unavailability of status of persons and the provisions of Article 953 CCiv (see section III. above).[62]

In short, because of the lack of rules and the different positions generated by this controversial issue, if an international surrogacy case comes before the Argentine authorities, the response from the authorities could be one or the other: recognition of the agreement and the legal parentage, based primarily on the best interests of the child; or the refusal to recognise the agreement and the filiation arising from it, because it is contrary to public policy.

---

of essential principles (see CSJN, 14/09/10, Boo, Héctor José s. sucesión testamentaria). Art 4 of the additional protocols to the *Tratados de Montevideo* (Treaties of Montevideo) Ms 1889/1940 establishes a specific rule that defines the exception of *ordre public*. The rule states that the law of other States shall never apply against political institutions, laws of *ordre public*, or principles of morality of the place of origin. The CNG also provides a rule for *ordre public* in Art 5: '[L]aw declared applicable by a convention on [PIL] may be denied application in the territory of a State Party that considers it manifestly contrary to the principles of its public policy (ordre public).' It should be noted that the CNG does not limit the exception of public policy to cases where application of foreign law contradicts public policy. Courts, when deciding, can consider whether the law manifestly contradicts the principles of public policy. (See P Lagarde, 'Public Policy' in *International Encyclopedia of Comparative Law, Private International Law*, vol III, Ch 11, 7–3.) 'Manifestly', as used in Art 5 CNG, clearly reflects a difference. This adverb restricts the rejection of regularly applicable law to cases where the application is 'manifestly' incompatible with the principles and provisions of *ordre public*. The difference deals with the limitation that the CNG includes. The application of foreign law is rejected because it would require a manifest violation of local juridical order and principles. See Dreyzin de Klor, above n 43.

[60] MJA Oyarzábal, 'El reconocimiento en la Argentina de la paternidad de hijos concebidos en el extranjero por inseminación artificial de pareja de homosexuales hombres' (2006) *La Ley* 1.

[61] Famá, above n 22.

[62] According to Zannoni, 'surrogacy is an immoral agreement contrary to public policy': E Zannoni, *Inseminación artificial y fecundación extrauterina* (Astrea, Bs As, 1978) 111.

However, it is important to emphasise that the situation of *public policy* in Argentina has changed with the reception and constitutional hierarchy of Human Rights Treaties.[63] Rights and principles included in those treaties are now part of the Argentine juridical system, occupying a paramount position. The incorporation of those treaties with constitutional hierarchy has expanded the application of foreign law.[64] Principles that previously were subject to debate or seen as contradicting Argentine legislation are now necessarily applied.[65]

Thus, despite this controversy, I think the best interests of the child would prevail, especially if we think of it as the right of the child to have a family and an identity. In this regard it is also important to stress that the best interests of the child have been considered as paramount by the CSJN and by the inferior courts.

As for the issue of nationality, if the child is born in Argentina, it will be an Argentinean citizen, since Argentinean nationality is attributed primarily through the *ius soli* principle. Those persons are called Argentine natives. This also includes Argentine natives by option, which comprises those born in foreign countries from Argentine natives and who opt for the citizenship of origin of their parents. This category is based on the principle of *jus sanguinis* and requires that at least one parent is Argentinean.[66]

So, under Argentine law,[67] if the intending parents were born in Argentina they may apply for the Argentine citizenship for their sons/daughters born abroad. This process may be effected at the Argentine Consulate by both parents when the child is under 18 years old, or it may be done directly in the Argentine Republic. In this case, both parents must attend in person at the National People Registry (RENAPER) and request the application in Decree 1601/04.

Once the child is 18 years old he or she may apply for Argentine nationality directly. He or she may do so at the Consulate, or directly in the Argentine Republic. In the latter case, he or she must personally attend at the National People Registry (RENAPER) and request the application in Decree 1601/04.

In all cases the following must be demonstrated:

(a) the parent–child relationship (*filiation*); and
(b) that the father/mother is or are Argentinean natives.

---

[63] Even when those rights were tacitly incorporated before the reform of 1994, since then they have been expressly included in the Argentine Constitution.

[64] In recent years, PIL has reflected the relevancy that TDDHHs (human rights treaties) have both in recent domestic laws (eg Law 26618 on Civil Marriage) and in judicial interpretation of international private law cases (eg the Convention on the Rights of the Child in cases of international child abduction). See A Dreyzin de Klor, 'Una vez más, los niños como prenda de conflicto' (2011) II *Revista de Derecho de familia* 132.

[65] Dreyzin de Klor, above n 43.

[66] This category differs from that of Argentine by naturalisation because in the former the option is a right that cannot be denied, while in the latter the right can be denied.

[67] Decree 3213/84, modified by Decree 231/95 and its similar Decree 1601/04.

The parent–child relationship (*filiation*) is proved by the birth certificate of the child issued by the corresponding authorities mentioning the parents' names. The question of surrogacy will arise only if the foreign authorities mention it in the birth certificate, or if the local authorities knew about the surrogacy agreement. In those cases the Argentinean authorities could deny the application based on public policy grounds.[68] If that happens, and the child is born in a State that considers the child to be the child of the intending parents and its citizenship rules are such that the child will not acquire its nationality, the child would be stateless (as in the case pending at the Argentinean courts analysed in section V. above).

Thus, sometimes nationality can be an issue if the child is born abroad, in light of a surrogacy agreement.

---

[68] Any reason would be based on the existence of the surrogacy agreement.

2

Australia

MARY KEYES

I. Introduction

Surrogacy is directly regulated in Australia by state and territory legislation.[1] It also involves many other areas of state, territory and federal law.[2] The surrogacy statutes in the Australian Capital Territory and the six states[3] are similar, in that they all permit altruistic surrogacy, subject to extensive and diverse requirements, and prohibit commercial surrogacy.[4] The distinction between commercial and altruistic surrogacy is based upon whether the intended parents[5] have agreed to pay the surrogate mother[6] for her services, beyond the reimbursement of reasonable expenses related to the pregnancy and birth.[7] There is no legislation in the Northern Territory that directly regulates surrogacy.

[1] Australia is composed of six states and 10 territories. This chapter covers the regulation of surrogacy in the six states and the two largest territories (the Australian Capital Territory (ACT) and the Northern Territory (NT)). The legislation which directly regulates surrogacy is the Parentage Act 2004 (ACT), Surrogacy Act 2010 (NSW), Surrogacy Act 2010 (Qld), Family Relationships Act 1975 (SA), Surrogacy Act 2012 (Tas), Assisted Reproductive Treatment Act 2008 (Vic), Status of Children Act 1974 (Vic) and Surrogacy Act 2008 (WA). There is no legislation specifically dealing with surrogacy in the Northern Territory.

[2] The most closely related areas are adoption law and the law of reproductive technology, which are largely regulated by the states and territories; and the laws of parental responsibility, immigration and citizenship, which are regulated nationally.

[3] New South Wales (NSW), Queensland (Qld), South Australia (SA), Tasmania (Tas), Victoria (Vic) and Western Australia (WA).

[4] Legislation with this effect was first enacted in the ACT in 2000. This legislation was based on the UK's Human Fertilisation and Embryology Act 1990. The ACT model has been followed in the Australian states. However, there are significant differences between the UK legislation and the Australian legislation: see J Millbank, 'The New Surrogacy Parentage Laws in Australia: Cautious Regulation or "25 Brick Walls"?' (2011) 35 *Melbourne University Law Review* 165, 178.

[5] In this chapter I use the term 'intended parent'. A variety of terms is used in the Australian legislation. 'Intended parent' is used in New South Wales, Queensland and Tasmania; 'arranged parent' is used in Western Australia; 'commissioning parent' is used in South Australia and Victoria; 'substitute parent' is used in the ACT.

[6] For the sake of consistency with the other chapters in this book, I use the term 'surrogate mother' in this chapter, although the term 'birth mother' is used in most Australian jurisdictions. The term 'surrogate mother' is used only in the Victorian legislation.

[7] See further below, section II.A.ii.

This chapter describes the current Australian law, referring in particular to the surrogacy legislation and to published surrogacy cases.[8] In Australia, commercial surrogacy is more common than altruistic surrogacy[9] and gestational surrogacy is more common than genetic surrogacy.[10] The chapter is presented in four sections: section II. describes the domestic regulation of surrogacy; section III. describes the law relevant to cross-border surrogacy, which is common in Australia; and section IV. presents a conclusion.

II. The Domestic Regulation of Surrogacy

A. Altruistic Surrogacy—The States and Australian Capital Territory

The states and the Australian Capital Territory have each recently regulated altruistic surrogacy in a way that is broadly similar. The legislation has two important legal consequences: first, it allows intended parents to apply to the court for a parentage order, which transfers parental status from the surrogate mother and her spouse or partner to the intended parents; secondly, it explicitly recognises the enforceability of the intended parents' obligation to reimburse the surrogate mother's expenses related to the surrogacy arrangement.

---

[8] There are very few data available in Australia about surrogacy. For this research, I analysed the published decisions of the Australian courts in surrogacy cases. Using the search terms 'surrogacy', 'surrogate' and 'parentage order' on the AustLII and LexisNexis Casebase databases, I identified 31 published cases of the Australian courts involving surrogacy arrangements. The earliest were decided in 1998 and the latest in 2012. In this chapter, I refer also to a recent study by Millbank, based on media reports between 2007 and 2010, from which she identified 69 arrangements: Millbank, above n 4, 168. Millbank's findings differ in various respects from the findings reported in this chapter. This may be partly because her study included prospective arrangements. Her sample consisted of 42 cases in which children had already been born, five cases in which the surrogate mother was pregnant, 15 cases in which surrogacy arrangements had been made but the surrogate mother had not yet conceived, and seven cases in which intended parents were pursuing surrogacy but had yet to find a surrogate mother: *ibid*, 169. The sample reported in each study is small but comprehensive.

[9] Of the 31 published surrogacy cases, 16 were commercial (51.6%), 12 were altruistic and in three cases it was unclear whether the arrangement was commercial or not. Millbank does not clearly indicate what proportion of the total number of arrangements in her study were commercial, although she reports a 'very strong correlation between international travel and commercial payment: of the 35 international arrangements it is striking that 32 parties reported payment to the [surrogate] mother': Millbank, above n 4, 192.

[10] Of the 31 published cases considered for this study, 19 involved gestational surrogacy (63.3%). Both intended parents were the genetic parents of the child in only three cases. In three cases, it was not clear whether the surrogacy was gestational or genetic. In Millbank's study, 51 of 69 (74%) arrangements clearly involved gestational surrogacy (in 13 it was not clear whether the arrangement was gestational or genetic). In her study, both intended parents were genetic parents in just over half of the gestational surrogacy cases: *ibid*, 173.

i. Parentage Orders

The principal effect of the surrogacy legislation is that intended parents can apply to the court for a parentage order, which has the effect of transferring the legal status and responsibilities of parents from the surrogate parents to the intended parents.[11] The surrogacy legislation therefore operates on the assumption that the surrogate parents are legally the parents of the child. This is often but not necessarily the case.[12] The point is irrelevant if the intended parents are able to satisfy the requirements of a parentage order, but if they are not able to satisfy those requirements then the general law will determine their parental status.

In most surrogacy cases, the child is conceived following a fertility procedure,[13] and the intended father is usually the biological father of the child.[14] Under Australian law, the surrogate mother is regarded as a parent, even if she is not genetically related to the child.[15] If the pregnancy was achieved by means of a fertility procedure and if the surrogate mother's partner or spouse consented to that procedure, that person will also be regarded as the parent of the child.[16] In such

---

[11] Parentage Act 2004 (ACT), s 29; Surrogacy Act 2010 (NSW), s 39; Surrogacy Act 2010 (Qld), s 39(2); Family Relationships Act 1975 (SA), s 10HB(13); Surrogacy Act 2012 (Tas), s 26(1); Status of Children Act 1974 (Vic), s 19; Surrogacy Act 2008 (WA), s 26(1). Once the order is made, the intended parents' status is recognised under the Family Law Act 1975 (Cth), s 60HB(1), Family Law Regulations 1984 (Cth), reg 12CAA.

[12] Parental status is determined by reference to evidentiary presumptions which are set out in federal, state and territory legislation. Most of these presumptions may be rebutted, usually by DNA evidence establishing paternity. However, the most relevant presumption in surrogacy cases, applicable when the child is conceived by a fertility procedure, is irrebuttable in most Australian jurisdictions: see below, n 17. The presumptions are broadly similar in the legislation of all jurisdictions. Most of the references in this section are to the presumptions in the federal Family Law Act 1975 (Cth), by way of example of the Australian law. The relevant legislation of the state and territories is Parentage Act 2004 (ACT); Status of Children Act 1978 (NT); Status of Children Act 1996 (NSW); Status of Children Act 1978 (Qld); Family Relationships Act 1975 (SA); Status of Children Act 1974 (Tas); Status of Children Act 1974 (Vic); Artificial Conception Act 1985 (WA). The presumptions may conflict, in which case the court should apply the presumption which seems most likely to be correct, eg Family Law Act 1975 (Cth), s 69U(2).

[13] Either by artificial insemination or by in vitro fertilisation. It is very unusual in Australia that both surrogate mother and her partner are the biological parents, but see *Lowe & Barry* [2011] FamCA 625.

[14] In the published surrogacy cases, the intended father was the genetic father in 26 of 31 cases (83.8%) (in three cases, it was unclear). In Millbank's study, the intended father was the genetic father in 47 of 69 cases (68%): Millbank, above n 4, 173.

[15] Family Law Act 1975 (Cth), s 60H(1), (2), incorporating reference to the prescribed laws of the states as to parental status. The prescribed laws are those referred to above at n 12. These presumptions were not developed with the circumstances of surrogacy in mind. They are part of a uniform legislative scheme that was intended to ensure that gamete donors did not acquire parental responsibilities, whereas in most surrogacy arrangements the parties intended the sperm donor to have parental responsibility and for the birth parents not to have such a responsibility: *Dudley & Chedi* [2011] FamCA 502, [30]; *Hubert & Juntasa* [2011] FamCA 504, [16]; *Johnson & Chompunut* [2011] FamCA 505, [16]. These presumptions have been applied in several surrogacy cases, with the result that the surrogate mother and her husband were found to be the parents: *Re Births, Deaths and Marriages Registration Act 1997* (2000) 26 Fam LR 234; *PJ v Director General Department of Community Services* [1999] NSWSC 340; *Re Michael (surrogacy arrangements)* [2009] FamCA 691.

[16] Family Law Act 1975 (Cth), s 60H(1), (3), referring to the prescribed laws of the states and territories, which are those laws referred to above at n 12.

situations, the biological parents are conclusively presumed not to be parents of the child. [17] An intended parent may be regarded as a parent if registered as such in a birth register,[18] or if that person has acknowledged parental status.[19]

The surrogacy legislation permits intended parents in altruistic surrogacy arrangements to apply for a parentage order after the child is born, subject to extensive requirements which are not identical in the different Australian jurisdictions.[20] In most jurisdictions, the responsibility for ensuring compliance with the requirements lies with the courts in dealing with post-birth applications for parentage orders. In two jurisdictions, state government authorities have a primary role in regulating surrogacy arrangements. In Western Australia, the court can make a parentage order only if the Western Australian Reproductive Treatment Council approved the surrogacy arrangement before the surrogate mother became pregnant.[21] In Victoria, registered artificial reproductive technology (ART) providers can carry out procedures in a surrogacy arrangement only if the arrangement has been approved by the Victorian Patient Review Panel.[22] In both states, further requirements must be satisfied before the court can make a parentage order.[23]

The most important requirements that are common to all seven jurisdictions are that the arrangement is not commercial,[24] that the surrogate mother consents to the transfer of parentage[25] and that the transfer is in the best interests of the

---

[17] The presumptions are stated to be conclusive in Parentage Act 2004 (ACT), s 11(5); Status of Children Act 1996 (NSW), s 14(4); Status of Children Act 1978 (NT), s 5D(2); Status of Children Act 1978 (Qld), s 17(3); Status of Children Act 1974 (Vic), s 10C(3)(a). Family Law Act 1975 (Cth), s 60H(1) has been held to have the same effect: *Re Michael (surrogacy arrangements)* [2009] FamCA 691, [25].

[18] Eg Family Law Act 1975 (Cth), s 69R.

[19] Eg Family Law Act 1975 (Cth), s 69T.

[20] In the ACT and New South Wales the application is made to the Supreme Courts. In Victoria, the application may be made either to the Supreme Court or to the county court. In Queensland, applications are made to the Childrens Court; in South Australia the Youth Court has jurisdiction; in Tasmania, applications are made to the Magistrates Court; in Western Australia, the Family Court of Western Australia has jurisdiction.

[21] Surrogacy Act 2008 (WA), ss 16(1), 17(e).

[22] Assisted Reproductive Treatment Act 2008 (Vic), s 39. This applies only where an ART provider is involved in the conception. In other cases, the intended parents can apply for a parentage order, in which case the court must ensure compliance with additional requirements: Status of Children Act 1974 (Vic), s 23.

[23] Status of Children Act 1974 (Vic), s 22(1); Surrogacy Act 2008 (WA), ss 19–22.

[24] Parentage Act 2004 (ACT), s 24(c); Surrogacy Act 2010 (NSW), s 23; Surrogacy Act 2010 (Qld), s 22(2)(e)(vi); Family Relationships Act 1975 (SA), s 10HA(2)(b)(ix); Surrogacy Act 2012 (Tas), s 16(2)(a)(ii); Status of Children Act 1974 (Vic), s 22(1)(d). This requirement is not explicit in the Western Australian legislation but it can be implied from the fact that commercial surrogacy is prohibited: Surrogacy Act 2008 (WA), s 8.

[25] Parentage Act 2004 (ACT), s 26(1)(b) (requiring also that the surrogate mother's spouse or partner consents); Surrogacy Act 2010 (NSW), s 31(1); Surrogacy Act 2010 (Qld), s 22(2)(h); Surrogacy Act 2012 (Tas), s 16(2)(j)(iii) (the NSW, Queensland and Tasmanian legislation also requires that the surrogate mother's spouse and the intended parents consent to the making of the parentage order); Family Relationships Act 1975 (SA), s 10HB(7) (requiring only the surrogate mother's consent); Status of Children Act 1974 (Vic), s 22(1)(e) (requiring only that the surrogate mother consents; if the surrogate mother's partner is a party to the surrogacy arrangement, that person's consent to the parentage

child.[26] In all jurisdictions, it is also required that the intended parents are resident in the jurisdiction,[27] and that the application must be made after the child was born but no later than six months after the birth.[28] The other requirements differ between the various jurisdictions on a range of issues.

The main protections in all seven jurisdictions are counselling requirements and age restrictions. All jurisdictions require that the parties have received counselling, and most require that the parties have also received legal advice about the surrogacy arrangement.[29] In six jurisdictions, counselling and legal advice must have been given before the parties entered into the arrangement.[30]

All jurisdictions impose minimum age requirements, but there is no consistency as to which parties must meet these requirements or as to the relevant age. Three jurisdictions impose minimum age requirements for the intended parents

order is also required: s 22(3)); Surrogacy Act 2008 (WA), s 21(2)(d) (this requires that the surrogate mother's partner or spouse also consents). The court may dispense with this requirement only if the surrogate parent is dead, incapacitated or unable to be contacted: Parentage Act 2004 (ACT), s 26(2); Surrogacy Act 2010 (NSW), s 31(2); Surrogacy Act 2010 (Qld), s 23(3); Family Relationships Act 1975 (SA), s 10HB(8); Surrogacy Act 2012 (Tas), s 16(4)(a); Status of Children Act 1974 (Vic), s 24(1); Surrogacy Act 2008 (WA), s 21(3)(c). In Western Australia, the court may make a parentage order even if the surrogate mother does not consent, but only if the surrogate mother is not the genetic mother and if at least one intended parent is a genetic parent: s 21(3)(c), (4). As to the requirement of consent, see *AP v RD* [2011] NSWSC 1389.

[26] Parentage Act 2004 (ACT), s 26(1)(a); Surrogacy Act 2010 (NSW), s 22(1); Surrogacy Act 2010 (Qld), s 22(2)(a); Family Relationships Act 1975 (SA), s 10HB(6); Surrogacy Act 2012 (Tas), s 16(2)(k); Status of Children Act 1974 (Vic), s 22(1)(a); Surrogacy Act 2008 (WA), ss 13(1), 21(2)(g). In Western Australia, the legislation creates a presumption that it is in the best interests of the child for the intended parents to be the parents of the child: Surrogacy Act 2008 (WA), s 13(2).

[27] In South Australia, the requirement is of domicile: Family Relationships Act 1975 (SA), s 10HA(2)(b)(iv). In the other jurisdictions, the requirement is of residence: Parentage Act 2004 (ACT), s 24(e); Surrogacy Act 2010 (NSW), s 32; Surrogacy Act 2010 (Qld), s 22(2)(g)(ii); Surrogacy Act 2012 (Tas), s 16(2)(j)(ii); Surrogacy Act 2008 (WA), s 19(1).

[28] In four jurisdictions, the child must be at least four weeks old at the time the application is made: Surrogacy Act 2010 (Qld), s 21(1)(a); Family Relationships Act 1975 (SA), s 10HB(5); Status of Children Act 1974 (Vic), s 20(2)(a); Surrogacy Act 2008 (WA), s 20(2), (3). In New South Wales and Tasmania, the child must be at least 30 days old (Surrogacy Act 2010 (NSW), s 16(1); Surrogacy Act 2012 (Tas), s 15(1)(a)) and in the ACT the child must be at least six weeks old (Parentage Act 2004 (ACT), s 25(3)).

[29] In the ACT there is no requirement that the parties received legal advice. In Western Australia, it is a requirement that any egg or sperm donor must also receive counselling and legal advice: Surrogacy Act 2008 (WA), s 17(c). This is not required in the other jurisdictions.

[30] Surrogacy Act 2010 (NSW), ss 35(1), 36(1); Surrogacy Act 2010 (Qld), s 22(2)(e); Family Relationships Act 1975 (SA), ss 10HA(2)(b)(vii), 10HA(6)(c); Surrogacy Act 2012 (Tas), s 16(2)(a)(i), (f); Assisted Reproductive Treatment Act 2008 (Vic), ss 40(1)(c), 43; Surrogacy Act 2008 (WA), s 17(c). Under the ACT legislation, the court must consider whether the parties have received counselling, but the time at which such counselling must be received is not stipulated and the consequences if they did not receive it are unclear: Parentage Act 2004 (ACT), s 26(3)(e). In Victoria, for pregnancies not commissioned with the assistance of registered ART providers, counselling and legal 'information' are required for all parties to the agreement, but it does not appear that they must have been received before the agreement was made: Status of Children Act 1974 (Vic), s 23(2)(b). In New South Wales, the surrogate mother and her spouse must also have received counselling after the child was born: Surrogacy Act 2010 (NSW), s 35(2). In Tasmania, the surrogate mother, her spouse and the intended parents must also receive counselling after the birth: Surrogacy Act 2012 (Tas), s 16(2)(f)(ii).

and the surrogate mother,[31] and another two also impose requirements for the surrogate mother's spouse or partner.[32] The two remaining jurisdictions impose minimum age requirements only for some parties.[33] In some jurisdictions, the minimum age is 18 years,[34] in others the minimum age is 25 years.[35] In New South Wales, the surrogate parents must be at least 25 years old but the intended parents need only be aged over 18;[36] and in Tasmania, the surrogate mother must be at least 25 years old and the intended parents must be at least 21 years old.[37]

Other requirements relating to the qualifications of the parties differ significantly between the different jurisdictions. Only two states require some of the parties to have undergone assessment to confirm their suitability to be involved in the surrogacy arrangement.[38] In three states, the surrogate mother must usually have already given birth to a live child.[39] Two jurisdictions mandate that one of the intended parents is genetically related to the child,[40] and one of those jurisdictions also requires that neither surrogate parent is genetically related to the child.[41] In Victoria, the surrogate mother must not be genetically related to the child.[42] In all

---

[31] In New South Wales, the surrogate mother must have been at least 25 and the intended parents must have been at least 18 when the agreement was made: Surrogacy Act 2010 (NSW), ss 27(1), 28(1). In Tasmania, at the time the arrangement was made the surrogate mother must have been at least 25 and the intended parents must both be at least 21: Surrogacy Act 2012 (Tas), s 16(2)(b), (c). In Western Australia, the surrogate mother and at least one of the intended parents must be at least 25 years old, apparently at the time of applying for parentage orders: Surrogacy Act 2008 (WA), ss 17(a)(i), 19(1)(a).

[32] In Queensland, all parties must have been at least 25 years old when the surrogacy agreement was made: Surrogacy Act 2010 (Qld), s 22(2)(f), (g). In South Australia the intended parents, the surrogate mother and her husband must all be at least 18 years old: Family Relationships Act 1975 (SA), s 10HA(2)(b)(ii).

[33] In the ACT, the intended parents must be at least 18, apparently at the time the application for parentage orders are made: Parentage Act 2004 (ACT), s 26(3)(b). There is no minimum age prescribed for the surrogate mother or her partner or spouse. Under the Victorian legislation, the surrogate mother must have been at least 25 at the time of entering the agreement: Assisted Reproductive Treatment Act 2008 (Vic), s 40(1)(b); Status of Children Act 1974 (Vic), s 23(2)(a). There is no age requirement relevant to the intended parents.

[34] Parentage Act 2004 (ACT), s 26(3)(b); Family Relationships Act 1975 (SA), s 10HA(2)(b)(ii).

[35] Surrogacy Act 2010 (Qld), s 22(2)(f), (g); Status of Children Act 1974 (Vic), s 23(2)(a); Surrogacy Act 2008 (WA), ss 17(a)(i), 19(1)(a).

[36] In New South Wales, the surrogate mother must have been at least 25 and the intended parents must have been at least 18 at the time the agreement was made: Surrogacy Act 2010 (NSW), ss 27(1), 28(1). In New South Wales, if an intended parent was under 25 years of age, the court 'must be satisfied that the intended parent is of sufficient maturity to understand the social and psychological implications of making a parentage order': *ibid*, s 29(1).

[37] Surrogacy Act 2012 (Tas), s 16(2)(b), (c).

[38] In South Australia, the surrogate mother must have been assessed and approved by an accredited counselling service: Family Relationships Act 1975 (SA), s 10HA(2)(b)(vi). In Western Australia, all parties must have undergone both psychological and medical assessment: Surrogacy Act 2008 (WA), s 17(c)(ii), (d).

[39] Surrogacy Act 2012 (Tas), s 16(2)(d); Assisted Reproductive Treatment Act 2008 (Vic), s 40(1) (ac); Surrogacy Act 2008 (WA), s 17(a)(ii).

[40] Parentage Act 2004 (ACT), s 24(d); Family Relationships Act 1975 (SA), s 10HA(2)(b)(viii)(B).

[41] Parentage Act 2004 (ACT), s 24(b).

[42] Assisted Reproductive Treatment Act 2008 (Vic), s 40(1)(ab).

jurisdictions except South Australia,[43] single people can be intended parents,[44] and no jurisdiction discriminates between de facto and married couples.[45] In South Australia and Western Australia, same-sex couples cannot be intended parents.[46]

In six jurisdictions, it must be shown that there was a need for the surrogacy.[47] Medical needs satisfy this requirement in all of these jurisdictions,[48] and in three states the requirement of a social need may be satisfied if the intended parent or parents are men.[49]

In four jurisdictions, the surrogacy agreement must be in writing.[50] In most jurisdictions, the agreement is between the surrogate mother, her spouse or partner, and the intended parents, but in Western Australia, if there is a third party egg or sperm donor, that party must also sign the agreement.[51] Three jurisdictions explicitly require that the agreement was made pre-conception.[52]

---

[43] Family Relationships Act 1975 (SA), s 10HA(2)(a)(ii).

[44] Surrogacy Act 2010 (NSW), s 25(1)(b); Surrogacy Act 2010 (Qld), s 21(6); Surrogacy Act 2012 (Tas), ss 5, 13(1); Status of Children Act 1974 (Vic), s 17(1) (definition of 'commissioning parent'); Surrogacy Act 2008 (WA), s 3. In the ACT, the surrogacy agreement must involve two intended parents, but the legislation allows for only one of those parents to apply for a parentage order: Parentage Act 2004 (ACT), ss 24(c), 25(2).

[45] In South Australia, the intended parents must be married, or in a de facto relationship of at least three years' standing prior to the date of the surrogacy agreement or for periods aggregating a total of three years over a four-year period immediately preceding the agreement: Family Relationship Act 1975 (SA), s 10HA(2)(b)(iii).

[46] Family Relationships Act 1975 (SA), s 10HA(2)(b)(iii); Surrogacy Act 2008 (WA), s 19(1)(b), (2).

[47] Surrogacy Act 2010 (NSW), s 30(1); Surrogacy Act 2010 (Qld), s 22(2)(d); Family Relationships Act 1975 (SA), s 10HA(2)(b)(v); Surrogacy Act 2012 (Tas), s 16(2)(h); Assisted Reproductive Treatment Act 2008 (Vic), s 40(1)(a); Surrogacy Act 2008 (WA), s 19(1)(b).

[48] Medical needs are satisfied if the intended mother is unable to conceive (Surrogacy Act 2010 (NSW), s 30(3)(a); Surrogacy Act 2010 (Qld), s 14(2)(a); Family Relationships Act 1975 (SA), s 10HA(2)(b)(v); Surrogacy Act 2012 (Tas), s 7(2)(a); Surrogacy Act 2008 (WA), s 19(2)) or sustain a pregnancy, or if she would face serious health risks if she were to undertake a pregnancy (Surrogacy Act 2010 (NSW), s 30(3)(b), (c); Surrogacy Act 2010 (Qld), s 14(2)(b); Surrogacy Act 2012 (Tas), s 7(2)(b), (c)). The requirement is also satisfied in some jurisdictions if there is a risk that any child of the intended mother would suffer from a serious genetic abnormality, disease or illness: Surrogacy Act 2010 (NSW), s 30(3)(d); Surrogacy Act 2010 (Qld), s 14(2)(b)(iii); Family Relationships Act 1975 (SA), s 10HA(2)(b)(v); Surrogacy Act 2012 (Tas), s 7(2)(d); Surrogacy Act 2008 (WA), s 19(2).

[49] Surrogacy Act 2010 (NSW), s 30(2)(a), (b)(ii); Surrogacy Act 2010 (Qld), s 14(1)(a), (b)(ii); Surrogacy Act 2012 (Tas), s 7(1)(a), (b)(ii).

[50] Surrogacy Act 2010 (NSW), s 34(1); Surrogacy Act 2010 (Qld), s 22(2)(d); Family Relationships Act 1975 (SA), s 10HA(6); Surrogacy Act 2008 (WA), s 17(b). There is no express requirement of writing in the Parentage Act 2004 (ACT) s 23, or in Victoria: Assisted Reproductive Treatment Act 2008 (Vic), s 3 (definition of surrogacy arrangement). The Tasmanian legislation states that a surrogacy agreement may be made orally or in writing (Surrogacy Act 2012 (Tas), s 5(6)). One of the requirements in the Tasmanian legislation that must be satisfied before the court can make a parentage order is that the agreement is in writing (Surrogacy Act 2012 (Tas), s 16(2)(e)). That requirement can be dispensed with if the court considers that making the parentage order is in the child's best interests: Surrogacy Act 2012 (Tas), s 16(3)(a).

[51] Surrogacy Act 2008 (WA), s 17(b).

[52] Surrogacy Act 2010 (NSW), s 24(1); Surrogacy Act 2010 (Qld), s 22(2)(e)(iv); Surrogacy Act 2012 (Tas), s 5(5)(a). It is an implicit requirement in the other jurisdictions: Parentage Act 2004 (ACT) s 23 (definition of substitute parent agreement); Family Relationships Act 1975 (SA) ss 10HA(2)(a)(i), 10HA(2)(b)(viii)(A); Assisted Reproductive Treatment Act 2008 (Vic), s 39; Surrogacy Act 2008 (WA), s 17(e). In Victoria, it is not even an implicit requirement in cases where the pregnancy was achieved without medical assistance.

It is a requirement in most jurisdictions that the child be living with the intended parents at the time the application for parentage orders is made.[53] In the other jurisdictions, the court must take into account whether the child is living with the intended parents at the time of the application.[54]

The regime in Western Australia is the most extensive and it incorporates requirements that are not included in the other jurisdictions. In particular, the surrogate parents and the intended parents must have agreed in writing to a plan regarding the child, which must 'adequately balance the rights and responsibilities of the parties to the plan', 'promote the child's long-term welfare' and 'be reasonable in the circumstances'.[55] The plan must detail the arrangements relating to the child's contact with the surrogate parents.[56]

In four jurisdictions, the courts have no discretion to grant a parentage order if the statutory requirements are not met.[57] In New South Wales, Queensland and Tasmania, the legislation permits the court to dispense with many of the requirements in exceptional cases, if that would be consistent with the child's best interests.[58]

ii. *The Enforceability of the Surrogacy Agreement*

At common law in Australia, surrogacy agreements were unenforceable as contrary to public policy. The surrogacy legislation has only slightly amended this position, recognising that the surrogate mother is entitled to enforce the intended parents' obligation to pay her reasonable expenses associated with the pregnancy and birth. The legislation in four states specifically provides that the agreement to reimburse the surrogate mother's expenses is enforceable.[59] In the Australian Capital Territory, Victoria and South Australia, the legislation does not directly recognise the surrogate mother's right to recover against the intended parents, but

---

[53] Surrogacy Act 2010 (NSW), s 33; Surrogacy Act 2010 (Qld), s 22(2)(b)(iii); Surrogacy Act 2012 (Tas), s 16(2)(j)(i); Status of Children Act 1974 (Vic), s 22(1)(c); Surrogacy Act 2008 (WA), s 22(1)(e).

[54] Parentage Act 2004 (ACT), s 26(3)(a); Family Relationships Act 1975 (SA), s 10HB(9)(a).

[55] Surrogacy Act 2008 (WA), s 22(1).

[56] Surrogacy Act 2008 (WA), s 22(2).

[57] Some requirements in the ACT scheme are clearly mandatory (Parentage Act 2004 (ACT), s 24), whereas others are not clearly mandatory from the wording of the statute: *ibid*, s 26(3) (stating only that the court must take various factors 'into consideration, if relevant').

[58] Surrogacy Act 2010 (NSW), s 18(2); Surrogacy Act 2010 (Qld), s 23(2); Surrogacy Act 2012 (Tas), s 16(3). In *BLH v MW*, a case involving a pre-commencement surrogacy agreement (ie an agreement made before the legislation permitting altruistic surrogacy commenced), Irwin DCJ dispensed with four requirements under the Act (the requirements that the parties had obtained independent legal advice and counselling, that the agreement was in writing before the child was conceived and that an affidavit of the counsellor be provided to the court), as is allowed under the Queensland legislation: Surrogacy Act 2010 (Qld), s 63(4) (relating specifically to pre-commencement surrogacy arrangements): [2010] QDC 439. This decision suggests that the Queensland courts may take a liberal approach to the requirements.

[59] Surrogacy Act 2010 (NSW), s 6(2); Surrogacy Act 2010 (Qld), s 15(2); Surrogacy Act 2012 (Tas), s 10(2); Surrogacy Act 2008 (WA), s 7(3).

it is consistent with the legislation that the surrogate mother should be entitled to enforce the agreement to pay her reasonable expenses.[60]

The specific expenses that may be recovered by the surrogate mother differ between the seven jurisdictions. In the Australian Capital Territory, the legislation specifically refers only to recovery of expenses connected with the pregnancy and the birth and care of the child.[61] In six states, expenses relating to medical and legal services are explicitly stated to be recoverable, and in five of those the legislation specifically allows recovery of costs related to counselling.[62] Reimbursement of insurance premiums and the recovery of lost income are expressly allowed in four states,[63] and travel costs associated with the surrogacy may be recovered in Tasmania and Victoria.[64]

The legislation in Queensland and Tasmania specifically provides that the surrogate mother has the same right to manage her pregnancy as any other pregnant woman, and that this right is not contractible.[65] The same result follows in the other jurisdictions, most of which explicitly provide that the surrogacy contract is not enforceable, aside from the surrogate mother's right to reimbursement.[66] Any provisions of the surrogacy agreement which restricted the surrogate mother's entitlement to manage her pregnancy would be unenforceable.

The right to terminate a pregnancy is not explicitly addressed by the surrogacy legislation.[67] In two states, the intended parents' obligation to reimburse is enforceable only if the surrogate mother has performed the agreement by consenting to the making of the parentage order.[68] The effect of this in Queensland would appear to be that, if the child was not born live, the surrogate mother would not be entitled to recover her expenses.[69] In the other jurisdictions, the

---

[60] Parentage Act 2004 (ACT), s 26(3)(d); Family Relationships Act 1975 (SA), s 10HA(2)(b)(ix); Assisted Reproductive Treatment Act 2008 (Vic), s 44(2).

[61] Parentage Act 2004 (ACT), s 40.

[62] The five states that expressly allow recovery of counselling expenses, in addition to medical and legal expenses are: Surrogacy Act 2010 (NSW), s 7(2)(a), (d), (4); Surrogacy Act 2010 (Qld), s 11(2)(a), (b), (d), (e); Surrogacy Act 2012 (Tas), s 9(3)(d); Family Relationships Act 1975 (SA), s 10HA(2)(b) (ix); Surrogacy Act 2008 (WA), s 6(1), (2), (3)(a), (c). In Victoria, counselling expenses are not expressly listed: Assisted Reproductive Treatment Act 2008 (Vic), s 44(2), Assisted Reproductive Treatment Regulations 2008 (Vic), reg 10(a), (b).

[63] Surrogacy Act 2010 (NSW), s 7(2)(c), (e); Surrogacy Act 2010 (Qld), s 11(2)(c), (f); Surrogacy Act 2012 (Tas), s 9(3)(c), (f); Surrogacy Act 2008 (WA), s 6(3)(b), (d).

[64] Surrogacy Act 2012 (Tas), s 9(3)(g); Assisted Reproductive Treatment Act 2008 (Vic), s 44(2), Assisted Reproductive Treatment Regulations 2008 (Vic), reg 10(c).

[65] Surrogacy Act 2010 (Qld), s 16; Surrogacy Act 2012 (Tas), s 11.

[66] Parentage Act 2004 (ACT), s 31; Surrogacy Act 2010 (NSW), s 6(1); Assisted Reproductive Treatment Act 2008 (Vic), s 44(3); Surrogacy Act 2008 (WA), s 7(1).

[67] The Tasmanian legislation refers to the possibility of termination of the pregnancy in the context of preserving the surrogate mother's entitlement to reimbursement of her expenses if the pregnancy is terminated in certain circumstances: Surrogacy Act 2012 (Tas), s 10(2)(b), (3)(b).

[68] Surrogacy Act 2010 (Qld), s 15(2)(b).

[69] The legislation in Tasmania makes specific provision for situations in which the surrogate mother has tried to become pregnant but no pregnancy ensues, or the pregnancy ceases: Surrogacy Act 2012 (Tas), s 10(2)(a), (b).

entitlement to reimbursement is not stated to be conditional on the surrogate mother performing her obligations.

In most jurisdictions, the surrogacy legislation does not specifically refer to the surrogate mother's entitlement to maintain contact with the child. This is a serious gap in the law; in applications in related areas of law, such as applications to adopt the child, the courts often refer to past and proposed ongoing contact between the surrogate mother and the child.[70] Ongoing contact between the child and the surrogate mother is referred to only in the legislation in Tasmania and Western Australia. In Western Australia, the plan that the intended parents and surrogate parents are required to make concerning the child must set out arrangements about the child's contact with the surrogate parents.[71]

In some jurisdictions, the surrogacy legislation regulates access to information concerning the surrogacy, particularly information recorded in birth registers after a parentage order has been made.[72] In most jurisdictions, children are entitled to access court records relating to applications for parentage orders, although the courts' leave to do so is required.[73] In most jurisdictions, the surrogacy legislation does not specifically incorporate requirements relating to recording of or access to genetic information.[74]

B. Parenting Orders and Adoption in Surrogacy Cases

Intended parents may use other areas of federal and state law to achieve some recognition of their parental responsibilities. The two most important are parenting orders and adoption. In the published surrogacy cases, the most common

---

[70] The child's contact with the surrogate mother is referred to in the following cases, which were applications for adoption: *W: Re Adoption* (1998) 23 Fam LR 538, 544; *Re D & E* (2000) 26 Fam LR 310, [10]; *Re A & B* [2000] NSWSC 640, (2000) 26 Fam LR 317, [12]. It is also referred to in applications for parenting orders in the Family Court (as to which, see below, section II.B.): eg *Lowe & Barry* [2011] FamCA 625, [55]; *Hutchens & Franz* [2009] FamCA 414, [10]; *Re Mark (an application relating to parental responsibilities)* [2003] FamCA 822, (2003) 31 Fam LR 162, [15]; *Rusken & Jenner* [2009] FamCA 282, [45].

[71] Surrogacy Act 2008 (WA), s 22(2). In Tasmania, the court may request a report from a counsellor, and may specify that the report address particular matters, including proposed arrangements for the child's contact with the surrogate mother, her spouse and any gamete donor: Surrogacy Act 2012 (Tas), s 18(2)(d).

[72] Surrogacy Act 2010 (NSW), ss 55–57; Surrogacy Act 2008 (WA), s 38.

[73] Surrogacy Act 2010 (NSW), s 53; Surrogacy Act 2010 (Qld), s 52; Family Relationships Act 1975 (SA), s 10HE; Status of Children Act 1974 (Vic), s 34; Surrogacy Act 2008 (WA), s 37(1).

[74] The New South Wales surrogacy legislation alone refers to the obligations upon ART providers to register information relating to donors of gametes under that state's Assisted Reproductive Technology Act 2007 (NSW): Surrogacy Act 2010 (NSW), s 37(1). Reproductive technology providers are under similar obligations in three other states (Reproductive Technology (Clinical Practices) Act 1988 (SA); Assisted Reproductive Treatment Act 2008 (Vic); Human Reproductive Technology Act 1991 (WA)), although those requirements are not specifically referred to in the surrogacy legislation. In the ACT, the Northern Territory, Queensland and Tasmania, there is no requirement to register this information.

application is for parenting orders under the federal Family Law Act.[75] Applications for parenting orders are made in the federal Family Courts. Parenting orders must be distinguished from the parentage orders that may be made under the state and territory surrogacy legislation.[76] Parenting orders do not create or recognise parental status but determine parental responsibilities.[77] Applicants for parenting orders need not be parents.[78]

Intended parents may in some cases be able to apply to adopt the child under state and territory adoption legislation.[79] This may be possible if the intended parents are related to the child.[80] If the surrogate mother is related to the intended parents, the intended parents may be able to adopt the child relying on the family relationship between them and the child. Alternatively, if one of the intended parents is presumed to be a parent of the child, that person's partner may be able to adopt the child in reliance on the provisions permitting adoption by a step-parent.[81]

The laws relating to parenting orders and to adoption operate independently of the surrogacy legislation.[82] The courts dealing with applications for parenting orders do not have jurisdiction to deal with the surrogacy legislation;[83] rather, their principal responsibility is to make a decision as to parenting responsibilities which is in the child's best interests.[84] The courts have repeatedly stated that

---

[75] Twenty of the 31 published surrogacy cases are applications for parenting orders (in one of these cases, applications were also made for a parentage declaration and for leave to adopt). Fewer cases concern applications for leave to adopt children (three cases); applications to adopt children (three cases); declarations as to parentage (two cases); and applications for parentage orders (three cases).

[76] As at January 2013, there were only three published cases in which intended parents have applied for parentage orders: *AP v RD* [2011] NSWSC 1389, *BLH v SJW* [2010] QDC 439, *MM & KF* [2012] NSWSC 445.

[77] Family Law Act 1975 (Cth), s 61D.

[78] Family Law Act 1975 (Cth), s 65C permits any 'person concerned with the care, welfare or development of the child' to apply for a parenting order.

[79] They must first be granted leave to apply to adopt the child by the federal Family Court, under the federal Family Law Act 1975 (Cth), s 60G, although applications to adopt children are made under state and territory law.

[80] The parties cannot make private arrangements for adoption, although in some jurisdictions, if the applicant adoptive parent is related to the child, or is the step-parent of the child, he or she may apply to adopt the child: eg Adoption Act 2000 (NSW), ss 29, 30; Adoption of Children Act 1994 (NT), s 15(1); Adoption Act 2009 (Qld), s 92(1)(a).

[81] In *Re Michael (surrogacy arrangements)* [2009] FamCA 691, Watts J refused leave to apply for adoption, as neither intended parent was legally recognised as the parent of the child. On the other hand, in the recent international altruistic surrogacy case of *McQuinn & Shure* [2011] FamCA 139, Murphy J held that the intended father was a parent of the child on the basis of his biological relationship to the child, and granted leave for the intended mother, who was his spouse, to apply to adopt the child.

[82] The surrogacy legislation does not specify its impact on adoption legislation. The surrogacy legislation does not indicate its intended interrelationship with the Family Law Act provisions relating to parenting orders.

[83] The surrogacy legislation invests state and territory courts with the jurisdiction to make parentage orders. The same courts have jurisdiction to deal with crimes under state and territory law. Most applications for parenting orders under the Family Law Act are heard by the federal Family Court, which lacks subject-matter jurisdiction to deal with state and territory laws.

[84] Family Law Act 1975 (Cth), ss 60CA, 65AA.

the surrogacy legislation is irrelevant to that determination.[85] Likewise, in several adoption cases decided before the current surrogacy legislation was enacted, the court emphasised that the best interests of the child must dominate any policy concern about surrogacy. In *Re D & E*, an application by intended parents to adopt the child born of an altruistic surrogacy arrangement in New South Wales, Bryson J stated:

> I do not regard surrogacy arrangements as an institution which should be encouraged by the law even where, as in this case, there is no commercial aspect of the arrangement.[86]

Even so, his Honour went on to determine that

> [c]onsideration of the welfare and interests of the child in this case outweighs, in an overwhelming way, any consideration that in order to serve public policy and discourage surrogacy arrangements an adoption order should be withheld or the court's response to the application should be modified to accommodate the view that surrogacy arrangements should not be encouraged, or should be discouraged.[87]

C. Commercial Surrogacy—States and Australian Capital Territory

In all Australian jurisdictions except the Northern Territory, various aspects of commercial surrogacy agreements are criminalised. In most jurisdictions, entry into a commercial surrogacy agreement is an offence, and the offence applies to all parties to the agreement.[88] In Queensland, the making and receiving of payments in excess of reimbursement of the surrogate mother's reasonable expenses are also criminalised.[89] In Victoria, the legislation does not criminalise entry into the agreement; the only offence in that state directly related to the surrogacy agreement is the receipt by the surrogate mother of payment for her services in excess of reimbursement.[90] In South Australia, the legislation does not criminalise entry into the surrogacy agreement or the payment or receipt of money under that agreement, but it provides that commercial surrogacy agreements are 'illegal and void'.[91]

The legislation in some jurisdictions is somewhat ambiguous as to the effect of a commercial surrogacy agreement, so far as the surrogate mother's entitlement to recover reasonable expenses is concerned. In three jurisdictions, the agreement

---

[85] Eg *Raines v Curtin* [2007] FamCA 1295, [3]; *Lowe & Barry* [2011] FamCA 625, [23].

[86] *Re D & E* [2000] NSWSC 646, (2000) 26 Fam LR 310, [21]. At the time, there was no legislation directly regulating surrogacy in New South Wales.

[87] *Ibid.* This statement was referred to with approval in the international commercial surrogacy case of *Ellison & Karnchanit* [2012] FamCA 602. See similarly *Re A & B* [2000] NSWSC 640, (2000) 26 Fam LR 317, [28], [52]–[54].

[88] Parentage Act 2004 (ACT), s 41; Surrogacy Act 2010 (NSW), s 8; Surrogacy Act 2010 (Qld), s 56; Surrogacy Act 2012 (Tas), s 40; Surrogacy Act 2008 (WA), s 8.

[89] Surrogacy Act 2010 (Qld), s 57.

[90] Assisted Reproductive Treatment Act 2008 (Vic), s 44(1). See also Surrogacy Contracts Act 1993 (Tas), s 4(4).

[91] Family Relationships Act 1975 (SA), s 10G(1). See similarly Surrogacy Contracts Act 1993 (Tas), s 7.

may be regarded as severable, so that the offensive aspect of the arrangement, under which the intended parents undertook to pay more than reimbursement of the surrogate mother's expenses related to the pregnancy and birth, is severed and the obligation to reimburse the surrogate mother for her expenses remains effective.[92] Even so, the intended parents could certainly not apply for parentage orders because it is a mandatory condition to making parentage orders that the arrangement is not commercial.[93]

i. Criminal Offences by Third Parties to the Surrogacy Arrangement

The surrogacy legislation also criminalises activities of third parties to the surrogacy agreement, particularly those involved in procuring surrogacy agreements, those involved in advertising related to surrogacy and those involved in providing services to assist in achieving a pregnancy in commercial surrogacy arrangements.

Five jurisdictions criminalise procuring or brokering surrogacy arrangements.[94] All seven jurisdictions criminalise advertising in relation to surrogacy.[95] In most jurisdictions it is prohibited to advertise that a person is willing to enter into a surrogacy agreement and that a woman is willing to act as a surrogate.[96] It is also an offence in five jurisdictions to advertise to seek, or attempt to induce, a person to act as a surrogate mother.[97]

Some jurisdictions differentiate advertising for commercial arrangements from advertising relating to altruistic arrangements. In the Australian Capital Territory, the maximum penalty is more severe for advertisements relating to commercial surrogacy than for those relating to altruistic arrangements.[98] New South Wales expressly exempts the advertisement of altruistic surrogacy agreements, but only if

---

[92] Surrogacy Act 2010 (NSW), s 6; Surrogacy Act 2010 (Qld), s 15; Assisted Reproductive Treatment Act 2008 (Vic), s 44(3).

[93] Parentage Act 2004 (ACT), s 24(c); Surrogacy Act 2010 (NSW), s 23; Surrogacy Act 2010 (Qld), s 22(2)(e)(vi); Family Relationships Act 1975 (SA), s 10HA(2)(b)(ix); Surrogacy Act 2012 (Tas), s 16(2)(a)(ii) Status of Children Act 1974 (Vic), s 22(1)(d). This requirement is not expressed in the Western Australian legislation but it is implied from the fact that commercial surrogacy is prohibited: Surrogacy Act 2008 (WA), s 8.

[94] Parentage Act 2004 (ACT), s 42(1) (s 42(2) specifically provides that it is not an offence under s 42(1) to procure someone to enter into a surrogacy agreement if that person intends to be a party to the agreement); Family Relationships Act 1975 (SA), s 10H(a); Surrogacy Act 2012 (Tas), s 41(2) (applies to altruistic as well as commercial arrangements); Surrogacy Act 2008 (WA), s 9(1) (applies to altruistic as well as commercial surrogacy arrangements).

[95] Parentage Act 2004 (ACT), s 43(1); Surrogacy Act 2010 (NSW), s 10(1); Surrogacy Act 2010 (Qld), s 55; Family Relationships Act 1975 (SA), s 10H(c); Surrogacy Act 2012 (Tas), s 41(2); Assisted Reproductive Treatment Act 2008 (Vic), s 45; Surrogacy Act 2008 (WA), s 10.

[96] Parentage Act 2004 (ACT), s 43(1)(b)(iii); Surrogacy Act 2010 (NSW), s 10(1)(a), (c); Surrogacy Act 2010 (Qld), s 55(1)(c), (d); Assisted Reproductive Treatment Act 2008 (Vic), s 45(1)(a); Surrogacy Act 2008 (WA), s 10(c) (this provision applies only to commercial surrogacy).

[97] Parentage Act 2004 (ACT), s 43(1)(a), (b)(i)–(ii); Surrogacy Act 2010 (NSW), s 10(1)(b), (d); Surrogacy Act 2010 (Qld), s 55(1)(a), (b); Assisted Reproductive Treatment Act 2008 (Vic), s 45(1)(b); Surrogacy Act 2008 (WA), s 10(a) (this provision applies only to commercial surrogacy).

[98] Parentage Act 2004 (ACT), s 43(1).

'no fee has been paid for the advertisement'.[99] In Western Australia, the publication of material relating to surrogacy is criminal only so far as commercial surrogacy is concerned.[100] In Queensland, South Australia, Tasmania and Victoria, the offences relating to advertising do not distinguish between commercial and altruistic surrogacy; but in Tasmania, the criminal offences only apply to paid advertising.

The provision of services in order to facilitate a pregnancy as part of a commercial surrogacy arrangement is criminalised in some jurisdictions.[101] In four states, it is prohibited to disclose information relating to surrogacy arrangements.[102]

D. Surrogacy in the Northern Territory

In the Northern Territory, surrogacy is not directly regulated. If the pregnancy results from a fertility procedure, the surrogate mother and her consenting spouse or partner would be regarded as the parents of the child.[103] If the intended parents were related to the child, they might apply to adopt the child.[104] Alternatively, they might apply for parenting orders under the Family Law Act.

It is unclear whether a surrogate mother would be able to enforce the intended parents' agreement to reimburse her expenses in the Northern Territory. It seems unlikely that a commercial surrogacy arrangement would be enforced by the courts in the Northern Territory, given the strength of opposition to commercial surrogacy in the other Australian jurisdictions.

III. Cross-border Surrogacy

The diversity in the regulation of surrogacy within Australia and internationally creates the possibility of a conflict of laws. Cross-border surrogacy appears to be common in Australia.[105] This usually occurs intentionally, when intended parents attempt

---

[99] Surrogacy Act 2010 (NSW), s 10(2).

[100] Surrogacy Act 2008 (WA), s 10.

[101] Surrogacy Act 2010 (Qld), s 58(1) (the provision of 'technical, professional or medical service' with the intention of assisting a person to become pregnant is an offence, if the provider of the service knows that that person is a party to a commercial surrogacy agreement). See similarly Parentage Act 2004 (ACT), s 44; Surrogacy Contracts Act 1993 (Tas), s 5 and Surrogacy Act 2008 (WA), s 11(1). The provision of a service after the woman has become pregnant is not an offence: Surrogacy Act 2010 (Qld), s 58(2); Surrogacy Act 2008 (WA), s 11(2).

[102] Surrogacy Act 2010 (NSW), s 52(1); Surrogacy Act 2010 (Qld), s 53(2); Surrogacy Act 2012 (Tas), s 42 (prohibiting reporting of surrogacy applications); Status of Children Act 1974 (Vic), s 33(2).

[103] Status of Children Act 1978 (NT), s 5D(1). This presumption is irrebuttable: *ibid*, s 5D(2).

[104] The legislation allows biological parents and relatives of the child to apply for adoption: Adoption of Children Act 1994 (NT), s 15(1).

[105] Twenty-one of the 31 published cases involve cross-border surrogacy (67.7%). International arrangements (18, or 58%) are more common than inter-state arrangements (only three of 31 cases). Millbank found that 44 of 69 arrangements reported in the media were cross-border cases (63.7%), and that 35 of those were international cases (50.7%): Millbank, above n 4, 191.

to avail themselves of a more attractive regime than that which applies in their home jurisdiction, usually by entering into a commercial surrogacy agreement in another country with a surrogate mother who conceives and bears the child in that other country. It may also occur incidentally, as a consequence of population mobility.[106] In some altruistic cases, the parties happen to live in different jurisdictions.[107]

A. Parentage Orders in Cross-border Cases

The surrogacy legislation in the mainland states and the Australian Capital Territory does not clearly indicate the circumstances in which the provisions relating to parentage orders are intended to apply, but in every jurisdiction the legislation requires various connections to the jurisdiction in which parentage orders are sought. In addition to the requirement that the intended parents must be resident in the jurisdiction, three jurisdictions require that the child must have been conceived as a result of a procedure carried out in that jurisdiction,[108] and in most jurisdictions other requirements effectively limit the scope of the legislation to local surrogacy arrangements.[109] The legislation in New South Wales and Tasmania explicitly contemplates that the child may not have been born within the state.[110]

In three states, the courts have a discretion to relax the requirement that the intended parents are resident in the state in exceptional circumstances, if that would be consistent with the child's best interests.[111] This would permit the courts

---

[106] This has occurred in several published cases. In *W: Re Adoption* (1998) 23 Fam LR 538 (NSWSC), the intended parents had entered into a commercial surrogacy agreement in California, where they lived at the time, and subsequently relocated with the child to New South Wales, where they applied to adopt the child under New South Wales legislation. In *Rusken & Jenner* [2009] FamCA 282, the intended parents had entered into a commercial surrogacy arrangement in South Africa, and subsequently relocated with the child to Australia. The intended father later applied for parenting orders as against the intended mother.

[107] The parties in the leading surrogacy case, *Re Evelyn* (1998) 23 Fam LR 53 (Fam), lived in different Australian states. There are other published cases involving altruistic surrogacy in which the parties were from different Australian states: *AP v RD* [2011] NSWSC 1389 (the first published application for parentage orders under the New South Wales surrogacy legislation); *Lowe & Barry* [2011] FamCA 625 (an application for parenting orders under the federal Family Law Act).

[108] Parentage Act 2004 (ACT), s 24(a); Family Relationships Act 1975 (SA), s 10HB(2)(c); Status of Children Act 1974 (Vic), s 20(1)(a).

[109] In Western Australia, the requirement that the Western Australian Reproductive Treatment Council pre-approved the arrangement effectively limits the scope of the legislation to local surrogacy arrangements: Surrogacy Act 2008 (WA), s 16(1). In South Australia, the surrogacy agreement must record the parties' intention to apply for parentage orders under local legislation: Family Relationships Act 1975 (SA), s 10HA(2)(b)(x). In some jurisdictions, counselling and legal advice must be provided by local practitioners, eg Surrogacy Act 2010 (NSW), s 36(1); Surrogacy Act 2010 (Qld), ss 19, 30(1); Family Relationships Act 1975 (SA), ss 10HA(1), 10HA(2)(b)(vi), 10HA(2)(b)(vii), 10HA(3), 10HA(4); Status of Children Act 1974 (Vic), s 23(3). These requirements will effectively exclude non-local arrangements.

[110] Surrogacy Act 2010 (NSW), s 38(2) (referring to registration of birth of a child born outside Australia), s 50(1) (referring to registration of birth of a child born in another Australian state or territory). See similarly Surrogacy Act 2012 (Tas), ss 35, 37(2)(b).

[111] Surrogacy Act 2010 (NSW), ss 18(2), 32; Surrogacy Act 2010 (Qld), ss 22(2)(g)(ii), 23(2); Surrogacy Act 2012 (Tas), ss 16(2)(j)(ii), 16(3)(a).

to grant parentage orders in some cross-border cases. In the other states and the Australian Capital Territory, the courts do not have any flexibility in relaxing the nexus requirements and would therefore not be able to grant parentage orders in some cross-border situations.

B. Parental Status in Cross-border Cases

The rules relating to parental status will remain relevant in surrogacy cases in which the requirements for parentage orders cannot be satisfied. In most juris-dictions, the relevant presumptions as to parental status when a child has been born following a fertility procedure are stated to apply irrespective of where those procedures occurred and irrespective of where the child was born.[112] The presumptions that arise from registration of a person as a parent in a birth reg-ister and from acknowledgments of paternity also apply to birth registers in, and acknowledgments made under the law of, proclaimed foreign countries.[113]

The courts have considered the issue of parental status in some international surrogacy cases in which intended parents have applied for parenting orders. The courts usually do not explicitly refer to choice of law for parental status. The Family Law Act states that when a court exercises jurisdiction under the Act, it must apply the Act.[114] This has been applied as a choice-of-law rule in favour of the law of the forum in a case concerning parental status which did not involve surrogacy.[115] In applications made under Australian legislation, the court might be expected to determine the meaning of the term 'parent' according to that legis-lation.[116] The courts sometimes take the view that it is not necessary to determine parental status in applications for parenting orders, and therefore have refrained from making such a determination.[117] When the issue is addressed, the courts

---

[112] Parentage Act 2004 (ACT), s 11(7); Status of Children Act 1978 (Qld), s 14(1); Family Relationships Act 1975 (SA), s 10B(1); Status of Children Act 1974 (Tas), s 10A(1); Artificial Conception Act 1985 (WA), s 4(1). The New South Wales and Northern Territory legislation apply irrespective of where the person was born and whether that person's parents have ever been domiciled in the jurisdiction, but do not specifically refer to the place the procedure occurred: Status of Children Act 1996 (NSW), s 4(1); Status of Children Act 1978 (NT), s 2A. The Victorian legislation states that the provisions apply irrespective of where the procedure occurred, but does not explicitly state that they apply irrespective of the place of birth: Status of Children Act 1974 (Vic), s 10B.

[113] Eg Family Law Act 1975 (Cth), ss 69R and 69T, applied in *Brianna v Brianna* (2009) 43 Fam LR 309.

[114] Family Law Act 1975 (Cth), s 42(1). This is subject to s 42(2), which is not presently relevant (it permits the court to apply foreign law if that would be consistent with common law choice of law rules, or the choice of law rules in the Marriage Act 1961 (Cth)).

[115] *Brianna v Brianna* (2010) 43 Fam LR 309, [65].

[116] *Re Mark (an application relating to parental responsibility)* [2003] FamCA 822, (2003) 31 Fam LR 162, [23].

[117] The courts take the view that is not necessary to do so because any person who has an interest in the child's welfare is able to apply for parenting orders, and intended parents satisfy this requirement: Family Law Act 1975 (Cth), s 65C. In one of the few extended discussions of parental status in an inter-national surrogacy case, Brown J carefully considered whether the biological and intended father of the child who was born in the US pursuant to a commercial surrogacy agreement, was the parent of that

usually apply Australian law in determining the status of the Australian intended father.[118] However, in some international surrogacy cases the court has referred to foreign law without explaining why it is relevant.[119] In several cases, the court has concluded that the Australian intended father is a parent of the child, even though this is not consistent with Australian law.[120]

i. Parental Status in Citizenship and Immigration Law

The citizenship and immigration status of children born in surrogacy arrangements outside Australia depends on their relationship with the intended parents. Children born outside Australia can apply for citizenship by descent if one of their parents was an Australian citizen at the time they were born.[121] 'Parent' is not defined in the relevant provisions of the citizenship legislation,[122] and its meaning in the context of that Act is not necessarily the same as under other federal, state and territory law.[123] Some applications for Australian citizenship for children

---

child under the Family Law Act 1975 (Cth): *Re Mark (an application relating to parental responsibility)* [2003] FamCA 822, (2003) 31 Fam LR 162. Ultimately, her Honour concluded that it was unnecessary to make a positive finding on that point, because the Act permits a person concerned with the welfare of the child to apply for parenting orders, although she considered that it was consistent with the ordinary meaning of the term 'parent' to find that the child's biological and social father was his parent: *ibid*, [60], [81]. Strictly speaking parental status remains relevant, because in making a parenting order, the child's welfare is the paramount consideration: Family Law Act 1975 (Cth), s 60CA. One of two primary considerations in determining what is in the child's best interests is 'the benefit to the child of having a meaningful relationship with both of the child's parents': *ibid*, s 60CC(2)(a). The Act requires the court to apply a rebuttable presumption that 'it is in the best interests of the child for the child's parents to have equal shared parental responsibility for the child': *ibid*, s 61DA(1).

[118] *Re Mark (an application relating to parental responsibility)* [2003] FamCA 822, (2003) 31 Fam LR 162, [103]; *Wilkie & Mirkja* [2010] FamCA 667, [6]; *Dudley & Chedi* [2011] FamCA 502, [27]; *Findlay & Punyawong* [2011] FamCA 503, [18]; *Gough & Kaur* [2012] FamCA 79, [7]. See similarly *Johnson & Chompunut* [2011] FamCA 505, [14]–[15].

[119] *Dudley & Chedi* [2011] FamCA 502, [25]; *Dennis & Pradchaphet* [2011] FamCA 123, [20] (Stevenson J noting that the Thai surrogate mother was the child's mother 'pursuant to Thai law'). In these cases, there was no conflict between Australian and foreign law on the issue of the status of the surrogate mother, both legal systems treating the surrogate mother as the child's parent.

[120] In most Australian jurisdictions, the biological father of the child is conclusively presumed *not* to be the child's father. See above n 17. In *McQuinn & Shure* [2011] FamCA 139, [19], [23], the Australian intended father, who was the biological father, was held to be the father of the child. See also *O'Connor & Kasemsarn* [2010] FamCA 987, [21] and *Collins v Tangtoi* [2010] FamCA 878, [16]. Cf *Gough & Kaur* [2012] FamCA 79, [7], in which Macmillan J held that the Australian intended father, who was the biological father, was not a parent for the purposes of the Family Law Act 1975 (Cth).

[121] Australian Citizenship Act 2007 (Cth), s 16(2).

[122] The term 'responsible parent' is defined (*ibid*, s 6), but that term is inapplicable to determining entitlement to citizenship under s 16(2).

[123] *H v Minister for Immigration and Citizenship* (2010) 188 FCR 393, [2010] FCAFC 119. In this case, the Full Court of the Federal Court held (*ibid*, [127]): 'There is nothing in the legislative text, or the legislative structure of the Citizenship Act that requires the court to conclude that, in the specific context of s 16(2) [of that Act], the word "parent" can only mean biological parent. Indeed, these considerations indicate that the better view is that the word "parent" in s 16(2) has the meaning it bears in contemporary English usage.' They stated (*ibid*, [129]): 'Typically, parentage is not just a matter of biology but of intense commitment to another, expressed by acknowledging that other person as

born overseas in surrogacy arrangements on the basis of their biological father's citizenship have been successful, whereas others have not.[124]

The surrogacy legislation does not directly address the effect of a parentage order on a child's citizenship status. The Citizenship Act requires that the child must be the child of an Australian citizen at the time of birth.[125] The surrogacy legislation does not clearly indicate whether it has retrospective effect, in transferring parental status to the intended parents, such that the status applies at the time of birth. Again, there is a diversity in the legislation of the different jurisdictions. For example, the wording of the Queensland legislation suggests that a parentage order has only prospective effect.[126] The New South Wales legislation suggests, inconsistently, that the order has both a prospective and a retrospective effect.[127]

If the child is not regarded as being an Australian citizen, the Hague Convention on Intercountry Adoptions, to which Australia is a party, will apply to any application to adopt the child.[128]

The Migration Regulations permit a visa to be granted to a 'dependent child' of an Australian citizen or permanent resident.[129] The Migration Act's non-exclusive definition of 'child' includes the meaning that word has under the Family Law Act.[130] Biological parents are apparently taken to satisfy this requirement under the Migration Regulations, even though under Australian law, the biological parents are conclusively presumed not to be the child's parents.[131]

C. Extra-territorial Effect of the Surrogacy Offences

In three jurisdictions, the surrogacy legislation incorporates nexus provisions in relation to the criminal offences.[132] In the Australian Capital Territory, New

---

one's own and treating him or her as one's own.' The latter interpretation is likely to be favourable to Australian intended parents in international surrogacy cases.

[124] In *Cadet & Scribe* [2007] FamCA 1498, [5], the court noted that the child, born in a commercial surrogacy arrangement in the US, obtained Australian citizenship by descent from his biological father. See also *Ronalds & Victor* [2011] FamCA 389, [2] (twins born in India) and *Re Mark (an application relating to parental responsibilities)* [2003] FamCA 822, (2003) 31 Fam LR 162, [14] (child born in the US). In a number of cases where children were born in Thailand, the court has noted that the Australian Embassy in Bangkok refused to process applications for citizenship by descent unless the applicant could produce a court order recognising that the surrogate mother has relinquished her parental rights: *Collins & Tangtoi* [2010] FamCA 878, [10]; *O'Connor & Kasemsarn* [2010] FamCA 987, [14]. See also *Dennis & Pradchaphet* [2011] FamCA 123, [6].

[125] Citizenship Act 2007 (Cth), s 16(2).

[126] Surrogacy Act 2010 (Qld), s 39(2).

[127] Surrogacy Act 2010 (NSW), s 39(1) (prospective), (2)(a) (retrospective).

[128] Eg Adoption Act 2000 (NSW), s 31.

[129] Migration Regulations 1994 (Cth), Sch 2, cl 101.21. The definition of 'dependent child' in the Migration Regulations does not further define the term 'child': Migration Regulations 1994 (Cth), reg 1.03.

[130] Migration Act 1958 (Cth), s 5CA(1).

[131] See above n 17.

[132] In the ACT and New South Wales, the surrogacy legislation states that these nexus provisions operate in addition to the general nexus provisions in the criminal law: Parentage Act 2004 (ACT),

South Wales and Queensland, the offences apply to local residents when they are acting outside the jurisdiction.[133] One purpose of these provisions is to prevent the exploitation of surrogate mothers in developing countries.[134] In the other jurisdictions, the general rules of the criminal law would be applied to determine the scope of operation of the legislation.

D. Cross-border Surrogacy Cases in Australian Courts

Most of the published surrogacy cases concern applications by intended parents to the federal Family Court for parenting orders under the federal Family Law Act, and in almost all of these cases there was a cross-border element.[135] Parenting orders have been made in several cases in which the surrogacy agreement was prohibited by state law.[136] Similarly, leave to adopt was granted in one international case in which the arrangement was prohibited by state law.[137] There is a significant tension between the dominant policy requiring decisions to be made in the child's best interests in most applications relating to children's welfare, and the policy of controlling altruistic surrogacy and prohibiting commercial surrogacy.[138]

There are only three published cases of intra-Australian surrogacy. In these cases, the cross-border element was irrelevant. Two cases were applications for parenting orders under the federal Family Law Act, so there was no conflict of laws.[139] The third case is one of only three published cases involving an

s 45(2); Surrogacy Act 2010 (NSW), s 11(1). Those general nexus provisions state that the law applies to acts done within the state and to acts done outside the state that have effects within the state: Criminal Code 2002 (ACT), s 64(1); Crimes Act 1900 (NSW), s 10C. Similar nexus provisions exist in other states' criminal law and would be applicable to crimes under the surrogacy legislation, eg Criminal Law Consolidation Act 1935 (SA), s 5G(2).

[133] Parentage Act 2004 (ACT), s 45(1); Surrogacy Act 2010 (NSW), s 11(2) (stating that the offences also apply to persons domiciled in the state); Surrogacy Act 2010 (Qld), s 54(b).

[134] Standing Committee of Attorneys-General, Australian Health Ministers' Conference, Community and Disability Services Ministers' Conference, Joint Working Group, *A Proposal for a National Model to Harmonise Regulation of Surrogacy* (January 2009), p 14; Ms Burney, Surrogacy Bill 2010, NSW Legislative Assembly, *Hansard*, 10 November 2010, p 27, 583.

[135] Of the 20 published cases in which the intended parents have sought parenting orders in surrogacy cases, 18 were cross-border cases. Sixteen of those cases involved the intended parents travelling outside Australia and only one of the international cases was an altruistic arrangement. Of the 18 cross-border cases, two were intra-Australian cases and both of these were altruistic.

[136] Eg *Re Mark (an application relating to parental responsibilities)* [2003] FamCA 822, (2003) 31 Fam LR 162, [94]; *Dudley & Chedi* [2011] FamCA 502; *Findlay & Punyawong* [2011] FamCA 503; *Ellison & Karnchanit* [2012] FamCA 602. These cases all involved international commercial surrogacy.

[137] *McQuinn & Shure* [2011] FamCA 139. See also *W: Re Adoption* (1998) 23 Fam LR 538, 543, involving an international commercial surrogacy situation, in which Windeyer J stated that in determining whether to make an order for adoption, 'the interests and welfare of each individual child ... are paramount. It is not the role of the court to make its decisions in order to act as a warning for others not to enter into surrogacy arrangements.'

[138] M Keyes, 'Cross-border Surrogacy Agreements' (2012) 26 *Australian Journal of Family Law* 28.

[139] In two cases, the applications were for parenting orders under the federal Family Law Act, so there was no conflict of laws: *Re Evelyn* (1998) 23 Fam LR 53; *Lowe & Barry* [2011] FamCA 625.

application for parentage orders under the surrogacy legislation.[140] In that case, the child was born in Victoria but the intended parents resided in New South Wales, which was where the application for parentage orders was made under New South Wales legislation.[141] Justice Brereton noted that the child was born outside the jurisdiction,[142] but that factor had no effect on his Honour's decision.

There is only one published case of international altruistic surrogacy.[143] In *McQuinn & Shure*,[144] intended parents who were resident in Queensland entered into an altruistic surrogacy arrangement with a surrogate mother who was resident in Alberta, Canada. The arrangement appears to have been legal in Alberta but was certainly criminalised in Queensland at the time.[145] In granting leave to the intended parents to apply for adoption, Murphy J of the Family Court did not refer to the fact that the intended parents' act in entering into a surrogacy arrangement was criminalised at the time.

Australian intended parents are increasingly engaging in international commercial surrogacy arrangements.[146] Typically, the Australian intended parents enter into commercial arrangements in other countries, where commercial surrogacy is either permitted or not policed, with a surrogate mother in that country. The surrogacy arrangement is usually gestational, and the intended father is typically the biological father. The child is born in the other country, and the intended parents then return to Australia with the child.

The most common relief sought by intended parents in Australian courts where the child has been born outside Australia is for parenting orders under the Family Law Act.[147] The material before the court generally indicates that the safeguards provided in the Australian legislation in relation to altruistic surrogacy are lacking.[148] The Australian courts do not even require evidence as to the surrogate mother's consent to the parenting orders being made. In most cases, the intended parents tendered evidence showing the surrogate mother's consent to the orders, but there are a number of cases in which judges have made adverse comments about the lack of participation of foreign surrogates in the proceedings in the

---

[140] There were only three published cases as at January 2013; see above, n 76.

[141] *AP v RD* [2011] NSWSC 1389.

[142] *Ibid*, [1].

[143] In one of the 18 international cases, it is not clear from the judgment whether the arrangement was altruistic or commercial.

[144] *McQuinn & Shure* [2011] FamCA 139.

[145] Surrogate Parenthood Act 1988 (Qld), ss 2 (definition of 'prescribed contract'), 3(1)(c).

[146] Of the 18 published cases which involved international arrangements, four were decided before 2010 (one each in 1998, 2003, 2007 and 2009); 14 have been decided since 2010 (four in 2010, eight in 2011 and two in 2012). Only one of the 18 cases was altruistic. Overseas clinics and agencies reported a trebling in the number of births in surrogacy arrangements involving Australian intended parents between 2008 and 2011: Australian Families Through Gestational Surrogacy, 'Statistics on Babies Born to Australians' (2011), cited in Millbank , above n 4, 192.

[147] Of the 18 international cases, 16 were applications for parenting orders. One was an adoption application, and one was an application for leave to adopt.

[148] *Dudley & Chedi* [2011] FamCA 502, [18]; *Findlay & Punyawong* [2011] FamCA 503, [16]; *Hubert & Juntasa* [2011] FamCA 504, [12].

Australian courts. In *Ronalds & Victor*, substituted service on the Indian surrogate mother had been ordered. Justice Dessau stated that the surrogate mother and her partner 'have chosen not only not to participate by attending, but also not to participate with any contact at all with the Court or with the [intended parents].'[149] In *Wilkie & Mirkja*, the Indian surrogate mother could not be served with process because she had given a non-existent address in the surrogacy contract.[150] Justice Cronin waived the requirements of service and made parenting orders in favour of the intended parents, even though the surrogate mother had no notice of the proceedings and there was no evidence that she consented to the arrangements. In *Edmore v Bala*, Cronin J noted the

> unusual feature of this particular application … that it has been served on the respondent [Indian surrogate mother] who I suspect, from looking at the signature, has very little knowledge of what this [application] is really all about.

Even so, his Honour relied on the fact that the birth mother had not appeared and that nothing had been filed on her behalf in making the parenting orders sought by the Australian intended parents.[151] In some cases, the nature of the evidence of the surrogate mother's consent to the parenting orders ought to raise grave concerns. For example, in three cases, the judge noted without comment that the material translated to the Thai surrogate mother included her own affidavit.[152]

Rusken & Jenner is the only published decision in which the foreign surrogate mother later resiled from her agreement to relinquish the child.[153] That case principally concerned parenting orders that should be made as between the intended parents of the child, who were from South Africa and had entered into a surrogacy arrangement there. After the child was born, the intended parents moved to Australia with the child. The surrogate mother, who was from South Africa, intervened in the proceedings, seeking an order that the child should be returned to her in South Africa, on the basis of her right of custody over the child under South African law. Justice Bell emphasised that the surrogate mother was paid for her services, and rejected her claim that the child should be returned to her on the basis that there was no evidence that this would benefit the child.[154]

The intended parents in cross-border surrogacy arrangements may attempt to adopt the child under Australian law. In *W: Re Adoption*, the intended parents entered into a commercial surrogacy in California, where they lived at the time. That arrangement was legal in California. They later moved to New South Wales and sought to adopt the child under New South Wales legislation. The relevant government department objected to the intended parents' application to adopt

---

[149] *Ronalds & Victor* [2011] FamCA 389, [6].
[150] *Wilkie & Mirkja* [2010] FamCA 667.
[151] *Edmore v Bala* [2011] FamCA 731, [2].
[152] *Dennis & Pradchaphet* [2011] FamCA 123, [11]; *Collins & Tangtoi* [2010] FamCA 878, [6]; *Ellison & Karnchanit* [2012] FamCA 602, [116].
[153] *Rusken & Jenner* [2009] FamCA 282.
[154] *Ibid*, [44]–[45].

the child on several bases, including that the arrangement would have breached the New South Wales adoption legislation if it had been entered into in New South Wales. Justice Windeyer rejected this concern, noting that the agreement was made in California, and that it was not 'entered into deliberately for the purposes of circumventing the law of New South Wales'.[155] His Honour seems to have regarded the application of Californian law as legitimate on the basis of the intended parents' residence in California at the time of entry into the agreement.[156] In *McQuinn & Shure*, the child was born in an altruistic surrogacy arrangement in Alberta, Canada. Justice Murphy granted leave to apply for adoption to the intended parents, who were from Queensland, relying on the genetic connection between the intended father and the child, which he took to create a step-parent relationship between the child and the intended mother.[157]

The surrogacy legislation in three jurisdictions specifically states that the criminal offences relating to commercial surrogacy have an extra-territorial application.[158] The possible illegality of the intended parents' acts under local surrogacy legislation has been noted in some cases, but usually the court has stated that the possible illegality of the arrangement was irrelevant to its decision about parenting orders.[159] In four decisions handed down in June 2011, Watts J took a stricter attitude to this issue. In all four cases, Australian intended parents had entered into commercial arrangements in Thailand and sought parenting orders in the Family Court. The intended parents were Queensland residents in two cases, and New South Wales residents in the other two cases. Justice Watts noted that the conduct of the intended parents who were Queensland residents appeared to breach Queensland criminal law,[160] and he directed that a copy of his reasons be conveyed to the Queensland Director of Public Prosecutions.[161] Nonetheless, he made the parenting orders sought by the intended parents, noting that the paramount consideration was the children's best interests, which were served by making the orders.[162] The New South Wales surrogacy legislation in force when the surrogacy agreements were entered into in the other two cases criminalised entry into commercial surrogacy agreements, and this applied to acts done outside the jurisdiction which had effects within the jurisdiction.[163] His Honour held that it was 'not clear that it could be said that the offence [of entry into an agreement]

---

[155] *W: Re Adoption* (1998) 23 Fam LR 538, 542.

[156] (1998) 23 Fam LR 538, 543.

[157] *McQuinn & Shure* [2011] FamCA 139.

[158] See above, section III.C.

[159] See the cases cited above, n 136.

[160] At the time the surrogacy agreements were entered into, the relevant legislation was the Surrogate Parenthood Act 1988 (Qld). Its provisions were not materially different from those of the current Surrogacy Act 2010 (Qld), so far as the criminalisation of commercial surrogacy and the extraterritorial effect of the offences were concerned.

[161] *Dudley & Chedi* [2011] FamCA 502, [44]; *Findlay & Punyawong* [2011] FamCA 503, [32].

[162] *Dudley & Chedi*, [38], [43]; *Findlay & Punyawong*, [23], [31].

[163] *Hubert & Juntasa* [2011] FamCA 504 and *Johnson & Chompunut* [2011] FamCA 505, considering Assisted Reproductive Technology Act 2007 (NSW), s 43, the scope of which was determined by Crimes Act 1900 (NSW), s 10CA.

has an effect in the State of New South Wales' and that it was unlikely that the intended parents had committed a crime under New South Wales law.[164]

In all four cases, Watts J declined to make a finding that the intended father was a parent, because of the illegality of the surrogacy arrangement under Queensland law[165] and on the basis of the public policy against commercial surrogacy in New South Wales.[166] Millbank suggested that the strict approach taken by Watts J in these cases was likely to cause Australian intended families who had engaged in commercial surrogacy outside Australia not to present to court.[167] The number of cases decided by the courts has declined noticeably since these four decisions were handed down.[168]

IV. Conclusion

Australian intended parents are increasingly seeking to access surrogacy arrangements. The legal response to surrogacy in Australia is partial and chaotic. The surrogacy legislation legalises altruistic surrogacy, subject to a number of requirements. Commercial surrogacy is widely prohibited, but this prohibition appears to be ineffective in preventing Australian intended parents from entering into commercial agreements abroad. It seems that the Australian surrogacy legislation is therefore largely ineffective. Intended parents have relied on other areas of law, especially federal family law, to gain recognition of their parental responsibilities. The lack of coordination between different areas of law creates uncertainty for the parties and their lawyers, and difficulties for courts in dealing with cases involving surrogacy.

Cross-border surrogacy appears to be more common than local surrogacy in Australia. In parliamentary and law reform commission reports that led to the enactment of the current legislation, the position of intended parents who have travelled outside their home jurisdiction in order to access surrogacy arrangements is often noted sympathetically.[169] Notwithstanding this recognition, the

---

[164] *Hubert & Juntasa* [2011] FamCA 504, [13]; *Johnson & Chompunut* [2011] FamCA 505, [12].

[165] *Dudley & Chedi* [2011] FamCA 502, [32]; *Findlay & Punyawong* [2011] FamCA 503, [20]. Cf *Ellison & Karnchanit* [2012] FamCA 602, in which Ryan J disagreed with Watts J's decision in *Dudley & Chedi* not to make a finding of parentage on public policy grounds.

[166] *Hubert & Juntasa* [2011] FamCA 504, [18]; *Johnson & Chompunut* [2011] FamCA 505, [18].

[167] Millbank, above n 4, 206.

[168] The number of cases was small until 2010, when there were four cases published. In 2011, eight cases were published. Since these four cases were handed down in June 2011 (19 months before this chapter was written), only three cases have been published.

[169] See NSW Legislative Council, Standing Committee on Law and Justice, *Legislation on altruistic surrogacy in NSW*, Report No 38 (May 2009), p 68; Queensland Parliament, Investigation into Altruistic Surrogacy Committee, *Report* (October 2008), p 11; Parliament of South Australia, *Inquiry into Gestational Surrogacy*, 26th Report of the Social Development Committee (2007), pp 27–28, 31, 63; Parliament of Tasmania, Legislative Council Select Committee, *Report on Surrogacy* (No 21, 2008),

surrogacy legislation does not clearly or effectively address cross-border situations. The priority that Family Court judges are required to give to the best interests of the child, in applications for parenting orders, has had the consequence of subverting the prohibition of commercial surrogacy. Urgent consideration needs to be given to improving the effectiveness of the regulation of surrogacy in Australia, especially in relation to cross-border arrangements.

---

pp 21–22; Western Australia Legislative Assembly Select Committee on the Human Reproductive Technology Act 1991, *Report* (Parliament of Western Australia, 1999), pp 243, 255.

3

Belgium

GERD VERSCHELDEN AND JINSKE VERHELLEN

I. Introduction

A. Absence of Specific Legislation on Surrogacy

Belgium currently[1] lacks specific legislation concerning surrogacy. Domestic substantive (family or medical) law does not regulate surrogacy, but Belgian private international law rules provide general mechanisms to regulate surrogacy issues (see below sections III.B. and IV.A.ii.a.).

Pending the adoption of appropriate legislation, one can rely to some extent on existing case law. At the end of the 1980s, case law was created with regard to the full adoption of children born through surrogacy. At the beginning of the twenty-first century, a number of parentage cases were brought to light and, more recently, there was a sharp increase in the number of cases involving issues of private international law.

i. Ethical Admissibility of the Phenomenon

Mid-2004, the Belgian Advisory Committee on Bio-ethics launched its opinion concerning pregnancy for another person (surrogacy).[2] This opinion was unique in the history of the Committee—notorious for its lack of conclusiveness—because, in spite of its moral polyphony, it was, for once, unequivocal as to the desirability of legal regulation. According to this Committee, pregnancy for another person is in principle ethically permissible, and needs to be regulated by law at both the Federal and Community levels.[3]

---

[1] This national report was finalised at the end of January 2012.

[2] Opinion no 30 *dd.* 5 July 2004, available only in French, 'relatif à la gestation-pour-autrui (mères porteuses)' and in Dutch 'betreffende zwangerschap-voor-een-ander (draagmoederschap)' at <www.health.belgium.be>.

[3] *Ibid*, p 24 *juncto* p 34. Belgium is a federal State, composed of Communities and Regions (Art 1, Belgian Constitution). Although justice is a federal matter, the Communities are (also) competent for personal matters, such as, for instance, adoption. Belgium comprises three Communities: the Flemish (Dutch-speaking) Community, the French Community and the German-speaking Community.

ii. Towards a Legal Framework for Surrogacy

At the beginning of 2012, various bills addressing surrogacy were discussed in the Belgian Federal Parliament, for the most part in the Senate and some also in the Chamber of Representatives.[4] A former bill aiming at the prohibition of every form of surrogacy[5] was not reintroduced. The actual bills range from straightforward punishment of the sale of children or 'commercial surrogacy',[6] including the publicity and mediation involved,[7] right up to legal regulation of (certain types of) surrogacy, involving modification of the law on affiliation[8] or a combination of the affiliation and adoption laws.[9]

None of the above-mentioned bills shows a real interest from the legislative side in the problems of private international law. A substantial (critical) report by the Council of State on a large number of earlier bills concerning surrogacy[10] strikingly illustrates the legislator's past failure to create a legal statute for surrogacy, which was mainly due to the lack of a global view on the issue.

iii. Recent Attention on the Cross-border Aspects of Surrogacy

Until recently, the Belgian legislator merely focused on the domestic regulation of surrogacy, without paying any attention to cross-border elements. As a result of the huge media exposure of a number of international cases that also involved Belgian citizens, the legislator's focus has been somewhat broadened. For example, a proposal for a resolution has been submitted to the Chamber of Representatives with regard to the international legal regulation of surrogacy, requesting, among other things, that the Belgian Government play a pioneer role in dealing with the issue of surrogacy on the international scene, for example by putting the issue on the agenda of the Council of the European Union, while at the same time urging the European Commission to take initiatives for a European ban on commercial surrogacy.[11] It is noteworthy that this proposal for a resolution mentions the

---

[4] All legislative documents are available in pdf-format (French-Dutch) at <www.senate.be> or <www.lachambre.be>.

[5] Proposition de loi (Nyssens, CdH) interdisant la maternité de substitution et le recours aux mères porteuses, Chamber 2007-08, no 52-0170/001 (4 October 2007).

[6] See section VII. below, 'Payments in Surrogacy'.

[7] See section VIII, below, 'Advertising'.

[8] Proposition de loi-Defraigne (MR) relative aux mères porteuses, Senate 2010, no 5-160/1 (23 September 2010); Proposition de loi-Mahoux (PS) relative à la maternité pour autrui, Senate 2010, no 5-236/1 (6 October 2010); Proposition de loi (Temmerman et Swennen, sp.a) portant organisation des centres de maternité de substitution, Senate 2010-11, no 5-929/1 (5 April 2011), also introduced into the Chamber (by Vanlerberghe *c.s.*, sp.a), Chamber 2010-11, no 53-1453/001 (12 May 2011).

[9] Proposition de loi (Tommelein *c.s.*, Open Vld) réglementant la maternité de substitution, Senate 2010, no 5-130/1 (9 September 2010).

[10] Opinions no 39.474/AG, 39.475/AG, 39.476/AG, 39.477/AG, 39.478/AG and 39.525/AG, Senate 2005-06, no 3-417/3, 93 pages (14 February 2006).

[11] Proposition de résolution concernant la réglementation internationale de la maternité de substitution, Senate 2010-11, no 5-1075/1 (9 June 2011).

European and not the global level, by not referring, for instance, to the Hague Conference on Private International Law.

The vacuum in Belgian substantive law does not safeguard the Belgian legal system from foreign surrogacy arrangements. The Belgian authorities are aware of this, as appears, for instance, from the travel advice given on the website of the Ministry of Foreign Affairs, where one reads for Ukraine:

> More and more Ukrainian hospitals offer surrogacy services. These services are completely legal in Ukraine, but we strongly advise against using them as there is a legal vacuum on this issue in Belgium. It is essential to consult a Belgian lawyer beforehand.[12]

The websites of the Belgian embassies in Ukraine and India also refer to this legal vacuum and the consequences this might have for the legal parenthood of Belgian commissioning parents. For India one reads:

> Belgian citizens who wish to approach a surrogate mother in India, have no assurance that their father- or motherhood will be recognised in Belgium—even when they respect the local rule. There is also no guarantee that a travel document will be issued to the child. ... We wish to remind you that, in view of the problems Belgian citizens may encounter by choosing surrogacy, the possibility of adoption is provided for in Belgian law and thus should be considered as an alternative.[13]

Recent case law in Belgium indicates an increase in not only the number of cross-border surrogacy cases, but also their variety. Table 1 below shows this variety in only five recent cases.

Also in the scientific community there has been an increased interest in the legal regulation of surrogacy. Ongoing PhD research (Ms Liesbet Pluym, Ghent University) aims at creating a legal statute for surrogacy in Belgium, reducing the risk of surrogacy tourism in Belgium as much as possible. The research project, entitled 'Family Law Regulation of Surrogacy in Belgium', focuses on a double perspective: domestic family law and private international law.[14]

For this chapter, the authors of the Belgian report opted to unite their efforts and to provide an overall picture using an integrated approach, starting from their own field of specialisation—Belgian substantive family law (Verschelden[15]) and Belgian private international law (Verhellen[16]).

---

[12] See <www.diplomatie.belgium.be> (authors' own translation).

[13] See <www.diplomatie.be/newdelhinl> (authors' own translation).

[14] This four-year research project (supervisor G Verschelden) started in 2011, funded by the Special Research Fund of Ghent University (BOF—Bijzonder OnderzoeksFonds). The dissertation will be written in Dutch: 'Een familierechtelijk statuut voor draagmoederschap in België'. All suggestions, comments and news on the issue will be greatly appreciated by the researcher at <lbpluym.pluym@ugent.be>.

[15] See also G Verschelden, 'Pleidooi voor een familierechtelijke regeling van draagmoederschap in België', *Tijdschrift voor Privaatrecht* 2011, vol 4, 1421–1510.

[16] See also J Verhellen, 'Intercountry surrogacy: a comment on recent Belgian cases', *Nederlands Internationaal Privaatrecht* 2011, vol 4, 657–62; and J Verhellen, 'Draagmoederschap en de grenzen van het Belgische IPR', *Tijdschrift voor Privaatrecht* 2011, vol 4, 1511–62.

Table 1: Cross-border Surrogacy Cases

Case	Place of birth	Nationality		Genetic links					Parent(s) in birth certificate			
		SM[1]	CP	SM	CM	CF	Egg donor	Sperm donor	CM & CF	CF & CF	CF & SM	CF no mother
H&E (2008)[2]	Ukraine	Ukr	Belgium			X			X			
M&M (2010)[3]	California	USA	Belgium		X	X	X (?)			X		
C (2010)[4]	India	India	Belgium			X	X					X
Samuel (2011)[5]	Ukraine	Ukr	Belgium	X		X					X	
AM&ND (2011)[6]	India	India	Belgium			X	X					X

Notes

[1] Abbreviations used: SM (surrogate mother), CP (commissioning parents), CF (commissioning father), CM (commissioning mother).

[2] Court of First Instance Antwerp, 19 December 2008, *Tijdschrift@ipr.be* 2010, vol 4, 140, comment by J Verhellen.

[3] Court of Appeal Liège, 6 September 2010, *Revue Trimestrielle de Droit Familial* 2010, vol 4, 1125, comment by C Henricot, S Saroléa and J Sosson, and the revised decision of the Court of First Instance Huy, 22 March 2010, *Revue de Jurisprudence de Liège, Mons et Bruxelles* 2010, vol 38, 1815, comment by P Wautelet and *Journal des Tribunaux* 2010, 420, comment by N Gallus.

[4] Court of First Instance Brussels, 6 April 2010, *Revue Trimestrielle de Droit Familial* 2010, vol 4, 1164.

[5] Court of First Instance Brussels, 15 February 2011, *Tijdschrift@ipr.be* 2011, vol 1, 125.

[6] Court of First Instance Nivelles 6 April 2011, *Actualités du droit de la famille* 2011, vol 8, p 162, comment by N Gallus and *Revue Trimestrielle de Droit Familial* 2011, vol 3, p 695.

B. The Non-regulation of Surrogacy in the Act on Medically Assisted Reproduction

The Act of 6 July 2007 concerning medically assisted reproduction and the use of superfluous embryos and gametes (hereafter 'Act on MAR')[17] has not regularised surrogacy. The legislator expected that surrogacy would subsequently be regulated by specific legislation. In the Act on MAR, the legislator did try to promote specific forms of intentional parenthood regulated by the Act, by stating that the 'rules of affiliation as stipulated in the Civil Code are in the favour of the intended parents' (Act on MAR, Articles 27 and 56).[18] In this (very vaguely formulated) correction to the existing affiliation rules, pending the passing of specific legislation with regard to the matter, the legislator simply disregarded the practice of surrogacy by assuming that the recipient of an embryo or gametes is always the intended mother. However, it is precisely because they want to transmit their own genes that intended parents have recourse to a surrogate mother. Although the donation of egg cells and sperm cells—as opposed to the donation of redundant embryos—can be done in a non-anonymous way following the consent of both the donor and the recipient(s), it is important to note that, within the context of surrogacy, the recipient will always be the surrogate mother, whereas the donors will most often be the commissioning parents.

On the level of doctrine, discussion is ongoing about whether or not the Act on MAR is applicable in cases where artificial procreation techniques are used in the execution of a surrogacy agreement,[19] and it has been advocated that 'high-tech' surrogate motherhood[20] is legally forbidden.[21] The Minister of Justice has clarified, in a response to a question from Parliament, that—although it does not regulate surrogacy—the Act on MAR has a wide scope. This entails that when the execution of a surrogacy arrangement involves the application of one of the medically assisted reproduction techniques which fall under the Act on MAR, this Act needs to be respected.[22]

It may be assumed that the Act on MAR makes adjustments to the law on affiliation only when donor material is used. In this case, a distinction is made between intended parenthood and genetic parenthood, whereby the law gives preference to

---

[17] *Belgian State Gazette*, 17 July 2007.

[18] From the moment of implantation of donated redundant embryos (Act on MAR, Art 27, first sub-s) or as from the moment of insemination of donated gametes (Act on MAR, Art 56, first sub-s).

[19] Affirmative: T Wuyts, 'De afstamming na medisch begeleide voortplanting' in P Senaeve, F Swennen and G Verschelden (eds), *De hervorming van het afstammingsrecht* (Antwerp, Intersentia, 2007) 303, no 518. Negative: J Sosson, 'Le droit de la filiation nouveau est arrivé !', *Journal des Tribunaux* 2007, 391, no 19 and fn 100.

[20] Whereby a deep-frozen redundant embryo, created using an egg cell of the commissioning mother, is implanted in a surrogate mother.

[21] T Wuyts, 'De afstamming na medisch begeleide voortplanting' in P Senaeve, F Swennen and G Verschelden (eds), *De hervorming van het afstammingsrecht* (Antwerp, Intersentia, 2007) 303, no 518 and fn 55.

[22] Chamber of Representatives 2010–11, 21 June 2011, COM 268, 13 (Question no 5163 asked by S Becq).

the former. This differentiation does not exist when medically assisted reproduction techniques are applied using gametes (egg-cells or semen) from the intended parents. In the latter case, the general affiliation rules from the Civil Code are fully applicable.[23] In any case, by application of the Act on MAR, donors are virtually excluded from the possibility of filing a claim regarding the affiliation of the child (Act on MAR, Article 27, second sub-section and Article 56, second sub-section), resulting in the commissioning parents' lack of ability *de lege lata* to go to court in order to have their genetic affiliation with the commissioned child legally determined on the basis of the Affiliation Law.

II. Legal Requirements for Surrogate Mothers/Commissioning Parents

In the absence of Belgian legislation concerning surrogacy, there are no legal requirements for surrogate mothers or for the commissioning parents.

Pending legislative action, it is the *ethical committees* of the hospitals who decide autonomously on the criteria with which surrogate mothers and commissioning parents must comply. A newspaper reported that as of recently, the Ethical Committee of Ghent University Hospital accepts (married or unmarried) gay couples as commissioning parents. The couple itself decides which of the two men is to donate his sperm, and can make its own arrangements for a surrogate mother in whom an embryo is implanted, created with the egg cell of an anonymous donor.[24]

Each of the four bills aimed at creating a legal framework for surrogacy[25] provides conditions with which the surrogate mother and the commissioning parents must comply. These conditions are summarised below. Those bills also contain provisions regarding medical and psychological pre-examinations, as well as the provision of information, education and assistance before and during the pregnancy for the persons involved, whether or not in a surrogacy centre. A discussion of these requirements falls outside the scope of this chapter.

A. Proposed Requirements for the Surrogate Mother

i. Age

All bills demand that the surrogate mother should at least have attained the age of majority: one bill sets the minimum age at 21 years,[26] the other ones stick to the age of 18. The *maximum allowed age* has been described twice in absolute terms: from

---

[23] P Senaeve, *Compendium van het personen- en familierecht* (Leuven/Den Haag, Acco, 2011) 280, no 707.

[24] I Ghijs, 'Draagmoederschap voor homo's mogelijk in Gent' ('Surrogacy for gay couples made possible in Ghent'), *De Standaard*, 3 June 2011, available at <www.destandaard.be>.

[25] Above nn 8 and 9.

[26] Art 10, 1° proposition Temmerman.

36 years[27] maximum up to younger than 45 years.[28] In two instances, the age limit also has been defined in variable terms: one bill proposes a maximum age of (in principle) 37 years old for surrogate mothers, but extendable to a maximum age of 45, provided that the surrogate mother is a first or second degree relative of either one of the commissioning parents;[29] while the second bill states that, in principle, the surrogate mother must not have attained the age of 45, except when the surrogate mother is the mother of either one of the commissioning parents, in which case the age limit is extended to under 50.[30]

The Act on MAR (see section I.B. above) stipulates that embryo implantation or gamete insemination is not allowed for women over 47 years of age.

ii. Civil Status

Only one bill sets requirements for the civil status of the surrogate mother, stipulating that she should be either single, or divorced or a widow.[31]

iii. Capacity to Contract

Only one bill explicitly stipulates that a (adult) surrogate mother must be legally competent.[32] In the other bills, the legal capacity to contract is presupposed, as the surrogate mother is a contracting party to the surrogacy agreement.

iv. Nationality or (Place of) Residence

Two out of the four bills contain requirements in this respect: one bill requires that both surrogate parents possess Belgian nationality or have a permanent residence in Belgium.[33] Another bill stipulates that the surrogate mother must either possess Belgian nationality, or be subject to Belgian personal law.[34]

v. Having Given Birth to Another Living Child

Three out of the four bills stipulate that a woman must have given birth to at least one living child before she can act as a surrogate mother;[35] the two most recent bills further require that said child must still be alive at the time of conclusion of the surrogacy contract.

---

[27] Art 9, 1° proposition Mahoux.
[28] Art 5, para 2, b) proposition Defraigne.
[29] Art 10, 1° proposition Temmerman.
[30] Art 4, para 2, A, first enumeration dash—proposition Tommelein.
[31] Art 5, para 2, a) proposition Defraigne.
[32] Art 10, 2° proposition Temmerman.
[33] Art 4, para 2, C, fifth enumeration dash—proposition Tommelein.
[34] Art 10, 3° proposition Temmerman. What this actually means is completely unclear.
[35] Art 4, para 2, A, second enumeration dash—proposition Tommelein; Art 9, 2° proposition Mahoux; Art 10, 6° proposition Temmerman.

vi. Health Condition

All bills contain provisions aimed at maximising the chances for a normal pregnancy and a healthy child. For instance, one of the bills contains the requirement that the obstetric anamnesis should not indicate any pathology that would imply an increased risk for complications during the next pregnancy.[36] According to a second bill, a surrogate mother must prove, by means of a certificate issued by a gynaecologist, that the scheduled pregnancy is free of any foreseeable risks, both to her own health and to the health of the child.[37] According to yet another bill, a candidate surrogate mother needs to submit a recent health report proving that a pregnancy would not entail any serious risks, either to herself or to the future child.[38] According to a fourth proposal, the surrogate mother must submit a certificate proving that there is no existing pathology that might lead to abnormal risks during pregnancy, either to herself or to the child.[39]

vii. Requirements Regarding Kinship

One bill states that the surrogate mother *must not be a relative*[40] of *both commissioning parents*, except if the surrogate mother is a sister or a fourth degree relative of either the husband, the cohabiting male partner or the female spouse.[41] Another bill stipulates that the surrogate mother is not allowed to donate gametes for the creation of the child, in order to *avoid any genetic kinship between the surrogate mother and the child*.[42]

B. Proposed Requirements for the Intended Parents

i. Age

Three out of the four Belgian bills propose a maximum age limit, while two of them require that the *minimum age* be set at the age of majority (ie the age of 18). One bill does not set any minimum age limit, but does however set different *maximum age limits* for the intended mother, depending on whether or not she is the genetic mother: in case of high-tech surrogacy, she must be under 43, and in case of low-tech surrogacy she must be under 45.[43] Another bill states that a commissioning parent must have reached the age of majority and imposes a maximum

---

[36] Art 4, para 2, A, third enumeration dash—proposition Tommelein.
[37] Art 5, para 2, e) proposition Defraigne. This bill also requires that the surrogate mother consulted a psychiatrist at least once (Art 5, para 2, d) proposition Defraigne).
[38] Art 9, 3° *juncto* Art 17, para 4, 2° proposition Mahoux.
[39] Art 10, 5° proposition Temmerman.
[40] It is not clear whether this refers to genetic kinship or legal kinship.
[41] Art 5, para 2, c) proposition Defraigne.
[42] Art 3, second sub-s *juncto* Art 2, 2° proposition Temmerman. The same ban on gamete donation also applies to her spouse or partner.
[43] Art 4, para 2, B proposition Tommelein.

age limit of 47 years old.[44] Yet another bill[45] also requires that the age of majority has been reached, with a maximum age limit set at no more than 45 years old, or subject to compliance with the age requirements as set forth in the Act on MAR.[46] Article 4 of this Act stipulates that gametes can be taken from adult women of a maximum of 45 years of age. A request for embryo implantation or for gamete insemination can be submitted by women who have reached the age of majority, with a maximum age limit of 45 years old.

ii. Civil Status and Sexual Inclination

The four bills are quite heterogeneous in this respect: two of these bills allow surrogacy for single mothers, while the two other bills reserve it for couples only. Two bills allow gay couples, while in the other two bills heterosexual couples are required. One of the bills accepts single persons and heterosexual couples.[47] Another bill requires a cohabiting couple or a married couple of husband and wife who do not in fact live apart.[48] In yet another bill, a 'commissioning parent' is described as any person who has decided to become a parent through resorting to the services of a surrogate mother;[49] the explanatory notes to the bill reveal that this definition refers to single persons and couples,[50] regardless of their sexual inclination. Lastly, a fourth bill requires that the commissioning parents must either be a married couple, or partners who have been cohabiting in a sustained and affectionate way for a minimum of three years,[51] regardless of their sexual inclination.[52]

iii. Capacity to Contract

Only one bill explicitly sets the condition that the commissioning parents must have legal capacity.[53] In the other bills such capacity to contract is presupposed, as the commissioning parents are a contracting party to the surrogacy agreement.

iv. Nationality or (Place of) Residence

Three of the four bills set conditions in this regard: one bill stipulates that the commissioning parent(s) must possess Belgian nationality or have a permanent

---

[44] Art 10, 1° proposition Mahoux.
[45] Art 9, 2° proposition Temmerman.
[46] See section I.B. above.
[47] *Cf* the definition of a 'commissioning parent' as the commissioning mother or the commissioning father, and the definition of 'commissioning father' as the partner of a *woman*, Art 2, 1° resp. 3° proposition Tommelein.
[48] Art 2, 1° en 2° proposition Defraigne.
[49] Art 2, 3° proposition Mahoux.
[50] Explanatory memorandum proposition Mahoux, Senate 2010, no 5-236/1, p 6.
[51] Art 9, 4° proposition Temmerman.
[52] Art 9, 4° proposition Temmerman.
[53] Art 9, 3° proposition Temmerman.

residence in Belgium.[54] A second bill requires that the commissioning parent(s) is (are) domiciled[55] in Belgium for at least two years.[56] The third bill requires that the commissioning parents possess Belgian nationality or be subject to Belgian personal law.[57]

v. *Physiological Impossibility to Have Children/Health Risks*

All the bills point out that a gynaecologist must have diagnosed a medical problem that would make it impossible for the commissioning parent(s) to have children. One bill requires a written confirmation that it is physiologically impossible for the commissioning mother to get pregnant because of a congenital or acquired absence of the womb, or as a result of a malfunctioning womb, or because of the fact that a pregnancy would be life-threatening for the mother, which by itself constitutes a contraindication for pregnancy, or because there is a risk that a pregnancy in the case of the said woman would be life-threatening for the child.[58] According to a second bill, a written confirmation by a gynaecologist is needed, stating that it is physiologically impossible for the female partner of the (heterosexual) couple to become pregnant from her husband or cohabiting partner, or that a pregnancy would entail severe health risks either to herself or to the child.[59] According to a third bill, a reasoned, dated and signed written document issued by a gynaecologist must confirm either that it is a physiological impossibility for the commissioning parent(s) to complete the pregnancy, or that a pregnancy might be seriously life-threatening for the woman and/or the future child, whereby such risk must be greater than the normal risk incurred by a pregnant woman belonging to the same age category as the commissioning parent.[60] The fourth bill also requires a similar written document issued by a gynaecologist, confirming a physiological impossibility or an absolute contraindication for the woman to get pregnant, except for male gay couples wishing to become commissioning parents.[61]

vi. *Genetic Relationship with the Child*

Three out of the four bills allow surrogacy only if there exists a genetic relationship between at least one commissioning parent and the child.[62] In other words, the representatives who have submitted these bills require that the commissioning parents possess usable egg cells or sperm cells.

---

[54] Art 4, para 2, C, fifth enumeration dash—proposition Tommelein.
[55] In the civil law sense.
[56] Art 10, 2° proposition Mahoux.
[57] Art 9, 1° proposition Temmerman. What is meant by the latter is completely unclear.
[58] Art 4, para 1 proposition Tommelein.
[59] Art 5, para 1 proposition Defraigne.
[60] Art 7 proposition Mahoux.
[61] Art 9, 7° proposition Temmerman.
[62] Art 2, 6° proposition Tommelein; Art 2, 2° *juncto* Art 8 proposition Mahoux; Art 3, first sub-s proposition Temmerman.

III. Enforceability of Surrogacy Arrangements

A. Surrogacy Without Cross-border Elements

In the Belgian doctrine a majority of the authors[63] assume that, in the absence of a legal framework, any surrogacy agreement containing arrangements concerning the affiliation of the child and/or parental authority is absolutely null and void. It is mainly the object and cause of a surrogacy agreement that are considered as problematic.

First, only goods or services that are being put on the market can be the *object* of a commercial agreement (Belgian Civil Code (hereafter 'BCC'), Article 1128). The human person cannot be commercialised and cannot as such be considered as an object, because it constitutes a physical and psychological entity. Any contractual obligation for a surrogate mother to surrender the child must be considered as problematic, given the inalienable right of a woman who has given birth to a child to be considered as the legitimate mother of that child (see also below, section IV.A.i.a.).

Furthermore, such surrogacy contract agreements have an illicit *cause* (Article 1131 BCC). The obligation entered into by the surrogate mother before the actual birth, or even prior to the conception of the child, for the purposes of giving up both her child and her parental rights, is contrary to Belgian public policy. No deviation is possible from the general rule that the delivery itself constitutes the basis for the establishment of legal motherhood, nor from the principle of parental authority as a consequence of legally-established parentage.

One of the consequences of the absolute nullity of the surrogacy agreement is that when one of the contracting parties concerned refuses to meet its obligations, the other party cannot enforce compliance with the agreement before a court. Until now, the nullity of a surrogacy agreement under Belgian law has never been contested in any Belgian court of law; neither have there been any legal proceedings aimed at imposing the compulsory execution of a surrogacy agreement.

B. Surrogacy with Cross-border Elements

Belgian rules of private international law regulate the recognition and enforceability in Belgium of cross-border surrogacy agreements. We shall elaborate on this in section IV. below.

---

[63] A Heyvaert, 'De nieuwe procreatietechnieken en de Afstammingswet van 31 maart 1987', *Vlaams Tijdschrift voor Gezondheidsrecht*, 1988, 233, no 17; N Massager, 'L'influence des techniques de procréation médicalement assistée sur la filiation de l'enfant à naître' in *10 années d'application du nouveau droit de la filiation*, vol 1 (Liège, Editions du Jeune Barreau de Liège 1997) 220–21, nos 75–77; G Verschelden, *Afstamming* in series *Algemene Praktische Rechtsverzameling* (Mechelen, Kluwer, 2004) 700—02, nos 1273–75; T Wuyts, 'De afstamming na medisch begeleide voortplanting' in P Senaeve, F Swennen and G Verschelden (eds), *De hervorming van het afstammingsrecht* (Antwerp, Intersentia, 2007) 363, no 592.

With regard to the element of internal Belgian public policy (see section III.A. above), recent cases illustrate how this element is countered in cross-border surrogacy arrangements by the interests of the child. In this way the Court of Appeal in Liège (*M&M* case[64]) recognised that surrogacy contracts which directly concern the human body are void under public policy principles. However, this illicit nature of a surrogacy contract cannot infringe the superior interests of the child. The original French quotation reads as follows:

> Le contrat de gestation pour autrui est contraire à l'ordre public en droit interne belge. ... Les principes de l'indisponibilité du corps humain, du statut des personnes et du droit pour la mère qui porte et met au monde un enfant de déterminer son lien de filiation, font obstacle à la reconnaissance d'effets juridiques à un contrat de gestation pour autrui dès lors qu'un tel contrat est frappé de nullité absolue pour contrariété à l'ordre public ... On peut toutefois considérer que l'illicite du contrat de gestation pour autrui—dont découlent les actes de naissance dont la reconnaissance est postulée—ne peut porter atteinte à l'intérêt supérieur des enfants.

Similar considerations may be found in other cases. In the *AM&ND* case,[65] the court concluded that a refusal to recognise Indian birth certificates which establish a parentage link with the biological father, would be contrary to the superior interests of the children, since it would deprive them of any link with their father and of '*tout état civil*', in light of the fact that there is no mother according to Indian law. In the case of child *C*,[66] the President of the Court of First Instance of Brussels found in summary proceedings that according to Indian law the Belgian commissioning parent was the legal father of the child and that there was no mention of a mother on the birth certificate. The judge considered that even when the surrogacy contract seems illegal, legal parenthood should be recognised in Belgium.[67] This is justified by the fact that it is not in the interests of the child to stay in India—a country with which the child does not seem to have any connection.

In the *Samuel* case,[68] the Brussels Court of First Instance even got round this public policy issue, taking into account the child's interests. The biological father requested the recognition of the Ukrainian birth certificate. By granting this request the court was of the opinion that it did not give effect to a surrogacy agreement that could possibly contravene the principles of Belgian public policy. According to the court, the request in fact only concerned the establishment of the biological father's paternity and had little to do with the surrogacy arrangement as such. The court merely saw a man who resorted to an artificial reproduction technique to fulfil his desire to have a child, and did not consider this to be illegal.

---

[64] See Table 1, Note 3 above.
[65] See Table 1, Note 6 above.
[66] See Table 1, Note 4 above.
[67] The recognition of the legal parenthood still had to be considered on the merits.
[68] See Table 1, Note 5 above.

IV. Legal Parenthood/Nationality of the Child

Given the absence of specific legislation regarding surrogacy, a delivery in Belgium will cause the surrogate mother and her male spouse (if any) to be considered as the legal parent(s) in application of current affiliation law (section IV.A. below). Commissioning parents will have to start an adoption procedure (section IV.B. below) to acquire parental rights. Parentage established by affiliation entails retroactive consequences starting from the date of birth of the child or from the date of its conception, depending on the interest of the child (*Infans conceptus pro jam nato habetur, quoties de commodis eius agitur*). On the other hand, parentage established by adoption merely entails legal consequences from the start of the adoption procedure, more particularly from the time of submission of the written request for adoption (Article 349-1 BCC). In section IV.C. below we shall briefly consider the consequences for the nationality of the child.

A. Legal Parenthood by Affiliation

i. *Surrogacy Without Cross-border Element*

a. Maternal Affiliation

Mentioning in the Birth Certificate the Name of the Woman Who Gave Birth to the Child

In Belgium, a birth certificate must mention the name of the woman who gave birth to the child (Article 57, 2° BCC), resulting in the fact that the woman who gave birth to that child becomes its 'legal mother' by mere operation of law (Article 312, § 1 BCC). This rule, called '*Mater semper certa est*', results in the legal motherhood of a surrogate mother, even though the genetic mother is another woman. A surrogacy agreement cannot alter the fundamental principle of proven descent from the mother's side. No derogation is possible from Article 312, § 1 BCC, relating to public order.

In Belgium, commissioning parents who want to avoid mentioning the name of the (surrogate) mother on the birth certificate will face nearly insurmount-able problems.[69] This is because of the double registration system, which ensures that the name of the woman who gave birth to the child will appear on the birth certificate. If the child has not been registered within 15 days following its birth, the obligation of notification of birth is converted into an obligation to register, on the basis of which the registration must be done by the staff of the institution where the child was born or, in other cases, by the physicians, midwives or

---

[69] A De Wolf, 'Draagmoederschap in België en Frankrijk: een stand van zaken' in K Boele-Woelki and M Oderkerk (eds), *(On)geoorloofdheid van het draagmoederschap in rechtsvergelijkend perspectief* (Antwerp, Intersentia, 1999) 105–06.

other persons who were present at the time of delivery, or by the person in whose residence the delivery took place (Article 56, §§ 1 and 2 BCC).

Any failure to comply with the registration and notification obligations is subject to criminal prosecution (Belgian Penal Code (hereafter 'BPC'), Article 361). If the woman who gave birth to the child does not state her own name but uses a false name instead, or if the commissioning mother had her own name recorded on the birth certificate,[70] both persons will face even more severe punishment (Article 363 BPC). The woman who gave birth to the child and provides a false name to the Registrar may furthermore be prosecuted for having adopted a false name (Article 231 BPC). Anyone who obstructs the drawing up of a birth certificate or destroys a completed birth certificate may also be subject to criminal prosecution (Article 363 BPC).

Voluntary Recognition by a Woman

If the name of the woman who gave birth to the child (the surrogate mother) is not mentioned in the birth certificate, or when there is no birth certificate available, motherhood may also be established through recognition (Article 313, § 1 BCC) by any woman, ie including the *commissioning mother*, subject to the approval of the parent with respect to whom affiliation has already been established (Article 329*bis*, § 2, first sub-section BCC).[71]

If the surrogate mother has given birth anonymously, nothing precludes the commissioning mother from recognising the gestational child. Furthermore, any *surrogate mother* who, *after having given birth anonymously*, refuses to surrender the child may recognise the child to whom she has given birth.

Although there is a legal obligation to mention the name of the mother in the birth certificate, the Belgian legislator has not precluded the *de facto* existence of birth certificates in which no mention is made of the name of the mother, as alternatives have been provided for the establishment of affiliation on the mother's side (*viz* recognition by a woman and the judicial establishment of motherhood (below)).[72]

Judicial Establishment of Motherhood

Where motherhood cannot be ascertained on the basis of the entry in the birth certificate of the name of the woman who gave birth, or when the child has been registered under false names without having been recognised by any woman, motherhood may be established by judicial decision (Article 314, first sub-section BCC). Both the surrogate mother and the commissioning mother can take the

---

[70] For an applied case, see n 92 below.

[71] This would, more particularly, require the approval of the man who has recognised the child prior to its birth; however, such maternal recognition does not require the consent of the husband of the woman who recognises the child.

[72] Court of Cassation, 29 January 1993, available at <www.cass.be> (homologation of the full adoption of a child whose mother had given birth anonymously in France).

initiative to start an investigation as to their respective motherhood (see Article 332*ter*, first sub-section BCC). If the surrogate mother has no affiliation ties with the child, she will probably first opt for a voluntary establishment of affiliation through recognition. However, the judicial establishment of motherhood offers more certainty, because a recognition that is not corroborated by a '*possession d'état*' may be successfully contested if the surrogate mother can prove that the commissioning mother did not give birth to the child. On the other hand, judicially-established motherhood can be challenged only through third party proceedings.

In order to establish maternity by court decision, the claimant must submit proof that the child in question is identical to the child to whom the alleged mother gave birth (Article 314, third sub-section BCC). This can be proved by showing that, with respect to such an alleged mother, the child is in a '*possession d'état*' relationship (Article 314, fourth sub-section BCC). This notion reflects the socio-affective reality, the actual perception of affiliation ties, rather than the biological reality. Whether or not there exists a true '*possession d'état*' in each separate case must be determined by a judge on the basis of the requirements described in Article 331*nonies* BCC, summarised as *nomen, fama et tractatus*.[73]

In the absence of '*possession d'état*', evidence of affiliation may be furnished by all legal means. The same applies to the furnishing of counter-evidence (Article 314, fifth sub-section BCC).

For the *commissioning mother*, this means that when the surrogate mother has anonymously given birth abroad, she can be designated as the legal mother by an order of court if she can prove that she has a '*possession d'état*' relationship with respect to the child, eg because she always behaved like a mother, whereas the surrogate mother never assumed a maternal role. In that case, any evidence that the commissioning mother did not give birth to the child is completely irrelevant and cannot serve as a ground for precluding the judicial establishment of the motherhood of the commissioning mother on the basis of '*possession d'état*'. The structure of the applicable legislation shows that '*possession d'état*' with respect to a woman constitutes irrefutable evidence as to the judicial establishment of motherhood. This is because from Article 314, fifth sub-section BCC it follows that if the gestational child is in a '*possession d'état*' relationship with the commissioning mother, it is impossible to furnish (counter-)evidence that this alleged mother did not give birth to the child.[74] In the absence of a '*possession d'état*' relationship vis-à-vis the

---

[73] Pursuant to Art 331*nonies* BCC, the '*possession d'état*' (the French expression is used because it is hard to find a satisfactory English translation) must be continuous and ongoing. This can be evidenced by facts that, as a whole or separately, demonstrate a relation of affiliation. These facts include, among others, that the name borne by the child has always been the name of the person it allegedly descends from; that the woman has always treated her child as her own; that she has provided for the livelihood and education of the child; that the child has treated her as its mother; that said child is recognised as the woman's child by her own family and relatives and by society; and that public authorities consider it as such.

[74] G Verschelden, *Origineel ouderschap herdacht* (Bruges, die Keure, 2005) 106–07 no 176.

commissioning mother, it makes no sense to resort to any and all legal means, eg through an expert examination, for the purpose of proving that the woman who provided the egg cell—most often the commissioning mother—is the genetic mother of the child. Any evidence of genetic affiliation is irrelevant for the establishment of motherhood; the surrogate mother who gave birth to the child is the legal mother of the child, even if she has no genetic ties with the child.

Besides the motherhood of the commissioning mother, the motherhood of the *surrogate mother* can also be judicially established, if the latter has given birth anonymously, if the name of a different woman—ie a false name—appears on the child's birth certificate, or if there simply is no birth certificate available and the child has not yet been recognised by another woman. By definition, the surrogate mother gave birth to the child. Also in this case, the primary source of evidence for proving that she actually gave birth to the child resides in the presence of a *'possession d'état'* relationship (between the child and the surrogate mother).

In the absence of a *'possession d'état'* relationship vis-à-vis the surrogate mother (eg because shortly after the birth the child was handed over to the commissioning mother who then took care of it), the proof of motherhood may be furnished by any and all legal means. However, a genetic examination, ordered in pursuance of Article 331*octies* BCC, whereby the DNA structure of the surrogate mother is compared with that of the child, does not in all cases give a decisive answer with regard to the legal grounds for claiming motherhood. Where the surrogate mother got pregnant in a natural way or has been impregnated by embryo transfer, then she is also the genetic mother. In such case, an expert examination whereby her genetic material is compared with that of the child does make sense in order to come to a conclusion as to the circumstances of the child's delivery and the corresponding affiliation on the mother's side. If the child was conceived using an egg cell of the commissioning mother or a donor, however, then the surrogate is not genetically related to the child. In such a case, a scientific examination establishing such absence of genetic affiliation is irrelevant and therefore insufficient for dismissing a claim for the judicial establishment of motherhood filed by the surrogate mother.

b. Paternal Affiliation

A Married Surrogate Mother Gave Birth to the Child

In application of the principle '*Mater semper certa est*', there is usually no doubt about the motherhood of a surrogate mother who gave birth in Belgium (see section IV.A.i.a. above). The question of legal paternity is in turn linked to this motherhood. A child born during the marriage of a surrogate mother, or within 300 days from the dissolution or nullification of said marriage, shall have the husband of the surrogate mother for its father (Article 315 BCC, '*Pater is est quem nuptiae demonstrant*').

This *presumption of paternity* does not apply for a limited list of cases where the paternity of the husband is unlikely because the child was born more than 300 days after a divorce based on facts, either proven before or granted by the judge, or following the initiation of a divorce proceeding (see Article 316*bis* BCC). In such cases the child will be fatherless, unless the (surrogate) mother and her husband make a joint declaration of preservation of paternity before the Registrar, no later than the time of registration of the birth.

A claim *contesting the husband's paternity* is not admissible if the husband has consented to artificial insemination or another action aimed at reproduction, unless the conception of the child cannot be a result of such actions (Article 318, § 4 BCC). This rule was key in a lawsuit where a married woman had artificially inseminated herself against the will of her husband, using the sperm of a homosexual friend of the family in order to fulfil the desire of this friend to have children. The Court of First Instance of Ghent had ruled that this legal provision is also applicable in surrogacy cases where insemination serves the purpose of procreation for another person. Nonetheless, the claim was *in casu* deemed admissible on the basis of a notarial deed containing a declaration stating that the child would not in any way be raised in the family of the surrogate mother and her husband. The judge could not conclude from that notarial deed that the husband of the surrogate mother had consented to the artificial insemination of his wife. As evidence had been adduced to prove that the child was not conceived by the husband, the claim was declared well-founded.[75]

In case of doubt as to the legal motherhood of a married surrogate mother—eg because she delivered abroad anonymously, as a result of which her name does not appear in the birth certificate, or in the absence of such birth certificate—then the affiliation on the father's side is regulated in different ways, depending on whether or not another woman (eg the commissioning mother) did manage to recognise the child or to have her motherhood legally established.

Following recognition by the commissioning mother, the paternity of her husband will automatically be legally established pursuant to Article 315 BCC, on condition that such recognition was notified to the husband (Article 313, § 3, first sub-section BCC); without such notification, the recognition is not opposable vis-à-vis said husband (Article 313, § 3, third sub-section BCC). In the event that the married commissioning mother managed to have her motherhood legally established, her husband will need to be summoned to appear before court (Article 332*ter*, fourth sub-section BCC) and will become the father of the child in application of Article 315 BCC.

If the affiliation of the child cannot be established as regards any woman at all, the child will not have a bond of affiliation based on the marriage but may still be recognised by a man, or the paternity may still be judicially established, just as would be the case for a child born from an unmarried surrogate mother.

---

[75] Court of First Instance Ghent, 31 May 2001, *Tijdschrift voor Belgisch Burgerlijk Recht—Revue Générale de Droit Civil Belge* 2002, 27, comment by G Verschelden.

An Unmarried Surrogate Mother Gave Birth to the Child

If the surrogate mother is an unmarried woman then the child is not automatically assigned to a father by mere operation of law. It is possible, however, for any man to recognise the gestational child, or there is the possibility of judicial establishment of paternity.

(1) Voluntary Recognition by a Man

Any man can recognise a child to whom an unmarried surrogate mother has given birth (Article 319 BCC) or is yet to give birth, on condition that pre-natal recognition takes place after the conception of the child (Article 328, second sub-section BCC), subject to the consent of the surrogate mother (Article 329*bis*, § 2, first sub-section BCC). In the case of such *pre-natal recognition*, the Registrar will normally request that a medical certificate is submitted which confirms that the (surrogate) mother has already been pregnant for at least six months. This is because no certificate of civil status can be drawn up for a foetus of less than 180 days old.[76]

This means that, *de lege lata*, it is impossible to recognise a child prior to its conception. However, in the notary world a suggestion *de lege ferenda* has been put forward, which was specifically aimed at regulating the affiliation issue following a surrogate pregnancy by means of a surrogacy contract drawn up prior to the conception of the child, whereby such contract would serve as proof of the (pre-conceptive) recognition of the child by the (two) commissioning parent(s).[77]

If the surrogate mother refuses to give her consent then the person seeking recognition (eg the commissioning father) will need to summon her to the Court of First Instance, which will first try to reconcile both parties. In the event that such a reconciliation attempt fails, the Court will rule whether or not it is possible to proceed with the recognition. If it is proven that the person seeking recognition is not the biological father then the request for recognition will be dismissed. As a rule, if non-paternity cannot be proven, recognition will be granted, unless this would manifestly interfere with the child's interests (Article 329*bis*, § 2, third sub-section BCC).[78] This affiliation rule is, however, eliminated by the Act on MAR: when the commissioning father wishes to recognise the child, the evidence of genetic non-paternity (evidence quite easy to furnish in cases where donor sperm was used) will not constitute a ground for dismissal of his request for recognition. This is a practical application of a principle from the Act on MAR (Article 56, first

---

[76] Circulaire n° 42 *dd* 22 mars 1849 du Ministre de l'Intérieur concernant l'inhumation des mort-nés, *Bulletin du Ministère de l'Intérieur* 1849, p 135: '[L]es dispositions relatives à l'état civil, doivent rester étrangères aux fœtus de moins de six mois.'

[77] Written opinion of the Commission on Family Law of the Royal Federation of Belgian Notaries on seven (former) bills concerning surrogacy, August 2006, unpublished.

[78] The legal text stipulates that in this context only the interests of children of more than one year of age may be taken in account by the judge; however, that age limit has been found unconstitutional (Constitutional Court, 16 December 2010, no 144/2010, available at <www.const-court.be>).

sub-section), according to which the affiliation rules as set forth in the Civil Code are in the favour of the commissioning parent who has received the gametes.

Whenever a *married man* recognises a child conceived with a woman to whom he is not married, this recognition must be notified to the male spouse or female spouse (Article 319*bis*, first sub-section BCC) by registered letter or by a process served by a bailiff, depending on whether the certificate of recognition was drawn up in Belgium or not (Article 319*bis*, second sub-section BCC). Failure to do so would entail non-opposability vis-à-vis the spouse of the recognising person and the joint children (Article 319*bis*, third sub-section BCC).

Before 1 July 2007, a married man wanting to recognise a child conceived with a woman to whom he was not married, had to submit his recognition act to be homologated by the Court before his recognition could enter into effect. Jurisprudence has confirmed that this obligation also applies to cases where surrogacy is involved. In a first lawsuit where a surrogate mother had anonymously given birth in France to a child conceived using the gametes of a recognising person and his spouse, the Court ruled that the words 'conceived with a woman other than the female spouse' encompass the situation wherein a woman other than the wife gives birth to a child generated from the genetic material of a married man.[79] In a second lawsuit, two embryos had been created using the gametes of a married couple and were implanted into a surrogate mother. The commissioning father did recognise the binovular twins prior to birth, however only one child was full-term and was actually born. The request for homologation of the recognition act was declared well-founded,[80] and later on the child was fully adopted by the genetic mother.[81]

(2) Establishment of Paternity by Judicial Decision

If it turns out to be impossible to find a person of the male gender who is prepared to recognise the child of an unmarried surrogate mother, the paternity may also be established judicially.

For instance, an unmarried surrogate mother may summon the man who, pursuant to a surrogacy agreement, was supposed to act as commissioning father but is refusing to accept the child, in order to have his paternity established by an order of the court (Article 322, first sub-section BCC). In the absence of a '*possession d'état*', the affiliation on the father's side can be demonstrated using any legal means of proof (Article 324, second sub-section BCC). If the gestational child was conceived with his sperm (eg following the implantation of an embryo created with his semen), his paternity can be established on the basis of the conclusions of an expert examination ordered in application of Article 331*octies* BCC. The same applies for the paternity of the partner of an unmarried surrogate mother who,

---

[79] Court of First Instance Hasselt, 27 March 2001, *Limburgs Rechtsleven* 2001, 323, with editorial note.
[80] Court of Appeal Brussels, 1 March 2007, *Revue trimestrielle de droit familial* 2007, 754.
[81] See below n 104.

during the execution of a surrogacy contract, has conceived a child through sexual intercourse and does not want to bear any responsibility for that child.

Any man may also take the initiative to have his paternity legally established. For instance, a commissioning father who behaves like a father can have his paternity established if he is able to demonstrate that the gestational child is in a '*possession d'état*' relationship with him (Article 324, first sub-section BCC), even though the child was not conceived using his sperm. The same possibility remains open to the partner of the unmarried surrogate mother, regardless of whether the child was conceived using his own genetic material or not.

ii. Surrogacy with Cross-border Element

We distinguish two scenarios here:

(a) surrogacy abroad for Belgian couples; and
(b) surrogacy in Belgium for couples resident abroad.

In both scenarios the Belgian rules of private international law (PIL) apply in order to determine questions related to the establishment of the legal parenthood: for the first scenario these are the rules on recognition of foreign judgments and authentic instruments; for the second scenario they are the jurisdiction and choice-of-law rules. As no international or European rules presently apply in this matter, the Belgian Code of Private International Law (PIL Code) is the only available legal instrument.[82]

a. Foreign Birth: Foreign Surrogate Mother, Belgian Commissioning Parent(s)

In practice Belgium is confronted with foreign surrogacy in two ways. First, commissioning parents request a passport for the child at the Belgian consulate or diplomatic post in the country where the child was born. This application implies the need to determine the nationality of the child and therefore the child's parentage. The child will be recognised as a Belgian national, and therefore as entitled to a Belgian passport, only if the parentage of (one of) the Belgian commissioning parents is confirmed. In PIL terms this boils down to the question whether the Belgian consular and diplomatic authorities can recognise the foreign birth certificates and/or judgments. Secondly, a child arrives in Belgium (eg with a foreign passport)[83] and the commissioning parents request the local authority to register the foreign birth certificate in their civil registry. This request implies the same PIL review. In both situations the recurring main issue is the recognition in Belgium of the parentage line established abroad. Belgian current legal

---

[82] Act of 16 July 2004 published in the *Belgian State Gazette* of 27 September 2004, which entered into force on 1 October 2004. For an English translation, see (2004) 6 *Yearbook of Private International Law* 319–75.

[83] This is possible when the child acquires the nationality of the State where he or she is born, eg the United States.

practice reveals that Belgian administrative authorities always refuse to recognise the documents submitted and that the issue is then presented to the court. This is the case despite the fact that the Belgian PIL Code provides for recognition without prior judicial control or special procedure. As will be illustrated below, the principled refusal of the non-judicial authorities is in stark contrast to the flexible approach of the courts.

For purposes of recognition, the Belgian PIL Code provides different regimes for foreign 'judgments' on the one hand and foreign 'authentic acts' on the other hand. The criteria for recognising foreign judgments are regulated by Articles 22–25 of the Code; those for recognising foreign authentic acts by Article 27. The main difference between the two recognition regimes is the review as to the substance of the foreign document: for the recognition of authentic acts a conflict-of-laws test applies, which is not the case for the recognition of judgments. Article 27, § 1 provides as follows:

> A foreign authentic instrument is recognised by any authority in Belgium without the need for any procedure if the validity is established in accordance with the law applicable by virtue of the present statute and more specifically with due regard to Articles 18 and 21.

Only the interpretation of Article 27 has so far been the subject of case law. Cross-border surrogacy cases have not yet been considered under the more flexible criteria for the recognition of judgments. However, in the case of the *M&M* twins[84] for instance, the judges were faced with Californian birth certificates that had been the subject of a prior judgment in that state. In this case two men, who married in Belgium in 2004, turned to a surrogacy agency in the United States. Before the birth of the children, the Californian Supreme Court declared both men to be the biological and legal parents. This judgment ordered the hospital to indicate the two men as parents on the birth certificates, and this was duly done. A few days after the twins were born, the couple returned to Belgium and asked the Belgian local authority to register these certificates in the civil register. The public prosecutor opposed this registration. The men then instituted legal proceedings for the recognition of the Californian birth certificates.[85] The Court of First Instance of Huy[86] did not take the distinction between authentic instruments and judgments into account because the legal regimes for both provide that recognition should be refused in cases of evasion of the law or a violation of public policy. The judge thus reverted immediately to public policy and evasion of the law, which is an understandable course to take. After all, the issue in question is the reviewing of parentage that can be formed abroad while this is impossible in Belgium. However, one cannot ignore the distinction introduced by the Belgian legislator: authentic instruments require a review as to the applicable law, while this is not the case for judgments.

---

[84] See Table 1, Note 3 above.
[85] It should be noted here that the public prosecutor in Belgium, like in France, has the role to guard over the best interests of children, also in civil cases.
[86] See Table 1, Note 3 above.

This so-called '*contrôle de la loi applicable*' induces an invasive analysis of the content of the foreign authentic instrument. In case of cross-border surrogacy, the Belgian authorities (administrative and judicial) must examine whether the foreign birth certificate respects Belgian choice-of-law rules. If its validity is established in accordance with the applicable law appointed by the PIL Code, the birth certificate can be recognised. This applicable law is the law of the nationality of the person whose parenthood is at stake (Article 62 PIL Code). Thus, when the commissioning parents are Belgian nationals, authorities have to determine whether the birth certificates could have been issued under Belgian law.

When reviewing Ukrainian birth certificates according to the conditions of Belgian law, the judge in the *H&E* case[87] used the following balanced consideration:

> It is hereby advisable to ascertain whether application of the forum conflict-of-laws rule and of the foreign law reach a similar result. The certificates should not be identical; it is the equivalence between the certificates that counts.

The conflict-of-laws test does indeed imply that the result reached abroad is taken into consideration; the result reached in the foreign act must have been possible according to Belgian PIL rules. In this case the judge in Antwerp did not recognise the Ukrainian authentic instruments as birth certificates. According to the Belgian principle *mater semper certa est*, the woman who gives birth is regarded as the legal mother (irrespective of the genetic link with the child). While the commissioning mother can be regarded as the legal mother under Ukrainian law, this is not possible under Belgian law. Where paternity is concerned, Belgian law presumes the mother's husband to be the father. As in this case Belgian law could not regard the commissioning mother to be the legal mother, this could also have consequences for the commissioning father's paternity. Here, the Antwerp judge made a creative finding: he did recognise the Ukrainian birth certificates as valid authentic instruments in so far as they established the formal recognition by the Belgian man that he was the father of the children. The judge did not consider this recognition to be contrary to international public policy.

Later rulings in other cross-border surrogacy cases reached similar results, for instance the judgment of the Court of Appeal in Liège,[88] which partially recognised the Californian birth certificates of the *M&M* twins. Only the parentage of the genetic father was recognised, not that of his (male) spouse. After all, current Belgian law does not permit double male parentage,[89] unless it is through adoption (see below, section IV.B.ii.).

---

[87] See Table 1, Note 2 above.

[88] See Table 1, Note 3 above.

[89] Moreover, Art 143, second sub-s BCC excludes the presumption of paternity in the case of same-sex marriage.

In this way Belgian judges end 'limping' legal situations for the children as far as paternal affiliation is concerned. At this time, the other (female or male) commissioning parent will have to turn to adoption.[90]

b. Birth in Belgium: Belgian Surrogate Mother, Foreign Commissioning
   Parents

In two well-known cases (*Baby D*[91] and *Baby J*[92]) a child born in Belgium was handed over to a Dutch couple in exchange for a sum of money.[93]

Baby D was born in February 2005 to a Belgian surrogate mother who also was the genetic mother. She agreed to carry a child for a Belgian commissioning couple. Contrary to the—initially purely Belgian—surrogacy arrangement, the surrogate mother handed the child over to a Dutch couple, with whom she had contact via the Internet before the birth of the child. She informed the commissioning parents that she had had a miscarriage. Since 2005 court proceedings have continued (first in Belgium, then in The Netherlands): Dutch courts ruled that Baby D could stay with the Dutch couple; she still lives with this foster family. DNA-testing revealed that the Belgian commissioning father is the genetic father of the child; he is still continuing proceedings in order to get contact rights with 'his' child. In Belgium criminal proceedings are still pending against the surrogate mother, the commissioning parents and the Dutch couple.

Baby J, being genetically linked with a Belgian woman and her partner, was born in Ghent in July 2008. After falsifying the hospital's admission records (the pregnant Belgian woman lied about her identity, pretending to be a Dutch woman and providing this Dutch woman's identity documents), a Dutch man registered the birth at the Ghent Civil Registry. The child then lived in The Netherlands for several months with the Dutch married couple. When the falsifications came to light, a criminal investigation was launched. The child was initially taken into care under guardianship of the Dutch child welfare system and was then placed in a Belgian foster home. The biological mother requested a Belgian court to rule that she was the mother of the child and not the Dutch woman, and therefore that the Dutch woman's husband was not the child's father as his paternity is only established by their marriage (thus by a presumption). The Ghent Court of First Instance, having jurisdiction based on the habitual residence of the child in Belgium (Article 61, 1° PIL Code), examined the applicable law and rightly found that Dutch law was applicable. Article 62 PIL Code indeed refers to the national law of the person whose maternity or paternity is being contested. According to Article 209 of the Dutch Civil Code, the parental link between a child and a

---

[90] Applying internal adoption rules, see Juvenile Court Antwerp, 22 April 2010, *Tijdschrift voor Familierecht* 2012, vol 2, 43, comment by L Pluym.

[91] Court of Appeal Gent 5 September 2005, *Tijdschrift voor Vreemdelingenrecht* 2006, vol 2, 163, comment by Th Kruger.

[92] Court of First Instance Gent, 24 December 2009, *Tijdschrift@ipr.be*, 2010, vol 4, 133, comment by J Verhellen.

[93] See the national report on The Netherlands by I Curry-Sumner and M Vonk in ch 17 of this book.

person cannot be contested if the facts confirm that person's status as parent as described in the birth certificate. The judge ruled that this was not the case for Baby J regarding the Dutch parents: the child had lived with the Dutch married couple for only a few months, after which he was removed and placed in a foster home. The biological mother could therefore contest the maternity and paternity of the Dutch couple.

The records of the criminal investigation clearly revealed that it was the Belgian woman who gave birth to the child and that false information was provided to the hospital. Moreover, the criminal records also showed that all parties involved (the Belgian woman and her partner, whose biological paternity was established, as well as the Dutch married couple) admitted that Baby J was born to the Belgian woman and prior to his birth was 'sold' on the Internet by the Belgian couple to the Dutch couple. According to the court, the Belgian woman successfully proved that it was not the Dutch woman who had given birth to Baby J. The court therefore accepted the contestation of maternity, which led to the implicit contestation of the Dutch husband's paternity at the same time.

This case has the 'advantage' that the real legal parenthood was clarified within a relatively short period of time: following the contestation of the maternity and paternity of the Dutch couple, the biological mother recognised the child before a Ghent civil servant. However, this case does make it obvious that very diverse matters are brought together under the surrogate motherhood concept. One could indeed argue that the Baby J case is not a matter of surrogacy but an example of the criminal offence 'fraud with a child's civil status',[94] and even of trade in children. Such illegal practices illustrate how people push and even transgress legal boundaries. It is clear that cross-border surrogacy contravenes the rules on inter-country adoption. In both the Baby D and Baby J cases the children were brought to The Netherlands without the required prior consent of the Dutch Minister of Justice, and thus without any prior procedural safeguards.

B. Legal Parenthood by Adoption

The singular nature of affiliation results in the fact that two women (eg the surrogate mother and the commissioning mother) or two men (eg homosexual commissioning parents) can never be bound by affiliation to one and the same child. It is however possible to supplement parentage by affiliation with parentage by adoption. Most often, full adoption is opted for in surrogacy cases, as this results in the severing of the bonds with the original family (including quite often the surrogate mother), whereas in the case of a simple adoption the ties with the original family are preserved, as only an additional adoptive relationship is being

---

[94] Punishable by Art 363 BPC, which reads as follows: 'He who exchanges one child with another child or attributes a child to a woman who did not give birth to that child is punishable with five to ten years of imprisonment.'

created between the adopting persons and the person adopted, as well as his or her descendants. In the present chapter we shall only elaborate on the basic conditions for adoption that are relevant in the context of surrogacy.

i. Lawful Reasons

Any adoption must always be based on lawful reasons; if an adoption involves a person aged under 18, such adoption can be done only in the higher interests of the child, while at the same time respecting his or her fundamental rights on the basis of international law (Article 344-1, first sub-section BCC).[95]

The Belgian courts have repeatedly been confronted with applications for adoption following surrogacy. In all cases, the central question was whether or not the adoption by the commissioning parent(s) of a child born from a surrogate mother was based on lawful reasons. A chronological overview of jurisprudence reveals that the latter, after having been more restrictive toward the matter in the past, has become more permissive over the years.

In 1989, the Court of Appeal in Ghent refused the homologation of a full adoption by a married couple of a child conceived through sexual intercourse between the person seeking to adopt and his girlfriend, who was at that time living with the married couple. The Court considered that it had not been the intention of the legislator to allow childless married couples to 'commission' a child through surrogacy, just in order to have it adopted and taken into the family following the birth of the child. The institution of adoption is not something to be exploited.[96]

In a 1996 case on the other hand, at the request of the genetic mother, the Juvenile Court of Brussels ruled that all legal conditions for full adoption had been met, as the (surrogate) mother—an unmarried sister to the (female) person seeking to adopt—had given her consent to the adoption and because, in social intercourse, the child was already being considered as the son of the requesting party; it was thus in the child's own interest that its legal situation be clarified and that fact and law be united. The judge considered that although the bond with the grandmother of the child would be severed at law, it would nevertheless be re-established on the facts, albeit in a different form (as an adoptive grandparent), as a result of which that bond would be preserved anyway. The child concerned had been conceived through in vitro fertilisation, using gametes from the commissioning parents, and had already been recognised by the commissioning father.[97]

---

[95] Since 1 September 2005; formerly Art 343, first sub-s BCC, stipulating that adoption is permitted when it is based on lawful reasons and if it is beneficial to the person concerned.

[96] Court of Appeal Ghent (15th chamber), 16 January 1989, *Tijdschrift voor Gentse Rechtspraak* 1989, 52. Another important point for consideration was that the bond with the mother would be legally severed as a result of the adoption and that, sooner or later, a breach in this factual 'ménage à trois' could arise.

[97] Juvenile Court Brussels, 4 June 1996, *Tijdschrift voor gezondheidsrecht—Revue de droit de la santé* 1997–98, 124, comment by E Montéro and *Jurisprudence de Liège, Mons et Bruxelles* 1996, 1182, with opinion of the Public Prosecutor.

In 2000, a married couple wanted to obtain full adoption of two children who had been conceived in vitro, using the gametes of both persons seeking to adopt. A married sister of the female person seeking to adopt had been found willing to act as a surrogate mother. The Juvenile Court of Turnhout considered that, starting from their birth, the children were raised exclusively by the adopters and that those children were their full genetic offspring. After having confirmed that the surrogate mother and her husband—as lawful parents—gave their explicit consent to the full adoption, and considering that the grandparents also had no objections, the full adoption of the gestational child by the commissioning parents was finally homologated. In the court's judgment it was stated in so many words that surrogate motherhood, as an expression of a person's own free will and being the responsibility of the person who is prepared to act as such without seeking personal profit, is not contrary to public policy.[98]

As recently as 2007, the Juvenile Court of Antwerp dismissed a request for full adoption in a case of intra-family surrogacy, because the bonds between the child, its surrogate mother and its commissioning mother could also be guaranteed without adoption. In 2008, this court judgment was overturned, however, by the Court of Appeal of Antwerp. The unmarried mother of the commissioning mother acted as a surrogate mother. She had become pregnant by implantation of an embryo created with the semen of the commissioning father (the spouse of the commissioning mother). The genetic father had eventually managed to recognise the child conceived with his mother-in-law.[99] The genetic mother wanted fully to adopt the child. At first instance, the Antwerp Juvenile Court ruled that surrogate motherhood as such is completely illegal under the current Belgian public policy rules and regulations. One cannot rent out one's own body, neither can a child be the object of any agreement. According to this court, surrogacy can be accepted as a lawful reason only when it is accepted, assisted and monitored by the authorities.[100] However, on appeal the Court of Appeal of Antwerp ruled that the full adoption had to be permitted. A surrogacy with no financial transaction attached to it, with the sole intention of the surrogate mother to fulfil the desire of her daughter to have children, could not, according to the court, be contrary to public policy. It was very much in the child's best interests that the genetic mother also became his or her legal mother. The Court further pointed out that it was not

---

[98] Juvenile Court Turnhout, 4 October 2000, *Rechtskundig Weekblad* 2001–02, 206, comment by F Swennen.

[99] Initially, full adoption was claimed by both commissioning parents, since paternal recognition was until recently forbidden because of an absolute obstacle to marriage for the mother and the recognising person (see Art 321 BCC). It is only after an exemption to the marriage impediment of persons directly related to each other was made possible (see Arts 161–164 BCC, as amended by the Act of 15 May 2007 regarding the modification of the Civil Code with regard to the marriage between related persons) that the commissioning father was able to recognise the child.

[100] Juvenile Court Antwerp, 11 October 2007, *Rechtskundig Weekblad* 2007–08, 1777.

the surrogate mother's intention to manifest herself as a mother towards the child; she simply wanted to remain the grandmother of the child.[101]

In 2009, the Juvenile Court of Brussels ruled that the full adoption by the genetic mother of a child who had been recognised by her husband prior to birth[102] was based on lawful reasons. The Public Prosecutor raised the question whether this was a request for affiliation or a request for adoption. He looked upon the conflict between bio-physiological motherhood and the genetic motherhood of the commissioning mother in terms of a dispute with regard to affiliation, for which the existing law does not provide any regulation and which must be settled by the court by establishing the most probable affiliation, using all legal means available (see Article 331*septies* BCC). The court did not adhere to this point of view and evaluated the request on the basis of the existing adoption legislation. Given the fact that a civil action contesting the motherhood of the surrogate mother cannot be filed (according to the court) because the surrogate mother gave birth to the child,[103] the adoption procedure is in this case being used in a certain way to fill up a gap in the legislation, or at least to try to satisfy a hypothesis that was by no means intended by the legislator. The court finally also stressed the superior interests of the child, which required that fact and law be united.[104]

ii. Civil Status of the Adopting Parents

For single-person adoptions, Belgian law does not provide any specific requirements regarding the civil status of the person seeking adoption. However, commissioning parents seeking joint adoption of a child as a couple must either be married or already have submitted a declaration of legal cohabitation, or have been *de facto* cohabiting in a permanent and affectionate way for at least three years prior to the request for adoption (Article 343, § 1, b) BCC). In Belgium, same-sex marriages have been valid since the Act of 13 February 2003. Since the Act of 18 May 2006, couples in a same-sex marriage are also entitled jointly to adopt a child. However, practice shows that same-sex couples face major problems with regard to obtaining joint adoption. Among other reasons, this is due to the non-recognition of the Belgian same-sex marriage in countries supplying adoptive children, as well as to the opposition of a number of local hospitals.[105]

---

[101] Court of Appeal Antwerp, 14 January 2008, *Rechtskundig Weekblad* 2007–08, 1774, comment by F Swennen.

[102] See n 80 above.

[103] This needs to be nuanced: a commissioning mother who has always behaved like a mother may very well lodge a dispute claim as a 'person claiming the motherhood of the child' (see Art 312, para 2 *in fine* BCC), and the actual delivery may also be proven by means of the '*possession d'état*' principle (*cf* Art 314, third and fourth sub-s BCC).

[104] Juvenile Court Brussels, 6 May 2009, *Jurisprudence de Liège, Mons et Bruxelles* 2009, 1083 and *Revue trimestrielle de droit familial* 2011, 172, with opinion of the Public Prosecutor and comment by J Sosson.

[105] In the past four years, no more than 18 same-sex couples have managed to adopt a child. It appears that conservative hospitals, either by themselves or through their gynaecologists, are on the search for heterosexual couples seeking adoption: see written question no 5-2454, asked by senator Bert Anciaux (sp.a) to the Minister of Justice *dd.* 1 June 2011, <www.senate.be> (in French and Dutch).

As a consequence gay couples, especially those where neither of the partners already has children of his own,[106] increasingly tend to resort to the services of a surrogate mother.

iii. *Conditions of Age, Capability and Suitability*

At the time of submission of the written request for adoption, the commissioning parents must have attained the age of 25 (18 for adoption of a stepchild) and must be at least 15 years older (10 years for adoption of a stepchild) than the surrogate child they wish to adopt (Article 345 BCC). Furthermore, they must also prove their capability and suitability as adoptive parents (Article 346-1 BCC). The suitability of the commissioning parent(s) will be assessed by the Juvenile Court on the basis of a social investigation ordered by it. This social investigation is not compulsory if the spouse or cohabiting partner of the commissioning parent has already recognised the child and therefore has become a first-degree relative of the child (see Article 346-2, third sub-section, 1° BCC), or if the surrogate mother has surrendered the child to the commissioning parent(s) shortly after birth, after which the surrogate child shares everyday life with its commissioning parent(s), and it will eventually become clear that the latter has/have a social and affectionate bond with the child (Article 346-2, third sub-section, 2° BCC).[107]

iv. *Consent to Adoption*

When the affiliation of the child is legally established, both legal parents need to give their consent to the adoption of their child (Article 348-3 BCC). The mother—most often the surrogate mother—and the father—her husband, if any—can give their consent to the adoption only after a period of two months following the birth of the child (Article 348-4, first sub-section BCC).

The latter clause, which is a typical illustration of the subsidiarity principle, is a clear indication of the fact that current Belgian adoption law is not in any way adapted to the issue of surrogate motherhood but is instead a hampering factor.

C. Nationality

The Belgian Act on Nationality provides that once legal parenthood, by birth or by adoption, is established, the child acquires Belgian nationality from his or her mother or father. According to Article 8 of the Act, a child born in or outside

---

[106] As a matter of fact, adoption of the child of the homosexual spouse/partner does indeed occur very frequently. In 2010, more than half (261 out of 460 = 56.7%) of all independent adoptions in Flanders (without the mediation of an adoption agency) were actually adoptions of a child by the 'co-mother' (260 cases) or the 'co-father' (1 case): see the *Activiteitenverslag 2010 van de Vlaamse Centrale Autoriteit inzake adoptie (Kind & Gezin)*, available at <www.kindengezin.be> (brochures) (only in Dutch).
[107] For an applied case, see Juvenile Court Brussels, 6 May 2009 (reference in n 104).

Belgium is automatically a Belgian citizen when born to a Belgian parent also born in Belgium.[108] A similar rule applies for an adopted child (Article 9 of the Act).[109]

In the *H&E* and *Samuel* cases,[110] for instance, the children born in Ukraine acquired Belgian nationality after the recognition by a Belgian court of the father-hood of one of the Belgian commissioning parents, as established in the foreign birth certificate. It was only after court proceedings that the children could be granted Belgian passports.[111]

V. Rights of the Child Born Through a Surrogacy Arrangement

A. Absence of Specific Legislation

In the absence of a legal framework for surrogacy, there is no specific Belgian legislation that protects the rights of the child in this connection. None of the present bills contains any textual content with regard to the rights of a child born following a surrogacy agreement. An annex is attached to one of the Belgian bills, containing a draft model (yet to be discussed, according to the submitters) for a surrogacy agreement, which includes a clause stating that the child has the right to request information from the justice of the peace concerning the obligatory preliminary psychological and medical examination of the surrogate mother (and her partner).[112]

When a child born through surrogacy is adopted afterwards, Belgian *adoption law* requires that the competent authorities keep a record of all data available to them with regard to the origin of the person adopted, in particular the data regarding the identity of his or her mother and father, as well as any data that may be necessary for the monitoring of his or her health, and data about the medical past of the person adopted and of his family or relatives, in view of the execution of the adoption and in order to allow the person adopted to find out about his or her origins later on, if he or she should wish to do so. The competent authorities guarantee access to the above-mentioned data for the person adopted and for his or her representative to the extent permitted by Belgian law, where appropriate assistance is being provided. Data collection and storage, as well as access to these

---

[108] If the Belgian parent is not born in Belgium, the Belgian nationality can be granted to the child only after a declaration of the parent within five years after the child's birth (Art 8, § 1, 2°, b Belgian Nationality Act of 28 June 1984).

[109] Belgian Nationality Act of 28 June 1984.

[110] See Table 1, Notes 2 and 5 above.

[111] The commissioning parents initiated court proceedings against the refusal by the Belgian embassy to recognise the birth certificate (Art 23 PIL Code).

[112] Section III draft model of surrogacy agreement attached to the proposition Temmerman and Swennen, Senate 2010-11, no 5-929/1, p 13.

data, are regulated by a Royal Decree determined after consultation in the Council of Ministers (Article 368-6 BCC).[113] This legal provision applies to both inter-country and domestic adoption.

B. Application of International Treaties by Belgian Judges

i. Cross-border Surrogacy Cases

In cross-border surrogacy cases, Belgian judges have to an important extent been guided by the UN *Convention on the Rights of the Child* (CRC) and the *European Convention on Human Rights* (ECHR). Courts apply the CRC, and more specifically Articles 3 and 7, in a rather ambiguous way. The CRC has been used both to refuse and to give effect to foreign birth certificates. This was clearly illustrated by the *M&M* case,[114] where the Court of First Instance and the Court of Appeal took very different stands. The lower court took the child's right to know his or her parents into consideration. Even though it is not clear whether the term 'parents' in the context of Article 7 CRC should be read to refer to the biological or the commissioning parents, the court considered that the CRC gives priority to the continuity between '*le milieu familial d'origine de l'enfant et celle de sa croissance et de son développement*'. The lower court also took a clear stand on the application of Article 3 of the CRC. It argued that

> if the Belgian legislator wishes to regulate surrogacy, it would have the obligation to put into place a balanced regime respectful of the fundamental rights and interests of all those involved, while attributing priority to the superior interests of the child. The child's interests override the legitimate desire of the commissioning parents to have a child.

This judge was of the opinion that by recognising the Californian birth certificates she would give effect to the surrogacy agreement and thus support the idea that children, from their birth, are objects which can be commercialised. It would also support procreative tourism on an international level, and encourage commercial practices breaching the interests of the child and human dignity. The Court of Appeal looked at the interests of the children from a different angle. It considered that public policy arguments could indeed impede the recognition of the Californian birth certificates, but such refusal would deprive the children of any parentage link with their biological father while at the same time they could not be considered the children of the surrogate mother. This would prejudice them in a severe way.

The interests of the child are also taken into consideration when applying Article 8 ECHR. In the case of the child *C*,[115] for instance, the court stated that the non-recognition of the Indian birth certificate—and thus letting the child stay in India—would infringe the right to family life. The biological father had been

---

[113] To date, this Royal Decree has not been adopted.
[114] See Table 1, Note 3 above.
[115] See Table 1, Note 4 above.

taking care of the child since its birth which created '*un lien priviligié*' and family life between the child and the commissioning father.

It is clear that by the time a surrogacy case comes before court, non-recognition of the foreign birth certificate could always be considered contrary to the best interests of that particular child. The child, born of and often genetically related to at least one of the commissioning parents, is often stateless and/or parentless. The question whether this 'fait accompli' should imply the recognition of all surrogacy arrangements is food for profound thought. The *Samuel* case, for instance, drew wide media attention and public outrage because the child was stuck in an orphanage in Ukraine. Much less attention was paid to the fact that the commissioning parents tried unlawfully to remove the child from Ukraine. The judge referred to this attempted abduction ('the unfortunate and even unlawful attempt by the claimant to fetch the child from Ukraine'), but immediately added that this was not an element that had to be taken into account when reviewing the legal validity of the birth certificate.

ii. Internal Affiliation Cases

In several internal affiliation cases the Belgian Court of Cassation judged that neither Article 8 ECHR nor Article 3 CRC is 'self-executing'.[116] It follows that Belgian judges cannot apply these treaty provisions in such a way that they would eliminate internal affiliation rules. Concerning Article 7.1 CRC, the Constitutional Court construes the term 'parents' in its biological sense, meaning the child's natural parents ('*verwekkers*' in Dutch; '*auteurs*' in French).[117]

VI. Rights of the Surrogate Mother

In Belgium, there exists no *specific legislation* from which the special rights of a surrogate mother may be deduced. Pursuant to the present affiliation law, she has the right to keep the child and to be named as the mother in the birth certificate of the child, which makes her the legal mother of the child (see section IV.A.i.a. above). In the absence of any (legal) affiliation bond with the child, she may have a right of access to the child, meaning that she will be entitled to maintain contact with the child only if she can prove that she has a special affectionate bond with the child; this access right may be refused in the interests of the child (Article 375*bis* BCC).

Two of the four *non-government bills* regarding the regulation of surrogacy do nevertheless contain provisions regarding the rights of the surrogate mother. For instance, a proposition is made to include a compulsory clause in every surrogacy

---

[116] Concerning Art 8 ECHR, see eg Court of Cassation, 19 September 1997 (establishment of paternity by judicial decision). Concerning Art 3 CRC, see eg Court of Cassation, 4 November 1999 (two decisions, contestation of voluntary recognition), both decisions available at <www.cass.be>.

[117] Constitutional Court, 17 December 2003, no 169/2003, B.5 *in fine* (prohibition against recognising an incestuous child), available at <www.const-court.be>.

contract, stating that the surrogate mother *has the last and decisive word if her life or health are endangered in the course of the pregnancy or during the delivery of the child.*[118] Another proposition is made to allow a period of reflection of three months for every surrogate mother, during which she may change her mind with regard to the surrogacy agreement concluded by her.[119] For 90 days following the implantation of the embryo, she can opt to either proceed to an abortion or keep the child.[120] Prior to the beginning of the pregnancy, she is also entitled to terminate the agreement unilaterally.[121] According to a draft model of a surrogacy agreement attached to this bill, the surrogate mother would need to submit a declaration stating that neither she nor her partner intend to build up a parent–child relationship with the child, and the possibility is provided for the elaboration of a form of access right. From this it also appears that the surrogate mother could unilaterally terminate the agreement during her pregnancy if her psychologist and her gynaecologist are of the opinion that the commissioning parents are no longer suitable candidates for parenthood.[122]

In the *M&M* case,[123] the lower court took Article 3 of the ECHR into consideration. It found that surrogacy '*pose de sérieuses objections du point de vue de la dignité et du bien-être de la femme porteuse*'. Commercial surrogacy arrangements could reduce the surrogate mother to '*une fonction de reproduction monnayable*'.

VII. Payments in Surrogacy ('Commercial' v 'Altruistic' Surrogacy)

If the surrogate mother receives financial compensation for her services that *exceeds* the normal amount for a *reimbursement of expenses*, a majority of the Belgian authors assume that, in the absence of specific legislation and in application of the general contract law, such surrogacy agreement has an illicit cause (Article 1131 BCC; see section III.A. above) as it is *contrary* to the *moral order*.[124]

All Belgian legislative initiatives aiming at the legal regulation of surrogate motherhood clearly are of the same purport: only entirely altruistic surrogacy is

---

[118] Art 4, para 4, eighth enumeration dash—proposition Tommelein.

[119] Art 12, para 1 proposition Temmerman.

[120] Section IX draft model of surrogacy agreement attached to the proposition Temmerman and Swennen, Senate 2010-11, no 5-929/1, p 18 (*juncto* pp 14–15 with more details about abortion).

[121] Art 12, para 2 proposition Temmerman.

[122] Section IV and section IX draft model of surrogacy agreement attached to the proposition Temmerman and Swennen, Senate 2010-11, no 5-929/1, p 14 and p 17.

[123] See Table 1, Note 3 above.

[124] See also G Baeteman, *Overzicht van het personen- en gezinsrecht* (Deurne, Kluwer, 1993) 642, no 1038; P Senaeve, 'Juridische aspecten van het draagmoederschap', *Vlaams Tijdschrift voor Gezondheidsrecht* 1988, 250, no 10; P Senaeve, 'Juridische implicaties van nieuwe ontstaansvormen van menselijk leven', *Rechtskundig Weekblad* 1985–86, 638, no 31. Against: E Guldix, 'De impact van de medische wetenschap en techniek op het personen- en gezinsrecht', *Rechtskundig Weekblad* 1993–94, 1106, no 11, who looks upon surrogacy as a form of service rather than the giving away or the selling of a baby.

permissible, while commercial surrogacy should be considered completely wrong. Two bills propose a total ban on financial compensation as such for any person acting as a surrogate mother.[125] Two other bills also start from the principle that a surrogate mother may not request any personal financial compensation from the commissioning parents that might be considered as a payment for the child, but those bills do however provide for the reimbursement to the surrogate mother of all expenses incurred, including all medical, legal and administrative costs, as well as certain types of insurance costs.[126] One of these bills even provides for compensation for miscellaneous expenses such as pregnancy clothing, travelling expenses, and compensation for lost wages.[127]

In addition, several bills have also been submitted with the aim of prohibiting commercial surrogacy through the introduction of a general criminalisation of the sale of children,[128] or a specific penal sanction for surrogate mothers and commissioning parents who offer commercial surrogacy services.[129]

VIII. Advertising

There currently exists *no legislation* which either permits or prohibits advertising for surrogacy. However, all non-government bills submitted for discussion with the aim of allowing certain forms of surrogacy contain provisions for the prohibition and punishment of advertising other than by the authorised fertility centres,[130] as well as restrictions regarding *instigation* towards adoption,[131] go-betweens[132] and/or mediation.[133]

---

[125] Art 5, first sub-s proposition Tommelein; Art 4, first sub-s proposition Defraigne.

[126] Art 4, first sub-s *juncto* Art 16, para 3, 3°–5° proposition Mahoux; Art 13 proposition Temmerman and Swennen.

[127] Sections VII and VIII draft model of surrogacy agreement attached to the proposition Temmerman and Swennen, Senate 2010–11, no 5-929/1, 16–17.

[128] Proposition de loi (de Bethune *c.s.*, CD&V) complétant le Code pénal en vue d'incriminer la vente d'enfants, Senate 2010–11, no 5-532/1 (24 November 2010), also introduced into the Chamber (by Lanjri *c.s.*, CD&V), Chamber 2010–11, no 53-0874/001 (22 December 2010).

[129] Arts 3 and 5 proposition de loi (Temmerman et Swennen, sp.a) tendant à réprimer la maternité de substitution à des fins commerciales et la publicité y afférente, Senate 2010–11, no 5-1074/1 (9 June 2011); Arts 4 and 3 proposition de loi (Beke *c.s.*, CD&V) complétant le Code pénal par des dispositions relatives à la commercialisation de la maternité de substitution et à la médiation aux fins de celle-ci, Senate 2010–11, no 5-932/1 (5 April 2011), also introduced into the Chamber (by Lanjri *c.s.*, CD&V), Chamber 2010–11, no 53-1429/001 (4 May 2011); Arts 3 and 5 proposition de loi (Vanlerberghe *c.s.*, sp.a) modifiant le Code pénal en ce qui concerne la maternité de substitution à finalité commerciale, Chamber 2010–11, no 53-0497/001 (28 October 2010).

[130] Art 5, first sub-s proposition Tommelein; Art 4, first sub-s proposition Defraigne; Art 5 proposition Mahoux; Art 4 *juncto* art 18, paras 1 and 3 proposition Temmerman and Swennen.

[131] Art 16, para 2 proposition Tommelein; Art 11, para 1 proposition Defraigne; Art 4, second sub-s proposition Mahoux; Art 18, para 2 proposition Temmerman and Swennen.

[132] Art 5, second sub-s proposition Tommelein; Art 4, second sub-s proposition Defraigne; Art 6 proposition Mahoux.

[133] Art 16, para 3 proposition Tommelein; art 11, para 2 proposition Defraigne.

Besides this, other *specific legislative initiatives* were taken—even in the absence of any legal regulation of (permitted) surrogacy—which are aimed at restraining commercial surrogacy, including punishments for persons offering or advertising commercial surrogacy,[134] or for anyone who pays a person, proposes to pay a person or makes publicity for a payment for commercial surrogacy,[135] as well as those who act as a go-between or mediator for such surrogacy.[136]

IX. Surrogacy v Anonymous Delivery (or Discreet Delivery)

Apart from the four bills discussed above, which aim at the regulation under strict legal conditions of surrogate motherhood in Belgium, no fewer than eight other bills have been submitted to the federal Parliament, which are aimed at departing from the current principle of establishment of maternity on the basis of the mother's name as mentioned in the birth certificate (*Mater semper certa est*), through the introduction of the possibility of anonymous delivery (two bills[137]) or of discreet delivery (six bills[138] and one resolution proposal[139]). The difference lies in the fact that in the case of the proposed anonymous delivery, registration of the personal details of the woman giving birth is either not required or impossible, while in the case of the proposed discreet delivery, this will always be done, so that the child concerned is offered the possibility, under certain conditions, to trace its own roots.

---

[134] Art 4 proposition Temmerman and Swennen, Senate 2010–11, no 5-1074/1; Art 4 proposition Beke *c.s.*, Senate 2010-11, no 5-932/1; Art 4 proposition Vanlerberghe *c.s.*, Chamber 2010–11, no 53-0497/001.

[135] Art 5 proposition Temmerman and Swennen, Senate 2010–11, no 5-1074/1; Art 3 proposition Beke *c.s.*, Senate 2010-11, no 5-932/1; Art 5 proposition Vanlerberghe *c.s.*, Chamber 2010–11, no 53-0497/001.

[136] Art 5 proposition Beke *c.s.*, Senate 2010–11, no 5-932/1.

[137] Proposition de loi (Brotchi *c.s.*, MR) relative à l'accouchement anonyme, Senate 2010-11, no 5-502/1 (18 November 2010), in which the woman who gave birth to the child decides whether her personal details are registered or not; Proposition de loi (Colen *c.s.*, VB) modifiant la réglementation afin de permettre l'accouchement anonyme, Chamber 2010-11, no 53-0701/001 (25 November 2010), which does not provide any possibility for the recording and storage of the personal details of the mother who gave birth to a child by anonymous delivery.

[138] Proposition de loi (Taelman, Open Vld) modifiant le Code civil en ce qui concerne l'accouchement discret, Senate 2010, no 5-46/1 (2 September 2010), also introduced into the Chamber (by Lahaye-Battheu *c.s.*, Open Vld), Chamber 2010-11, no 53-1404/001 (27 April 2011); Proposition de loi (Swennen and Temmerman, sp.a) modifiant le Code civil afin de permettre l'accouchement discret, Senate 2010, no 5-258/1 (8 October 2010), also introduced into the Chamber (by Detiège and Vanlerberghe, sp.a), Chamber 2010-11, no 53-0829/001 (15 December 2010); Proposition de loi (Lanjri *c.s.*,CD&V) modifiant le Code civil en ce qui concerne l'accouchement discret, Chamber 2010-11, no 53-0349/001 (12 October 2010), also introduced into the Senate (by de Bethune *c.s.*, CD&V), Senate 2010, no 5-347/1 (15 October 2010).

[139] Proposition de résolution (Lahaye-Battheu *c.s.*, Open Vld) relative à la création d'un service d'enregistrement des accouchements discrets, Chamber 2010-11, no 53-1354/001 (1 April 2011).

The submitters of all these bills do not seem to realise that the intended legal amendments will strongly facilitate the application of surrogate motherhood in Belgium. This is because, if the legal motherhood of the surrogate mother is no longer ascertained, the commissioning mother can simply recognise the child (Article 313 BCC), whereas at present such maternal recognition is possible only after a child's delivery in another country where the name of the mother does not need to be mentioned in the birth certificate (eg France) (see section IV.A.i.a. above).

4

Brazil

NADIA DE ARAUJO, DANIELA VARGAS AND
LETÍCIA DE CAMPOS VELHO MARTEL

I. Domestic Law

A. Introduction

Brazilian regulation allows only altruistic surrogacy. Neither the Constitution nor the Civil Code has a specific rule on the issue. The only existing regulation was enacted not by Congress but by the Federal Medical Board (*Conselho Federal de Medicina*—CFM),[1] which passed a resolution with rules for surrogacy:[2]

VII—SURROGACY (TEMPORARY DONATION OF UTERUS)

The Clinics and centres for reproductive services can use assisted reproductive techniques to create a situation identified as surrogacy, as long as there is a medical problem that prevents the intended mother from having a baby.

1—The surrogate mothers must belong to the same family as the intended mother, up to the second degree. All other cases are subject to authorization of the Regional Medical Board.

2—The surrogate situation cannot be commercial.

Resolution no 1957/2010 establishes the rules for all matters on assisted reproductive technology (ART), including surrogacy. The resolution creates rules that apply to almost all legal aspects of surrogacy, although by its nature and scope it should cover only medical practice and ethics. These rules must respect constitutional principles when setting the legal framework of surrogacy.[3]

---

[1] While not a regulatory agency, nor a private entity, the CFM is a federal agency and has the power, conferred by law, to regulate the medical profession. Therefore its regulations are binding on the medical professionals.

[2] RESOLUÇÃO CFM no 1957/2010 (published in the *Official Journal* of 6 January 2011).

[3] Although there may be some debate over the nature of CFM resolutions, with some scholars pointing out that the norms enacted by CFM are in the field of ethics and not in the field of law, it is hard to deny their legal and administrative character. As stated above, the legislative branch has delegated powers to the CFM. So the debate is not about the ethical or juridical nature of the resolutions, but about the delegation and its limits, and the validity of each resolution when contrasted

In Brazil, family relations are regulated by federal uniform rules valid country-wide and embodied in the Civil Code. The first Brazilian Civil Code, enacted in 1916, with numerous amendments throughout the years, remained in force until 2002, when it was replaced by a new Code.

Assisted reproductive techniques raise an issue that is not expressly regulated by Brazilian law: Who is the mother? In Brazilian legal thinking the presumption is that the identity of the mother is always certain, and that the child's mother is the woman who gave birth. A federal law entitled the Statute of Children applies to every situation related to children. According to that Statute too (Article 10, II), the mother is the one who delivers the baby. There are rules on the determination of paternity but not of maternity. Surrogacy challenges these old rules on the certainty of motherhood, and there is no specific regulation for these new cases.

The Brazilian Ministry of Health has approved a standardised form that must be filled in by the health professional at the public or private health facility where the birth occurred. In that document, the field concerning the mother refers to the woman who gave birth to the child, with information on her marital status, age, previous illnesses, pregnancies and childbirths. Surrogacy situations are not contemplated. The information contained in this form will be transcribed by the Registry that will issue the birth certificate.

Registration of all births in Brazil is directly regulated by the Law of Public Registry (Law no 6015/1973). It determines that if the registrar has any doubt whilst engaged in the registration of a birth certificate, he or she must send the case to the assigned judge. Parties who disagree with the registrar may also request a judge to grant a protective measure to amend the registration.

An exception to the general rule of having a father and a mother on the birth certificate is adoption by a same-sex couple, where the registration officer has been authorised by the judge to include more than one father or mother on the child's birth certificate. This situation could be used as an analogy to surrogacy cases, thus permitting registration in the name of a person (the intended mother) different from the one who gave birth.

Since the Brazilian Civil Code establishes a presumption of paternity in favour of the husband, if the woman who gave birth is married, the husband's name will be included on the child's birth certificate. If the husband proves in a court procedure that he is not the genetic father, the birth certificate will be amended to exclude such paternity.

In a case of an unmarried woman, it is necessary for the child's father to declare his paternity at the Registry. Otherwise, it is possible to initiate a paternity investigation in the family court. To date, the genetic link between father and child prevails over other factors.

---

with the legislation or even with the Constitution. For example, CFM has regulated the withholding and withdrawing of life-support systems from critically ill patients. A Federal Court, asked to decide about the legality of the particular resolution, deemed it legal and the decision was final, without any appeal. See Federal District Court of Brasilia, action no 2007.34.00.014809-3, Judge Roberto Luis Luchi Demo, 9 December 2010, available at <www.trf1.jus.br>.

Paternity may be established by any means of proof. DNA tests, albeit secure and subsidised by the Government in family cases, will be performed only if voluntary. If there is a refusal to submit to the test, courts are forbidden to force the alleged father to comply, but nonetheless can determine paternity based on other sources of evidence.

According to the principles embodied in the Federal Constitution, Article 226, paragraph 7 assures the right to family planning, and the family is considered as the foundation of society with special protection from the State. In spite of this wording, abortion is prohibited and considered to be a felony, except in two cases: when the mother's life is at risk; or when the pregnancy resulted from rape.

B. Legal Requirements on a Surrogate Mother/The Intended Parents

The CFM Resolution no 1957/2010 prescribes two types of requirements:

(a) general requirements;
(b) specific requirements.

In the first case, the legal capacity of all parties is asserted, according to the rules of the Civil Code. In the latter, each party is subject to a different group of requirements according to his or her role in the procedure.

The physician who performs the procedure must be certified and licensed by the Regional Medical Board, and the clinic or centre of assisted reproduction must be accredited by federal and regional agencies. Amongst other duties, the physician is to give full, clear and correct information to the parties on the procedure, stating all risks involved.

The surrogate and the intended mother must be close relatives (first- or second-degree relatives). This means that the surrogate may be the mother, the sister or the daughter of the intended mother. This is the only specific requirement imposed on the surrogate, who does not have to meet any other requirements, such as marital status, sexual orientation or medical condition.

The intended mother must fulfil two extra requirements:

(a) she must have a medical condition that prevents her from carrying the child or getting pregnant;
(b) she must be the egg donor.

These requirements make gestational surrogacy the only kind allowed by Brazilian rules. Nonetheless, and despite the wording used in Resolution no 1957/2010, at least one Regional Medical Board has disregarded this requirement and authorised a surrogacy with eggs from an anonymous donor.[4]

---

[4] Decision by Santa Catarina Judge Gerson Cherem III, Sucession Court of Florianópolis. Decided on 9 August 2010.

Nevertheless, if the intended mother does not have relatives who are available or willing to act as a surrogate mother, the Regional Medical Boards[5] may authorise a surrogate that does not have family ties with the intended mother, as long as the request is justified. Although this rule comes from the federal Regulation, its implementation by the Regional Boards may vary from state to state.[6]

The intended mother may be single and use a sperm donor, since there is no special requirement with regard to the intended father. Therefore, surrogacy arrangements for female same-sex couples are possible, while for male same-sex couples they are not; and only surrogacy with the intended mother's genetic material is admitted by the CFM Resolution.[7]

C. Enforceability of Surrogacy Arrangements

Private surrogacy agreements with commercial purposes are not permitted in Brazil.[8] This ban does not cover reimbursement by the intended parents to the surrogate of all the expenses incurred during the ART procedures, pregnancy and delivery. Child maintenance in Brazil is also due to pregnant women, according to Law no 11804/2008. The surrogate might be entitled to obtain a maintenance order during pregnancy if the intended parents do not comply with their obligations.

The CFM regulation for all ART procedures requires a written document in which express consent is given by all parties involved in the medical procedure. This binding instrument must be entered into by the surrogate and the intended mother. If one of the parties involved is married, although the Regulation does not mention it expressly, it is current practice for the husband to sign the consent form too.

To date, neither the Superior Court of Justice, which decides on the uniform interpretation of all federal law, nor the Supreme Court, which decides on constitutional inquiries, has been asked to rule on the issue of surrogacy. Thus there is no authoritative guidance on the subject matter and no prediction as to how courts will react. It is important to note that Brazilian law is strongly resistant to commoditisation of the human body.

---

[5] In the Brazilian federal system, there are 26 states and one federal district. Each one has a Regional Medical Board (CRM). The Regional Boards are guided by general rules edited by CFM. They usually supervise the application of CFM general rules and perform administrative processes, and have permission to enact complementary rules since they are in compliance with the general ones. On surrogacy, some Regional Boards have complemented the CFM Resolution, setting up more requirements, such as psychological evaluation of the intended parents and the surrogate.

[6] The Regional Boards can authorise other family members and even friends to act as surrogates, if there is no suspicion of commercial elements in the agreement.

[7] The indirect prohibition of surrogacy by male same-sex couples may give rise to relevant constitutional inquiries concerning the equal protection clause and the recent Supreme Court decision about the rights of homosexuals.

[8] No advertising is permitted. Brazilian legislation is very restrictive on advertising in general for medical procedures, and even for certain types of treatment or medical care.

D. Legal Parenthood

There are no specific rules with regard to surrogate births, but the Civil Code has rules on the presumption of legal parenthood for children born in Brazil in Article 1597. For the mother, the presumption is that the childbirth defines motherhood. For the definition of 'fatherhood', there are three different scenarios:

(a) the father is the husband, if the woman was married at the time the child was conceived;
(b) the father is the sperm donor, if he consented to the ART procedure and was married to the woman at the time of birth (in this case, marriage at the time of conception is not relevant);
(c) the father is the husband of the woman who gave birth, having given prior consent for his wife to undergo an ART procedure with a sperm donor.

None of these rules specifically addresses the issue of surrogacy and all are interpreted to include civil partnership and cohabitation.

When a child is born as a result of a surrogacy agreement, the lack of specific regulation prevents the registration of the child in the name of the intended mother, since she did not give birth. The Brazilian Criminal Code considers it to be a felony for a woman to claim to have given birth to the child of another woman. It is also a felony, committed by health professionals, to indicate in the hospital records that the mother is a different woman from the one who gave birth. In this scenario, the intended mother would have to seek judicial authorisation for the child to be registered as hers.[9]

Brazilian case law on surrogacy so far has dealt only with issues regarding the registration of birth of newborns. Comprehensive research in state courts has shown no results as to:

(a) disputes between the surrogate and the intended parents;
(b) inquiries about the legality and constitutionality of altruistic surrogacy agreements;
(c) the validity and enforceability of surrogacy contracts.

Thus far, the cases found have addressed the registration of the newborn by the intended parents.[10] In all cases the outcome was similar, with no reference

---

[9] As for the intended father, it is plainly legal to register the child in his name, even if the newborn is not genetically related to him.

[10] Because all the decisions are from first instance judges, and some are protected by confidentiality, it is accordingly difficult to quote from them: 1st Decision by Santa Catarina Judge Gerson Cherem III, from the Sucession Court of Florianópolis, decided 8 August 2010; 2nd Decision by Rio Grande do Sul State Judge Luís Antônio de Abreu Johnson, decided 3 January 2011; 3rd Decision by Minas Gerais State Judge Átila Andrade de Castro, decided 14 June 2004; 4th Decision from the Office of São Paulo State Court, Opinion no 82, 2010 has regulated the question in Case no 104323, from 2009 (no information on the judge is available); 5th Decision on Case 0188 11 001069-4, from Nova Lima, 2ª Civil Court, State of Minas Gerais (also there is no information on the judge).

to a dispute between the intended parents and the surrogate, or to commercial elements in the agreement; the first instance judge ordered the registration of the newborn by the intended parents, sometimes after a DNA test. Only one decision was appealed, and it was affirmed.[11] One of these cases had an interesting outcome: the first instance judge authorised an order similar to a pre-birth order which is something entirely new in our system.[12]

E. Rights of the Child Born through a Surrogacy Arrangement

According to the Brazilian Constitution, any legal distinction between legitimate and illegitimate children is forbidden. There is a constitutional clause specifically addressed to banishing 'any discriminatory designation' of children born inside or outside of wedlock, as well as natural and adopted children. The clause also applies to children born of an ART procedure. Therefore, a child born through a surrogacy arrangement is entitled to an equal status of filiation.

It is worth mentioning that Brazilian law recognises children as subjects of several basic rights (eg, the rights to life, health, nourishment, education, rest and leisure, professional training, culture, dignity, respect, freedom, and family and community life), and the Constitution declares that the family and the State have the duty to safeguard children from abuse, violence, cruelty, oppression, exploitation and discrimination.[13]

II. Private International Law and Nationality Issues in Surrogacy

A. Choice of Law: Domicile

There is no specific rule in Brazilian private international law for international surrogacy cases in Brazil. The conflict rule that applies to all cases of international family law is the domicile rule. It has many flaws, as it does not specify what to do in a case where two domiciles are involved.

Brazil is a party to various Inter-American Conventions on Private International Law, sponsored by the Organization of American States,[14] and some of them deal with family issues, including child abduction and maintenance. There is no specific rule for surrogacy in any of them. Brazil is also a party to two Hague Conference on Private International Law Conventions, on inter-country adoption

---

[11] 4th Decision, above n 10.
[12] 2nd Decision, above n 10.
[13] Art 227 of the Brazilian Constitution.
[14] For more details, see <www.oas.org>.

and on child abduction, often applied by the Brazilian judicial system, but these do not apply to surrogacy arrangements.[15]

Since Brazilian family law is applicable to all private persons, foreigners or Brazilians, who are permanent residents of Brazil, one issue that must be addressed is as regards the effects of surrogacy arrangements made abroad. If the intended parents are domiciled abroad, and the child is born abroad, the applicable law on the surrogacy agreement will not be Brazilian law but the local law, and a commercial surrogacy agreement may be legal according to the *locus regit actum* rule. Nonetheless, if Brazil is the permanent residence of the intended parents, a surrogacy arrangement made abroad that does not comply with the limitations of Brazilian law may be considered a *fraude à la loi*, and may even prevent registration for nationality purposes.[16] If the intended mother discloses the existence of a commercial surrogacy, or if this information is revealed in the birth certificate, the Brazilian Consulate or the Brazilian Registry may infer that there was an explicit intent to evade Brazilian law and therefore not allow registration of the birth in the intended mother's name. To date, no such cases have been reported.

B. Nationality

The Brazilian system of assigning nationality is twofold. The main rule is the *ius soli* principle, whereby a child born in Brazil will be a Brazilian national. When the child is born abroad, he or she can still be a Brazilian national through the *ius sanguinis* rule, in the situations set out in Article 12, I, C of the Brazilian Constitution, if either the father or the mother is a Brazilian national at the time of the child's birth. If the Brazilian parent registers the child in the Brazilian Consulate of the place of birth, Brazilian nationality is automatic. Otherwise, although the child is always recognised as a Brazilian national, a request to confirm the nationality will have to be made before a Federal Judge, according to the Brazilian Constitution. Issues regarding Brazilian nationality will therefore only arise if the child is born abroad.

Since the traditional *ius sanguinis* rule values the genetic link between the child and the parents for nationality purposes, one issue that arises in surrogacy is whether the child will be a Brazilian national if neither one of the intended parents is genetically related to the child. This would be the case in surrogacy arrangements with egg and sperm donors, not permitted in Brazil but possible in some jurisdictions. As regards adoption, the child adopted by a Brazilian national will be entitled to Brazilian nationality in view of the new paternity or maternity link with a Brazilian national. The same rationale may be applied to surrogacy

---

[15] For more information, see <www.hcch.net>.

[16] We emphasise that the CFM Regulation on the subject matter does not apply to medical professionals in countries other than Brazil, This is not our point here. We are speculating that a commercial surrogacy agreement made abroad may be considered a breach of the Brazilian system that bans almost all forms of commodification of the human body.

arrangements, but only if the intended parents manage to obtain a proper birth certificate issued by the place of birth. The child will be entitled to Brazilian nationality only if the father or mother shown on the birth certificate is a Brazilian national. Otherwise, the child will have the nationality of the gestational mother or the nationality of the country of birth, but will not be a Brazilian national.

As mentioned above, one problem that intended parents may face is the refusal of the Brazilian Consulate to register a child born abroad as a result of a surrogacy arrangement, or of the Brazilian Registrar to accept a foreign birth certificate that mentions a surrogacy arrangement. If the child born abroad does not have a Brazilian parent on his or her birth certificate, Brazilian nationality will not be asserted through the *ius sanguinis* rule.

The risk in this case is that the foreign surrogacy arrangement may be considered a *fraude à la loi*, since there is a precedent in Brazilian family law. If a *fraude à la loi* issue is raised, the birth certificate could be deemed ineffective, and this may impact the child's nationality. Before the Divorce Law of 1977, divorce was not admitted in Brazil. Many couples that were permanent residents in Brazil divorced abroad and tried to have the decision recognised and enforced in Brazil. The Brazilian Supreme Court considered that in cases where one or both parties to the divorce were Brazilian nationals and residents of Brazil, there was an explicit intent to evade Brazilian mandatory laws that did not allow for divorce, and denied recognition of the foreign divorce proceedings.

C. Jurisdiction and Recognition and Enforcement

Since 2004, jurisdiction over all cases involving international judicial cooperation has been transferred from the Federal Supreme Court to the Superior Court of Justice. The Supreme Court viewed the matter of public policy very strictly, as seen in the divorce cases mentioned above. This change of venue may present a brighter scenario for future surrogacy cases. The Superior Court of Justice has taken a liberal approach in family issues, especially regarding children's rights.

In Brazil, the 'best interests of the child' is always interpreted as favouring the inclusion of the child in a family, preferably the child's biological family. The family is highly valued in Brazilian society, and the right to a family is protected. For example, as regards same-sex couples, not only is adoption permitted, but the names of both fathers or both mothers are included on the birth certificate. Therefore, it seems likely that a surrogacy situation originating abroad would be validated, as long as the local applicable law had been respected. Brazilian courts have traditionally respected foreign law in cases where the question involved related to an obligation that was enforceable abroad. If we continue in the path laid down by the courts in adoption cases, foreign surrogate agreements would be enforceable in the name of the 'best interests of the child'.

5

The People's Republic of China[*]

ZHENGXIN HUO

I. Current Chinese Law on Surrogacy

On 22 September 1996, a surrogate mother gave birth to a test-tube baby in the Third Hospital of Peking University in Beijing. It was the first time in mainland China that a test-tube baby, conceived in a laboratory using the parents' sperm and egg, had been carried and delivered by someone other than the biological mother.[1] Since then, China has quietly emerged as one of the most active countries in the world when it comes to surrogacy. According to the estimation of Guangzhou-based *Southern Metropolis Weekly* newspaper, around 25,000 surrogate children had been born in mainland China up to April 2009.[2] Nevertheless, it should be noted that most surrogate pregnancy services in China operate underground, as the Chinese Government banned surrogacy of both the commercial and altruistic varieties in 2001.

On 20 February 2001, the Ministry of Public Health of the People's Republic of China issued 'Administrative Measures for Assisted Human Reproductive Technology' (hereinafter 'Administrative Measures').[3] Effective as of 1 August 2001, this administrative rule bans all forms of trade in fertilised eggs and embryos, and prohibits medical institutions and medical staff from performing any form of surrogacy procedure. It also stipulates that the use of assisted reproductive technology shall conform to China's family planning policy, ethical standards and laws.[4] Moreover, it states that any medical institution which abets a surrogacy arrangement in violation of the Administrative Measures shall be warned and punished by a fine of not more than 30,000 yuan (RMB), and that the

---

[*] This chapter is supported by the Program for New Century Excellent Talents in University sponsored by the Ministry of the People's Republic of China.

[1] Tan Bintao and Duan Yong, 'Daiyun Shengyu zhong de Qinzi Guanxi [The Parent–child Relationship in Surrogacy Arrangements]' (2010) 13 *Renmin Sifa [People's Judicature]* 66, 67.

[2] See <www.nf.nfdaily.cn/nanfangdaily/ndzk/200904140115.asp>, last visited 9 July 2011.

[3] Renlei Fuzhushengzhi Jishu Guanli Banfa, Zhonghua Renmingongheguo Weishengbu Ling No 14 of 2001 [Administrative Measures for Assisted Human Reproductive Technology, Order of the Ministry of Public Health of the People's Republic of China, No 14 of 2001], 22 February 2001 (PRC).

[4] Administrative Measures, above n 3, at Art 3.

relevant responsible personnel shall be subject to administrative liabilities, and when committing a crime, shall be prosecuted for criminal liabilities.[5]

In order to complement the Administrative Measures, the Ministry of Public Health amended the Ethical Principles of Assisted Human Reproductive Technology and Human Sperm Bank (hereinafter 'Ethical Principles') on 23 June 2003.[6] Pursuant to the amended Ethical Principles, the principle of protecting children is established as one of the seven fundamental ethical principles of assisted human reproductive technology which is guaranteed and implemented by, inter alia, the prohibition on medical staff performing surrogate surgery.[7]

These two administrative rules issued by the Ministry of Public Health outlaw surrogacy arrangements, from which several important conclusions may be drawn. First, surrogacy arrangements, whether commercial or altruistic, are void and unenforceable in China. Pursuant to the Contract Act of the People's Republic of China, effective as of 1 October 1999, a contract shall be null and void if it offends against public policy or violates a mandatory provision of any law or administrative regulation;[8] surrogacy contracts of both the commercial and non-commercial varieties shall therefore be void and unenforceable as they violate the mandatory provisions of the administrative rules, and Chinese People's Courts usually deem them to be contrary to the public policy of the State.[9]

Secondly, the existing administrative rules impose sanctions only on the medical institutions and the medical staff; neither the surrogate parties (ie, the intended parents and the surrogate mothers) nor the intermediaries are penalised. There are two suggested reasons why the surrogate parties and the intermediaries are excluded from sanctions. The first is a legal reason, ie under the Legislation Act of the PRC, the Ministry of Public Health, as a department within the State Council, has no authority to promulgate administrative ordinances that may

---

[5] Administrative Measures, above n 3, At art 22.
However, it is worth noting that performing surrogacy procedures does not constitute a crime under the Criminal Law of the People's Republic of China; therefore, stating the possibility of criminalising surrogacy-related activities by Art 22 of the Administrative Measures is meaningless from the perspective of legal analysis.

[6] Renlei Fuzhu Shengzhi Jishu he Renlei Jingziku Lunli Yuanze [Ethical Principles of Assisted Human Reproductive Technology and Human Sperm Bank, Order of the Ministry of Public Health of the People's Republic of China, No 176 of 2003]. Under the Legislative Act, orders issued by various ministries and commissions, the People's Bank of China, the Auditing Agency, or other administrative organs directly under the State Council are classified as 'administrative rules'. The administrative rules are a source of legal norms under the current Chinese legislative system. As the Ethical Principles and the amended Ethical Principles were promulgated by the Ministry of Public Health as the Orders of the Ministry, they enjoy the status of administrative rules which are authoritative within the scope of the authority of the Ministry of Public Health. Zhonghua Renmin Gongheguo Lifafa [Legislation Act] arts 71,82 (2000) (PRC).

[7] Ethical Principles, above n 6, at Chapter One, Section 3(5).

[8] Zhonghua Renmin Gongheguo Hetongfa [Contract Act] art 52 (1999) (PRC); see Yongping Xiao and Zhengxin Huo, 'Ordre Public in China's Private International Law' (2005) 53:3 American Journal of Comparative Law 653, 658.

[9] The details of a Chinese domestic case on surrogacy will be discussed in section II. below.

impose sanctions on subjects other than medical institutions and medical staff.[10] The second reason is rooted in the Chinese cultural tradition. As Mencius (*c* 372 BC–289 BC), one of the most influential philosophers and sages in the Chinese history, and one of the principal interpreters of Confucianism, taught more than 2,000 years ago, '[t]here are three ways to be unfilial, the worst is not to produce off-spring':[11] those who suffer from reproductive dysfunction are morally and psychologically disadvantaged in Chinese society; therefore, penalising infertile people who resort to surrogacy to remedy the situation would not be in line with traditional Chinese values. Against this background, it is natural that the intended parents, and the surrogate mothers as well as the brokers who abet surrogacy arrangements, are not directly sanctioned by law.

Thirdly, the overarching rationale for banning surrogacy is the interests and welfare of children, as unambiguously manifested by the amended Ethical Principles. Surrogacy arrangements present enormous complications for the legal status of the child born through a surrogacy arrangement, such as: Who are the legal parents of the newborn child? How should we determine the nationality of the child, if the surrogate parties are of different nationalities or the child is born in a foreign jurisdiction? What are the rights of the child born through a surrogacy arrangement? So far, China has not enacted any law to regulate such issues; there-fore, legalising surrogacy may put children born through surrogacy arrangements at risk. In this light, it is not surprising that the Chinese Government believes that the interests of children (the weaker party) are of paramount concern and far outweigh the interests of any adult party.

In addition to protecting the interests of children, the Chinese Government argues that banning surrogacy is also a way of avoiding the legal, social and ethical chaos that would otherwise be caused by legalising it. For example, what require-ments are imposed on a couple if they apply for a surrogate mother's services? What kind of woman may serve as a surrogate mother? Is she entitled to payment for the services rendered? Who is responsible for a possible miscarriage or abor-tion? What is to be done if the surrogate mother becomes critically ill or refuses to give the baby to the intended parents after delivering it? Currently, no law or regulations exist in China to cover these questions. In such circumstances, it seems necessary for a complete ban on surrogacy, as the spokesman for the Ministry of Public Health retorted: '[W]e understand the feelings of the infertile couples; but what should we do if these questions arise?'[12]

Fourthly, China has hitherto not enacted any national law to regulate sur-rogacy, the existing legal documents that outlaw surrogacy arrangements being the administrative rules promulgated by the Ministry of Public Health. Under the Constitution and the Legislative Act of the People's Republic of China, the Ministry of Public Health, as a department directly under the State Council,

---

[10] Legislative Act, above n 6, at Art 71.
[11] Mencius, *Mengzi [Mencius]* (*c* 280 BC) Book 7, ch 26.
[12] See <www.china.org.cn/english/2001/Jun/15215.htm>.

has the power to enact administrative rules within the scope of its authority;[13] however, the legal status of such administrative rules is rather low within the Chinese legislative system, in so far as they can contravene neither the Constitution nor national laws enacted by the National People's Congress (NPC) or its Standing Committee.[14] Thus, it follows that it is still possible that the Chinese legislature would enact national law to legalise surrogacy in the future.

Indeed, banning all types of surrogacy by the administrative rules might raise the issue of constitutionality.[15] Under Article 49 of the Constitution, both husband and wife have the duty to practise family planning;[16] moreover, the Act of Population and Family Planning of the People's Republic of China, effective as of 1 September 2002, provides, in Article 17, that Chinese citizens have the right to reproduction as well as the obligation to practise family planning.[17] Article 18(1) of the Act goes on to stipulate that couples are encouraged to have only one child; however, where the requirements specified by laws and regulations are met, couples are entitled to request to have a second child. This article states in the second paragraph that specific measures in this regard shall be formulated by the peoples' congress or the standing committee of a province, autonomous regions or municipality directly under the central government.[18] So far, all local authorities except Tibet Autonomous Region have issued specific measures to implement the Act of Population and Family Planning.[19] Though local regulations are not identical on the specific requirements for having a second child, they share some common grounds, for example in rural areas, if the first child is a girl, and the couple is entitled to have the second child, in urban areas, 'only-child' couples can have two children, etc.[20]

---

[13] Zhonghua Renmin Gongheguo Xianfa [Constitution] Art 90 (1984) (PRC); Legislative Act, above n 6, at Arts 78, 79.

[14] Under the 1982 Constitution, The NPC is the highest organ of State power. Nevertheless, unlike the parliament in a western country, the NPC is in session for only a very short time of less than 20 days a year; therefore the NPC has a standing committee exercising almost all the powers of the NPC while it is not in session. Hence both the NPC and the SCNPC exercise the legislative power of the State. Constitution, above n 13, at Arts 57, 58; Legislative Act, above n 6, at Arts 77, 78, 79; See also Zhengxin Huo, 'A Tiger without Teeth: The Antitrust Law of the People's Republic of China' (2008) 10:1 *Asian-Pacific Law & Practise Journal* 32, 41–42.

[15] See, eg, Wang Guisong, 'Zhongguo Daiyun Guizhi de Moshi Xuanze [On the Choice of Legislative Model of Surrogacy in China]' (2009) 88 *Fazhi yu Shehui Fazhan [Legislation and Social Development]* 118, 124, 125.

[16] Constitution, above n 13, at Art 49.

[17] Zhonghua Renmin Gongheguo Renkou yu Jihuashengyufa [Act of Population and Family Planning], Art 17 (2001) (PRC).

[18] At the level immediately below the central government, mainland China is divided geographically into 31 administrative divisions. According to the terms used to describe these administrative divisions and their relationship with the central government, they may be classified into three categories: provinces; municipalities directly under the Central Government; and ethnic minority autonomous regions. At present, there are 22 provinces, four municipalities and five autonomous regions. See Lin Feng, *Constitutional Law in China* (Hong Kong, Sweet & Maxwell, 2000) 145–48.

[19] <www.chinapop.gov.cn/xxgk/zcfg/index_1.html>.

[20] See, eg, Beijingshi Jihua Shengyu Tiaoli [Regulations of Family Planning of Beijing], Art 17 (revised in 2003).

Hence, Chinese citizens are entitled to have at least one child under the Constitution, the Act of Population and Family Planning as well as the local regulations; in this respect, banning all forms of surrogacy may take away the statutory right to have a child from those who suffer from infertility or other medical issues which may make pregnancy or delivery impossible, risky or otherwise undesirable. This means that the administrative rules promulgated by the Ministry of Public Health are in conflict with the Constitution and the Act of Population and Family Planning enacted by the National People's Congress. In this respect, it is argued that the State Council should repeal the administrative rules which contravene the Constitution and the national law through the process provided by the Legislative Act of the Peoples' Republic of China.[21]

II. Chinese Judicial Practice in Surrogacy

Though the Ministry of Public Health of the PRC banned surrogacy in 2001, underground surrogacy businesses are thriving in the world's most populous country. Today, there are numerous surrogacy agencies in mainland China, most of which are located in big cities such as Beijing, Shanghai, Guangzhou, Wuhan and so on. Notwithstanding the tight control over the Internet by the Chinese Government, the websites of such agencies can easily be accessed.[22] In the city of Beijing where the author lives, surrogacy advertisements are posted along the streets. The Chinese Government seems to turn a blind eye to the underground surrogacy industry in spite of the prohibition of surrogacy arrangements.

The considerable demand by many couples in desperate need of a child and the loopholes in the existing regulations are the basic reasons for the poor implementation of the administrative rules and the booming underground surrogacy industry in China.

According to the statistics provided by the Science & Education Department of the Ministry of Public Health of the PRC, around 10–15 per cent of Chinese couples suffer from reproductive dysfunction, among whom 10 per cent are seeking to use assisted human reproductive technology.[23] Given the massive population of China, experts generally believe that there is a huge demand for the surrogacy market in China. Therefore, a complete prohibition on all types of surrogacy arrangements ignores the reasonable need of infertile couples and dispossesses them of the right to become parents. As Fan Liqing, Vice Director of the Human Reproductive Engineering Institute at Xiangya Medical School of Zhongnan University, remarked: '[A]ll people are on an equal footing. Why

---

[21] Legislative Act, above n 6, at Arts 88, 90, 91.

[22] If you search '代孕', the Chinese characters for surrogacy, in <www.baidu.com>, China's largest search engine, you will find 5,380,000 results, many of which are the websites of surrogacy agencies.

[23] See <www.news.sina.com.cn/c/212466.html>, last visited 14 July 2011.

should we deprive those patients of the rights to have their own children when medical science means we can remedy the situation?'[24]

In addition to those infertile couples who desperately need surrogacy to have children, there emerges another type of woman who applies to use the gestational surrogate mother's services only because she wishes to keep her figure or to avoid labour pains.[25] As the population of wealthy people is growing rapidly in China, the demand for gestational surrogacy arrangements by this type of woman is on the increase. In this light, the prohibition of all types of surrogacy arrangements does not accord with the social reality of China, and therefore its poor implementation is almost inevitable.

Furthermore, the existing administrative regulations sanction only the medical institutions and the medical staff that perform surrogacy surgery; such an arrangement cannot but lead to the consequence that surrogacy surgeries will have to be performed underground, or surrogate mothers will have to have sexual relations with the intended father.[26] As a matter of fact, these are the two salient features of surrogacy arrangements in China. For gestational surrogacy arrangements, intermediary agents usually arrange surrogacy surgery secretly in hospitals where they have established underground partnerships with the doctors; for traditional surrogacy, surrogate mothers sometimes have to have sex with the intended father if they have no access to surrogacy surgery in hospitals.[27] Both these scenarios, clearly, will present legal and ethical problems—the very consequences that the administrative rules purport to avoid.

Since surrogacy contracts are void and unenforceable, and the surrogacy industry exists underground, most of the disputes arising from surrogacy arrangements in China have been settled through private channels; seldom have the parties to the arrangements submitted their disputes to the courts. Nonetheless, there was a famous case, heard by the People's Court of Jiangnan District, Nanning City, Guangxi Zhuang Autonomous Region in 2008, in which the surrogate and biological mother of a baby boy refused to cede custody to the couple with whom she had made the surrogacy agreement.[28] This case has been proven to be very influential in China: it not only provided an opportunity to see how Chinese People's Courts dealt with surrogacy arrangements, but also issued in a wave of study and debate on the legality of surrogacy by Chinese scholars.

In 2004, the plaintiff, Ms Chen, a 20-year-old girl, entered into a surrogacy agreement with the defendants, Mr and Mrs Zhao, pursuant to which Chen would conceive and bear a child for the Zhaos (by having sex with Mr Zhao); she would then relinquish her legal rights over the child when it was born. In return,

---

[24] Wang Linfang, 'Daiyun Beiliang Hongdeng Yinfa Zhongduo Zhengyi [Banning Surrogacy Raises Hot Debate]' *Beijing Qingnianbao [Beijing Youth Daily]*, 21 March 2001; see also <www.gmw. cn/01wzb/2001-03/25/GB/2001%5E1834%5E0%5EWZ3-2522.htm>.

[25] Wang, above n 24.

[26] Wang, above n 15, 126.

[27] See <www.news.sina.com.cn/s/2005-12-30/14567860736s.shtml>.

[28] www.lawyee.net/OT_Data/LawyeeCase.asp?MailID=716.

Chen would receive 150,000 yuan (RMB) for carrying and delivering the child. In December 2005, Chen gave birth to a boy. After delivering the baby, Ms Chen transferred custody to the Zhaos as required by the contract. In April 2008, Chen asked for the boy to be given back to her for a few days, as she hoped to take a short visit to her home town together with him. The Zhaos agreed. However, after going back to her home town, Chen did not come back as she promised and refused to return the boy to the Zhaos. Mr Zhao subsequently went to Chen's home town and persuaded her to give the boy back to him. After Zhao left, Ms Chen regretted very much losing custody of the boy, and thus brought the action against the Zhaos in the People's Court of Jiangnan District, Nanning City, to claim custody.

The trial judge held that:

(a) the surrogacy agreement between the plaintiff and the defendants was null and void, as it manifestly violated Chinese public policy;
(b) under the Chinese Marriage Act, both the father and the mother have custody of the child;[29] and
(c) the issue of which parent the child should reside with shall be determined in accordance with the best interests of the child.

The judge went on to reason that in the present case, awarding custody to the Zhaos conformed to the best interests of the boy for the following reasons. First, Chen had entered into a commercial surrogacy contract voluntarily and transferred custody of the boy to the Zhaos after delivering the baby; and on the other hand, suffering from infertility, the Zhaos signed a contract with Chen, the surrogate mother, to have a child, and they exercised custody after the boy was born. Though the surrogacy contract per se was null and void, the above facts demonstrated that the Zhaos had a stronger intent to have and raise the child. Secondly, Chen was an unemployed girl who lived in a poor and remote village, whereas the Zhaos had a stable, high income and lived in Nanning, the capital of Guangxi Zhuang Autonomous Region; therefore, the Zhaos had an obvious advantage in terms of economic status. Hence the Court awarded custody of the boy to the Zhaos on a 'best interests of the child analysis'.[30]

From the above case, we might summarise the position and practice of the Chinese People's Courts on surrogacy arrangements as follows:

(a) Surrogacy arrangements, at least commercial arrangements, are null and void, as they offend the public policy of China.
(b) Invalidating surrogacy arrangements does not affect the legal status and rights of surrogate children.
(c) When judging which party shall be awarded custody, the courts usually employ the standard of 'best interests of the child'.

---

[29] Zhonghua Renmin Gongheguo Hunyinfa [Marriage Act], Arts 21, 23 (2001) (PRC).
[30] See Wang, above n 15, 118.

III. Suggestions for Choice-of-Law Rules
for Surrogacy

On 1 April 2011, China's first statute on Conflicts Law came into force.[31] This is considered to be an historic event in Chinese legislative history, as it indicates that China has finally modernised its conflict-of-law rules after so many years of unremitting efforts made by legislators and scholars alike.[32] However, the Act does not contain any choice-of-law rules regarding international surrogacy. As China adheres to the position that all types of surrogacy arrangements are illegal, it is natural that its Conflicts Law Act remains silent on surrogacy.

Nevertheless, the article in the Act reflecting the doctrine of public policy, *ordre public*, may have a bearing on international surrogacy. Pursuant to Article 15, the application of a foreign law shall be excluded if such application is offensive to the public policy of the PRC, and the law of the PRC shall apply.[33] Though the Chinese People's Courts have not hitherto made decisions on cases concerning international surrogacy, the decision in the domestic case, analysed in section II. above, shows that Chinese judges tend to hold that surrogacy contracts offend the public policy of the State. In this light, the author believes that if the surrogate parties choose a foreign law which upholds the legality and validity of a surrogacy contract, Chinese courts will probably exclude the application of that foreign law and invalidate the contract by applying Chinese law.[34]

In addition, the choice-of-law rules on parent–child relationships and guardianship provided by the Conflict of Laws Act may also be relevant when such relationships arise in a surrogacy dispute. Article 25 of the Act provides a flexible solution to determine the law governing personal and property relationships between parents and children. According to this article, such relationships shall be governed by the law of the place where the parents and children have a common habitual residence; in the absence of such common habitual residence, the law which is more favourable to protect the interests of the weaker party, as between the national law and the law of the habitual residence of either party, shall apply. Under Article 30 of the Act, international guardianship shall be governed by the law of the habitual residence or *lex patriae* of either party that favours the rights and interests of the ward. Needless to say, both articles are the reflection of the standard of 'best interests of the child' in the Conflicts Law.[35]

As analysed in sections I. and II. above, the administrative rules banning all types of surrogacy ignore the cultural tradition and the practical reality of Chinese

---

[31] Zhonghua Renmin Gongheguo Shewai Minshi Falvguanxi Shiyongfa [Act on the Application of Laws over Foreign-related Civil Relationships] (2010) (PRC).

[32] For detailed discussion, see Zhengxin Huo, 'An Imperfect Improvement: The New Conflict of Laws Act of the People's Republic of China' (2011) 4 *International & Comparative Law Quarterly* 1065–92.

[33] Act on the Application of Laws over Foreign-related Civil Relationships, above n 31, Art 15.

[34] See Xiao and Huo, above n 8, at 660–72.

[35] See Huo, above n 32, at 1081–82.

society, and deprive a large number of people of the statutory right to have their own children; moreover, they are in conflict with China's Constitutional Law and relevant national law, and have produced undesirable consequences. Therefore, it is argued that the competent Chinese authority should repeal the administrative rules and legalise surrogacy arrangements, with certain necessary restrictions, in the future. Those restrictions include:

(a) surrogate parties shall enter into the surrogacy agreement voluntarily;
(b) intended parents shall be heterosexual couples who suffer from infertility or other medical issues which may make pregnancy or delivery impossible, risky or otherwise undesirable;
(c) surrogate mothers shall be single, widowed or divorced women who have no medical issues which may make the pregnancy or delivery risky or otherwise undesirable.

It is submitted that if only these mandatory restrictions were enforced, surrogacy arrangements, including commercial surrogacy, would not undermine the State's core moral standards and the value that society attaches to family units.[36] After all, surrogacy promises a virtually irresistible solution for many infertile couples who are yearning for a child. Their reasonable demand and statutory rights cannot be ignored or rejected.

It should be mentioned that though the Chinese Government and society have become more and more tolerant towards homosexuality, same-sex marriage is still outlawed, and there is no indication that the Chinese legislature will legitimise same-sex marriage in the foreseeable future.[37] Under the Marriage Act, marriage is the legal union between a man and a woman, which is regarded as one of the fundamental principles of the Chinese marriage system.[38] In addition, the Chinese Government requires parents adopting children from China to be in heterosexual marriages; indeed, in responding to the question whether homosexual couples are entitled to adopt children in China, the Chinese Central Government states forcefully that as homosexuality offends the basic principles of the Chinese Marriage Act and good morals of Chinese society, homosexual couples are strictly prohibited from adopting children in China.[39] In this light, permitting only heterosexual couples access to surrogacy is justified under current Chinese law.

---

[36] See, eg, Tan and Duan, above n 1, at 68; Wang, above n 15, at 127.
[37] As a matter of fact, Li Yinhe, a sexology scholar of the Chinese Academy of Social Sciences, proposed a Chinese Same-Sex Marriage Bill as an amendment to the Marriage Act, to the Chinese People's Political Consultative Conference in 2003, 2005, 2006 and 2008. All four proposals failed because she was unable to find enough co-sponsors for a place on the agenda. A government spokesperson, when asked about Li Yinhe's gay marriage proposal, said that same-sex marriage was still too 'ahead of time' for China. He argued that same-sex marriage was not recognised even in many Western countries, which are considered much more liberal on social issues than China. See <www.news.163.com/07/0225/17/386PF5TU000127B0.html>.
[38] Marriage Act, above n 29, Art 2.
[39] See <www.gov.cn/banshi/2005-10/12/content_76246.htm>.

Moreover, as we are living in a globalised world where human affairs freely cross State boundaries and different States adopt very different attitudes towards surrogacy, the author advocates that Chinese legislators should enact choice-of-law rules for international surrogacy once surrogacy arrangements have been legalised by Chinese domestic law. Depending on the categories of surrogacy arrangements, the suggested choice-of-law rules are:

1. Disputes arising from altruistic surrogacy are governed by the applicable law of the surrogacy contract.
2. Disputes arising from commercial surrogacy are governed by the law chosen by the parties; in the absence of a choice of law, the law which is more favourable to the interests of the surrogate mother shall be applied among those that have material relations with surrogacy.
3. Parent–child relationships and guardianship arising from surrogacy shall be governed by the relevant articles in the Act on the Application of Laws over Foreign-related Civil Relationships.
4. However, the domestic mandatory rules on surrogacy arrangements and the protection of foetuses and children shall be applied irrespective of which law is applicable to the surrogacy contract.

For an altruistic surrogacy, the surrogate mother does not provide her services for money, the surrogacy parties are generally on an equal footing; therefore, their disputes arising from the surrogacy shall be governed by the applicable law of their contract, which reflects the principle of party autonomy. Under Chinese law, a contract shall be governed by the law chosen by the parties, and in the absence of an effective choice of law, the law which has the closest connection with the contract shall be applied. In determining which law is most closely connected to the contract, Chinese courts will employ the characteristic performance test.[40] Thus, an altruistic surrogacy would usually be governed by the habitual residence of the surrogate mother if the parties fail to select an applicable law.

For a commercial surrogacy, the surrogate mother is usually poor, and carries and delivers the child for the intended parents for money; therefore, the former, generally, is the weaker party who needs special protection. In this light, if the parties cannot reach an agreement on the applicable law, the law which is more favourable to the surrogate mother among those that have material relations with the surrogacy shall be applied.

As noted above, China's Conflict of Laws Act has contained the choice-of-law rules for parent–child relationships and guardianship respectively; therefore, issues regarding such relationships arising in a surrogacy dispute shall be governed by the corresponding rules in the Conflicts Act.

Nonetheless, as surrogacy often concerns the core moral standards and the social values of the forum as well as the interests of foetuses and children, most

---

[40] Contract Act, above n 8, Art 126; Act on the Application of Laws over Foreign-related Civil Relationships, above n 31, Art 41.

States impose mandatory rules on surrogacy arrangements and on the protection of foetuses and children. In order to implement the legislative policy behind those mandatory rules, the suggested choice-of-law rules contain a proviso, pursuant to which those mandatory rules shall be applied no matter which law governs the surrogacy contract.

6

Czech Republic

MONIKA PAUKNEROVÁ[*]

I. Domestic Law on Surrogacy

A. General Introduction

Legal and ethical issues relating to surrogate maternity have been for many years the subject-matter of various debates and proposals on how to solve them.[1] Surrogate maternity has not yet been specifically regulated, which should have been changed relatively recently. The legal regulation of surrogacy ought to have been included in the Act on Specific Medical Services, which was adopted in November 2011 as part of a comprehensive medical and health reform.[2] However, at the very last moment of its drafting—at the end of June 2011—the decision was made that the legal regulation of surrogate maternity would not be included in the said Act. The reason for the removal of surrogacy from the law was concern that it could give rise to various ramifications brought in by the suggested legal concept that the mother in a legal sense would be the woman who is the genetic mother of a child, ie 'the donor of the genetic substance', and not the woman who gave birth to the child, as has been accepted traditionally by Czech law. Examples of problematic situations were provided, such as when a child is born with a certain handicap and the commissioning couple is no longer interested in keeping such a child, the surrogate mother decides to keep the child, or the commissioning

---

[*] The author wishes to thank her doctoral student Magdalena Pfeiffer for her valuable contribution in collecting and researching materials for this paper.

[1] See inter alia S Radvanová, 'Kdo jsou rodiče dítěte—zdánlivě jednoduchá otázka' ['Who are parents of a child—ostensibly a simple question', in Czech] (1998) 5 *Zdravotnictví a právo [Public Health and Law Review]* 7; D Melicharová, 'Určení a popření mateřství, problematika surogačního mateřství' ['Determination and denial of maternity: the issue of surrogate motherhoo', in Czech] (2000) 7-8 *Zdravotnictví právo* 24; J Skácel, 'Est mater semper certa?' (in Czech) (2011) 6 *Bulletin advokacie* 26; K Smolíková, 'Institut matky hostitelky' ['The institution of a host mother', in Czech] (2009) 11 *Zdravotnictví a právo* 6; I Stará, 'Právní a etická otázka pronájmu dělohy' ['Legal and ethical issues of the womb for rent', in Czech] (2010) 4 and 5 *Právo a rodina [Law and Family]* 19 and 17.

[2] Act No 373/2011 Sb, the Act on Specific Medical Services ('Sb'—Collection of Laws of the Czech Republic).

couple get divorced or even die before the birth of the child, etc. Concerns were expressed that some deputies would be unable to vote for the reform draft due to their conscientious objections.[3]

Grounds for the deferral of this regulation in the Czech Republic are not only legal, since many issues have been reliably solved by the aforementioned Act, but also moral and political, as the whole medical and health reform has been a subject of sharp political disputes. Nevertheless, the issue of surrogate motherhood and 'the womb for rent' has been both vital and topical in the Czech Republic; a former (female) Minister of Justice and a former (female) Minister of Health were actively engaged in the legislative embedding of its basic principles.[4] However, the recent removal of the surrogacy regulation from the reform Act seems likely to delay the expected revolutionary change in the understanding of a surrogate and genetic mother for a long time.

B. General Legal Background

As has already been mentioned, at present there is no specific regulation in the Czech Republic, and it is necessary to refer generally to the framework provided by Czech law, both private and public, including international treaties binding on the Czech Republic. Surrogacy has not been explicitly permitted in any piece of valid legislation, but it has not been explicitly forbidden either. Therefore, we can rely on one of the fundamental constitutional principles, namely, what is not prohibited by the law is allowed.[5] As a result, surrogacy is not unlawful in the Czech Republic contrary to, for example, the legislation in Slovakia,[6] whose legal order is otherwise quite close to that of the Czech Republic due to the split of Czechoslovakia in 1992.

Considering international treaties, the Convention on the Rights of the Child and the 'best interests of the child' rule (Article 3) should be mentioned, as well as the principle that the child shall have the right from birth to a name, the right to acquire a nationality and, as far as possible, the right to know and be cared for by his or her parents (Article 7). Other significant principles are stipulated by the European Convention for the Protection of Human Rights and Fundamental Freedoms, such as the prohibition of discrimination (Article 14) and the right to

---

[3] See R Nohl, 'Revoluce se zasekla. Právo na náhradní matku se odkládá' ['The revolution is blocked. The right to surrogate mother has been deferred', in Czech] *Aktuálně.cz* 29.6.2011, at <www .aktualne.centrum.cz/domaci/zivot-v-cesku/clanek.phtml?id=705653>.

[4] The press release of the Ministry of Health and the Ministry of Justice of the Czech Republic (CR) of 2 September 2009; in English see 'Battle looms over parents' rights', *Prague Daily Monitor*, Reuters, 31.8.2009, at <www.aktualne.centrum.cz/czechnews/clanek.phtml?id=646152>.

[5] Art 2(4) of the Constitution of the CR: 'All citizens may do that which is not prohibited by law; and nobody may be compelled to do that which is not imposed upon her by law.' Constitutional Act No 1/1993 Sb.

[6] The Slovak Family Act (Act No 36/2005 Zz) in s 82 expressly and clearly provides that the mother is a woman who gave birth to the child and that any agreements and contracts to the contrary are invalid ('Zz'—Collection of Laws of the Slovak Republic).

respect for private and family life (Article 8). The Convention on the Elimination of All Forms of Discrimination against Women is also relevant, particularly from the perspective of unmarried women. Specific regulation is contained in the Convention on Human Rights and Biomedicine, which is based on the principle that the interests and welfare of the human being shall prevail over the sole interest of society or science (Article 2), and also stipulates the equitable access to health care (Article 3), and prohibits financial gain from the human body and its parts (Article 21). Basic significance in private international law is assigned to the Convention on the Protection of Children and Cooperation in respect of Intercountry Adoption and to the European Convention on the Adoption of Children.

General principles are also incorporated in the Charter of Fundamental Rights and Freedoms,[7] which ensures basic rights and liberties for everyone irrespective of gender (Article 3), the right to the protection of health (Article 31) and the right of parenthood and family to be protected by the law, and the provision for the special protection of children and juveniles to be guaranteed (Article 32). The basic formal source for the issues relating to assisted reproduction is the National Health Care Code 1966, amended many times, including an amendment relating to assisted reproduction.[8] Another law relevant from the health perspective is the Act on Human Tissues and Cells.[9] Public law regulates certain relevant aspects, namely, the Act on the Protection of Personal Data,[10] the Act on Public Health Insurance[11] and the Criminal Code.[12]

The main domain for surrogate maternity is private law; the applicable law is the Family Act (FA),[13] stipulating the principle that the mother of a child is the woman giving birth to the child (section 50a FA). General private law is governed by the Civil Code,[14] which is relevant with respect to legal acts considered in relation to surrogacy arrangements. Conflict-of-law rules to determine the applicable law are provided by the Act on Private International Law and the Rules of Procedure Relating Thereto ('PIL Act').[15]

Currently, the process of comprehensive recodification of Czech private law has drawn to a close. The changes include, inter alia, the new Civil Code (Act No 89/2012 Sb) and the new Act on Private International Law (Act No 91/2012 Sb).[16]

---

[7] Act No 2/1993 Sb, the Charter of Fundamental Rights and Freedoms.

[8] Act No 20/1966 Sb, the National Health Care Code.

[9] Act No 296/2008 Sb, the Act on Human Tissues and Cells. See in detail M Kalvach, 'Asistovaná reprodukce ve světle současné legislativy' ['Assisted reproduction in the light of existing legislation', in Czech] (2010) 3 *Zdravotnictví a právo* 21.

[10] Act No 101/2000 Sb, the Act on the Protection of Personal Data.

[11] Act No 48/1997 Sb, the Act on Public Health Insurance.

[12] Act No 40/2009 Sb, the Criminal Code.

[13] Act No 94/1963 Sb, the Family Act.

[14] Act No 40/1964 Sb, the Civil Code.

[15] Act No 97/1963 Sb, the Private International Law Act.

[16] In English see M Pauknerová, 'Codification of Czech Private Law in the Middle and on the Outskirts of Europe' in *Private Law, Liber Amicorum Valentinas Mikelenas* (Vilnius, Justitia, 2008) 239.

The Civil Code, which has been subject to quite intensive critical debates—newly includes a comprehensive regulation of family law and is to replace the existing Family Act in full. Both Acts will come into force on 1 January 2014.

It is assumed that surrogacy has been recently dealt with by several medical centres in the Czech Republic in cases when the egg-donor is the woman of the commissioning couple, ie in the case of so-called full (or gestational) surrogacy. The estimate has been that about 15 women a year become surrogate mothers in the Czech Republic.[17]

C. Legal Requirements for a Surrogate Mother/The Intended Parents

Surrogate maternity has been considered as one of the forms of assisted reproduction regulated in detail in the amended National Health Care Code.[18] The Code stipulates several legal conditions and restrictions with respect to both the so-called 'infertile couple' and the donor.

In general, assisted reproduction may be carried out only upon the written application of a man and woman intending to undergo the treatment together (the infertile couple), if it appears to be unlikely, due to medical reasons, that the woman can become pregnant in a natural way, or where a material risk exists that genetic defects or diseases may be transferred. The application contains the consent of the man to in vitro fertilisation (IVF) of the woman; the consent must be expressed before every trial of IVF: the Code aims to prevent situations when the man in the couple changes. The application may not be older than 24 months.

For the purposes of treatment, a man and a woman may not be considered an 'infertile couple' if a relationship exists between them within the prohibited degrees, excluding their entering into marriage under the Family Act. Thus assisted reproduction is fully excluded with respect to couples who are related in a direct line (ascendants/descendants) and in a collateral line (siblings); the same applies to a relationship formed by adoption. The Family Act further excludes any marriage with a person who has already entered into a registered partnership if the partnership still exists (sections 11 and 12 FA).[19] Considering section 27d of the National Health Code, attention is drawn to the fact that an 'infertile couple' may be a man and a woman intending to undertake the treatment in common; however, the provision does not expressly provide that the man and the woman should be partners at the same time. This leads to quite careful inferences that a certain possibility has been opened to infertile women without a partner or to homosexual women;[20] however, such considerations relate only to IVF and not to adoption.

---

[17] Eg Stará, above n 1, 20.
[18] See ss 27c, 27d and 27e of the National Health Care Code.
[19] Registered partnerships are regulated by the Registered Partnership Act No 115/2006 Sb.
[20] Kalvach, above n 9, 22.

Assisted reproduction may be implemented only with respect to women in their fertile years and if their health allows for it (both aspects are diagnosed by a specialist doctor); thus these two conditions must be fulfilled by a surrogate mother as well. The donor of the embryonic cells for assisted reproduction is generally understood as a person who is not a member of the infertile couple. A medical centre dealing with assisted reproduction is subject to the statutory duty to keep anonymous the identity of both the donor and the infertile couple. These are general rules for assisted reproduction.

These rules can apply by analogy to a surrogate mother and the commissioning couple. Requirements published by the Clinic for Reproductive Medicine and Gynaecology in Zlin, which is the only institution in the Czech Republic openly admitting that it assists surrogate maternity, state that the woman of the commissioning couple must suffer from an anatomic reason for her infertility and, at the same time, she must be the donor of the egg. The donor may not be a surrogate mother since, under the law, the egg-donor must remain anonymous in relation to the egg-recipient; moreover, should a third woman be the egg-donor, it would cause more complications in the opinion of the Clinic. A surrogate mother, if married, must have the consent of her husband.

A surrogate mother undergoes the treatment of IVF when she is implanted with an egg of the woman from the commissioning couple fertilised with her husband's sperm. The procedure following the confirmation of pregnancy includes the recognition of paternity of the conceived child by the man from the commissioning couple, with the consent of the pregnant woman. At the moment of the birth of a child, the surrogate mother gives up the child and the child is automatically entrusted to the custody of the father. Both the recognition of paternity by the father and the giving up of the child by the surrogate mother must be done before the competent authorities in compliance with relevant Czech legislation. The woman from the commissioning couple subsequently applies for adoption of the child.[21] Such procedure has been often criticised as rather cumbersome and as implying certain risks, but it is in compliance with the existing legal premise that only the woman giving birth to a child legally becomes its mother.

D. Enforceability of Surrogacy Arrangements

A general agreement exists in Czech jurisprudence that any contract on surrogacy would be considered invalid under the mandatory provision of section 39 of the Civil Code due to its conflict with good morals and/or evasion of the law.[22] Such surrogacy arrangements would not be legally enforceable. Apparently, some

---

[21] 'Surrogate mothers have given birth to dozens of children at our clinic.' The interview (in Czech) with the director of the Clinic for Reproductive Medicine and Gynaecology in Zlin D Rumpík and D Císařová, Faculty of Law, Charles University Prague, 10.07.2011, at <http://nahradni-materstvi .webnode.cz/news/nahradni-matky-porodily-uz-i-u-nas-desitky-deti/>, 16.7.2011.

[22] See eg Melicharová above n 1, 27; Smolíková, above n 1, 7.

contracts have been made in practice as innominate contracts in accordance with section 51 of the Civil Code.

Czech law is based upon the principle that the mother of a child is the woman having given birth to the child; therefore, what is relevant in the case of surrogacy is the consent of the surrogate mother to surrender the child to its genetic parents and the consent to the child's adoption. Courts have repeatedly decided that the consent to the adoption of a child can only be declared by the mother in person before a judge. Moreover, before the decision of a court on the child's adoption, the child must be in the custody of its future adoptive parent for at least three months (*cf* section 69 FA).

In the case of surrogacy based upon a commercial purpose, it is assumed that such a contract would be against good morals and would degrade a woman—the surrogate mother—to the position of a mere 'carrier'; on the other hand, gratuitous contracts on surrogacy do not seem to be against good morals. This is why the conclusion of gratuitous surrogate agreements (for no payment) has been tolerated, although their performance is legally unenforceable.[23]

E. Payments in Surrogacy ('Commercial' v 'Altruistic' Surrogacy)

The Czech Republic is well-known for the fact that there are many reproduction centres, both as departments of university hospitals and private clinics. It is generally understood that public financing of infertility treatment is substantial. There is also a significant foreign clientele: Czechs, many of whom are not religious, generally support reproductive medicine.[24]

In the case of surrogacy, the woman in the commissioning couple pays by herself for acts of IVF, ie for the taking of her egg and fertilising it with her husband's sperm. An additional amount should be added for pharmaceuticals used before the collection (retrieval) of eggs to stimulate the ovaries to produce eggs. Some health insurance companies are willing to cover these expenses, provided the woman fulfils certain legal requirements, ie she is younger than 40 and the procedure is recognised as one of the trials of IVF paid by the insurance.[25]

Under section 95 of the Family Act, an unmarried mother (in whose place the surrogate mother stands in the view of the existing Czech law) may claim against the father of her child the reimbursement of costs accrued with respect to pregnancy and delivery and the maintenance that would cover all her justified expenses. These are claims the mother can quite successfully raise before the

---

[23] See K Mottlová, 'Určování mateřství', diplomová práce ['Determination of maternity', diploma thesis, in Czech] (Brno, Faculty of Law, Masaryk University, 2008) 17.

[24] For details, see F Křepelka, 'Commercialized assisted reproduction' in J Schencker (ed), *Ethical dilemmas in assisted reproductive technologies* (Berlin, Walter de Gruyter—Medicine, Sciences, 2011) 366.

[25] An interview with D Rumpík at <www.nahradni-materstvi.webnode.cz/news/nahradni-matky-porodily-uz-i-u-nas-desitky-deti/>.

court too. The financial burden relating to pregnancy and delivery may depend on individual circumstances; the amount may be paid as a lump-sum, so the father of the child (or the commissioning couple) is (are) therefore legally permitted to pay quite a substantial amount of money to the surrogate mother.

The case can be more complicated if the surrogate mother is married; here, the new presumption of paternity applies, which was incorporated into the Family Act by the amending Act No 227/2006 Sb. If a child is conceived through IVF of a woman within the assisted reproduction procedure under the special law (ie the National Health Care Code), the father of that child is the man who consented to artificial fertilisation under that Code, unless a different cause of pregnancy has been proved (section 54(3) FA).

The above-mentioned Article 21 of the Convention on Human Rights and Biomedicine should be noted in connection with payments, under which the human body and its parts shall not, as such, give rise to financial gain, ie any financial gain is prohibited. Should the mother take any payment for carrying the foetus in her uterus (pregnancy), she could be prosecuted for trafficking in children (section 168 of the Criminal Code) or for the entrusting of a child into the power of another for the purposes of paid adoption (section 169 of the Criminal Code).

F. Legal Parenthood of the Child

Czech civil law lays down the rule that the mother of the child is the woman who gave birth to the child (section 50a FA). This provision was included in the Family Act by the amendment of this Act in 1998 in relation to developments in the field of assisted reproduction.[26] The new Civil Code also includes this principle (section 775 of the new Civil Code). The Explanatory Report to the Civil Code states that the legal principle under which the delivery of a child is the only relevant fact for the decision on the issue of maternity, corresponds to Article 2 of the European Convention on the Legal Status of Children Born out of Wedlock.[27] According to this Explanatory Report, there are no doubts that an action filed by a woman who was the donor of the genetic substance against the woman who gave birth to the child could not be successful.[28] Such an approach has been the subject of criticism, with some of the legal profession claiming that it is in the interests of the health of a child to prefer the woman who provided the genetic material over the woman who gave birth to the child and who is not the provider of the genetic material. Therefore, a proposal has been made to include an exception to

---

[26] Act No 91/1998 Sb, amending and supplementing the Family Act.

[27] Maternal affiliation of every child born out of wedlock shall be based solely on the fact of the birth of the child.

[28] See Parliament CR, the Chamber of Deputies, Print no 362, the Government Bill to pass the Civil Code (in Czech), at <www.psp.cz/sqw/historie.sqw?o=6&t=362.>; and the Senate, Print no 259, at <www.senat.cz/xqw/webdav/pssenat/original/63016/53258>.

this rule for the genetic mother of a child.[29] As expected, the classical solution has been preserved.

The determination of paternity is regulated in the Family Act (sections 51–62a FA); in Part Two 'Parents and Children', Chapter Three 'Determination of Parenthood', it systematically follows the determination of maternity. The father of a child is the husband of a surrogate mother, if married (*cf* section 51 FA); the husband of a surrogate mother may surrender his paternity by declaration. If a surrogate mother is not married, the man of the commissioning couple is considered the father if he makes the consenting declaration of paternity together with the surrogate mother. This declaration can be made before the birth of the child (sections 52(1) and 53 FA), or upon the decision of a court in the proceedings for the determination of paternity (section 54(3) FA). The woman of the commissioning couple subsequently adopts the child (as the wife of the father of a child) in adoption proceedings before a court.

Generally, the consent of a statutory representative of a child is needed for adoption. Intercountry adoption of a child is subject to the consent of the Office for International Legal Protection of Children (section 67 FA). If parents are statutory representatives of an adoptive child, their consent is not required in certain qualified cases (section 68 FA). Further, parents may give their consent to adoption in advance without any link to specific adoptive parents. The advance consent must be made in person by the parent before a court, or before a competent authority in charge of the social and legal protection of children. The consent may not be given earlier than six weeks after the birth of a child. It may be withdrawn only until such time as the child is placed in the custody of future adoptive parents upon the decision of a court (section 68a FA). Only spouses are permitted to adopt someone as a common child; where the husband is an adoptive father, the consent of the other spouse is required (section 66 FA): it is not possible for a commissioning couple intending formally to adopt a child to be unmarried. The age difference between an adoptive parent and the adoptive child should be reasonable (section 65(1) FA). Irrevocable adoption, which is desirable in this type of adoption, is permitted at the age of one year of the child (section 75 FA); before this age-limit, adoption may only be revocable, which can later be changed to irrevocable.

The existing Czech legislation does not permit adoption of a relative, which means that a surrogate mother may not be a relative of the woman in the commissioning couple. The new Civil Code has brought in a significant change, since there is an express stipulation that adoption is excluded among relatives in the direct line and among siblings *with the exception of surrogacy* (section 804 of the new Civil Code). The Explanatory Report states that the exception applies to surrogacy where a child is born to a woman who is not its genetic mother. However, the Roman law principle still applies, that the mother of a child is the woman who gave birth to the child.

---

[29] Skácel, above n 1, at 32.

Under section 13(1) of the Registered Partnership Act, it is not permitted that either of the partners may become an adoptive parent. Therefore it is not possible that the institution of adoption for the purposes of surrogacy could be used by a homosexual couple.

Arrangements for adoption may be carried out only by authorities in charge of the social and legal protection of children. However, the official procedure in that sense is not implemented where the application for adoption is filed by the spouse of the parent of a child, which is the case in surrogacy (*cf* section 20(3) of the Act on the Social and Legal Protection of Children[30]).

G. Nationality of the Child

Czech law has been quite liberal with respect to the acquisition of State citizenship (nationality). The nationality of the Czech Republic is acquired by a child born out of wedlock if the mother (in our case a surrogate mother) is a foreign national and the father is a national of the Czech Republic on the date of the consenting declaration of the parents on the determination of paternity, or on the date of the legal effect of the paternity judgment (section 4 of the Czech Citizenship Act[31]).

Next, Czech nationality is acquired by a child if at least one adoptive parent is a national of the Czech Republic on the date of the legal effect of the adoption judgment (section 3a of the Czech Citizenship Act).

Other possibilities include the acquisition of Czech nationality by birth, if the parents of the child are natural persons without citizenship, at least one of them has permanent residence in the territory of the Czech Republic and the child was born in its territory (section 3(1), Czech Citizenship Act). Moreover, a natural person found in the territory of the Czech Republic shall be a citizen of the Czech Republic, except when it is proved that he or she has acquired citizenship of another State by birth (section 5 of the Czech Citizenship Act).

H. Advertisement

In practice, the Internet is used for advertising: both types of advertisements may be found—those by women offering the services as a surrogate mother, as well as those posted by couples looking for a suitable surrogate mother. The publishing of advertisements relating to surrogacy would be contrary to the Act on the Regulation of Advertisement.[32] Under section 2 of that Act, any advertisement must not be against good morals; section 5c expressly prohibits adverts in support of the donation of human tissues or cells for any financial compensation.

---

[30] Act No 359/1999 Sb, the Act on the Social and Legal Protection of Children.
[31] Act No 40/1993 Sb, the Czech Citizenship Act.
[32] Act No 40/1995 Sb, the Act on the Regulation of Advertisement.

A natural person or legal entity publishing such an advertisement may be liable to a fine, imposed in administrative proceedings.

I. Rights of the Child Born Through a Surrogacy Arrangement

Where the adoption of a child as I explained in section I.F. above has been carried out, all rights and duties of parents pass to the adoptive parents. The legal effect of a judgment on adoption terminates the existence of rights and duties between the adopted child and its biological family (including inheritance rights; section 72 FA). In the case of irrevocable adoption, the adoptive parent, ie in surrogacy the wife of the father of a child, is recorded in the register of births instead of the woman who gave birth to the child, ie instead of the surrogate mother. The original records of the parents remain untouched in the book of births. This fact is not reflected in the birth certificate of a child where the adoptive parent takes the place of the parent; however, upon reaching majority, the child may examine his or her birth records in the birth register (sections 5 and 24 of the Act on the Birth, Marriage and Death Registers[33]). The child's right to know his or her biological or gestational mother is preserved, as this is in compliance with international conventions.

J. Rights of the Surrogate Mother

Generally speaking, there is no statutory provision preventing a mother from keeping the child after delivery. This will also apply in the future: the Explanatory Report, in its part relating to the above-mentioned section 775 of the new Civil Code on the determination of parenthood, states that is it without any doubt that any action by a woman donor of the genetic material against the woman who gave birth to the child cannot be successful. On the other hand, there is no statutory provision preventing the woman in the commissioning couple from applying for adoption. If the adoption becomes irrevocable, all legal and other bonds between a child and its surrogate mother are cancelled, and the surrogate mother has no legal right to contact with the adopted child.

The mother of a child, ie the surrogate mother, may apply to court for the determination of paternity. Other rights of a surrogate mother include her right to the reimbursement of her costs incurred in relation to her pregnancy and delivery, and to maintenance which would cover all her justified needs.

There is no specific law restricting the surrogate mother's right to terminate her pregnancy. There has been a case reported in which a surrogate mother decided to terminate her pregnancy in the fourth month after it was discovered that the child was suffering from an incurable disease.[34]

---

[33] Act No 301/2000 Sb, the Act on the Birth, Marriage and Death Registers.
[34] See Z Kodriková, 'Matka vždy jistá?' ['Mater semper certa?' in Czech] (2006) 10 *Právo a rodina* 13.

II. Private International Law Rules in Relation to Surrogacy

The Private International Law Act (PIL Act) contains no conflict-of-law rules specifically aimed at the case of surrogacy. As to the law applicable to the determination of maternity, with regard to systematic classification in the Family Act, the conflict rules relating to the determination of paternity could be applied accordingly. Under section 23 of the PIL Act, determination (ascertainment or denial) of paternity shall be governed by the law of the State whose citizenship the child acquired by birth. If the child lives in the Czech Republic, paternity may be determined under Czech law, if this is in the child's interest. As early as in 1970, Czech legal literature expressed the opinion that the law of the State whose citizenship the child acquired by birth should also be applied in cases concerning the determination of maternity.[35] The nationality principle is the basis for the conflict regulation in the new Private International Law Act (new PIL Act), introduced in Parliament together with the new Civil Code.[36] Under section 54 of the new PIL Act, the determination and denial of parenthood shall be governed by the law of a State whose nationality the child acquired by birth. If the child has acquired by birth more than one nationality, Czech law will be the applicable law. If it is in the interests of the child, the law of a State where its mother had habitual residence at the time of the conception of the child shall apply. If a child has its habitual residence in the Czech Republic and if it is in the child's interest, Czech law shall apply in the process of determination or denial of parenthood.

Czech law governing the acquisition of Czech nationality is a combination of the principles *ius sanguinis* and *ius soli*; Czech nationality can be acquired in many cases. In addition, if it is in the interests of a child, Czech law will apply in other cases. As has been suggested earlier, Czech law does not contain any strict prohibitions with respect to surrogacy, and its quite broad applicability can be considered positive.

Since the leading principle, which seems likely to be applicable in the future as well, is that the mother of a child is the woman who gave birth to the child, it appears to be quite obvious that the genetic mother—donor of the genetic substance—in order formally to become the mother of the child, subsequently will have to adopt the child. The above-indicated scheme supports the significance of conflict-of-law rules for adoption. Pursuant to section 26 of the PIL Act, adoption shall be governed by the law of the State whose citizen is the adopter. If adopting spouses are citizens of different States, the conditions set for adoption by the laws

---

[35] See J Fiala and V Steiner, 'Teoretické otázky určení mateřství podle českého práva' ['Theoretical Questions of Determination of Maternity under Czech Law', in Czech] (1970) 1 *Právník* [*The Lawyer*] 33.
[36] See Parliament CR, the Chamber of Deputies, Print no 364, the Government Bill to pass the Private International Law Act (in Czech), at <www.psp.cz/sqw/text/tiskt.sqw?O=6&CT=364&CT1=0>; and the Senate, Print no 260, at <www.senat.cz/xqw/webdav/pssenat/original/63004/53251>.

of both States must be met. If a law which either does not permit adoption or does so under extremely difficult conditions would have to be applied, but the adopter or at least one of the adopting spouses has been living in the Czech Republic for a longer period of time, Czech law shall be applied. This approach is essentially taken by the new PIL Act based on the premise that, for adoption, it is necessary to meet all requirements set by the law both of a State whose national the adopted child is, as well as of the State whose national is the adoptive parent. In the case of different nationality of each of the adopting spouses, the requirements of the law of the state of each of them should be respectively met, as well as the law of the State whose national the child is. If foreign law has been used which does not permit adoption or allows for it only under extremely hard circumstances, the law of the Czech Republic shall apply if the adoptive parents, or at least one of them, or the adoptive child have their habitual residence in the Czech Republic (section 61 of the new PIL Act).

The initial connecting factor is nationality, in the case both of the determination of parenthood and adoption. Nationality has been a traditional connecting factor in Czech international family law, which the Czech legislature can hardly abandon. At first sight it might be suggested that the modern point of contact—in the light of European and global trends too—would be habitual residence, which should be given preference over nationality; but this seems doubtful in this context. It should be noted that due to today's increased mobility of persons, habitual residence of a person in a particular State may be somewhat incidental to the main focus of that person's life, even if lasting for, say, two years. Protection should be provided to the person having certain legitimate expectations under the law of the State of which that person is a citizen. Moreover, the criterion of habitual residence is used as a complementing connecting factor for the expanded application of Czech law, thus providing a certain balance to the relationship between nationality and habitual residence.

The recognition of foreign decisions on adoption is regulated traditionally in Czech law; it may be refused predominantly only if the adoption is contrary to public policy (see sections 63–64 of the PIL Act and Article 24 of the Intercountry Adoption Convention). Foreign decisions in matters involving determination of parenthood, in which at least one of the parties is a Czech citizen, shall be recognised in the Czech Republic, unless barred by the provisions of sections 63–64 of the PIL Act, only on the basis of a special decision pronounced by the Supreme Court of the Czech Republic (section 67 of the PIL Act). Under the new PIL Act, the recognition will be pronounced by a competent district court (for details, see section 63(1) and section 16(2) of the new PIL Act).

No special conflict-of-law regulation exists in Czech law with respect to surrogacy arrangements. Even here, though, we can find relatively firm and unambiguous support in the existing legislation. Arrangements of such nature, in my opinion, should be based upon the fulfilment of requirements set by the law of both contracting parties (nationality and/or habitual residence of the surrogate mother as well as of the commissioning couple); otherwise the risk of invalidity of such an act may occur. As a subsidiary possibility, the application of *lex fori* to surrogacy arrangements may be used, ie Czech law; however, the risk of invalidity would not thereby be removed. It should be taken into consideration that surrogacy arrangements are not a type of contract of only a material nature stipulating compensation for the surrogate mother. The essence of such a contract should be particularly and principally the specific rights and obligations of the contracting parties, primarily the fact that the surrogate mother shall give up the child after its birth and surrender the child to the commissioning couple. The risk that such a contract would be invalid under some of the relevant legal systems appears to be quite high. A possibility to allow party autonomy, ie a possibility to admit the choice of applicable law, seems inappropriate. This also begs the question whether a surrogate mother may be considered a weaker party to the surrogacy arrangement: probably not, as most laws lay down the statutory presumption of maternity in favour of the surrogate mother.

III. Reported Domestic and Cross-border Cases of Surrogacy

In the recent cases of surrogacy, the procedure in practice includes the recognition of paternity and a subsequent so-called pseudo-adoption by the wife of the child's father; however, the question may be raised whether such an approach may be perceived as the fraudulent evasion of the law. No cases have been reported so far to be considered by the courts, and information on legal assistance in surrogacy cases is reported only by the media and in interviews, which is difficult to verify properly. No case with an international element seems to have been dealt with yet. It is difficult to ascertain the actual legal practice: the problem is that only decisions of the highest courts and the Constitutional Court are published regularly, and no mention of surrogacy has been found in their court reports.

7

France

LOUIS PERREAU-SAUSSINE AND NICOLAS SAUVAGE[1]

I. Introduction

In April 2011, the French *Cour de cassation*, the highest court for civil matters in the country, clarified the position of French law regarding the recognition of surrogacy arrangements pursued by French couples abroad.[2] This decision had been expected for several years, and states that it would be contrary to public policy to give effect to any foreign surrogacy agreements. That being said, limiting this contribution to such a statement would be giving a false overview of French law. Indeed, the reality is much more complex. According to informal statistics, at least 150 to 200 children are born abroad every year thanks to surrogacy treatment undertaken by French couples abroad. Only a small proportion of these couples seem to encounter serious difficulties in returning to France with their children and in establishing their legal status as parents.

To provide a comprehensive picture of the current situation in France, it is necessary, first, to introduce current French law concerning domestic surrogacy, secondly, to describe and analyse the treatment given by French law to surrogacy agreements taking place abroad and, lastly, to give an overall picture of the current debate on this issue.

II. Domestic Cases

While surrogacy agreements are void in civil law, the practice of surrogacy treatment is prohibited by criminal law.

---

[1] We should like to thank Professor Paul Beaumont and Katarina Trimmings for organising the workshop that provided a unique opportunity not only to exchange information, but possibly also to find common ground in order to protect children and families from the harmful effect of the lack of coordination of legal systems in international surrogacy cases.

[2] Cour de cassation, civile, Chambre civile 1, 6 avril 2011, 09-66.486, Publié au bulletin and Cour de cassation, civile, Chambre civile 1, 6 avril 2011, 10-19.053, Publié au bulletin; *Rev Crit DIP* 2011.722, note P Hamje; *Gaz Pal* 12 mai 2011, p 13; X Labbé, 'La gestation pour autrui devant la Cour de cassation', *Dalloz* 2011.1064.

A. Surrogacy Agreements in Civil Law

Article 16-7 of the Civil Code[3] provides: 'Any agreements relating to procreation or gestation for a third party are void.'[4] This article, to which there exists no exception, makes all domestic surrogacy agreements void.

This provision was inserted into the Civil Code in 1994. Unlike many States, such a provision did not result from an Act on human reproduction but from an Act on bioethics, the official title of which might be translated as the 'Act concerning respect for the human body'.[5] Such a title indicates that France's approach to this issue is much more focused on the protection of fundamental principles of bioethics rather than on the regulation of human reproduction techniques. The Act itself arose from a typical domestic surrogacy case before the *Cour de cassation* in 1991. In that case, the *Cour de cassation* decided that any agreements, even altruistic ones, by which a woman binds herself to conceive and bear a child in order to give it up at birth are contrary to two public policy principles, ie neither the human body nor the civil status of persons may be subject to private agreements.[6]

As for the first public policy principle, the idea that the human body may not be subject to private agreements (in French '*l'indisponibilité du corps humain*') derives from the idea that the body is not a standard thing, and, as such, should not be subject to traditional contract law and party autonomy. In surrogacy cases, neither the body of the surrogate mother nor the body of the new-born child should be subject to a contract. This concept may similarly apply in the context of child trafficking and non-regulated adoption.

The second public policy principle presented by the *Cour de cassation* in this decision was that the legal status of persons may not be subject to private agreement (in French '*l'indisponibilité de l'état des personnes*'). This principle is much more specific to the French legal system than the principle on the protection of the human body. In France, the legal status of persons is a matter for the State to regulate. The French King François I made the registration of births on French soil mandatory as early as 1539,[7] more than four centuries before the United Nations Convention on the Rights of the Child (UNCRC).[8] Since that time, the law on civil status, along with the State administration, has been developed with the aim of providing a single document, of the highest standard of proof,

---

[3] An English version of the Civil Code, as well as some other codes, can be found on the following governmental website, <www.legifrance.gouv.fr/>.

[4] Translation by the authors.

[5] *Loi no 94-653 du 29 juillet 1994 relative au respect du corps humain.*

[6] Cass Ass plén, 31 mai 1991, D 1991, p 417, rapp Y Chartier, note D Thouvenin; RTDCiv 1991, p 517, obs D Huet-Weiller; JCP G 1991, II, no 21752, comm J Bernard, concl Dontewille, note F Terre; Defrénois 1991, p 1267, obs J-L Aubert; LPA, 23 oct 1991, no 127, p 4, note Gobert.

[7] Ordonance of Villers-Cotterêts, 10 August 1539.

[8] Adopted by the General Assembly of the United Nations on 20 November 1989. See in particular Art 7(1).

containing information on legal status, including birth, names, marriage, divorce and death. Such record of civil status, called in French '*les registres de l'état civil*', is kept by a qualified civil servant, called '*officier d'état civil*', in each municipality. The information registered by the civil status officer may result from events, the operation of law, judgments or administrative decisions, and may not be changed by private agreement. For instance, a birth certificate is filled in by the civil status officer on the basis of the statement of anyone present at the birth. The civil status officer must accordingly record the name of the person who gave birth to the child as the mother, which establishes maternity (Article 311-25 of Civil Code). As a result of the 1991 decision (above), confirmed by the Parliament in the Act on Bioethics, any replacement of the name of the woman who gave birth by the name of another woman, through any private agreement, including surrogacy, is without effect.

B. Prohibition of Surrogacy Treatments in Criminal Law

While surrogacy arrangements are not given effect under civil law, the 1991 decision also raised the question of the prohibition of surrogacy treatments in French criminal law. At that time, the French Penal Code did not explicitly provide for the prohibition of surrogacy treatment. However, surrogacy treatment does fall under the prohibition of concealing or simulating birth, which is currently provided by Article 227-13 of the French Penal Code. Such an offence consists of simulating birth or concealing birth in such a way that it modifies the civil status of the child concerned, such as identifying someone other than the birth mother as the legal mother of the child. In surrogacy cases, the surrogate mother would be considered to be concealing a birth, the intending mother to be simulating one. Today, such an offence is severely punished by up to three years' imprisonment and a fine of up to €45,000.

Following the 1991 decision, the 1994 Act on Bioethics created a new offence as regards intermediaries such as agencies, clinics or doctors. According to Article 227-12, paragraph 3, it is an offence to act as an intermediary between a person or a couple willing to foster a child and a women agreeing to bear this child with a view to delivering up the child to them. Such an offence is penalised by up to one year's imprisonment and a fine of up to €15,000, which is doubled if such an activity is performed on a regular basis or for financial purposes. Agencies or clinics may be sanctioned for committing such an offence by fines of up to €450,000 in accordance with Article 227-13.

Lastly, Article 511-24 of the Penal Code condemns any medically-assisted reproduction activities that would not be allowed by the Public Health Code, which includes any surrogacy activities, punishable by up to five years' imprisonment and a fine of up to €75,000.

As a result, whether it be full or partial, altruistic or commercial, surrogacy is prohibited under French law.

III. International Cases

Surrogacy being prohibited in domestic law, international surrogacy cases encountered in France involve French citizens or residents performing surrogacy abroad. The burning question currently faced by intending couples and French authorities is to what extent parentage established abroad may be recognised in French law.

A. Treatment of Civil Status Records Made in a Foreign Country

Under French law, any records of civil status of French persons and foreigners made in a foreign country are considered truthful, unless 'sufficient elements establish that they are irregular, forged or that the facts declared therein do not correspond with reality' (Article 47 of the Civil Code).[9] In surrogacy cases, such foreign civil status records may therefore be presented to any French authorities as proof of the fact that parentage is established between the intending parents and the child. French authorities must take such foreign civil certificates as truthful, unless one of the three exceptions listed in Article 47 applies. The Ministry of Justice and the *Conseil d'Etat,* which is the highest court for administrative matters, including nationality and entry to French territory, recently reiterated that only these three exceptions may apply and confirmed, therefore, the liberal French approach to foreign records.

In its decision of 4 May 2011,[10] the *Conseil d'Etat* was seized by a French genetic father who entered into a surrogacy arrangement in India. Following the birth, the legal mother, who was the Indian surrogate, legally gave up the child to his father. French authorities in India refused to provide the child with travel documents, arguing that it would be contrary to French public policy to recognise parentage between an intending father and a child born out of surrogacy. In addition, Indian authorities did not provide nationality to the child due to the abandonment of the child by the mother and the absence of *ius soli.* The child concerned being stateless, the French father urgently requested the *Conseil d'Etat* to provide the child with a French passport. By its decision of 4 May 2011, the *Conseil d'Etat* responded to the urgency of the situation by providing *laissez-passer* to the child, but refused to provide a passport. (A *'laissez-passer'* is a provisional measure, generally used in cases of loss of travel documents, allowing entrance to the

---

[9] Such a truthful foreign record may be the basis for applying conflict-of-law rules (eg marriage, maintenance, parental responsibility) or for its enforcement (eg divorce), depending on the legal nature of the document issued. Factors on which the choice of methods (conflict of law or enforcement) should be based are still debated by the legal doctrine. See *Journal du Droit International* 2008.145. G Cuniberti and P Callé, 'L'acte public en droit international privé' *Economica,* 2004. In relation to surrogacy, courts and the *Ministère public* have focused the legal debate on the truthful character of the foreign record (eg cited decisions of the *Conseil d'Etat*). Today, a general public policy exception is also favoured by the *Ministère public:* see section III.C. below and Cour d'appel de Rennes, 29 mars 2011, 10/02646.

[10] Conseil d'Etat, 4 Mai 2011, requête n°348778.

country for a one-way trip and in exceptional circumstances, on the presumption that the person concerned is of French nationality.)[11]

To provide such a travel document, the *Conseil d'Etat* adopted a two-stage process of reasoning. First, it applied Article 47 of the Civil Code and admitted that the Indian birth certificate was real and truthful, especially by stating that the French father was the biological father of the child, which was confirmed before the court by DNA testing. The Indian birth certificate was therefore taken as a true factual element according to Article 47 of the Civil Code, which allowed the *Conseil d'Etat* to presume that the child was French and therefore entitled to a *laissez-passer*. In addition, the *Conseil* noted that the legal mother according to Indian law legally ended her parental rights for the benefit of the father.

Secondly, the *Conseil d'Etat* stated that

> the circumstances, by which the children of Mr ... and Ms ... were conceived through a contract that might be void according to French public policy, shall not have any consequences on the obligation of the administrative authorities to give primary consideration to the best interests of the child in all actions concerning children ...

in accordance with Article 3, paragraph 1 of the UNCRC. In other words, the *Conseil d'Etat* did not decide whether this contract would be void, but decided that, even if such a contract was void, the French Administration must allow the presumed child of a French person to enter French territory on the basis of the child's best interests.

The *Conseil d'Etat* confirmed the approach in its decision of 8 July 2011 by which, following the same reasoning in a similar case, it refused to issue a *laissez-passer* to the children concerned, considering that further inquiries were necessary to establish the truthful character of the Indian civil status records due to contradictions in the declarations of the presumed father and mother. By taking such a decision, the *Conseil d'Etat* confirmed that public policy cannot be invoked to deny the effects of Article 47 of the Civil Code where the birth certificate is truthful, which means that the father can prove his genetic paternity and that the mother clearly consents to give up the child.

Taking a similar approach, on the 25 January 2013 the Ministry of Justice issued a memorandum on the interpretation of Article 47 of the Civil Code and recalled that, as soon as the conditions of this article are fulfilled, a certificate of French nationality should be issued if requested. In particular, the memorandum states that if the foreign records of civil status—which establishes the parentage with a French national,—are truthful according to Article 47 of the Civil Code, the sole presumption of the use of a surrogacy agreement abroad is not sufficient to refuse requests for a certificate of French nationality. In practice, the local records of civil status will not be considered as truthful in relation to maternity established with the intending mother. However, they will be considered as truthful in relation to the paternity of the French father if DNA tests are positive. Without a doubt, the

---

[11] Decree No 2004-1543 of December 2004.

memorandum responds to the need to avoid the child being stateless and allows the child to enter and remain in France.

B. Parentage Established by Foreign Judgments

French law is also liberal in giving effect to foreign judgments. Indeed, foreign judgments concerning the personal status of a French or foreign person have been recognised by operation of law, *de plano*, since 1900, according to a famous *Cour de cassation* decision in the *De Wrède* case.[12]

The enforcement of foreign judgments may be refused on three grounds only, since a *Cour de cassation* decision in the *Cornelissen* case (2007):[13]

- (a) when the case does not have sufficient links with the foreign judge seized (*'l'absence de competence indirect du juge étranger'*); or
- (b) when the judgment has been obtained to circumvent French law (*'fraude à la loi'*); or
- (c) when such a foreign decision is contrary to public policy on procedure or on substance (*'non-conformité à l'ordre public international de fond et de procedure'*).

On this last basis, the *Cour de cassation* refused the enforcement of two American surrogacy orders in April 2011.[14]

Both cases involved French married couples who had children as a result of surrogacy agreements made in the United States of America—one in California, the other one in Minnesota—and in which parentage was established by judgment. In both cases, enforcement of these judgments was requested by the intending parents before the French consular authorities in order to provide French civil status records to the children. Such a French civil status record was obtained in each case. However, the French Government took action later on in order to void these registrations on the basis of their being contrary to public policy.

Unlike in the *Conseil d'Etat* cases cited above, the children concerned were not stateless but United States citizens, thanks to their birth on US soil. As a result, the children concerned could enter French territory, which was not the case for the children born in India. This highlights the serious impact that the law on citizenship of the State of birth may have on the outcome of international surrogacy cases. However, following the issuance of the memorandum of 2013 mentioned earlier (Section III.A.), a certificate of French nationality can be issued for the child of a French genetic father. This significantly reduces the impact of the law

---

[12] Cass Ch Civ 9 mai 1900, in Ancel & Lequette, *Grands arrêts de la jurisprudence française de droit international privé*, no 10.

[13] Cour de cassation, civile, Chambre civile 1, 20 février 2007, 05-14.082, Publié au bulletin.

[14] Above n 1.

on citizenship of the State of birth on the outcome of international surrogacy case involving French intending parents.

Eventually, the *Cour de cassation* accepted the request of the French Government, by two decisions of 6 April 2011, and voided these registrations, indicating that,

> *according to current law*, it is contrary to the principle by which the status of persons may not be subject to private agreements, ... to give effect, in relation to parentage, to an agreement on surrogacy. (emphasis added)

The Court added that such an agreement 'is void on a mandatory basis according to Article 16-7 and 16-9 of the Civil Code, even if the agreement is legal according to foreign law.'

Therefore, the *Cour de cassation* clearly rejected the enforcement of surrogacy orders, and even broadly rejected any legal consequences that surrogacy agreements might have in French law. As a result, the children concerned could not be registered in the French civil status records as the children of both French intending parents.

One might notice that the *Cour de cassation* abided by the same argument as for domestic surrogacy agreements. However, compared to the 1991 decision (section II.A. above), the principle by which the human body may not be subject to private agreement was no longer raised by the Court, because such a principle was not upheld by Parliament at the time of the adoption of the 1994 Bioethics Act because it was considered as having too broad a scope (eg, it would have banned organ donation for instance). Instead, the Court focused on the status of persons which may not be subject to private agreements, which is much less universal and much more specific to the French legal system than the reference to the protection of the human body.

It is also worth comparing the approach of the *Cour de cassation* with that of the *Conseil d'Etat*. First of all, the *Conseil d'Etat* and the *Cour de cassation* do not have the same jurisdiction *ratione materiae*. The former has jurisdiction for administrative law, including entry into the territory and delivery of passports, while the latter has jurisdiction over civil, commercial and criminal matters, including civil status and parentage. The decisions of these two highest courts started a dialogue in relation to the treatment of surrogacy cases. Their approaches appear to be in contradiction. However, it would be more appropriate to say that they do not deal with the same legal issues, nor with the same circumstances.

Indeed, the *Conseil d'Etat* did not have to face the dilemma of determining who was the legal mother as between the intending mother and the surrogate mother, unlike the *Cour de cassation*. The main issues faced by the *Conseil d'Etat* were whether the French applicant was the genetic father and whether the birth mother agreed to leave the child with the father. The *Conseil d'Etat* responded positively to these questions in its first decision, and added that the interest of the child prevails over public policy in such circumstances. It is worth noting here that under French law, paternity disputes are resolved through DNA testing, while disputes over maternity are resolved by the principle *mater semper certa est*, which favours the birth mother over the genetic mother. Would the *Conseil d'Etat* have taken the same approach if it was the intending (and the genetic) mother only who requested a *laissez-passer* for the child? This is not so evident, because a choice would have had to be made between the intending mother, who would have been the genetic mother, and the surrogate mother, who would have been the birth mother, while this choice, according to French law, is made in favour of the birth mother, namely, the surrogate mother.

By taking decisions on paternity only, the *Conseil d'Etat* does not respond to the core issue: Should the effect of surrogacy agreements be recognised as regards maternity? Instead, the *Conseil d'Etat* limits the impact of the position of the *Cour de cassation* towards (intending) fathers. By doing so, the *Conseil d'Etat* necessarily invited the *Cour de cassation* to refine its position towards genetic fathers.

While the *Conseil d'Etat* and the Ministry of Justice in its memorandum had a rather pragmatic approach, the *Cour de cassation* maintained a theoretical position consisting in banning any effect of surrogacy agreements. In this regard, it is worth noting that the *Cour de cassation* did not have the opportunity to make a distinction between paternity and maternity, because the questions raised before the Court focused on the enforcement (the transcription) of a judicial surrogacy order as such. In terms of private international law methods, French courts may decide on partial enforcement only when the judgment in question can be divided into two distinct rulings. If a judgment cannot be divided into distinct rulings, its enforcement must be rejected or approved in its entirety according to the prohibition on the review of the merits that has been adopted since the early twentieth century. Yet a surrogacy order cannot be divided in respect of paternity and maternity. Therefore, the *Cour de cassation* was technically not in a position to adopt a distinct ruling for paternity and maternity.

C. Transcription Procedure

Following detailed comments on the treatment of foreign civil status records and of foreign judgments concerning French citizens as well as foreigners, it is necessary to introduce the *transcription* procedure that permits French nationals to transcribe foreign judgments or foreign civil status records into French civil status records. This *transcription* is not mandatory and a child may obtain nationality or travel documents without such transcription (see section III.A. above). Its purpose is to establish a French public document of the highest standard of proof that firmly establishes parentage according to French law (see section II.A. above). In practice, it facilitates any procedure before French administrative authorities. Therefore, the most common thing for a French citizen to do following the birth of his or her child abroad, is to apply to the French consulate for the registration of the foreign birth certificate or the foreign judgment in the French civil status records (Articles 48 and 49 of the Civil Code).

Nevertheless, the consulate may refuse this registration if the foreign records cannot be considered as truthful on the basis of Article 47 of the Civil Code (see section III.A. above), or if, in the case of foreign judgments, the enforcement may be refused (see section III.B.). A couple may appeal this decision before the *Tribunal de Grande Instance*, and ultimately before the *Cour de cassation*. If the consulate does register the child, which seems to happen in the majority of surrogacy cases, the *Ministère public* may also request this registration to be void on the same basis and before the same courts. As of today, it seems that, in practice, courts have been very tolerant, and have rejected a number of requests made by the *Ministère public* on the basis of Article 47 of the Civil Code.

However, responding to the resistance of some lower courts, the *Cour de cassation* facilitated the action of the *Ministère public* by clarifying the possibility of using a more general ground of action: the *Ministère public* may generally act to protect public policy in any circumstances, on the basis of Article 423 of the Civil Procedure Code, which includes the possibility of requesting the registration to be void in surrogacy cases.[15] It is worth mentioning that the memorandum of 25 January 2013 only applies to the issuance of a certificate of French nationality and therefore does not have any effect in relation to *transcription* procedure.

In practice, a number of French attending parents avoid using this procedure due to the efficient enquiries of the French Minister in the course of such a procedure. Acting on this ground, the *Ministère public* has been successful in the decisions published by the *Cour de cassation* on the 6 April 2011.[16]

IV. Current Debates

Over the past few years, the prohibition on surrogacy has been called into question and debated by the highest authorities, due to the high number of French couples performing surrogacy abroad. On one hand, an extremely well-documented report by a Senate commission in 2008 arrived at the conclusion that surrogacy should be allowed in specific circumstances and strictly regulated.[17] As a result, two surrogacy bills were introduced before the Senate in early 2010,[18] but they have not been discussed since. On the other hand, revision of the Bioethics Act took place in 2011. In the course of this revision, the *Conseil d'Etat*, acting as adviser to the

---

[15] Confirmed by the Cour de cassation in the case of foreign judgments: C cass Chambre civile 1, 17 décembre 2008, 07-20.468, Publié au bulletin; *Rev crit DIP*. 2009.320, note P Lagarde; *JDI* 2009.9, note S Bollée; *JCP G* II. 2009.10020, notes A Markovic et L Davout. Such a ground for action may also apply in the absence of a judgment: Cour d'appel de Rennes, 29 mars 2011, 10/02646.

[16] See n 1 above.

[17] *Rapport d'information de Mme Michèle André, MM Alain Milon et Henri de Richemont, fait au nom de la commission des lois et de la commission des affaires sociales du Sénat no 421 (2007–2008)—25 juin 2008.*

[18] *Propositions de loi no 233et 234 (2009–2010) tendant à autoriser et encadrer la gestation pour autrui.*

Government, published in May 2011 a study on the revision of the Bioethics Act of 1994, where it questioned the prohibition on surrogacy but concluded that the prohibition on the establishment of maternity between the intending mother and the child should be maintained while legal alternatives should be found to facilitate family life without legal parentage between the intending mother and the child.[19] The Revision of the Bioethics Act was eventually adopted in July 2011,[20] but did not bring about any changes regarding the prohibition of surrogacy and maintained the law in place. However, the memorandum issued by the Ministry of Justice on 25 January 2013, which does not amend the current law, clarifies that a child born of a French genetic father is French even in surrogacy cases. This memorandum is in keeping with the spirit of the 2011 Study of the *Conseil d'Etat* which did not exclude the establishment of paternity, but only the establishment of maternity between the intending mother and the child.

It is worth noticing that the *Cour de cassation*, as well as the *Conseil d'Etat* mentioned above, intervened in the context of the revision of the Bioethics Act. It might be noticed that the *Cour de cassation* decision opened with the words 'according to current law', and highlighted, therefore, that the law might change through the revision of the Bioethics Act. By doing so, the *Cour de cassation* highlighted that it was not for the Court to modify the law on surrogacy but for Parliament in the course of revision of the Act. A month later, the *Conseil d'Etat* took a different position in relation to paternity, and confirmed its position on 8 July (ie a day after the adoption of the Act reviewing the Bioethics Act). A year and a half later, the memorandum of 2013 clarifies the interpretation of the law in relation to nationality.

The current state of law, based on the elements described above, has given rise to a complex question in practice. Over the past decades, intending parents have tried through various mechanisms to circumvent the prohibition. The establishment of maternity has been consistently refused to the intending mother by the *Cour de cassation*, a position confirmed by the *Conseil d'Etat* in its official report on the review of the Bioethics Act. In contrast, the *Conseil d'Etat*, in its report, surprisingly suggested that the intending mother be granted, upon request, some rights of custody, provided the surrogate mother agrees.[21] On the other hand, paternity may legally be established through acknowledgement, which actually allows the child to obtain French nationality if the father is French according to Article 18 of the Civil Code. According to the *Conseil* in its report, acknowledgement of paternity should become the main alternative to the prohibition on surrogacy. This distinct treatment of maternity and paternity seems confirmed by the decisions of the *Conseil d'Etat* mentioned earlier. Favouring the establishment of paternity in surrogacy cases at least has the advantage of solving passport and

---

[19] 'La révision des lois de bioéthique', étude du Conseil d'État parue à la Documentation française, esp 47–54.
[20] Loi no 2011-814 du 7 juillet 2011.
[21] 'La révision des lois de bioéthique', above n 19, 52 and 53.

nationality issues, as confirmed by the memorandum of the Ministry of Justice issued in 2013.

Today, the position of Parliament and the *Cour de cassation* raises serious questions in relation to human rights, including those of children.[22] In this regard, the Court stated that the voiding of such registrations does not prevent the children from having such maternal and paternal affiliation as the laws of the United States provide to them. In addition, the Court considered that such a decision does not prevent the children from living in France with the couples in question. In particular, the intending fathers, unlike the intending mothers, can still establish paternity according to French law, by acknowledgement, and thus the child may even obtain French nationality. The Court thus expressly rejected the idea that such a decision would contravene Article 8 of the European Convention on Human Rights or Article 3, paragraph 1 of the UNCRC.[23]

This position has been criticised by the legal doctrine on several grounds:

— for not being able to sever the situation of the intended parents and the child;[24]
— for giving to the concept of 'international public policy' a scope that is much too broad;
— for not taking into account the fact that, if Article 16-7 of the Civil Code were strong enough to imply the surrogacy to be void under international public policy, it is a common principle of French conflicts of laws that public policy should not be applied as strictly when the foreign situation is closely linked to the French legal system (*inlandsbeziehung*), which is the case here;[25]
— as not being in accordance with the case law of the European Court of Human Rights.[26] (In this context, one of the couples concerned is currently preparing a case against France before the European Court of Human Rights.)

It is worth mentioning that the memorandum issued by the Ministry of Justice on 25 February 2013 has little effect on these issues since it has no effect on the establishment of paternity or maternity. Indeed, the memorandum ensures only that the child obtains French nationality if he was born of a French genetic father.

The two series of judgments that we have considered in this chapter, that of the *Cour de cassation* and that of the *Conseil d'Etat*, as well as the recent memorandum of the Ministry of Justice, raise some important distinctions and questions with

---

[22] See D Berthiau and L Brunet, 'L'ordre public au préjudice de l'enfant' in *Dalloz* 2011, 1522.

[23] To compare with Conseil d'État, Juge des référés, 04/05/2011, 348778, in relation to a child blocked in India.

[24] P Lagarde, note sous C cass Chambre civile 1, 17 décembre 2008, 07-20.468, Publié au bulletin; *Rev crit DIP* 2009.320.

[25] P Hamje, note sous: Cour de cassation, civile, Chambre civile 1, 6 avril 2011, 09-66.486, Publié au bulletin and Cour de cassation, civile, Chambre civile 1, 6 avril 2011, 10-19.053, Publié au bulletin; *Rev Crit DIP* 2011.722.

[26] *Ibid.*

which we conclude below, and which it would be worth considering carefully in the possible development of an international instrument on surrogacy:

(a) Should the recognition of paternity and the recognition of maternity be treated separately?

(b) Should gestational surrogacy involving sperm and egg donors be treated differently from gestational surrogacy with the embryo of the intending couple?

(c) Does a distinction need to be drawn between surrogacy involving a judicial order and surrogacy that does not? If there is no judicial order, how should applicable law rules intervene to establish parentage, especially in civil law States?

(d) There would certainly be a need for rules on visas and entry to the territories in addition to rules on the recognition of parentage.

(e) How should an international surrogacy arrangement be defined? Does the international character of the agreement relate to the nationality of the intending couple, or to their country of residence or to both?

8

Germany[1]

SUSANNE L GÖSSL

I. Overview

Due to the lack of federal competence for reproductive medicine, in 1989 and 1990 the first attempts of the German legislator to regulate surrogacy were limited to its criminal law aspects.[2] Therefore the Adoption Placement Act (AdVermiG)[3] and the Embryo Protection Act (ESchG)[4] consist only of prohibitions, confirming the case law of the 1980s treating surrogacy as a form of illegal adoption which violates the child's and mother's human dignity.[5] Although federal competence for reproductive medicine was established in 1994 in Article 74 No 26 *Grundgesetz* (GG),[6] these rules about surrogacy itself have not been changed—yet.

The Embryo Protection Act prohibits the undertaking of surrogacy (section 1, paragraph 1, number 2, 6, 7, and paragraph 2 ESchG; for details see section II.A. below). The Adoption Placement Act prohibits commercial actions supporting surrogacy, such as placement, advertising for placement (sections 13c, 13d, 14b)

---

[1] Special thanks to C Budzikiewicz.

[2] C Müller-Götzmann, *Artifizielle Reproduktion und gleichgeschlechtliche Elternschaft* (Berlin, Springer, 2009) 235 f; J Taupitz, 'Rechtspolitische und rechtliche Grundlagen' in H-L Günther, J Taupitz and P Kaiser (eds), *Embryonenschutzgesetz* (Stuttgart, Kohlhammer, 2008) 17.

[3] Gesetz über die Vermittlung der Annahme als Kind und über das Verbot der Vermittlung von Ersatzmüttern (*Adoptionsvermittlungsgesetz*) revised 22 December 2001, Bundesgesetzblatt I 354; amended by Art 8 Law 10 December 2008, Bundesgesetzblatt I 2403. The provisions on surrogacy (ss 13a–14b) were introduced in 1989, Gesetz zur Änderung des Adoptionsvermittlungsgesetzes, 27 November 1989, Bundesgesetzblatt I 2014.

[4] *Embryonenschutzgesetz* 13 December 1990, Bundesgesetzblatt I 2746, amended 23 October 2001, Bundesgesetzblatt I 2702.

[5] OLG Hamm 7 April 1983—3 Ss OWi 2007/82, (1985) *Neue Juristische Wochenschrift* 2205; BVerfG 6 December 1983—2 BvR 878/83, not published; VGH Kassel, 23 December 1987—11 TH 3526/871, (1988) *Neue Juristische Wochenschrift* 1281; undecided AG Gütersloh 17 December 1985—5 XVI 7/85, (1986) *Zeitschrift für das gesamte Familienrecht*, 718; KG Berlin 19 March 1985—1 W 5729/84, (1985) *Neue Juristische Wochenschrift* 2201. Decision: OLG Hamm 2 February 1985—11 W 18/85 (1985) *Neue Juristische Wochenschrift* 781; LG Freiburg 25 March 1987—8 O 557/86 (1987) *Neue Juristische Wochenschrift* 1486, 1488.

[6] *Gesetz zur Änderung des Grundgesetzes*, 27 October 1994, Bundesgesetzblatt I 3146.

and the public search for parties (section 14a, paragraph 1, number 2, letter c; for details see section II.B. below).[7]

Some further provisions in criminal and civil law disapprove undertakings in the context of surrogacy.[8] Section 1591 *Bürgerliches Gesetzbuch* (BGB) defines a 'mother' solely as the person giving birth. The federal 'Guidelines for the Undertaking of Assisted Reproduction 2006',[9] which have been adopted by several States' Medical Associations as binding rules of conduct, prohibit surrogacy as well. Health insurers never have to pay for treatment 'such as surrogacy'.[10]

Those courts which have been concerned with surrogacy since the codification extended these provisions to a general disapproval of surrogacy in the legal system.[11]

The main reason for prohibiting surrogacy is the violation of the child's and the surrogate mother's human dignity,[12] reducing both to objects of (commercial) contracts.[13] Furthermore, grave psychological damage might occur to a child growing up with one mother who gave birth and another from whom it originates genetically ('split' biological motherhood). In contrast to adoption or sperm donation, both also leading to 'split' parenthood, the birth procedure creates not only a social but also a special biological bond between child and birth mother. Both are thus considered as victims.[14] Their mutual bond, as well as the traditional picture of motherhood,[15] has to be protected.[16]

---

[7] M Coester, 'Ersatzmutterschaft in Europa' in H-P Mansel, T Pfeiffer, H Kronke, C Kohler and R Hausmann (eds), *Festschrift für Erik Jayme* (Munich, Sellier, 2004) 1243, 1245.

[8] *Ibid*; H Grziwotz, 'Beurkundungen im Kindschaftsrecht' in G Brambring and HU Jerschke (eds), *Beck'sches Notar-Handbuch*, 5th edn (Munich, CH Beck, 2009) 80; R Dettmeyer, *Medizin & Recht. Rechtliche Sicherheit für den Arzt*, 2nd edn (Heidelberg, Springer, 2006) 174.

[9] (2006) 103 *Deutsches Ärzteblatt* A1392, 3.1.2 (commentary).

[10] *Bundestagsdrucksache* 11/6760 p 14; R Brandts 'SGB V § 27a Künstliche Befruchtung' in S Leitherer (ed), *Kasseler Kommentar Sozialversicherungsrecht*, 69th supplement (Munich, CH Beck, 2011) 30.

[11] Violating public policy: VG Berlin 5 September 2012—VG 23 L 283.12, (2012) *BeckRechtsprechung* 56424; AG Düsseldorf November 2010—not published, 5; AG Frankfurt am Main 29 December 2010—49 XVI 108/08—not published, 5; AG Hamm 22 December 2010—49 XVI 108/08—not published 5 f; no tax deductibility: FG München 21 February 2000—16 V 5568/99, (2000) *BeckRechtsprechung* 30813399; FG Düsseldorf, 9 May 2003—18 K 7931/0, (2003) *Deutsches Steuerrecht—Entscheidungsdienst* 145; no health insurance: LG Köln, 4 July 2007—23 O 347/06 (2008) *NJW Rechtsprechungs-Report* 542; heterologous insemination is deductible as an extraordinary financial burden as long as the distinction from illegal practices, 'such as surrogacy' remains clear: Niedersächsisches FG, 5 May 2010—9 K 231/07, (2011) *Deutsches Steuerrecht—Entscheidungsdienst* 82, 86; C Budzikiewicz, 'Duitsland' in K Boele-Woelki, I Curry-Sumner, W Schrama and M Vonk (eds) *Draagmoederschap en illegale opneming van kinderen* (Utrecht, WODC, 2011) 228.

[12] Art 1, para 1, s 1 GG: Human dignity shall be inviolable.

[13] A Eser and H-G Koch, 'Rechtsprobleme biomedizinischer Fortschritte in vergleichender Perspektive' in Professors of Criminal Law Tübingen and Ministry of Justice Baden-Württemberg (eds), *Gedächtnisschrift für Rolf Keller* (Tübingen, Mohr Siebeck, 2003) 15, 24; M Kettner, 'Neue Formen gespaltener Elternschaft' (2001) B 27 *Aus Politik und Weltgeschichte* 34, 38; H-G Koch, 'Fortpflanzungsmedizin im europäischen Rechtsvergleich' (2001) B 27 *Aus Politik und Weltgeschichte* 44, 57.

[14] M Bals-Pratsch, R Dittrich and M Frommel, 'Wandel in der Implementation des Deutschen Embryonenschutzgesetzes' (2010) 7 *Journal für Reproduktionsmedizin und Endokrinologie* 87, 93 f; Koch, above n 13, 49.

[15] Eser and Koch, above n 13, 19; Kettner, above n 13, 38; Müller-Götzmann, above n 2, 248.

[16] Eser and Koch, above n 13, 24; Kettner, above n 13, 38.

There is no distinction between commercial and altruistic surrogacy.[17] The law differentiates in terminology but not in treatment,[18] whether or not the genetic material comes from the surrogate mother (*Ersatzmutter*[19]—genetic material from the surrogate mother; *Tragemutter* or *Leihmutter*[20]—genetic material not from the surrogate mother).[21] For the intended parents the law uses the term 'commissioning parents' (*Bestelleltern*). In the literature the term 'intended parents' (*Wunscheltern*) is more common.

II. Criminal Law

A. Embryo Protection Act

The Embryo Protection Act of 1990 (ESchG) bans medical procedures used for reproduction regarded as 'abusive' by the legislator or leading to 'split' motherhood (see section I. above).[22] The following methods are forbidden:

(a) the medical undertaking of egg donation (section 1 paragraph 1 number 1);
(b) egg fertilisation with the intention of transferring the egg to a woman other than the one who produced it (number 2);
(c) the removal and transfer of an embryo from one woman to another (number 6); and
(d) artificial fertilisation of or embryo transplantation into a surrogate mother (number 7).

The intended and surrogate parents are not punished (paragraph 3).

A surrogate mother is defined as a woman who is prepared to give up her child permanently after birth. The Act focuses on the intention of the parties. Embryos created to be implanted into the woman who produced the ovule may be implanted into another woman if for some reason the first woman is unable to

---

[17] Budzikiewicz, above n 11, 226.
[18] Coester, above n 7, 1251.
[19] 'Substitute mother'.
[20] 'Carrying mother' and 'mother-to-rent'.
[21] Eg AK Diefenbach, *Leihmutterschaft Rechtliche Probleme der für andere übernommenen Mutterschaft* (Frankfurt aM, self-published, 1990) 17; H-L Günther, '§ 1 Abs 1 Nr 7 ESchG' in H-L Günther, J Taupitz and P Kaiser (eds), *Embryonenschutzgesetz* (Stuttgart, Kohlhammer, 2008) 6–8; H Grziwotz, 'Beurkundungen im Kindschaftsrecht' in G Brambring and H-U Jerschke (eds), *Beck'sches Notar-Handbuch*, 5th edn (Munich, CH Beck, 2009) 78; A Hieb, *Die gespaltene Mutterschaft im Spiegel des deutschen Verfassungsrechts* (Berlin, Logos, 2005) 10; U Wanitzek, *Rechtliche Elternschaft bei medizinisch unterstützter Fortpflanzung* (Bielefeld, Gieseking, 2002) 221 ff.
[22] Bundestagsdrucksache 11/5460, 25 October 1989, 6, 7, 9; Coester, above n 7, 1245; M Frommel, J Taupitz, A Ochsner and F Geisthövel, 'Rechtslage der Reproduktionsmedizin in Deutschland' (2010) 7 *Journal für Reproduktionsmedizin und Endokrinologie* 96, 100.

carry the child. The essential question is whether this was foreseeable or planned at the moment of the embryo's creation.[23]

B. Adoption Placement Act

The Adoption Placement Act (AdVermiG) prohibits commercial actions supporting surrogacy, ie:

  (a) placement;
  (b) advertising for placement (sections 13c, 13d, 14b); and
  (c) a public search for parties (section 14a, paragraph 1, number 2, letter c).[24]

As mentioned above, the Act defines a surrogate mother as a woman who agrees to give up her child permanently after birth. The word 'agreement' seems to require a contractual, ie legally valid, agreement,[25] but it is understood as referring to an actual agreement only. Thus in order to fulfil the requirements for a 'surrogate mother', it does not matter if the underlying agreement is void.[26]

III. Civil Law

A. Validity of Contracts

i. Contracts with Placement Company or Doctor

Legal transactions violating a statutory prohibition are void *ab initio* (section 134 BGB). Contracts between a surrogate mother or intended parents and a surrogacy placement company or the doctor undertaking such a procedure violate the prohibitions of the Embryo Protection Act 1990 and the Adoption Placement Act, and thus are void.[27]

---

[23] Coester, above n 7, 1245 f; Dettmeyer, above n 8, 175; Frommel, *et al*, above n 22, 104.

[24] Coester, above n 7, 1245.

[25] 'Legal transaction' in commentary on draft, Bundestagsdruckssache 11/4154 9.

[26] H-U Maurer, 'Anhang zu § 1744' in D Schwab (ed), *Münchener Kommentar zum Bürgerlichen Gesetzbuch Vol 8*, 4th edn (Munich, CH Beck, 2008) 32 f: consistency with s 1, para 1, no 7 ESchG; Coester, above n 7, 1244: agreement would be voidable.

[27] B-R Kern, '§ 38 Der Arztvertrag' in A Laufs and B-R Kern (eds), *Handbuch des Arztrechts*, 4th edn (Munich, CH Beck, 2010) 62.

ii. National Public Policy

Commercial contracts between the intended parents and the surrogate mother, as well as adoption placement contracts, are contrary to German public policy and therefore void (section 138, paragraph 1 BGB).[28]

Non-commercial contracts do not make anyone the object of a commercial transaction, so the agreement could be regarded as valid.[29] Instead, the prevailing part of the doctrine regards all contracts about artificial procreation which lead to a 'split' motherhood as contrary to the values of the German law and therefore as contrary to public policy.[30]

All claims against surrogate mothers who kept the child have failed for reasons of public policy: such claims covered issues such as custody of the child, unjust enrichment for received payments and compensation for fraud.[31]

B. Parentage

German law protects the family not only as a genetic but also, in particular, as a social relationship.[32] Maternity and paternity are regarded as different, not immediately related, bonds to the child.[33] This differentiation is justified by the natural difference between men and women, the birth process.[34]

Section 1598a BGB provides for the possibility to determine genetic parentage without legal consequences. The rule was enacted with regard to fatherhood,[35] but its wording applies to motherhood as well.[36]

---

[28] AG Düsseldorf, above n 11, 4; AG Frankfurt am Main, above n 11; AG Hamm, above n 11; Grziwotz, above n 8, 80; D Looschelders '§ 138' in T Heidel, R Hüßtege, H-P Mansel, U Noack (eds), *Anwaltkommentar BGB Band 1: Allgemeiner Teil*, 2nd edn (Bonn, Deutscher Anwaltverlag, 2012) 175 f.

[29] Diefenbach, above n 21,160.

[30] Eg OLG Hamm, above n 5; LG Freiburg, above n 5, 1488; Kern, above n 27, 62; Maurer, above n 26, 33; R Sack, '§ 138 BGB' in *J von Staudingers Kommentar zum BGB, Allgemeiner Teil* (Munich, Sellier/de Gruyter, 2003) 450 f; a less strict, minor opinion still regards the contract as not enforceable and voidable by the surrogate mother and the intended parents until eight weeks after birth, similar to adoption, eg Coester, above n 7, 1251.

[31] OLG Hamm, above n 5; LG Freiburg, above n 5 1488; KG, above n 5, 2201.

[32] K Muscheler and A Bloch, 'Das Recht auf Kenntnis der genetischen Abstammung und der Anspruch des Kindes gegen die Mutter auf Nennung des leiblichen Vaters' (2002) *Familie Partnerschaft Recht* 339, 339; M Dittberner, *Lebenspartnerschaft und Kindschaftsrecht* (Frankfurt aM, Peter Lang, 2004) 188; T Rauscher, '§ 1591 BGB' in J von Staudinger, *Kommentar zum BGB, vol 4 Familienrecht* (Munich, Sellier/de Gruyter, 2011) 24; A Spickhoff, 'Der Streit um die Abstammung—Brennpunkte der Diskussion' in A Spickhoff, D Schwab, D Henrich and P Gottwald (eds), *Streit um die Abstammung— ein europäischer Vergleich* (Bielefeld, Gieseking, 2007) 13, 18.

[33] Gesetzentwurf 5 October 2007, Bundestagsdrucksache 16/6561 15.

[34] Koch, above n 13, 48; Muscheler and Bloch, above n 32, 340; B Schwarz, *Die Verteilung der elterlichen Sorge aus erziehungswissenschaftlicher und juristischer Sicht* (Wiesbaden, VS Verlag, 2011) 50; critical Hieb, above n 21, 202; Eser and Koch, above n 13, 23 f; see also OLG Stuttgart 7 February 2012—8 W 46/12, (2012) 389 *NJW-Rechtsprechngs Report* 390.

[35] Bundestagsdrucksache 16/6561 9; BVerfG, 12 February 2007—1 BvR 421/05 (2007) *Neue Juristische Wochenschrift* 753; Muscheler and Bloch, above n 32, 342 f; Rauscher, above n 32, 25; Schwarz, above n 34, 60.

[36] Rauscher, above n 32, 25 f; Spickhoff, above n 32, 28.

i. Motherhood

The mother is the woman who gives birth (section 1591 BGB). This rule was enacted in 1998 to create a clear determination[37] and to deter reproduction treatments leading to 'split' motherhood (see section I. above).[38] Motherhood is not contestable or dispensable,[39] even in the more theoretical case of embryo implantation against the woman's will.[40] It alone creates a legally relevant relation between mother and child.[41] A differing genetic mother has no rights and no legal relationship with the child.[42]

The only possible way to dissolve the bond between the legal mother and a child, and create one between intended mother and child, is by adoption.[43]

ii. Fatherhood

Legal fatherhood is regulated more liberally than motherhood. The mother's husband primarily is the father (section 1592, number 1 BGB). If the mother is unmarried or the husband's fatherhood has been contested successfully before a court, the legal father is whoever acknowledges paternity (section 1592, number 2) or whose paternity has been judicially established (section 1592, number 3).[44] Whenever the child has a legal father, a contestation of paternity is always necessary to acknowledge a different paternity, even in cases where the legal father obviously is not the genetic father.[45]

One person's fraudulent acknowledgement of parenthood may be contested by a competent authority,[46] such as the public prosecutor.

---

[37] Schwarz, above n 34, 41; Spickhoff, above n 32, 19; Wanitzek, above n 21, 434.

[38] Gesetzentwurf 13 June 1996 Bundestagsdrucksache 13/4899 82; Rechtsausschuss des Deutschen Bundestages, Beschlussempfehlung und Bericht, 12 September 1997 Bundestagsdrucksache 13/8511 69; Schwarz, above n 34, 41.

[39] Gesetzentwurf 13 June 1996, Bundestagsdrucksache 13/4899 82; KG, above n 5, 2201; OLG Stuttgart, above n 34, 389; Dettmeyer, above n 8, 175; Grziwotz, above n 21, no 80; Rauscher, above n 32, 16; Schwarz, above n 34, 41.

[40] Rauscher, above n 32, 18.

[41] Exceptions: s 1307 BGB (marriage between relatives) and s 173 Strafgesetzbuch (incest), both referring to genetic relations; Coester, above n 7, 1247; Muscheler and Bloch, above n 32, 340 f; Rauscher, above n 32, 19; H Seidl, 'Anfechtung bei der homologen und heterologen Insemination' (2002) *Familie Partnerschaft und Recht* 402. See also J Gernhuber and D Coester-Waltjen, *Familienrecht*, 5th edn (Munich, CH Beck, 2006) 625; Schwarz, above n 34, 41.

[42] BVerfG, 13 February 2007—1 BvR 421/05 (2007) *Neue Juristische Wochenschrift* 753; 18 January 1988—1 BvR 1589/87, (1988) *Neue Juristische Wochenschrift* 3010; 31 January 1989—1 BvL 17/87 (1989) *Neue Juristische Wochenschrift* 891; OLG Stuttgart, above n 34, 389; Frommel *et al*, above n 22, 97; Rauscher, above n 32, 17, 23.

[43] VG Berlin, above n 11; Gernhuber and Coester-Waltjen, above n 41, 625; Rauscher, above n 32, 17; Schwarz, above n 34, 41.

[44] OLG Stuttgart, above n 34, 390; eg Gernhuber and Coester-Waltjen, above n 41, 626; Schwarz, above n 34, 41.

[45] P Eckersberger, 'Auswirkungen des Kinderrechteverbesserungsgesetzes auf Vereinbarungen über eine heterologe Insemination' (2002) *Mitteilungen des Bayerischen Notarvereins* 261, 262.

[46] Section 1600, para 1, no 5 BGB.

iii. Adoption

Through adoption, a child becomes the child of the adoptive parents or the adoptive person under German substantive law (section 1754 BGB). The former parents lose all rights with respect to the child,[47] therefore their consent, or exceptionally a judicial decision,[48] is required (section 1748 BGB).[49] A promise to consent is against public policy and void.[50] A spouse[51] can adopt the other spouse's child to become the second parent ('stepchild' adoption or *Stiefkindadoption*).

Adoption should not be permitted if the adoptive parents took part in a procurement which is unlawful or contrary to public policy (section 1741, paragraph 1, phrase 2 BGB). Surrogacy may involve a procurement prohibited by the Adoption Placement Act[52] and is against public policy (see section II.B. above). Therefore, adoption might be permitted only if absolutely necessary for the child's well-being.[53] Here most courts apply a strict standard: if the intended parents already live in a stable (gay or hetero) partnership and one of them is recognised as the legal parent, usually an adoption by the other partner is not regarded as necessary.[54] Only a few courts have decided that this strict standard might not be in the child's best interests.[55]

IV. Cross-border Issues

A. Competence for Passport Issues

An administrative directive determines the competence for passport issues for children born outside of German territory. To avoid abusive methods 'such as surrogacy', the diplomatic representative at the place of birth exclusively is competent to issue the first passport or related documents, even if the child's habitual residence has been transferred to German territory, eg if the child entered on another passport, or if the child had an entry permit for a country within the Schengen

---

[47] Schwarz, above n 34, 58 f.

[48] BVerfG 27 April 2006—1 BvR 2866/04, (2006) *Das Standesamt* 322; Schwarz, above n 34, 58 f.

[49] Schwarz, abvoe n 34, 46.

[50] Coester, above n 7, 1249; Wanitzek, above n 21, 230.

[51] Or partner in a homosexual partnership according to s 9 para 7 Lebenspartnerschaftsgesetz, 16 February 2001, BGBl I 266.

[52] AG Hamm, 22 February 2011—XVI 192/08 (2011) *BeckRechtsorechung* 25140.

[53] Coester, above n 7, 1250.

[54] AG Düsseldorf, above n 11, 5; AG Frankfurt am Main, above n 11, 5; AG Hamm, above n 11, 5 f; AG Hamm, above n 52.

[55] LG Frankfurt a. M. 3 August 2012—2-09 T 50/11 (2012) *Neue Juristsche Wochenschrift* 3111; LG Düsseldorf 15 March 2012—25 / 758/10 (2012) *BeckRechtsprechung* 19794.

area[56] or if the child has been brought in illegally.[57] The Federal Foreign Office issues special warnings that surrogacy cases are to be handled very strictly.[58] In fact, German authorities have refused to issue passports if there was any indication of surrogacy and therefore doubt that under German law the intended parents would be the legal parents. Indications of surrogacy are, for example, unusual travel behaviour, a lack of parturition documentation or a maternal age at which childbirth is already complicated.[59]

B. International Scope of Surrogacy Criminal Law

The Embryo Protection Act and Adoption Placement Act apply to acts undertaken within German territory.[60] Furthermore, courts have also applied the provisions in cases where the illegality of an agreement was a preliminary question of substantive German adoption law, no matter what law applied to the agreement itself, so the provisions seem to be considered as internationally mandatory.[61]

C. Mandatory Rules in Surrogacy Contracts

Contracts on surrogacy have been declared void without analysis if German law actually applied.[62] As the criminal law provisions do not have extraterritorial effects,[63] courts seem to interpret the disapproval of surrogacy contracts as internationally mandatory.

---

[56] See eg 'The Schengen Acquis', as referred to in Art 1(2) of Council Decision 1999/435/EC of 20 May 1999, [2000] OJ L239/1.

[57] Appendix to s 19 19.3. of Art 1.19 Allgemeine Verwaltungsvorschrift zur Durchführung des Passgesetzes (*Passverwaltungsvorschrift*—PassVwV), 17 December 2009, *Gemeinsames Ministerialblatt* 2009 no 81 p 1686.

[58] See <www.auswaertiges-amt.de/EN/Infoservice/FAQ/GermanFamilyLaw/Leihmutterschaft. html?nn=479790>.

[59] VG Berlin 15 April 2011—23 L 79.11—published only online, eg, at *juris—Das Rechtsportal*; VG Berlin, above n 11; personal experiences of attorney who was involved in surrogacy cases, personal e-mail 22 June 2011 to the author; AG Nürnberg 14 December 2009—UR III 0264/09, UR III 264/09 1, (2010) *Das Standesamt* 182183.

[60] Section 3 Strafgesetzbuch; JL Backmann, *Künstliche Fortpflanzung und Internationales Privatrecht* (Munich, CH Beck, 2002) 87; H-L Günther 'Vor § 1 ESchG' in H-L Günther, J Taupitz and P Kaiser (eds), *Embryonenschutzgesetz* (Stuttgart, Kohlhammer, 2008) 16 f.

[61] AG Düsseldorf, above n 11; AG Frankfurt am Main, above n 11; AG Hamm, above n 11.

[62] AG Nürnberg, above n 59, 183; Fachausschuss-Nr 3579, 18/19 May 2000 (2000) *Das Standesamt* 310, 311.

[63] Backmann, above n 60, 91.

D. Nationality

German law applies to the question of German nationality.[64] Section 3, number 1, 4 *Staatsangehörigkeitsgesetz* (StAG) follows the principle of *paterni et materni*: if one legal parent is German, the child automatically has German nationality.[65]

E. Private International Law: Parentage[66]

Article 19, paragraph 1 *Einführungsgesetz zum Bürgerlichen Gesetzbuche* (EGBGB) determines the applicable law on questions of legal and genetic[67] parentage. There are three equally relevant connecting factors:[68]

(a) the law of the child's place of habitual residence;
(b) in relation to each parent, the nationality of said parent; and
(c) in case of the mother's marriage, the law applicable to the marriage at the time of the child's birth or, if earlier, the moment of the marriage's dissolution.

Whether the establishment of parentage requires a special approval of a third party, and how this approval has to occur, is also governed by the child's nationality's law (Article 23 EGBGB).

To determine the habitual residence of a newborn child, the prevailing view in doctrine applies the mother's habitual residence, that is the residence of the person who gave birth.[69]

The law applicable to marriage is determined by section 14 EGBGB.[70] Marriage is governed by the mutual nationality law of the spouses, subsidiarily by the law of

---

[64] Eg AG Nürnberg, above n 59, 183.

[65] If fatherhood is established before the child's 23rd birthday. See Gernhuber and Coester-Waltjen, above n 41, 643; F Sturm, 'Dürfen Kinder ausländischer Leihmütter zu ihren genetischen Eltern nach Deutschland verbracht werden?' in JF Baur, O Sandrock, B Scholtka and A Shapira (eds), *Festschrift für Gunter Kühne* (Frankfurt, Recht & Wirtschaft, 2009) 919, 920, fn 9.

[66] In relation to Greece, Luxemburg, The Netherlands, Spain, Switzerland and Turkey, the CIEC Convention no 6 on the Establishment of Maternal Descent of Natural Children of 12 September 1962 applies in cases where the motherhood has been officially registered. Its relevance is so small in the surrogacy context that it is disregarded here.

[67] R Hepting, 'Die Feststellung der Abstammung' in R Hepting and B Gaaz (eds), *Personenstandsrecht*, vol 2 (Frankfurt aM, Verlag für Standesamtswesen, 2006) IV-273.

[68] Against, B Heiderhoff, 'Art 19 EGBGB' in HG Bamberger and H Roth (eds), *Beck'scher Online Kommentar BGB*, 20th edn (Munich, CH Beck, 2011) 9. Not supported by history or wording.

[69] VG Berlin 26 November 2009—11 L 396.09 Vdoc, 11 L 396/09 (2009) *BeckRS 42145*; Hepting, above n 67, IV-169. First applying law of claimed mother's nationality: D Henrich, 'Das Kind mit zwei Müttern (und zwei Vätern) im internationalen Privatrecht' in S Hofer, D Klippel and U Walter (eds), *Perspektiven des Familienrechts. Festschrift für Dieter Schwab* (Bielefeld, Gieseking, 2005) 1141, 1146. Against: Fachausschuss-Nr 3579, 18/19 May 2000, (2000) *Das Standesamt* 310 f: law of the State where the child was supposed to live.

[70] Homosexual partnership—s 17b *Lebenspartnerschaftsgesetz*: registry of the partnership, limited by scope of substantial German law (para 4); eg Heiderhoff, above n 68, 18; Sturm, above n 65, 932, fn 93.

the mutual habitual residence during the marriage or sub-subsidiarily by the law of the closest mutual relationship.

If the alternatives deliver contradictory results, the law best for the child in the instant case applies. That is the law leading most efficiently and quickly to resolution of a clear parental situation.[71] In questions of surrogacy, a part of the German literature applies only alternatives supporting the motherhood of the person giving birth.[72] Article 19 EGBGB's wording does not support this interpretation. More convincing is the opinion which applies Article 19 EGBG with no such valuation but later uses *ordre public* (Article 6 EGBGB) to correct unacceptable results.[73] This might happen if one of the parties is German but travelled outside Germany to circumvent the prohibition on surrogacy, and if the intended parent–child relation has not yet been established.[74] The Expert Committee of German Registrars and one court refused the application of foreign law to a surrogacy case for these reasons.[75]

On the other hand, the AG Nürnberg refused to apply the public policy exception in a surrogacy case in respect to fatherhood and applied the foreign (Russian) law, which led to a valid acknowledgement.[76] As the acknowledgement of paternity is more liberal under German law, the public policy exception seems to be handled less strictly than in questions of motherhood as a whole.

Contestation of parentage is governed by the law which determined the parentage (Article 20 EGBGB). Contestation by the public prosecutor is internationally mandatory.[77]

The prevailing opinion generally applies a *renvoi*. An exception is made in cases where the *renvoi* reduces Article 19's alternative connecting factors, that is by leading to a law which is already applicable because of another of the three connecting factors. In this case, *renvoi* is excluded.[78]

---

[71] Eg AG Nürnberg, above n 59, 182; AG Karlsruhe 14 June 2007—UR III 26/07 (2008) *Praxis des Internationalen Privat- und Verfahrensrechts* 549; VG Berlin, above n 11; unclear OLG Stuttgart, above n 34, 389 f; Henrich, above n 69, 1148 f; D Henrich, 'Art 19 EGBGB' in J von Staudingers *Kommentar zum BGB, EGBGB/IPR* (Berlin, Sellier/de Gruyter, 2008) 78; H Klinkhardt, 'Art 19 EGBGB' in FJ Säcker and R Rixecker (eds), *Münchener Kommentar zum Bürgerlichen Gesetzbuch Vol 10*, 5th edn (Munich, CH Beck, 2010) 14; Sturm, above n 65, 920 f; against R Hepting, 'Konkurrierende Vaterschaften in Auslandsfällen' (2000) *Das Standesamt* 33, 35: law of the probable biological father.

[72] Hepting, above n 67, IV-281 f; Klinkhardt, above n 71, 14; D Looschelders, 'Alternative und sukzessive Anwendung mehrerer Rechtsordnungen nach dem neuen internationalen Kindschaftsrecht' (1999) *Praxis des Internationalen Privat- und Verfahrensrechts* 420, 423; F Wedemann, *Konkurrierende Vaterschaften und doppelte Mutterschaft im Internationalen Abstammungsrecht* (Munich, Nomos, 2006) 141 f.

[73] LG Düsseldorf (above n 55); Henrich, above n 69, 1151; Heiderhoff, above n 68, 25 f; Backmann, above n 60, 128 f.

[74] Henrich, above n 69, 1151; Heiderhoff, above n 68, 25 f; Backmann, above n 60, 128 f.

[75] VG Berlin, above n 11; Fachausschuss-Nr 3579, 18/19 May 2000 (2000) *Das Standesamt* 310 f.

[76] AG Nürnberg, above n 59, 183.

[77] Gesetzentwurf, 1 September 2006, BR-Drucks 624/06 19; Spickhoff, above n 32, 62.

[78] Eg OLG Nürnberg 25 April 2005—7 WF 350/05 in (2005) *Zeitschrift für das gesamte Familienrecht* 1697; Heiderhoff, above n 68, 30; Klinkhardt, above n 71, 23; T Rauscher 'Vaterschaft auf Grund Ehe mit der Mutter' (2002) *Familie Partnerschaft Recht* 352, 356; against D Henrich, 'Kollisionsrechtliche Fragen bei medizinisch assistierter Zeugung' in T Helms and JM Zeppernick (eds), *Lebendiges*

F. Private International Law: Adoption

Adoption is governed by the law of the nationality of the adoptive person. To adoption by spouses the law governing the marriage applies.[79]

G. Recognition of Foreign Decisions on Surrogacy or Adoption

Recognition of decisions or acts of the competent foreign authority is refused if contrary to public policy.[80] There is almost no case law. Most likely the same assessment will apply as in the question of applicable law on parentage. Recognition of a Turkish adoption was refused in 2007. But this was not a representative case of surrogacy, as the surrogate mother and her husband were the genetic parents and promised to hand over the child to the intended parents. This violated German public policy.[81] In 2009 a court recognised the decision about the acknowledgement of fatherhood as not against public policy, although there was suspicion of surrogacy.[82] So, the public policy exception seems to apply in questions of fatherhood less strictly than in questions of motherhood. The general prevention of split motherhood leads to the negation of motherhood of any person other than the one giving birth.[83]

V. Facts and Figures

There are no official figures about the incidence of surrogacy. According to unofficial estimations by the Federal Association of Reproductive Centres (BRZ),[84] the need for ovule donors is around 1,000 per year, but of these only one requests surrogacy. Destinations for surrogacy abroad are mainly India, Ukraine and the

---

Familienrecht: Festschrift für Rainer Frank (Frankfurt aM, Verlag für Standesamtswesen, 2008) 249, 254; Sturm, above n 65, 920, fn 9.

[79] Art 22, para 1 EGBGB.

[80] Eg s 328 para 1 no 4 *Zivilprozessordnung* (ZPO) or s 109 para 1 no 4 Act on Proceedings in Family Matters and in Matters of Non-Contentious Jurisdiction (FamFG).

[81] AG Hamm 19 March 2007—XVI 23/06 in (2007) 87 *Rechtsprechung zum Internationalen Privatrecht* 259, 260; affirmative LG Dortmund 13 August 2007—15 T 87/07, (2008) *BeckRS* 15835.

[82] AG Nürnberg, above n 59, 183.

[83] VG Berlin, 26 November 2009—11 L 396.09 Vdoc, 11 L 396/09, (2009) *BeckRS* 42145; Heiderhoff, above n 68, 36; for a different opinion and in favour of a less strict use of the public policy exception, K Siehr 'Vertrauensschutz im IPR' in A Heldrich, J Prölss, I Koller (eds), *Festschrift für Claus-Wilhelm Canaris zum 70. Geburtstag*, vol 2 (München, CH Beck, 2007), 815, 819.

[84] Bundesverband Reproduktionsmedizinischer Zentren Deutschlands eV.

USA.[85] The German Embassy in Ukraine estimates the number of surrogacy cases within their competence as fewer than five *per annum*.[86]

VI. Outlook

A part of the literature pleads for a more liberal approach to surrogacy,[87] but not so strongly that legal change is likely,[88] at least under the current Government. The legislator had the chance to update the provisions of reproductive medicine as a whole, as a Supreme Court decision led to a renovation of provisions on pre-implantation diagnostics,[89] but only reformed absolutely necessary parts. Statements of politicians confirm a general reluctance in that area.[90] The Grand Chamber of the European Court of Human Rights (ECHR) did not confirm[91] the ECHR's first decision on Austrian egg donation law.[92] An upholding of the first decision most probably would have necessitated reform of German egg donation law. As egg donation and surrogacy are regulated under the same German rule, this might have led to a reform of surrogacy law. But as the Grand Chamber did not confirm the decision, there was no obligation to reform. Thus, German surrogacy law most likely will remain unchanged for the next few years.[93]

---

[85] P Thorn and T Wischmann, 'Leitlinien der BKiD' (2010) *Journal für Reproduktionsmedizin und Endokrinologie* 394, 397.

[86] E-mail, 15 August 2011 by German Embassy Kiev to the author.

[87] Eg Günther, above n 21, 19; W Heun, 'Restriktionen assistierter Reproduktion aus verfassungsrechtlicher Sicht' in G Bockenheimer-Lucius, P Thorn and C Wendehorst (eds), *Umwege zum eigenen Kind* (Göttingen, Universitätsverlag Göttingen, 2008) 49, 53; Hieb, above n 21, 204; Müller-Götzmann, above n 2, 279 ff; Thorn and Wischmann, above n 85, 401.

[88] Conclusion Congress Umbrella Association Reproduction Biology and Medicine (DVR-Kongress), 13 November 2009; Frommel *et al*, above n 22, 105; Koch, above n 13, 52.

[89] BGH 6 July 2010—5 StR 386/09, (2010) *Neue Juristische Wochenschrift* 2672.

[90] Budzikiewicz, above n 11, 235; F Geisthövel, 'Aktuelle Fragen aus reproduktionsmedizinischer Sicht' (2010) 7 *Journal für Reproduktionsmedizin und Endokrinologie* 515; representative of the Federal Ministry of Health (*Bundesministerium für Gesundheit*), e-mail, 26 August 2011, to the author.

[91] Grand Chamber, *SH et al v Austria*, app no 57813/00 (2 November 2011).

[92] *SH et al v Austria*, app no 57813/00 (1 April 2010), referred to Grand Chamber.

[93] Personal statements to the author by representatives of the Academy for Civil Status Matters (*Akademie für Personenstandswesen*); BRZ, German Ethics Council (*Deutscher Ethikrat*).

9

Greece[1]

KONSTANTINOS A ROKAS

I. Introduction

In 2002, Greece promulgated innovative legislation in the field of medically assisted reproduction. The basic idea underlying these changes was that it is preferable to regulate and try to police medical activity in the reproductive services than to adopt absolute and therefore futile prohibitions. In line with this reasoning, it was deemed opportune to allow surrogacy. There are of course several other factors that have contributed to the support of such pro-natalist legislation. Perhaps the most important is the very low fertility rate of the country.[2]

In Greek law this procedure is permitted under a specifically designed system necessitating the intervention of the judiciary. In this chapter we shall first present the structure of the Greek model, explaining its different requirements (section II. below). Besides the basic aspects of surrogacy that have already been explored in legal literature, we shall discuss certain practical issues of the procedure, such as the content of Greek birth certificates following surrogacy, and proceed to an evaluation of this model bearing in mind solutions chosen by other countries. Secondly, we shall investigate how and to what extent internationality issues arise in the context of surrogacy, and how these are perceived and treated in law. Lastly, we shall evaluate

[1] This contribution draws partly upon the doctoral thesis currently being prepared by Konstantinos A Rokas under the title *La procréation médicalement assistée en droit international privé comparé* at the University Paris 1-Panthéon-Sorbonne under the supervision of Professor Étienne Pataut. The author gratefully acknowledges the significant support of the Swiss Institute of Comparative Law and of the Max-Planck-Institut für Ausländisches und Internationales Privatrecht where part of the research for this article was carried out. The author is also grateful to Mr Takis Vidalis, legal officer of the National Bioethics Commision—Greece, for his guidance and his valuable insight, and to Mr Pantelis Ravdas for kindly sharing the valuable information that resulted from wide-scale research, conducted jointly with Ms Archontiki Chlomou and Ms Irini Kourou, on surrogacy decisions (for which see more below) and for our passionate discussions. The author would like, in connection with the same research, to thank Ms Archontiki Chlomou for her availability and help. The usual disclaimer applies.
[2] K Nygren and G Lazdane, 'Current trends of fertility—and infertility-in Europe' (2006) 63 *Entre nous, The European Magazine for Sexual and Reproductive Health* 10; J Gautier, 'Human Rights Considerations in Addressing Low Fertility' (2006) 63 *Entre nous, The European Magazine for Sexual and Reproductive Health* 8; The ESHRE Capri Workshop Group, 'Europe the continent with the lowest fertility', *Human Reproduction Update*, Advance Access published 4 July 2010, 1, 3, 8.

this treatment and propose alternative approaches (section III. below). Data from judicial practice, which have been unavailable up to now, comprise valuable material that will help us to formulate a representative picture of the functioning of the regulatory framework. (It should be noted this is the first time these data have been scrutinised and commented on from a private international law perspective.)

II. The Greek Legal Framework for Surrogacy[3]

A. The Regulatory Framework for Surrogacy

The Greek regulation of surrogacy results mainly from two pieces of legislation, namely, Law no 3089/2002 on Medically Assisted Reproduction and Law no 3305/2005 on Application of Medically Assisted Reproduction (hereafter 'LAMAR'). The core of the regulation of assisted human reproduction is to be found in the first piece of legislation, which provides the requirements for access to various reproductive techniques and reforms the law of parentage. A systematic examination of the adopted provisions incorporated in the Greek Civil Code (hereafter 'GCC') reveals the basic principles governing access to medical assistance to human reproduction. Crucial is the altruistic character of the process (Articles 1458, 1459 GCC; Article 8 LAMAR) and the necessity for a medical reason justifying recourse to the help of a practitioner (Article 1455 GCC). The second piece of legislation completes the legal requirements for the application of medically assisted reproduction and provides for administrative and penal sanctions for violations of the legal conditions. Furthermore, an independent Authority is instituted, which is responsible for policing the correct application of the legal provisions and the activity of clinics as well as genetic material banks.[4]

---

[3] For surrogacy in general see, among others: AC Papachristou, 'Le don d'utérus et le droit hellénique' in F Monéger (ed), *Gestation pour autrui: Surrogate Motherhood* (Paris, Société de Législation Comparée, 2011) 169; E Kounougeri-Manoledaki, 'Surrogate Motherhood in Greece (According to the New Law on Assisted Reproduction)' in A Bainham (ed), *The International Survey of Family Law* (published on behalf of the International Society of Family Law (Bristol, Jordan Publishing Limited, 2005) 267; N Koumoutzis, 'Arts 1457–1458 GCC' in A Georgiades and M Stathopoulos (eds), (2007) VII *Commentary of the Greek Civil Code* 582 (in Greek); E Kounougeri-Manoledaki, *Artificial Fertilisation and Family Law*, 2nd edn (Athens-Thessaloniki, Sakkoulas, 2005) 57; P Agallopoulou, 'Surrogate Motherhood', *Digesta* 1 (2004/A) (in Greek); P Filios, *Family Law*, 4th edn (Athens-Thessaloniki, Sakkoulas, 2011) 199 (in Greek); A Koutsouradis, 'Die gerichtliche Erlaubnis zur unterstützten Fortpflanzung durch eine Leihmutter in Griechenland' (2004) *Zeitschrift für das gesamte Familienrecht—Ehe und Familie im privaten und öffentlichen Recht* 1426; V Vathrakokilis, *ERNOMAK, Interpretation—Case law of the Greek Civil Code*, Arts 1346–1694, vol V, 'Family Law' (Athens, 2004) (in Greek); K Pantelidou, 'Reflections about the New Institution of Surrogate Motherhood' in *Studia in Honorem Loucas Theocharopoulos et Dimitra Kontogiorga—Theocharopoulou*, vol I, 503 (Thessaloniki, Aristotle University of Thessaloniki, 2009) (in Greek); AC Papachristou, *Manual of Family Law*, 3rd edn (Athens-Komotini, Ant N Sakkoulas Publishers, 2005) (in Greek); E Kounougeri Manoledaki, *Family Law*, 4th edn (Athens-Thessaloniki, Sakkoulas, 2008) (in Greek).

[4] Information as to the supervision of reproductive services reveals that it remains quite insufficient due to technical and financial difficulties. This conclusion results basically from an announcement

Presidential decrees, ministerial decisions and occasional decisions of the Greek Authority complete the regulatory framework of surrogacy.

Greece has also transposed into its internal law the European Union directive on standards of quality and safety for the donation, procurement, testing, processing, preservation, storage and distribution of human tissues and cells (Directive 2004/23/EC of the European Parliament and of the Council of 31 March 2004) and Commission Directive 2006/86/EC of 24 October 2006 implementing Directive 2004/23/EC of the European Parliament and of the Council as regards traceability requirements, notification of serious adverse reactions and events and certain technical requirements for the coding, processing, preservation, storage and distribution of human tissues and cells.[5]

B. Legal Requirements for a Surrogate Mother/ The Intended Parents

Greek law allows only gestational surrogacy. Access to it, as with all other reproductive techniques, is permitted only when there is a medical problem preventing people from having children by natural means or in order to avoid a hereditary disease (Article 1455 GCC). It requires the informed, written consent of all the participants (Article 1456 GCC). Surrogacy is subject to additional requirements, among which is judicial authorisation issued prior to the embryo transfer (Article 1458 GCC). Candidates for surrogacy may be married or unmarried couples and single women. The text of the legislation indicates by its wording that the applicant must be a woman. According to the prevailing view in theory, homosexual couples and single men are not permitted to have recourse to surrogacy (Articles 1456, 1458 GCC).[6] Despite that, there have been two recent decisions—one of which has finally been reversed- giving permission to single

---

made by the Greek Authority (No 44/24-6-2010, available at: <http://www.iya.gr/templ/inc_givefile. cfm?fid=16> in Greek) as well as from discussions with specialists in this sector and field research that started in September 2011 which focuses on fertility clinics in Greece. It is conducted on the basis of personal interviews with the responsible doctors at the fertility centres. To date, more than 15 clinics in the Athens area have been solicited and 11 questionnaires have been collected. The goal of this attempt is to assess questions of internationality in cases of reproductive services, as well as to investigate other practical issues such as the cost of procedures or the insurance of practitioners in this field. The research will be presented upon completion of the PhD.

[5] Presidential Decree 26/08 (*Official Gazette* [hereafter 'OG'] 51 A/24-3-2008).

[6] Papachristou, *Manual of Family Law*, above n 3, 203–04; Koumoutzis, above n 3, 589, 607; *contra* G Vellis, 'Issues from the Law no 3089/2002 on medically assisted reproduction (artificial fertilisation)' (2003) Θ *Chronicles of Private Law* 495, 497 (in Greek); G Daskarolis, 'Observations after the law on assisted reproduction (n° 3089/2002)' (2004) Δ *Chronicles of Private Law* 193, 200 (in Greek). Art 1458 § 2 provides: 'The court authorisation is issued following an application of the *woman* (emphasis added) who wishes to have a child, provided that evidence is adduced not only with regard to the fact that she is medically unable to conceive but also that the surrogate mother is in good health and able to conceive.' From the wording of the provision it may be inferred that the legislator did not provide for a similar possibility for single men (The translation of the Greek Law no 3089/2002 is available at: <http://ciecl.org/legislation.htm>).

men to proceed with surrogacy on the basis of analogy with the provisions already existing for women.[7] Moreover, only adults—with one exception[8]—are allowed to make use of techniques of assistance in reproduction.

Women may have recourse to surrogacy up to their reproductive age limit. This upper limit is fixed at 50 years (Article 4 §1 LAMAR). In relation to donors, they must be adults with full legal capacity (Article 8 § 7 LAMAR).[9] The woman who will bear the child has to submit to medical screening, and in particular to a detailed psychological evaluation of her capability to serve as a gestational carrier (Article 13 § 2 LAMAR). Intended parents are also medically screened (Article 13 § 3 in combination with Article 4 §§ 2–3 LAMAR). Moreover, according to Article 8 of Law no 3089/2002, the two women involved must be domiciled in Greece. The meaning and gravity of this condition will be analysed below.

As regards the requirements for the granting of judicial authorisation by the Court of First Instance, the woman who wishes to have a child files an application before the Court. The one-member Court in the jurisdiction of which either the intended mother or the gestational carrier has her habitual residence is competent to determine the issue (Article 799 Code of Civil Procedure). The Court examines the request in a non-adversarial procedure (Article 121 of the Introductory Law of

---

[7] Decision 2827/2008, one-member Court of First Instance of Athens, (2009) Θ *Chronicles of Private Law* 817, observations by AC Papachristou (in Greek); Decision 13707/2009, one-member Court of First Instance of Thessaloniki, published in DSANET (the database of the Bar Association of Athens) (in Greek). See also the legal opinion 261/2010 of the Legal Council of the State at <www.nsk.gov.gr/webnsk/> on the issue of the inscription of the legal parents on the birth certificate (in Greek). However, the Attorney of the Court of First Instance of Athens has lodged an appeal against the decision 2827/2008 of the one-member Court of First Instance of Athens. The Court of Appeals of Athens has reversed the first decision but the surrogacy procedure had by that time already taken place. Decision 3357/2010, Court of Appeals of Athens, [2012]60 *Nomiko Vima* 1437; Furthermore, information recently came to light concerning the impossibility for one man to be named as parent on the birth certificate of a child conceived through surrogacy abroad, due to the fact that he was in a couple with another man. More precisely, the case concerned an unmarried couple comprising two Greek-Australian men, who lived for many years in Australia. The two men managed seven years ago to have a child in the United States through a surrogacy procedure. Recently one of them, who had both Greek and Australian citizenship, wished for his child to obtain Greek citizenship despite the fact that the family was not established in Greece. Therefore he tried to have his name put on the birth certificate so that the child could also get Greek citizenship based on the *ius sanguinis* principle. The Greek authorities opposed this. We should thank Ms Bliati Maria, senior investigator at the Greek Ombudsman, for bringing this information to our attention (<www.new.synigoros.gr/langs?i=stp.en>).

[8] Art 4 § 1 second subpar LAMAR, providing that exceptionally minors may also have access to techniques of assistance in human reproduction in the event of a medical problem threatening them with permanent infertility.

[9] Recovery is permitted of certain expenses involved in the procedure for extracting the genetic material. The law specifically provides for the type of expenses that may be recovered. These are: the medical, laboratory and hospital expenses which are necessary before and after extracting the genetic material, as well as the cost of the stay at the hospital; the donor's travel and accommodation expenses; and any actual losses of the donor due to his absence from work. The amount of money that is acceptable by law to be paid to the donor is determined by a decision of the Greek Authority on Assisted Reproduction (Art 8 § 5 LAMAR).

the Civil Code), during which it proceeds only to consideration of the legal conditions. Judges cannot evaluate the fitness of the intended parents.[10]

C. The Surrogacy Arrangement

i. Enforceability of the Surrogacy Arrangement

In Greek law the centre of gravity in surrogacy does not lie, as in other countries, in the arrangement between the parties but in the judicial authorisation (Article 1458 GCC). The required agreement provides only for those issues that are not covered by law. These can be significant, because the procedure of surrogacy takes time and involves very complex issues with regard to the participants. These aspects, however, should not contradict the law, which means that the parties cannot provide for terms contrary to public policy. If, for instance, a provision limits the autonomy of the gestational carrier in an unacceptable way, it will be held to be illegal and it will not be possible to have it legally enforced. In practice, this can mean, for instance, that the surrogate mother has the right to abort, irrespective of the existence of a clause to the contrary. The parties to the agreement will not be able to prevent her from exercising her rights to her body. Neither will clauses be enforceable that provide for money exceeding the legally-determined amount.

The above assumptions are not confirmed by case law since courts so far have not been required to deal with the parameters of the surrogacy agreements other than the minimum legal conditions. No case has been reported where a surrogate mother has been opposed to the intended parents on any point.

ii. Payments in Surrogacy

As already pointed out, only altruistic surrogacy is permitted. The surrogate can receive no fee for her involvement in the whole process. She is permitted, though, to receive an indemnity for loss of income for those days she does not work. The legislation provides that expenses and actual damage such as loss of income must be paid to her (Article 13 § 4 LAMAR).[11] The total amount cannot exceed the

---

[10] Papachristou, *Manual of Family Law*, above n 3, 213.

[11] In Art 2 of Ministerial Decision no 36 [*OG* B´ 670/16.04.2008], it is provided: 'The woman who gestates and gives birth for another woman is compensated for all the expenses which are necessary for achieving pregnancy, the gestation and the parturition, provided that those are not covered by her social security fund. The amount that will be paid results from the receipts issued in conformity with tax law. Those expenses are recoverable only if the judicial permission necessary for surrogacy has been granted.' Further, art 4 provides: 'The woman who bears a child for another woman, is compensated for her absence from her work, which is necessary to achieve pregnancy, the gestation, the parturition and the puerperium. If the gestating woman is in an employment relationship, compensation is due only if during the aforementioned absence from her work no salary or any other remuneration is paid for any reason to her. The amount of the compensation results from a formal declaration of the gestating woman, in which the exact time of absence from her work as well as the loss of income is stated. If the gestating woman is unemployed, the amount of her compensation covers the fee which she, in accordance to her professional qualifications, would receive if she was working. In no case shall the compensation exceed the amount of €10,000. The compensation is due only if the judicial authorisation required by law is granted.'

limit determined by the Greek Authority on Assisted Reproduction. Nonetheless, it appears[12] that parties in surrogacy arrangements with a gestational carrier who is a stranger to the family agree on the payment of extra money under the table. Thus, the altruistic character of the surrogacy may be compromised on occasion.

D. Legal Parenthood

Legal parenthood in the context of surrogacy is dealt with in a clear-cut way. Although Greek law does not depart from the principle that a mother is considered to be the one who bears and gives birth to a child, an exception is introduced. Article 1464 § 1 GCC provides that the woman who acquires the judicial authorisation for a surrogacy is presumed to be the mother of the child. This authorisation will suffice for her to be indicated as the mother of the child in the birth certificate. When the intended mother is married, her husband will also be considered as the father of the child due to its birth in wedlock (Article 1465 GCC). In the case of an unmarried couple, the companion of the intended mother will be held to be the father of the child, provided that he has given his consent before a notary (Articles 1456 § 1, 1463, 1475 § 2 GCC). This consent is deemed by the law to be a legal acknowledgement of the child (Article 1475 § 2 GCC). The Greek solution as to the parentage indicates that once the judicial authorisation has been granted and the child is born, the regulation of the parentage cannot be modified by the participants in the surrogacy. Parties cannot alter the agreement and differently regulate the legal link of the child, nor can the surrogate mother change her mind so as to claim the child. The only exception afforded to the regulation of the motherhood issue following surrogacy is when the ova of the surrogate are used in the process. In this case, either the intended mother or the surrogate has the right to file an application within six months after the birth of the child to contest the established parentage (Article 1464 § 2 GCC).

The regulation of parentage discussed above has considerable advantages. The parentage issue is solved prior to the birth of the child. Thus any undesirable twist in the surrogacy process will not operate against the child. If, for instance, the intended parents die in a car accident before the birth of the child, the child will not be considered as legally parentless and the surrogate will not be exposed to any risk. The same will be true in the event that the child is born with a handicap. The parents cannot withdraw their consent to the process, abandoning the child to the surrogate or to an institution; they have to assume their responsibility towards the child and the gestational surrogate. Further, this regulation cuts short any later attempt by the surrogate to blackmail the couple, asking for additional

---

[12] This information cannot be substantiated in legal literature, but it has been crosschecked through personal inquiries with specialists in the field of assisted reproduction as well as through contacting foreign couples seeking surrogacy services in fertility clinics in Greece.

money for giving up the child to the intended parents. The clarity from the outset of the role of all the participants, as to their rights and duties before and during the surrogacy, as well as after the birth of the child, helps everyone to realise the seriousness and the difficulty of the whole process. It must always be borne in mind, however, that there is no such thing as simple surrogacy. Each case presents hurdles to be overcome. Participants and practitioners alike have to be extremely cautious.

Lastly, concerning the granting of nationality to the child, this will not differ from any other case in Greece. Consequently, a child will obtain Greek citizenship when either of the intended parents is a Greek citizen (Article 1 § 1 of Law no 3838/2010) or has a strong link with the Greek legal order (see Articles 1 *et seq*, Law no 3838/2010).[13] If this is not the case, the law of citizenship of the foreign intended parents will govern the issue. Difficulties might arise when the intended parents come from restrictive countries in relation to surrogacy. There is, however, a strong chance that the authorities of the foreign country will not be in the position to discover that the child is born as a result of a surrogacy procedure—since there is no explicit mention of the surrogacy procedure in the birth certificate[14]— which could present hurdles to the acquisition of citizenship.

E. Advertisement of Surrogacy Services

Advertisement of surrogate services is prohibited and is subject to criminal sanctions. According to Article 26 § 8 LAMAR:

> Whoever participates in the procedure of obtaining a child through surrogacy without complying with the terms of Article 1458 [GCC], [Article] 8 of [Law] no 3089/2002 and [Article] 13 of [Law] no 3305/2005 faces imprisonment of at least two (2) years and a minimum penalty of €1,500.00. The same punishment is given to whoever publicly or with the circulation of documents, pictures or by representation announces, promotes or advertises, even covertly, obtaining a child through a third woman or provides professional services of brokerage with any counterpart or offers his own services or the services of another person for the same purpose.

---

[13] According to Art 1 § 2 of Law no 3838/2010, a child who is born in Greece also acquires Greek citizenship if: (a) one of its parents is born in Greece and he is, from his birth, permanently resident in Greece; (b) it does not acquire foreign citizenship upon its birth or cannot acquire such citizenship with a declaration of its parents for that purpose in the competent foreign authority, provided that the law of the citizenship of the parents requires such a declaration; (c) it is of unknown citizenship, provided that the impossibility to ascertain citizenship upon birth is not due to a lack of cooperation by the parents. These provisions could be found relevant in cases of children who face difficulty in obtaining the nationality of the country of their parents due to a prohibition on surrogacy. Nevertheless, no such case has been reported so far.

[14] This finding is supported by the Law on Civil Registry (Arts 20 § 1 and 22 § 1 of Law no 344/1976), as well as by information obtained from the department dealing with births of the Civil Registry Services of the City of Athens.

F. Rights of the Child and of the Surrogate

i. *Rights of the Child*

No specific provision exists providing for the rights of children born following surrogacy. As a principle, it must be accepted that these children enjoy the same rights as any other child born naturally. Furthermore, Greek law does not provide for the anonymity of the surrogate. Consequently, if the child finds out that it was born through surrogacy, it might have a legitimate interest in seeking its origins. Under the existing rules, the child could force the clinic to reveal the identity of the surrogate as well as other information about her. Therefore, it appears reasonable to provide that the child has the right to seek the identity of the gestational carrier. Such a right could be substantiated in Article 5 of the Greek Constitution, providing for one's right to develop one's personality freely. Knowing one's biological origin can be considered an important aspect of the freedom to develop personality, since it can be interpreted as a factor in bonding with other relatives.[15] A problem that arises here is that the gestational surrogate has also the right to her privacy. Of course the right of the child is not unconditional. Thus conflicts of interest must be solved on a case-by-case basis after an evaluation of all the relevant facts.[16]

On the other side, the child has no right to contest the legal bond with the intended mother even if the whole process did not fulfil all the legal requirements. Only the two women participating in the process have the right to contest motherhood within the limits determined by the law (Article 1464 § 2 GCC).

ii. *Rights of the Surrogate*

As said in section II.C.i. above, the surrogate mother enjoys full protection of her personal autonomy, which means that she is fully responsible for the labour. Essentially, this entails that she has the ability to terminate her pregnancy at any time.[17] Of course the surrogate, like any other woman, can abort a pregnancy only within the terms of the law, ie freely in the first three months (Article 304 § 4 α of the Greek Penal Code) and after this period only when there is an imminent danger to her life and her health (Article 304 § 4 (β), (γ), (δ) of the Greek Penal Code). The surrogate cannot relinquish her right to abort and she cannot be forced to do so, because both options would mean a loss of control of biological functions, which is contrary to Article 2 § 1 of the Greek Constitution guaranteeing human dignity.[18]

---

[15] T Vidalis, *Life With No Face. The Constitution and the Use of Human Genetic Material*, 2nd edn (Athens-Komotini, Ant N Sakkoulas Publishers, 2003) 157 (in Greek).

[16] *Ibid*, 153–62.

[17] See Art 1 LAMAR, entitled 'General Principles', in which the safeguarding of the freedom of the person and the protection of personality constitutes a major consideration in the way the various methods of assisted reproduction take place.

[18] Vidalis, above n 15, 123–24.

Of course it is reasonable to expect from the surrogate a minimum degree of care concerning her acts during pregnancy, which will be determined according to objective criteria.[19] As to the reasonable limitations on the surrogate's rights, one should examine codes of medical ethics as well as other texts specifying the rights of pregnant women. Any other demand or clause in a contract exceeding the standard care required for any other pregnancy will not be enforceable against the surrogate.

Besides that, the surrogate has no rights in relation to the child. No visitation rights or any other relationship with the child are granted to her. Notwithstanding this, the law does not exclude the contact of the surrogate mother with either the child or the intended parents, though such contact will be rare. The regulation of the surrogate's rights does not differ according to the existence or not of a genetic relationship with the intended parents.

Apart from the relationship between the surrogate, the parents and the child, we have to take into account the relationship between the surrogate and the treating physician. A contract of medical services between her and the doctor exists, on the basis of which she is entitled to specific rights. The physician has an obligation to specifically inform her (Article 5 § 1 LAMAR) about the nature, the possible complications and risks of the treatment, as well as all the potential parameters of the whole operation.[20] The information about the risks of the surrogacy process is crucial. Any violation of these obligations can give rise to a lawsuit against the doctor or the fertility clinic.[21] Possible liability of the doctor may also be based on a violation of the legal conditions of the practice of assisted reproduction, for instance for implanting more embryos than is allowed (Article 6 § 1 LAMAR).

III. Private International Law Aspects of Surrogacy

We shall now explore the extent of foreign elements in surrogacy practice in Greece, and how and to what extent the existing provisions on assisted reproduction deal with this (section III.A.), and how this international dimension in surrogacy procedure has been perceived and treated (section III.B.). For this purpose we shall evaluate the existing legal provisions and the already large number of decisions granting authorisation for surrogacy. Lastly, we shall propose what we consider to be an appropriate private international law approach in relation to

---

[19] *Ibid*, 119–22.

[20] For potential liability issues, see also C Spivack, 'USA' in F Monéger (ed), *Gestation pour autrui: Surrogate Motherhood* (Paris, Société de Législation Comparée, 2011) 257, 273.

[21] For the contract of medical reproductive services, see in general I Androulidaki-Dimitriadi, 'The Contract of Medical Assistance in Human Reproduction (Ärztliche Behandlung bei künstlicher Insemination)' in M Stathopoulos, K Beis, F Doris and I Karakostas (eds), *Genethlion Apostolou S Georgiadi*, vol I (Athens-Komotini, Ant N Sakkoulas Publishers, 2006) 26 (in Greek).

an institution the regulation of which varies significantly from one country to another (section III.C.).

A. Rules Influencing Cross-border Surrogacy

Despite the high probability that surrogacy cases will have an international dimension, no specific conflict-of-law rule has been enacted.[22] The only provision dealing directly with the issue of the internationality is Article 8 of Law no 3089/2002, which provides that the women involved in a surrogacy arrangement should both be domiciled in Greece. In particular it provides: 'Articles 1458 and 1464 are applicable only in so far as the claimant (woman) and the surrogate mother have their domicile in Greece.' Doubts exist as to the exact nature of this provision.

The provision is primarily aimed at preventing fertility tourism,[23] and in particular at stopping women from poorer countries travelling to Greece to serve as surrogates. No underlying private international law justification is to be found in the explanatory note to the aforementioned statute.[24] This provision exhibits similarities with domicile and habitual residence requirements adopted in other countries in relation to other family law institutions such as the civil partnership, which have been qualified as 'connecting jurisdictional links'.[25] An assessment, however, as to the degree of functional equivalence between these provisions requires extensive research which is outside the scope of the present contribution. Moreover, one might ask whether this provision lays down a unilateral rule indicating when the rules of substantive law of the forum are applicable.

We should be reluctant to read such a statutist approach into Article 8, ie one determining the scope of application of the Greek legislation on parentage in the presence of a foreign element.[26] To assimilate Article 8 with a unilateralist

---

[22] Koutsouradis, above n 3, 1427.

[23] P Agallopoulou and A Koutsouradis, *Medical Assistance in Human Reproduction, Law no 3089/2002, Preparatory works—Parliamentary Discussions*, 238 (in Greek); E Kounougeri-Manoledaki, *Artificial Fertilisation and Family Law*, 2nd edn (Athens-Thessaloniki, Sakkoulas, 2005) 64 (in Greek).

[24] A Koutsouradis, 'Issues in Relation to Surrogacy, Especially After the Adoption of the Law no 3305/2005' (2006) 54 *Nomiko Vima* 337, 341 (in Greek).

[25] HM Watt, 'European Federalism and the "New Unilateralism"' (2007–2008) 82 *Tulane Law Review* 1983, 1986. The Greek domicile requirement should, though, be clearly distinguished from the notion of domicile as it is understood in common law countries.

[26] See E Kounougeri-Manoledaki, 'Surrogate Motherhood in Greece (According to the New Law on Assisted Reproduction)' in A Bainham (ed), *The International Survey of Family Law* (published on behalf of the International Society of Family Law) (Bristol, Jordan Publishing Limited, 2005) 267, 272. Professor Kounougeri-Manoledaki contends that when Greek law is designated as applicable by a conflict-of-law rule, Art 8 should not be applied. Understanding the full meaning of this position is not possible without a clarification of whether she refers to Greek conflict-of-law rules or only foreign ones. If she refers also to Greek conflict-of-law rules, this would mean that she rejects a unilateralist function. On the other hand, if she conceives this possibility only from the point of view of a foreign legal order, it is logical to assume that she accepts, or at least that she does not exclude, such a function of a unilateral designation of the scope of application of Greek law. On the contrary, Professor Koutsouradis believes that if Greek law is designated as applicable by a foreign conflict-of-law

methodology approach seems to contradict the way 'domicile', is proved in the context of surrogacy cases, as decisions, which will be examined below, indicate.

Additionally, it has been claimed that Article 8 could be interpreted as a private international law rule of a substantive nature,[27] ie a rule of domestic law providing for the specific regulation of an international situation. More precisely, this provision is considered to determine the scope *ratione personae* of the relevant substantive surrogacy rules, in such a way that it would prevent, among others, Greek women domiciled abroad having access to the process.[28] Except for the above, one could assert that the rule of Article 8 is reminiscent of the phenomenon of *self-limiting statutes*.[29]

Even so, and irrespective of the categorisation of the aforementioned provision, it can legitimately be stated that its existence has prevented people from other countries seeking surrogacy, and fertility clinics from engaging in cross-border reproductive activity. For this reason we could assert that this provision serves indirectly the private international law goal of the avoidance of the creation of limping legal relationships, i.e. parentage of children born through surrogacy recognised in one country and not in another.

The deterrent role of Article 8 is completed with Article 26 § 8 subparagraph a LAMAR, which provides that people who participate in a surrogacy process violating, among other provisions, Article 8 of Law no 3089/2002, face a minimum of two years' imprisonment and a minimum fine of €1,500. So far, no decision imposing any penalty in this respect has been reported.

The set of rules which influences, at least indirectly, surrogacy cases that can be qualified as objectively international has been examined above. No other specific private international law provision has been enacted. Nonetheless, the private international law evaluation of surrogacy practice demands further analysis. The character of Article 8 and more generally of the Greek system of private international law will be analysed further below in light of the large number of surrogacy decisions.

B. Case Law on Surrogacy and the Treatment of Internationality

Prior to the entry into force of the Greek law on medically assisted reproduction, a number of surrogacy cases had already come before the courts. At that stage,

---

provision but the domicile condition is not met, the presumption in favour of the intended mother does not arise. One could take from this that Art 8 is part of the substantive legislation: Koutsouradis, above n 3, 1427. As seen further below, Professor Koutsouradis does not recognise a unilateralist function in this provision. As to the solution of the applicable law question, he adopts a different position, for which see section III.B. below.

[27] Koutsouradis, above n 24, 341 (in Greek).

[28] *Ibid.*

[29] L Collins *et al* (eds), *Dicey, Morris & Collins, The Conflict of Laws*, 14th edn (London, Sweet & Maxwell, 2006), 23.

couples who had had recourse to the process filed an application for adoption of the child after its birth which was then granted.[30] Between the acceptance and regulation of surrogacy in the Greek legal order in 2002 and now, a significant number of processes have taken place, none of which presented any problems as between the participants.

Extensive research conducted with the support of the Greek Bioethics Commission provided valuable data on the number and important features of surrogacies entered into all over Greece.[31] The significance of this research is manifold. It brings to the surface a large number of decisions that have not been published. From the data retrieved it is estimated that approximately only 10 per cent of the decisions granting permission for surrogacy are published. Furthermore, a significant number of processes take place *in camera* for the protection of the privacy of the participants (Article 799 § 2 Code of Civil Procedure). In addition, this research was an opportunity to evaluate data which normally do not appear in the text of published decisions, such as testimonies and court minutes. Court minutes are significant because they contribute towards the better assessment of the existence of foreign elements in a given case. Lastly, the fact that this research covers an extensive period, namely, from the date of entry into force of the Greek law up to the present, allows us to form an idea of the treatment of internationality by Greek judges in the context of voluntary jurisdiction.

The research has inventoried 128 (out of 136) decisions granting authorisation.[32] However, the actual number is estimated to be much higher.[33] It is worth mentioning that in 24 per cent of the cases the gestational carrier was a member of the family,[34] namely, the mother, the sister or the sister-in-law of the intended parents.

---

[30] Decision 5803/1999, multi-member Court of First Instance of Iraklion, Decision 31/1999, multi-member Court of First Instance of Iraklion, *Kritiki Epitheorissi* (2000) 236 (in Greek).

[31] The research was conducted from November 2009 to December 2011 and covers the period from the entry into force of Law no 3089/2002 on Medically Assisted Reproduction. The data of the archive of the Court of First Instance of Athens (which is the biggest court in the country in terms of its annual workload), of the Court of First Instance of Piraeus, as well as those of the electronic databases NOMOS and ISOKRATIS of the Bar Association of Athens, have been scrutinised. Research of the decisions has been carried out by A Chlomou and P Ravdas. The recording, indexing and statistical analysis of the data have been done by I Kourou and P Ravdas. The findings are analysed in the following study: P Ravdas, 'Surrogate Motherhood: Legislator's expectations under the challenge of statistical data' in AC Papachristou and E Kounougeri-Manoledaki (eds), *Family law in the 21ˢᵗ Century, from incidental to structural changes*, (Athens-Thessaloniki, Sakkoulas, 2012) 67, 68, fn 4 (in Greek). This study examines surrogacy from a substantive law perspective. The private international law observations made in this chapter are the result of our independent examination of the case law.

[32] Ravdas, above n 31, 68, fn 4.

[33] As explained to us by Mr Pantelis Ravdas, (see above n 31), due to the system of indexing of the Greek courts it is not possible to be absolutely certain as to the exact number of the decisions relating to surrogacy processes.

[34] Ravdas, above n 31, 81 ; See also the conclusion from a study in a Belgian clinic, which reports that in '62 per cent of cases, the gestational carrier was a relative of the intended parents': C Autin, ML Gustin and A Delvigne, 'In vitro fertilization surrogacy: experience of one Belgian centre' (2011) 26 *Human Reproduction* (suppl 1) i80–i82. This article appears in *Abstracts of the 27th Annual Meeting of the European Society of Human Reproduction and Embryology*, Stockholm, Sweden,

Thanks to the possibility to study the full text of all the aforementioned decisions as well as the minutes,[35] we can proceed to some interesting observations. Decisions examined reveal that individuals who are connected with a foreign country due to their nationality or their origin, are involved in the majority of the cases.[36] The internationality element most often concerns the gestational carrier, who in 54 per cent of the cases has a foreign citizenship.[37] In a small number of cases more than one person[38] in the process had a strong link with a foreign legal order, mainly due to his or her nationality, an observation which is crucial. Yet the existing data do not permit us to conclude that there is a cross-border reproductive care phenomenon in relation to surrogacy. Judges have found in all the applications filed that the surrogate and the intended mother had, as is required by law, their domicile in Greece. Doubts could be raised in relation to the permanence of this domicile, but a general overview seems to confirm that in almost all these cases the centre of gravity of the arrangement was in Greece. This position is supported by the fact that the citizenship or the origin of the individuals involved in the surrogacy arrangement corresponds to countries which have primarily constituted the source of the recent immigration influx into Greece. Nonetheless, there are some cases at least where the cross-border element is undeniable.[39] Similarly, it is beyond doubt that, irrespective of the domicile of the individuals, the judges were in the majority of these cases technically confronted with situations which could be qualified as objectively international.[40]

This finding is highlighted because internationality in private law relationships is widely seen as the principal or sufficient precondition for the intervention of private international law.[41] This observation does not underestimate the fact that it remains a huge issue to determine the conditions under which the application of foreign law, or more generally the intervention of private international

---

3–6 July 2011, Selected Oral Communication Session, Session 53: 'Cross Border Reproductive Care & ART in Developing Countries', Tuesday, 5 July 2011, consulted in <www.humrep.oxfordjournals.org/content/26/suppl_1/i80.abstract?etoc>.

[35] Thanks to the people who have conducted this research and the Greek Bioethics Commission that kindly permitted us to have full access to the materials in their entirety.

[36] Ravdas, above n 31, 75-80.

[37] *Ibid*, 78.

[38] There were several decisions where a link with a foreign legal order existed, but the following decisions are perhaps the most characteristic and the less controversial in that sense. They are all of the one-member Court of First Instance of Athens: Decisions 1484/08.03.2006, 5243/13.09.2006, 5261/31.08.2007—not published (all in Greek).

[39] Personal research leads to the conclusion that there are clinics that offer such services to people travelling to Greece for that purpose. Indications can be found also in the international press: see eg J Mills, 'Triplets make it a grand total of 12 babies for the super-surrogate mother', 25 March 2008, available at <www.dailymail.co.uk/news/article-543948/Triplets-make-grand-total-12-babies-super-surrogate-mother.html#>; information found in Ravdas, above n 31, 73, fn 24.

[40] P Mayer and V Heuzé, *Droit international privé*, 10th edn (Paris, Montchrestien, 2010) 5–6.

[41] P Mayer, 'Le phénomène de la coordination des ordres juridiques étatiques en droit privé' *Recueil des Cours de l'Académie de Droit International*, vol 327 (The Hague, Martinus Nijhoff Publishers, 2007) 80–88.

law reasoning, is deemed necessary.[42] Depending on the legal tradition, different answers are provided for this problem. Thus, in a common law jurisdiction, the relevance of internationality is largely dependent on the parties, who have to plead for the application of foreign law.[43] Consequently, it would be inconceivable, for instance, in England to have parties in a voluntary jurisdiction procedure pleading for the application of a foreign law which might eventually prohibit the surrogacy process. On the other hand, in many Continental countries, including Greece, the application of foreign law, in principle, takes place *ex officio*.[44] The existence of a foreign element in a private law case must normally give rise to a question of applicable law. The problem of the identification of the competent legal order can arise also at the stage of the creation of a juridical situation or of a right. For example, for the celebration of a marriage in Germany, it is required that the legal officer confirms that people with a connection with more than one country comply with the substantive requirements of the laws applicable in accordance with the relevant conflict-of-law rule.[45]

For the aforementioned reasons, it is reasonable that judges dealing with cases containing foreign elements must conduct a private international law thinking process prior to the conclusion that Greek law is generally applicable. In Greece, judges, as already mentioned, have been confronted in the context of surrogacy with some objectively international situations without giving a legally-grounded answer about the law that they have finally considered as applicable. With the exception of one recent decision,[46] in all the surrogacy cases inventoried judges applied Greek law, even when the existence of an internationality element has been undeniable.[47] In the light of the above remarks one might wonder about the meaning of this case law in terms of private international law.

This unilateralist approach would interpret the 'domicile' requirement as a determining factor for the designation of the applicable law. Through domicile,

---

[42] TC Hartley, 'Pleading and Proof of Foreign Law: The Major European Systems Compared' (1996) 45 *ICLQ* 272.

[43] M Sychold, 'England', in Swiss Institute of Comparative Law (ed), *The Application of Foreign Law in Civil Matters in the EU Member States and its Perspectives for the Future, Part I Legal Analysis* (2011), 507 et *seq* available at <http://ec.europa.eu/justice/civil/files/foreign_law_en.pdf>; Hartley, above n 42, 292.

[44] See Art 337 of the Greek Code of Civil Procedure; E Vassilakakis and V Kourtis, 'Greece', in C Esplugues, J Iglesias and G Palao (eds), *Application of Foreign Law* (Sellier, Munich, 2011) 201, 203; KA Rokas, 'Greece', in Swiss Institute of Comparative Law (ed), above n 43, 209 et *seq.*

[45] See Art 13 of EGBGB. Similarly, for other countries like Italy, see GP Romano, 'Is Multilateral Conflict Rule on Capacity to Marry in Line with the Italian Constitution? Some Observations Suggested by Two Recent Conflict Cases Submitted to the Italian Constitutional Court' (2005) 7 *Yearbook of Private International Law* 205.

[46] One-member Court of First Instance of Iraklion: Decision 13/16.01.2012—not published (in Greek). For this decision, see more in detail below n 60.

[47] There have been a significant number of cases where there is explicit reference to the foreign nationality of the participants in the surrogacy. Among these cases are the following: one-member Court of first Instance of Athens: Decisions 5284/27.08.2003 (3812/13.09.2005); 5246/13.10.2004; 27/05.01.2005; 3141/13.05.2005; 4189/29.06.2005; 1484/08.03.2006; 596/30.01.2007; 2064/03.04.2007; 5261/31.08.2007; 219/14.01.2008—not published (all in Greek).

a delimitation of Greek provisions would take place. In our opinion it is quite improbable that Greek judges relied consciously on domicile to give an answer to the issue of the competent legal order for the different private law questions and, more precisely, to the most crucial one, ie parentage. An argument in support of this view can be identified by the absence in these decisions of a uniform interpretation of 'domicile'. Judges seem to have relied on many different kinds of evidence to prove its existence. The testimony of a friend[48] or of the intended parents,[49] tax declarations,[50] a residence permit,[51] a work permit,[52] a contract for the lease of an apartment in Greece[53] are some of the means used to prove that the condition of Article 8 was met. Further, no analysis or indication of the degree of permanence of the residence is given in the decisions. Accordingly, it may be deduced that even provisional residence in the country could suffice for a woman wishing to apply for surrogacy. The provisional character of the domicile is contrary to the opinion expressed by the Rapporteur-General of the Government for the law on assisted reproduction (Law no 3089/2002), deputy Mr Thanos Askitis, who, during the introductory discussion for its adoption, made reference to a permanent residence.[54] Notwithstanding this, the judgments show that surrogacy seekers, habitually residents in other countries, are not excluded in practice due to the lack of sufficient control of the domicile requirement. This finding indicates that the means used to prove 'domicile' before the courts, widens the field of application of the Greek legislation in a manner that makes it difficult to support an argument that Article 8 has a private international law function. Therefore, to identify in the stance of the judges a unilateralist methodology as opposed to the traditional choice-of-law rules would not be irrefutable.

Such a change in the perspective of solving private international law problems— from bilateral conflict rules to unilateral ones—cannot be confirmed for one

---

[48] One-member Court of First Instance of Athens, Decisions 6662/02.12.2003, 4878/06.09.2004—not published (in Greek).

[49] One-member Court of First Instance of Athens, Decision 5243/13.09.2006—not published (in Greek).

[50] One-member Court of First Instance of Athens, Decisions 27/05.01.2005, 219/14.01.2008—not published (in Greek).

[51] One-member Court of First Instance of Athens, Decision 5868/31.10.2003—not published (in Greek); in this case the residence permit was valid till 10 March 2004.

[52] One-member Court of First Instance of Athens: Decision 4392/03.07.2003—not published (in Greek); in this case the work permit was valid till 3 January 2004.

[53] One-member Court of First Instance of Athens, Decision 2064/03.04.2007—not published (in Greek).

[54] It should be added, however, that the deputy Mr Askitis does not extensively develop his opinion on how Art 8 should be interpreted or how the term 'permanent residence' should be construed in practice. He merely indicated that the residence should be understood as a permanent one. His position is to be found in Agallopoulou and Koutsouradis, above n 23. In the absence of further indication in the law it can be inferred that domicile in this context should be understood in the same way as in arts 51–56 GCC, ie as a permanent settlement in a place with the intention to remain; In that sense see Ravdas, above n 31, 72 fn 19; For the notion of domicile in civil law see V Vathrakokilis, above n 3, *arts 1-286, vol. A', General Principles*, (Athens, 2001) 255-261, K Fountedaki, Arts 51 et *seq* in A Georgiades (ed), *Concise Interpretation of the Greek Civil Code, vol. I arts 1-946* 120-124 (Athens, P N Sakkoulas, 2010) (in Greek).

more reason. The fact that we are dealing with a new institution could mean that the legislator simply did not take into account the probability of private international law issues so as to provide for the appropriate private international law rules. The adoption of such rules could occur at a subsequent stage, as is often the case with innovative institutions of family law. Thus to claim that there is a shift from a bilateral conflict-of-law rule methodology to a unilateral one would be premature. For all these reasons it seems that a different understanding of the case law is more likely.

Neither can a justification be found in an implicit application of the existing conflict-of-law rules concerning parentage. There has been only one case applying the Greek conflict-of-laws rules.[55] The rest did not apply, nor even allude to, the application of the Greek conflict-of-laws rules for parentage.[56] It seems more probable that judges neglected the private international law issue based on, on the one hand, the absence of an explicitly created choice-of-law rule and the consideration that the centre of gravity in these cases lied in Greece and, on the other hand, an implicit assumption that all internationality issues are solved with Article 8.[57]

Another explanation for the absence of a choice-of-law argument could be the fact that the object of the application before the Court of First Instance is not the determination of a private law right, such as the parentage between the mother and the child, but just permission to proceed to a surrogacy. Although the process is conducted in the civil courts, its nature is, at least partially, similar to an administrative one. The decision does not grant parentage to the intentional mother but simply creates a presumption in her favour. However, this is not entirely accurate, because the decision rendered is the basis upon which the registrar will proceed to the inscription of the intended mother as the legal mother of the child. If private international law is absent at this phase, private international law issues disappear once and for all, as it would be unrealistic to expect the registrar to proceed to such an evaluation when the decision is brought before him. Besides, failure to take into account the private international law issue at the outset of the process, when the same issue can arise in a subsequent phase, such as in the event of contestation of motherhood or when the intended parents, having proceeded to the surrogacy in violation of the legal conditions, hope to establish a legal link by adoption, seems to be unreasonable.

The second set of facts has already appeared once before the Greek courts. A Greek couple, with the help of an Albanian married woman, had recourse to surrogacy in violation of the legal conditions. Once the child was born, the couple sought to adopt it. The judges had no objection in principle to granting this. They did, however, identify foreign elements in the case, and thus tried to determine

---

[55] One-member Court of First Instance of Iraklion: Decision 13/16.01.2012. For this decision, see more details below, n 60.

[56] Of course these rules do not take into account the evolution of medically assisted reproduction.

[57] Despite the fact that Art 8 may be understood as a rule of a substantive nature regulating an international aspect, its role is not to provide an answer to the question of applicable law.

the law applicable to the adoption by applying the relevant conflict-of-law rule (Article 23 GCC). For the adoptive parents this would be Greek law. Albanian law was found to be applicable concerning the adoptee. In accordance with the applicable law, the consent of the natural parents of the child was required. Consequently, a prerequisite was to answer the incidental question concerning who the parent was. The legal nature of the question seems to dictate the determination of the applicable law. The court, however, considered automatically—and without further analysis—the incidental question of parentage in light of Greek law. The Albanian couple were regarded as the parents. Of course, this position could be seen as the result of an implicit application of the law governing the main question. This aspect set aside, the court focused on the conditions of Albanian law that should be complied with. One of these conditions provided that the child should have been included in a list maintained by the Albanian State for a given period of time, and that every possibility of an adoption in Albania should have been exhausted prior to permission being given for an international adoption. The judges did not apply this set of Albanian provisions due to contravention of public policy (Article 33 GCC) and granted the adoption.[58]

This case shows that private international law problems can easily arise in the context of litigation, or when parties attempt to establish the parentage following a surrogacy process that has been conducted in violation of the legal conditions. In the context of litigation, one of the parties may be tempted to invoke the foreign law parameter—in particular when this prohibits surrogacy—to blackmail the other participants. This would happen, for instance, if someone brought an action claiming parentage against the intended parents after the completion of the process. To reinsert the conflict-of-law process in this context would seem problematic and self-contradictory. Of course there would be means to react against such a devious and dishonest tactic. The litigant who pleaded the application of foreign law could be opposed on the ground of public policy enhanced by the situation's close connection with the Greek legal order and by arguments based on a 'legitimate expectations' test. Notwithstanding this, it seems reasonable for a legal order to try to anticipate potential private international law problems. Admittedly, to pretend that the granting procedure will, by taking into account the international dimension of a case, guarantee an internationally valid legal status would be a far-reaching aim. However, this does not preclude us from trying to follow a consistent approach within the same legal order, both at the moment of permission being granted and at a subsequent stage in the event of litigation. Therefore we believe that the nature of the authorisation process should not be interpreted as barring the examination of private international law issues.

---

[58] Multi-member Court of Chania 122/2008 legal database Nomos; and multi-member Court of Chania, Decision 20/09.10.2008 (not published) (in Greek). See the commentary on the first decision of the court by Chr Panou, 'Panorama critique de la jurisprudence hellénique de droit international privé (année 2008)' (2009) 62 *Révue Héllenique de Droit International* 297.

Moreover, it is necessary to note at this point that the lack of a specially created conflict-of-law rule for surrogacy does not necessarily mean a lack of private international law regulation. Thus, in relation to surrogacy, one should identify the private law question at stake, which will most frequently be the one of parentage of the child. Once the question is identified, the existing conflict-of-law rules providing for the law applicable to parentage should be consulted. The relevant provisions would be the ones found in the Greek Civil Code in Articles 14, 17 et *seq*.[59] Accordingly, the lack of an explicitly designed conflict-of-law rule for surrogacy is not sufficient to explain in legal terms the total absence of private international law considerations. In this respect a recent provisional decision of the one-member Court of First Instance of Iraklion seems to confirm this point of view.[60]

It has been argued, however, that provisions of Law no 3089/2002, and especially Article 1458 of the Civil Code, should be construed as internationally mandatory rules (*lois de police, règles d'application immediate*).[61] This position might

---

[59] In such a case we would most probably speak of application of these provisions by analogy. For these provisions in general, see: S Vrellis, *Private International Law*, 3rd edn (Athens, Nomiki Vivliothiki, 2008) 321 (in Greek); Z Papassiopi-Passia, 'Relations among parents and children' in A Grammatikaki-Alexiou, Z Papassiopi-Passia and E Vassilakakis (eds), *Private International Law*, 4th edn (Athens-Thessaloniki, Sakkoulas, 2010) 223-224 [In Greek]; G Kalavros, 'Arts 3–33' in A Georgiades and M Stathopoulos (eds), *Commentary of the Greek Civil Code* (Athens, PN Sakkoulas Publishing, 1978) 30-37, A Metallinos, 'Arts 3–33 Civil Code' in A Georgiades (ed), *Concise Interpretation of the Civil Code* (Athens, PN Sakkoulas, 2010) 50-53.

[60] One-member Court of First Instance of Iraklion: Decision 13/16.01.2012—not published (in Greek). In this provisional decision the applicant couple were Italians. The surrogate was also a foreigner. In the presence of these internationality elements the Court applied Arts 17 and 14 GCC so as to determine the law applicable to the parentage issue. Art 17 provides that the applicable law as to the status of a child born in wedlock is determined according to the law that governs the personal relations of the spouses at the moment of the birth of the child. The law applicable to the personal relations is to be found in Art 14 GCC, which provides: 'The personal relations between spouses shall be governed in the following order of decreasing priority by 1. the law of their last common citizenship during their marriage, provided that one of them has preserved it, 2. by the law of their last common habitual residence during their marriage, 3. by the law with which the spouses have the closest connection.' The approach of the Court in examining the aforementioned provisions is correct, although these cannot have been considered to have been adopted with surrogacy in mind'. There are two problems in the approach followed, though. The first consists of the fact that the Court does not justify why in applying the aforementioned articles it takes as 'spouses' the intended parents instead of the couple of the surrogate and her husband. The second is that it does not explain the reason why the relevant provisions apply. This could have been done by indicating an application of these rules by analogy. An adaptation of the provisions to the circumstances could also have been deemed necessary. Such adaptation could consist in a direct choice of the third connecting factor, ie the law with which the spouses had the closest connection. This approach would permit taking into account all the persons involved and would result in the application of Greek law. Nevertheless, the Court, proceeding in the way it did, has ordered the parties to produce legal information from the Hellenic Institute of International and Foreign Law as to the content of the provisions of Italian law regulating the substantive conditions for such judicial permission and the consequences in case the intended parents did not fulfil them. It has further sought an official translation of the passports of the intended parents and the certificate of the marital situation of the surrogate, who apparently is a foreigner but not Italian. Nonetheless, the Court has in its final decsision found that Italian law should not be applied and, thus, granted the autorisation to proceed.

[61] Koutsouradis, above n 24, 343, 346 (in Greek).

appear consistent with the text of the decisions examined, where we have seen that judges proceeded to the direct application of Greek law without even considering the possibility of applying foreign law. Despite that, one might object that there is no such imperative reason justifying the existence of a mandatory rule. Moreover, in the decisions reviewed, there is not a single hint supporting such an interpretation. The lack of an explicit determination of the scope of the law irrespective of a potential link with other legal orders, as well as the absence of a clear explanation of judicial construction, creates reasonable doubts as to whether this opinion is well founded. Another interpretation which seems more conceivable in terms of conflicts justice will be provided.

In most of the cases that have resulted from the aforementioned research, there is a very close connection with the Greek legal order. The most important elements with regard to the couples or the participants in general seem to be located in Greece. Even when one of the participants has foreign citizenship, it could be assumed convincingly that the people involved are established and work in Greece, and thus that the centre of gravity of the relations created is also to be found there. As a consequence, only exceptionally will the circumstances in which the relationships are created be screened before a foreign legal order's jurisdiction. There is, nonetheless, one argument that contests this assumption. It derives from the adoption case presented above. The facts in this case are similar to those in a significant number of the surrogacy cases examined. More precisely, as in the surrogacy decisions, the people involved in this case were also from a country that has traditionally been a principal source of immigration towards Greece, namely Albania, and they were at the same time residing and working in Greece.[62] Despite the similarity of the circumstances in this adoption case with the majority of the surrogacy cases with a foreign element, the judges proceeded to the identification of the applicable law through the existing bilateral conflict-of-law rule. Thus, the absence of private international law considerations in the surrogacy cases examined is not consistent with the judicial approach in other fields of family law practice where the centre of gravity can also be found in Greece. Notwithstanding this observation, we believe that the absence of a conflict-of-laws rule explicitly created for surrogacy—contrary to adoption where such a rule exists in article 23 GCC—indicates that the most reasonable explanation for the application of Greek law is the fact that Greece was the most closely connected legal order in the majority of the surrogacy cases.

This analysis is not totally satisfying and thus brings us inevitably to the question of how private international law issues might be approached and eventually treated better in these kinds of cases.

---

[62] Similar circumstances existed also in other ordinary adoption cases: See for instance Multi-member Court of First Instance of Syros 19 ΕΠ/2006, [2007] 55 *Nomiko Vima* 2057 (in Greek); multi-member Court of First Instance of Athens 921/2005 [2006] 54 *Nomiko Vima* 104 (in Greek). These cases did not concern a surrogacy procedure.

C. Private International Law Treatment *de Lege Ferenda*

The issue of the correct approach in terms of conflicts of justice remains. The intervention of private international law, or more generally taking into account issues that arise from the involvement of more than one legal order, is necessary.

One of the potential propositions could consist of the adoption of a conflict-of-law rule providing for the distributive application of the national law of all the people involved in a surrogacy.[63] One would ascertain what the personal law of each of the intended parents provides regarding the issue of surrogacy and the parentage issue. If these laws permit the procedure, it should be allowed.

The fact that this solution could be seen as rather restrictive of surrogacy makes it necessary to examine whether it is proportionate in relation to the goal pursued. Thus one should answer three questions. First, whether this rule is adequate to satisfy the purpose for which it is adopted. Secondly, whether it creates more problems than those that it is supposed to solve, and thirdly whether there are other alternative solutions that better serve the avowed aim. Certainly among other factors that must be taken into account one should check whether the adoption of a specific proposal would lead to burdensome and impracticable procedures. In relation to the proposition suggesting a distributive application of the national laws of the involved parties, this seems to be a valid objection. There are serious reasons to believe that it would limit access to surrogacy beyond an acceptable degree and there are several reasons not to wish such a result.

One reason derives from a human rights approach. How could a State limit access to a technique that is considered to provide an answer to a medical problem and which, it is claimed, enjoys constitutional protection?[64] In Greece medical assistance of human reproduction enjoys constitutional protection under Article 5 protecting one's right freely to develop one's personality. This fact strengthens the argument that limitations should be specifically justified.

Nonetheless, a legitimate purpose pursued by restricting access through a conflict-of-law rule is to avoid the creation of limping family law relationships. The first objection to this aim would be uncertainty regarding the frequency of such a phenomenon.[65] The level of improbability should be measured in relation to the number of foreign surrogacies that take place. Further, one should carefully consider the stance of restrictive States. It is interesting to observe

---

[63] For a proposition for a choice-of-law rule taking into account the law applicable to the capacity of the intended mother, see A (Teun) VM Struycken, 'Surrogacy, a New Way to Become a Mother? A New Pil Issue' in K Boele-Woelki, T Einhorn, D Girsberger and S Symeonides (eds), *Convergence and Divergence in Private International Law—Liber Amicorum Kurt Siehr* (The Hague, Eleven International Publishing, 2010) 357, 371.

[64] Vidalis, above n 15, 124–25 (in Greek); Koutsouradis, above n 24, 343, 347 (in Greek); Papachristou, *Manual of Family Law*, above n 3, 215 (in Greek).

[65] See B Audit, *Droit international privé* (Paris, Economica, 2006) 597, who in relation to adoption seems to imply that where the danger of limping situations is not as high as it is believed, this fact can legitimately lead to bypassing the law of the adoptee when it forbids adoption.

that even in the strictest States—perhaps with some exceptions, one of which is Germany[66]—the couple is never obstructed from assuming parental responsibility for the child, raising the child and generally taking care of it.[67] There will be legal difficulties but the couple almost always obtains custody of the child. This picture is totally different from situations in the past like limping marital status, or illegitimate children. The result of decisions granting authorisation to foreign couples for surrogacy does not lead to a dead end in the country of origin. The solutions of receptive legal orders do not differ as fundamentally from the solutions of restrictive countries as is thought, or at least do not in a way that would exclude or significantly obstruct the goal of coordination of legal systems. Therefore, access should not be conditioned on the basis of a conflict-of-law rule that requires the distributive application of the personal law of all the parties.[68]

This does not mean that a conflicts rule is superfluous. It will have worth particularly in situations where litigation arises and people invoke different laws in order to support their interests. In this event, and especially when the process did not take place in the Greek forum, it will be important to assess the country or the countries that have a close connection with the process. We suggest that the applicable law should be the one of the seat of the clinic where the process has been conducted. This is justified by the fact that people from foreign countries prior to their journey seek information about the legal framework of the country that is their destination.[69] Accordingly, such law would seem to correspond to the legitimate expectations of all the parties and it has the advantage of stability.

---

[66] For the difficulties that couples face in their efforts to return back to Germany with the child born through surrogacy, see S L Goessl, in the chapter about Germany; N Satkunarajah, 'Surrogate child denied German passport' (09/05/2011) 605 *Bionews*. It is reported in this article that a German couple having recourse to India for surrogacy, were refused visas for the children. Despite that, there have been couples who, after a judicial battle, managed to bring children back to Germany with them.

[67] See Supreme Court of France, 1st chamber Civ, 6 April 2011, App No 10-19053; in that sense see also J Verhellen, 'Intercountry surrogacy: a comment on recent Belgian cases' [2011] *Nederland Internationaal Privaatrecht* 657, 659; D Gruenbaum, 'Foreing Surrogate Motherhood: *mater semper erat*' [2012] *American Journal of Comparative Law* 475, 504.

[68] See also M Jänterä-Jareborg, 'Parenthood for Same-Sex Couples: Challenges of Private International Law from a Scandinavian Perspective' in J Erauw, P Volken and V Tomljenovic (eds), *Liber Memorialis Petar Šarčević Universalism, Tradition and the individual* (Munich, Selier European Law Publishers, 2006) 75, 90, where she argues against limiting joint parenthood of lesbian couples having recourse to assisted reproduction to purely domestic cases. According to the author, limiting access would mean that the limits of legal developments would be dictated by the States which are more restrictive.

[69] For a similar answer regarding the law applicable to the parentage of lesbian couples having joint recourse to assisted reproduction in a public hospital in Sweden, see *ibid*, 89 and fn 64: justifying the application of *lex fori*—which will coincide with the law where the clinic has its establishment—by invoking the novelty of the Swedish institution. Of course it has to be borne in mind that the application of *lex fori* in parentage issues in Sweden happens frequently. At the same time, however, it is easier to have parentage established abroad recognised in Sweden than in other countries. For a comprehensive presentation of Swedish private international law on parentage, see esp KJ Saarlos, *European private international law on legal parentage?, Thoughts on a European instrument implementing the principle of mutual recognition in legal parentage* (Maastricht, University Library Maastricht, 2010) 129, 176 *et seq*, the full text of which is available at <www.arno.unimaas.nl/show.cgi?fid=19540>.

It does not constitute a mobile connecting factor. Further, this law will coincide in most of the cases with the national law of the surrogate mother, and although her personal law should not always apply, we think that this will be a positive factor since she is by definition or often the vulnerable party in the arrangement. This law has the advantage of cutting short any attempt by the parties involved to move and establish themselves in another jurisdiction so as to take advantage of the difference in legislation to get rid of the obligations assumed under the surrogacy contract. Further, this law has advantages due to the fact that we are in a personal status field. This rule promotes the desirable permanence of personal status. Lastly, the law of the country where the clinic is located can be applied in the course of a permission process.

This specific conflict-of-law rule designating as applicable the law of the country where the fertility clinic is situated would also have advantages as a solution that might be proposed for adoption in the context of an international convention for surrogacy procedures. One of the advantages of this conflict-of-law rule is that it reflects the reality of the practice. This means that the proposal of such a rule would be easier to accept by countries that permit surrogacy and earn huge amounts of money from cross-border reproductive care. Of course this might seem like a compromise for restrictive or less liberal States who could, however, deal with their concerns by the adoption of other rules of a substantive nature that would protect, in a more effective way, the interests of gestational surrogates as well as of all the people involved in the process. Besides, major destination countries, like some states of the United States, Ukraine and India,[70] would boycott a convention that would restrict access to their jurisdictions to a great extent. The other relatively liberal countries, like the United Kingdom and Greece—if we suppose that they would be eager to adopt such a convention—cannot by themselves exercise any important influence towards adopting it, since they attract only a minor percentage of surrogacy seekers. A convention that would be signed only by prohibiting countries and some relatively open countries would, eventually, have a disproportionate cost in relation to the result that could be attained in terms of practice.[71]

Lastly, this specific conflict-of-law rule, suggested above, would reflect to a certain extent considerations similar to the ones which exist among scholars who advocate the extension of the 'recognition' methodology in the field of private international law.[72]

---

[70] It is reported that surrogacy is expected by 2012 to generate £1.5 billion for India annually: L Donnelly, 'Surrogacy: The Brave New World of Making Babies' (2011) *Daily Telegraph*, 22 January, available at <www.telegraph.co.uk/family/8276156/Surrogacy-the-brave-new-world-of-making-babies.html>.

[71] If, however, more European countries legalised surrogacy, eventually on the basis of a judicial authorisation system the balance of power between the negotiating parties would alter considerably in favour of those that wish to promote an international regulation.

[72] In relation to this see in particular G Cuniberti, in his commentary of Cass civ (1) 17 December 2008, *Journal du Droit International* 2008, 146, 149–53; P Lagarde, in his commentary on the aforementioned decision, *Révue Critique de droit international privé* 2009, 321, 330–31; P Lagarde, 'La gestation

In any event, people must be informed of the potential diversity of laws in a subject as sensitive as surrogacy and parenthood, so as to be in the position to assess the risks associated with the operation in which they are involved.[73] This position is similar to the one adopted by other States in relation to institutions such as marriage[74] or *pacs* (*Pacte civil de solidarité*: the French equivalent for civil partnership),[75] which consider that it is not possible to limit beyond a reasonable level People's access to institutions which might be considered as involving the exercise of a fundamental right, such as the creation of a family. In those cases it is admitted that the legal order has the duty to inform the parties involved about the risks linked to the international dimension of the situation, but not to restrict unduly their access to the institution.

IV. Conclusion

Greece has enacted a modern regulation for medically assisted reproduction, allowing gestational surrogacy. This regulation has given one more reproductive alternative to infertile couples in an environment of legal security. The almost complete non-existence of judicial controversies in relation to surrogacy in past years constitutes an indication that this new institution is functioning well in the country. This assumption does not neglect the intricacy of the method. It remains a highly-complicated procedure, for which the special attention of all the involved

---

pour autrui: problèmes de droit interne et de droit international privé' (2009) 62 *Révue Héllenique de Droit International*, Special File: Law and Multiculturalism—Contemporary Challenges, International Congress organised by the Hellenic Institute of International & Foreign Law in celebration of its 70 years of service, Athens, 26–27 November 2009 511, 519–20; *contra* L d'Avout, in his commentary on the same decision (2009) *Jurisclasseur Périodique* 39, 41. Recently, discussion concerning the issue of the 'recognition methodology' and the possibilities of its expansion has been passionate. Despite the importance of the topic, it is not discussed in this context. For this, see also among others: P Lagarde, 'Développements futurs du droit international privé dans une Europe en voie d'unification : quelques conjectures' (2004) 68 *RabelsZeitschrift* 225; P Mayer, 'Les méthodes de la reconnaissance en droit international privé' in *Le droit international privé: esprit et méthodes, Mélanges en l'honneur de Paul Lagarde* (Paris, Dalloz, 2005) 547 *et seq*; Y T Marzal, 'The Constitutionalisation of Party Autonomy in European Family Law' (2010) 6 *Journal of Private International Law* 155.

[73] About the particular attention that parties should pay to this issue, see also the website of the UK's Human Fertilisation and Embryology Authority. On this issue with regard to lesbian couples having recourse to assisted reproduction and having their parenthood established, see Jänterä-Jareborg, above n 68, at 91.

[74] See Art 13 § 2 EGBGB.

[75] See 'Pacs enregistré à l'étranger', *Répertoire international Dalloz*, latest information of 2009, concerning an order of the *Conseil d'État* of 18 December of 2007 partially suspending an administrative circular suggesting diplomatic agents should oppose the conclusion of a *pacs* when this could contradict local public policy. Thus French citizens can conclude a *pacs* even with foreigners in the consular authorities of France when this might be prohibited in the hosting country. The ambassador or the consul will only have the obligation to inform them about the legal problems they might encounter.

parties is indispensable. Despite the existing difficulties, Greece's judicial authorisation system constitutes an interesting example of regulation of surrogacy.

As regards the private international aspects of surrogacy in Greece, one might observe that the country has not been a major destination for couples from other countries. Nonetheless, judges have been confronted with cases affected with foreign elements. The existing provisions, and more precisely Article 8 of Law no 3089/2002, do not allow us to have a clear picture on the position of the legislator on private international law issues. The correct reading of this article, which seems not to fulfil a specific conflicts justice purpose, is that women wanting to have recourse to surrogacy must have a permanent residence in Greece. Notwithstanding this, case law reveals loose control of this condition. Besides that, judges have not paid specific attention to the internationality issues, but this has not ultimately had the consequence of inequitable results in terms of substantive justice. The internationality issues should be subject to specific consideration. Parties having a link with a foreign legal order should be specifically informed of the inherent risks, without necessarily being obstructed from having access to this process. Lastly, as regards the most appropriate conflict-of-law rule for the applicable law in parentage issues, this should be the law of the seat of the clinic where the whole procedure takes place. The place where the fertility centre is situated is a connecting factor reflecting the actual practice of surrogacy and that finally designates as competent a legal order with a close connection to the whole procedure.

10

Guatemala

JAIME TECÚ AND ELEONORA LAMM

I. Legal Framework

In Guatemala, there is no general law for assistive reproductive techniques (ARTs), nor a law that regulates surrogate motherhood, socially understood as the fact of hiring a woman in order to introduce into her womb genetic material that belongs to other people, with the purpose of using the woman's womb during the pregnancy and to create a child who is not genetically her own child but the child of the people who provide the genetic material, or otherwise the child of those who arrange for the contribution of the genetic material.

Since the Guatemalan legal system wholly lacks any regulation of surrogacy, and as surrogacy is not forbidden by law, this could leave those participating in the process extremely vulnerable.

II. The Current Situation in Guatemala Due to Lack of Legal Regulation

In Guatemala the mother is the woman who gives birth to the child, and if she is married, the child will be registered in the name of her husband as father. It is presumed that the mother's husband is the father of the child (Article 199 of the Civil Code (CCiv)). Thus, according to the Civil Code the legal parent of the child will be the surrogate mother (and her husband), not the 'intending parents'.

What happens in Guatemala (there are no research works on this—it is an open secret) is that during a woman's pregnancy, she and the intending parents agree (but not in writing) that when the baby is born (as a result of a sexual relationship, not of an ART), he or she shall be registered as a child of the intending parents. In Guatemala, this behaviour constitutes a crime,[1] but there is no way to identify

---

[1] Art 238 Penal Code, 'Supposition of birth: The person who pretends pregnancy or birth in order to obtain non applicable rights, shall be punished by imprisonment for three to five years and a fine of

these cases since there is no effective control by the people certifying the birth of children.[2]

In these cases, the woman is already pregnant when she reaches agreement with the intending parents, and in general the agreement provides that the intending parents will pay for any expenses incurred during the mother's pregnancy and the medical expenses of birth.[3]

Although there is no official knowledge of any such case, it is estimated that this mechanism is also used in surrogacy cases. Thus, once the surrogate mother gives birth to the child, the child is registered as that of the intending parents, thereby committing the crime decribed above.

Another mechanism that is used to determine parentage in favour of the intending parents would be adoption by direct delivery, although it is currently prohibited in Guatemala by the Adoption Act[4] (Decree 77-2007[5]). Guatemala

---

ten thousand to one hundred thousand quetzals. The physician, nursing staff or midwives who cooperate with the execution of this crime in addition to the imposed punishment shall be punished by special inhabilitation in the exercise of their profession by twice the imposed punishment.' Art 240 Penal Code, 'Suppression and adulteration of legal status. This article punishes by imprisonment for three to eight years and a fine of ten thousand to one hundred thousand quetzals the person who: 1. Falsely denounced or had it registered in the corresponding registry of civil status any fact which created or changed the civil status of a person, or knowingly took advantage of the false registration. 2. Hid or exposed a child with the purpose of making him/her lose his/her rights or legal status. 3. Registered or had registered a non existent birth or provided false data about his/her biological parents.'

[2] See Arts 70, 71, 72, 73, 74, 75 and 76 of Ley del Registro Nacional de las Personas. Decreto No 90-2005 (National Civil Registration Act. Decree Number 90-2005, passed on 14 December 2005). The Regulation of inscriptions/registrations of the National Registry of People of Guatemala (RENAP): Agreement of the Board of the National Registry of People no 176-2008, in its Art 17 stipulates that if the birth occurs in any of the Municipalities of Guatemala, the following documents and other items shall be presented in order to register that birth: the identity cards of the father and the mother (original and a photocopy), or, if applicable, only that of of the mother (the identity card of the mother is essential); the identity card of the informant (original and a copy); the medical certificate of birth, issued by the physician or midwife, previously filed in the Registry of Civil Status; where the midwife is non-registered, the certificate shall be presented with her or his authenticated signature and the authenticated signatures of both parents, or, if applicable, only that of the mother; a maintenance fee; and a valid passport in the case of foreign parents.

[3] 'A Guatemalan couple decided to adopt a child because they were not able to procreate. A close friend of the couple told them about a lady who was pregnant and wanted to give away her child at the moment of birth because she already had three children and she cannot afford to raise another one. The couple paid all the expenses (medical expenses, vitamins, food, etc) with the condition that all the tests were done using the name of the future adoptive mother. When she was going to give birth, the biological mother was hospitalized under the name of the adoptive mother. Thus, the couple requested the child's birth certificate without any inconvenience.' M Grajeda and E Cardona, *Estudio sobre adopciones y los derechos de los niños y niñas en Guatemala. La Adopción como última Opción* (Guatemala, PRONICE, 2006).

[4] The Report of the Comisión Internacional contra la Impunidad en Guatemala (CICIG— International Commission Against Impunity) states in its concluding section: '[I]n this report, however, a number of anomalies that may be being committed in the new adoption procedures were identified. Among the anomalies are the following: The registration of the child under the substitute family's surnames by order of the Childhood and Adolescence Judges before the end of the adoption process...' See *Informe sobre actores involucrados en el proceso de adopciones irregulares en Guatemala a partir de la entrada en vigor de la Ley de Adopciones (Decreto 77-2007)* [*Report on the involved parties in the irregular adoption process in Guatemala as of the effective day of the Adoption Act (Decree 77-2007)*], presented 1 December 2010 by the International Commission Against Impunity in Guatemala.

[5] Decreto 77-2007, adopted 11 December 2007; passed on 27 December 2007.

previously had almost no protection in the field of adoptions and weak legislation on childhood. The procedures for adoption did not involve many requirements and were performed by a notary public without proper supervision by the State. This situation changed with the enactment of Decree 77-2007. The main objective of this law is to ensure the best interests of the child, guaranteeing transparent adoptions with legal certainty.

According to this new law, the surrogate mother can neither hand over (deliver) the child directly to the family applying for the adoption, nor specifically stipulate who will adopt her child. The potential adoptive parents are also prohibited from having any contact with the biological parents of the child or with any person who might influence the consent of the surrogate mother.[6]

This is a fairly common practice in Guatemala. It is believed that under the previous system of adoption,[7] many mothers gave their children to certain selected families and even promised them before birth; some mothers also attempted to charge for their consent.[8] Despite its being prohibited now, this is still being done (although with less frequency). In these cases, and without prejudice to what has been said above, a person might also commit the crime of irregular adoption[9] or undertaking an irregular adoption procedure.[10]

Another way to elude the lack of regulation and current legislation is directly to cause the pregnancy of a woman. After the intending father has recognised the child as his own, his wife would seek a spousal adoption, regulated in Decree 77-2007 and its respective regulations.[11]

---

[6] Art 10, Decree 77-2007. Further, under Art 10 g), it is forbidden for the biological parents give their consent to the adoption before the child's birth, or that such consent should be granted before six weeks after the child's birth.

[7] Prior to the enactment of Decree 77-2007, recurring irregularities as to the origin of the child, the payment of large amounts of cash, replacement of biological mothers, rented wombs and other anomalous events were known. See Consejo Nacional de Adopciones. Plan Operativo Anual. Ejercicio Fiscal 2011. [National Board for Adoption. Annual Operating Plan. Fiscal Year 2011], available at <www.cna.gob.gt/plai/doc/direccion/POA2011.pdf>.

[8] In different circumstances, in particular adolescents with difficult life histories are involved in getting pregnant over and over again, with the purpose of giving their babies up for adoption. In exchange, they receive an economic benefit and care during pregnancy: Grajeda and Cardona, above n 3.

[9] Art 241 *bis* Penal Code: 'Irregular Adoption: The person who in order to obtain the adoption of a person for herself/himself, gave or promised an economic benefit to a person or third person, or a benefit of any nature, regardless of how she/he achieves the purpose, shall be punished by imprisonment for three to five years and a fine of twenty thousand to one hundred thousand quetzals. The penalties shall be imposed without prejudice to the penalties that may be available for the commission of other crimes.'

[10] Art 241 *ter* Penal Code: 'Irregular adoption procedure: The public servant who knowingly undertook a procedure, authorized or registered an adoption, using documents or registration in false public registries or in which the filiation of a child has been altered, or any other information required by law for the validity of the adoption, shall be punished with imprisonment for six to ten years and a fine of fifty to one hundred thousand quetzals'.

[11] Among other requirements, it is required to present a certified photocopy of the personal identification of the adoptive parent; criminal and police records; a certificate of marriage or, if this is the case, a certificate of common law marriage; a record of employment or income; a medical certificate of non-infectious contagious diseases and good mental health; two photographs evidencing that she or he is cohabiting with the child; a notarial record in which the biological father or mother expresses that he or she has the guardianship and custody of the child and his or her express acceptance of the

If the surrogate mother is an unmarried woman,[12] she would be inseminated with genetic material that belongs to the intending father, or the intending father would make her pregnant in the normal way[13] (he has to be the biological/genetic father, given that DNA testing is now required[14]).[15] Also, the surrogate mother could be implanted with an embryo comprising the intending parents' genetic material. Once the child is born, the intending father would recognise him or her as his child. Later, the wife of the intending father would request spousal adoption, being a much simpler process than for other adoptions, in that the interested parties may formalise it by public deed.[16]

Notwithstanding the foregoing, surrogacy, as it was defined, could be penalised by the law against sexual violence, exploitation and trafficking in persons,[17] which regulates a number of crimes to protect children from exploitation, ie that a mother receives an economic benefit or some other kind of benefit from the fact that her child is delivered to another person. Some authors argue that if a woman is committed to deliver her biological child by virtue of the legal business of surrogate motherhood, her act is no different from 'trafficking in human beings'.[18]

III. The Need for Urgent Measures

In the absence of legislation, in principle surrogacy as such is not legal, although it is not prohibited.

---

child's adoption by his or her spouse; and to submit a notarial record in which the biological parents state their consent for the adoption, unless one of them has died or has lost his or her parental rights. Prior to a favourable decision of the General Direction, the interested parties may formalise the adoption through public deed. See Art 48 of the Regulations of the Adoption Act, Act No 182-2010, issued on 24 June 2010.

[12] If she is a married woman, the paternity of the surrogate mother's husband is presumed; therefore he needs to contest his paternity in order for the intending parent to recognise the child: Arts 199, 200 and 201 CCiv.

[13] A new practice is beginning in Guatemala: a married man has an alleged affair with another woman of a lower economic status. When the child is born, the biological father's wife initiates the process of spousal adoption of the child. This masks a prior agreement to avoid the adoption process.

[14] As of 2011, DNA testing is performed on all children declared adoptable and on the parents who have given their consent for their children's adoption. See Consejo Nacional de Adopciones (2011), above n 7.

[15] In these cases, the woman who provides her pregnancy may also provide her genetic material.

[16] Art 39, Decree 77-2007.

[17] Decree 9-2009, Ley Contra la Violencia Sexual, Explotación y Trata de Personas [Law against Sexual Violence, Exploitation and Trafficking in Persons], passed on 18 February 2009.

[18] F Alarcón Rojas, 'El Negocio de maternidad por sustitución en la gestación' in E González de Cansino (ed), *Memorias del Primer Seminario Franco-Andino de Derecho y Bioética* (Bogotá, Centro de Estudios sobre genética y Derecho- Universidad Externado de Colombia, 2003) 125.

The fact is that in the case of surrogacy there is no legal mechanism (with the exception of the spousal adoption method[19]) for a child to be registered as the son or daughter of the intending parents. This child could only be registered as the son or daughter of the woman who has given birth to him or her (the surrogate mother).

In addition, according to our analysis, surrogacy in Guatemala (meaning the fact of hiring a woman in order to introduce into her womb genetic material of other people, with the purpose of using the woman's womb during the pregnancy and creating a child who is not genetically her own child) could lead to the commission of criminal offences, regardless of whether there is economic remuneration or not. It could constitute the crime of trafficking in persons, together with other crimes, or the crime of suppression or adulteration of legal status or alleged birth. It could even constitute the crime of irregular adoption or undertaking an irregular adoption procedure.

If Guatemala wishes to prevent the obtaining of children through abusive measures and/or violating their human rights, or through surrogacy which is not regulated, it is considered that efforts need to be made in different areas.

One of those areas is the registration of children, in order to prevent their being registered as their own children by those who are not their true biological parents. For this, it is necessary to amend the regulation in force in order to exercise better control over the birth registration process in hospitals (both public and private) and also over midwives.

The other area that requires further regulation is spousal adoption, where a previous agreement between the parties or even a benefit of any kind for the biological mother can exist.

IV. International Surrogacy Cases in Guatemala

Karen Smith Rotabi, Assistant Professor of Social Work at Virginia Common wealth University, maintains that surrogacy in Guatemala is replacing international adoptions from that country.[20] She states that in response to concerns regarding child sales and theft,[21] a new era of reform has been underway in Guatemala, in accordance with the Hague Convention on Intercountry Adoption, ratified by Guatemala. With this new system, intercountry adoption has undergone a radical

---

[19] It is not a completely 'legal' mechanism as the parties would be avoiding the procedural adoption rules.

[20] See K Smith Rotabi, 'Human Rights and the Business of Reproduction: Surrogacy Replacing International Adoption from Guatemala', *RH Reality Check*, available at <www.rhrealitycheck.org/blog/2010/05/20/human-rights-business-reproduction-surrogacy-begins-replace-international-adoption-guatemala>.

[21] In Guatemala it is believed that payments to birth mothers for their infants have become routine. It was estimated that at the peak of this practice, Guatemala sent 17 children a day to other countries as intercountry adoptees.

decline, and it is no longer the opportunity it once was for building families. Thus, she observes in the reproductive health blog *RH Reality Check*:

> As adoption has become more difficult, the global surrogacy industry has begun to surge to meet the fertility demands of individuals and couples seeking to secure healthy infants.

A handful of adoption agencies and service providers with prior significant interests in Guatemala have been shifting to meet this need. Because Guatemala has no regulatory laws on surrogacy, 'expertise' on such matters is more about the *how to*, *where to* and *with which* (vulnerable) woman to contract the service.

Smith Rotabi argues that a political and policy response is needed, as Guatemala has no legislation governing surrogacy. She emphasises that very little is currently known about how widespread it is, about the exact nature of Guatemalan surrogacy services and the mechanics of such arrangements: how women get impregnated, by whose sperm, and with whose eggs and so on. However, it is possible to find websites offering these services and providing many details.[22]

It is time for Guatemala to review its surrogacy legislation, before this new industry reaches the same level as the old one.

V. Private International Law

In Guatemala there are two sources of private international law, the conventional rules[23] and the autonomous rules, although regarding surrogacy there is no autonomous or conventional rule governing this specific matter.

In Guatemala, private international law rules are set out in chapter II of the Judicial Authority Act[24] but, as said, there is no specific rule for international surrogacy cases.

According to Article 24 of the Judicial Authority Act, the civil status and capacity of the person and family relations are governed by the law of their domicile. It is clarified in Article 26 that the civil status and capacity of foreign persons acquired under their personal law shall be recognised in Guatemala if it is not contrary to public policy.

---

[22] See among others <http://www.advocatesforsurrogacy.com/guantemala_program.php>; <www.surrogacypartners.com/guatemalasurrogacy.html>. 'Advocates for Surrogacy' say that Guatemala is an excellent and ethical source of cheap babies. It describes its programme as 'A Great Opportunity for Surrogates' who are 'extraordinary women who bring to you the gift of life'.

[23] Guatemala is a signatory to two Hague Conventions: one on intercountry adoption (passed by Decree 31-2007) and one on child abduction (passed by Decree 24-2001). Guatemala has also ratified the Bustamante Code by Decree 1575. Guatemala is a party to the Inter-American Convention on Letters Rogatory and Additional Protocol; the Inter-American Convention on Proof of and Information on Foreign Law; the Inter-American Convention on the Taking of Evidence Abroad; the Inter-American Convention on International Commercial Arbitration; and the Inter-American Convention on Support Obligations.

[24] Passed by Decree 2-89. In force since 31 December 1990.

With regard to external and intrinsically formal aspects, Articles 28 and 29[25] of the Judicial Authority Act state that these are governed by the laws of the place where the act was entered into. If the juridical act has to be performed in a place different from the one where it was entered into, all matters relating to its compliance are governed by the law of the place of execution (Article 30 of the Judicial Authority Act).

Regarding content, Article 31 of the Judicial Authority Act regulates a 'pact of submission', according to which 'legal acts are governed by the law to which the parties have submitted them, unless this submission is contrary to express prohibition laws or public policy'. Thus, in regard to the content and effects of the surrogacy agreement, it might be possible to take into account the rule established under Article 31 which allows for the autonomy of the parties, provided that the submission is not contrary to express legal prohibitions or public policy.

Consequently, if the parties chose a foreign law that permits surrogacy (the law of a country where surrogacy is legal) as the applicable law,[26] and the agreement complies with the foreign law, in principle the surrogacy agreement and its consequences/effects[27] should be valid in Guatemala, unless contrary to mandatory rules or public policy.

Regarding this, it is considered that if the child is born abroad as a consequence of a surrogacy agreement and the intending parents ask for the registration of the child in Guatemala (before the National Registry of People of Guatemala (RENAP) in Guatemala once they are back in the country or at the consular authorities[28]), the principle would be that because of the lack of regulation on surrogacy, the RENAP or the consular authority would deny the registration on the basis of public policy grounds according to Article 30 of the Judicial Authority Act and Article 44, which states:

> The laws, regulations and judgments of other countries as well as documents or particular dispositions from abroad have no validity or whatsoever effect in the Republic of Guatemala if they undermine national sovereignty, contradict the Constitution of the Republic or are contrary to public policy.

Also, because of the lack of regulation, the authorities would not be entitled to register the child because they can do only what the law entitles them to do (the principle of legality in administrative matters).[29]

It is important to remember that in Guatemala a mother is the woman who gives birth to the child. Thus, no physician can legally certify that a child is the son or daughter of a woman who is not the one who gave birth. Even where the child

---

[25] The formal validity of acts is governed by the law of the place where they were entered into.

[26] See Art 35 of the Judicial Authority Act.

[27] If the intending parents ask for the recognition of the surrogacy agreement (or the recognition of its consequences).

[28] See Art 85 of the National Civil Registration Act.

[29] Art 154 of the Constitution of the Republic of Guatemala states: 'Officials are depositories of authority, legally responsible for their official conduct, subject to the law and never above it.'

was born abroad and the foreign birth certificate could certify as the child's parent a person other than the birth mother, since in Guatemala that is not possible, this birth certificate could not be registered by the Guatemalan authorities.

As explained in chapter one of this book, the question of surrogacy will arise only if the foreign authorities mention it in the birth certificate, or if the local authorities knew about the surrogacy agreement. If it is not the case, it is possible that the intending parents could inscribe the child as their own. In those cases, if a Guatemalan national goes to the Consulate of Guatemala where the child was born and declares that it is his or her child, the child will be registered as that person's own child. The consular agent will notify the birth to the RENAP and it will be registered in the database. In other words, if the intending parents say nothing about the surrogacy agreement, it is possible that they could inscribe the child born as a consequence of a surrogacy agreement as if he or she had born abroad 'naturally'. Thus, it is important to regulate surrogacy in order to prevent this kind of situation which implies a violation of children's rights.

11

Hungary

CSONGOR ISTVÁN NAGY

I. Domestic Law on Surrogacy

In Hungary, there is no specific regulation on surrogacy. Act CLIV of 1997 on Health Care ('Act on Health Care') deals with reproductive procedures but does not touch upon the question of surrogate motherhood.

A. The Unborn Child of the Act on Health Care: The Rules on Surrogacy that Never Entered into Force

The original version of the Act on Health Care,[1] as adopted by the Hungarian Parliament on 15 December 1997, did contain provisions on surrogacy, but these rules never entered into force: first their entry into force was postponed[2] and then later the Parliament repealed these provisions.[3] It is to be noted that the question of surrogacy was highly controversial in the 1997 parliamentary debate regarding the Act.[4]

In the Hungarian language there are two terms for surrogacy; the difference between the two designations depends on whether the surrogacy is undertaken for monetary consideration or not (ie whether it is commercial or altruistic). The first term is 'nurse-pregnancy' ('*dajkaterhesség*') and refers to altruistic surrogacy arrangements, ie the surrogate mother receives no monetary consideration for her cooperation. The second term is 'hired mother' or 'hired motherhood' ('*béranya*' or '*béranyaság*'): here the mother is receiving a fee for her service.[5]

---

[1] On the original 1997 version of the Act on Health Care in general, see J Sándor, *Medical Law. Hungary* (Alphen aan den Rijn, Kluwer Law International, 2003) 120–21.

[2] Section 1 of Act XXXVII of 1998.

[3] Section 32(1) of Act CXIX of 1999.

[4] J Sándor, 'Reproductive Rights in Hungarian Law: A New Right to Assisted Procreation?' (2000) 4(2) *Health and Human Rights* 196, 213.

[5] Cf *ibid*, 213, fn 24 (designating commercial surrogacy ('*béranyaság*') as motherhood for salary and non-commercial surrogacy ('*dajkaterhesség*') as nurse-motherhood, and emphasizing that the

The original version of the Act CLIV of 1997 on health care dealt exclusively with 'nurse pregnancy' (altruistic surrogacy). According to section 183(1), surrogacy was to be allowed if the couple were married or they were partners-in-life (cohabitants), and if:

(a) the genetic mother, due to her bodily condition, was unable to bear the child; or

(b) the child-bearing would endanger the genetic mother's life or bodily integrity; or

(c) it is very probable that no child would be born from the embryo if it was implanted into the genetic mother's body.

The Act also posed strict requirements on who might act as a surrogate mother ('nurse mother', in Hungarian '*dajkaanya*'). Only a close relative of the genetic couple could be a surrogate mother, provided she had legal capacity, was capable of bearing a healthy child and was at least 25 years old but not older than 40 years at the time when the embryo was implanted, and had given life at least to one child (who was born alive).[6]

Surrogacy presupposed the proposal (recommendation) of a specialised physician and an administrative permission. The couple had to submit a joint request; the surrogate mother was to submit a declaration of assent, and if she was married or had a partner-in-life, the permission presupposed the assent of the husband or the partner-in-life as well.[7] The declaration of assent was to be included in a private deed with full evidentiary force,[8] or in a public deed.[9]

All the detailed issues were to be tackled in a ministerial decree, which, however, was never adopted.[10]

Section 184(1) of the Act provided that the surrogate mother could not receive any payment for her activity and thus enabled only altruistic surrogacy. The language of this provision was not completely clear: it prohibited any kind of payment or fee but it did not touch upon the issue of remuneration for the costs of the surrogate mother.

Furthermore, section 184(2) prohibited the advertising of the application or use of surrogate motherhood, or of the procedure in any sense.

---

latter term 'has no pejorative connotation; on the contrary, it has an emotionally positive association with wet-nursing').

[6] Section 183(2).

[7] Section 183(3).

[8] Under Hungarian law, the term 'private deed with full evidentiary force' encompasses, among others, the following documents: the document was autographed and signed by the person who made the declaration, the document was signed by two witnesses, the signature of the person who made the declaration is authenticated by a court or a public attorney, the document was prepared and countersigned by an attorney-at-law, a qualified electronic signature was placed on the electronic document. Section 196 of the Code on Civil Procedure.

[9] Section 183(4).

[10] Section 183(6).

B. Is Surrogacy Lawful in Hungary?

Surrogacy as such is not lawful in Hungary, ie it cannot be practised on the territory of Hungary. The Act on Health Care contains an exhaustive enumeration of those reproductive procedures that are lawful in Hungary; since surrogacy arrangements are not so listed, they are not lawful.[11]

Interestingly, before the entry into force of the 1997 Act on Health Care, due to 'the lack of any explicit legal prohibition, surrogacy already existed in Hungary'.[12]

It is doubtful whether surrogacy is contrary to Hungarian criminal law.[13] The majority opinion seems to be that the surrogacy itself is not prohibited. At the same time, it is to be noted that surrogacy may still amount to a criminal act in Hungary, although it should be stressed that the relevant provisions of the Criminal Code[14] have not been tested in this context.

Section 173/I of the Hungarian Criminal Code prohibits the 'illegal use of the human body'. It provides that

> the person who illegally acquires a human gene, cell, gamete, embryo, organ, tissue, dead body or part of it, as well as who releases these or trades with them, commits a felony.

The maximum punishment is in general three years in prison, but in certain aggravating circumstances this may increase up to eight years. The Criminal Code also provides that it is a misdemeanour if someone prepares to commit the above crime.

The conduct of surrogacy procedures may come under the purview of section 173/I of the Hungarian Criminal Code, as it may amount to the acquiring of a human cell, gamete or embryo. In this regard, 'acquiring' means seizing the human cell, gamete or embryo, etc. Although section 173/I applies only to acts that are illegal, since the Act on Health Care does not list surrogacy among the lawful reproductive procedures, it qualifies as an illegal act.

Another provision of the Hungarian Criminal Code that may have relevance in the context of surrogacy is section 193, entitled 'Change of family status'. It provides that 'the person who changes the family status of another, in particular if he or she replaces the child or brings him or her into another family, commits a felony'. The maximum punishment is in general three years in prison, but in certain aggravating circumstances this may increase up to five years. (Note that according to section 49(2) of the Hungarian Family Code, an adoption must not be approved if it confers any profit on the parties, or on any person or organisation that is instrumental in the process.)

---

[11] Chapter IX of the Act on Health Care.

[12] Sándor, above n 4, 213.

[13] Z Navratyil, *A varázsló eltöri pálcáját? A jogi szabályozás vonulata az asszisztált humán reprodukciótól a klónozásig* (Budapest, Gondolat, 2012) 164–65.

[14] Act IV of 1978 on the Criminal Code.

The Hungarian court applied section 193 of the Hungarian Criminal Code to a matter where the Hungarian defendants made, for financial consideration, adoption declarations and waivers of parental rights in the US and in Canada. Although these declarations were valid under US and Canadian law, the court applied Hungarian law to these declarations because the newborn babies were Hungarian citizens. It held that the above declarations were invalid under Hungarian family law.[15] Accordingly, the court established violation of section 193 of the Hungarian Criminal Code.

In another case, the Hungarian court interpreted section 193 of the Hungarian Criminal Code in the context of an arrangement whereby pregnant Hungarian women travelled to the US in order to give birth to their children and have them adopted there in exchange for financial consideration. The Hungarian court held that the persons instrumental in this scheme (organisers, intermediaries and abettors) had violated section 193, and imposed criminal sanctions on the defendants.[16]

Although the cases above did not involve surrogacy arrangements, the decisions are telling about the potential application of section 193 to such schemes.

Of course, the above rules are applicable only in cases that come under Hungarian criminal jurisdiction. According to sections 3–4 of the Hungarian Criminal Code, Hungarian criminal jurisdiction covers criminal acts committed on the territory of Hungary, including Hungarian ships and aircrafts residing abroad, irrespective of the person of the perpetrator (principle of territoriality), as well as criminal acts committed abroad by Hungarian citizens (principle of nationality).[17] In addition, Hungarian criminal law recognises the principles of protection and universality; but in such cases the criminal procedure has to be instituted by the chief public prosecutor.[18]

Accordingly, the above criminal rules may cover not only those acts committed on the territory of Hungary, but also acts committed by Hungarian citizens abroad. Section 173/I of the Hungarian Criminal Code ('Illegal use of human body') seems not to be applicable to acts committed outside the territory of Hungary: although the criminal rules have such a purview, these rules are essentially applicable only to conduct that is illegal under the Hungarian Act on Health Care, and this Act is applicable only on the territory of Hungary.[19] On the other hand, the territorial scope of section 193 of the Hungarian Criminal Code ('Change of family status') is probably not confined to the territory of Hungary, especially in those cases when the parents attempt to enter the child in the Hungarian birth register.

---

[15] Case Bf.V.1.917/1999 (Supreme Court).
[16] Case B0015303 (Budapest Court of Appeals).
[17] Section 3 of the Criminal Code.
[18] Section 4(3) of the Criminal Code.
[19] Section 4 of the Act on Health Care.

C. Enforceability of Surrogacy Arrangements

As surrogacy is illegal in Hungary, surrogacy agreements, under Hungarian law, amount to contracts for the pursuance of illegal activity and are, as such, void.[20] Although there is no guidance given by courts in this respect, it is assumed that such agreements are null and void and legally unenforceable.[21]

D. Legal Parenthood and the Nationality of the Child

Under Hungarian law, there is no specific provision on whether the biological or the genetic mother is to be regarded as the child's legal mother. However, it is probable that under Hungarian law the legally recognised mother is the biological mother.[22] This is further supported by the fact that the new Hungarian Civil Code[23] (not yet in force) expressly provides that the mother is the woman who bore the child.[24]

Under section 44 of the Hungarian Family Code,[25] the child may request the court to establish who his or her mother is. At the same time, it must be stressed that if there is no evidence in respect of the child-bearing (for instance, witnesses who were there at the time of the child-bearing, public or private deeds available at the hospital where the child was born), it is probably impossible to prove who the biological mother is, since courts normally use genetic evidence in lineage matters.

Interestingly, if the biological mother is married, her husband is presumed to be the father of the child due to his marital relationship with the mother.[26] The presumed father has the right to rebut this presumption by attacking it before the court.[27]

Accordingly, the parents of the child are probably the genetic father (provided there is no presumption of fatherhood or it is rebutted) and the biological mother (surrogate mother), while it may be difficult to prove who the biological mother was.

---

[20] Section 200(2) of the Hungarian Civil Code.

[21] Cf J Sándor, 'A humán reprodukciós orvosi eljárások jogi szabályozásáról' ['Regulating assisted procreation'] (1996) 25 *Acta Humana* 29, 45 (contending that surrogacy agreements are normally legally not enforceable; arguing that the judicial enforcement of surrogacy agreements would amount to the illegal restriction of personality rights if the surrogate mother, on changing her mind, were required to endure child-bearing against her will).

[22] See J Sándor, 'A terápiától a szelekcióig: Jogi és etikai viták a reprodukciós beavatkozások új módszereiről' ['From therapy to selection: legal and ethical debates on the new methods of assisted reproduction'] (2005) 16(4) *Acta Humana* 3, 12; Z Navratyil, *A varázsló eltöri pálcáját? A jogi szabályozás vonulata az asszisztált humán reprodukciótól a klónozásig* (Budapest, Gondolat, 2012) 163.

[23] Act IV of 1959 on Hungarian Civil Code.

[24] Section 3:122(1) of the new Hungarian Civil Code.

[25] Act IV of 1952 on the Hungarian Family Code.

[26] Section 35(1) of the Hungarian Family Code.

[27] Section 43(1) of the Hungarian Family Code.

This implies that the child may be entitled to maintenance from the father. Under sections 69/A–69/D of the Hungarian Family Code, a parent has to maintain his or her child; if the parent does not live with the child, he or she has to pay monetary maintenance (while the parent who lives with the child has to provide maintenance in kind). This rule seems to be applicable irrespective of whether the father provided the gamete in the context of a surrogacy arrangement or not. If the surrogate mother refuses to hand over the child (remember that surrogacy agreements are null and void and, hence, unenforceable under Hungarian law), the child becomes entitled to maintenance from the father. Since the child is a minor, he or she has no legal capacity, so the maintenance must be paid into the hands of the statutory representative, ie the parent having custody over the child, which may be the surrogate mother in this case.

The father may ask the court to place the child with him. In this case, he would care for the child in his own household and provide maintenance in kind; likewise, he may, on behalf of the child, sue the surrogate mother for maintenance.

If the intended mother wants to become the legal parent of the child, she has to adopt him or her.[28] In this case the adoption is to be accomplished under the general rules, ie there are no provisions that would take into account the peculiar situation that in fact it is the genetic mother who wants to adopt her genetic child. The genetic mother would be required to adopt the child as if she had no tie with him or her. As a matter of practice, surrogacy arrangements may be managed under the veil of adoption procedures. The intended parents agree with the surrogate mother, and after the birth they adopt the child under the general rules as if they had no connection to the child at all. The Hungarian authorities do not permit the adoption, among other reasons, if either the parties or any person or organisation participating in the procedure acquire(s) any profit due to the adoption.[29]

The rights of the child born through a surrogacy arrangement, for example the child's right to know his or her genetic mother, are not recognised under Hungarian law. Since there are no specific provisions in Hungarian law on surrogacy, children born under such arrangements are afforded no special treatment. The legal mother is the biological mother; the genetic mother is not granted any legal status and has absolutely no legally recognised relationship (rights or obligations) with the child.[30]

Likewise, the rights of the surrogate mother are not recognised either, as there are no specific provisions in Hungarian law on surrogacy.

Hungarian citizenship law follows the principle of *ius sanguinis* and provides that the descendents of a Hungarian citizen automatically acquire Hungarian citizenship by birth.[31]

---

[28] Navratyil, above n 22, 164.
[29] Section 49(2) of the Hungarian Family Law.
[30] Navratyil, above n 22, 164.
[31] Section 3(1)–(2) of Act LV of 1993 on Hungarian Citizenship.

II. Surrogacy in Hungarian Private International Law

Hungarian private international law contains no specific provisions on surrogacy; hence, the general rules are applicable.

A. Jurisdiction

Lineage matters concerning the personal status of Hungarian citizens fall under exclusive Hungarian jurisdiction. According to section 62/B of the Hungarian Act on Private International Law:[32]

> The Hungarian court and administrative authority always has jurisdiction over procedures concerning the personal status of Hungarian citizens. This jurisdiction is exclusive.[33]

Similarly, according to section 62/D, '[t]he Hungarian court and other authority has no jurisdiction over procedures concerning the personal status of non-Hungarian citizens'. Nevertheless,

> [t]he Hungarian court has jurisdiction over law-suits between non-Hungarian citizens concerning personal status if either party has his place of living or habitual residence in Hungary.

B. Applicable Law

Section 42 of the Hungarian Act on Private International Law deals with family status and provides that the child's personal law at the time of birth shall apply to the establishment of fatherhood or motherhood, as well as to the rebuttal of the presumption of fatherhood. In respect of the recognition of the child by the father, the child's personal law at the moment of recognition is to be applied. Since the conceived-but-not-born child has, in most legal systems, no legal personality, in such cases the child's recognition is governed by the mother's personal law at the moment of recognition. Section 42(3) provides that

> [t]he recognition cannot be regarded as formally invalid if it is formally valid under Hungarian law or under the law in force at the place and time of the recognition [ie *locus regit actum*].

The Act on Private International Law employs four connecting factors for determining the personal law of natural persons, applying them in the following order: citizenship, place of living, closest connection and habitual residence. The principal

---

[32] Law-Decree (Act) 13 of 1979 on Private International Law.
[33] Notwithstanding the above, there are five exceptions to the exclusive Hungarian jurisdiction, which, however, do not concern surrogacy.

connecting factor used by the Act for defining a natural person's *lex personae* is nationality (citizenship). If a person has multiple citizenships, and one of them is Hungarian, Hungarian law is to be applied. The personal law of persons having multiple citizenships, if none of them is Hungarian, as well as of stateless persons, is determined by their place of living (irrespective of whether the place of living is in the country of citizenship or not). In case of multiple places of living, if one of them is in Hungary, Hungarian law is to be applied; otherwise, the law of the country is to be applied with which the person has the closest connection. In the absence of such a connection, the law of the country of habitual residence is applicable.[34]

The above provisions may, in certain matters, cause a vicious circle when the child's family status is to be determined under the law of citizenship. Under Hungarian conflicts law, family status is governed by the child's personal law; nevertheless, the child's personal law may in certain matters depend on who the child's parent is or parents are. Personal law is, in principle, determined by the person's citizenship; if someone has dual citizenship and one of them is Hungarian, his or her personal law is Hungarian. Hungarian citizenship law (similarly to several other Continental laws) follows the principle of *ius sanguinis* and provides that the child acquires the citizenship of his or her parents, without any measure being required.[35] The problem is that the identity of the alleged parent, ie the person whose parental status serves as the subject matter of the dispute, may have a decisive influence on the child's personal law through national citizenship law's following the principle of *ius sanguinis*.

Assume that both Hungarian law and the law of country 'B' follow the principle of *ius sanguinis*, follow the principle of citizenship in respect of personal law, and provide that if a person has dual citizenship and one them is domestic, domestic law is to be applied; Hungarian law adopts the biological mother principle, while the law of country 'B' adopts the genetic mother principle. The genetic mother is Hungarian, the biological mother is from country 'B'. In order to simplify the analysis, assume that the father is the citizen of a third country.

In this case, the question is who the legal mother is. If applying Hungarian law (under the hypothesis that the mother is the Hungarian citizen), the child's personal law would be Hungarian law (it is irrelevant how many other citizenships he or she may have; if he or she is also a Hungarian citizen, his or her personal law is Hungarian law). Hungarian law follows the biological mother principle; hence the mother is from country 'B', and this entails that the child has no Hungarian citizenship (legally speaking: neither of his or her parents is Hungarian). Since the child gets the citizenship of the mother, his or her personal law would be the law of country 'B' which, in turn, follows the genetic mother principle and does not treat the child as its own citizen; hence, the child's personal law is not the law of country 'B'. The same problems emerge if we proceed from the hypothesis that the mother is the citizen of country 'B'.

---

[34] Section 11 of the Act on Private International Law.
[35] Section 3(1)–(2) of Act LV of 1993 on Hungarian Citizenship.

Fortunately, the above vicious circle would normally not emerge in practice, as in cases coming before Hungarian courts (and administrative agencies) usually both intended parents are Hungarian citizens; hence, the child would qualify as a Hungarian citizen at least on the right of the father.

C. Recognition Matters

The recognition of the family status of the child born by a surrogate mother is governed by the general rules of private international law.

According to section 70 of the Act on Private International Law,

> [t]he decision of a foreign court or other authority rendered in a matter over which the Hungarian court or other authority has exclusive jurisdiction cannot be recognised in Hungary.

In the light of the jurisdictional rules described above, this provision may serve as a serious impediment to recognition of judgments dealing with the personal status of children born to a surrogate mother.

In a recent case,[36] the Hungarian court recognised a Ukrainian birth certificate concerning a child who might have been born as a result of a surrogacy procedure. The facts were as follows. The parents whose names were entered into the Ukrainian birth register were a Hungarian couple, who stated that they took part in a test-tube baby programme in Ukraine. The Hungarian Migration and Citizenship Office refused to settle the child's legal status. The judgment contained no reference to gestational surrogacy, probably due to the lack of evidence suggesting use of this arrangement; nonetheless, it is to be noted that the legal analysis below is also applicable to cases involving gestational surrogacy, provided this circumstance is not revealed to the court or the administrative agency.

In this case, the Hungarian court found that the father indicated in the Ukrainian birth certificate was the plaintiff and that the Ukrainian birth certificate was to be recognised in Hungary. Furthermore, when the child was born, there was a marital relationship between the plaintiff and the mother, hence, according to section 35(1) of the Hungarian Family Code, the plaintiff was presumed to be the father of the child. Lastly, it was also proved before the court that the person indicated in the birth register as the father was the child's genetic father: genetic evidence proved the plaintiff's fatherhood (DNA examination).

The court held that parentage is, in principle, to be established on the basis of the Ukrainian birth certificate, because there is a bilateral treaty on legal assistance between Hungary and Ukraine.[37] If the question of parentage cannot be settled

---

[36] 5.P.III.20.970/2011/2.

[37] See Treaty on legal assistance between the Hungarian Republic and Ukraine in civil matters, signed in Budapest on 2 August 2001 (promulgated by Law XVI of 2002) (in Hungarian: '*a Magyar Köztársaság és Ukrajna között a polgári ügyekben történő kölcsönös jogsegélyről szóló, Budapesten, 2001. augusztus 2-án aláírt szerződés (kihirdette a 2002. évi XVI. tv.)*').

through the birth certificate, the fatherhood of the man is to be presumed, if he was in a marital relationship with the mother at the time of conception. If this marital presumption is not applicable, the father may make a 'full force declaration of fatherly recognition'; in this case, the man making the declaration is to be regarded as the father. The declaration acquires full force only if it is approved by the mother, the minor's statutory representative and the child, provided the child is at least 18 years old.[38] Since fatherly declarations are usually made at the time when the child is a minor, and the child's statutory representative is normally the parent with whom he or she lives (usually the mother), as a matter of practice, the approval of the mother, in general, suffices to confer full force on the fatherly recognition.

It is to be noted that the interested party may request the establishing of fatherhood, thus rebutting the presumption of parenthood emerging from the Ukrainian birth certificate or the marital relationship.

Albeit that in gestational surrogacy cases it is normally not the status of the father but that of the mother that raises doubts (as the father gives the gamete, he is to be regarded as the father anyway), the above case shows that if the surrogacy procedure takes place in a country where the legal mother is the genetic mother, in Hungary—although Hungarian law follows the biological mother rule—the genetic mother will be, in principle, automatically recognised for documentary reasons. Nonetheless, the presumption entailed by the foreign public deed (birth certificate) can be rebutted. Lastly, in the context of the above case, as already mentioned, there was a bilateral treaty on legal assistance between Hungary and Ukraine, entailing the recognition of the Ukrainian birth certificate.

It should be remembered that causing a 'change of family status' is a felony under section 193 of the Hungarian Criminal Code (see section I.B. above). Hence, it may amount to a crime if someone enters another person (not the real parent) or causes this person to be entered in the birth register. Although the entry of the genetic mother in the birth register may be lawful in Ukraine, the Hungarian Criminal Code's purview may cover the acts of Hungarian citizens irrespective of the place of occurrence.

III. Summary

In conclusion, surrogacy is not specifically regulated in Hungary and its status is dubious. This much is certain—that surrogacy is illegal on the territory of Hungary. Although it is not clear whether it is also covered by criminal law, and it is to be noted that there is no judicial practice in this regard, surrogacy does raise serious criminal law concerns. Accordingly, surrogacy arrangements seem not to

---

[38] Section 37(4) of the Hungarian Family Code.

be enforceable under Hungarian law. However, surrogacy arrangements may be implemented under the veil of adoption.

Hungarian law follows the biological mother rule. Nonetheless, if the child is born in a foreign country to a surrogate mother and the foreign birth certificate indicates the name of the genetic mother without any reference to the woman who gave birth to the child (because the foreign country follows the genetic mother rule), the case law suggests that Hungarian courts may recognise the foreign birth certificate for documentary reasons, without *ex officio* investigating the circumstances of the conception and of the birth.

12

India

USHA RENGACHARY SMERDON

I. Introduction

Although the number of surrogate births in India is not known, anecdotal evidence indicates that the number continues to rise as the numerous assisted reproductive technology (ART) facilitators continue to streamline the process for prospective commissioning parents. India has never prohibited surrogacy, but in recent years India has increasingly recognised the need to regulate the industry. Regulation to date has taken the form of non-binding guidelines promulgated by the medical industry, but it is expected that more formal regulation will be enacted at the national and state levels. Given the number of problematic cases that continue to be reported with respect to cross-border surrogacy arrangements where the child's citizenship and parentage status are undefined, and given the concerns about adequate protections for surrogate mothers, the need for regulation is evident.[1]

II. On the Cusp of Regulation

Regulation of surrogacy has been considered for several years but has not yet been formalised. At the federal level, several versions of surrogacy bills have been proposed but legislation has not yet been enacted. Currently, the Assisted Reproductive Technologies (Regulation) Bill 2010 ('Draft Bill') is pending with the Parliament of India. The 2010 Bill grants rule-making authority to the Central Government of India. The Central Government has developed the Assisted Reproductive Technologies (Regulation) Rules 2010 ('Draft Rules').

---

[1] See eg Law Commission of India, 'Need for Legislation to Regulate Assisted Reproductive Technology Clinics as Well as Rights and Obligations of Parties to a Surrogacy', Report No 228, 5 August 2009 (recognising the need for surrogacy to be addressed by comprehensive legislation, stating: 'The need of the hour is to adopt a pragmatic approach by legalising altruistic surrogacy arrangements and prohibiting commercial ones.').

One state also has a bill pending. The Maharashtra Assisted Reproductive Technology (Regulation) Act 2011 was recently introduced in the state legislature of the State of Maharashtra.[2] The draft of the bill has not been publicly released, but it is reported to include the following provisions:

(a) a surrogate would have to register as a patient at a state government-run ART clinic in order to establish transparency;

(b) only a married woman (25–35 years) may become a surrogate;

(c) surrogacy would be prohibited for women who have more than five children;

(d) the state government will certify the medical fitness of women serving as surrogates; and

(e) international clients would have to obtain a letter from their embassy stating that surrogacy is accepted in the country concerned.[3]

Currently in place are non-binding National Guidelines for Accreditation Supervision & Regulation of ART Clinics in India, promulgated by the Ministry of Health and Family Welfare, Government of India, and the Indian Council of Medical Research and the National Academy of Medical Sciences (India) in 2005 ('Guidelines'). Most provisions of the Guidelines mirror the provisions of the Draft Bill discussed below. Also in place are Ethical Guidelines for Biomedical Research on Human Subjects, which provide a number of protections to surrogate mothers not contained in the Guidelines or the Draft Bill and Draft Rules, including that:

(a) surrogacy should be resorted to only when it is coupled with authorised adoption wherever applicable;

(b) it should be rebuttably presumed that a woman who carries the child and gives birth to it is its mother;

(c) the intending parents should have a preferential right to adopt the child subject to six weeks' post-partum delay for the necessary maternal consent;

(d) the contract for surrogacy, despite permitting reasonable payment of compensation on completion of adoption, is valid subject to the surrogate's right to retain the baby if she so desires;

---

[2] M Porecha, 'Surrogacy Bill Tabled', *The Free Press Journal* (Mumbai, 18 December 2011), at <www.freepressjournal.in/news/38089-Surrogacy-Bill-tabled.html>; M Porecha, 'Surrogates May Get Respite with Bill in the Offing: Experts', *The Free Press Journal* (Mumbai, 20 December 2011), at <www.freepressjournal.in/news/38465-Surrogates-may-get-respite--with-bill-in-the-offing--Experts.html>.

[3] There have been some attempts to implement cross-border pre-clearance of surrogacy arrangements. In 2010, the Consul Generals of Belgium, France, Germany, Spain, Italy, The Netherlands, Poland and the Czech Republic notified several IVF clinics by a joint letter not to provide surrogacy options to citizens of their countries unless the commissioning parties consulted with their embassy first. See 'IVF Centres Direct Foreigners to Consulates Over Surrogacy Issue', *Hindustantimes* (New Delhi, 15 July 2010). www.hindustantimes.com/India-news/Mumbai/IVF-centres-direct-foreigners-to-consulates-over-surrogacy-issue/Article1-572534.aspx.

(e) the only remedy for the genetic parent is to make a claim for custody on the grounds of the best interests of the child; and

(f) abortion under the abortion law on medical grounds should be the inviolate right of the surrogate, and in that event, the adopting parents have no claim over the amounts already paid.[4]

In addition, on July 9, 2012, the Ministry of Home Affairs sent a letter to the Ministry of External Affairs which sets forth the procedure for granting visas to foreign nationals who visit India for the purpose of engaging in surrogacy arrangements; the only type of visa available for this purpose is a medical visa and not a tourist visa which is considered a violation of visa conditions.[5] The visa guidelines indirectly regulate surrogacy by setting forth the conditions on which foreign nationals can travel to India for surrogacy 'to ensure that the surrogate mother is not cheated.'[6] Specifically, a medical visa for purposes of surrogacy may only be granted if:

(a) The foreign man and woman are married and have been married for at least two years;

(b) The visa application must include a letter from the Embassy of the foreign country in India or the Foreign Ministry of that country stating that (1) the country recognises surrogacy, and (2) the child/children born to the commissioning couple through the Indian surrogate mother will be permitted entry into their country as a biological child/children of the commissioning couple;

(c) The commissioning couple furnish an undertaking that they will take care of the child/children born through surrogacy;

(d) Medical treatment will be performed only at a registered ART clinic recognised by ICMR; and

(e) The commissioning couple must produce a notarised agreement between the couple and the prospective Indian surrogate mother.[7]

For purposes of drawing up the surrogacy contract, the commissioning couple may enter India on a tourist visa, but they cannot provide any samples to any clinic during this preliminary visit.[8]

The remainder of this section will discuss specific provisions of the Draft Bill and Draft Rules.

---

[4] Statement of Specific Principles for Assisted Reproductive Technologies: Ethical Guidelines for Biomedical Research on Human Subjects, Indian Council of Medical Research, 97 (2006).

[5] India clarifies stand on Surrogacy VISA Regulation (21 August 2012), <www.blog.indiansurrogacylaw.com>.

[6] *Ibid.*

[7] *Ibid.*

[8] *Ibid.*

A. Requirements of the Parties Involved with Surrogacy

The Draft Bill contains restrictions on any woman undergoing an ART procedure, which would include surrogate mothers, intended mothers and egg donors. No ART procedure may be performed on a woman younger than 21 years.[9] In addition, no woman may be treated with gametes or embryos originating from the gametes of more than one man or one woman during any one treatment cycle.[10]

i. Requirements Specific to Gamete Donors

Under the Draft Bill, men donating sperm must be between the ages of 21 and 45.[11] Woman donating eggs must be between the ages of 21 and 35.[12] There is no proscription on the number of times a man may donate sperm, but a woman cannot donate eggs more than six times in her life, with an interval between egg retrieval no shorter than three months.[13] Eggs from a single retrieval may be shared with only two recipients, as long as at least seven eggs are available for each recipient.[14] However, only one semen sample from an ART bank may be used for only one recipient.[15] In no event may the donor learn the identity of the recipient.[16]

ii. Requirements Specific to Surrogate Mothers

The Draft Bill requires that a surrogate mother must be an Indian citizen between the ages of 21 and 35.[17] A woman may not be sent abroad to act as a surrogate.[18] A woman who is married requires the consent of her spouse to be a surrogate.[19] A relative, a person known to the commissioning party or a stranger may serve as a surrogate, but if she is a relative, she must belong to the same generation as the commissioning mother.[20]

A surrogate mother may not also donate her eggs to the intended party seeking surrogacy (nor may her husband's sperm be used).[21] A woman may not serve as a surrogate for more than five successful live births in her life, including her biological children, and she may not undergo an embryo transfer more than three times for the same couple.[22]

---

[9] Section 20(14) of the Draft Bill.
[10] Section 23(3) of the Draft Bill. In addition, an ART clinic may not mix semen from two individuals before use. Section 23(4) of the Draft Bill.
[11] Section 26(3) of the Draft Bill.
[12] *Ibid.*
[13] Section 26(8) of the Draft Bill.
[14] Section 26(9) of the Draft Bill.
[15] Section 26(11) of the Draft Bill.
[16] Section 33(5) of the Draft Bill.
[17] Sections 2(bb), 34(5) and 34(22) of the Draft Bill.
[18] Section 34(18) of the Draft Bill.
[19] Section 34(16) of the Draft Bill.
[20] Section 34(18) of the Draft Bill.
[21] Sections 2(aa), 2(bb) and 34(13) of the Draft Bill.
[22] Sections 34(5) and 34(9) of the Draft Bill.

A surrogate mother is required to be medically tested and declare that she has not received a blood transfusion or product in the previous six months.[23] She is bound to not engage in any act that would harm the foetus during pregnancy or the baby after birth.[24] The surrogate mother must register at the hospital in her own name, and must clearly disclose that she is a surrogate mother and provide the names and addresses of the persons for whom she is acting as a surrogate.[25]

iii. Requirements Specific to Commissioning Parties

Commissioning parties must be unable to carry a baby to term.[26] It is not entirely clear whether surrogacy for commissioning gay and lesbian parties is permitted. The Draft Bill provides that ART shall be available to all persons, including single persons, married couples and unmarried couples.[27] The Bill defines 'couple' as 'two persons living together and having a sexual relationship that is legal in India', which suggests that gays and lesbians may be unable to engage in surrogacy arrangements.[28] However, the Bill defines an 'unmarried couple' as two persons, both of marriageable age, living together with mutual consent but without getting married, in a relationship that is legal in the country/countries of which they are citizens.[29]

Although the surrogate may be known to the commissioning couple, gametes may not be donated by a relative or known friend of the commissioning parties.[30] However, the retrieval of gametes of a person whose death is imminent is permissible if the dying person's spouse intends to avail himself or herself of ART to have a child.[31] Commissioning parties cannot use the services of more than one surrogate mother simultaneously.[32] Neither can the commissioning parties have embryos transferred simultaneously to both a surrogate mother and the commissioning mother.[33] The commissioning parties must provide the

---

[23] Section 34(6) of the Draft Bill.
[24] Section 34(23) of the Draft Bill.
[25] Section 34(8) of the Draft Bill.
[26] Section 20(1) of the Draft Bill.
[27] Section 32(1) of the Draft Bill.
[28] Section 2(h) of the Draft Bill. However, the Supreme Court of India is currently considering petitions challenging a Delhi court verdict decriminalising homosexual acts between consenting adults in private. See J Venkatesan, 'Homosexuality Should Be Construed an Offence: Counsel', *The Hindu* (Chennai, 16 February 2012), at <www.thehindu.com/news/national/article2900751.ece>. With regard to surrogacy, Justice GS Singhvi stated (*ibid*): 'Homosexuality should be seen in the context of changing society, as many things which were earlier unacceptable have become acceptable with passage of time. Phenomena of live-in relationship, single parents, artificial fertilisation and surrogacy have become normal. There is a case where a man is unmarried but wants to be a father and engage a surrogate mother. Thirty-four years ago it was against the order of nature but now artificial fertilisation is a thriving business. Many things which were considered immoral 20 years ago have become acceptable as society is changing.'
[29] Section 2(dd) of the Draft Bill.
[30] Section 20(12) of the Draft Bill.
[31] Section 23(6) of the Draft Bill.
[32] Section 34(20) of the Draft Bill.
[33] Section 34(21) of the Draft Bill.

surrogate mother with a certificate stating clearly that she has acted as a surrogate for them.[34]

Consistent with existing Indian law proscribing sex selection, the Draft Bill prohibits ART clinics from offering a couple a child of a predetermined sex.[35] Determining the sex of the child to be born through ART is considered a criminal offence.[36]

B. Enforceability of Surrogacy Arrangements

Surrogacy in India is permissible because no Indian law prohibits it.[37] The Indian Contract Act would apply with respect to the legality of surrogacy agreements.[38] Under section 10 of the Contract Act, all agreements are contracts if they are made with the free consent of parties competent to contract, for a lawful consideration and with a lawful object, and are not expressly declared void. It is possible that a court could find a surrogacy contract unenforceable on public policy grounds or unconstitutional under Article 23 of the Constitution of India, which prohibits forced labour and trafficking in human beings.[39] However, thus far, no Indian court has declared a surrogacy contract unenforceable.[40]

The Draft Bill specifically provides that surrogacy agreements are legally enforceable.[41] The Draft Rules contain forms of agreements for:

(a) surrogacy;
(b) consent for donation of eggs;
(c) consent for donation of semen/sperm;
(d) information on the semen donor, oocyte donor and surrogate mother;
(e) contracts (including the financial arrangements) between the ART Bank, on the one hand, and the semen donor, oocyte donor, surrogate mother, patient or the ART clinic, on the other hand; and
(f) the contract (including financial arrangement) between the patient and the surrogate.

C. Payments in Surrogacy

The Draft Bill contemplates that gamete donors and surrogates may be compensated financially by the ART Bank.[42] However, compensation for the surrogate mother is generally a matter between the surrogate mother and the commissioning

---

[34] Section 34(17) of the Draft Bill.
[35] Section 25 of the Draft Bill.
[36] *Ibid.*
[37] Section 3.5(a) of the Law Report, above n 1.
[38] Section 3.5(c) of the Law Report, above n 1.
[39] Constitution of India, Art 23, § 1.
[40] *Cf Yamada v Union of India*, 2008 INDLAW SC 1554 (29 September 2008) (noting that commercial surrogacy is 'legal' in India).
[41] Section 34(1) of the Draft Bill.
[42] Section 26(6) of the Draft Bill.

parties.[43] The Model Contract between the ART Bank and the Surrogate appended to the Draft Rules provides that:

> The surrogate clearly understands that the consideration for the surrogacy is to be paid by the parents and the Bank will not be responsible for any demand by the surrogate in the form of compensation. The Bank shall also not be responsible for payment to the surrogate for any expenses incurred during the surrogacy period.[44]

The Model Contract between the surrogate mother and commissioning parties sets forth a payment plan for the surrogate mother's compensation.[45] A first instalment of at least 5 per cent of the total agreed compensation is payable when the embryo transfer occurs; a second instalment of at least 5 per cent is due when the surrogate becomes pregnant; a third instalment of at least 5 per cent is due at the end of the first trimester; a fourth instalment of at least 10 per cent is due at the end of the second trimester and the remaining 75 per cent is due just after delivery. If the first embryo transfer does not succeed, for each subsequent embryo transfer within six months of the first, the surrogate is to receive an additional 50 per cent of the total initial price paid in the preceding instalments.

The commissioning parties must ensure that the surrogate mother is 'appropriately insured' until the child is handed over and until the surrogate mother is free from all health complications arising from the surrogacy.[46]

D. Legal Parenthood/Nationality of the Child

In the light of several publicised cases concerning the parentage and citizenship of children born through surrogacy, the Draft Bill contains relatively extensive provisions on these matters. It spells out that a child born to a married couple through ART is presumed to be the legitimate child of the couple, born in wedlock with the consent of both spouses, and shall have the same legal rights as a legitimate child born through sexual intercourse.[47] A child born to an unmarried couple through ART shall be considered the legitimate child of both parties.[48] A child born to a single parent will be considered the legitimate child of that parent.[49] If the married or unmarried couple separate or divorce after consenting to ART but before the child is born, the child shall still be considered the legitimate child of the couple.[50] The birth certificate issued with respect to the child born through surrogacy will bear the names of the commissioning parties as the child's parents.[51]

---

[43] Section 34(3) of the Draft Bill.
[44] Draft Rules, Form R2.
[45] Draft Rules, Form U.
[46] Section 34(24) of the Draft Bill.
[47] Section 35(1) of the Draft Bill.
[48] Section 35(2) of the Draft Bill.
[49] Sections 35(3) and 35(4) of the Draft Bill.
[50] Section 35(4) of the Draft Bill.
[51] Sections 34(10) and 35(7) of the Draft Bill.

Commissioning parties from countries other than India must ensure and establish to the ART clinic through proper documentation (ie, a letter from either the embassy of the relevant country in India, or from the foreign ministry of the country), clearly and unambiguously, that:

(a) that country permits surrogacy; and
(b) the child born through surrogacy in India will be permitted entry into that country as a biological child of the commissioning couple/individual.[52]

Non-residents of India must appoint a local guardian, who will be legally responsible for taking care of the surrogate during and after the pregnancy until the child is delivered to the commissioning parties or the local guardian.[53] The commissioning parties are legally bound to accept the custody of the child, regardless of any abnormality of the child.[54]

Refusal to take delivery of the child is considered an offence, punishable by imprisonment for up to three years, or a fine or both.[55] If the foreign commissioning party fails to take delivery of the child born to the surrogate mother, the local guardian will be legally obligated to take custody of the child, and is free to hand the child over to an adoption agency if the commissioning party or their legal representative fails to claim the child within one month of the child's birth.[56] During the transition period, the local guardian is responsible for the well-being of the child.[57]

Children born through surrogacy to foreign commissioning parties shall not be Indian citizens even though they are born in India.[58] However, in cases where commissioning parties refuse to take delivery of the child and the child is adopted or is raised by the legal guardian, the child will be granted Indian citizenship.[59]

E. Advertisement

Under the Draft Bill, an ART Bank may advertise for gamete donors and surrogates on a commercial basis, but advertisements may not contain any details relating to the caste, ethnic identity or descent of any of the parties involved in the surrogacy.[60] No ART clinic is permitted to advertise for surrogacy for its clients.[61]

---

[52] Section 34(19) of the Draft Bill.
[53] Section 34(19) of the Draft Bill.
[54] Section 34(11) of the Draft Bill.
[55] Section 40 of the Draft Bill.
[56] *Ibid.*
[57] *Ibid.*
[58] Section 35(8) of the Draft Bill.
[59] Section 34(19) of the Draft Bill.
[60] Sections 26(6) and 34(7) of the Draft Bill.
[61] Section 34(7) of the Draft Bill.

F. Rights of the Child Born Through a Surrogacy Arrangement

The Draft Bill prohibits the child born through surrogacy from learning the identity of the gamete donor or surrogate mother.[62] The trail of secrecy begins with the ART Bank. The ART Bank must obtain necessary information about the gamete donor or surrogate, including their identities and addresses, but must promise the donor or surrogate that their identities will remain confidential.[63] The ART Bank must obtain a written agreement from the ART clinic that in no circumstances (except if asked by a court) will the ART clinic reveal the identity of the donor to the recipient couple or anyone else.[64] The identity of the gamete donor or surrogate donor may be released only in cases of life-threatening medical conditions which require physical testing or samples of the gamete donor or surrogate mother, but only upon the prior informed consent of the gamete donor or surrogate mother.[65] In addition, the identity of gamete donors or surrogate mothers may be disclosed to a central database to be maintained by the Department of Health Research.[66] Divulging the identity of donors/surrogate mothers in violation of the Draft Bill is a punishable offence under the Act.[67]

Other than the identity of the gamete donor or surrogate mother, the parents or legal guardian of a minor child have the right to access other information about the donor, 'when and to the extent necessary for the welfare of the child'.[68] The commissioning parties are entitled to information about the donor including the donor's height, weight, ethnicity, skin colour, educational qualifications and medical history.[69] When the child reaches age 18, he or she may request information about the donor or surrogate mother, except their personal identity.[70]

G. Rights of the Surrogate Mother

Donors and surrogate mothers are required to relinquish all parental rights over the child.[71] Pursuant to the Model Surrogacy Agreement appended to the Draft Rules, the surrogate mother agrees to hand over the child after delivery.[72] She

---

[62] The Draft Bill is somewhat inconsistent in this regard since the commissioning parties are required to contract directly with the surrogate mother. The surrogate mother's identity (and that of her spouse) would be disclosed in the contract. See above n 45.

[63] Section 26(12) of the Draft Bill.

[64] Sections 20(2) and 26(13) of the Draft Bill.

[65] Section 36(3) of the Draft Bill.

[66] Section 20(9) of the Draft Bill.

[67] Section 26(14) of the Draft Bill.

[68] Sections 32(3) and 36(1) of the Draft Bill.

[69] Section 20(4) of the Draft Bill.

[70] Section 36(1) of the Draft Bill.

[71] Sections 34(4) and 35(6) of the Draft Bill.

[72] Draft Rules, Form J.

must agree to foetal reduction if asked by the party seeking surrogacy, if she is carrying more than one foetus. The surrogate mother has the right to terminate her pregnancy at will pursuant to the Medical Termination of Pregnancy Act of 1971.[73] If the surrogate mother terminates her pregnancy, she is required to refund all certified and documented expenses incurred during the pregnancy, unless the pregnancy is terminated on the basis of expert medical advice.[74]

H. Requirements of ART Clinics

Under the Draft Bill, all ART facilities (including ART Banks and research organisations) are required to register with a registration authority.[75] Clinics performing certain enumerated ART functions must also receive a certificate of accreditation issued by a state board.[76]

The use of individual brokers or paid intermediaries to obtain gamete donors or surrogates is considered an offence punishable by imprisonment for a term up to three years and a specified fine.[77]

III. Reported Problematic Cases

Due to the citizenship and parentage status issues with respect to children born through surrogacy arising both in India and in the country of the commissioning party, the number of reported cases involving cross-border surrogacy arrangements far outweigh the number of reported domestic cases involving difficulties in the surrogacy process. This section highlights reports of both types of cases.

A. Cross-border Cases

Problems with cross-border surrogacy arrangements have involved commissioning parties from multiple countries, primarily owing to the restrictiveness of the commissioning parties' country with respect to the legality of surrogacy.

---

[73] *Ibid.* Under the Medical Termination Act, a woman may generally terminate her pregnancy where the pregnancy does not exceed 12 weeks, or if the pregnancy does not exceed 20 weeks in the case of risk of life or grave injury to her physical or mental health, or where there is substantial risk that the child will suffer from such physical or mental abnormalities as to be seriously handicapped. Section 3(2) of the Medical Termination Act of 1971.

[74] Draft Rules, Form J.
[75] Section 13(1) of the Draft Bill.
[76] Section 13(4) of the Draft Bill.
[77] Section 38(6) of the Draft Bill.

i. Japan

The 2008 *Baby Manji* case involved a child conceived with the gametes of a Japanese man and an anonymous Indian egg donor. The man, Ikufumi Yamada, and his wife elected to try to have a baby using a surrogate mother.[78] The couple travelled to India in November 2007 and arranged for the surrogacy with Dr Nayna Patel at the Akanksha Infertility Clinic in Anand, India.[79] The baby was born on 25 July 2007 and named Manji.[80] However, earlier that month the couple had divorced.[81] The man's ex-wife chose not to make any claim to Manji, and that factor is most likely what led to Manji's case being given special scrutiny.[82]

Initially there was a delay in issuing Manji's birth certificate because of doubt as to how to address a mother for Manji on the certificate.[83] After receiving guidance from the chief registrar, the Anand municipal office issued a provisional birth certificate with only the father's name on it.[84] Apparently, difficulties with citizenship first arose because the Japanese Foreign Ministry told Yamada that in order to bring the baby to Japan, he would have to adopt Manji pursuant to Japanese and Indian laws and obtain an Indian passport.[85] Yamada encountered difficulties both in obtaining travel documents from the Indian Government and in obtaining a visa from the Japanese Government.[86]

Due to bomb blasts in Gujarat, Yamada moved his daughter to Jaipur to remain in the care of his mother who had travelled from Japan.[87] In Jaipur, a non-governmental organisation (NGO) called Satya filed a petition in Rajasthan High Court, seeking to prevent Yamada from taking Manji to Japan.[88] Satya's petition alleged that in the absence of a surrogacy law in India, the legitimacy of the baby could not be claimed by anyone, thus the NGO claimed custody could not be assumed by Manji's grandmother.[89] The petition also challenged the legality of commercial

---

[78] 'Father Eager to Bring Daughter to Japan', *Daily Yomiuri Online* (Osaka, 9 August 2008).

[79] *Ibid*. B Prakash, 'Conceived in Japan, Abandoned in Jaipur', *Times of India* (New Delhi, 6 August 2008), at <www.articles.timesofindia.indiatimes.com/2008-08-06/jaipur/27946017_1_girl-child-surrogate-mother-ikufumi-yamada>.

[80] 'Father Eager to Bring Daughter to Japan', above n 78.

[81] 'India Surrogate Baby's Fate Still Unknown', *Daily Yomiuri Online* (Osaka, 17 August 2008).

[82] 'No Entry For Surrogate Baby/Divorce of Japanese Couple Leaves Girl Stranded in India', *Daily Yomiuri Online* (Osaka, 8 August 2008).

[83] 'Japanese Baby Finally Gets Birth Certificate', *Times of India* (New Delhi, 10 August 2008), at <www.articles.timesofindia.indiatimes.com/2008-08-10/jaipur/27897780_1_certificate-japanese-baby-manji-yamada> (quoting a municipal office official as saying: 'The issue was complicated as the baby technically has three mothers—her biological father Dr Ikufumi Yamada's ex-wife, the egg donor and the surrogate mother—and we had no experience of issuing a birth certificate in such cases.').

[84] *Ibid*; 'Manjhee Gets Provisional Birth Certificate', *Times Now* (Mumbai, 9 August 2008).

[85] 'No Entry For Surrogate Baby/Divorce of Japanese Couple Leaves Girl Stranded in India', above n 82.

[86] 'Indian Surrogate Baby in Legal Limbo After Parents Divorce', *Daily Times* (Lahore, 7 August 2008), at <www.dailytimes.com.pk/default.asp?page=2008%5C08%5C07%5Cstory_7-8-2008_pg4_14>.

[87] 'Japanese Parents' Surrogate Child Stuck in India's Jaipur', *earthtimes.org* (Ripon, 6 August 2008).

[88] *Satya v Union of India et al*, Habeas Corpus Petition 7829 of 2008, Rajasthan High Court.

[89] 'Suit Filed to Stop Manji From Leaving India', *Times of India* (New Delhi, 13 August 2008), at <www.articles.timesofindia.indiatimes.com/2008-08-13/jaipur/27924116_1_surrogate-mother-manji-surrogacy>.

surrogacy, and alleged that Dr Nayna Patel and her clinic were engaged in an illegal trade in infants and selling them to foreigners.[90] The Rajasthan High Court issued notices to the Union Home Ministry and Department of Home of the state government to produce Manji within four weeks.[91] In response, Manji's grandmother filed a writ petition on Manji's behalf in the Supreme Court of India.[92] On 14 August 2008, the Supreme Court granted Manji's grandmother temporary custody, restrained the police from taking any steps to produce Manji before the Rajasthan High Court, and sought the assistance of the Solicitor General of India to examine surrogacy and nationality issues resulting therefrom in India.[93]

In an order disposing of the case dated 29 September 2008, the Supreme Court of India stated that the commission organised under the Protection of Children Act, 2005 was the appropriate authority to hear complaints of the type made by Satya.[94] On that basis, the Supreme Court disposed of Satya's proceedings in the Rajasthan High Court.[95] With respect to commercial surrogacy, the Court effectively validated the procedure in India:

> [Commercial surrogacy] is legal in several countries including India where due to excellent medical infrastructure, high international demand and ready availability of poor surrogates it is reaching industry proportions. Commercial surrogacy is sometimes referred to by the emotionally charged and potentially offensive terms 'wombs for rent', 'outsourced pregnancies' or 'baby farms'.[96]

With respect to Baby Manji's travel, the Supreme Court noted the Solicitor General's statements that if a comprehensive application for travel documents for Baby Manji was filed, the application would be disposed of expeditiously and not later than four weeks.[97] After the Supreme Court's judgment was issued, the Jaipur passport office gave special dispensation and issued a 'certificate of identity' to Manji.[98] Thereafter, the Japanese Embassy in New Delhi issued her a one-year

---

[90] *Ibid.*

[91] 'Produce Surrogate Child Manji in Court: Rajasthan HC', *Zee News* (Noida, 12 August 2008).

[92] *Baby Manji Yamada v Union of India et al*, Writ Petition No 369 of 2008, Supreme Court of India.

[93] 'Manji Snub for NGO', *The Telegraph* (Calcutta, 21 August 2008), at <www.telegraphindia.com/1080821/jsp/frontpage/story_9722522.jsp>; R Bhatnagar, 'Manjhi's Fate Depends on Centre's Decision', *DNA* (Mumbai, 16 September 2008), at <www.dnaindia.com/india/report_manjhis-fate-depends-on-centres-decision_1190487>.

[94] *Yamada v Union of India*, 2008 INDLAW SC 1554, 13 (29 September 2008).

[95] *Ibid*, 18.

[96] *Ibid*, 9. The Supreme Court also noted that payment to a woman serving as a surrogate varies widely from 'almost nothing' above expenses to over $30,000. *Ibid*, 12.

[97] *Ibid*, 17.

[98] 'Baby Born to Surrogate Indian Mother, Japanese Father Allowed to Leave India', *Mainichi Daily News* (Osaka, 18 October 2008); 'Japan Gate-Pass for Baby Manji', *The Telegraph* (Calcutta, 18 October 2008), at <www.telegraphindia.com/1081018/jsp/nation/story_9984517.jsp> (according to the passport officer involved, a certificate of identity is granted to people who are stateless or who cannot get a passport from their own country, and this was the first one issued from the Jaipur passport office); 'Japanese Grandmother Files Papers for Migration of Surrogate Baby', NewKerala.com (Kerala, 13 October 2008); see also Indian Passports Act 1967, § 4(2)(b).

visa on humanitarian grounds, and Manji arrived in Japan with her grandmother on 2 November 2008.[99]

ii. Germany

Another surrogacy case, this time involving German commissioning parents, has also reached the Indian Supreme Court.[100] The petitioner, Jan Balaz, a resident of Germany, and his wife, Susanne Anna Lohle, entered a surrogacy arrangement with Dr Nayna Patel's fertility clinic in Anand. The twins were conceived with Balaz's sperm and an egg from an Indian citizen.[101] The suit commenced at the Gujarat High Court and stemmed from the couple's difficulty in securing a visa for the twins.[102]

After the twins' birth on 4 January 2008, the Anand Municipality listed Jan Balaz and Susanne Lohle as the twins' parents on their birth certificates, although this did not conform with the names in the birth register maintained by the hospital. It was explained that the names of the commissioning parents were given to the Anand Municipality pursuant to the parents' wishes, and 'no attempt [was] made by either of the parties to play a foul game or [that] the same has been done with any ulterior motive'.[103]

In an interim order dated 2 April 2008, the Gujarat High Court expressed a desire that the Assistant Solicitor General of India appear for Respondent No 4, Regional Passport Office, and that the Assistant Solicitor General and two other learned counsel assist the court as *amici curiae*, 'considering certain larger issues found in the matter'.[104] Because 'there [were] a number of areas that may be required to be addressed,' the Gujarat High Court decided to keep the case open but grant interim relief with respect to the petitioner so that the twins could travel with Balaz out of India. The surrogate mother, who was also named in the petition, gave her consent that if the substantive relief prayed for by the petitioner was granted, she would cooperate with the petitioner in having the children taken out of India.

The Gujarat High Court directed that the twins' birth certificates be changed to reflect the name of the surrogate mother as the mother of the twins and remove Susanne Lohle's name.[105] The Gujarat High Court noted that a legal professional in Germany said it would be more convenient for both infants to have the correct names of their surrogate mother in the birth register, as German law recognises

---

[99] 'Baby Manjhi arrives in Japan', NDTV.com (New Delhi, 3 November 2008), at <www.ndtv.com/convergence/ndtv/story.aspx?id=NEWEN20080071002>.

[100] *Jan Balaz v Anand Municipality*, No 3020, Special Civil Application (Gujarat HC 2008).

[101] *Balaz v Anand Municipality*, No 3020, Special Civil Application (Gujarat HC 11 November 2009).

[102] *Ibid.*

[103] *Balaz v Anand Municipality*, No 3020, Special Civil Application, Interim Order 6 (Gujarat HC 2 April 2008).

[104] *Ibid*, 4.

[105] *Ibid*, 7.

the woman who has actually delivered the child, 'like that of ours'.[106] The Gujarat High Court further stated that

> the hospital authorities should not have mentioned the name of the wife of the petitioner as the mother of the said babies. Sometimes, the professional will have to prevail over the wishes of the client or consumers.[107]

Finally, the Gujarat High Court ordered the petitioner on the next hearing date to update the court about the progress in the matter, and further requested that the state government and central Government

> express their views as some important issues are involved in the matter where a policy decision of both the respective Governments obviously shall play an important role.[108]

Notwithstanding the Gujarat High Court's orders, Balaz reportedly continued to encounter difficulty in obtaining Indian passports for the twins. He subsequently had to approach the Gujarat High Court to have the twins' birth certificates further modified to remove all references to the court case so that the passport office would agree to issue the passports.[109]

Balaz was also obliged to seek a declaration from the Gujarat High Court that he had sole custody of the twins.[110] The Gujarat High Court declared unequivocally that absolute and exclusive custody already lay with Balaz and continued with him, such that Balaz 'is entitled to take the children wherever he wants to go and settle down and may determine the domicile of the children'.[111] The Gujarat High Court specifically directed the Union of India to create no obstruction of any nature with respect to Balaz's intention to take the twins out of India.[112]

However, Balaz continued to encounter troubles. The twins were initially issued Indian passports reflecting Jan Balaz as the father and the surrogate mother's name as the mother.[113] However, by a letter dated 6 May 2008, the Government of India, Ministry of External Affairs, Regional Passport Office requested a surrender of the Indian passports until the High Court handed down a final decision.[114] Balaz surrendered the Indian passports under the direction of the Gujarat High Court.

After further involvement of the Gujarat High Court, the Indian Passport Office issued the twins identity certificates and they were given a provisional visa from

---

[106] *Ibid.*

[107] *Ibid*, 10.

[108] *Ibid.*

[109] See *Balaz v Anand Municipality*, No 4791, Civil Application, Oral Order (Gujarat HC 21 April 2008).

[110] *Balaz v Anand Municipality*, No 3020, Special Civil Application, Oral Order (Gujarat HC 13 May 2009).

[111] *Ibid*, 5.

[112] See *Balaz v Anand Municipality*, No 6046, Civil Application, Oral Order (Gujarat HC 13 May 2008).

[113] *Balaz v Anand Municipality*, No 3020, Special Civil Application (Gujarat HC 11 November 2009) 4.

[114] *Ibid.*

the British Government.[115] The German couple had relocated to the UK, reportedly because they could not bring the twins into Germany due to Germany's surrogacy laws.[116] After surrendering the Indian passports, Balaz moved the Gujarat High Court to get the passports back in order to be able to bring the twins to Germany.[117] Balaz alleged that the denial of the passports violated Article 21 of the Constitution of India.[118]

The position of the Regional Passport Officer at Ahmedabad was that the surrogate mother could not be treated as the mother of the children, and that children born of surrogacy in India cannot be treated as Indian citizens within the meaning of section 3 of the Citizenship Act, 1955. Therefore, the children, as non-Indian citizens, could not apply for Indian passports under section 6(2)(a) of the Passport Act, 1967. In contrast, counsel for Balaz asserted that the twins were Indian citizens by birth under section 3 of the Citizenship Act, in that the children were born to a surrogate mother who herself was an Indian citizen. Balaz pointed out that since the children were not born in Germany they would not get German citizenship, especially because Germany does not recognise surrogacy.[119]

At the outset, the Gujarat High Court pointed out that the citizenship issue was a momentous question which had no precedent in India.[120] In addition, the Gujarat High Court noted that there were many legal, moral and ethical issues arising for its consideration in the case, also without precedent.[121] The Gujarat High Court stated that its primary concern lay with the rights of the two innocent babies more than the rights of any of the others involved, although it did recognise that the emotional and legal relationship of the babies with the surrogate mother and the donor of the ova was also of vital importance:

> Surrogate mother is not the genetic mother or biologically related to the baby, but, is she merely a host of an embryo or a gestational carrier? What is the status of the ova (egg) donor, which in this case is an Indian national but anonymous. Is the ova donor the real mother or the gestational surrogate? Are the babies motherless, can we brand them as legal orphans or Stateless babies? So many ethical and legal questions have come up for consideration in this case for which there are no clear answers, so far, at least, in this country. True, babies conceived through surrogacy, encounter a lot of legal complications on parentage issues, this case reveals. Legitimacy of the babies is therefore a live issue. Can we brand them as illegitimate babies disowned by the world[?][122]

[115] 'Despite HC Order, Surrogate Kids Yet to Get Passports', *Times of India* (New Delhi, 18 November 2009), at <www.articles.timesofindia.indiatimes.com/2009-11-18/ahmedabad/28075730_1_passport-office-surrogate-kids-surrogate-mother>.

[116] *Ibid.*

[117] S Murari, 'Children Have Right to Surrogate Mother's Citizenship, Says Indian Court', *Asian Tribune* (Hallstavek, 15 November 2009), at <www.asiantribune.com/news/2009/11/15/children-have-right-surrogate-mothers-citizenship-says-indian-court>.

[118] *Balaz v Anand Municipality*, No 3020, Special Civil Application (Gujarat HC 11 November 2009) 5.

[119] *Ibid.*

[120] *Ibid*, 1.

[121] *Ibid*, 9.

[122] *Ibid.*

Throughout the Gujarat High Court's opinion were repeated exhortations for comprehensive legislation to be enacted to define the rights of the respective parties.[123] In the absence of such legislation, the Gujarat High Court stated that it was more inclined to view the gestational surrogate as the natural mother, not the anonymous egg donor or the wife of the biological father, who had neither donated the ova nor conceived or delivered the children:

> Reluctantly, the only conclusion that is possible is that a gestational mother who has blood relations with the child is more deserving to be called as the natural mother. She has carried the embryo for [the] full 10 months in her womb, nurtured the babies through the umbilical cord. Even if we assume the egg donor is the real natural mother, even then she is an Indian national so revealed before the learned Single Judge, we are told. Both the egg donor as well as the gestational surrogate are Indian national[s], and hence the babies are born to an Indian national.[124]

Therefore, the Gujarat High Court concluded that the children were citizens by birth pursuant to section 3(1)(c)(ii) of the Citizenship Act, 1955.[125] Thus, the twins were entitled to Indian passports, and in the opinion of the Court, denial of these would violate Article 21 of the Constitution of India.[126]

After reaching its decision, the Gujarat High Court went on to express its hope that its views would pave the way for legislation to address surrogacy.[127] The Gujarat High Court went on to opine that under the Indian Evidence Act,

> no presumption can be drawn that a child born out of a surrogate mother, is the legitimate child of the commissioning parents, so as to have a legal right to parental support, inheritance and other privileges of a child born to a couple through their sexual intercourse.[128]

Thus, in the Gujarat High Court's view, the only remedy was the enactment of proper legislation:

> Whether the babies born out of a surrogate mother have any right of residence in or citizenship by birth or mere State orphanage and whether they acquire only the nationality o[f] the biological father has to be addressed by the legislature.[129]

Despite the Gujarat High Court's order directing the passport authorities to release the twins' passports, the regional passport office still refused to issue the twins Indian passports without consultation with the Union Home Ministry.[130]

---

[123] *Ibid*, 14, 19–21.

[124] *Ibid*, 16.

[125] *Ibid*, 17. Section 3(1)(c)(ii) of the Citizenship Act, 1955 provides: 'Except as provided in subsection (2), every person born in India, ... (c) on or after the commencement of the Citizenship (Amendment) Act, 2003 ... (ii) one of whose parents is a citizen of India and the other is not an illegal migrant at the time of his birth, shall be a citizen of India by birth.'

[126] *Balaz v Anand Municipality*, No 3020, Special Civil Application (Gujarat HC 11 November 2009), 17.

[127] *Ibid*, 19.

[128] *Ibid*, 20.

[129] *Ibid*.

[130] 'Despite HC Order, Surrogate Kids Yet to Get Passports', above n 115.

Balaz approached the Gujarat High Court again, claiming that the passport office was in contempt of court by not following the Gujarat High Court's order.[131]

On the heels of a notice issued by the Gujarat High Court demanding an explanation of why contempt of court proceedings should not be initiated against the passport office for not issuing passports, the central Government challenged the Gujarat High Court's ruling at the Supreme Court of India in November 2009.[132] The Government questioned whether a surrogate mother could be treated as a parent under the Citizenship Act, 1955, especially in light of the Law Commission's recommendation that birth certificates of surrogate children should contain only the names of the commissioning parents.[133] The Government also asked if a surrogacy contract executed within India would be upheld among the contracting parties in the absence of legislation.[134] Lastly, the Government asked the Supreme Court to decide whether the surrogate mother has any parental rights to the surrogate child, notwithstanding a valid surrogacy contract stipulating to the contrary.[135]

The Supreme Court stated that it considered the issues to be of 'grave importance', stayed the Gujarat's High Court's order and stated its view that the issues raised in the petition needed the earliest consideration.[136]

The Supreme Court had yet to rule on the substantive issues raised in the central Government's petition. Instead, the Court spent several months, through a series of hearings, concerning itself with figuring out a mechanism by which the children could travel to Germany. Initially, the Government indicated that it would issue travel documents within 48 hours of an application from Balaz, and suggested that Balaz could apply for a German visa.[137] The Supreme Court directed Balaz's return if the visa was refused.

The Solicitor General subsequently made his position opposing Indian citizenship more clear, by asserting that Indian citizenship should not be used as a temporary step to get acceptance in another country and that citizenship for the purpose of transit should not be permitted.[138] The Solicitor General also expressed the view that such issues do not present themselves if the commissioning

[131] *Ibid.*

[132] 'HC Seeks Explanation from Passport Officer for Contempt of Court', *Times of India* (New Delhi, 19 November 2009), at <www.articles.timesofindia.indiatimes.com/2009-11-19/ahmedabad/28085633_1_passport-officer-regular-passports-balaz>.

[133] D Mahapatra, 'German or Indian? Surrogate Twins in Legal No-Man's Land', *Times of India* (New Delhi, 1 December 2009), at <www.articles.timesofindia.indiatimes.com/2009-12-01/india/28087428_1_surrogate-twins-surrogacy-agreement-surrogate-mother>; *Union of India & ANR v Jan Balaz and others*, Special Leave to Appeal (Civil) No 31639/2009.

[134] *Union of India & ANR v Jan Balaz and others*, Special Leave to Appeal (Civil) No 31639 of 2009 Supreme Court of India (order dated 25 November 2009).

[135] *Ibid.*

[136] *Ibid* (orders dated 25 November 2009 and 30 November 2009).

[137] *Ibid* (order dated 24 December 2009). 'Centre Rules Out Passport to Babies of Surrogate Indian Mothers', *Deccan Chronicle* (Secunderabad, 30 November 2009); 'Give Passports to Surrogate Indian Mother's Twins: Apex Court', *IANS* (New Delhi, 4 December 2009).

[138] K Rajagopal, 'SC Enters Surrogacy Debate, Asks if an Indian Baby is a "Commodity"', IndianExpress.com (New Delhi, 16 December 2009), at <www.indianexpress.com/news/SC-enters-surrogacy-debate-asks-if-an-Indian-baby-is-a-commodity-/554760>.

parties are Indian, but when it comes to 'foreign nationals' the Indian Government was concerned about exploitation of the children and whether India is perceived as a country where people are going to enter into a contract to buy or sell children.[139]

According to press reports, the Supreme Court made a number of significant comments concerning the twins' citizenship status at a subsequent hearing:[140]

> Statelessness cannot be clamped upon the children. There must be some mechanism by which they get citizenship of some country. Children should be allowed to leave the country after an assurance of their citizenship has been given.[141]

The Supreme Court also affirmed its own role in the debate by stating:

> We want to know since when this matter has been debated in public or even in the media. We are on a side issue of judicial activism. In such matters, the People's representatives should step in to preserve the interest of the people as this involves largely poverty-stricken people. But if this area remains unoccupied with both the legislature and executive having not stepped in, under the Constitution, who should step in.[142]

At the next hearing, the Supreme Court instructed Balaz to submit an appropriate undertaking to assure his full compliance with any directions given by the Supreme Court or any other court in India.[143] The undertaking was to consist of Balaz's pledges to continue to abide by all orders of the Supreme Court, as the issue involved was the safety of the children, to use the travel documents only for the purpose of taking the children to Germany, to carry out an adoption in Germany and to produce a document from a suitable agency from Germany certifying that the children were in good condition.[144] It was at this stage that Balaz informed the Court of a pending appeal he had filed with the High Administrative Court in Berlin which was deciding the issue of whether the twins could be allowed to be brought into Germany for a paternity test and subsequent adoption.[145]

---

[139] *Ibid.*

[140] 'German Couple's Surrogate Kids May End Up Stateless', *Times of India* (New Delhi, 16 December 2009), at <www.articles.timesofindia.indiatimes.com/2009-12-16/india/28087928_1_surrogate-children-surrogate-mother-german-couple>.

[141] *Ibid.*

[142] *Ibid.*

[143] *Union of India & ANR v Jan Balaz and others*, Special Leave to Appeal (Civil) No 31639 of 2009 Supreme Court of India (order dated 17 December 2010).

[144] R Bhatnagar, 'Centre Will Ask Germany to Grant Visa to Surrogate Twins', *DNA* (Mumbai, 18 December 2009), at <www.dnaindia.com/india/report_centre-will-ask-germany-to-grant-visa-to-surrogate-twins_1324813>; 'Berlin Court to Have Final Say On Surrogate Twins Fate?', *Times of India* (New Delhi, 18 December 2009), at <www.articles.timesofindia.indiatimes.com/2009-12-18/india/28071461_1_german-couple-balaz-undertaking>.

[145] 'Berlin Court to Have Final Say on Surrogate Twins Fate?', above n 140. On 26 November 2009, the German Administrative Court of Berlin issued an interim decision on Balaz's request for visa-free entry, or alternatively a request for granting of a visa for family reunification, as well as a travel permit allowing a temporary stay: 'Verwaltungsgericht Berlin Beschluss', 26 November 2009, available at <www.berlin.de/imperia/md/content/senatsverwaltungen/justiz/gerichte/vg2/entscheidungen/11_1_0396_09_v____beschluss___anonymisiert.pdf?start&ts=1259758337&file=11_1_0396_09_v____beschluss___anonymisiert.pdf>. The German Court rejected the children's travel to Germany on the

Balaz filed the affidavit pursuant to the Supreme Court's order.[146] As part of the undertaking, Balaz agreed to deposit his passport with the Indian Consulate in Berlin and provided the details of an NGO in Berlin which would report back to Indian authorities and the Supreme Court periodically about the well-being of the children.[147]

The Solicitor General's next suggestion in January 2010 was to propose an intercountry adoption. Through an intercountry adoption, the Solicitor General reversed his previous objection to limited citizenship with a view to travel, by indicating that the Indian Government could consider granting Indian citizenship to the twins under section 20 of the Citizenship Act, 1955 for a limited purpose to travel and gain entry into Germany as the adopted children of the couple. The Solicitor General asked Balaz to approach the Central Adoption Resource Authority (CARA), the agency under the Ministry of Women and Child Development charged with regulating adoption, for an intercountry adoption, and pledged that all possible measures would be taken to expedite the adoption process.[148]

With respect to an intercountry adoption, the German Embassy submitted a letter on 14 January that stated in part:

> Contestation in court of paternity by the mother and her husband is not permitted according to Section 1600(5) of the German Civil Code, if the child was conceived by means of artificial insemination with the consent of the mother and her husband. Thus, under German law, a child born by an Indian woman who is married to an Indian national has no legal relationship with the German commissioning parents.[149]

Though it expressed its inability to issue visas to the twins on the ground of the paternity suit by Balaz, the German Embassy said:

> Issuing the children with a visa for the purpose of adoption in Germany could be considered. For this purpose, an application filed to the concerned agency in Germany would be considered in line with the 1993 Hague Convention on the Protection of Children and Cooperation in respect of Intercountry Adoption.[150]

---

basis that the question of parenthood and origin is judged under Indian law (*ibid*). Even though India's surrogacy rules are not yet clear, the Court noted that pursuant to s 112 of the Indian Evidence Act of 1872, Indian law provides that children are assumed to be the children of the married couple when they are born during the marriage. Therefore, in the Court's view, the husband of the surrogate mother is the father of the children (*ibid*). The fact that Balaz was listed in the Indian birth certificate did not change this fact. Such a birth certificate is not acknowledged by German law since it is clearly contrary to the fundamentals of German law which prohibits surrogacy (*ibid*). Under the Gujarat High Court decision, the Court concluded that the twins were citizens of India (*ibid*).

[146] *Union of India & ANR v Jan Balaz and others*, Special Leave to Appeal (Civil) No 31639 of 2009 Supreme Court of India (order dated 4 January 2010).

[147] 'German Dad to Deposit Passport as Collateral', *Times of India* (New Delhi, 5 January 2010), at <www.articles.timesofindia.indiatimes.com/2010-01-05/india/28139026_1_stateless-citizens-balaz-indian>.

[148] *Union of India & ANR v Jan Balaz and others*, Special Leave to Appeal (Civil) No 31639 of 2009 Supreme Court of India (order dated 4 January 2010).

[149] *Ibid*.

[150] *Ibid*.

Balaz's counsel raised the concern that intercountry adoption is normally a cumbersome and time-consuming process. The Supreme Court agreed with the concern and said that the Government needed to act speedily, since the children had been in India for nearly two years.[151] In light of the above, the couple's counsel suggested that the Indian Government help the couple by initiating the adoption procedure.

In February 2010, the Indian Government stated that it was in discussion with CARA.[152] It was represented that normally a surrogate child is not subject to adoption, but keeping in view the facts of the case, the Supreme Court said CARA might consider the issue of adoption in this case with sympathy.[153] The Government told the Court that it was willing to waive some of the restrictions on adopting children born through surrogacy.[154] The Supreme Court therefore asked the Government to file an affidavit on its willingness to relax these adoption norms.[155]

By the next hearing in March 2010, CARA had not filed the requested affidavit. The Solicitor General suggested that the Court direct CARA to process the adoption of the twins as a special case, even if it was not treated as a precedent in the future.[156] At first, Balaz's counsel opposed the proposed adoption because she was concerned that nothing tangible would happen.[157] The Supreme Court proposed that it consider the merits of the petition the following day. However, the following day Balaz's counsel submitted that she had had second thoughts, because she felt that the offer made by the Solicitor General was reasonable and deserved consideration, because it might finally resolve the controversy, at least in part.[158] In view of the above, the Supreme Court adjourned the case to 3 May and directed CARA to consider and process the case of adoption of the children and take appropriate action, including consultation within the authorities of the Government of Germany, within a maximum period of four weeks, keeping in view the peculiar facts of the case.[159]

---

[151] Parliament soon to enact Surrogacy Law (21 January 2010), <www.blog.indiansurrogacylaw.com>.

[152] *Union of India & ANR v Jan Balaz and others*, Special Leave to Appeal (Civil) No 31639 of 2009 Supreme Court of India (order dated 25 February 2010).

[153] *Ibid.*

[154] 'German Surrogate Twins: Government to Relax Adoption Norms', *India News Magazine* (25 February 2010).

[155] *Ibid.*

[156] *Union of India & ANR v Jan Balaz and others*, Special Leave to Appeal (Civil) No 31639 of 2009 Supreme Court of India (order dated 16 March 2010); 'India Judiciary Asks Government to Consider German Couple Surrogacy Plea', *Bernama* (Kuala Lumpur, 17 March 2010), at <www.bernama.com/bernama/v6/newsworld.php?id=483207>.

[157] *Union of India & ANR v Jan Balaz and others*, Special Leave to Appeal (Civil) No 31639 of 2009 Supreme Court of India (order dated 16 March 2010).

[158] *Ibid* (order dated 17 March 2010).

[159] *Ibid.* The Court also asked the Solicitor General to pursue independently with the ministry concerned the question of extending the visa of the German father when it learned that officials had refused to extend it; 'German Couple Make U-Turn, Accept Govt's Adoption Offer', *Times of India* (New Delhi, 17 March 2010), at <www.articles.timesofindia.indiatimes.com/2010-03-18/india/28138778_1_german-couple-susan-lohle-surrogate-babies>.

At a subsequent hearing, the Solicitor General indicated that CARA had taken all steps to facilitate an intercountry adoption and would issue a 'no objection' certificate as soon as it received evidence of the willingness to act of an agency in Germany.[160] The Supreme Court agreed that given the peculiar facts of the case, it would continue the proceedings over its summer vacation.[161]

Finally and somewhat unexpectedly, in May 2010, the Government of India provided identity documents for the children, the Ministry of External Affairs issued an exit permit and the twins were cleared for travel from the Indian side.[162] Despite its prolonged refusal to issue a visa, the German Government relented and made a one-time exception by granting the twins visas.[163] Balaz travelled with the twins to Germany with a view to adopting the children in Germany, which would be a precursor to their obtaining German citizenship.[164] The Supreme Court said: 'We can only wish good luck to them.'[165] The Supreme Court case has been converted to a civil appeal which is still pending, to address the substantive issues raised in the case.[166]

The long-running saga of the Balaz case has not deterred other German citizens from pursuing surrogacy in India. A court in Berlin ruled in 2011 that the German Embassy in India was within its rights to refuse to issue a German passport to a child born in December 2010 in India through surrogacy, even though the child's biological father is a German citizen, where the birth certificate for the child listed the commissioning parties as the child's parents and the place of birth was listed as an ART clinic.[167] The court ruled that doubts about the child's German citizenship were appropriate grounds for denying the passport application, and that the German father's citizenship was not legally relevant.[168] The commissioning couple are able to appeal the decision.[169]

iii. United Kingdom

Immigration issues also arose with respect to infants born at Dr Nayna Patel's Akanksha Fertility Clinic in Anand in 2004.[170] The twins were conceived with the

---

[160] *Union of India & ANR v Jan Balaz and others*, Special Leave to Appeal (Civil) No 31639 of 2009 Supreme Court of India (order dated 5 May 2010).

[161] *Ibid*.

[162] 'Twins Head for Germany, Apex Court Seeks Law on Surrogacy', *The Economic Times* (New Delhi, 26 May 2010), at <www.articles.economictimes.indiatimes.com/2010-05-26/news/27567157_1_surrogate-twins-surrogacy-german-court>.

[163] 'Germany Relents, Admits Twins with Indian Surrogate Mother', *earthtimes.org* (Ripon, 26 May 2010).

[164] *Ibid*.

[165] *Union of India & ANR v Jan Balaz and others*, Civil Appeal No 8714 of 2010 Supreme Court of India.

[166] *Ibid*.

[167] 'Surrogate Children Have No Right to German Passport, Court Rules', *The Local* (Berlin, 28 April 2011), at <www.thelocal.de/article.php?ID=34681&print=true>.

[168] *Ibid*.

[169] *Ibid*.

[170] S Pook, 'Twins Born to Their Granny Win Entry to UK', *Daily Telegraph* (London, 27 July 2004), at <www.telegraphindia.com/104728/asp/nation/story_3551289.asp>.

gametes of a British commissioning couple and the surrogate mother was the twins' genetic grandmother.[171] The twins were initially denied passports by the British High Commission because they were born in India and their surrogate mother was an Indian citizen; the British High Commission opined that visas were necessary for the twins' return.[172] After waging a six-month legal battle, the commissioning couple were able to secure the twins' entry into the country on a fixed-term entry visa for one year.[173] It was speculated that the British parents would have to obtain a parental order under the Human Fertilisation and Embryology Act 1990 or legally adopt the children, with citizenship becoming obtainable only thereafter.[174]

British citizens engaging in international surrogacy may seek parental orders under the Human Fertilisation and Embryology Act 1990, as amended by the Human Fertilisation and Embryology Act 2008, provided they pay the surrogate mother only expenses reasonably incurred.[175] More recently, the Family Division of the High Court ruled that payments of £3,000 as compensation for lost wages to each of two surrogate mothers, one of whom earned £130 per month as a housekeeper and the other who earned £160 a month as a maid, were not 'disproportionate'.[176] In total the couple paid the fertility clinic about £27,000.[177] In the court's view, although the payments exceeded reasonable expenses, it was plainly in the best interests of the two children born through surrogacy that they be brought up by the commissioning couple, where the couple were acting in good faith with no attempt to defraud the authorities.[178]

The Human Fertilisation and Embryology Act 2008 also requires that the woman who carried the child consents to the making of the parental order.[179] In one case, a gay couple could not obtain the consent of an Indian surrogate mother because she vanished after delivering twin boys for the couple.[180] The High Court who heard the case granted the parental order despite the lack of consent, finding that the couple had taken all reasonable steps to obtain the woman's consent.[181] The couple had given the clinic involved a deadline to provide the surrogate's

---

[171] *Ibid.*

[172] *Ibid.*

[173] *Ibid.*

[174] 'Twins Born to Own Granny Fly Home', *BBC News* (London, 26 July 2004), at <www.news.bbc.co.uk/2/hi/uk_news/england/london/3927321.stm>.

[175] Human Fertilisation and Embryology Act 2008, s 30.

[176] 'Couple Did Not "Overpay" Indian Surrogate Mothers', *AsianImage* (Lancashire, 6 December 2011), at <www.asianimage.co.uk/news/9404325.print>; M Beckford, 'Childless Couple Allowed to Keep Babies Born Through Indian Surrogate', *Telegraph* (London, 7 December 2011), at <www.telegraph.co.uk/news/newstopics/lawreports/893514/ Childless-Couple-Allowed-to-Keep-Babies-Born-Through-Indian-Surrogate>.

[177] 'Childless Couple Allowed to Keep Babies Born Through Indian Surrogate', above n 176.

[178] *Ibid.*

[179] Human Fertilisation and Embryology Act 2008, s 54(6).

[180] 'Gay couple win right to keep twins even though surrogate mother vanished without giving formal consent', *London Evening Standard* (London, 2 October 2012), at www.standard.co.uk/incoming/gay-couple-win-right-to-keep-twins-even-though-surrogate-mother-vanished-without-giving-formal-consent-8194329.html.

[181] *Ibid.*

consent and they hired an inquiry agent to try to locate the woman.[182] The judge relied on the provision of the Human Fertilisation and Embryology Act 2008 which provides that the surrogate mother's consent is not required where she 'cannot be found or is incapable of giving agreement.'[183] The judge believed it was the first time this provision was used by a court in England or Wales.[184]

Another case was decided on equitable grounds in the case of a British couple who applied for a parental order which was not granted before the genetic father's death from liver cancer.[185] The commissioning mother was not believed to be genetically related to the child.[186] The judge in the case allowed a parental order to be made in favour of both commissioning parents because, *inter alia*, no other order would recognise the child's status as the child of both parties, the identity of the child would be protected and it was in the child's best interests.[187] As in the case discussed above, the court also found the payment of £4,500 to the surrogate mother likely exceeded expenses reasonably incurred, but concluded that there was no evidence the couple acted 'in anything other than the utmost good faith' or that the payments could have been said to have overborne the will of the surrogate mother.[188]

iv. *Australia*

Although some Australian states have banned commercial surrogacy, the Department of Immigration and Citizenship has adopted the practice of conferring citizenship on children born through surrogacy overseas where there is a genetic relationship with at least one commissioning parent.[189] Once in Australia, some commissioning parties seek parental responsibility orders. Approximately 14 cases are reported to have reached the Family Court of Australia for such orders.[190] In one case, a gay couple approached the Family Court seeking a parental responsibility order for the non-genetic commissioning father.[191] In granting the order, the Court stated:

> As a matter of law, the word 'parent' tends to suggest some biological connection, but …
> biology does not really matter; it is all about parental responsibility.

---

[182] *Ibid.*

[183] *Ibid.*

[184] 'Gay couple win right to keep twins even though surrogate mother vanished without giving formal consent', *London Evening Standard* (London, 2 October 2012), at www.standard.co.uk/incoming/gay-couple-win-right-to-keep-twins-even-though-surrogate-mother-vanished-without-giving-formal-consent-8194329.html; Human Fertilisation and Embryology Act 2008, s 54(7).

[185] *A and A v P, P and B* [2011] EWHC 1738 (Fam).

[186] *Ibid.*

[187] *Ibid.*

[188] *Ibid.*

[189] A Horin, 'Concern Over Complex Laws on Surrogacy', *The Sydney Morning Herald* (Sydney, 9 February 2012), at <www.smh.com.au/national/concern-over-complex-laws-on-surrogacy-20120208-1reyy.html>.

[190] *Ibid.*

[191] M Dunn, 'Twins Victory for Gay Melbourne Couple After Indian Surrogate Gives Birth', *Herald Sun* (Melbourne, 22 January 2011), at <www.heraldsun.com.au/news/national/twins-win-for-gay-dads/story-e6frf7l6-1225992667107>.

v. Norway

A Norwegian woman spent over a year attempting to take twins born in India in 2009 to Norway, but encountered tremendous difficulties because the children were not Norwegian citizens and could not be issued with Norwegian passports.[192] The twins were born to a surrogate mother in India at the direction of the Norwegian single woman, who commissioned the pregnancy with the use of an Indian egg donor and a Scandinavian sperm donor.[193] Under Norwegian law, a woman who gives birth to a child is the child's mother.[194] According to the Norwegian authorities, the only way motherhood can be transferred in such a situation is through adoption.[195] After many months of negotiation, the Norwegian Government granted the twins a residence permit in Norway in April 2011.[196] It was expected that the twins would obtain Norwegian citizenship after their legal adoption there.

vi. Israel

There are several reported cases of homosexual men from Israel, with babies born to surrogates in India, who have been denied permission by a family court in Israel to proceed with paternity tests at the Israeli Consulate to show they are the biological fathers of the children, which is required for the children to obtain Israeli citizenship.[197] Surrogacy within Israel is permitted only by heterosexual commissioning parties.[198] Although gay Israeli men have been able to emigrate to Israel children born through Indian surrogacy in the past, the family court judge in one case stated that the court had no jurisdiction over children who were not in Israel and whose 'affinity to Israel has not been proven'.[199] In that case, the couple appealed to the Jerusalem District Court, which appointed a legal guardian to represent the children and remanded the case to the family court.[200] After several months had elapsed, the appellate court ordered a paternity test, and the twins were permitted to be registered by the Israeli Consulate in India as Israeli citizens and were issued passports to travel to Israel.[201]

---

[192] 'Norsk Kvinne I India Med Tvillinggutter Født A v Surrogatmor', Ministry of Children, Equality and Social Inclusion (9 April 2010), at <www.regjeringen.no/nb/dep/bld/aktuelt/nyheter/2010/Norsk-kvinne-i-India-med-tvillinggutter-fodt-av-surrogatmor.html?id=600042>.

[193] *Ibid*; S Deb Roy, 'Norwegian Stuck in Limbo with Twins Not Genetically Her Own', *Times of India* (New Delhi, 21 July 2010), at <www.articles.timesofindia.indiatimes.com/2010-07-21/mumbai/28288884_1_surrogacy-norwegian-embassy-clinic>.

[194] *Ibid*.

[195] *Ibid*.

[196] M Vikås and LM Glomnes, 'Volden-Tvillingene Komme Til Norge', *VG Nett* (Oslo, 15 April 2011), at <www.vg.no/nyheter/innenriks/artikkel.php?artid=10084386>.

[197] A Glickman, 'Judge Keeps Homosexuals' Kids Abroad', ynetnews.com (Tel Aviv, 9 May 2010), at <www.ynetnews.com/articles/0,7340,L-3886827,00.htm>l.

[198] *Ibid*.

[199] *Ibid*.

[200] *Ibid*; T Zarchin, 'Gay Father of Twins Born to Indian Surrogate Denied Permission to Bring His Sons Home', Haaretz.com (Tel Aviv, 9 May 2010), at <www.haaretz.com/print-edition/news/gay-father-of-twins-born-to-indian-surrogate-denied-permission-to-bring-his-sons-home-1.289128>.

[201] R Medzini, 'Gay Father Lands in Israel with Twins', ynetnews.com (Tel Aviv, 29 May 2010), at <www.ynetnews.com/articles/0,7340,L-3895445,00.html>.

vii. Canada

A reported case of twins born through surrogacy in India and then abandoned arose in connection with a Canadian couple who paid an Indian surrogate to bear twins from their fertilised eggs.[202] When the commissioning couple applied for travel documents from the Canadian High Commission, they were required to produce DNA tests.[203] The DNA tests revealed that the twins were not genetically related to either of the commissioning parents.[204] Canadian officials indicated that the commissioning parties' request to treat the surrogate case as a request to adopt was rejected.[205] The couple reportedly left India without the children, and their custody arrangements are not clear.[206]

It took years for another Canadian couple to emigrate their children to Canada. The Canadian couple used an Indian surrogate, who gave birth to twins in 2006.[207] DNA tests revealed that one of the children was genetically related to the commissioning father, but the other child was not related to either of the commissioning parents, due either to medical error or to fraud.[208] The Canadian Government would permit entry into the country by the child related to the Canadian citizen but not by the child who was not genetically related, despite a declaration of parentage for both children from an Ontario family court.[209] The Canadian couple remained in India with the twins for six years. Eventually, the Canadian Government granted the non-biological child an entry visa, and the couple planned to file an application for Canadian citizenship for the non-biological child based on humanitarian and compassionate grounds.[210]

At a fertility conference in Canada, a story was circulated about a Canadian couple who contracted with a surrogate mother in India. Genetic tests revealed that the child had Down's Syndrome.[211] The commissioning couple requested an immediate abortion, but the surrogate mother resisted, saying she would raise the child if they would just help her with expenses.[212] The commissioning couple said the baby would be the surrogate mother's entire responsibility.[213] The surrogate

---

[202] R Westhead, 'Troubling Questions Surround Surrogate-Born Children in India', thestar.com (Toronto, 26 April 2010), at <www.thestar.com/news/world/article/800791--troubling-questions-surround-surrogate-born-children-in-india?bn=1>.

[203] *Ibid.*

[204] *Ibid.*

[205] *Ibid.*

[206] *Ibid.*

[207] R Aulakh, 'Baby Quest Traps Couple in India', thestar.com (Toronto, 21 December 2010), at <www.thestar.com/news/article/910085--baby-quest-traps-couple-in-india>.

[208] *Ibid.*

[209] *Ibid.*

[210] R Aulakh, 'Couple Fights Surrogacy Policy to Bring Their Boy Back to Canada', thestar.com (Toronto, 20 August 2011), at <www.thestar.com/news/article/1042222--couple-fights-federal-surrogacy-policy-to-bring-their-boy-back-to-canada>.

[211] S Weatherbe, 'Whose Life Is It Anyway?', *National Catholic Register* (Kettering, 24 October 2010), at <www.ncregister.com/site/print_article/27138>.

[212] *Ibid.*

[213] *Ibid.*

mother was a single mother of two other children, and she ended up reluctantly agreeing to the abortion.[214]

A Canadian commissioning couple spoke to the media about corrupt practices they encountered with an ART facility in New Delhi with which they contracted for a surrogate child. The couple were quoted a fee in 2009 of USD $12,500, offset by credits for referring other commissioning parties to the business.[215] The commissioning mother set up the referral of six others to the clinic, but just before the baby was born, the doctor said the total fee would be USD $7,000 more than originally quoted.[216] The couple claimed that the doctor also refused to pay outside hospital bills for the caesarean section and instead presented a hospital bill three times the actual amount.[217] The couple said the doctor further tried to frustrate their attempt to get the child an exit visa from Indian immigration authorities.[218] According to the commissioning mother, '[t]hey jacked it up, knowing intended parents are quite desperate. I was extremely nervous, scared and angry'.[219]

viii. France

Indian media reported the story of a gay French father who encountered difficulty in emigrating to France his twins who were born in 2010 through surrogacy in Mumbai.[220] For him, trouble began when he took the twins' Indian birth certificate to the French Consulate and asked for the children to be entered on the French birth register so that he could obtain French passports for them.[221] The father was delayed in India for at least four months trying to sort out the issues.[222]

Another father with twins born in India through surrogacy subsequently encountered difficulties in France, after he brought the children to the country via Spain.[223] The father took the children to a physician who observed that the children were underweight and reported the father to the police. The children were taken into foster care, and the issue of the father's parentage and fitness were scheduled to be decided by a French court.

The difficulties in emigrating children born of surrogacy to France led to the operation of a scam in which a 22-year-old woman posed as the biological mother

---

[214] *Ibid.*

[215] M Magnier, 'A Bundle of Joy With Baggage', *Los Angeles Times* (Los Angeles, 18 April 2011), at <www.articles.latimes.com/print/2011/apr/18/world/la-fg-india-surrogacy-20110418>.

[216] *Ibid.*

[217] *Ibid.*

[218] *Ibid.*

[219] *Ibid.*

[220] S Deb Roy, 'French Gay Dad May Lose Surrogate Kids', *Times of India* (New Delhi, 9 June 2010), at <www.timesofindia.indiatimes.com/india/French-gay-dad-may-lose-surrogate-kidsiplarticleshow/6025936.cms>.

[221] *Ibid.*

[222] *Ibid.*

[223] M Janwalkar, 'Surrogacy Woes: Indian-Born Baby in French Foster Care', *DNA* (Mumbai, 27 July 2010), at <www.dnaindia.com/mumbai/report_surrogacy-woes-india-born-baby-in-french-foster-care_1415164>.

of surrogate children and the companion of at least two French men seeking to emigrate those children to France.[224] The scam came to light when immigration officials recognised the woman as having accompanied a different French national three months earlier. The children from both men were born at the same hospital and had birth certificates issued listing the same woman as their mother. Investigating authorities suspected the woman to be part of a larger racket involving gangs, civil officials and medical professionals. The second French man admitted that the children were born through surrogacy and that the woman was simply helping him complete the formalities of bringing the children to France. When he had applied for passports for the children at the French Consulate in Mumbai, his application was denied. Earlier, the French man went to France and filed a case to appeal the denial of the issuance of passports; the local court directed the French Government to issue passports to the children. Thereafter, at the French Consulate, the French man claimed that all that was needed to obtain French passports was a 'no objection' certificate from Indian immigration authorities. After four days in custody for presenting false documents, the French man was granted bail and was able to fly back to France with the children.

ix. Iceland

The first baby born through Indian surrogacy to Icelandic commissioning parents encountered lengthy delays in emigrating to Iceland. The baby was born in November 2010, but only after the intervention of a senator was the child granted a social security number by the Icelandic Parliament a month later.[225] According to the Iceland Ministry of Interior Affairs, even though the baby was granted Icelandic citizenship, there was a delay in issuing the child an Icelandic passport because Iceland had requested data from the Indian authorities about the child's parentage.[226] In interviews with the Indian media, the commissioning parents attributed the delay to an attempt by the Icelandic Government to thwart cross-border surrogacy arrangements.[227] The child was granted an Icelandic passport and left India in February 2011.[228]

---

[224] A Sathe, 'Indo-French Baby Trade Commission', MumbaiMirror.com (Mumbai, 27 July 2011), at <www.mumbaimirror.com/index.aspx?page=article&sectid=15&contentid=201107272011072703 4425397d905d6d8>.

[225] S Kurjan, 'Iceland Accepts Surrogate Baby Born in Thane', *Hindustan Times* (New Delhi, 21 December 2010), at <www.hindustantimes.com/India-news/Maharashtra/Iceland-accepts-surrogate-baby-born-in-Thane/Article1-640934.aspx>.

[226] 'Interior Minister: Surrogate Baby Issue Blocked in India', *Iceland Review* (Reyjavik, 17 January 2011), at <www.icelandpulse.com/icelandreview/1102-interior-minister-surrogate-baby-issue-blocked-in-india>.

[227] 'India's Icelandic Surrogate Baby Due Home Soon', *IceNews* (Reykjavik, 29 January 2011), at <www.icenews.is/index.php/2011/01/29/indias-icelandic-surrogate-baby-due-home-soon/>.

[228] 'Baby Joel Finally En Route to Iceland', *IceNews* (Reykjavik, 2 February 2011), at <www.icenews.is/index.php/2011/02/02/baby-joel-finally-en-route-to-iceland/>.

x. New Zealand

In New Zealand there is no formal immigration policy to facilitate the entry of a child born to a surrogate mother overseas.[229] It is reported that there are at least two babies in New Zealand who had been born to surrogate mothers in India, but the babies have not been recognised as citizens in either country. In one case, a certificate of identity had to be issued so that the child could travel to New Zealand. It is not clear whether adoptions will be permitted in either case.

xi. Ireland

The biological daughter of an Irish commissioning couple was born to an Indian surrogate on 25 September 2010.[230] In India, at the Irish Embassy, the couple received an emergency travel document for the child which they used to bring their daughter to the UK where they were residing at the time. When the baby was three months old, the couple relocated to Ireland, where they attempted to obtain a passport for the child which was refused. The commissioning father attempted to seek a declaration of parentage in June 2011, but the court refused to hear the application, stating that it was a High Court matter since it involved surrogacy.[231] Approximately 30 other children born through surrogacy abroad are reported to be in similar predicaments since the surrogate mother is regarded as the legal mother.[232]

xii. Spain

Commercial surrogacy is prohibited in Spain and the Spanish registration of children born to surrogates overseas has been called into question.[233] However, the Indian media have reported on cases of children born through surrogacy arranged by Spanish commissioning parents.[234] The Delhi Commission for Protection of Child Rights made an inquiry of one fertility clinic, seeking details about assisting a gay couple from Spain to have twins through surrogacy, and whether the

---

[229] S Dastgheib, '"Rent-a-womb" Babies Could End Up Stateless', stuff.co.nz (Wellington, 20 August 2011), at <www.stuff.co.nz/national/health/5477716/Rent-a-womb-babies-could-end-up-stateless>.

[230] E Hourican, 'Official Catch 22 That Blights This Baby's Life', Independent.ie (Dublin, 23 October 2011), at <www.independent.ie/lifestyle/official-catch-22-that-blights-this-babys-life-2914282.html>.

[231] S O'Connor, 'Surrogacy in Ireland—A Legal Quagmire', *Irish Medical Times* (Dublin 23 November 2011), at <www.imt.ie/opinion/2011/11/surrogacy-in-ireland-%E2%80%94-a-legal-quagmire.html>.

[232] F McPhillips, 'My Fight to Bring Home My Baby. . . Born to a Surrogate Mum in India', *Herald. ie* (Dublin, 3 January 2013), at www.herald.ie/lifestyle/my-fight-to-bring-home-my-baby-born-to-a-surrogate-mum-in-india-3341778.html.

[233] Hb, 'Valencia Gay Male Couple Told They Cannot Register as Parents of Twins: The Twins Were Born Legally to Surrogate Mother in the United States', typicallyspanish.com (Málaga, 17 September 2010), at <www.typicallyspanish.com/news/publish/article_27222.shtml#ixzzUs5i4s>.

[234] See, eg, D Nandan, 'IVF Brings Two-Fold Joy to Spanish Businessman', *Times of India* (New Delhi, 4 January 2012), at <www.articles.timesofindia.indiatimes.com/2012-01-04/delhi/30588363_1_surrogate-mothers-surrogacy-ivf>.

children were adopted and whether any adoption complied with the Juvenile Justice (Care and Protection) Act, 2000.[235]

xiii. Jamaica

An American woman created a stir when she left a baby at a passport office in Secunderabad on 25 January 2012 out of frustration at being unable to secure an Indian passport for the child who was born in December 2011.[236] The police traced the woman, through documents left with the baby, to an ART clinic.[237] The American woman stated that she brought seven samples of her husband's sperm from New York.[238] The child was reportedly conceived with eggs from an Indian egg donor and the sperm of the woman's husband, a Jamaican citizen, using a surrogate mother in Hyderabad.[239] The woman was unable to secure a Jamaican passport for the baby because there is no Jamaican Embassy in India; she approached the Honorary Consul of the Jamaican Government in Delhi, who referred her to the passport office in Hyderabad.[240] The woman said she believed that the baby was an Indian citizen since he was born on Indian soil.[241] Before she flew to India from New York, the woman reportedly approached the Jamaican Embassy in New York for guidance as to the baby's exit procedures.[242] She claimed she was advised that the baby would be issued with an Indian passport which she could use to fly the child to Jamaica, and that she would not need a visa for the child since India does not require visas to fly to Jamaica.[243]

The passport office in Hyderabad sought the advice of the Ministry of External Affairs. Because an egg donor's identity is confidential under a surrogacy arrangement, the Ministry of External Affairs advised that the only means for the child to be issued an identity card was proof of the husband's DNA linking the child biologically to him, or legal adoption documents.[244] The American woman countered

---

[235] 'Child Rights Panel Seeks Report On Surrogate Twins of Gay Spanish Couple', *The Hindu* (Chennai, 19 February 2011), at <www.thehindu.com/todays-paper/tp-national/tp-newdelhi/article1470919.ece?css=print>.

[236] M Ramu, 'American Woman Causes a Flutter at Passport Office in Secunderabad', *The Hindu* (Chennai, 26 January 2012), at <www.thehindu.com/news/states/andhra-pradesh/article283463.ece?css=print>.

[237] *Ibid.*

[238] *Ibid.*

[239] *Ibid.*

[240] *Ibid.*

[241] 'Parents' Mixed Nationality Led to Surrogacy Chaos', *Times of India* (New Delhi 27 January 2012), at <www.articles.timesofindia.indiatimes.com/2012-01-27/hyderabad/30670001_1_indian-passport-passport-application-surrogacy>.

[242] *Ibid.*

[243] *Ibid.*

[244] 'US Woman Advised to Bring Husband or Adopt Surrogate Baby', *DNA* (Mumbai, 29 January 2012), at <www.dnaindia.com/print710.php?cid=1643457>; 'Submit Adoption Papers: MEA', *Deccan Chronicle* (Secunderabad, 30 January 2012), at <www.deccanchronicle.com/channels/cities/hyderabad/submit-adoption-papers-mea-070>.

that her husband could not fly to India for DNA testing due to a fear of flying prompted by his father's death in an air crash.[245]

The police did not charge the American woman with abandonment, and she was eventually able to leave India with the baby after the US Consulate intervened.[246]

B. Domestic Cases

There have been a few reports of surrogate mothers suffering extreme medical complications from surrogate pregnancy. For example, after being pressured by her husband to become a surrogate for money, one young woman died after giving birth in Coimbatore in 2009.[247] In Ahmedabad, a woman died in 2012 during her eighth month of pregnancy allegedly due to the negligence of a clinic.[248]

Another woman who agreed to become a surrogate mother lost her uterus, developed other health complications and was divorced by her husband after being a surrogate three times.[249] The woman began serving as a surrogate after she had been approached by an agent who said she would be paid Rs. 2.25 lakh.[250] Her first surrogate pregnancy attempt failed after 45 days, for which she got Rs. 10,000, of which the agent took Rs. 2,000.[251] The second pregnancy failed after 50 days. She attempted to decline a third attempt, but the woman said that the agent demanded that she pay Rs. 25,000 to decline, so she felt she had no other choice.[252] For the birth of the child, the woman suffered placenta previa, placenta accreta, gestational diabetes and had to undergo a hysterectomy.[253]

There have been isolated reports of surrogate mothers demanding additional monies from Indian commissioning parents. One commissioning mother reported that a surrogate mother threatened to abort the baby if an additional

[245] 'Surrogate Baby to Soon Get ID Paper', *Deccan Chronicle* (Secunderabad, 27 January 2012), at <www.deccanchronicle.com/channels/cities/hyderabad/surrogate-baby-soon-get-id-paper-317>.

[246] GS Radhakrishna, 'Mom Dumps Surrogate Baby, Gets Him Back', *Telegraph* (London, 29 January 2012), at <www.telegraphindia.com/1120129/jsp/frontpage/story_15065100.jsp>; M Srinivas, 'All's Well for the Emperor Boy' *The Hindu* (Hyderabad, 1 March 2012), at http://www.thehindu.com/news/cities/Hyderabad/alls-well-for-the-emperor-boy/article2946984.ece

[247] S Carney, *The Red Market: On the Trail of the World's Organ Brokers, Bone Thieves, Blood Farmers and Child Traffickers* (New York, William Morrow, 2011).

[248] N Lal, 'Risks Flagged in India's Fertility Tourism', Asia Times Online (Hong Kong, 1 August 2012), at www.atimes.com/atimes/South_Asia/NH01Df01.html.

[249] K Srivastava, 'Woman Loses Uterus After Becoming Surrogate Mother Thrice', *DNA* (Mumbai, 27 December 2011), at <www.dnaindia.com/print710.php?cid=1630429>. 2.25 lakh is approximately USD $4,500.

[250] *Ibid.*

[251] *Ibid.*

[252] *Ibid.*

[253] *Ibid.*

sum of Rs. 100,000 was not paid.[254] In another case, a surrogate mother insisted on keeping one of the twins she was carrying for a commissioning couple unless the couple paid an additional Rs. 1 lakh.[255]

In August 2008, an Indian couple were detained at Mumbai airport and jailed when they attempted to take a 16-month-old child to Canada to visit relatives.[256] The couple were charged with carrying a fraudulently obtained passport for the child, which listed the couple as parents instead of the child's biological mother.[257] The baby was handed over to the child's biological mother, who was the couple's neighbour and who had agreed to bear them a child since they had been childless for a long time.[258] Fraudulent documents are also a factor in a case where an Ahmedabad gynaecologist has been charged with arranging fake surrogacy documents and incorrect birth certificates in the case of an infant that was sold to a Rajkot-based couple.[259] Cases such as these may be indicative of widespread rackets being investigated in Ahmedabad, Anand, Nadiad and Saurashtra.[260]

Legal parentage and related issues with respect to Indian citizens who have children born through a surrogate have also been questioned. For example, in 2005 a single man in Kolkata commissioned a pregnancy with a surrogate using a donor egg and his sperm. Lawyers interviewed opined that his parenthood would not be recognised under Indian law unless the court allowed him to adopt the boy, and that both the surrogate and the egg donor could claim the baby as well as the father, notwithstanding the Guidelines. The Juvenile Welfare Board indicated it had not encountered such a case before, and it was not clear to the Board what the status of the child would be.[261]

---

[254] R Martins, 'Two Women and a Baby', *Telegraph* (London, 17 October 2007), at <www.telegraphindia.com/1071017/asp/others/print.html>.

[255] *Ibid.*

[256] 'Baby Girl's Fake Passport Lands Couple in Trouble', *Times of India* (New Delhi, 15 August 2008), at <www.timesofindia.intiatimes.com/articleshow/3367440.cms>.

[257] *Ibid.*

[258] *Ibid.*

[259] 'Accused Doc Sold Babies on Forged Surrogacy Papers,' DNA (Mumbai, 3 January 2013), at www.dnaindia.com/india/report_accused-doc-sold-babies-on-forged-surrogacy-papers_1785170-all.

[260] U Nayudu, 'Surrogacy as Cover for Trading in Babies,' *The Indian Express* (New Delhi, 8 January 2013), at www.indianexpress.com/story-print/1055849.

[261] S Bhaumik, 'IVF Son for Single Indian Father', *BBC News* (London, 4 October 2005), at <www.news.bbc.co.uk/2/hi/south_asia/4309332.stm>; S Dhar, 'First Single Father: But What about the Laws?', *DNA* (Mumbai, 3 October 2005), at <www.dnaindia.com/report.asp?newsid=4408>. Similar issues have been encountered by single women who have conceived through IVF with anonymous sperm donation. See R Bhasin and R Chitlangia, 'Birth Certificates Elude Single IVF Moms', *Times of India* (New Delhi, 13 December 2008), at <www.articles.timesofindia.indiatimes.com/2008-12-13/delhi/27940614_1_ivf-certificate-icmr>.

IV. Conclusion

Although regulation of surrogacy in India draws near, surrogacy to date has operated in a largely unregulated environment, leading to a number of complications and lack of protections for children born through surrogacy, surrogate mothers and commissioning parties. The extent that regulation, when and if enacted in the form currently contemplated, will protect the parties remains an open question. What is certain is that problems will continue to abound in the Indian environment where surrogacy is permitted to flourish without check.

13

Ireland

I. Domestic Law

A. Lack of Regulation

Assisted reproduction, including in vitro fertilisation (IVF) and embryo donation, is carried out in Ireland,[1] but there is no Irish legislation on surrogacy or assisted reproduction. This is an area in urgent need of reform.

In the absence of legal regulation, clinics operate under the guidelines of the Medical Council of Ireland.[2] Surrogacy services are not widely available in Ireland, although there have been isolated incidents of clinics providing such services.[3] As IVF is available, it is unclear if surrogacy is being carried out but going undetected.

The legality of provision of surrogacy services within Ireland caused controversy in 2009 when a paper documenting the first Irish surrogacy case was published.[4] The surrogacy treatment had been carried out at the SIMS Institute, Ireland's largest fertility clinic, which has been providing fertility treatment since 1997. There is no legal ban on surrogacy services in Ireland, but in 1999 the Assisted Reproduction Sub Committee of the Institute of Obstetricians & Gynaecologists concluded the 'ethical and legal problems raised by surrogacy ... outweigh any possible benefit'.[5] The SIMS Institute, claimed that the clinical deployment of surrogacy had been sanctioned by the Institute of Obstetricians &

---

[1] *Report of the Commission on Assisted Human Reproduction* (2005) 20–28, available at <www.dohc. ie/publications/cahr.html>.

[2] Medical Council, *Guide to Professional Conduct and Ethics*, 7th edn (Dublin, Medical Council, 2009) 20–21.

[3] ES Sills, APH Walsh and DJ Walsh, 'First Irish pregnancies after IVF with gestational carrier' (2009) 102 *Irish Medical Journal* 56–58; E Donnellan, 'Twins born after possible first surrogate pregnancy in State', *The Irish Times* (Dublin, 26 February 2009).

[4] ES Sills, APH Walsh and DJ Walsh, 'First Irish Pregnancies after IVF with Gestational Carrier Author Response Letter' (2009) 102 *Irish Medical Journal* 126.

[5] *Report of assisted reproduction sub-committee of the executive council of the Institute of Obstetricians & Gynaecologists* (Dublin, Royal College of Physicians of Ireland, 1999) 1–15.

Gynaecologists in 2006.[6] The Institute of Obstetricians & Gynaecologists denied giving any such assent, stating that the issue was outside their remit and should be dealt with by the appropriate authorities, presumably the Medical Council of Ireland and the Irish Medicines Board.[7] When the EU Human Tissues and Cell Directive[8] was implemented in 2006,[9] the Irish Medicines Board became the competent authority to authorise sites carrying out prescribed activities involved in the donation, preservation, storage and distribution of human tissues and cells. This includes fertility clinics.

There is no Irish court judgment, to date, on domestic surrogacy or cross-border surrogacy.[10] One set of parentage rules applies to all children, regardless of the circumstances of their birth. Ireland considers the genetic father to be the 'natural father'. When, in *McD v L*,[11] fatherhood rights were given to an informal sperm donor, there were renewed calls for the regulation of assisted reproduction.

Although many Irish cases refer to the rights of the 'natural mother', there is no Irish case establishing whether the 'natural mother' is the gestational mother or the genetic mother.

Fertility services are available in Northern Ireland under the regulation of the Human Fertilisation and Embryology Authority (HFEA). Eligibility for treatment by a HFEA fertility clinic is policed by the individual clinics, but there is no *legal* impediment to Irish couples making use of these services. The HFEA guidelines allow foreign nationals both to donate gamete material and avail themselves of assisted reproductive technologies.[12] Where Irish parents are permitted to use HFEA surrogacy services, the UK courts do not have jurisdiction to grant a parental order regularising parentage unless one of the intended parents is domiciled in the UK.[13] Anecdotal evidence suggests that Irish couples most frequently travel to the Ukraine and California to make use of surrogacy services.

In 2005, the Commission on Assisted Human Reproduction (CAHR) published a report[14] in favour of the regulation of surrogacy. This report represents the most serious attempt to come up with a legislative framework for assisted reproduction, including surrogacy. It does not consider cross-border surrogacy,[15] inheritance, nationality or the scope of the proposed new parentage rules. The report was

---

[6] Above n 3.

[7] R O'Connor, 'First Irish Pregnancies after IVF with Gestational Carrier Letter to the Editor' (2009) 102 *Irish Medical Journal* 126; G Culliton, 'IVF surrogacy is not under RCPI's remit', *Irish Medical Times* (Dublin, 4 March 2009).

[8] Directive 2004/23/EC of the European Parliament and of the Council of 31 March 2004, [2004] OJ L102/48.

[9] European Communities (Quality and Safety of Human Tissues and Cells) Regulations 2006, SI 156/2006.

[10] Such a case has recently been heard by the Irish High Court. Judgment has been reserved by Mr Justice Abbott. F Gartland, 'Judgment later in landmark surrogacy case' *Irish Times* (Dublin, 1 February 2013).

[11] *McD v L* [2009] IESC 81.

[12] HFEA, *Code of Practice* (2011), note 6:1.

[13] Human Fertilisation and Embryology Act 2008, s 54 (UK).

[14] Above n 1.

[15] This issue had previously be raised in Parliament; O'Rourke, *Seanad Eireann Debate*, 27 November 2002, vol 170, col 1252.

examined by the Oireachtas Health Committee, but to date there has been no legislative action.

A potential barrier to the regulation of assisted reproduction was posed by the legal protection given to the unborn child under Article 40.3.3° of the Irish Constitution. This Article acknowledges the right to life of the unborn child and requires the State to defend and vindicate that right. If the right to life of the unborn required the State to ensure that all embryos created during assisted reproduction were implanted, this would severely limit the provision of reproductive services within Ireland. However, in *Roche v Roche*,[16] where a woman sought to have her three frozen embryos implanted against the wishes of her estranged husband, the Supreme Court held that the State was under no constitutional obligation to ensure the implantation of embryos created outside the womb. Calls for regulation of the parentage of children born using assisted reproduction have been part of parliamentary debates since the 1980s,[17] but little progress has been made. In 1982, the Law Reform Commission considered artificial insemination to be outside the remit of its report on illegitimacy.[18] A Private Member's Bill calling for the regulation of surrogacy was debated and defeated in 1999.[19]

Regulation of the parentage of children born using assisted reproduction is on the current programme of government for the Irish Labour–Fine Gael Government.[20] The Government has indicated that the issue of parentage is being addressed as a matter of urgency.[21] In February 2012, the Department of Justice issued guidance on establishing parentage and citizenship of children born through foreign surrogacy arrangements for the purposes of applying for travel documents and indicated that future legislation would be forthcoming.[22] The Irish Law Reform Commission is in the early stages of a project to suggest law reform in this area.[23]

B. Enforceability of Surrogacy Arrangements

Surrogacy agreements are not binding or enforceable as contracts in Ireland, as they are considered against public policy.[24] If a dispute between a surrogate and

[16] *Roche v Roche* [2010] 2 IR 321.
[17] Collins, *Dáil Eireann Debate*, 14 October 1987, vol 374, cols 248–52.
[18] Law Reform Commission, *Report on Illegitimacy* (LRC 4—1982), [387].
[19] Henry, *Seanad Eireann Debate*, 7 July 1999, vol 160, 566–69.
[20] Available at <www.taoiseach.gov.ie/eng/Publications/Publications_2011/Programme_for_Government_2011.pdf>.
[21] Shatter, *Dáil Éireann Debate*, 19 July 2011, vol 739, col 388; Gilmore, *Dáil Éireann Debate*, 13 July 2011, vol 738, col 491.
[22] The Ministry for Justice, Equality and Defence, 'The Minister for Justice, Equality and Defence announces the publication of guidance for Irish couples on surrogacy arrangements made abroad' (Press Release, 21 February 2012) available at <http://www.justice.ie/en/JELR/Pages/PR12000035>.
[23] *Report on the Third Programme of Law Reform 2008–2014* (LRC 86—2007), Project 31, Legal Aspects of Assisted Human Reproduction.
[24] D Madden, 'The Challenge of Surrogacy in Ireland' (1996) 14 *Irish Law Times* 34.

the intended parents were to appear before the Irish courts, it would be treated, like any other dispute between parents over who should care for a child, as a private guardianship and custody case where the welfare of the child is paramount.[25]

It has been argued that the Irish Supreme Court could extend the right to marital privacy[26] to incorporate the right of a married couple to have a child by surrogacy. This could prevent a surrogacy agreement from being struck down as against public policy.[27] In *McGee v Attorney General*,[28] the Irish ban on contraception was considered to be an unjustified violation of the plaintiff's right to make private decisions relating to the procreation of children and matters of married life. Therefore it could be argued that public policy is preventing the enforcement of a contract that is merely allowing a married couple to have their own genetic children is a similar unjustified violation. A similar argument in favour of the enforcement of surrogacy agreements relies on a constitutional right to procreate, as established in *Murray v Ireland*.[29]

It is submitted that these arguments have overstated both the right to marital privacy and the right to beget children as understood by Irish constitutional law. The right to marital privacy prevents State interference within the marital unit, but does not require the State to take positive action to give effect to marital decisions which affect the rights of third parties such as a surrogate mother or the child created through surrogacy. *Murray v Ireland* (above) holds that the right to beget children can be limited and so the State is permitted to put restrictions on that right. In *Roche v Roche*,[30] it was explicitly stated that the mother's constitutional right to beget children could be limited by her husband's wishes not to procreate.[31]

The arguments that surrogacy agreements are not against public policy presume that the only obstacle to contractual enforcement is a disapproval of surrogacy as a form of reproduction. However, in Irish law, it is not possible for the courts to enforce private agreements between adults over the upbringing of children, regardless of how those children are conceived.[32] Neither is it possible for the status of legal parent to be accorded by agreement.

Where the child is being cared for by individuals considered by Irish law to be married parents, Articles 41 and 42 of the Irish Constitution create a protective zone of parental autonomy into which the judicial arm cannot reach, unless the parents have failed in their constitutional duties towards the child. This constitutional protection attaches to the people presumed in law to be legal parents, ie

---

[25] Guardianship of Infants Act 1964, s 3.
[26] *McGee v Attorney General* [1974] IR 284.
[27] GW Hogan and GF Whyte, *JM Kelly: The Irish Constitution*, 4th edn (Dublin, Tottel, 2003), [7.6.55].
[28] Above n 26.
[29] *Murray v Ireland* [1991] ILRM 465.
[30] Above n 16.
[31] *Ibid*, [115].
[32] *McD v L*, above n 11.

the gestational mother and her husband. For example in *Z v Y, X*,[33] the court held that it could interfere with a married couple's decision not to tell their child that the husband was not her real father only where the couple had failed in their duty towards the child. Therefore, the Irish courts could not make a gestational mother and her husband give up a child merely because they had agreed to. It would have to be shown that they had failed in their constitutional duties towards the child, or it would have to be established that they were not in fact the child's parents.

Section 3 of the Guardianship of Infants Act 1964 requires any question concerning the upbringing of a child to be resolved in the best interests of the child, not in order to give effect to adult intentions. There is a strong gloss on the welfare test that remaining with the child's parents is in the best interests of the child.[34] Parents have a constitutional duty to care for their children which cannot easily be abandoned.[35] This is particularly the case where the child is born to married parents.[36] Therefore in cases where the parents have entrusted their children to the care of third parties and an adoption order has not been made, the child-centred welfare test will generally result in the child being returned to its birth parents, regardless of what was originally agreed.[37]

The Commission on Assisted Human Reproduction did not expressly consider the matter of binding surrogacy agreements, preferring to deal with the consequences of surrogacy by changing the rules of legal parenthood.[38] This approach meant that the general principle that adults cannot privately agree to give up parental duties or to transfer parental status remained unaltered. This position is reiterated in the Department of Justice guidelines which states that '..family relationships and rights and responsibilities that flow from them cannot be subjected to the ordinary law of contact and cannot, in particular, be transferred to another person, bought or sold.'[39]

C. Legal Parenthood in Ireland

The recently released, Department of Justice guidelines on establishing the parentage and citizenship of children born through foreign surrogacy arrangements state categorically that Irish authorities are bound to apply the Irish law of

---

[33] Unreported HC judgment of Laffoy J, 23 May 2008.
[34] *N v HSE and others* [2006] 4 IR 374; IESC 60, [104].
[35] *G v An Bord Uchtála* [1980] IR 32, 55.
[36] *Western Health Bord and An Bord Uchtala*, unreported SC judgment of Hamilton CJ, 10 November 1995; *Southern Health Board v An Bord Uchtála* [2000] 1 IR 165; *Northern Area Health Board v An Bord Uchtála* [2002] 4 IR 252.
[37] *Western Health Bord and An Bord Uchtala*; *Southern Health Board v An Bord Uchtála*; *Northern Area Health Board v An Bord Uchtála*, above n 36.
[38] Above, n 1.
[39] Department of Justice, 'Citizenship, Parentage, Guardianship and Travel Document issues in Relation to Children born as a result of Surrogacy Arrangements entered into outside the State' (21 February 2012) available at <http://www.justice.ie/en/JELR/20120221%20Guidance%20Document.pdf/Files/20120221%20Guidance%20Document.pdf>2.

parentage and that foreign birth certificates or court orders will not necessarily be binding in Irish law.[40] In Irish Law, legal fatherhood is based on a series of rebuttable presumptions found in the Status of Children Act 1987. These presumptions are based on the traditional common law presumptions of legitimacy[41] and were given legislative form following the abolition of illegitimacy.[42]

Where the mother is married, her husband will be presumed to be the father of the child, unless this can be rebutted on the balance of probabilities.[43] A married father has automatic guardianship rights.[44]

Where a man is named on an Irish birth certificate, he is presumed to be the legal father and must be treated as such for all notification purposes, unless a statutory declaration of parentage is made stating that he is not the father.[45]

If the father is not named on the Irish birth certificate, he will have to go to court to prove his status as legal father. The issue of parentage may be raised before the Irish court under sections 35 or 38 of the Status of Children Act 1987.[46] Section 38 allows the court to order blood tests to assist it in determining whether or not a named person is the parent, and all orders are subject to the welfare principle in section 3 of the Guardianship of Infants Act 1964. A declaration by the court is binding on all parties to the proceedings, and the child's birth can be re-registered to reflect the reality of the child's parentage.[47] Even where the unmarried father is named on the Irish birth certificate or has a declaration of parenthood in his favour, he does not have automatic guardianship rights, which must be acquired.[48]

The Department of Justice guidelines state categorically that, under Irish law, the woman who gives birth to a child is the legal mother of the child.[49] No legal source is cited to back up this assertion. Many legal systems have introduced a legal presumption in favour of the gestational mother in legislation regulating assisted reproduction.[50] No such legislation is present in the Irish legal system, and it is argued that the definition of the legal mother or 'natural mother' remains unresolved.[51]

---

[40] Ibid.

[41] Co Litt 244a. Approved by the Irish courts in *Yool v Ewing* [1904] 1 IR 434, 440–41.

[42] The abolition of legitimacy meant that these presumptions were converted to presumptions of parenthood, and it was necessary to reinforce the rules with statute. n 13 [207].

[43] Status of Children Act 1987, s 46.

[44] Guardianship of Infants Act 1964, s 6(1).

[45] *FP v SP and the Attorney General*, unreported judgment of Smith J, IEHC, 31 July 1999; *BM v MG*, unreported judgment of McGuinness J, IECC, 30 November 1999.

[46] *JPD v MG* [1991] ILRM 217, IESC.

[47] Civil Registration Act 2004, s 23.

[48] Guardianship of Infants Act 1964, s 6A; *K v W* [1990] 2 IR 437; *W'O'R v EH* [1996] 2 IR 248; *McD v L* [2009] IESC 8.

[49] Above, n 39, 2.

[50] Eg Human Fertilisation and Embryology Act 2008, s 33 (UK).

[51] In *G v An Bord Uchtala* [1980] 1 IR 32-101, 97–98, Kenny J notes the ambiguous nature of the term 'natural mother'.

While a presumption in favour of the gestational mother is present in Roman law,[52] there is no such principle in the common law tradition.[53] Common law texts set out principles of legitimacy which make reference only to the father.[54] In *O'B v S*, Walsh J suggests, obiter, that a presumption of *mater semper certa est* is found in Irish law by reason of sections 1, 7 and 28 of the Births, Death Registration Act (Ireland) Act 1880.[55] However, the Law Reform Commission did not consider adding a presumption in favour of the gestational mother to the Status of Children Act 1987.[56]

Some support for an Irish presumption in favour of the gestational mother may be found in section 19 of the Civil Registration Act 2004, which makes a person who witnessed a birth a qualified informant who can register the birth. In contrast, sections 35 and 38 of the Status of Children Act 1987 support the idea that the genetic mother can apply for a declaration of parenthood and that genetic evidence is relevant when the court makes a declaration of maternity. If there is indeed a presumption in favour of the gestational mother in Irish law, it is rebuttable by a declaration of maternity based on genetics in exactly the same fashion as the presumption of paternity in favour of a husband.[57]

Under Irish law the 'natural mother' is given automatic guardianship[58] and a personal right to custody of the child under Article 40 of the Constitution.[59] As guardian the mother retains full responsibility for the child unless this is permanently removed by an adoption order. She is presumed to act in the best interests of the child and the court is reluctant to intervene.[60]

In the case of surrogacy, it is unclear whether the Irish court would find the gestational mother or the genetic mother to be the 'natural mother'.[61] The Department of Justice has indicated that the surrogate mother will have automatic guardianship for life but this position is inconsistent with sections 35 and 38 of the Status of Children Act 1987. The mere intended mother will have no right to guardianship or custody but merely a limited right to apply for access. Whoever is given the status of 'natural mother' will become automatic guardian and be required to consent to applications for passports, medical treatment, etc.

A genetic father will be able to establish his status as legal parent through a declaration of parenthood,[62] but will be accorded guardianship only if it is in the

---

[52] Found in Justinian's *Corpus Juris Civilis*.

[53] C Baldessi, '*Mater est quam gestation demonstrate:* A Cautionary Tale' (27 June 2007), available at SSRN: <http://ssrn.com/abstract=927147>, accessed 31 October 2011.

[54] Above n 41. In the *Amphill Peerage Case* [1976] 2 All ER 411, 423, Lord Glaisdale clarified that there is no presumption of motherhood which is merely a fact: '[M]otherhood, although also a legal relationship, is based on a fact, being proved demonstrably by parturition. Fatherhood, by contrast, is a presumption.'

[55] *O'B v S* [1984] IR 316, 338.

[56] Above n 18, [206]. The Report states that maternity is not regarded as raising a question of fact.

[57] Above n 18, [254]; *I O'T v B* [1998] 2 IR 32.

[58] Guardianship of Infants Act 1964, s 6(4).

[59] *G v An Bord Uchtála* [1980] IR 32, 55.

[60] Above n 11, [36].

[61] Above n 10.

[62] This is accepted by the Department of Justice guidelines, n 39, 3.

best interests of the child. However, if the intended father does not have a genetic link to the child, he will not be able to establish the status of legal parent unless he is married to the 'natural mother' and can rely on the marital presumption.

If the intentional parents lack the status of parent, they cannot be given sole parental authority over the upbringing of the child while a parental guardian remains alive.[63] A recent Law Reform Commission report has suggested legal reform to allow non-parents to be awarded guardianship and custody, but this will be in addition to the automatic guardianship held by the child's legal parents.[64] Transfer of parentage is possible under the Irish system only through adoption. This may be used only where the adopters are habitually resident in Ireland.[65] It may prove impossible to regularise a surrogacy situation using Irish adoption law due to the problems posed by private placement of the child,[66] payment[67] and proper consent of the birth mother.[68]

Under the CAHR's proposed reforms, intended parents were presumed to be the child's legal parents from the moment of birth.[69] This would give the intended mother constitutional rights and make it very difficult for the surrogate mother to gain custody or guardianship. This allowed the intention of the parties to be given effect without interfering with the principle that parenthood is a State-controlled status, or with the general presumption that it is in the best interest of the child to be cared for by its parents. This solution requires more statutory safeguards to work in a satisfactory manner. Clear evidence that there is a surrogacy agreement is required in order for the presumption to apply. Yet no guidelines were given in the Report as to what would constitute valid consent from the surrogate mother, or what would happen if the intended parents were unsuitable. If this solution were limited to a purely domestic situation, these issues perhaps might be resolved, but as a means of recognising foreign surrogacy this solution seems extremely difficult to put into practice.

D. Nationality of the Child

In the past, the Irish Department of Foreign Affairs has refused to issue passports for babies born through surrogacy arrangements in the Ukraine, even where DNA tests have shown the Irish intended father to be the genetic father.[70] This has delayed return to Ireland for the families involved. In 2011, 19 families were

---

[63] Guardianship of Infants Act 1964, s 8(1).
[64] Law Reform Commission, *Report: Legal Aspects of Family Relationships* (LRC 101—2010), 33–45.
[65] Adoption Act 2010, s 37.
[66] Private placement is illegal under s 125 of the Adoption Act 2010, unless the child is placed with a relative for adoption.
[67] Payment is illegal under s 145 of the Adoption Act 2010.
[68] Adoption Act 2010, ss 14 and 26.
[69] Above n 1, 53.
[70] Gilmore, *Dáil Éireann Debate*, 13 July 2011, vol 738, col 491.

in contact with the Department of Foreign Affairs over travel documents. In some instances families obtained a travel document from another country, such as the USA, which allowed them entry to Ireland.[71] Applications for passports were considered on a case-by-case basis, and the Minister warned that intended parents should prepare to remain in the country of birth for some time.[72]

The new guidelines from the Department of Justice now provide some certainty for intended parents. Submission of a foreign birth certificate will not always provide sufficient evidence of citizenship. Regularising the citizenship status of children born through foreign surrogacy may involve one or more applications to the Irish courts and reliable DNA evidence can be requested. Intended parents are advised to seek legal advice before entering into an international surrogacy arrangement.[73]

Under the Irish Nationality and Citizenship Act 2004, citizenship of children born on the island of Ireland is now dependent on the citizenship and residency status of their parents. A person born outside Ireland is automatically an Irish citizen by descent if one of his or her parents is an Irish citizen who was born in Ireland.[74]

The Department of Justice has stated categorically that before a passport can be issued it must be proved that the child's genetic father or surrogate mother is an Irish citizen.[75] If the citizenship link exists only through the child's genetic mother, this will cause problems due to the uncertain state of the law.

In order for an Irish passport to be issued all guardians must agree or necessary consent must be dispensed with by an Irish Court. As the Department of Justice are currently operating on the assumption that the surrogate mother is the child's automatic and permanent guardian, obtaining her consent is a necessary step in obtaining an Irish passport for a child born abroad through surrogacy. This consent must be free and informed and comply with the guidelines from the Department of Justice.[76]

E. Advertisement

There are no advertising or information restrictions on access to foreign surrogacy services, which contrasts with advertisement of foreign abortion services which is strictly controlled.[77]

---

[71] Gilmore, *Dáil Éireann Debates*, 21 July 2011, vol 739, col 53.
[72] *Ibid*.
[73] Above, n 39, 7.
[74] Irish Nationality and Citizenship Acts 1956 to 2004.
[75] Above, n 39, 4.
[76] Above, n 39, 7.
[77] Regulation of Information (Services Outside the State for Termination of Pregnancies) Act 1995.

It is not an offence to advertise surrogacy in Ireland, nor to advertise surrogacy on a commercial basis in other countries. Some websites specifically target Irish intended parents.[78]

The issue of advertising was not addressed by the CAHR. However, section 144 of the Adoption Act 2010 makes it an offence to advertise that a parent or guardian of a child desires to have a child adopted, or that a person wishes to adopt a child.

F. Payments in Surrogacy ('Commercial' v 'Altruistic' Surrogacy)

There is no explicit bar on payment for surrogacy services in Irish law, but legislative policy is clearly against commercial surrogacy. The CAHR Report recommended that participants in surrogacy should not profit from the arrangement but that reasonable expenses should be paid. All members of the Commission were strongly against commercialisation of surrogacy. Concern was expressed that recognition of the legitimacy of surrogacy even in tightly-controlled circumstances would give rise to the growth of commercial surrogacy agreements.[79]

Payment for surrogacy services can create an additional barrier to domestic adoption. Section 145 of the Adoption Act 2010 makes it illegal to make or receive any payment or other reward in consideration of an adoption. Payment of money to a surrogate could be construed as being in 'consideration of an adoption' and thus illegal. This has yet to be tested by a court. The CAHR suggested that payment of reasonable and legitimate expenses to the surrogate mother would not be seen as contravening the Adoption Act.[80] There is some anecdotal evidence to suggest that such practices do happen in Ireland.[81]

Payment may also flag the situation as one violating child trafficking laws. Section 2(2) of the Criminal Law (Human Trafficking) Act 2008 criminalises the acts of selling a child, or offering or exposing the child for sale, or inviting the making of an offer to purchase a child.

G. Rights of the Child Born Through a Surrogacy Arrangement

No guidance currently exists as to the right of the child born through a surrogacy to know his or her biological/gestational mother. Irish constitutional law has created a limited right to know one's origins,[82] but this has yet to be used in an

[78] Eg <www.circlesurrogacy.com/index.php/en/international/Ireland, www.surrogatepathways.co.uk/ andwww.information-on-surrogacy.com/surrogacy-in-ireland.html>.

[79] Above n 1, 49.

[80] This was the view of the English courts in cases pre-dating the Human Fertilisation and Embryology Act 2008; *Re Adoption Application (payment for adoption)* [1987] Fam 81.

[81] ES Sill and CM Healy, 'Building Irish families through surrogacy: medical and judicial issues for the advanced reproductive technologies' [2008] *Reproductive Health* available at <http://www.reproductive-health-journal.com/content/5/1/9>.

[82] *I O'T v B* [1998] 2 IR 321, 349.

assisted reproduction case. A limited amount of information is retained by the IVF clinics under the Irish Medical Council guidelines and to comply with EU Directive 2004/23/EC.

The CAHR recommended that information about donor gametes should be maintained and given to the child when he or she reaches 18.[83]

H. Rights of the Surrogate Mother

There is no current legal guidance as to the rights of the surrogate mother, for example to terminate the pregnancy or to maintain contact with the child. Neither of these issues was addressed in the CAHR Report.

Irish law permits abortion in cases only where there is a direct risk to the life of the mother.[84] The 'natural mother' of a child has a constitutional right to custody of that child as against other individuals.[85]

I. Legal Requirements on a Surrogate Mother/the Intended Parents

No requirements currently exist.

The CAHR suggested that surrogate mothers should be aged over 18 and within the normal reproductive age range. No prohibitions based on marital status, gender or sexual orientation would be permitted by Irish anti-discrimination law.[86] The CAHR found no compelling reason to impose a residency requirement.[87] Ultimately the clinic would be required to ensure that the welfare of the child was prioritised in the decision to undergo treatment.

II. Private International Rules on Surrogacy

There are no Irish private international rules specifically regarding surrogacy. This aspect of surrogacy was entirely ignored by the CAHR Report.

It is argued that Irish law as it stands views parentage as a matter of fact rather than as a matter of law. The Irish courts have had to determine if they would recognise the legitimate status of a child born outside Ireland.[88] In such cases, the courts have established parentage as a matter of fact[89] and then looked to see if the

---

[83] Above n 1, 51.

[84] Art 40.3.3°, Irish Constitution; *X v Attorney General* [1992] 1 IR 1.

[85] Above n 59.

[86] Above n 1, 50–51.

[87] *Ibid*, 50.

[88] Originally under the Succession Act 1965, illegitimate children could not inherit property as 'issue'. This was later rectified by the Status of Children Act 1987.

[89] *AB v AG* (1868) IR 4 Eq 56.

parents are married as a matter of law. It is only for the second inquiry that the issue of application of foreign law has been entertained. The Irish courts should consider a child as legitimate if the *lex domicilii* of either parent would confer legitimate status on the child.[90]

It is likely that in any case involving the establishment of a child's parentage, the courts would apply Irish law to the question of the definition of parenthood and then undertake an enquiry to establish, on the facts, who the parent is. This approach is supported by Irish constitutional jurisprudence, which gives inalienable rights to individuals classed by the Irish courts to be 'parents'. It is also consistent with the approach taken by the Department of Foreign Affairs. This approach proves unproblematic for a genetic father, but it means that until the Irish definition of 'natural motherhood' is clarified by the courts, the position of the intended mother is uncertain.

In the absence of any international regulation, another possible approach, modelled on illegitimacy, is to use the foreign definition of parenthood where, on the facts, the child was born of a parent (whether intended, genetic or gestational) domiciled outside Ireland and this is in the best interests of the child.[91]

If parental status was conferred by parental order or another type of process occurring after the child's birth, this could be recognised by the Irish courts in a similar fashion to the recognition of legitimation. Thus an English parental order would be recognised by the Irish courts where it was recognised by the *lex domicilii* of either parent's domicile.[92] This second approach would allow the Irish courts to avoid situations of limping parenthood, where the child is considered to have different parents in Irish law to the parents recognised by the *lex domicilii* of its parents.

It is submitted that the Irish courts would be unlikely to use the common law private international rules for the recognition of foreign contracts[93] to recognise surrogacy agreements. In the same way that the Irish courts cannot give effect to foreign pre-nuptial agreements that are not compatible with the constitutional obligation for the court to ensure that there is proper provision for a spouse,[94] they cannot give effect to private agreements that do not reflect the position that the court is under a constitutional obligation to rule in the best interests of the child where there is a question over a child's upbringing.[95]

---

[90] W Binchy, *Conflict of Laws* (Dublin, Butterworths 1988) 352; *Bond v Pidding* [1933] IR 198.

[91] Before 1991, foreign adoptions were recognised in Ireland only where the adopters were domiciled in the place where the adoption was granted. Today, s 9 of the Adoption Act 2010 brings the Hague Convention on Protection of Children and Cooperation in Respect of Intercountry Adoption into force in Ireland. The 2010 Act also provides for the recognition of foreign adoptions through bilateral agreements.

[92] *Maghee v M'Allister* (1853) Ir Ch Rep 604, 606; *Bond v Pidding* [1933] IR 198.

[93] The recognition of civil and commercial contracts is now governed by the provisions of Regulation (EC) No 593/2008 (Rome I). Art 1(2)(a) and (2)(b) seem to exclude surrogacy agreements from its scope. Therefore, if there was any question that the courts would consider recognising a foreign surrogacy agreement as a foreign contract, the common law doctrine of the proper law of contract would be used.

[94] Art 41.3.2° Constitution of Ireland.

[95] Art 42A.4.1° Constitution of Ireland.

14

Israel

SHARON SHAKARGY

I. Introduction

Surrogacy is regulated in Israel under the Embryo Carrying Agreement Act (Agreement Authorization & Status of the Newborn Child), 5756-1996.[1] The Act is based on the recommendations of a public Commission,[2] though its provisions are somewhat more conservative than the Commission's suggestions.[3] The Act deems itself to be the only legal way to perform surrogacy in Israel, as entering into a surrogacy arrangement which is not in accordance with the Act is a criminal offence.[4]

II. Domestic Law

A. Initiating a Surrogacy—Making a Valid Agreement

According to the Act, surrogacy agreements must be approved by a State-appointed Committee, composed of seven members: two physicians specialising

---

[1] Hereafter 'the Act'. The Act is also known, in unofficial publications, as Surrogate Motherhood Agreements (Approval of Agreement and Status of the Newborn) Law. For an unofficial translation of the Act, see D Kelly Weisberg, *The Birth of Surrogacy in Israel* (Gainesville, University Press of Florida, 2005), App B, 219–28.

[2] The Aloni Commission. For further details regarding the Commission, see R Schuz, 'Surrogacy in Israel: An Analysis of the Law in Practice' in R Cook, S Day Schlater, F Kaganas (eds), *Surrogate Motherhood: International Perspectives* (Oxford, Hart Publishing, 2003) 36.

[3] This is manifested as follows: (i) The Act requires the surrogate be single for religious law reasons, although experts considered it better for the surrogate to have the most stable and strong support system possible. (ii) The Act determines legal procedure for establishing the child's status, while the Commission suggested the child would be legally considered as the natural child of the intended parents without any legal procedure, thus predetermining that there will be no familial relations between the surrogate and the child. See further Weisberg, above n 1, 134–37.

[4] Sections 2(1) and 7 of the Act. Such an offence is punishable with imprisonment. See s 19 of the Act, which applies to: creating a surrogate pregnancy without the Approval Committee's authorisation; offering, asking, giving or accepting money or other compensation that was not authorised by the Approval Committee; publishing any information that might identify a surrogate, intended parents or a child, or any information regarding the content of an approval process or a surrogacy agreement; giving or receiving a child without the presence of a social worker or not according to a court order.

in gynaecology and obstetrics, a physician specialising in internal medicine, a clinical psychologist, a social worker, a public representative who is a jurist by training, and a person of the clergy of the parties' religion.[5] There must be at least three males and three females on the Committee.[6]

When deciding a case, the Committee should examine the following:

(a) medical evaluations demonstrating the intended mother's inability to carry a pregnancy (including cases when carrying a pregnancy would be dangerous to her health);
(b) medical and psychological evaluations demonstrating all of the parties' compatibility with the process;[7]
(c) a psychologist's or social worker's confirmation that the intended parents have received adequate counselling, including with regard to other parenting options.

If the parties were mediated by an agency, the Committee should also examine the mediation agreement.

The Committee is required to hear the parties. It is authorised to demand any other relevant information and hear whomever else it sees fit.[8] The Committee should also make sure the agreement between the parties was obtained through informed consent and free will, that there is no foreseeable harm in the process to the surrogate or the child to be born through it, and that the agreement does not deprive any of the parties' rights.[9]

The Committee composed *Guidelines* which operate as de facto law. The *Guidelines* specify a list of clauses that must be encompassed in the agreement:

(a) The parties must name an agreed mediator for any disagreements regarding the execution of the agreement,[10] and specify a physician to settle medical disagreements.[11]
(b) The agreement must also stipulate the medical facilities that will be used in the process.[12]
(c) The agreement must detail the number of attempts at implantation the parties agree upon (the maximum number being six),[13] the agreed time-span

---

[5] Section 3(a).

[6] Section 3(b).

[7] In reality, intense counselling and reviewing is carried out. See E Teman, *The Birth of a Mother: Mythologies of Surrogate Motherhood in Israel* (PhD paper, Hebrew University of Jerusalem, 2006) 64. Teman also discusses in detail the medical tests conducted.

[8] Section 4.

[9] Section 5.

[10] Embryo Carrying Agreements Approval Committee, Recommendations and Legal Guidelines, ref no 72320, August 2006 (hereafter 2006 Guidelines), para 8, available at <www.health.gov.il/Services/Committee/Embryo_Carrying_Agreements/DocLib/pon_mishpati.pdf> (in Hebrew)·

[11] *Ibid*, para 29.

[12] *Ibid*, para 34.

[13] *Ibid*, para 11.

for them to take place,[14] the number of embryos the surrogate is willing to carry and the medical procedure that will be undertaken if the pregnancy exceeds this number.[15]

(d) The agreement should limit termination of the pregnancy to medical reasons only, and specify the special compensation for pain and suffering caused by such a procedure, as well as its ramification on the overall compensation to the surrogate. The agreement must also specify the ramifications of a termination by the surrogate for reasons other than medical necessity.[16]

(e) It should be noted in the agreement that informed consent of the surrogate must be obtained prior to any medical procedure.[17]

(f) Other provisions must state the surrogate's right to approach the court and demand compensation for further suffering or expenses endured,[18] and specify a procedure that would apply in the case of a breach of the agreement by any of the parties.[19]

(g) The agreement must also contain provisions as to the custody of the child in case one or both of the intended parents die during the pregnancy, or in the event of their divorce.[20]

The Committee is very sensitive to details, and reviews agreements with the utmost attention.[21] It makes decisions only following hearings and deliberations. Approval by a majority is sufficient.[22] The Act does not create an appeal procedure, but the usual practice is that a refusal to approve an agreement may be brought before the Committee for review; and if the Committee upholds its prior decision, the parties may petition the High Court of Justice.[23]

B. The Procedure

Once the agreement is approved, the parties transfer from the Committee's regulation and control to that of the welfare and medical authorities, as well as to limited court supervision.

The procedure must be carried out in a public hospital authorised to conduct surrogacy procedures, and only according to the approved agreement. This

---

[14] *Ibid*, para 30.
[15] *Ibid*, para 32.
[16] *Ibid*, para 36.
[17] *Ibid*, para 28.
[18] *Ibid*, para 43.
[19] *Ibid*, para 40.
[20] *Ibid*, para 27.
[21] Teman, above n 7, 65.
[22] Section 3(5).
[23] This practice was affirmed at a rather late stage by the Family Court. See FC (Tel Aviv) 26140/07 *Dr SM v Tel Aviv DA's office* (19.11.2008). To this day, 16 years after the enactment of the Act, there are only a few reported cases that have been brought before the Supreme Court (while presiding as the High Court of Justice). See section IV. below for a detailed account of those cases.

ensures supervision by the State through medical authorities.[24] The Act demands that the welfare authorities be notified of the pregnancy, the estimated date of the birth and the planned place of birth, all by the end of the fifth month of the pregnancy.[25]

Notice regarding the actual birth must be given no later than 24 hours after its occurrence.[26] Once such notice is given, the welfare authorities step in: the intended parents receive the child temporarily[27] in the presence of a governmental welfare agent,[28] but the agent is the guardian of the child until a court decides otherwise.[29] The intended parents must initiate proceedings for a decree called a Parenthood Order within seven days of the birth, otherwise the welfare agent will initiate such a procedure.[30] A decree is granted unless the child's best interests demand otherwise,[31] and so far no case in Israel has so demanded, thus the court's role largely concerns approving the parties' arrangement and granting the decrees. A surrogate's wish to keep the child is not in itself a reason not to grant a decree. However, if a social worker's review demonstrates that there has been a change in circumstances which justifies the surrogate's change of heart, and that it would not harm the best interests of the child, the court may grant her request.[32] The Committee recommends that circumstances such as would justify a change be stated in the original surrogacy agreement.[33] So far no petition has ever been filed by a surrogate requesting to keep the child.[34]

When the decree is granted, the intended parents become the child's legal parents and sole custodians.[35] Such a decision is final.[36] If a decree is not granted and the surrogate wants to keep the child, the court makes her the child's legal parent and sole custodian, but may also make an order as to the future relationship and legal status of the child with regard to the intended parents. In such a case the court may also order reimbursement or payments by and to any of the parties as it sees fit.[37] If a decree is not granted and the surrogate does not want to keep the

---

[24] Section 7.

[25] Section 9(a).

[26] Section 9(b).

[27] Section 10(a). The Ordinances state that if the agent finds that in the current circumstances it is inappropriate to give the intended parents custody, the agent will ask the court for instructions. In the meantime the agent is authorised to decide who shall have the child for the time being. See Ordinance no 9 of the Embryo Carrying Agreement Ordinances (Agreement Authorization & Status of the Newborn) (Notifications, Requests and Orders), 5758-1998.

[28] Section 10(c).

[29] Section 10(b).

[30] Section 11(a).

[31] Section 11(b).

[32] Sections 13(a), 13(c) and 14(a).

[33] *2006 Guidelines*, above n 10, para 9.

[34] An interview with the Committee's coordinator, Ms Aviva Nimrodi-Botzer, 3 August 2011 (hereafter 'Nimrodi-Botzer interview').

[35] Section 12(a).

[36] Section 13(b).

[37] Section 15.

child, the court has full discretion to order as it sees fit.[38] All such decisions are to be registered in a special registry run by the Ministry of Justice.[39]

C. Legal Requirements on a Surrogate Mother/ the Intended Parents

i. The Intended Parents

According to the Act, surrogacy in Israel is available only to couples composed of a man and a woman. The law does not specify that they should be married and thus includes unmarried couples.[40] Single people, as well as homosexual couples, are currently unable to use this law, and thus have no access to domestic surrogacy.[41]

The intended parents must be over 18 years of age and habitually residing in Israel.[42] The sperm used in the process must be the intended father's,[43] but the egg does not have to be the mother's and could be a donor's (but not the surrogate's).[44] According to the Committee's policy, the intended mother must be unable to carry a pregnancy, or be at high risk if she does, and both intended parents must be otherwise healthy and not over 52 years of age, but the Committee has discretion to deviate from this policy.[45]

---

[38] Section 14(b).

[39] Section 16.

[40] Indeed, in practice, several unmarried couples were approved by the Committee. See Schuz, above n 2, 45.

[41] The exclusion of single people was affirmed, for the time being, by the Insler Commission (the Commission Report is available in Hebrew at <www.health.gov.il/pages/default.asp?pageid=25 65&parentid=10&catid=6&maincat=1>). A High Court of Justice case brought by a gay couple was recently dismissed due to the establishment of the Public Commission for Revision of the Legislative Regulation of Fertility and Childbearing in Israel (the 'Mor-Yossef Commission'). This Commission, instituted on 7 June 2010, published its Report on 20 May 2012. The Report is available in Hebrew at <www.health.gov.il/PublicationsFiles/BAP2012.pdf> (hereafter 'Mor-Yossef Report'). The Mor-Yossef Report suggested vast changes to the legal regime regarding the regulation of assisted reproduction in general, and surrogacy in particular. Among other things, it suggested allowing family members to act as surrogates under minimal limitations; eliminating or narrowing some of the restrictions regarding the surrogate; and allowing surrogacy for singles as well as for gay couples, but limiting gay men to fully altruistic (which appears to mean uncompensated) surrogacy only. Since this Report has no official standing at the moment, and until it is incorporated into the law, I have discussed only the most notable changes suggested in it. Since it suggests massive changes, it might be assumed that attempts to legislate those changes would encounter at least some political opposition.

[42] Section 2(2).

[43] Section 2(4).

[44] Section 2(3)(b).

[45] Para 2 of the Committee's internal regulations, available in Hebrew at <www.health.gov. il/Services/Committee/Embryo_Carrying_Agreements/DocLib/pundInfo0210.pdf. p.6> (hereafter 'Committee Regulations'). Like the *Guidelines*, the Regulations were created by the Committee. They do not have a clear and official legal status, but they act as the de facto law on the matter. The Committee's discretion is rather flexible, as the age limit was readjusted from 48 to 52 years in light of petitions to the Committee, and it seems that in reality it is required that the intended mother be 48 years old or younger, and the intended father 59 years old or younger. See Schuz, above n 2, 45. However, the Committee will approve an intended parent who is over 52 years of age only in rare cases based on the intended parents' circumstances (Nimrodi-Botzer interview, above n 34). The court

ii. The Surrogate

Religious law is a key player in the Act, since it is the personal law in Israel to this day.[46] Particular attention was given to Jewish law requirements. According to Jewish law, a birthmother is a child's actual mother. Thus, the surrogate is the natural legal parent of the child. A married woman's child fathered by a man other than her husband is a *Mamzer*. '*Mamzer*' is a religious status under Jewish law which entails severe ramifications.[47] Since the surrogate would be impregnated by the intended father, if the surrogate were married the future child might be considered a *Mamzer*.[48] Therefore, the Act deems that the surrogate be unmarried.[49] The Committee is authorised to waive this demand if no other solution can be found for the intended parents.[50] Indeed, in 2006 there was one such case, in which the intended parents found a married woman who was willing to carry their child altruistically when they were unable to find any other surrogate due to financial difficulties. After long deliberations that involved the Chief Rabbi of Israel and the Knesset (Israeli Parliament), the procedure was approved.[51] Since then, and due to the great difficulty in finding suitable surrogates, a few married surrogates have been approved.[52]

Another religion-based rule is that the surrogate must also not be one of the following blood relatives of the parents: mother, daughter, sister, cousin.[53] This limitation is not subject to the Committee's discretion according to the Act. Naturally, the outcome of this limitation is that commercial surrogacy is practically inevitable.[54]

---

reaffirmed this practice in FC (Tel Aviv) 26140/07 *John Doe v Tel Aviv DA's office* (5.2.2010), which will be discussed in section IV below.

[46] J Schenker, 'Legitimising Surrogacy in Israel: Religious Perspectives' in Cook *et al* (eds), above n 2, esp at 244 (religious law as personal law) and 255–59 (religious considerations regarding assisted reproduction). See also Teman, above n 7, 69.

[47] Eg, a *Mamzer*, as well as his or her descendants, is not allowed to marry any Jew except for other *Mamzers*. Since religious law governs marriage in Israel to this day, this is a severe outcome.

[48] See Schuz, above n 2, 47; Shenker, above n 46, 259. See further on this concept M Elon, 'Mamzer' in F Skolnik and M Berenbaum (eds), *Encyclopedia Judaica*, 2nd edn (Detroit, Mich, Macmillan Reference USA in association with the Keter Publishing House, 2007); and in general DJ Bleich, 'Surrogate Motherhood: Survey of Recent Halakhic Periodical Literature' (1998) 32 *Tradition* 146.

[49] Section 2(3)(a). This line of reasoning is clearly demonstrated in the Knesset's discussions regarding the Act, dated 11 December 1995 and 7 March 1996, and despite the Aloni Commission's majority suggestion not to encompass the Jewish rules regarding *Mamzer* into the Act but to give the parties relevant information and allow them to decide.

[50] Section 2(3)(a).

[51] The case was reported in the *Yediot Ahronot* newspaper of 15 August 2006. The decision was said to be limited to that case's circumstances.

[52] Nimrodi-Botzer interview, above n 34. This was done only as a last resort in cases where the intended parents could not find any other suitable surrogate in a reasonable amount of time.

[53] Section 2(3)(2), together with s 1 (definition of a relative). This is another case where the Act has preferred the more cautious minority opinion of the Aloni Commission (by Rabbi Dr Halperin) over that of the majority.

[54] Schuz, above n 2, 36. She notes there that this is so even though the intention of the Aloni Commission was that surrogacy would be mainly altruistic.

The surrogate must be of the same religion as the intended mother (since in Jewish law religion is determined by the identity of the mother), but if all parties to the agreement are non-Jews, this demand may be waived, based on the discretion of the Committee's clergy representative.[55] The Act further requires that the surrogate must not be the egg donor,[56] based on the best interest of the child in having a minimal connection to the woman who 'gave him (or her) up'.[57]

According to the Committee's policy, the surrogate should be between the ages of 22 and 38 years old.[58] If she is a divorcée, at least seven months must have passed since the divorce.[59] She must have given birth to at least one child whom she has raised,[60] but to no more than three,[61] and must not have undergone childbirth during the year prior to her application.[62] A surrogate who has participated in more than two surrogacy procedures, including procedures that have failed, would be disqualified.[63] So will surrogates who are or were in psychiatric care or are heavy smokers, who use drugs or alcohol, or who have a criminal record. All of these requirements are in addition to the very elaborate medical conditions.

D. Enforceability of Surrogacy Arrangements

i. *Enforcement Regarding Handing the Child Over*

Surrogacy agreements approved according to the Act are binding, first and foremost, since the procedure is—to a large extent—taken out of the parties' hands and given to the State. As mentioned above, the State's organs oversee handing over the child, and priority is given to enforcing agreements and granting intended parents custody. It is only when both the surrogate mother wants to keep the child *and* there has been a notable change in circumstances that the intended parents might not receive the child in spite of their wishes. Clearly, the governing principle is the best interests of the child, but so is upholding the agreement. The legitimate interests of the surrogate are considered only when there has been an unforeseeable change of circumstances, and when the best interests of the child would not be compromised.[64]

---

[55] Section 2(5) of the Act. It appears that a clergyman of the parties' religion must be consulted. Nimrodi-Botzer interview, above n 34.

[56] Section 2(4).

[57] This was Halperin's minority opinion in the Aloni Commission's Report. His opinion was later preferred and enacted, despite the majority's view. See Schuz, above n 2, 46.

[58] Para 3 of the *Committee Regulations*.

[59] *Ibid*, para 4. This is meant to provide a disincentive to women divorcing only so that they could act as surrogates.

[60] *Ibid*, para 8.

[61] *Ibid*, para 1 of the second part of the Regulations.

[62] *Ibid*, para 9.

[63] *Ibid*, para 6.

[64] As mentioned in section II.B. above, s 13 allows the surrogate to demand the child, but only when there is a change of circumstances to support her change of heart, and only when it would not affect the best interests of the child.

ii. Enforcement of Payments

Though the Act does not specify the fact that the agreement is to be enforceable, the *2006 Guidelines* include a provision according to which the parties must state a procedure to be applied in the case of breach, thus making the agreement enforceable. Furthermore, all sums mentioned in the agreement have to be entrusted by the intended parents to a bank account run by a trustee,[65] thus promoting enforceability.

E. Payments in Surrogacy ('Commercial' v 'Altruistic' Surrogacy)

The Act authorises the Committee to approve monthly compensation payments to the surrogate for pain and suffering, as well as reimbursement of expenses resulting from the agreement such as time spent for the procedure, loss of income or temporary inability to work, and any other reasonable compensation.[66] The Act does not require that the surrogate be compensated and does not specify minimal or maximal payable sums, leaving it to the parties and the Committee's discretion. In practice, payments to the surrogate are currently around US $35,000–$45,000,[67] with a total cost of US $50,000–$75,000 in unmediated agreements, and approximately an extra US $10,000 in mediated ones.[68]

The financial requirements that apply to the intended parents are specified in the Committee's *2006 Guidelines*, according to which the parties must agree upon sums of compensation for the surrogate in case she loses her job, or some of her income or government welfare or other support. She must also be reimbursed for any taxation that might apply to the money she receives in the surrogacy process.[69] The *Guidelines* also describe the compensation payable to the surrogate as including, but not limited to, pain and suffering, discomfort, loss of income, travel, clothing, household help and childcare. The sums payable must be specified in the agreement.[70] In case of bed-rest or hospitalisation, additional sums would be paid.[71]

The Act authorises payments to the surrogate for legal counselling, insurance and other relevant costs.[72] The *Guidelines* further provide that the intended parents must pay for 10 hours of separate legal counselling for the surrogate, by an

---

[65] *2006 Guidelines*, above n 10, paras 44–45.
[66] Section 6.
[67] Nimrodi-Botzer interview, above n 34.
[68] In unmediated procedures, Schuz (above n 2, 42) found payments to surrogates in 2003 were between US $20,000–$25,000. Various Internet surrogacy forums updated the figures to $24,000–$42,000 for a single child (with an extra $10,000 in case of twins, and an extra $1,500–$5,000 if a Caesarean section was needed). The forums also contained information regarding mediated procedures, and noted that the real sums are sometimes not reported to the Committee, in order to avoid questions regarding unfair influence and over-commercialising the procedure.
[69] Para 21 of the *2006 Guidelines*.
[70] *Ibid*, para 39.
[71] *Ibid*, para 38.
[72] Section 6.

attorney of her choice.[73] They must also pay for any relevant medical counselling or treatment given to the surrogate, if it is not covered by the Israeli National Medical Insurance.[74] The surrogate and her children would also be entitled to psychological counselling throughout the duration of the process and for six months after the birth.[75] In order for the agreement to be approved, the intended parents must take out a life and risk insurance for the surrogate. The insurance is to last for the duration of the process and for six months after the birth, and have the maximum possible coverage. It must cover loss of ability to work, sickness and disability due to an accident.[76] It appears that though the surrogate is entitled to all of the above-mentioned sums, she is allowed to waive them if she convinces the Committee she is doing so willingly.

As previously mentioned, the Committee demands that all sums stipulated in the agreement must be entrusted by the intended parents to a bank account run by a trustee. Any remaining money would be returned to them only six months after the birth, or after a complete failure of the procedure.[77]

i. Public Support

Both the intended parents and the surrogate mother are also entitled to the regular governmental support given to parents upon the birth of a child. Since a surrogacy involves two 'sets' of parents, the rights would be divided between them. The surrogate is entitled to unpaid maternity leave of 26 weeks, and must take a minimum of three weeks in order to recover from the birth.[78] She might also receive payment for up to 12 weeks of leave from the national insurance funds, but such decisions are made on case-by-case basis.[79] Otherwise she might take paid sick leave. The surrogate would also be entitled to birth and hospitalisation grants.[80] The intended parents would be entitled to 12 weeks of paid maternity leave.[81]

F. Legal Parenthood/Nationality of the Child

As described above, in Israeli surrogacy cases there is no natural parenthood, and even legal parenthood is susceptible to changes and declared *ex post*. Legal parenthood of a child born through surrogacy is determined only by a court order

---

[73] Para 15 of the *2006 Guidelines*.

[74] *Ibid*, para 17.

[75] *Ibid*, para 19.

[76] *Ibid*, para 20.

[77] *Ibid*, paras 44–45.

[78] Sections 6(b)(1) and 6(e) of the Woman Employment Act, 5714-1954.

[79] Available at <www.btl.gov.il/benefits/maternity/an_Adopting_Parent/Pages/default.aspx> (in Hebrew, the English version of the page does not contain this information).

[80] This is the practical interpretation that is currently given to s 42 of the National Insurance Act, 5755-1995, according to online surrogacy forums.

[81] Section 9c(b) of the Woman Employment Act, 5714-1954, which applies s 7a of that Act to intended parents.

given after the birth, while in the meantime the child does not have parents but only guardians. The court order regarding parenthood over the child is regarded as constitutive of parenthood, rather than merely declaratory.

Once a Parenthood Order is issued, the child is considered the legal child of the intended parents, and if a decree is not granted, the court is required to name other parent(s), whether the surrogate or others. Such parenthood covers all aspects, including nationality.[82] In the unlikely event that both of the parents are Israeli residents but not citizens, and the child does not match any of the other provisions of the Nationality Act, 5712-1952, the child would have, from an Israeli perspective, the (foreign) nationality of the parents. There is no documentation showing that such a question has ever arisen, and it is safe to assume that the Committee would avoid such cases, or demand clarification in case of any doubt, prior to approving the agreement in such a case.

Note that according to the Act, the surrogate is not allowed to be genetically related to the child, but the intended father is required to be. The Act does not differentiate between cases where the intended mother is genetically related to the child and cases where egg donation is used. According to Israeli legislation, the egg donor has no legal standing whatsoever.[83]

G. Advertisement

The Act, though forbidding publication of details of the parties or of hearings held by the Committee and the courts, does not discuss the issue of advertising. Private advertising for a surrogate is a common practice, both online and offline, often recommended to the parties by agencies and other mediators. Agencies advertise themselves massively online, mainly by managing forums on the matter, but also by ads.

Surrogacy agencies are not regulated by the Act but only mentioned. The Committee's *Guidelines* require only that if an agency is involved, the parties' agreement with the agency be presented to the Committee and the amounts paid be reported.[84] Since the Act bans all surrogacy procedures other than those approved by the Committee, the agency-run procedures are subject to the same rules and limitations as the private ones.

H. Rights of the Child Born Through a Surrogacy Arrangement

Once the court assigns parents to a child, that child has all the rights that a natural child has, such as maintenance, inheritance, etc. With regard to the child's

---

[82] According to s 4 of the Nationality Act, 5712-1952, a child born in Israel would be a citizen of the State if the one of the parents was Israeli.

[83] Section 42 of the Egg Donation Act, 5770-2010.

[84] Para 10 of the *2006 Guidelines*.

special situation as being born via surrogacy, the Embryo Carrying Agreement Ordinances (Agreement Authorization & Status of the Newborn) (Registry), 5758-1998, creates a registry in which all successful surrogacy procedures are registered. The registry must contain the names and details of the child, surrogate and intended parents, as well as details of the court case and any orders made by the court regarding future relationships between the parties. All changes and updates must also be submitted to the registrar.[85]

This registry is not open to the public; however, when a person born through surrogacy reaches his or her majority (18 years), he or she may obtain a social worker's permission to see the record. A social worker's refusal to grant access to the record may be contested in court.[86]

I. Rights of the Surrogate Mother

The surrogate's rights are mainly protected with regard to financial compensation and protection of her mental and physical health, and her children's mental health. There is very little in the Act and accompanying documents to suggest that the surrogate has any other protected rights. Thus, for example, the surrogate is allowed to terminate the pregnancy only in the event of a medical risk; termination on other grounds might entail restitution and any other remedies the parties choose to include in the agreement.

Though the Act does not declare the intended parents as legal patents *ex ante*, it clearly prioritises them and their wishes. Therefore, a surrogate's wish to keep the child is only secondary to the intended parents' will and to the best interests of the child.

As mentioned, the court is authorised to make orders as to the future relationship with the child only for the intended parents' benefit, in the event that they are denied custody of the child.[87] There are no provisions ensuring a future relationship between the surrogate and the child when the intended parents are granted parenthood. However, when a third party is granted parenthood, the court is free to make any provisions with regard to the child's status it sees fit; it could even make an order regarding the child's relationship with the surrogate. The Committee's *Guidelines* state that the intended parents and the surrogate are to specify in the agreement what their relationship will be during and after the pregnancy.[88]

---

[85] Ordinance no 3.
[86] Section 16(c) of the Act, which refers to s 30 of the Child Adoption Act, 5741-1981 (hereafter 'Adoption Act').
[87] Section 13(c) of the Act.
[88] Para 12 of the *2006 Guidelines*.

III. Private International Law

The Israeli regulation is unlikely to have private international law aspects, as the Act allows only those habitually residing in Israel to participate in a surrogacy process as intended parents or surrogates. The basic norm of the Act is that all involved parties would also be of the same religion, thus avoiding inter-religious questions too. This is particularly important in Israel, due to the aforementioned fact that the personal law in Israel is religious law.

There is no official arrangement regarding foreign surrogacy, and currently there is no recognition of foreign surrogacy agreements, at least with regard to status.[89] It seems, though, that the monetary aspects of such agreements could be a valid cause of action and enforceable in Israel.

All children born to Israelis abroad are entitled to enter Israel and receive Israeli citizenship based on their genetic connection to their parents. Normally, Israeli births abroad are registered on the Israeli birthmother's declaration as to giving birth to the child, with no need for genetic testing. Since foreign surrogacy involves birth of a child by a third party (who is not Israeli), this procedure cannot apply.[90] Furthermore, it appears that foreign birth certificates do not suffice for proving parenthood.[91] Therefore, in order to grant an Israeli citizenship, the Ministry of Interior demands parenthood to be proven by genetic testing.[92] Note that in Israel, a genetic test aimed at determining family relations is possible only with a court's permission,[93] and the Ministry demands that the actual test be done in Israel, though the sample may be retrieved abroad.

Once a genetic relationship is proven with regard to either of the parents, the child is considered their natural child and registered accordingly, and the surrogacy is disregarded. There is no registration of the procedure. The fact that a foreign surrogacy is not registered is ironic, since one of the motivations for enacting the Israeli Act was to avoid parents have their children via foreign surrogacy and registering them in Israel without any indication of any other parties involved in their birth.[94]

---

[89] According to Ms Moria Cohen, the surrogacy's referent in the Ministry of Justice, the matter is currently under deliberation (copy of the correspondence on file with the author).

[90] According to procedure number 2.2.0004 of 1 January 2008, called Registry of Births Abroad by Israeli Mothers Procedure (available at <www.piba.gov.il/Regulations/3.pdf> (in Hebrew)).

[91] Adv Rina Nesher of the Ministry of Interior's legal department. (Replay dated 4 August 2011, on file with the author.)

[92] It appears that to date the Ministry of Interior has not allowed intended mothers to prove their relation to the child by a genetic test, due to the fact that there was no such procedure for mothers in the foreign births procedure. A recent decision by the Tel Aviv Family Court has ruled that genetic tests must be accessible in such cases to intended fathers and mothers alike: FC (Tel-Aviv) 10509-10-11 *IP v The Attorney General* (5.3.12).

[93] Section 28A of the Genetic Information Act, 5561-2000. This is due to the fear that such tests would reveal *Mamzers* (see section II.C.ii. above), thus operating against the child's best interests.

[94] Teman, above n 7, 70–71.

Since Parenthood Orders are possible only in domestic surrogacy cases, a spouse who is not genetically related to the child may be deemed a parent only following an adoption, which would entail proving that the surrogate has waived her rights regarding the child.[95] As opposed to foreign surrogacy, such an adoption requires registration.[96]

IV. Domestic Surrogacy Statistics and Case Law

There are no formal statistical reports regarding domestic surrogacy. Data is released by the Ministry of Health on a sporadic basis. By 2001 there had been 108 applications to the Approval Committee, out of which 90 were approved, and 30 babies were born in 22 births. Between 2001 and 2006 there were 360 applications, 287 of which were approved, and out of which 156 babies were born in 125 births, including one of triplets.[97] By the end of 2010, the Committee had received a total of 723 applications, out of which 327 babies were born in 260 births.[98]

Domestic surrogacy was discussed in the courts with regard to the following issues:

(a) *The constitutionality of the law's limitations regarding the inaccessibility of the procedure.* This was brought to the court by a single intended mother and a gay couple of intended parents. Both cases were discussed in a High Court of Justice petition.

In the case of the single intended mother,[99] the court has deemed the limitation constitutional for the time being and denied the petition while referring the issue to the legislators. Indeed, the Insler Public Commission of 2004 addressed the issue, but its recommendations reaffirmed the court's decision.[100]

---

[95] Section 28L of the Adoption Act, regarding foreign adoptions. According to this section, the birthmother's waiver must be documented by her country's general adoption agency. Some agencies use court orders that eliminate the surrogate's custody and transfer it to the intended parents.

[96] This situation would change if the Mor-Yossef Report were enacted. The Commission suggested regulating cross-border surrogacy by an international convention, and suggested applying the Israeli procedure of Parenthood Decrees to all surrogacy procedures performed in clinics that were supervised and authorised by Israeli authorities, while maintaining the current arrangement for procedures conducted in other facilities. See Mor-Yossef Report, above n 41, 66–69.

[97] D Shapira and J Shapira, 'A decade of Embryo Carrying Agreement Act (Agreement Authorization & Status of the Newborn Child), 5756-1996: Reality and Desirable Alternatives' (2007) 36 *Medicine and Law* 26 (in Hebrew).

[98] Nimrodi-Botzer interview, above n 34. Formal database is currently under construction.

[99] HCJ 2458/01, *New Family v The Approval Committee* (23.12.02). Another, somewhat related interesting case has dealt with a single man's request to have a surrogacy arrangement using embryos created with his sperm and his ex-wife's eggs. This request was denied on various grounds, including the woman's objection and the man's being single (FA 228/08 *John Doe v Jane Doe at el* (7.6.2010).

[100] The Commission Report is available at <www.health.gov.il/pages/default.asp?pageid=2565&parentid=10&ca tid=6&maincat=1> (in Hebrew).

The second case, which dealt with the disqualification of a couple comprising two men,[101] was not discussed by the court due to the establishment of yet another commission—the Public Commission for Revision of the Legislative Regulation of Fertility and Childbearing in Israel (the Mor-Yossef Commission). This Commission has discussed the matter of gay parents, among other issues, and suggested allowing such male couples only altruistic surrogacy, a term which appears to mean uncompensated surrogacy, due to the shortage of surrogates in Israel.[102] At this point it is up to the legislator to decide whether to accept this recommendation.

(b) *The Committee's discretion and relevant factors.* Cases were brought regarding disqualifications by the Committee based on an intended parent's age and on the number of children an intended parent already has. In the maximal age limit case, [103] the Committee disapproved of a couple comprising a 53-year-old woman and a 58-year-old man (at the time of their first application to the Committee; they were 57 and 63 respectively by the time they got to court). The court reaffirmed the Committee's discretion regarding age limits, based on the best interests of the child, and dismissed the case. The court also mentioned six cases in which the Committee approved couples where the wife was over 51, as a sign for the Committee's to adopt a balanced approach toward age, amongst other factors. This decision was appealed to the Court of Appeals and to the Supreme Court, both of which found the age limitation to be justified and reasonable, and both of which upheld the Committee's decision.

In the case dealing with the issue of how childless the intended parents should be,[104] the Committee has rejected a couple of intended parents who already had three natural children before the wife lost her ability to sustain a pregnancy. The court overturned the Committee, ruling that the fact that the parents already had three children should not, by itself, disqualify them from surrogacy.

(c) *Publication of surrogacy procedures.* Two cases were brought by parties who wanted to waive the secrecy of the procedure and allow television crews to accompany them, despite section 19 of the Act, which lists actions forbidden under the act, including unauthorised publication of any personal information regarding surrogacy procedures. The first case was brought regarding one of the first surrogacy procedures in Israel, and the request was denied.[105] A second case, brought on similar grounds a few years later, was successful, so a television crew was allowed to follow and document the procedure, as long as measures were taken to make sure that the identity of

[101] HCJ 1078/10 *Pinkas v The Approval Committee* (30.6.10)).
[102] Mor-Yossef Report, above n 41, 60–65.
[103] FC (Tel Aviv) 26140/07 *John Doe v Tel Aviv DA's Office* (15.2.2010).
[104] HCJ 625/10 *John Doe v The Approval Committee* (27.6.11).
[105] FC (Tel Aviv) 4570/98 *Jane Doe v The Attorney General* (18.2.1998).

the parties was not revealed.[106] One last case involved a petition by a man who wanted, after divorcing his wife, to impregnate a surrogate using frozen embryos created during the marriage from his sperm and his ex-wife's eggs. This case was dismissed.[107]

(d) *Parenthood in surrogacy between same-sex partners.* In a recent case, a woman who donated an egg to her female spouse under the Egg Donation Act[108] was later given access to a Parenthood Order procedure which, once completed, would give her the status of a second mother to the child. In donations under the Egg Donation Act, all familial ties between the donor and the child are severed.[109] Therefore, in this case the donor was legally disconnected from the egg upon donation, and once the child was born it was registered as the birthmother's legal child, according to the Egg Donation Act. At that point the donor asked the Ministry of Interior to register her as the child's second mother (by disregarding the donation detachment clause). The Ministry of Interior refused her request and demanded that she adopt the child. The court decision on the matter was that though the birthmother's status was based on this being a donation case, the donor's petition should be discussed as if this was a surrogacy case. This was based on the fact that the donation was made within a familial structure in which the 'donor' was the birthmother spouse and was acting as the child's parent. Accordingly, the court initiated a Parenthood Order procedure, ruling that unless the 'donor' was found to be unfit, a decree would be issued and she would be registered as the child's second mother.[110] This case is of particular importance, since it appears to be leaping towards allowing same-sex couples access to surrogacy in Israel.

V. Cross-border Surrogacy Statistics and Cases

There are no formal statistical reports regarding cross-border surrogacy. According to unofficial data, including online advertisements of agencies, it appears that Israeli agencies mainly work with surrogates from Armenia, Georgia, India, Moldova and the Ukraine. The eggs used are mostly those of Caucasian Americans.

Cross-border surrogacy has been discussed in Israeli courts with regard to the procedure of registering the children as being those of the intended parents. Since Israeli law demands a court authorisation prior to any genetic test designed

---

[106] FC (Tel Aviv) 51740/06 *Chaya et al v The Attorney General* (19.4.07).
[107] See above n 99.
[108] Egg Donation Act, 5770-2010.
[109] *Ibid*, s 42(a) and (c), but affinity rules would apply should the child wish to marry the donor or members of her immediate family (subs (b)).
[110] FC 60320-07 *TZ v Tel Aviv DA's Office* (4.3.12).

to determine parenthood, there are many cases of intended parents asking for such permission. Those cases are normally highly technical, but one of them has recently gained public attention. In this case, the family court refused genetic testing of a gay man who was the intended father of twins born in India. The court decided that there could be doubts regarding whether or not the parents were fit to be parents due to their lifestyle, and therefore that the babies must be separately represented in the case.[111] Due to the fact that the lifestyle the judge referred to was that the parents were two homosexual men, the Court of Appeals quickly intervened and authorised the principle of the separate representation for the babies as a general rule, based on Article 28b(a)(1) of the Genetic Information Act, 5561-2000, while strongly opposing the judge's reasoning.[112]

Another case currently being discussed is that of a homosexual couple who petitioned the High Court of Justice to revoke the procedure that forces parents of surrogate children to undergo genetic testing, so that parenthood can be registered based on birth certificates. This petition has not yet been decided.[113]

---

[111] FC (Jerusalem) 28240/09 *DG v Jerusalem DA's Office* (19.3.10).

[112] FA (Jerusalem) 14816-04-10 *John Doe et al v The State of Israel* (6.5.10). Another recent notable case is the one mentioned earlier in n 92, which clarified the situation of intended mothers, entitling them to the same genetic procedure in cases of surrogacy, exempting them from the Ministry of Interior's requirement that the child be adopted by such mothers even when they are genetically related to the child.

[113] HCJ 566/11 *DM-M et al v The Ministry of Interior.*

15

Japan

MARCELO DE ALCANTARA[*]

I. Introduction

Japan is one of the countries where surrogacy remains legally unregulated.[1] The first child to be born to a surrogate mother in Japan was delivered in 2001 at Suwa Maternity Clinic in Nagano Prefecture.[2] This was a gestational surrogacy case in which the sperm and the egg were provided by the intended couple, and a sister of the intended mother volunteered to act as the surrogate. After this case was made public, different sectors of society, including medical associations and courts, sought to discourage the practice of surrogacy. However, no legislative proposal has ever been introduced in the Japanese legislature (the Diet) to regulate the practice.

Japan is a civil law country, and the establishment of parentage and other family law matters are defined and governed by the terms of the Civil Code. According to the Japanese Civil Code, the woman who gives birth to a child is the legal mother.[3] If she is married, her husband is presumed to be the legal father of the child.[4] Moreover, Japan is a country that follows *ius sanguinis* principles. Japanese citizenship law is governed by the provisions of the Nationality Law of 1950, which states that a child shall be a Japanese citizen if the father or mother is a Japanese citizen at the time of the child's birth.[5]

---

[*] This work was supported by JSPS KAKENHI Grant Number 22730080. The author is grateful to an anonymous reviewer for helpful suggestions.

[1] See generally M de Alcantara, 'Surrogacy in Japan: Legal Implications for Parentage and Citizenship' (2010) 48 *Family Court Review* 417; RB King, 'Redefining Motherhood: Discrimination in Legal Parenthood in Japan' (2009) 18 *Pacific Rim Law & Policy Journal* 189; Y Semba *et al*, 'Surrogacy: Donor Conception Regulation in Japan' (2010) 24 *Bioethics* 348.

[2] 'First Surrogate Mom Gives Birth: Controversial Doctor Helps Sister Break Ground in Japan', *Japan Times* (20 May 2001), at <search.japantimes.co.jp/cgi-bin/nn20010520a3.html>.

[3] Supreme Court, Second Petty Bench, 27 April 1962, 16.7 *Minshū* 1247.

[4] Art 772 (Presumption of Child in Wedlock): '(1) A child conceived by a wife during marriage shall be presumed to be a child of her husband. (2) A child born after 200 days from the formation of marriage or within 300 days of the day of the dissolution or rescission of marriage shall be presumed to have been conceived during marriage.' Available at <www.japaneselawtranslation.go.jp>.

[5] Art 2(1), Nationality Law (Law No 147 of 1950). Available at <www.japaneselawtranslation.go.jp>.

II. Domestic Law on Surrogacy

Although surrogacy is not legally prohibited in Japan, medical associations and government commissions have strongly condemned its practice. The general view is that the practice of surrogacy is undesirable from the point of view of the welfare of the child, and because it involves physical and emotional exploitation of women.

In 2003, a committee attached to the Ministry of Health, Labour and Welfare[6] and another one attached to the Ministry of Justice[7] recommended that surrogacy be discouraged. Also in 2003, the Japan Society of Obstetrics and Gynecology (JSOG) adopted guidelines prohibiting surrogacy and stating that doctors should not be involved in any surrogacy arrangements.[8]

In 2006, the Science Council of Japan (SCJ) established a committee of experts (Assisted Reproductive Technologies Review Committee) in response to a request by the Government to consider the issues relating to assisted reproductive technology, especially surrogacy. Its final report, entitled *Issues Related to the Assisted Reproductive Technologies Centered on Surrogate Pregnancy—Toward a Social Consensus,*[9] was published on 8 April 2008. This report recommended that surrogacy arrangements should be prohibited and that doctors and agents should be disciplined for their involvement in commercial surrogacy.[10] Furthermore, the report states that

> [w]ith respect to the legal status of the born child as a result of surrogacy pregnancy, the surrogate mother shall be regarded as the mother .... [T]his shall also apply to instances where a surrogate pregnancy is conducted overseas.[11]

In an apparent contradiction, it also states that

> [w]ith respect to a married couple commissioning a surrogate pregnancy and the child born as a result of that pregnancy, parenthood is established by way of an adoption or special adoption .... [T]his shall also apply to instances where the surrogate pregnancy is conducted overseas.[12]

In other words, the report of the SCJ recommends the prohibition of domestic surrogacy but suggests that couples might seek cross-border surrogacy and subsequent adoption in order to achieve their goal of becoming the child's legal parents.[13]

---

[6] Available at <www.mhlw.go.jp/shingi/2003/04/s0428-5.html> (in Japanese).

[7] Available at <www.moj.go.jp/MINJI/minji07_00071.html> (in Japanese).

[8] Available at <www.jsog.or.jp/about_us/view/html/kaikoku/H15_4.html> (in Japanese).

[9] Science Council of Japan Assisted Reproductive Technologies Review Committee, *Issues Related to the Assisted Reproductive Technologies Centered on Surrogate Pregnancy—Toward a Social Consensus* (8 April 2008), <www.scj.go.jp/ja/info/kohyo/pdf/kohyo-20-t56-1e.pdf>.

[10] *Ibid*, 39.

[11] *Ibid*, 40.

[12] *Ibid*.

[13] See de Alcantara, above n 1, 426.

Considering this lack of a legal framework, the fact that surrogacy is likely to be banned and that the existing laws have not been interpreted by Japanese courts as supporting the practice of surrogacy, as will be shown in the following discussion of reported cases of international surrogacy, it is possible to draw certain conclusions about the current status of Japanese domestic law on surrogacy:

(a) *Legal requirements of a surrogate mother and/or the intended parents.* In principle, each fertility clinic is free to set its own policies and requirements.

(b) *Enforceability of surrogacy arrangements.* Japanese courts will probably declare any surrogacy arrangement void and unenforceable as contrary to public policy.

(c) *Payments in surrogacy arrangements.* Any surrogacy arrangement involving payment will probably be considered a criminal offence.

(d) *Legal parenthood/nationality of the child.* The surrogate mother will be the legal mother of the child by virtue of bearing the child, and the intended parents will need to adopt the child in order to establish parentage. The child will acquire Japanese citizenship at birth if one legal parent is a Japanese national.

(e) *Advertisement.* Advertising for a surrogate, or advertising to be a surrogate or to promote surrogacy, will probably be considered a criminal offence.

(f) *The rights of the child born through a surrogacy arrangement.* The rights and best interests of the child will be paramount in any court proceedings.

(g) *The rights of the surrogate mother.* As the legal mother, the surrogate has the right to keep the child and to refuse to give her consent to the adoption.

III. Reported Domestic Cases on Surrogacy

The guidelines of the JSOG prohibiting doctors from involvement in domestic surrogacy were successful, and almost all Japanese obstetricians and gynaecologists follow them. One exception is Yahiro Netsu. He is a 70-year-old doctor at the Suwa Maternity Clinic[14] in Nagano Prefecture, and probably the only Japanese doctor who openly offers surrogacy treatment in the country.

Dr Yahiro Netsu performs surrogacy only in strict accordance with his clinic's guidelines.[15] According to these guidelines, only gestational surrogacy may be performed, and both the egg and sperm should be from the intended couple. They should be legally married, and the intended mother should not be more than 45 years of age and she should not have her uterus. The surrogate mother should be a family member (the wife's mother, or the husband's or wife's sister),

---

[14] <e-smc.jp/en/>.
[15] Suwa Maternity Clinic guidelines on surrogacy are available at <e-smc.jp/special-reproduction/sr/surrogate/guideline.php> (in Japanese).

no money should be involved, and the resulting child should be registered as the surrogate mother's child and, afterwards, adopted by the intended couple.

Between 2001 and 2009, 13 children were born through surrogacy at Suwa Maternity Clinic. In four cases (in which six children were born), the surrogate was a sister of the husband or wife, and in seven cases (in which seven children were born) the surrogate was the mother of the wife.[16]

IV. Reported Cross-border Surrogacy Cases

Given the absence of clinics offering surrogacy services and the strong rejection and disapproval of surrogacy by the Government and medical associations, foreign couples are not attracted to Japan, and Japanese couples are encouraged to go abroad for surrogacy. For this reason, all reported cross-border cases involve Japanese couples who achieved surrogacy abroad in welcoming jurisdictions. We describe here three important cross-border surrogacy cases; two of these took place in the US and the third in India. Only the first two cases have been decided by Japanese courts. The third case involved a Japanese couple but has not been heard in a court in Japan.

The most influential case in Japan regarding cross-border surrogacy is the Aki Mukai surrogacy case.[17] Aki Mukai, a Japanese TV personality, and her husband, Nobuhiko Takada, a former professional wrestler, travelled to the state of Nevada in the US to have a baby through surrogacy. She had suffered from cervical cancer some years before and her womb had been removed. In a clinic in Nevada, their gametes were fertilised in vitro, and the embryos were implanted in an American surrogate who gave birth to twin boys in 2003. A court order by the state recognised the Japanese couple as the legal parents of the twins, and birth certificates recording Mukai and Takada as the parents were issued. When the twins were brought to Japan on US passports, and the Japanese couple wanted their US birth certificates to be registered in Japan, their applications were refused by the Japanese Government and the case went to court. (It is important to note that many intended couples who hide the fact that their children have been born through surrogacy are able to register them, but Mukai and Takada had spoken publicly about their decision to opt for surrogacy.)

The final decision came in 2007, when the Japanese Supreme Court ruled that

[a] judicial decision rendered by a foreign court acknowledging the establishment of a natural parent–child relationship between persons who are not eligible for such relationship under the Civil Code is contrary to public policy as prescribed in Article 118, item 3 of the Code of Civil Procedure and therefore not effective in Japan.[18]

---

[16] Y Netsu and R Sawami, *Haha to musume no dairi shussan* (Tokyo, Harushobo, 2009) 275–77.

[17] See de Alcantara, above n 1, 418–23.

[18] Supreme Court, Second Petty Bench, 23 March 2007, 61.2 *Minshū* 619. An English version of the decision in available at <www.courts.go.jp/english/judgments/text/2007.03.23-2006.-Kyo-.No..47.html>.

Under Japanese law, the legal mother is the woman who gives birth to the child.[19] For this reason, the Court said that a mother–child relationship could not be established between the twins and the woman who had not conceived and delivered them, even though the children are genetically related to the intended mother.

The second reported cross-border case took place just before the Aki Mukai surrogacy case and involved a couple from Kobe. Yasunao and Yoko Kondo, a Japanese couple in their 50s, went to a California fertility clinic and underwent a gestational surrogacy using a donated egg and the Japanese husband's sperm. The embryos were placed into an American surrogate and she gave birth to twin boys in 2002. A California court granted the Japanese couple the right to have their names placed on the birth certificates as the legal parents. Soon after the birth, while they were still in California, the intended parents applied through the Japanese consulate to have the children's births registered, and consequently to have legal parentage and citizenship recognised, but their application was rejected by the Japanese Government.[20] In this case, the fact that they had used a surrogate emerged because of an administrative instruction that requires authorities to check births by women over the age of 50.

Yasunao and Yoko took their case to the Japanese courts. In 2004, a family court upheld the Government's decision to reject their application on the grounds that the woman who gave birth to the twins is their legal mother. In 2005, both the Osaka High Court and the Japanese Supreme Court affirmed the family court's ruling.[21]

In both the Aki Mukai and Yoko Kondo's cases, US state courts recognised the intended parents as the legal parents. However, the approaches taken by Japanese courts to those two cases were different from each other. In the Yoko Kondo case, the courts adopted the applicable law approach and, in accordance with Articles 17 and 18 of Japan's old Private International Law Act (Articles 28 and 29 of the new Act),[22] applied Japanese law to deny legal parentage to the intended couple. In the Aki Mukai case, the courts adopted the recognition approach, and considered whether the Nevada court's order should be recognised in Japan under Article 118, item 3, of the Code of Civil Procedure.

The third cross-border case reported was one of gestational surrogacy involving a Japanese couple and an Indian surrogate. Ikufumi and Yuki Yamada travelled to India in 2007 and entered a surrogacy agreement with an Indian woman. She was implanted with embryos that had been fertilised in vitro with the Japanese husband's sperm and an egg from an unknown donor, and a baby girl, named Manji, was born in India in 2008. However, before the birth of Manji, the Japanese couple divorced and the intended mother refused to take the child, as she was not genetically related to the baby. The intended father went to India to bring Manji to Japan, but he was not allowed to do so. Since the Japanese Government refused

---

[19] See n 3 above.
[20] K Hall, 'Surrogate-born Duo in Citizenship Morass', *Japan Times* (6 December 2003), <search. japantimes.co.jp/cgi-bin/nn20031206b7.html>; K Hall, 'Japanese Couple Fight for Son's Citizenship', *Los Angeles Times* (28 December 2003), <articles.latimes.com/2003/dec/28/news/adfg-jcitizen28>.
[21] Only the Osaka High Court's decision was published. See Osaka High Court, 20 May 2005, 1919 *Hanrei Jihō* 107.
[22] See section V. below.

to recognise the intended couple as the legal parents, and as India does not grant citizenship via *ius soli*, the child did not acquire any nationality at birth. Without legal travel documents, Manji was unable to leave India and enter Japan.[23]

After facing numerous problems, including an Indian NGO filling a petition[24] seeking to prevent the intended father from taking the child to Japan, Indian officials finally issued the child with an identity certificate, and this document allowed the Japanese embassy to issue a visa for the child to enter Japan.

V. Private International Law Rules

Japan's private international law rules are codified in the Act on the General Rules of Application of Laws (Law No 78 of 21 June 2006).[25] There are two articles in the Law that may have implications for surrogacy: Article 28, concerning the establishment of parentage of legitimate children; and Article 29, concerning the establishment of parentage of illegitimate children:

Article 28 [Establishing the Parent–Child Relationship Where the Child is Legitimate]
(1) A child shall be legitimate where at the time of the child's birth the child was legitimate under the national law of one of the spouses.

...

Article 29 [Establishing the Parent–Child Relationship Where the Child is Illegitimate]
(1) Where a child is illegitimate, establishment of the parent–child relationship with regards to the father (paternity) shall be governed by the father's national law at the time of the child's birth, and with regards to the mother (maternity) by the mother's national law at that time. In these cases, when establishing the parent–child relationship by acknowledgment, where the national law of the child at the time of acknowledgment requires the agreement or consent of the child or a third party as a condition of acknowledgment, this requirement must also be satisfied.

... [26]

In the case of Japanese couples who go abroad for surrogacy, Japanese courts have, in accordance with Articles 28 and 29, applied domestic law (Japanese law) to

[23] See UR Smerdon, 'The Baby Market: Crossing Bodies, Crossing Borders: International Surrogacy Between The United States and India' (2008) 39 *Cumberland Law Review* 15, 69–72; M Ryznar, 'International Commercial Surrogacy and its Parties' (2010) 43 *The John Marshall Law Review* 1009, 1022.

[24] See *Satya v Union of India et al*, Rajasthan High Court (19 May 2012) Habeas Corpus Petition No 7829; *Baby Manji Yamada v Union of India & ANR*, Supreme Court of India (29 September 2008) Writ Petition (C) No 369, available at <judis.nic.in/scwelcome.htm>.

[25] English translation by K Anderson and Y Okuda, 'Translation of Japan's Private International Law: Act on the General Rules of Application of Laws [*Hō no Tekiyō ni Kansuru Tsūsokuhō*], Law No 10 of 1898 (as newly titled and amended 21 June 2006)' (2006) 8 *Asian-Pacific Law & Policy Journal* 138, also available at <blog.hawaii.edu/aplpj/archives>. See also <www.japaneselawtranslation.go.jp>.

[26] Anderson and Okuda, above n 25, 154–55.

solve disputes concerning the establishment of parentage. As we have seen, under Japanese law the woman who gives birth is the legal mother and her husband the legal father. For this reason, private international law has not been beneficial to Japanese intended couples, as in the case of Yoko Kondo.

In addition, even when the parent—child relationship is established by a court decision in the country where the surrogacy took place, the recognition and enforcement of this foreign judgment in Japan is likely to be denied. Article 118 of the Code of Civil Procedure (1996) sets forth the conditions that any foreign judgment must satisfy in order to be entitled to recognition and enforcement in Japan:

Article 118 [Effect of final and binding judgment rendered by foreign court]

A final and binding judgment rendered by a foreign court shall be effective only where it meets all of the following requirements:

(i) The jurisdiction of the foreign court is recognized under laws or regulations or conventions or treaties.
(ii) The defeated defendant has received a service (excluding a service by publication or any other service similar thereto) of a summons or order necessary for the commencement of the suit, or has appeared without receiving such service.
(iii) The content of the judgment and the court proceedings are not contrary to public policy in Japan.
(iv) A mutual guarantee exists.[27]

Courts have interpreted, as in the Aki Mukai case, that such a foreign judgment violates public policy and therefore, in accordance with Article 118, is not entitled to recognition and enforcement in Japan.

---

[27] Available at <www.japaneselawtranslation.go.jp>.

16

Mexico

ELEONORA LAMM*

I. General Legal Framework

The Political Constitution of the Mexican United States ('Constitution of Mexico')
provides, in Article 4, that

> every person has the right to decide in a free, mature and informed way, the number and
> spacing of their Children.

That implies the recognition of reproductive rights and of reproductive freedom,
which could include surrogacy.[1]

In regard to this, although the *Suprema Corte de Justicia de la Nación* (Mexico's
Supreme Court) has not yet deliberated on the subject of surrogacy, it is important to emphasise that it has ruled on landmark cases that have gained international attention for putting the country at the forefront of the advancement of
sexual and reproductive rights,[2] and this makes one consider the possibility that
Mexico's Supreme Court could rule in favour of surrogacy in future. For example,
since 2007, Mexico's Supreme Court has sanctioned the decriminalisation of

---

* I should like to thank Dr Ingrid Brena, Dr Alejandra Olay Cheu, Dr Jorge Alberto Silva Silva and
Dr Nuria González Martín for their contributions.

[1] The view might be taken that surrogacy is a form of access to those reproductive rights enshrined
in the Constitution. Thus, surrogate motherhood would involve the exercise of the constitutional right
given to couples and individuals to decide freely and responsibly on the formation of their family, and
on the procreation of children (or not) and their number and spacing. The foundation of so-called
sexual and reproductive rights is twofold: the right to reproductive and sexual health and care; and the
right to reproductive and sexual self-determination.

[2] A 1994 constitutional amendment overhauled the Supreme Court and, to a somewhat lesser
extent, reformed the rest of the judiciary. It expanded the Court's constitutional jurisdiction by
incorporating two new procedures allowing access to judicial review—*acciones de inconstitucionalidad*
(actions of unconstitutionality) and *controversias constitucionales* (constitutional controversies)—and
generally restructured the administration of the judiciary. Thus began what is officially called the
Ninth Era of the Supreme Court. Each time a legal reform changes the structure and jurisdiction of
the federal judiciary, a new *época*, or era, begins.

first-trimester abortion[3] and the legalisation of gay marriage and adoption,[4] and it has established the fundamental right of transgender individuals to change their officially recognised sex without public registration of their previous sex.[5]

Also, although the *Ley General de Salud* (General Health Law) says nothing about surrogacy, it regulates the State's obligations for providing health services, family planning and the coordination of research for human health.[6] It is considered that assisted reproductive techniques (ART), including surrogacy, are within this framework of support to family planning and health research, as their main goal is to achieve human reproduction, which implies family planning.[7]

Now, specifically, surrogacy in Mexico is regulated by the Civil Codes[8] of Coahuila, Queretaro and Tabasco, and by the surrogacy law for Mexico City, although this last law has not entered into force yet.

II. Civil Codes

In Mexico, each state is responsible for regulating civil matters according to Articles 73[9] and 124[10] of the Constitution of Mexico. Consequently there is a Federal Civil Code of Mexico and each state (constituent part of the federal whole) has enacted its own Civil Code.

A. Federal Civil Code of Mexico

The Federal Civil Code of Mexico (CCF) has only general rules on ART relating to the right to make free, responsible and informed decisions about the number and spacing of children (Article 4111 CCF), the need for the informed consent of the woman and the agreement of her husband, if married (Article 4112 CCF), the banning of cloning or any other procedures to select race (Article 4114 CCF),

---

[3] Acción de inconstitucionalidad 146/2007 & acumulada, resolved by the Plenary Supreme Court on 28 August 2008 (Ninth Era).

[4] Acción de inconstitucionalidad 2/2010, resolved by the Plenary Supreme Court on 10 August 2010 (Ninth Era).

[5] Amparo directo civil 6/2008, relacionado con la facultad de atracción 3/2008-PS, resolved by the Plenary Supreme Court on 6 January 2009 (Ninth Era). See further A Madrazo and E Vela, 'The Mexican Supreme Court's (Sexual) Revolution?' (2011) 89 *Texas Law Review* 1863.

[6] See Arts 1, 3 and 27, Ley General de Salud [General Health Law], *Diario oficial de la Federacion* (DOF) (*Official Gazette*) 07-02-1984.

[7] D Rodríguez López, 'Nuevas técnicas de reproducción humana. El útero como objeto de contrato' (2005) 11 *Revista de Derecho Privado* 97.

[8] In San Luis Potosi, Arts 1160 and 1474 of the Civil Code allow access to assisted reproductive techniques, but they do not expressly regulate surrogacy.

[9] Art 73 of the Constitution of Mexico establishes which are the matters of federal jurisdiction, and it does not mention civil matters.

[10] Art 124 of the Constitution of Mexico states that: 'The powers not expressly granted by this Constitution to federal officials are understood to be reserved to the states.'

and donor anonymity (Article 4115 CCF). It does not contain any provisions on surrogacy.

B. States' Civil Codes

Surrogacy has been expressly regulated in three states' Civil Codes, but they provide different solutions.

i. Civil Code of the State of Coahuila

Articles 489 and 491 of the Civil Code of the State of Coahuila stipulate:

Article 489 Any agreement or Convention dealing with procreation or gestation done on behalf of another person is without force.

Article 491 A surrogate motherhood contract is without force and therefore will not produce any legal effect. If a fertilized egg were implanted in a woman who has not provided the genetic material, motherhood will attribute to this woman and not to the woman who has contributed it.

Thus, the Civil Code of Coahuila expressly establishes the unenforceability of surrogacy contracts, so that any agreement, covenant or convention of this kind is regarded as if it has not happened. Surrogacy does not produce any effect, and the Civil Code clarifies that the mother is the person who has given birth.

ii. Civil Code of the State of Queretaro

Article 400 Couples that adopt embryos cannot resort to assisted motherhood or surrogate motherhood, or hire a third woman's womb for the gestation of the embryo.

Thus, the Civil Code of Queretaro prohibits surrogate motherhood.

iii. Civil Code of the State of Tabasco

Article 92 of the Civil Code of Tabasco, in its third, fourth and fifth paragraphs, makes explicit reference to surrogacy, differentiating between surrogate motherhood and substitute gestational motherhood, depending on whether the surrogate mother contributes her genetic material or not. Therefore, the third and fourth paragraphs of Article 92 expressly state:

In the case of children born as a result of the participation of a substitute gestational mother, the maternity of the intending mother who presents it[11] will be presumed, since that fact implies its acceptance. In cases involving a surrogate mother, the same requirements must be complied with as in a full adoption.

---

[11] The law says '*que la presenta*'. It is not clear in the wording and does not specify who or what should be presented.

A substitute gestational mother is the woman who carries the pregnancy to term and provides the gestation, but not the genetic material. On the other hand, the surrogate mother provides both: the genetic material and the pregnancy. An intending mother is the woman who agrees to use the services of the substitute gestational mother or surrogate mother, according to the case [in issue].

In accordance with this Article, a substitute gestational mother is a woman who carries the pregnancy but who does not contribute the genetic material. In these cases, motherhood corresponds to the intending mother, whose maternity is presumed.

This presumption applies regardless of whether the intending mother has provided her own genetic material or not, according to what is established under Article 347 of the Civil Code:

> When a second woman takes part in the reproductive process the former will be presumed as the legal mother who hires the surrogate mother, whether or not she provides the egg. That is, when the gestational mother is not the biological mother of the child born as a result of an embryo transfer, the intending mother shall be considered as the legal mother of the child and the child shall be considered as the legitimate child of that woman.

Furthermore, in its fifth paragraph Article 92 provides:

> [E]xcept in the case involving a child born of a substitute gestational mother, when the child is born of a married woman who lives with her husband, the Civil Registry officer cannot register as the father a person other than her husband, except where he has disowned the child and there is a final judgment that so declares it.

Thus, in the cases of substitute gestational mother, if the substitute gestational mother is married, her husband's paternity of the child will not be presumed; rather, as the motherhood of the intending mother is presumed, and she should be considered the legal mother, the intending mother and her husband will be the child's parents.

What is expressed in this Article is also confirmed by Article 360 of the Civil Code, which maintains:

> Except in the case of a child born as a result of a surrogacy contract, the child of a married woman may not be recognised as a child by a man other than her husband, unless the child has been disowned by him and a final judgment has ruled that he/she is not his child.

On the other hand, a surrogate mother contributes both the gestation and her own genetic material. Thus, in accordance with Article 92, in order to establish the motherhood of the intending mother, a full adoption procedure must be used.[12]

---

[12] Art 398 CCiv Tabasco: 'Legal Effects. Because of full adoption the adoptee joins a family as a legitimate child, giving him/her the surname of the adoptive parents and the same rights, obligations and kinship as blood filiation.'

In this regard, Article 399 of the Civil Code stipulates that for full adoption to take place, it is required

> [t]hat the child to be adopted ... be the result of a pregnancy achieved as a consequence of the use of artificial insemination or fertilization in vitro with the participation of a surrogate mother who had agreed with the intended parents to put the child up for adoption.

Consequently, as the Article refers to the rules of full adoption, the intending parents necessarily must meet the requirements demanded by law to adopt, such as being a married heterosexual couple or a couple who live as husband and wife (Articles 399 ff, Civil Code of Tabasco).[13] In these cases, this adoption would be a kind of adoption by special consent, ie in favour of certain people—the intending parents who agreed the surrogacy and the delivery up for adoption.

It is worth clarifying that the Civil Code of Tabasco—nor any other law in Tabasco—does not specify or regulate the essential characteristics or requirements of surrogacy agreements, that is, whether they must be altruistic or may also be commercial. Moreover, there is no special paragraph or amendment in the Civil Code contracts section to cover this. Tabasco's congressmen, in 1997, simply left open the possibility that a woman could hire another woman's womb, but never established how or in what circumstances this might be carried out. The Civil Code states only that in the case of a substitute gestational mother, the maternity of the intending mother is presumed and she will be the legal mother— which seems to imply that the intending mother would be able to register the child as her own—and that in the case of surrogate motherhood, the intending parents must resort to adoption—ie an adoption in favour of certain people: the intending parents—but without more details.

It is known that surrogacy is carried out in practice, and different clinics or medical centres in this state offer this service.[14] In general, it is done through a contract before a notary public, but there is no official knowledge of any case.

C. Mexico City

Mexico City is the only Mexican state to have approved a rule (Surrogacy Law for Mexico City) that expressly regulates surrogacy, but, because of the reasons that I will explain below, it didn't come into force. Consequently, given that it has not entered into force and, as we shall see, is still under review, the following sections first analyse the current legal framework in Mexico City (the provisions of Mexico City's Civil Code (CCDF) and the Criminal Code for the Federal

---

[13] It should be considered that Art 165 recognises the right of a married couple and of common law marriage (unmarried cohabiting parents) to employ any artificial reproduction methods to create their own descendants.

[14] See, among others, Centro de Cirugía Reproductiva y Ginecología de Villahermosa Tabasco, at <http://reprogyn.com.mx/estatic/tratamientos.php; http://reprogyn.com.mx/estatic/nota7.php>.

District (CPDF)[15]) and the present reality in Mexico City according to the current legislation. The Surrogacy Law for Mexico City is examined in section II.C.iii. below.

i. Current Legal Framework in Mexico City

In the Federal District, ARTs are allowed for heterosexual or same-sex married couples under the terms of Article 162 CCDF, which states that

> the spouses, by mutual agreement, have the right to decide in a free, mature and informed way, the number and spacing of their children, and to employ any artificial reproduction methods to achieve their own descendants ...

Taking into account Article 291 *Ter* CCDF, a couple in a common law marriage may also make use of these techniques.

Berna understands that according to what is stated under Articles 162 and 291 CCDF, as surrogacy is a method of ART, in principle it would be authorised for spouses and parties to a common law marriage, but not for single people, regardless of gender.[16]

Nevertheless, under the current legislation, motherhood is based on the principle that the mother is the woman who gives birth to the child (Article 340 CCDF). The quality of 'mother' lies in the biological fact of procreation, which is proved by the birth certificate or otherwise with the proof of birth.[17] Moreover, paternity is established on the basis of legal presumptions. If the woman is married, according to the legal presumption, her husband is the father of the child; and even if he denies being the father, it will be necessary to undertake a special judicial procedure to rebut the presumption.[18]

If we add the provisions of Article 338 CCDF, which state that

> filiation is the relationship between parent and child, forming the primary social nucleus of the family; therefore it cannot be subject to agreement between the parties or to a transaction, or subject to arbitration, so that no one can enforce it under current legislation. then, under the current legislation, surrogacy would be prohibited.[19]

Thus, under current legislation in Mexico City, there is a risk for people who are obliged to declare the birth (Article 55 CCDF) that they could be subject to

---

[15] In October 2002 the Criminal Code for the Federal District (CPDF) was amended, and the reform incorporated a second title called 'Assisted Reproduction and Artificial Insemination' in the second book, called 'Assisted Reproduction, Artificial Insemination and Genetic Engineering'. The new articles punish different offences relating to the practice of assisted reproduction.

[16] I Brena, 'La maternidad subrogada ¿es suficiente la legislación civil vigente para regularla?' (2009) 23 *Revista de Derecho Privado del Instituto de Investigaciones Jurídicas de la Universidad Nacional Autónoma de Mexico* 141.

[17] R Villegas, *Derecho Civil Mexicano. Derecho de Familia*, 5th edn (Mexico, Porrúa, 1980) 600.

[18] Arts 324, 325 ff CCDF.

[19] I Brena, 'La gestación subrogada ¿una nueva figura del derecho de familia?' in I Brena (ed), *'Fertilización Asistida' Memorias del Coloquio celebrado en octubre de 2010* (Mexico, Instituto de Investigaciones Jurídicas de la Universidad Nacional Autónoma de Mexico, 2010).

sanctions if it is discovered that they declared the intending mother as the mother who gave birth to the child. Doctors or any other persons who attend childbirth are at the same risk if they sign a birth certificate giving false information.[20]

Furthermore, a person who delivers his or her child for a payment, or who is involved somehow in this delivery, may commit a crime penalised by the Criminal Code.[21]

Under current legislation, surrogacy agreements in Mexico City are not legal.

ii. The Current Reality in Mexico City

In the absence of specific rules on surrogacy, and taking into account the current legislation in Mexico City, some scholars consider that the delivery of the child from the surrogate mother to the intending parents could be justified through adoption. It will be necessary, in that case, for the participants in a surrogacy agreement to meet all the requirements and follow all the procedures regulated for adoption, as set out in Articles 390 ff CCDF.[22]

If the surrogate mother is single and the intending father provided his genetic material, he should recognise the child instead of adopting him or her. If the surrogate mother is married, the paternity of her husband must have been previously contested in order for the intending father to recognise the child as his son or daughter.[23]

In both cases, after the recognition of the child by the intending father, if he is married, his wife should adopt the child (spousal adoption). As analysed in the Argentinean report in chapter one of this book, the inconvenience of this mechanism lies in the facts that not only would it imply an 'infringement' of the adoption rules, but also, if the intending mother is the genetic mother too—cases of gestational surrogacy—we would be asking her to adopt her own genetic child.[24]

Without prejudice to the disadvantages or problems already identified in this study, what would happen to the child if the intending parents do not meet the requirements established by law for adopters? Or what if they refuse to use adoption? Or what if the surrogate mother refuses to give up the child for adoption? It may also be that the Public Prosecutor opposes the adoption,[25] among many other inconveniences.

---

[20] Brena, above n 16.

[21] See Art 169 CPDF that punishes the person who illegally delivers a child to a third party for final custody in exchange for an economic benefit.

[22] In Mexico City's Civil Code, two types of adoptions are available: adoption by single people and adoption by couples, whether married, in common law marriage, or in civil unions. See Arts 390–391 CCDF (stating the requirements that singles and couples, respectively, must meet in order to adopt).

[23] Art 374 CCDF. The child of a married woman cannot be recognised as the child of a man other than her husband unless the child has been disowned by him and a final judgment has ruled that the child is not his child.

[24] Without prejudice to the difference in treatment between men and women: the man, if he contributed with his genetic material, is not required to adopt the child as his recognition of the child is sufficient. (See ch 1 of this book, section II.)

[25] Art 398 CCDF.

Hence the desirability and necessity for the Surrogacy Law for Mexico City finally to enter into force.

iii. Surrogacy Law for Mexico City

a. Brief Explanation of the Parliamentary Situation of the Law

The Surrogacy Law for Mexico City was approved (passed) by the *Asamblea Legislativa del Distrito Federal* (Legislative Assembly of the Federal District) on 30 November 2010, and should have entered into force on 1 January 2011, but was not published in the *Official Gazette*. As set by the authorities, the time fixed by the Legislative Assembly for the entry into force of this Law (1 January 2011) gave no opportunity to make the appropriate legal and medical consultations, and thereby precluded its subsequent publication.

The first Bill, approved on 30 November 2010, was reviewed by the head of government of Mexico City. On 9 November 2011 a new Bill was submitted, considering and contemplating the observations made by the head of government of Mexico City.[26] This new Bill was approved in committees of the Legislative Assembly on 9 December 2011, in order to submit it for approval by the Plenary Session.[27]

On 20 December 2011 the Plenary Session of the Legislative Assembly, instead of passing the Law, approved a 'motion of censure', which means that the Bill must return to the commissions for their consideration.[28] Thus, the text that is analysed in this chapter is not a definitive one. We shall have to wait to see what happens with both Bills.

As the Bill approved on 30 November 2010 and the one submitted on 9 November 2011 are largely the same (they have just a few, albeit important, differences, which are the issues that were modified or added as a result of the observations made by the head of government of Mexico City), I shall go on to analyse the text of the Bill submitted in 9 November 2011, stressing those aspects and rules that are different from the one approved on 30 November 2010.

---

[26] According to Maricela Contreras, President of the Health Committee of the Legislative Assembly, what was sought with the amendments and adjustments to the legislative proposal was to meet the observations made by the head of government of Mexico City, and to include the requests made by civilian organisations on issues of fairness and non-discrimination. Contreras said that the amendments to the Bill aimed at avoiding the possibility of an *acto de inconstitucionalidad* (unconstitutional act) by the Attorney General's Office or the National Commission on Human Rights. *Source*: Website of the Ministry of Health of Mexico City, at <www.salud.df.gob.mx/ssdf/>.

[27] For more information on the difficulties regarding the parliamentary procedure of this Law, see the Preamble to the Bill submitted on 9 November 2011, available at the website of the Legislative Assembly of the Federal District at <www.aldf.gob.mx/>.

[28] The Plenary Session stated, among other reasons, that the head of government's observations were made out of time according to Art 12 second base, II inc. b of the Consitution of Mexico, which lays down a 10-day time limit. The time taken to make the observations (around nine months) also violated Art 48 of the *Estatuto de Gobierno del DF* (Statute of Government of the Federal District) and Art 92 of the *Ley Orgánica de la Asamblea Legislativa del DF* (Organic Law of the Legislative Assembly of the Federal District).

b. Analysis of the Surrogacy Law for Mexico City

Definition

According to the Bill,

> surrogacy will be done through the transfer of human embryos, resulting from the fertilization of an egg and sperm, to a person to carry the pregnancy to term. This process will be done in favour of one or two applicants (intending parent(s)), with whom the child to be born will generate bonds of filiation.

The Bill regulates only what is known as 'gestational surrogacy': the surrogate mother does not contribute her genetic material; such material can be[29] provided by the intending mother or by another woman (a donor).

System—Notary Public and Surrogacy Instrument

The surrogacy agreement will be made in the form of a contract before a notary public, who will be responsible for verifying the compliance with the requirements of the parties who will participate in the surrogacy practice. Thus:

(a) the consent of the parties shall be given before a notary public through a surrogacy instrument that will be elaborated by the Juridic and Legal Services Counsel of the Federal District;

(b) all the parties shall give their consent before the transfer of any embryo;

(c) the surrogacy instrument must provide for the surrogate's obligation to deliver the child after birth to the intending parent(s) and for the intending parent's or parents' obligation to receive him or her, setting a deadline for compliance;

(d) the surrogacy instrument must not contain provisions that contravene international treaties ratified by the Mexican State, or federal and local laws concerning the protection of children and women. It must safeguard the best interests of the child and cannot contain clauses that limit the right of the child or children born as a result of surrogacy to know their identity.

Characteristics

(a) *Altruism.* The Bill emphasises that surrogacy must be altruistic. This requirement is confirmed by the provisions of Article 16 which state that, in order to preserve the altruistic spirit, the surrogate mother should, preferably, be related by blood or affinity to the parties involved in the surrogacy practice, since these cases are most often entered into for emotional reasons.

Notwithstanding the above, the surrogacy agreement may provide for compensation for moral damages and, where appropriate, for the payment of damages for the possible death or permanent disability of the surrogate

---

[29] I say 'can be' because the new Bill submitted in November 2011 does not require the intending parent(s) to provide their genetic material, unlike the previous Bill approved in November 2010.

mother resulting from this practice, in accord with the economic abilities of the intending parent(s).

(b) *Confidentiality.* The Secretary of Health will maintain a register of women (surrogates) and people who want to undergo surrogacy, and must keep confidential the identity of the parties. Furthermore, the attending physician shall maintain professional secrecy regarding the identity of the parties.

Intervention by the Secretary of Health

The Bill provides that before any procedure, the intending parent(s) and the surrogate mother must go to the Secretary of Health to express their intention to carry out surrogacy. The Secretary of Health must make an assessment of their psychological ability to perform this procedure.

If the assessment approves the procedure, the Secretary of Health will issue a certificate to be presented to the notary public.

Judicial Intervention

Any conflict arising from the application of the surrogacy instrument must be resolved by the Family Judge.

In addition, the Family Judge will resolve the situation of the child or children born as a result of surrogacy, according to the rules on parental rights, custody and guardianship established by the Civil Code, in the case of separation or death of one or both intending parent(s).

Medical Intervention

Article 4 clarifies that the practice of surrogacy may only take place in public or private health institutions certified by the competent authority.

With respect to the obligations of physicians, besides acting in accordance with professional secrecy, as noted above, they must inform the involved parties of the medical and biological consequences of the practice and its possible risks.

Before proceeding with the practice, the physician must request from the parties the documents that prove that they comply with the legal and physical requirements. The Bill also stress that physicians cannot proceed without having received the surrogacy instrument.

It is the physician who must certify that:

(a) the intending parent(s) and the surrogate mother are wholly determined to carry out the practice of surrogacy and have received all the necessary information; and

(b) the surrogate mother is in good physical and mental health.

Parties

(1) Surrogate

As noted above, the surrogate mother should, preferably, be related by blood or affinity to one of the parties involved in the surrogacy arrangement. If there is no candidate who meets this condition, any woman who can carry a baby to term may act as a surrogate.

The surrogate mother must not have been pregnant for 365 days prior to embryo implantation, and cannot have participated more than twice as a surrogate.

The notary public must consult the surrogacy register (which must be created under the jurisdiction of the Secretary of Health—see 'Characteristics' above) to verify that the woman who wishes to act as a surrogate mother has not done so before on more than two occasions. On the one hand this requirement protects the surrogate's physical health; on the other hand it ensures that she has no commercial interest in the practice.

The Bill provides that a social worker will conduct a home visit to ensure that the surrogate's home environment is free from violence and is favourable for the proper development of the pregnancy.

As mentioned above, the surrogate mother does not contribute her genetic material.

(2) Intending parent(s)

It is important to note that this issue (who can be an intending parent) has been one of the most hotly debated and controversial aspects of the Bill.

The Bill approved in November 2010 allowed access to surrogacy only to heterosexual couples—married or not—who contribute their genetic material and suffer from a permanent failure or a medical contraindication to being able to gestate. Thus, the following were not included:

(a) single men (the Bill did allow single women if they comply with the requirements set out for the intending mother);
(b) heterosexual couples who cannot contribute their genetic material, or who do not suffer from such a permanent failure or medical contraindication;
(c) homosexual couples.

It is important to emphasise that in December 2009, the Legislative Assembly of the Federal District reformed its Civil Code and redefined marriage to allow same-sex marriage.[30] This change allowed gay couples access to adoption as married couples.[31] The reform was challenged by the Federal Attorney-General's

---

[30] In Mexico City there are now three legal structures for recognising couples, all accessible to both gay and straight couples: (i) civil unions (*sociedades de convivencia*), which are tailored not just for sexual couples but for cohabitants who decide to make a contract to regulate their relationship; (ii) common law marriage (*concubinato*), which is acquired with the passage of time (2 years of cohabitation) or when there is both cohabitation and a child in common, and which is regulated in a manner similar to marriage; and (iii) marriage in a strict legal sense. See Art 146 CCDF (setting out the prerequisites for formal marriage) and Art 291 *bis* (common law marriage); Art 2, *Ley de Sociedad de Convivencia para el Districto Federal* (Law on Civil Union for the Federal District (LSCDF)) (civil unions). See also Madrazo and Vela, above n 5.

[31] As explained above, in Mexico City's Civil Code there are two types of adoption: (i) adoption by single people; and (ii) adoption by couples, whether married, in common law marriage or in civil unions. In both cases, prior to the reform there was no specific prohibition that banned gay couples (or gay single people) from adopting. See Madrazo and Vela, above n

office.[32] As mentioned above, the Supreme Court upheld the reform: same-sex marriage and adoption are both constitutional.[33]

It was understood that after the Supreme Court upheld the reform of the Civil Code for the Federal District regarding same-sex marriage, and after the enactment of the Decree published in the *Official Journal* of the Federation on 10 June 2011 that amends the title of Chapter I of Title I of the Political Constitution of the Mexican United States, incorporating into the Constitution the catalogue of human rights protected by international instruments ratified by Mexico and conferring on them a new hierarchy in the Mexican legal system, those limitations of the Bill approved in November 2010 were discriminatory and in violation of Articles 1 and 4 of the Constitution of Mexico. Thus, under the new Bill submitted in November 2011, the intending parent(s) can be heterosexual or homosexual couples, married or not, or single persons.

Also, the new Bill does not require the intending parent(s) to contribute to the surrogacy with their genetic material or that they have a permanent failure or a medical contraindication to being able to gestate. The elimination of these two requirements by the new Bill submitted in 9 November 2011 has the aim of extending the possibility to be an intending parent(s) to as many people as possible, in order to comply with the rules regarding same-sex marriage and the international human rights instruments ratified by Mexico.

Further, the intending parent(s) must be responsible for all medical expenses until the full recovery of the surrogate, regardless of whether the birth was achieved or not.

Filiation

The filiation of the child born as a result of surrogacy is established with the intending parent(s), and he or she or they will appear on the birth certificate.[34]

The intending parent(s) are the legal parents from the birth of the child. The Bill clarifies that the bonds of filiation are generated at the end of the pregnancy.

---

[32] Acción de inconstitucionalidad 2/2010, SCJN, above n 4.

[33] Regarding marriage, the court's holding rested on two rights: (i) the right to the recognition and protection of one's family; and (ii) the right to the free development of one's personality. For the Court, Art 4, para 1 of the Mexican Constitution, which mandates the legal protection of the family, meant that the law has to protect the family as a social reality and not as an ideal model. From this perspective, same-sex marriage is a new form of relationship that demands recognition. Regarding adoption, the Court held that the best interests of the child were to be determined case by case and not through an *a priori* ban on gay adoption. Furthermore, it held that simply posing the question, with nothing to distinguish one couple from another but their sexual orientation, was discriminatory in itself, and thus the question could not be answered by the Court. See Madrazo and Vela, above n 5.

[34] The child's birth certificate is the document issued by the physician under the terms of the Ley de Salud para el Distrito Federal [Health Law of the Federal District], *Diario oficial de la Federacion* (DOF) (*Official Gazette*) 15-01-1987.

Abortion

The surrogate mother can decide on the termination of pregnancy in the terms established by the criminal and health laws in Mexico City.

In 2007, Mexico City's Assembly once again reformed its criminal code and its health law by redefining the crime of abortion as the interruption of pregnancy after the twelfth week, and establishing that prior to that time, voluntary abortion would be part of the health services granted free of charge by the state.[35] For second- and third-trimester abortions, the reform left untouched the series of exceptions to the rule that abortions constituted criminal conduct.[36]

As mentioned above, the decriminalisation of abortion was challenged before the Supreme Court by both the Federal Attorney-General's Office and the head of the National Commission of Human Rights through two independent *acciones de inconstitucionalidad*.[37] The two main arguments they advanced to strike down the new law were:

(a) that it violated the fetus's right to life; and
(b) that it violated men's rights to procreation and to equality (because it placed the final decision entirely in the hands of women).

The Court decided the issue in August 2008 and found the decriminalisation of abortion to be constitutional.[38]

iv. Rules of Private International Law of Mexico City

The Bill approved in November 2010 required that both the intending parent(s) and surrogate mother be inhabitants of Mexico City. That fact needed to be accredited through a certificate of residence issued by the competent authority.

Although this requirement would have prevented reproductive tourism, it is no longer demanded under the new Bill (9 November 2011).

---

[35] See Art 144 CPDF and Art 16, Health Law of the Federal District.

[36] Art 148 CPDF. The exceptions are: (i) when the pregnancy is the result of rape or an artificial insemination that was not consented to; (ii) when the fetus has a congenital malformation; (iii) when the woman's health is at risk; or (iv) when the pregnancy is the result of imprudence (ie, accident).

[37] Acción de inconstitucionalidad 146/2007, & acumulada SCJN, above n 4.

[38] It did so by focusing on a technical aspect of criminal law—the principle of strict legality—according to which there is no crime unless expressly and clearly stated in a written text. The majority of the Court held that the right to life of a fetus was not enshrined in the Constitution. Rather, the majority found that the State had an obligation to promote and secure the conditions of an already existing life. It found that the question of when life began remained unanswered by the Constitution and the international treaties signed by Mexico. With this, the Court basically reversed its holding from 2002 (Acción de inconstitucionalidad 10/2000, resolved by the Plenary Supreme Court on 29 and 30 January 2002 (Ninth Era)), which had established that the Constitution protected the right to life from the moment of conception. Further—and more importantly—it held that 'the mere existence of a constitutional right does not imply an obligation to criminalise a type of conduct that affects it'. With this, the Court basically determined that enshrining the right to life (even if life begins at conception) does not imply that abortion must be criminalised. See Madrazo and Vela, above n 5.

In Mexico City, private international law rules are set up in the preliminary norms of the Civil Code for the Federal District, but there is no specific rule for international surrogacy cases.

According to general rules, the principle would be that if a Mexican citizen enters into a surrogacy agreement abroad (in a State where surrogacy is legal), according to the Civil Code for the Federal District, if the agreement has been made according to the foreign law that allows surrogacy (Article 13 inc I[39]) and has fulfilled its formalities (Article 13 inc IV[40]), then, in principle, the surrogacy agreement and its consequences/effects[41] should be recognised in Mexico City, unless this constitutes a fraud on the law (Article 15 inc I[42]) or a violation of public policy (Article 15 inc II[43]).

If the Surrogacy Law for Mexico City enters into force, it is understood that if a Mexican citizen enters into a surrogacy agreement abroad (under the foreign law) which also conforms to the provisions of the Surrogacy Law for Mexico City, and then the intending parent(s) seek its recognition (or the recognition of its consequences, eg the recognition of the birth certificate granted in the foreign State recognising the intending parents as legal parents, or the foreign judgment recognising the intending parents as legal parents) in Mexico City, this should be feasible without it being possible to invoke public policy. The public policy grounds might be invoked only if the surrogacy agreement entered into abroad would be contrary to the principles established under the Surrogacy Law for Mexico City, for example if it were a commercial surrogacy agreement. But it might be possible that even in these cases, the surrogacy agreement and its effects/consequences could be admitted or recognised in Mexico City, taking account of the best interests of the child. Public policy could yield to the best interests of the child, which, according to the Surrogacy Law, should be considered paramount.[44] (It should be noted that the Family Judges usually take into account the principle of the best interests of the child in their rulings.)

---

[39] Art 13 inc I CCF—the legal situations validly created in the federal entities of the Republic or in a foreign State under its law should be recognised.

[40] Art 13 inc IV CCDF—the form of legal acts is governed by the law of the place where they are entered into. However, those entered into outside the Federal District, may be attached to the forms prescribed in this Code if the effects of the act will occur in the Federal District.

[41] Eg birth certificate granted in the foreign State recognising the intending parents as legal parents, or foreign judgment recognising the intending parents as legal parents.

[42] Art 15 inc I CCDF—when fundamental principles of Mexican law have been fraudulently evaded, the judge must determine the fraudulent intention of such evasion.

[43] Art 15 inc II CCDF—where the provisions of foreign law or the result of their application are contrary to fundamental principles or institutions of Mexican public policy.

[44] Art 3, Surrogacy Law for Mexico City. It provides that 'best interests of the child' mean 'the paramount consideration that has to be given to the full exercise of the rights of the child or children born as a result of surrogacy and the development of these rights with respect to the rights of any other person, as guiding principles for the development of standards and their implementation in all aspects related to life of the child in the manner specified under the international treaties ratified by Mexico and the laws applicable in the matter'.

III. Mexican Private International Law

The starting point regarding private international law is that there is no specific rule of Mexican private international law for international surrogacy cases in Mexico.

Also, although unofficially one hears of couples who have gone to the United States (or to other States where surrogacy is legal or permitted, often with little or no internal regulation) and entered into surrogacy agreements, there is no official notice of such cases.

The system of sources of Mexican private international law has a dual genesis,[45] ie the conventional[46] rules and the autonomous rules.

Considering the legislative system that prevails in Mexico given its federal structure,[47] it should be noted that there is no consensus in the way that each state has regulated international relations regarding the family, and it is thus possible to find three categories of treatment:[48]

(a) local legislators have regulated the family relations with a foreign element. For example, Mexico City's legislators have prescribed some private international law rules for such situations;

(b) local legislators have chosen to link local regulation of the matter to what is resolved or indicated by the Mexico City legislators (reference to the Civil Code of the Federal District must be interpreted as if referring to the Federal Civil Code). The problem is that state codes have not amended their texts in order to insert the current name of the code. For example, this occurs in the case of marriages in the Civil Codes of Durango[49] or Campeche,[50] or in the case of international adoption in the Civil Code of Coahuila;[51]

(c) local legislators regulate certain parts of family relations, while other parts are delegated to the federal legislature. For example, the civil status and

---

[45] M Rábago Dorbecker, 'Capítulo Tercero. Fuentes del derecho internacional privado' in N González Martín (ed), *Lecciones de derecho internacional privado. Parte general* (Mexico, Porrúa-UNAM, 2007) 100.

[46] Mexico is a party to several treaties, conventions, agreements and accords. Among others: Convention on Elimination of the Requirement of Legalisation of Foreign Public Documents (Apostille) (Hague, 5 October 1961); Inter-American Convention on General Rules of Private International Law (Montevideo, 1979); Inter-American Conventions on Extraterritorial Validity of Foreign Judgments and Arbitrational Awards and On Domicile of Natural Persons in Private International Law (Montevideo, 1979); Inter-American Convention on Letters Rogatory; Inter-American Conventions on Status and Legal Capacity of Judicial Persons in Private International Law and on International Competence for Extraterritorial Validity of Foreign Judgments (La Paz, 1984); United Nations Convention of the Recognition and Enforcement of Foreign Arbitral Awards (1958), etc.

[47] See section II. of the present chapter.

[48] JA Silva. 'Los convenios internacionales relacionados con el derecho de familia: su falta de recepción en el derecho interno mexicano' in *XXVIII Seminario Nacional de Derecho Internacional Privado y Comparado* (Pachuca (Mexico), 2004), publication pending.

[49] Art 156 CCiv Durango.

[50] Art 172 CCiv Campeche.

[51] Art 511 CCiv Coahuila.

capacity of the person are regulated under the state codes, but as regards foreign persons or the marriage of Mexican people celebrated abroad, those issues are delegated by the state codes to the federal regulator. See the Civil Codes of Colima,[52] Nayarit[53] and Puebla,[54] among others.

To sum up, as the states have jurisdiction over family relationships, that gives rise to a number of encodings equal to the number of states that make up the Mexican federation. The same is true for international family relationships.[55]

A proposal to alleviate the normative dispersion that characterises Mexico, partly as a result of its being a federation, is the *Proyecto de Código Modelo de Derecho Internacional Privado* (Project for a Model Code of Private International Law),[56] promoted by the Mexican Academy of Private International and Comparative Law, that took shape after the work sessions conducted at the Academy's Twenty-Ninth National Seminar on Private International and Comparative law, held in Puebla, Mexico, in November 2005.[57]

This Project, with its 2011 amendments,[58] although it does not have a norm that expressly regulates international surrogacy, stipulates rules regarding filiation that could be very useful in a surrogacy case:

Article 20

The constitution of filiation by blood or by artificial insemination, its existence and the right to contest it are governed by the law of the place of the birth of the child. This same rule applies for the disownment of the state of child.

The insemination, its prior acts and those that follow it until the birth are governed by the law of the residence of the biological mother.

If the child was born in a place different from the domicile or residence of the mother or legal representative, the last will apply.

Parenthood relationships are governed by the law of the common domicile of the spouses, and if it does not exist, by the law of the child's residence or place of birth, always taking into account that most favourable to the child.

Article 21

... The effects of filiation are governed by the law of the place of the child's residence.

---

[52] Art 12 CCiv Colima.
[53] Art 12 CCiv Nayarit.
[54] Art 313 CCiv Puebla.
[55] Silva, above n 48.
[56] To view the Project, see 'Proyecto de Código Modelo de Derecho Internacional Privado' (2006) 20 *Revista Mexicana de Derecho Internacional Privado y Comparado* 73–75. Since its publication in 2006, the Project has been under constant review by Drs Pérez Nieto Castro and Silva Silva.
[57] N González Martín, *Familia internacional en Mexico. Adopción, alimentos, restitución, tráfico y trata* (Mexico, Porrúa/UNAM, 2009).
[58] The second version of the Project was presented in the Seminar on Private International and Comparative Law, held in Puebla, Mexico, in 2011.

Article 22

Parental custody, the right to claim it, its suspension and guardianship are governed by the law of the child's residence or by the law of the place of the birth of the child, that most favourable to the child should be applied.

This Project for a Model Code of Private International Law is specifically not intended to draft a single law for all Mexico, but to serve as a model for each state.

In the current system, since there is no law for international surrogacy cases, it would be necessary to resort to general rules.

It is important to stress that Mexican legislation does not establish which law determines filiation. There are no private international law provisions regarding filiation. This means that reference must be made to the general rule of private international law, according to which filiation is governed by the law that regulates civil status, except in those cases in which the *favor fili*, the most favourable law, should be applied. Thus, the conflict rule that would apply would be the domicile rule in some federal entities, while in other federal entities the conflict rule that would apply would be the *lex fori* rule. If surrogacy is regarded as a contract, the conflict rule that would apply would be the law of the contract, which would be the general rules.

With regard to the formal aspects, the form of the surrogacy agreement (the form of the act) would be governed by the law of the place where the act was entered into. It is important to emphasise that all federal entities follow this rule.

On the other hand, as regards the content and effects of the surrogacy agreement, it might be possible to take into account the rule established under Article 13 inc V (CCF) that states that

the legal effects of acts and contracts are governed by the law of the place where they have to be executed, unless the parties have validly designated the applicability of another law.

Thus, it admits autonomy of the will, and in the absence of agreement the surrogacy is governed by the law where its effects take place, provided that the law applicable is not a fraud on the law or contrary to public policy (Article 15 CCF).

Consequently, if the parties choose as the applicable law a foreign law that permits surrogacy (the law of a country where surrogacy is legal), and the agreement complies with the foreign law, in principle the surrogacy agreement and its consequences/effects should be valid in Mexico. Thus, if the intending parent(s) ask for the recognition of the surrogacy agreement (or the recognition of its consequences) in Mexico,[59] this should be feasible unless it is a fraud on the law (Article 15 inc I CCF) or in violation of public policy (Article 15 inc II CCF).

It is important to note that the possibility that the public policy exception could operate depends on each federal entity. In relation to that, the tendency of

---

[59] Or they ask for its recognition before Mexican consular authorities, if this is the case.

Mexico's Supreme Court should be stressed, which, as analysed above, in the last few years has been adopting 'progressive' (liberal) rulings,[60] which suggests that it could rule in favour of surrogacy in a future case.

Also to be considered is the constitutional reform made by Decree, published in the *Official Journal* of the Federation on 10 June 2011, mentioned in section II. C.iii.b. above, that incorporated into the Constitution the catalogue of human rights protected by international treaties to which Mexico is a party. Its importance is that it grants the international treaties on human rights a new constitutional status in the Mexican legal system, thereby strengthening the obligation of every authority of Mexico to know these rights and to respect them. It is considered that this constituti onal reform should have some influence in favour of surrogacy in future rulings.

---

[60] See Acción de inconstitucionalidad 146/2007 & acumulada SCJN; Acción de inconstitucionalidad 2/2010, SCJN. and Amparo directo civil 6/2008, SCJN, explained in section I. above, available at <www.scjn.gob.mx>.

17

The Netherlands

IAN CURRY-SUMNER AND MACHTELD VONK

I. Introduction

The Dutch Government operates a very restrictive policy with respect to commercial surrogacy. Incidents in recent years have led to numerous parliamentary questions being raised in the Second Chamber of the Dutch Parliament. The Minister of Justice has responded to the Dutch Parliament by commissioning research to be conducted into the nature and scope of the problems related to commercial surrogacy and the unlawful placement of children. The aim thereby is to ensure that more clarity can be gleaned as to what actually occurs in the countries where the possibilities are greater than in The Netherlands, as well as providing information with regard to the Dutch response upon the return of the commissioning parents to The Netherlands.

From April 2010 until January 2011, researchers from the Utrecht Centre for European Research into Family Law (UCERF) at the Molengraaff Institute for Private Law of Utrecht University conducted the research commissioned by the Minister of Justice.[1] The resulting report was published on 2 March 2011.[2] The report contains an in-depth study of Dutch criminal and civil law on the consequences of surrogacy, and a detailed analysis of the way Dutch private international law does and could regard international surrogacy. Furthermore, it contains reports from four jurisdictions that allow surrogacy, namely, California (USA), India, Greece and Ukraine, and eight reports from European countries that are faced with the same problems as The Netherlands, namely, Belgium, England, Germany, France, Norway, Poland, Spain and Sweden. In these country reports, answers are provided as to whether specific rules exist regulating surrogacy and which measures have been adopted to ensure the enforcement of those rules.

In legal literature a distinction is drawn between different types of surrogacy. High-technology surrogacy makes use of in vitro fertilisation (IVF) and always

---

[1] The research team consisted of Professor Katharina Boele-Woelki (chair of the research group), Ian Curry-Sumner, Wendy Schrama and Machteld Vonk.

[2] This contribution is largely based on that report: K Boele-Woelki, I Curry-Sumner, W Schrama and M Vonk, *Draagmoederschap en illegale opneming van kinderen* (The Hague, WODC, 2011).

requires the involvement of a reproductive expert. This form of surrogacy offers commissioning parents the possibility to conceive a child that is genetically related to both of them. This is not, however, a requirement. Alongside IVF-surrogacy, low-technology surrogacy is also possible. In this case the surrogate is always genetically related to the child. The commissioning father may or may not be genetically related, depending upon whether the couple have used his sperm or that of a donor.[3] In low-technology surrogacy the egg will be fertilised by means of artificial insemination. Furthermore, parties may be involved in do-it-yourself surrogacy, where the child is conceived by natural means or self-insemination. In this last scenario the child could be genetically related to the surrogate and her husband. Another important distinction concerns the difference between altruistic and commercial surrogacy. In general, it would appear difficult to draw a distinct line between these two forms of surrogacy arrangements. In both cases, financial payments will be made. However, the financial payments in commercial surrogacy arrangements are often (if not always) concerned with profit, whereas in altruistic surrogacies the main object is to help another couple have a child.

In this chapter, Dutch law on surrogacy and the legal consequences of surrogacy for the intended parents, the surrogate mother and above all the child will be discussed, in the context both of domestic surrogacy and of cross-border surrogacy. In order to illustrate the legal rules, we introduce a Dutch married heterosexual couple, Charlotte and Michael, who dearly wish for a child of their own. They have undergone fertility treatment, but to no avail. They have considered international adoption, but were daunted by the intense screening and the subsequent long waiting period. A close friend, Tania, has offered to become their surrogate mother. This is the start of a long and uncertain journey towards possible parenthood.

II. Domestic Surrogacy

The first step Charlotte and Michael take is to collect information about the legal consequences of a surrogacy arrangement for the child that Tania wants to bear for them. They face many complicated legal issues regarding the validity and enforceability of the agreement they intend to draw up with Tania, the amount of money they may pay her for her services and, most importantly, the question of acquiring parental status.

---

[3] Given the present guidelines issued by the medical profession on surrogate motherhood, it seems very unlikely that hospitals knowingly provide low-technology surrogacy treatment. This means that in a case of domestic surrogacy (which means there is no international element in the procedure), the couple will either have had IVF-surrogacy treatment or been involved in some form of do-it-yourself surrogacy.

A. Legal Issues: Contracts and Payment

There has been a lot of discussion regarding the validity of surrogacy contracts in The Netherlands.[4] Such contracts may contain many different kinds of clauses, ranging from the surrogate mother agreeing that she will not smoke during the pregnancy, to her agreement to abort the child if serious birth defects are discovered.[5] However, the main clause concerns the obligation of the surrogate mother to surrender the child to the commissioning parents after the birth. Whereas not all authors agree on the validity of the subsidiary clauses and the possibility for damages if the surrogate mother does not fulfil her obligations, they all agree that the main clause is void and cannot be enforced.[6] Under Dutch law, juridical acts (including agreements) that violate mandatory statutory provisions or are contrary to good morals will result in the agreement being regarded null and void, which means that it is treated as if it had never came into being and thus cannot be enforced.[7] Contracts concerning the surrender of children after birth are considered to be a breach of good morals. Contracting about the legal position of children, for instance who will be the child's legal parent, may violate the mandatory statutory provisions of parentage law and parental responsibility, which would render such a contract illegal and void.[8] Nevertheless, there are authors who propose that under certain conditions surrogacy contracts should play a role in the process of transferring parental rights from the surrogate mother to the intended couple.[9]

At present, however, adults cannot legally enter into contracts concerning the status of legal parenthood if this deviates from mandatory statutory provisions, and they cannot be obliged on the basis of a contractual provision to surrender 'their' child to the other contractual party. This does not mean that such contracts are completely without meaning. For instance, one of the licensed IVF centres that

[4] AML Broekhuijsen-Molenaar, 'Geoorloofdheid van draagmoederschap naar Nederlands (wenselijk) recht' in K Boele-Woelki and M Oderkerk, *De (on)geoorloofdheid van het draagmoederschap in rechtsvergelijkend perspectief* (Antwerpen, Intersentia, 1999); JBM Vranken, 'Contractualisering en draagmoederschap' (1997) 4 *Tijdschrift voor Privaatrecht* 1751; K Boele-Woelki and M Oderkerk, *De (on)geoorloofdheid van het draagmoederschap in rechtsvergelijkend perspectief* (Antwerpen, Intersentia, 1999); JH Nieuwenhuis, 'Promises, promises' (2001) 37 *Nederlands Juristenblad* 1795; SM Dermout, *De eerste logeerpartij: Hoogtechnologische draagmoedershap in Nederland*, PhD Thesis (Groningen, 2001); P Vlaardingerbroek, 'Mens en maatschappij: Draagmoederschap: een gecompliceerde constructie' (2003) 52 *Ars Aequi* 171; M Van den Berg and C Buijssen, 'Hoogtechnologisch draagmoederschap, De techniek staat voor niets, nu het recht nog' (2004) *Nederlands Juristenblad* 724; JG Klijnsma, 'De verzakelijking van het menselijk lichaam' (2008) 1 *Ars Aequi* 11.

[5] See, eg, K Boele-Woelki and M Oderkerk, above n 4, 23, for a list of such clauses; see also P Vlaardingerbroek, above n 4.

[6] For an overview of the discussion, see P Vlaardingerbroek, above n 4.

[7] Art 3:40(2) Dutch Civil Code (DCC).

[8] See Asser-De Boer 2006, No 696. With regard to parental responsibility, see for instance Art 1:121 lid 3 DCC.

[9] M Van den Berg and C Buijssen, above n 4; JBM Vranken, above n 4; and MJ Vonk, *Children and their Parents: A comparative study of the legal position of children with regard to their intentional and biological parents in English and Dutch law* (Antwerpen, Intersentia, 2007) 276–77.

recently opened a surrogacy centre, requires the parties to draw up a contract. The contract itself cannot alter the legal status of the parties involved, but the idea is that it can give a court supportive evidence about the intentions of the parties involved at the time the contract was drawn up, and thus may facilitate decisions in the adoption process.[10]

Regarding the issue of payment, it is difficult to acquire precise information. It is clear that Charlotte and Michael are allowed to reimburse Tania for the expenses that she makes with regard to the pregnancy, but how much more they may pay her is unclear. The regulations in the Dutch Criminal Code ('DCrC') relating to 'commercial' surrogacy concern acting as a go-between for surrogate and intentional parents, and not so much the issue of payment to the surrogate mother. The Government wants to avoid the coming into being of commercial go-betweens or surrogacy brokers. The legislation was specifically not aimed at making surrogates and intended parents liable to criminal prosecution.

B. Legal Issues: Transfer of Full Parental Status

The transfer of full parental rights in surrogacy arrangements will not occur against the will of any of the parties involved. This means that the surrogate mother has no legal duty to hand over the child, nor are the intended parents under a legal duty to accept the child. This also applies where a contract has been drawn up in which parties have agreed on the placement of the child in the family of the intended parents. If the child is not yet six months old, the intended parents may take the child into their home only with the consent of the Child Protection Board.[11]

Under Dutch law, the woman who gives birth to the child is the child's legal mother, whether or not she is also the child's genetic mother.[12] This is a mandatory statutory provision from which parties cannot deviate.[13] Whether the child born to the surrogate mother will automatically have a legal father depends on the surrogate's marital status.[14] It will be obvious that the surrogate mother's marital status is of great relevance where the transfer of parental rights to the intended parents is concerned. The marital status of the intended parents may also play a role where the transfer of parental status is concerned. [15] In the discussion below,

---

[10] For an overview of how Dutch courts have taken contracts into consideration when judging on the voluntary transfer of rights from the surrogate mother to the commissioning parents, see MJ Vonk, 'The role of formalised and non-formalised intentions in legal parent-child relationships in Dutch law' (2008) 4(2) *Utrecht Law Review*.

[11] Art 1:241(3) DCC and Art 1 Foster Children Act (*Pleegkinderenwet*).

[12] Art 1:198 DCC.

[13] Rb Den Haag, 11 December 2007, *LJN* BB9844.

[14] Art 1:199 DCC.

[15] However, as is clear from the policy guidelines of the surrogacy centre established at the VU Medical Centre (VUMC), only married intended parents at present have access to gestational surrogacy services.

the starting point will be the placement of the child in the family of the intended parents. This means that there is still agreement between the surrogate mother and the intended parents that the child will grow up with the intended parents. Where relevant, the genetic connection between child and intended parents will be discussed. Table 1 shows the possibilities for the transfer of parental rights. First the situation will be discussed where the surrogate mother is married and then where she is unmarried.

Table 1: Transfer of Full Parental Status

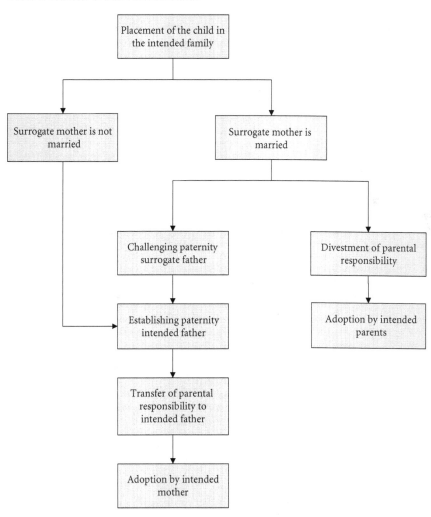

i. Surrogate Mother is Married: The Child has Two Legal Parents at Birth

The surrogate mother will be the child's legal mother, and if she is married her husband will be the child's legal father[16]; both will have parental responsibility for the child by operation of law.[17] In the very unlikely situation that the surrogate mother's husband did not consent to the conception of the child, he may challenge his paternity.[18] Unless the surrogate father was completely unaware of fact that his wife was acting as a surrogate for another couple, he is highly unlikely to succeed. In most surrogacy arrangements the surrogate's husband will play a role. In cases of surrogacy in combination with IVF, the requirements are such that the surrogate mother's husband's consent is required.[19] In a recent case the paternity of the surrogate's husband was challenged in the name of the child through an *ad hoc* guardian (*bijzonder curator*). The child may challenge the paternity of any non-biological father and is not bound by the consent of adults or their marital status.

All this means that full parental status can be transferred to the intended parents only through joint adoption. However, before the child can be adopted by the intended parents, the surrogate parent(s) will first have to be divested of their parental responsibility.[20] Divestment of parental responsibility is a measure of child protection used in cases where parents are unable or unfit to look after their child.[21] Parents cannot apply to the court to be divested, only the Child Care and Protection Board and the Public Prosecution Service can apply to the court to have parents divested of their responsibility.[22] In the late 1990s there had been discussion in Parliament whether parents themselves should not be given a right to apply for divestment, but the Minister of Justice at that time was against such a measure as it would introduce the possibility for parents to relinquish their parental rights.[23]

The outcome of a divestment procedure is uncertain as the Dutch Supreme Court has not yet had the opportunity to decide on divestment in the context of surrogacy.[24] However, decisions by various courts of appeal allow for the

---

[16] Art 1:198 DCC (mother) and Art 1:199(a) DCC (father).

[17] Art 1:251(1) DCC.

[18] Art 1:200(3) DCC.

[19] *Richtlijn hoogtechnologisch draagmoederschap* [*Guidelines on high-technology surrogacy*], NVOG 1998, para 3.3. VUMC treatment protocol: 'If the surrogate mother has a partner, the partner has to give his written agreement to the surrogate mother's decision to carry a surrogate pregnancy.' See <www.vumc.nl/communicatie/folders/folders/IVF/Hoog-technologisch%20draagmoederschap%20. pdf>.

[20] Art 1:1228(1)(g) and Art 1:266 DCC.

[21] LE Kalkman-Bogerd, 'Ontheffing en draagmoederschap' (1998) 9 *Tijdschrift voor Familie- en Jeugdrecht* 198.

[22] Art 1:267 DCC.

[23] Eg, *Dutch Second Chamber* 1994/1995 answers by the then Secretary of State to questions submitted by Member of Parliament Boris Dittrich, attachment 622 to Parliamentary Debates.

[24] The Dutch Supreme Court did however judge in a case unrelated to surrogacy that parents may be unable or unfit to take care of a specific child (HR 29 June 1984 *NJ* 1984/767). This judgment has been used by courts of appeal to justify divestment in surrogacy cases.

divestment of the surrogate parents on the ground that they are unable or unfit to care for this particular child since they did not intend to have it for themselves.[25] If the divestment procedure is successful, the intended parents may be attributed with joint guardianship, which is very similar to parental responsibility. Normally, when parents are divested of parental responsibility, guardianship will be attributed to an institution for family guardianship.[26] However, in the surrogacy cases that have been published, guardianship was attributed to the intended parents if the court considered this to be the best possible solution for the child concerned. If the intended parents have taken care of the child together for a year, they may file for an adoption order with the court, provided they have been living together for three years on the day the adoption request is filed. There is no special post-surrogacy adoption procedure, which means that the normal criteria for adoption apply in such cases. These criteria require the adoption to be in the child's best interests and state that adoption cannot take place if the child's parents object. Only in a very limited number of circumstances may a court disregard parental objections.[27] The court may, for instance, disregard a parental objection if the child has not lived with the parents since its birth. In an IVF-surrogacy pilot that took place in the 1990s, all the children were adopted by the intended parents a year after their birth.[28] No legal problems were reported. Nevertheless, in particular where parents have not involved the Child Protection Board before the birth of the child, transferring parental rights from the surrogate parents to the intended parents may be a lengthy procedure of which the outcome is uncertain.

ii. Surrogate Mother is Not Married: Child has One Legal Parent at Birth

If the surrogate mother is not married, the child will have only one legal parent by operation of law: the surrogate mother. She will also be the only holder of parental responsibility. The intended father may recognise the child with the surrogate mother's consent. Once the intended father has acquired the status of legal parent through recognition, he may apply for sole parental responsibility, to the exclusion of the surrogate mother.[29] The intended father can file such an application only if the surrogate mother is the sole holder of parental responsibility.[30] The intended mother may subsequently adopt the child after she has been taking care of that child with the intended father for a year and where all the other criteria for adoption have been met.

---

[25] Hof Amsterdam, 19 February 1998, *NJ Kort* 1998/32 and Hof 's Gravenhage, 21 August 1998, *NJ* 1998, 865.

[26] Art 1:275 DCC.

[27] Art 1:228(2) DCC.

[28] SM Dermout, *De eerste logeerpartij: Hoogtechnologische draagmoedershap in Nederland*, PhD Thesis (Groningen, 2001).

[29] Art 1:253c DCC.

[30] Dutch law is ambivalent on this point; an in-depth discussion of this issue may be found in MJ Vonk, above n 9, ch 6 on partially genetic primary families.

It is unclear whether the unmarried intended mother will be attributed with parental responsibility by operation of law through partner adoption. If one follows the system of the law regarding parental responsibility, joint parental responsibility does not come about by operation of law for cohabiting couples as a result of adoption. However, in particular in the case of joint adoption, it would be rather awkward to attribute parental responsibility to only one of the adoptive parents, while the other can obtain it only through registration in the parental responsibility register (as is normally the case for cohabiting parents). In the case of partner adoption, it might be more defensible not to attribute parental responsibility to the adopting partner by operation of law, although it might well be contrary to the adopter's expectations.[31]

C. Surrogacy in Practice

Charlotte and Michael's first stop is the only hospital that offers IVF-surrogacy treatment in The Netherlands: VU Medical Centre in Amsterdam.[32] The hospital offers such treatment in accordance with the legal and professional framework set out in ministerial guidelines and the *Guidelines on IVF-surrogacy* issued by the Dutch Society for Obstetrics and Gynecology.[33] These *Guidelines* are based on the IVF Regulation Statement issued by the Government in 1997,[34] which allows for IVF-surrogacy to take place under very strict conditions in one of the 18 licensed IVF clinics. The 1997 IVF Regulation Statement determines that IVF-surrogacy must take place in accordance with the *Guidelines on IVF-surrogacy*[35] of the Dutch Society for Obstetrics and Gynaecology. These *Guidelines* require IVF clinics to draw up their own protocols regarding IVF surrogacy.

The *Guidelines* contain a number of requirements to be met by the surrogate mother (Tania) and a number of requirements to be met by the intended mother (Charlotte) and her partner (Michael). When discussing the requirements for surrogates and intended parents, it is very important to make a distinction between IVF-surrogacy, which at present is carried out only at the Amsterdam VU Medical Centre, and surrogacy that takes place out of sight of the reproductive experts.

---

[31] J Kok, 'Gezamenlijk gezag en voorkinderen' (2006) *Tijdschrift voor Familie- en Jeugdrecht* 209, who refers to JE Doek, *Losbladige personen- en familierecht* (Titel 14, aant 2A bij art 1:251 DCC) (Deventer, Kluwer, 2006) Titel 14, aant 2A for Art 1:251 DCC.

[32] In the early 1990s a trial was started to study whether or not surrogacy should be allowed as a means to help a certain group of infertile couples to have children of their own (SM Dermout, above n 4). The intake centre that was established as a result of this trial was forced to close in July 2004, as Dutch IVF clinics turned out to be unwilling to participate in gestational surrogacy. However, in April 2006 one of the Dutch-licensed IVF clinics announced that it would make gestational surrogacy services available to married couples (VUMC, 6 April 2006).

[33] *Hoogtechnologisch draagmoederschap*, Richtlijn Nederlandse Vereniging voor Obstetrie en Gynaecologie, No 18 January 1999, at <www.nvog.nl/> (*Guidelines on IVF-surrogacy* by the Dutch Society for Obstetrics and Gynaecology).

[34] Planningsbesluit in-vitrofertilisatie, Staatscourant 1998/95, 14–18.

[35] *Guidelines*, above n 33.

For the latter group there are no requirements, because do-it-yourself surrogacy is unregulated.

i. IVF-Surrogacy

One of the most important requirements listed in the *Guidelines* is that IVF-surrogacy treatment may be provided only for intended parents whose own genetic material (the woman's eggs and the man's sperm) can be used. A direct consequence of this requirement is the fact that only heterosexual couples are eligible for IVF-surrogacy in The Netherlands. Furthermore, intended parents have to bring their own surrogate mother, preferably a relative or a close friend, since advertising in the context of surrogacy or bringing intended parents and surrogate mothers together is a criminal offence.[36] Before IVF-surrogacy treatment is provided, both the surrogate mother and the intended parents will have to undergo psychological screening and be informed of their legal position regarding the child after its birth.

The *surrogate mother* will at least have to meet the following criteria: she may not be over 44 years of age, must be in good health, have given birth to one or more children for herself and regard her own family as complete. Her previous pregnancies and deliveries must have been uncomplicated, she must have a strong personality, a strong desire to provide this service to the intended parents, and she must be able and willing to surrender the child after birth. Both the surrogate mother and her partner need to be Dutch nationals, live in The Netherlands and be fluent in the Dutch language.

The *intended mother* must be incapable of carrying a pregnancy to term, either because she has no or a non-functioning uterus, or because a pregnancy would endanger her life. She may not be older than 40 years of age at the time of the IVF treatment. Moreover, the Dutch Child Care and Protection Board, which is involved in the whole process from the beginning, requires proof that the intended parents do not have a criminal record, as this may frustrate the transfer of parental status to the intended parents at a later stage.

Charlotte and Michael meet all the criteria, but their prospective surrogate mother, Tania, delivered her first child by C-section and therefore does not meet the 'uncomplicated pregnancy and delivery' requirement. Charlotte and Michael are willing to forgo the possibility of having a child genetically related to both of them, as this seems impossible in The Netherlands, but Tania has problems with giving up her own genetic child. Egg donation in combination with surrogacy is not allowed in The Netherlands (in this case Tania could give birth to a child conceived with a donor egg). Charlotte and Michael find no one else among their friends and family willing to be a surrogate and carry their genetic child or give up her own genetic child.

---

[36] See for more detailed information SM Dermout, H Van der Wiel, P Heintz, K Jansen and W Ankum, 'Non-commercial surrogacy: an account of patient management in the first Dutch centre for IVF Surrogacy, from 1997 to 2004' (2010) 25(2) *Human Reproduction* 443.

ii. Advertising for a Surrogate

Charlotte and Michael consider advertising for a surrogate mother on the Internet, but soon they discover this to be illegal. A number of different aspects of surrogacy are illegal in The Netherlands. Table 2 indicates the relevant provisions that might be utilised in criminal proceedings.

In the end they search the Internet and find there are possibilities for them in a number of foreign jurisdictions, such as Ukraine, India and California. They go to their chosen destination, and find a surrogate mother who gives birth to their

Table 2: Table of Criminal Provisions in Surrogacy Context

Criminal provision	Maximum fine	Maximum prison sentence
Art 151a DCrC Illegal mediation for placement of child	€7,600	6 months
Art 442a DCrC Illegal placement of a child younger than 6 months	€3,800	3 weeks
Art 151b DCrC Mediation and publicising wish for surrogacy	€19,000	1 year
Art 151c DCrC Mediation and promotion of abandoning a child	€7,600	6 months
Art 236 DCrC Fraud in relation to status	€19,000	5 years
Art 225 DCrC Misrepresentation	€76,000	5 years
Art 228 DCrC False declaration with regard to birth by doctor or midwife	€19,000	3 years
Art 278 DCrC (International) human trafficking	€76,000	12 years
Art 279 DCrC Removal of minor from parental authority	€19,000	6 years
Art 20 Foster Child Act Placement of child without notification (Art 5 Foster Child Act)	€3,800	In cases of repeat offending within 2 years, a prison sentence may be imposed (2 months)

child. The question then arises how The Netherlands deals with the couple upon their return.

III. Cross-border Surrogacy

A. Introduction

The question arises what happens when a Dutch couple return to The Netherlands with a child conceived through surrogacy. At this stage a distinction should be made based upon the legal procedure that has taken place abroad. Although the scenario utilised in this chapter focuses on the judicial determination of parentage coupled with the subsequent issuance of an amended birth certificate, there are jurisdictions and situations in which surrogacy arrangements ultimately lead to the issuance of a judicial adoption order. Accordingly, the applicable private international law rules can and often will be very different. Nonetheless, the rules applicable to these different procedures will not all be dealt with here. This chapter will concentrate on the situation of the vast majority of surrogacy cases entering into The Netherlands, namely, on the basis of the alleged creation of legal familial ties, ie parentage.

B. Variety of Possible Procedures

i. *Initial Contact with Dutch Authorities Abroad*

The diversity of the situations in which surrogacy arrangements come to light negates the possibility of dealing with all cases in depth in this chapter. However, it is possible to illustrate the variety of routes along which surrogacy cases may come to the attention of the Dutch authorities. One possibility is that the case first arises outside The Netherlands at the Dutch Consulate. Roughly speaking, these cases may be divided into three main categories:

  (a) *Passport application.* The Dutch commissioning parents may wish to apply for a Dutch passport. In this scenario, the Dutch commissioning parents will argue that the relationship of parentage established abroad has resulted in the child acquiring Dutch nationality. Although such a request must be submitted to the Dutch Consulate or Embassy abroad, it is ultimately the Dutch Ministry of Foreign Affairs in The Hague that is competent to issue the passport. The application of the Dutch rules on private international law is, however, executed in the first instance by the consular registrar abroad.
  (b) *Residence permit.* Dutch commissioning parents may also wish to apply for a provisional permission to remain in The Netherlands (the so-called

machtiging tot voorlopig verblijf (MVV)). This is necessary, however, only if the child possesses the nationality of a country with an MVV obligation.[37] The United States of America is not one of these countries, and so these requests are not received with regard to children with American citizenship (ie all children born on US soil).

(c) *Short stay visa.* Dutch commissioning parents may also wish to request a short stay visa. This visa is also known as a 'tourist visa' and is only issued via the Dutch Immigration and Naturalisation Service (*Immigratie en Naturalisatie Dienst* (IND)).

In short, the IND or the consular registrar will always be the first authority to assess any request made by Dutch commissioning parents abroad, irrespective of whether this request concerns an issue relating to nationality or immigration. The relevant statutory rules applied by the various civil servants in these cases are always the same, namely:

— Articles 92–101, Book 10, Dutch Civil Code, previously contained in Private International Law (Parentage) Act (in Dutch: *Wet Conflictenrecht Afstamming* (hereinafter Wca))[38]
— Articles 103–111, Book 10, Dutch Civil Code, previously contained in Private International Law (Adoption) Act (in Dutch: *Wet Conflictenrecht Adoptie* (hereinafter Wcad))[39]
— Placement of Foreign Children for Adoption Act (in Dutch: *Wet Opneming van Buitenlandse Kinderen ter Adoptie* (hereinafter Wobka)).

ii. Initial Contact with Authorities in The Netherlands

Alongside the procedures that may be started abroad, there are also situations in which a surrogacy arrangement may surface after the Dutch commissioning parents have returned to The Netherlands, without prior contact with Dutch consular services abroad. In these situations, initial contact is with the Registrar of Births, Deaths, Marriages and Registered Partnerships ('the Registrar') in a municipality in The Netherlands. This can happen in the following situations:

(a) If the child possesses the nationality of a country that does not have an MVV obligation (eg the United States of America) and has obtained valid travel

---

[37] On the basis of §4.1.1, Part B, Chapter 1, Aliens Circular 2000 (*Vreemdelingencirculaire 2000*), an application for the issuance of a residence permit will not be rejected on the basis of Art 17(1) of the Aliens Act (*Vreemdelingenwet*) as due to the absence of an MVV, if the child has the nationality of one of the following countries: Australia, Canada, Japan, Liechtenstein, New Zealand, Vatican City, the USA and South Korea. (This is also the case for citizens of the European Union and the Schengen Area.)

[38] As of 1 January 2012, these rules will be codified in Title 5, Book 10, DCC (namely, the codification of private international law).

[39] As of 1 January 2012, these rules will be codified in Title 6, Book 10, DCC (namely, the codification of private international law).

documentation from that country (eg a passport),[40] the child may enter The Netherlands without prior contact with Dutch authorities abroad.

(b) The commissioning parents may also arrive in The Netherlands from a country within the Schengen Area.[41] This may happen, for example, when a Greek–Dutch couple travel to Greece and conceive a child through the legally-available surrogacy possibilities there.[42] According to Greek law, the commissioning parents would be the legal parents of the child, whereby the child would obtain Greek nationality. Accordingly, the commissioning parents would be permitted to travel with the child without an MVV. Furthermore, the commissioning parents would be able to travel freely within the Schengen Area without prior consultation with the Dutch consulate.

Whether the child will subsequently be granted permanent residency will depend on the individual circumstances. However, the fact that the child is now in The Netherlands plays an important role in the subsequent approach of the Dutch judiciary.

iii. Summary

According to the given circumstances, the question whether the commissioning parents have become legal parents of a child conceived by means of a surrogacy arrangement can present itself in a variety of different settings. Furthermore, the request made by the commissioning parents may also arise with respect to an application for a Dutch passport,[43] the registration of a foreign birth certificate[44] or the determination of child maintenance.[45] On the basis of research into the law of California, Greece, India and Ukraine,[46] it is clear that commissioning parents involved in a surrogacy arrangement in one of these jurisdictions can return to The Netherlands with a variety of different documents, for example an original birth certificate, an amended birth certificate, a judicial decision, an administrative decree or an adoption order. Nevertheless, despite the variety of situations, legal questions and documents, the same Dutch rules will apply in all cases. Due to space restrictions, in this chapter attention will be paid only to the situation in which the commissioning parents return to The Netherlands and allege that they are already the legal parents of the child as result of the rules of parentage. We therefore shall not deal with the situation in which the parents have adopted their child abroad.

---

[40] The USA utilises the *ius soli* principle, meaning that all children born on American soil acquire American citizenship: 8 USC §1401.

[41] These countries are also exempt from the obligation to obtain an MVV. See §4.1.1, Part B, Chapter 1, Aliens Circular 2000, in combination with §2.2, Section B, Chapter 10, Aliens Circular 2000.

[42] K Boele-Woelki *et al*, above n 2, 137–43.

[43] Eg, HR (Supreme Court) 27 May 2005 *LJN*: AS5109 en HR 28 April 2006, *LJN*: AU9237.

[44] Eg, Rb's-Gravenhage 21 June 2010, *LJN* BN1330.

[45] K Saarloos, *European private international law on Legal parentage? Thoughts on a European instrument implementing the principle of mutual recognition in legal parentage* (Maastricht, Océ, 2010) 210.

[46] K Boele-Woelki *et al*, above n 2, 91–162.

It is generally the case that commissioning parents who utilised proceedings, for example in California, will possess a judicial determination of parentage (so-called *judgment of parentage*), as well as an amended or original birth certificate. If the commissioning parents allege that parentage has already been established abroad, the steps they are required to take will depend on whether the alleged parentage has been established abroad by virtue of a legal fact (eg birth) or legal act (eg recognition) (both issues discussed in (section C), or in a judicial decision (section D). In the following sections the rules with regard to these different situations will be dealt with, in order to explain how Dutch law currently deals with parentage that has been established abroad in surrogacy cases.

C. Confirmation of Alleged Parentage: Legal Acts or Facts

i. General Criteria

Due to the lack of specific private international law rules in cases of surrogacy, reference must be made to the general rules laid down in Book 10 of the Dutch Civil Code, previously contained in the Private International Law (Parentage) Act (Wca). Article 10:101 DCC stipulates the conditions that must be satisfied in order to recognise a foreign legal act or fact in The Netherlands. Before dealing with the criteria themselves, it is important to appreciate that two different situations fall within the purview of this provision, namely, legal facts (*rechtsfeiten*) and legal acts (*rechtshandelingen*).

First, as already described above, Dutch commissioning parents may return to The Netherlands with a birth certificate according to which they are the legal parents of the child. The birth certificate would appear to provide *prima facie* evidence of legal parentage. In California the birth certificate *may* refer to an underlying judicial decision, namely, the judgment on parentage, but this is not always the case. The question is whether this 'legal fact' that has been recorded on the birth certificate can be recognised in The Netherlands according to the criteria laid down in Article 10:101 DCC. The birth certificate in this sense is to be regarded as confirmation of a legal fact. The second scenario that falls within the ambit of this provision is that of the legal act. An example is the recognition of a child by a man. The recognition also ultimately leads to the acquisition of a formal confirmation of the act that has taken place. In The Netherlands, for example, recognition by the father of a child leads to the acquisition of a deed or certificate of recognition.

The criteria that apply in both situations are that the deed or certificate must:

(a) have been issued by a competent authority;
(b) have been issued abroad;
(c) be laid down in a legal document;
(d) have been made in accordance with local law; and
(e) not be contrary to Dutch public policy.

The majority of these conditions do not raise specific issues within the context of surrogacy, with the exception of two aspects in particular, namely, that the deed or certificate must have been issued 'in accordance with local law' and that recognition of the deed must not be contrary to Dutch public policy.

ii. 'In Accordance with Local Law'

A Dutch civil servant confronted with the question whether a foreign deed can be recognised in The Netherlands will first need to determine whether the legal familial ties have been created in accordance with foreign law. With respect to this question, it would appear that the civil servant must determine whether the legal facts have been registered in accordance with the rules applicable in the relevant jurisdiction. Generally speaking, the civil servant is to assume that this is the case, and only when the civil servant has 'sufficient doubt' that this is not the case can he or she request further supplementary evidence to support the claims made in the foreign deed.[47] With respect to the criterion of 'sufficient doubt', it is important that two questions be answered separately. First, what circumstances can give rise to 'sufficient doubt'? Secondly, what steps need to be taken once the civil servant has established that he or she has sufficient doubt?

With respect to the first question, one must refer to the general starting point in relation to the recognition of foreign deeds, namely, that the Dutch civil servant should display trust when confronted with foreign documents. The civil servant can determine that he or she has 'sufficient doubt' only on the basis of objective indications to the contrary. It is also necessary to know in relation to what the Dutch civil servant may have 'sufficient doubt'. The sufficient doubt in this context must relate to the correct application of the rules applicable in the jurisdiction in which the deed or certificate was issued. Accordingly, a distinction must be made between jurisdictions in which surrogacy is permitted and jurisdictions that do not permit surrogacy.

If a jurisdiction permits surrogacy arrangements, and furthermore also permits commissioning parents to be registered on the original birth certificate, then a birth certificate upon which Dutch commissioning parents have been registered as the legal parents has been issued in compliance with the applicable rules of the jurisdiction issuing the deed. In Ukraine, for example, it is permitted for a birth certificate to be issued to commissioning parents, as long as one of the parents is genetically related to the child.[48] In this situation, the civil servant must determine whether he or she has doubt that the deed or certificate has been issued contrary to the proper observance of this rule. The fact that the civil servant thinks that the persons registered on the birth certificate have used a surrogate is not a sufficient ground (with regard to this condition) to refuse recognition of the

---

[47] Vonken (Personen- en Familierecht. Het internationale afstammingsrecht), Art 10 Wca, note 1, p 2173.

[48] K Boele-Woelki *et al*, above n 2, 159.

birth certificate. This may, however, nonetheless provide sufficient grounds for non-recognition with respect to the application of the public policy exception.[49]

If, however, the foreign jurisdiction does not permit surrogacy, and the civil servant has sufficient objective indications that the commissioning parents have used a surrogate, then the civil servant may take the necessary steps to discover whether the deed has been drawn up in accordance with the locally applicable rules. The question arises, however, of when the civil servant can state that he has sufficient objective indications to believe that the local law has not been observed. This question can best be answered using an illustration. If, for example, two white Caucasian commissioning parents wish to register their child in a Dutch municipality, and the child is not Caucasian but instead of a different ethnic origin, then the civil servant will have sufficient objective indications to doubt that the local rules have been followed if, according to local law, both commissioning parents need to be genetically related to the child.

Once the civil servant has determined that he has sufficient doubt to question whether the local rules have been applied correctly, the next question is which steps he or she can then take. The normal procedure will be for the civil servant to request supporting documentation. According to Ukrainian law, for example, the registration of the child in the registers of the local municipality requires a certificate in which the genetic relationship of the child is determined with respect to at least one parent. This certificate does not, however, state that use has been made of a surrogate. The commissioning parents will generally also be in possession of a surrogacy contract wherein all the agreements between the commissioning parents and surrogate parents are set out. Should the commissioning parents not possess such a contract (or refuse to hand it over), it would seem very difficult on this ground to determine that the parents have used a surrogacy arrangement. Nonetheless, the inability to deny recognition on the basis that local law regulations have been followed does not exclude the subsequent possibility of non-recognition on grounds of public policy.

iii. Grounds for Refusal

Despite satisfying the abovementioned criteria, a foreign legal act or legal fact may also be denied recognition.[50] With respect to the non-recognition of foreign legal acts and facts, the public policy exception is the most important exception and will form the basis of the rest of section III.C. The aim of the public policy exception is to block the application of foreign law and the recognition of legal facts and acts concluded abroad, if the application or recognition would lead to a situation contrary to the fundamental principles and values of the Dutch legal system.[51] Article 10:101(2) DCC lists three specific cases which will always be deemed to be

---

[49] See further below at section III.C.
[50] Art 10:101(1) DCC.
[51] L Strikwerda, *Inleiding tot het Nederlands Internationaal Privaatrecht* (Deventer, Kluwer, 2008) 53.

contrary to Dutch public policy. These situations will be dealt with first, prior to an analysis of the general public policy grounds for non-recognition.

iv. Specific Public Policy Grounds

In Article 10:101(2) DCC three specific situations are listed in which a foreign legal act or legal fact will be regarded as contrary to Dutch public policy, namely:

(a) if the recognition of the child is made by a Dutch national who, according to Dutch law, would not have been entitled to recognise the child;
(b) if, where the consent of the mother or the child is concerned, the legal requirements applicable pursuant to Article 10:95(4) DCC were not complied with; or
(c) if the instrument manifestly relates to a sham transaction.

It would appear that the last two conditions have not provided any real problems with respect to surrogacy arrangements. The first condition has, however, raised a number of problems that will be discussed further here.

If a Dutch man recognises a child abroad, yet according to Dutch law he would not have been permitted to recognise the child, then the foreign recognition will not be recognised in The Netherlands. The aim behind this non-recognition clause is that otherwise Dutch fathers would easily be able to circumvent the adoption legislation by recognising children abroad. The conditions for recognition may be found in Article 1:204 DCC. The condition listed in Article 1:204(1)(e) DCC is of crucial importance in the context of surrogacy. This provision determines that a recognition will be regarded as null and void if made

> by a man who is married at the time of the recognition to another woman unless the district court has *prima facie* held that there is or has been a bond between the man and the mother which may, to a sufficient degree, be regarded as sufficiently equivalent to a marriage, or that there is a close personal relationship between the man and the child.[52]

Prior to discussing the intricacies of the exceptions, it is first important to explore the extent of the prohibition itself. The Court of Appeal Amsterdam has, for example, determined that the prohibition does not apply if the man is involved in a registered partnership with another woman,[53] whilst the District Court Arnhem has applied this prohibition in a case when a man was married to another man.[54] Furthermore, the prohibition does not apply to a non-Dutch man who is permitted according to the law of his nationality to recognise a child of another woman.[55]

---

[52] Translation provided by H Warendorf, R Thomas and I Curry-Sumner, *Civil Code of The Netherlands*, (Deventer, Kluwer 2009) 75.
[53] Hof Amsterdam 18 August 2002, *LJN* BG2522.
[54] Rb Arnhem, 26 April 2008, *LJN* BI3495.
[55] HR (Supreme Court) 28 April 1986, *NJ* 1987, 926. Reference will always be made to the law of the nationality of the non-Dutch man in accordance with Art 10:95(1) DCC.

With respect to the exceptions to this prohibition, two separate questions must be posed, namely:

(a) When are the conditions for the exceptions satisfied in an international context?
(b) Does prior permission need to be requested from the district court in order to satisfy the exception provided for in Article 1:204(1)(e) DCC?

In answering the first question, reference may be made to the decision of the Supreme Court on 27 May 2005. This case was discussed extensively in the Chapter on Dutch Law in the 2006 Issue of the International Survey of Family Law.[56] As stated in the 2006 Survey, the case revolved around a child born in 2001 in Turkey. The Dutch father had provided a notarial instrument in 2001, in which he had stated that he was the biological father of the child. A problem arose because at the time the father was married to another woman (and had been since 1973). The Dutch Supreme Court held that the mandatory nature of the public policy exception must lead to the conclusion that the man was not competent to recognise this child. The Supreme Court referred to a number of facts and circumstances that were relevant in determining whether a married man is competent to recognise a child, namely,

> the man's evidenced interest and commitment to the child both before as well as after the birth. Furthermore, more is required than simple contact during a limited period of time.[57]

The District Court Assen has, moreover, determined that no close personal relationship can exist between an unborn child and a man, since this relationship can develop only after the child is born.[58]

With respect to the second question, the Dutch Supreme Court has also provided clear directions in 2006. In this case, the central question was whether recognition in Vietnam by a Dutch national could be recognised in The Netherlands. The child was born to an unmarried Vietnamese mother and recognised by a Dutch national who was married to another woman at the time. According to the district court, the man satisfied the requirement of Article 1:204(1)(e) DCC and therefore the Vietnamese recognition could be recognised in The Netherlands. However, the man had not requested *prior* permission from the district court, as required by Article 1:204(1)(e) DCC. The Supreme Court held that this was not required, as long as the man could prove that he substantively satisfied the necessary requirements.[59] On 30 November 2007, the Supreme Court provided even more clarity in explaining that the relationship between the man and the child

---

[56] I Sumner and C Forder, 'The Dutch Family Law Chronicles: Continued Parenthood notwithstanding divorce' in A Bainham (ed), *International Survey of Family Law 2006 Edition* 264–65.

[57] Hof Den Haag, 27 May 2009, *LJN* BI1434. See also MJ Vonk, 'Een, twee of drie ouders?' (2003) 122 *Tijdschrift voor Familie- en Jeugdrecht* 124–25.

[58] Rb Assen 15 June 2006, *LJN* AY7247.

[59] HR 28 April 2006, *LJN* AU9237

can be evidenced on the basis of the agreements and circumstances surrounding the case.[60]

The two abovementioned questions raise particular problems with respect to surrogacy cases. If the commissioning father satisfies the substantive criterion of a 'close personal relationship' with the child, then it is possible to recognise the child in the country of origin, regardless of whether or not he is married to another woman. Since it is also not required that the man who recognises the child be the biological father, this route would appear to be a rather 'simplified' route should adoption prove to be too difficult, too expensive or procedurally impossible.

v. General Public Policy Grounds

Alongside the specific public policy grounds discussed above, Article 10:101(1) DCC provides for a general public policy exception. The question arises whether international surrogacy arrangements will fall foul of this exception. In discussing this topic, a number of different scenarios must be distinguished. Due to restrictions on space, only one of those scenarios will be discussed here, namely, whether the lack of a birth mother on the birth certificate should lead to non-recognition.

Two cases have dealt with the issue of a birth certificate upon which no mother is listed. The first case concerned three Dutch persons, two men (in a relationship) and a woman who acted as the surrogate. The surrogate did not wish to have any role in the child's life, but she knew that if she gave birth in The Netherlands she would be regarded as the child's legal mother. As a result, the parties decided that the surrogate should give birth in France, since anonymous birth is possible according to French law. After the birth they returned to The Netherlands, with a French birth certificate upon which only the biological father was listed. The Dutch registrar refused to register the birth certificate, stating that this was contrary to Dutch public policy. The District Court of The Hague[61] agreed with the registrar, basing its conclusion on Article 7 of the United Nations Convention on the Rights of the Child. On the basis of this provision, every child has a right to know his or her parents and be raised by them. The district court held that in recognising the birth certificate, upon which no details were provided with regard to the mother, the identity of the mother would in this way be withheld from the child. Consequently,

> the child should be granted the choice to be able at a later age to give form to his or her identity. In doing so, he or she needs, as far as possible, full access to details of his or her parentage. Registration of the French birth certificate therefore contravenes Dutch public policy.[62]

---

[60] HR 30 November 2007, *RvdW* 2007, 1023.
[61] The District Court of The Hague, 14 September 2009, *LJN*: BK1197.
[62] The District Court of The Hague, 14 September 2009, *LJN*: BK1197.

In another unpublished decision of the District Court of The Hague,[63] the judge decided that a birth certificate from the United States of America upon which two men were registered as the parents also contravened Dutch public policy. It was held that the principle *mater certa semper est* rule is fundamental public policy, and therefore a birth certificate naming two men could not be recognised in The Netherlands.

D. Confirmation of Alleged Parentage: Judicial Decisions

i. *General Criteria*

In similar vein to Article 10:101 DCC, Article 10:100 DCC lays down the specific conditions according to which a foreign judicial decision on legal parentage may be recognised in The Netherlands. The conditions with respect to an enforceable decision, jurisdiction of the foreign judge and adherence to the rules of a fair trial do not appear to have presented any particular problems for Dutch judges and civil servants in light of the specific complexities in surrogacy cases. These conditions will therefore not be discussed further here.

ii. *Competence of the Civil Servant*

If the Dutch civil servant is unsure whether a foreign judicial decision should be recognised, he or she is obliged to request the advice of the Advice Committee for Issues relating to Civil Status and Nationality (*Commissie van Advies voor de Zaken betreffende de Burgerlijke Staat en de Nationaliteit*).[64] The civil servant must request this advice the moment that he or she has 'sufficient doubt' that the judicial decision does not meet the required criteria laid down in Dutch law. There are, however, no cases with respect to when the civil servant may assume that he or she has 'sufficient doubt'.[65]

iii. *Public Policy*

If the recognition of the foreign judicial decision would be contrary to Dutch public policy then the decision will not be recognised. According to the law of California, for instance, parties can request the judge to determine parentage prior to the birth of the child. In a recent unpublished decision of the District Court of The Hague, the court was confronted with such a case.[66] Parentage between the applicants and two children had been determined by the Superior Court of

---

[63] The District Court of The Hague, 23 November 2009, Case no 328511/FA RK 09-317 (unpublished).

[64] Art 1:29c DCC.

[65] It is suggested that the same criteria and reasoning would apply here as are applicable with regard to the recognition of foreign legal facts and legal acts (see section III.C. above).

[66] See n 53 above.

California prior to the birth of the children. After the birth of the twins, the civil registrar drew up the birth certificate in accordance with the pre-birth judicial decision. The Californian court also ordered that the civil servant draw up the birth certificate accordingly upon the birth of the children. The District Court of The Hague refused to recognise and register the birth certificates in the relevant registers in The Netherlands, stating that the underlying judicial decision could not be recognised. The District Court argued:

> The judicial decision from the Superior Court of California of 15th April 2008 cannot be recognised since this is contrary to Dutch public policy, bearing in mind the afore-mentioned fundamental rule of family law (*mater certa semper est*) and the fact that the judicial decision was ordered without the legal mother first being determined.[67]

Question marks may be placed, however, with respect to this line of reasoning. The determination of paternity is not always dependent upon the prior determination of maternity. Especially when considering that the applicant in the case was also the biological father of the children, why is the recognition of a decision with regard to the determination of paternity of the biological father contrary to Dutch public policy? Furthermore, according to Californian law, all parties must have provided consent prior to the issuance of a judicial determination of parentage.[68] If the biological mother had already been consulted and provided consent to the judgment of parentage, why is the recognition of such a decision contrary to Dutch public policy? Furthermore arguments and reasoning is absolutely essential.

E. Summary

It is to be hoped that this section of the chapter has illustrated the complexity surrounding the recognition of foreign birth certificates and judicial decisions regarding parentage. The current private international law rules in the field of parentage have not been designed to deal with the complex issues that present themselves in surrogacy cases. Specific recognition rules need to be designed that show deference to the complexity of the cases, as well as the diversity of relevant factors.

---

[67] Authors' own translation.
[68] K Boele-Woelki *et al*, above n 2, 134.

18

New Zealand

CLAIRE ACHMAD

I. Introduction

When considering surrogacy in New Zealand, a crucial starting point to bear in mind is that altruistic surrogacy is legal; however, commercial surrogacy is illegal under New Zealand law.[1] There is no one dedicated piece of legislation in New Zealand addressing surrogacy, and at this time there is no official New Zealand government policy on cross-border surrogacy.[2] However, there may be said to be a legislative framework in New Zealand which governs domestic surrogacy, made up of four key pieces of legislation, which are introduced and discussed in section II. of this chapter. This legislative framework also has an impact on cross-border surrogacy, and these impacts are discussed in section IV. below.[3]

Section III. of this chapter highlights some significant domestic surrogacy cases from the New Zealand courts. Whilst domestic surrogacy through artificial reproductive technology (ART) is able to be practised in New Zealand under a strong regulatory framework (pursuant to the Human Assisted Reproductive Technology Act 2004), New Zealanders have been amongst those (predominantly developed-world) citizens taking up cross-border surrogacy in the past three to four years in particular. Many of the known cases of cross-border surrogacy involving New Zealand citizens or residents as intending parents have not occurred without some difficulty, and a small number of these cases have now reached the New Zealand Family Court.[4] The cases heard by the Court to date which have been publicly reported are identified and discussed in section IV. These cases have so far demonstrated a cautious judicial approach to the rapidly-emerging issue of

---

[1] Human Assisted Reproductive Technology Act 2004, s 14(3).

[2] See generally for some helpful (albeit now somewhat outdated) contextual background on New Zealand domestic surrogacy policy, K Daniels, 'The Policy and Practice of Surrogacy in New Zealand' in R Cook and S Day Sclater (eds), *Surrogate Motherhood: International Perspectives* (Oxford, Hart Publishing, 2003).

[3] Note also that a fifth piece of legislation, the Citizenship Act 1977, may also be relevant in situations of cross-border surrogacy, available at <www.legislation.govt.nz/act/public/1977/0061/latest/DLM443684.html?search=ts_act_citizenship+act_resel&p=1&sr=1>.

[4] At <www.justice.govt.nz/courts/family-court/>.

cross-border surrogacy, but are important in this discussion as they highlight many of the most pertinent and difficult issues regarding surrogacy in a cross-border context.

II. The Legislative Framework

As mentioned above, a legislative framework setting some standards and limitations on surrogacy in New Zealand may be said to exist, despite there being no one piece of legislation dealing with surrogacy in New Zealand (or surrogacy arrangements involving New Zealand citizens or residents) in a holistic, over-arching manner. The four key pieces of legislation which can be said to create this framework due to the bearing they have on surrogacy arrangements which take place in New Zealand—and to some extent those which involve New Zealand citizens or residents undertaking cross-border surrogacy arrangements—are as follows:

— Human Assisted Reproductive Technology Act 2004;[5]
— Status of Children Act 1969;[6]
— Care of Children Act 2004;[7] and the
— Adoption Act 1955.[8]

These pieces of legislation have all been applied to some extent in the various surrogacy cases which have come before the New Zealand courts to date. It is also important to mention that the New Zealand Family Court, in considering cases of cross-border surrogacy involving New Zealand citizens or residents, has in some instances to date also considered the potential relevance and application of the Adoption (Intercountry) Act 1997; however, this point will be returned to in section IV. below addressing cross-border cases to date. This current section identifies the key legislative provisions relevant to surrogacy in New Zealand, impacting on issues such as legal parenthood, surrogacy payments, the legal requirements on parties to a surrogacy arrangement, advertisement, and the rights of the child born through such an arrangement and those of the surrogate mother.

---

[5] At <www.legislation.govt.nz/act/public/2004/0092/latest/DLM319241.html?search=ts_act_human+assisted+reproductive_resel&p=1&sr=1>.
[6] At <www.legislation.govt.nz/act/public/1969/0018/latest/DLM390654.html?search=ts_act_status+of+children_resel&p=1&sr=1>.
[7] At <www.legislation.govt.nz/act/public/2004/0090/latest/DLM317233.html?search=ts_act_care+of+children_resel&p=1&sr=1>.
[8] At <www.legislation.govt.nz/act/public/1955/0093/latest/DLM292661.html?search=ts_act_adoption+act+1955_resel&p=1&sr=1>.

A. Human Assisted Reproductive Technology Act 2004

The Human Assisted Reproductive Technology Act 2004 (HART Act) has a number of stated purposes, set down in section 3 of the Act, all of which are worth restating here:

(a) to secure the benefits of assisted reproductive procedures, established procedures, and human reproductive research for individuals and for society in general by taking appropriate measures for the protection and promotion of the health, safety, dignity, and rights of all individuals, but particularly those of women and children, in the use of these procedures and research;

(b) to prohibit unacceptable assisted reproductive procedures and unacceptable human reproductive research;

(c) to prohibit certain commercial transactions relating to human reproduction;

(d) to provide a robust and flexible framework for regulating and guiding the performance of assisted reproductive procedures and the conduct of human reproductive research;

(e) to prohibit the performance of assisted reproductive procedures (other than established procedures) or the conduct of human reproductive research without the continuing approval of the ethics committee;

(f) to establish a comprehensive information-keeping regime to ensure that people born from donated embryos or donated cells can find out about their genetic origins.[9]

The HART Act is the main piece of New Zealand legislation which has provisions specific to surrogacy. In this respect the most pertinent provisions are as follows.

Section 4 sets out a number of principles intended to guide any actions under the HART Act. For example:

(a) the health and well-being of children born as a result of the performance of an assisted reproductive procedure or an established procedure should be an important consideration in all decisions about that procedure:[10]

(c) ... the health and well-being of women must be protected in the use of these procedures:[11]

(e) donor offspring should be made aware of their genetic origins and be able to access information about those origins ...[12]

Section 5 defines the term 'surrogacy arrangement'. It states that it means

an arrangement under which a woman agrees to become pregnant for the purpose of surrendering custody of a child born as a result of the pregnancy[.][13]

---

[9] HART Act 2004, s 3(a)–(f).
[10] HART Act 2004, s 4(a).
[11] HART Act 2004, s 4(c).
[12] HART Act 2004, s 4(e).
[13] HART Act 2004, s 5.

Section 14 is the core provision governing the legal status and enforceability of surrogacy arrangements in New Zealand, providing:

> A surrogacy arrangement is not itself illegal, but is not enforceable by or against any person.[14]

Regarding payments for surrogacy in New Zealand, section 14 also explicitly prohibits commercial surrogacy arrangements, section 14(3) making commercial surrogacy a criminal offence:

> Every person commits an offence who gives or receives, or agrees to give or receive, valuable consideration for his or her participation, or for any other person's participation, or for arranging any other person's participation, in a surrogacy arrangement.[15]

Committing such an offence carries liability of imprisonment for a term not exceeding one year or a fine not exceeding New Zealand $100,000, or both.[16] 'Valuable consideration' is defined as including 'an inducement, discount or priority in the provision of a service'.[17]

However, it should be noted that section 14(4) provides exceptions to the prohibition set out in section 14(3). It states that the prohibition does not apply to a payment made to the provider for 'any reasonable and necessary expenses incurred for any of the following purposes',[18] those purposes being collecting, storing, transporting or using a human embryo or gamete;[19] counselling one or more parties in relation to the surrogacy agreement;[20] insemination or in vitro fertilisation;[21] and ovulation or pregnancy tests.[22] It also does not apply to a payment made to 'a legal adviser for independent legal advice to the woman who is, or who might become, pregnant under the surrogacy arrangement'.[23]

Regarding advertising, section 15 of the HART Act prohibits advertising pertaining to actions which are illegal under the Act, and gives a wide meaning to such advertising. Section 15(1) provides:

> No person may, with the intention of obtaining responses from members of the public, publish or arrange for any other person to publish, any material that invites persons to participate, or to inquire about opportunities for participating, in actions that are prohibited by section 8 or section 13 or section 14.[24]

The word 'publish' is given a wide meaning and explicitly defined by section 15(2) (for example, to give a flavour of what is captured by the word 'publish' in the

---

[14] HART Act 2004, s 14(1).
[15] HART Act 2004, s 14(3).
[16] HART Act 2004, s 14(5).
[17] HART Act 2004, s 5.
[18] HART Act 2004, s 14(4)(a).
[19] HART Act 2004, s 14(a)(i).
[20] HART Act 2004, s 14(a)(ii).
[21] HART Act 2004, s 14(a)(iii).
[22] HART Act 2004, s 14(a)(iv).
[23] HART Act 2004, s 14(4)(b).
[24] HART Act 2004, s 15(1).

HART Act, this is said to include, among other things, newspaper or magazine publications,[25] broadcast,[26] inclusion in film,[27] inclusion in any disk for use with a computer,[28] dissemination via the Internet or any other electronic medium,[29] or distribution by any means[30] or by being brought to the notice of the public in New Zealand by any other means[31]). Committing such an offence in respect of advertising carries a penalty on summary conviction of 'imprisonment for a term not exceeding 3 months or a fine not exceeding $2,500, or both'.[32]

It is important to note briefly that the HART Act establishes a bifurcated supervisory system for matters under the Act, comprising a Ministerial Advisory Committee (ACART)[33] and the Ethics Committee on Assisted Reproductive Technology (ECART).[34] A number of guidelines on surrogacy have been issued by ECART. For example, in 2007 ECART published its 'Guidelines on Surrogacy Arrangements Involving Providers of Fertility Services'.[35] The Guidelines reinforce the principles set out in section 4 of the HART Act,[36] and specify those requirements that ECART must establish are present when it considers an application for ethical approval of a surrogacy arrangement involving a provider of fertility services. Some of the most important requirements are:

(a) at least one of the intended parents will be the surrogate child's genetic parent;[37]
(b) the intended mother must have a medical reason for not undertaking pregnancy;[38] and
(c) there has been discussion, understanding and declared intentions between the parties regarding day-to-day care, guardianship, adoption and any ongoing contact.[39]

Interestingly, the Guidelines also include a number of 'relevant factors' that ECART must take into account when considering an application. For example, '[w]hether the relationship between the intending parents and the intending

---

[25] HART Act 2004, s 15(2)(a).
[26] HART Act 2004, s 15(2)(d).
[27] HART Act 2004, s 15(2)(e).
[28] HART Act 2004, s 15(2)(f).
[29] HART Act 2004, s 15(2)(g).
[30] HART Act 2004, s 15(2)(h).
[31] HART Act 2004, s 15(2)(j).
[32] HART Act 2004, s 15(3).
[33] See, for further information on ACART, <www.acart.health.govt.nz/>.
[34] See, for further information on ECART, <www.ecart.health.govt.nz/>.
[35] Ethics Committee on Assisted Reproductive Technology, *Guidelines on Surrogacy Arrangements Involving Providers of Fertility Services* (2007), available at <www.ecart.health.govt.nz/moh.nsf/pagescm/6799/$File/surrogacy-fertitlity-providers-nov08.pdf>.
[36] *Ibid*, at para [1].
[37] *Ibid*, at para [2](a)(i).
[38] *Ibid*, at para [2](a)(ii).
[39] *Ibid*, at para [2](a)(iii).

surrogate safeguards the wellbeing of all parties and especially any resulting child'[40] and '[w]hether the intending surrogate has completed her family'.[41]

Thus it is fair to say that the policy around IVF surrogacy in New Zealand which goes through the ethics approval process under the HART Act is robust and sets out a number of specific, rigorous standards and requirements. Of course, practically speaking, an informal altruistic surrogacy arrangement in New Zealand would not be subject to the safeguards of the legislative regime, leaving those involved potentially vulnerable.

i. *The HART Act and the Rights of Children to Know Their Biological Origins*

New Zealand law does make some provision for the rights of children born from assisted human reproduction (AHR) situations, and these may be applied by analogy to surrogacy situations. Most notably, one of the HART Act principles is that 'donor offspring should be made aware of their genetic origins and be able to access information about those origins'.[42] Moreover, the HART Act creates a rigorous information-keeping and information accessibility regime regarding donors of embryos and cells, and donor offspring.[43] Once such a child turns 18, he or she is entitled to access information about his or her donor.[44] However, informal surrogacy arrangements would not fall under this regime, and therefore a real potential exists for an information lacunae to develop regarding those children born from such surrogacy arrangements. Furthermore, these safeguards for biological information to be preserved and made available would not apply to cross-border surrogacy cases involving New Zealand citizens and residents, and this therefore raises important questions around giving effect to a child's identity rights under Articles 7 and 8 of the United Nations Convention on the Rights of the Child.

B. Status of Children Act 1969 and Legal Parenthood in New Zealand

Turning now to consider the highly pertinent issue of legal parenthood in the context of surrogacy in New Zealand, the core piece of legislation governing legal parenthood in New Zealand is the Status of Children Act (SOCA) 1969. The SOCA 1969 treats children born in New Zealand and those born elsewhere equally.[45] There is no mention of the term 'surrogacy' in the Act, but this piece of legislation does have profound impacts on the legal parenthood of children born from surrogacy arrangements.

---

[40] *Ibid*, at [2](b)(ii).
[41] *Ibid*, at [2](b)(i).
[42] HART Act 2004, s 4(e).
[43] See HART Act 2004, Pt 3.
[44] HART Act 2004, s 50(1).
[45] SOCA 1969, s 3(4). See also s 5(3) of the same Act.

Applying this legislation to surrogacy situations, the surrogate mother is the legal mother of any child born, regardless of whether the child is conceived through sexual intercourse or artificial insemination.[46] The consequence of this status is that the surrogate mother bears all rights and liabilities of motherhood until the child is adopted. Under section 17 of the SOCA 1969, even where a woman becomes pregnant as a surrogate via an ovum or embryo donated by or derived from another woman, it is the woman who becomes pregnant who is 'for all purposes the mother of any child of the pregnancy'.[47] The implications of this position for a surrogate mother and the intending parents (and, by extension, for the child) are that if the surrogate changed her mind about the surrogacy agreement and sought to keep the child, she is already seen to be the legal mother in the eyes of New Zealand law. The flip side of this, of course, is that if the intending parents changed their minds and backed out of the surrogacy agreement, the surrogate mother would be liable for all legal responsibilities relating to the child.

Given its extensive implications, section 5 of the SOCA 1969, 'Presumptions as to parenthood', is worth restating in full:

(1) A child born to a woman during her marriage, or within 10 months after the marriage has been dissolved by death or otherwise, shall, in the absence of evidence to the contrary, be presumed to be the child of its mother and her husband, or former husband, as the case may be.
(2) Every question of fact that arises in applying subsection 1 of this section shall be decided on a balance of probabilities.
(3) This section shall apply in respect of every child, whether born before or after the commencement of this Act, and whether born in New Zealand or not, and whether or not his father or mother has ever been domiciled in New Zealand.

The effect of section 5 is that even if a surrogacy occurs via sexual intercourse between the surrogate mother (who is married) and the intended father, the surrogate's legal husband is presumed to be the legal father of the child born, and the surrogate herself is presumed to be the legal mother. As provided in section 5(2) however, the presumption may, if a question of fact arises, be rebutted. This would be decided on the standard of the balance of probabilities.[48] Under section 8(2) of the Act, a statutory mechanism formalising paternity of the child is available, if the surrogate mother and the intended father sign 'any instrument ... acknowledging that he is the father of the child',[49] if executed as a deed by and in the presence of a solicitor. The SOCA 1969 states that this will be 'prima facie evidence that the person named as the father is the father of the child'.[50]

In surrogacy arrangements where the surrogate mother is artificially inseminated with the intended father's sperm, sections 18 and 21 of the 1969 Act have

---

[46] SOCA 1969, ss 5(1) and 17(2).
[47] SOCA 1969, s 17(2).
[48] SOCA 1969, s 5(2).
[49] SOCA 1969, s 8(2).
[50] *Ibid.*

implications for legal parenthood. These provisions pertain to the procedures in AHR situations specifically. The effect of section 18 is that where a woman acts as a surrogate and becomes pregnant through an AHR procedure, with her partner's consent and via the use of semen from a man who is not her partner, the surrogate's partner is, 'for all purposes, a parent of any child of the pregnancy'.[51] Section 21 pertains to the situation of a woman acting alone, and specifies that the non-partner ovum donor is not for any purpose a parent of any child of an AHR pregnancy.[52] If these provisions were to be applied to surrogacy situations, the effect would be that the intended father would be free of any legal status or responsibility in respect of the surrogate child should the arrangement break down (and any partner of the surrogate who consents would take on the legal responsibilities of parenthood). A New Zealand Family Court judge observed in 2008 that the presumption that the mother of the child is the person who gives birth to that child, even in the face of that woman having no genetic relationship to the child, means that in surrogacy situations in New Zealand, 'the true reality of the situation, that is, the genetic reality, is not recognised at law'.[53]

C. Adoption Act 1955 and the Care of Children Act 2004—Regularising the Parental Relationship

In New Zealand, the key method of regularising the parental relationship between intending parents and a surrogate child is via an adoption under the Adoption Act 1955. This is the only avenue available in New Zealand to create full legal parenthood in a surrogacy situation. Guardianship or a parenting order are two other options which exist to create a legal parental relationship. These options are both able to be applied for under and governed by the Care of Children Act (COCA) 2004.[54] The 2004 Act legislates in New Zealand the principle that the best interests of the child are paramount.[55] However, unlike in the case of adoption, the full legal parental relationship between the surrogate (and her partner) and the surrogate child is not extinguished with a guardianship or parenting order.[56]

---

[51] SOCA 1969, s 18(2).

[52] SOCA 1969, s 21(2).

[53] *In the matter of C [Adoption]* [2008] *New Zealand Family Law Reports* 141, para [31], per Judge Walsh.

[54] See COCA 2004, ss 15–29 regarding guardianship, and ss 47–57 regarding parenting orders.

[55] COCA 2004, s 4, which states that the welfare and best interests of the child must be the first and paramount consideration "in the administration and application of this Act," and "in any other proceedings involving the guardianship of, or the role of providing day-to-day care for, or contact with, a child."

[56] See, for helpful discussion of these and other issues, New Zealand Law Commission, 'New Issues in Legal Parenthood', *Report 88* (Wellington, New Zealand Law Commission, 2005) at 78ff.

III. Domestic Case Law on Surrogacy—Non Cross-border Cases

Reported case law on domestic surrogacy arrangements in New Zealand is limited. This section therefore outlines two key domestic surrogacy cases which have been reported in New Zealand.

One of the earliest surrogacy cases reported in New Zealand is *Re P (adoption: surrogacy)*.[57] This case concerned a couple who advertised for a child in a newspaper in 1985. A woman, M, responded to the advertisement, and a surrogacy arrangement was agreed between the intending parents and M; a child was subsequently born.[58] The Nelson District Court held that the payments the intending parents had made to M were to be regarded as maintenance payments only, and were not in the nature of a profit transaction.[59] Judge McAloon, bearing in mind the paramount consideration in any matter of adoption being the welfare of the child, held that the child's welfare would be best served in this case if the intending parents were to adopt the child, and accordingly an adoption order was made.[60]

It is worth noting at this juncture that the cases on surrogacy reported in New Zealand—both the cases concerning domestic surrogacy arrangements and those concerning cross-border surrogacy—have come before the courts in the form of either adoption applications under the Adoption Act 1955, or parenting order or guardianship applications under the COCA 2004. Therefore the primary issue put before the court in these cases is often the legal status of the parental relationship between the intending parents and the child born from the surrogacy arrangement, and how this might be regularised.

Another domestic surrogacy case is *In the Matter of C [Adoption]*.[61] In this case, the intending parents applied to adopt the child, C, who was fully genetically related to both intending parents but was born by way of altruistic surrogacy.[62] Given the effect of the SOCA, in that the surrogate was regarded as C's legal mother since she gave birth to him (and her partner considered the legal parent too), the intending parents applied for an adoption order under the Adoption Act 1955. The complicating factor in this case was that the intending parents were in a de facto relationship (unmarried), whereas the Adoption Act refers only to the term 'spouse'.[63] Judge Walsh made far-reaching comments in his decision that the New Zealand adoption legislation is outdated and in need of reform.[64] Judge Walsh therefore interpreted the legislation in a modern context, stating that New

---

[57] *Re P (adoption: surrogacy)* [1990] *New Zealand Family Law Reports* 385.
[58] *Ibid*, 386.
[59] *Ibid*, 390.
[60] *Ibid*.
[61] *In the Matter of C [Adoption]* [2008] *New Zealand Family Law Reports* 141.
[62] *Ibid*, para [15].
[63] *Ibid*, para [9].
[64] *Ibid*, paras [71] and [76].

Zealand society had changed dramatically since 1955, the year of the Act.[65] He thus adopted a meaning of the word 'spouse' interpreted in the light of considerations of the time of the judgment (2008), saying it is permissible to interpret 'spouse' as meaning two persons in a relationship in the nature of marriage.[66] An adoption order was thus made in favour of the intending parents, despite their not being married.[67]

IV. New Zealand and Cross-border Surrogacy— A Snapshot of the Situation to Date

Before proceeding to highlight some of the cases which have come before the New Zealand courts concerning cross-border surrogacy arrangements, it is helpful to highlight the situation relative to New Zealand concerning cross-border surrogacy. It has become clear over the past few years in particular that New Zealand citizens and residents are taking up cross-border surrogacy as an option. At the time of writing, since 2010, Child, Youth and Family, the New Zealand Government child welfare and protection agency, is reported to have received 63 inquiries from New Zealand citizens or residents considering commissioning, or already having commissioned, a surrogate child overseas,[68] and is reportedly aware of 15 children born overseas as a result of an arrangement with New Zealand intending parents.[69] In terms of practical issues arising out of the cross-border surrogacy cases which have reached the New Zealand courts to date involving New Zealand intending parents, immigration issues, including visa and entry, have been reported as difficult. One New Zealand couple who commissioned and had a child born in Thailand via a cross-border surrogacy arrangement, had their story reported in the New Zealand media.[70] Currently in New Zealand there is no immigration policy which specifically facilitates the entry of children born out of a cross-border surrogacy arrangement into New Zealand. The decision to grant a visa in this situation to allow entry to New Zealand would therefore technically have to be considered by the Minister of

---

[65] *Ibid*, para [64] ff.

[66] *Ibid*, paras [73] and [77].

[67] It should be noted that to date, the Adoption Act 1955 has not been amended or reformed, despite ongoing criticism of the Act from the judiciary; for a recent example, see *Re KJB and LRB [Adoption]* [2010] *New Zealand Family Law Reports* 97, para [39], per Judge von Dadelszen.

[68] As reported by Television New Zealand, *Parents warned over international 'baby farms'* (Saturday, 20 August 2011), at <www.tvnz.co.nz/national-news/parents-warned-over-international-baby-farms-4357823>.

[69] *Ibid*.

[70] 3 News, *Parents of surrogate born daughter battle to bring her home* (28 August 2009), at <www.3news.co.nz/Parents-of-surrogate-born-daughter-battle-to-bring-her-home/tabid/817/articleID/118792/Default.aspx>.

Immigration (under an existing statutory discretion), and on this basis there would be no guarantee that entry would be possible. In making such a decision, the Minister has discretion as to what matters and information will be considered. For example, it is arguable that perhaps it might be important for such a decision-maker to consider DNA information in relation to the child's genetic (or lack thereof) relationship to the intending parents, the intention of those intending parents to adopt the child (again, or lack thereof) and any criminal records held by either of the intending parents.

Secondary practical issues also highlighted in the New Zealand reported cross-border cases which will be discussed shortly include the parental relationship to the child (in fact the issue given the most consideration and attention by the New Zealand courts to date) and citizenship (which may be gained through adoption, or alternatively by grant based on descent or on an exception to policy which may be made by the Minister of Internal Affairs on a case-by-case basis). For example, such a case-by-case decision might be made for public interest reasons or on humanitarian grounds.[71]

In the context of highlighting these practical issues thrown up by New Zealand cross-border surrogacy cases to date, it is interesting to note that the New Zealand Central Authority under the Hague Convention on Protection of Children and Cooperation in Respect of Intercountry Adoption 1993, along with some other central authorities, raised cross-border surrogacy as an issue of concern with the Hague Conference on Private International Law.[72] This was the first important step in getting the issue on the agenda of the Hague Conference work programme, which it now is.[73] The New Zealand government agencies which have concerned themselves with cross-border surrogacy are Child, Youth and Family, Immigration New Zealand and the Department of Internal Affairs. As such, they have published an information sheet directed at New Zealanders considering a cross-border surrogacy arrangement.[74] This information sheet provides a comprehensive overview of factors of which intending parents should be aware, indicates important aspects which intending parents may wish to investigate further before undertaking such an arrangement, and includes advice to seek independent legal advice on any such arrangement.[75]

---

[71] Citizenship Act 1977, s 9(1)(c).

[72] As reported by Permanent Bureau of the Hague Conference on Private International Law, *Private International Law Issues Surrounding the Status of Children, Including Issues Arising from International Surrogacy Arrangements* (Preliminary Document no 11, 2011) at fn 5.

[73] Hague Conference on Private International Law, *Press Release: Cross-frontier surrogacy issues added to Hague Conference work programme* (7 April 2011), at <www.hcch.net/index_en.php?act=events.details&year=2011&varevent=216>.

[74] Child, Youth and Family, Department of Internal Affairs and Immigration New Zealand, *International Surrogacy Information Sheet*, available at <www.cyf.govt.nz/documents/adoption/international-surrogacy-information-sheet.pdf>.

[75] *Ibid.*

A. Cross-border Cases

This section discusses four cross-border surrogacy cases which have been reported in the New Zealand courts. The first case which may be considered in this category is *Re application by L*.[76] Mr and Mrs L applied to adopt the baby born to Mrs L's sister, Mrs G, who had acted as a surrogate with the use of Mr L's sperm and Mrs L's egg, because Mrs L could not carry a child to term.[77] Therefore this was a full or gestational surrogacy. Mrs G lived in Australia, and it was there that the child was born.[78] The question before the Family Court focused on which adoption regime—domestic or intercountry—was the appropriate one to govern the adoption. More specifically, the Court considered whether the adoption needed to be effected under the Adoption (Intercountry) Act 1997,[79] and therefore the case turned on whether the child was held to be habitually resident in Australia or New Zealand. Judge von Dadelszen held that Mr and Mrs L always intended the child to travel back to New Zealand after birth, and that was where they intended to raise the child.[80] Therefore it was the opinion of the Court that the child's place of habitual residence was New Zealand. In making this finding, Judge von Dadelszen observed:

> Not only were Mr and Mrs L present at H's birth, but Mrs L chose to breast-feed the child from that time until he was six weeks of age. When he was seven days old he travelled to New Zealand in the applicant's care. It is very clear from all the information before the Court that the arrangements made between the L's and the G's [*sic*] were entered into with full knowledge of all the implications and in an open, frank and loving way.[81]

A final adoption order was therefore made in favour of Mr and Mrs L under the Adoption Act, as the case was found to fall outside of the jurisdiction of the Adoption (Intercountry) Act.[82]

At the time of writing, during the past year there have been three cross-border cases reported in the New Zealand Family Court, all brought before the Court by way of adoption applications. Given the quick succession of these cases in the New Zealand courts, they can perhaps be considered the beginning of what may turn into a new wave of cross-border surrogacy cases with which the New Zealand courts—in particular the Family Court—might continue to be confronted. These are considered chronologically below.

---

[76] *Re application by L* [2003] *New Zealand Family Law Reports* 529.

[77] *Ibid*, para [3].

[78] *Ibid*, para [4].

[79] Section 4 of the Adoption (Intercountry) Act 1997 incorporates the Hague Convention on Protection of Children and Cooperation in Respect of Intercountry Adoption 1993 into New Zealand law, and gives it the force of law in New Zealand.

[80] *Re application by L* [2003] *New Zealand Family Law Reports* 529, paras [15]–[16].

[81] *Ibid*, para [6].

[82] *Ibid*, para [19].

i. *Re KJB and LRB [Adoption]*[83]

In this case, intending parents living in Australia who were unable to carry a child to term, arranged for a surrogate, the sister of the intending father, to carry the child, who was fully genetically related to the intending parents.[84] The surrogate lived in New Zealand, but she travelled to Australia for the IVF procedure. She subsequently returned to New Zealand, and that is where the child, John, was born.[85]

The main issue dealt with by Judge von Dadelszen in this case was again whether the child was habitually resident in Australia or New Zealand, and therefore which piece of adoption legislation was to be applied.[86] The Judge held that John's habitual residence was in Australia,[87] and it was only because the surrogate mother had a family of her own to care for in New Zealand that he was born there.[88] The intending parents habitually resided in Australia, and had also cared for him since birth (albeit in New Zealand).[89]

The Judge also held that the welfare and best interests of John were best served by speedy resolution of his legal status. He therefore said that the adoption application should be heard by the Family Court under the Adoption Act 1955, but commented that the adoption legislation was, given its age, unsuited to dealing with issues such as cross-border surrogacy given their contemporary nature.[90] Furthermore, interestingly, the Judge explicitly stated his view that the decision 'should not be regarded as setting a precedent' but reached purely having regard to the particular circumstances of the case.[91]

ii. *Re an Application by KR and DGR to Adopt a Female Child*[92]

This case signals a real shift in complexity in terms of the nature of cross-border surrogacy cases confronting the New Zealand courts. Here, a child, S, was born in Thailand via a surrogacy arrangement through the fertility clinic and the SriSiam Hospital in Bangkok.[93] Her genetic father, DGR, appeared as her legal father on the Thai birth certificate issued in S's name.[94] S's genetic mother was an egg donor (therefore S is not genetically linked to either her intending mother, KR, or her surrogate mother, who was therefore a gestational surrogate).[95] The case highlights difficult issues of nationality and citizenship; the method by which

---

[83] *Re KJB and LRB [Adoption]* [2010] *New Zealand Family Law Reports* 97.
[84] *Ibid*, para [1].
[85] *Ibid*, para [3].
[86] *Ibid*, para [4].
[87] *Ibid*, para [25].
[88] *Ibid*, para [24].
[89] *Ibid*, para [25].
[90] *Ibid*, para [39].
[91] *Ibid*, para [37].
[92] *Re an application by KR and DGR to adopt a female child* [2011] *New Zealand Family Law Reports* 429.
[93] *Ibid*, para [4].
[94] *Ibid*.
[95] *Ibid*, para [5].

S was able to enter New Zealand was through a 12-month visitor's visa.[96] DGR and KR applied to adopt S through the New Zealand adoption system. Judge Ryan held that the Adoption (Intercountry) Act did not apply,[97] and that 'the evidence satisfies me on the balance of probabilities that S' welfare and best interests will be promoted by the making of an adoption order' under the Adoption Act 1955.[98]

Perhaps most interestingly, Judge Ryan made the following comment on public policy considerations related to the case:

> There is no doubt that with less children being made available for adoption in New Zealand and with the advances and refinements in human assisted reproduction and the ready availability of egg donors in foreign countries, it is essential that some control is exerted over the processes that may be used by New Zealand citizens or those wishing to become permanent residents in this country. However, these are policy considerations that are not within the role of this court to impose. It is for the Parliament in consultation with the appropriate government agencies both in New Zealand and overseas to put in place rules and protocols surrounding IVF procedures undertaken in foreign countries by New Zealanders.[99]

iii. Re an Application by BWS to Adopt a Child[100]

This is another complex case, with the added legal complication of the intending parents being a homosexual male couple in a civil union, who are United States citizens living in New Zealand with New Zealand residency status.[101] They had twin boys, born in California to a friend who acted as a gestational surrogate. An anonymous egg donor provided two eggs, one of each of the eggs was fertilised by one of the intending parents and both were implanted into the surrogate mother.[102]

The main issues considered in the decision on the adoption application made by the intending parents to the New Zealand Family Court were:

(a) whether the adoption needed to be effected as an intercountry adoption;

(b) whether the egg donor's consent to adoption was required;

(c) if the intending parents were fit and proper to parent the twins;

(d) whether the payment made to the surrogate was in breach of section 25 of the Adoption Act 1955 (which prohibits payments in consideration of adoption); and

(e) if the children's best interests and welfare would be promoted by the making of an adoption order.

---

[96] *Ibid*, para [8].

[97] *Ibid*, para [14].

[98] *Ibid*, para [19].

[99] *Ibid*, para [20].

[100] *Re an application by BWS to adopt a child* [2011] *New Zealand Family Law Reports* 621.

[101] *Ibid*, at para [6].

[102] *Ibid*, at para [9].

The Superior Court of California had issued a pre-birth order pertaining to the surrogacy, which declared both the intending parents to be the legal parents of the twins.[103] This carried through to their birth certificates.[104] The twins were able to enter New Zealand on 12-month visitors' visas (as had been the case with the child S in *Re an application by KR and DGR to adopt a female child*).[105] Judge Walker found that the intending parents always intended to bring the twins back to New Zealand and raise them there, and extrapolated the habitual residence of the twins as being New Zealand. The Judge described them in this respect as 'party to the intention of their parents'.[106] The Judge held that consent of the surrogate to the adoption had been obtained validly, and that the payments made to the surrogate were not in consideration for adoption.[107]

Therefore an adoption order was made under the Adoption Act 1955; however, in the course of doing so Judge Walker voiced some strong policy considerations, such as expressing concern that, given the egg donation was anonymous, it remained highly uncertain that the twins would ever be able to trace their genetic mother.[108] This was seen by the Judge to be of concern in terms of the twins' sense of identity, and may be seen as a small step in the New Zealand courts towards beginning to touch on the myriad of human rights issues raised by cross-border surrogacy arrangements. Furthermore, the Judge noted with concern that

> [t]he Applicants' payment to the surrogate mother, while not illegal in the United States, does not sit well with New Zealand's efforts to 'prohibit certain commercial transactions relating to human reproduction'[109]

and expressed doubt that the intending parents would have had the same surrogacy arrangement approved under the New Zealand legislation and policy.[110]

V. Conclusion

New Zealand does have some important legislation which has an impact on surrogacy arrangements, despite these pieces of legislation for the most part not being explicitly directed at surrogacy issues. Of particular relevance in light of the growing prevalence of present-day cross-border surrogacy arrangements, New Zealand does not have any legislation or official government policy on cross-border surrogacy. The New Zealand Minister of Justice has recently publicly stated that there

---

[103] *Ibid*, para [10].
[104] *Ibid*.
[105] *Ibid*, para [15].
[106] *Ibid*, paras [53]–[54].
[107] *Ibid*; see on consent paras [58] ff, and on payment paras [63] ff.
[108] *Ibid*, para [82].
[109] *Ibid*, para [83].
[110] *Ibid*, para [85].

are no plans to create a legislative ban on international surrogacy, but noted that New Zealand law and policy generally does not allow children born overseas as a result of international surrogacy to be brought into New Zealand, except where relevant ministers choose to exercise an existing statutory discretion.[111] However, New Zealand citizens and residents do appear to be actively pursuing cross-border surrogacy, and the case law to date on this issue, as discussed in this chapter, shows that the New Zealand courts are taking tentative steps towards adjudicating these highly complex situations.

It must be recognised, though, that the current case law (at the time of writing) is limited in the sense that cross-border surrogacy has been considered by the Family Court alone, and the issue has come before the Court only by way of adoption applications. This surely raises concern as to the potential that in the absence of dedicated surrogacy legislation and policy, to some extent a de facto policy around cross-border surrogacy may be developed through case law. The cross-border surrogacy decisions of the Family Court to date have rejected the application of New Zealand's intercountry adoption legislation, and this appears to be in line with the conclusions adopted by the most recent Special Commission of the Parties to the Hague Intercountry Adoption Convention in 2010.[112] What is also clear in New Zealand's case law to date on this issue is that the welfare and best interests of the child are considered to be the paramount concern, and that where the Family Court is satisfied that to stay in the care of the intending parents serves the child's best interests, it appears that a domestic adoption order will likely be granted. This may lead to perverse outcomes and encourage potential intending parents to embark on cross-border surrogacy arrangements, believing that they can simply have the parental relationship regularised via an adoption order should they be able to return to New Zealand with a surrogate child. However, as Judge Ryan observed in *Re an application by KR and DGR to adopt a female child*, this is a matter for which Parliament and relevant government agencies are most appropriately positioned to develop the necessary procedures and policy.

It is positive that initial steps have been taken by the Family Court (for example in *Re an application by BWS to adopt a child*) to highlight some of the relevant human rights issues—especially those of the rights of the child; nevertheless, potential exists for much greater engagement with these issues should future cross-border surrogacy cases come before the New Zealand courts.

---

[111] See text after n 70 above.

[112] Permanent Bureau of the Hague Conference on Private International Law, *Conclusions and Recommendations and Report of the Special Commission on the Practical Operation of the 1993 Hague Intercountry Adoption Convention* (Preliminary Document no 4, 2011), para [60].

19

Russia

OLGA KHAZOVA

It is an old idea that the more pointedly and logically we formulate a thesis, the more irresistibly it cries out for its antithesis.

Hermann Hesse, *The Glass Bead Game*

I. Introduction

Russia has been placed within the third category with regard to its approach to surrogate motherhood—'countries with a relatively neutral approach to surrogacy where surrogacy is regulated'—because there is at least some regulation of these matters in Russian law. However, those few provisions on surrogate motherhood that exist in the Russian law hardly correspond to the meaning that we associate with the word 'regulation'. Until very recently there were just two short articles in the Russian Family Code 1995, and these were, in fact, the only regulatory provisions in this field. A new Law was adopted in November 2011—the Federal Law on the Basis of Protection of Citizens' Health (hereafter 'the Law on Citizens' Health'), which added new rules on surrogate motherhood. Even if we take into account these new provisions, there are still more gaps than regulation of assisted reproduction in general and surrogate motherhood in particular in Russian law. Current regulation is, undoubtedly, not enough, especially bearing in mind the complexity of the issues related to surrogacy. Nevertheless, the articles that we do have are very important, as they opened the door to legal application of surrogate motherhood in the country and to a certain extent defined a general national legal framework for surrogacy. The first case of full ('gestational') surrogacy in Russia took place in December 1995, when two girls were born by a surrogate mother in the Saint Petersburg IVF centre.[1]

Before moving to a more extensive discussion of the surrogate motherhood issues, a few introductory comments are necessary concerning the main Russian

---

[1] VS Korsak, EV Isaakova, OA Vorobjeva *et al*, 'The First Experience in Russia of Conducting a Programme of Surrogate Motherhood' (in Russian) (1996) 2 *Problems of Reproduction* 46.

legal sources on the topic and the basic Russian legal concepts that exist with regard to surrogacy.[2]

Despite a wide application of assisted reproduction technologies (ART), and particularly those that include surrogate motherhood, in Russian medical practice,[3] there is still, as has been already pointed out, little regulation in the field, and those legal rules that exist do not cover all the variety of problems arising therefrom. There are three federal laws and one governmental legal act, which contain provisions relevant to the theme of surrogacy:

(a) The Family Code 1995, mentioned above, contains two articles, one of which concerns the order of registration of legal parents of a child born using a surrogate (section 51, paragraph 4(2)) and the other the issues of contesting paternity and maternity with regard to a child conceived through IVF and born to a surrogate (section 52, paragraph 3(2)).

(b) The second legal source at the federal level, also mentioned above, which is directly relevant to our theme, is the new Law on Citizens' Health 2011, which replaces the previous Law on Citizens' Health 1993.[4] It gives a definition of surrogate motherhood and contains some other important provisions.

(c) There is also a provision on surrogate motherhood in the Federal Law on the Acts of Registration of Civil Status 1997, which, having followed the legal rule contained in the Family Code, merely clarifies some details concerning registration of the birth of a child born by a surrogate mother (section 16(5)).

(d) Lastly, at the ministerial, or governmental, level there is a Ministry of Health Order 2003, which approved regulation of the application of assisted reproduction methods.[5] Although this document deals mostly with

---

[2] On this matter see also AY Ivanyushkin, 'Bioethics and New Reproductive echnologies in Russia' in D Evans (ed), *Creating the Child* (The Hague, Kluwer Law International, 1996) 267; OA Khazova, 'Genetics and Artificial Procreation in Russia' in M-T Meulders-Klein and P Vlaadingerbroek (eds), *Biomedicine, the Family and Human Rights* (The Hague, Kluwer Law International, 2002) 377, 383; GR Kolokolov, 'Legal Foundations of Medical Interference in Human Reproductive Activity (Artificial Insemination)' (2005) 2 *Russian Law: Theory and Practice* 210.

[3] In 2008, the number of IVF cycles carried out in Russian infertility centres constituted 49.1% of all ART cycles (in 2007—47.1%). As to the surrogacy programmes, 430 cycles with the participation of surrogate mothers, carried out in 38 centres in 2008, ended in embryo transfer (in 2007—367 cycles carried out in 33 centres; in 2006—300 cycles). See VS Korsak, 'ART in Russia. Report for 2008' (in Russian) (2010) 6 *Problems of Reproduction* 15, 15–16; VS Korsak, 'ART in Russia. Report for 2007'(in Russian) (2009) 6 *Problems of Reproduction* 14, 14–15.

[4] The full title of the previous Law is the Fundamentals of Legislation on Protection of Citizens' Health 1993. The new Law on Citizens' Health 2011 established different dates of entry into legal force of its provisions. Section 55, on application of assisted reproduction, entered into legal force on 1 January 2012.

[5] RF Ministry of Health Order No 67 of 26.02.2003 'On Application of Assisted Reproductive Technologies (ART) to the Therapy of Female and Male Infertility' (*Prikaz Ministerstva zdravoohranenija RF No 67 of 26.02.2003 'O primenenii vspomogatelnykh reproduktivnykh tehnologyi (VRT) v terapii zhenskogo i muzhskogo besplodia'*).

medical issues, it also contains important 'non-medical' provisions, which have been largely included in the new Law on Citizens' Health 2011.

As far as the basic concepts of Russian law regarding surrogate motherhood are concerned, it is necessary from the outset to point out the following. First, only full, or gestational, surrogacy is allowed in Russia. The new Law on Citizens' Health 2011 introduced a clear prohibition of so-called 'partial', or 'traditional', surrogacy, when it stated that 'a surrogate mother shall not be an oocytes donor' (section 55(10)). Before that, although there was no such prohibition, 'partial' or 'traditional surrogacy' was not permitted anyway.[6] It was done through strict regulation of the adoption procedure. The point is that what is called 'traditional surrogacy' is, in fact, a method of artificial insemination with a donor's sperm (whether anonymous or not), and the 'traditional' surrogate mother is a biological or genetic mother of a child to whom she will give birth. Therefore, she is not a 'surrogate' but a true mother. Under the Russian law, if a woman wants to get rid of her child, she may do that only by giving her consent to place the child for adoption. Adoption procedure is very special and very strict; it is not applicable in case of surrogate motherhood, and violation of this procedure is a serious offence.

Secondly, the Family Code provision that concerns the order of registration of legal parents of a child born using a surrogate stipulates that

> a married couple that has given its consent in written form to implantation[7] of an embryo into another woman for the purpose of its gestation, can be registered as the child's parents only with the consent of this woman (surrogate mother).[8]

This provision is based on the concept that a woman who gives birth to a child is considered at law as the mother of this child—a modern modification of the old Roman law principle *'mater semper certa est'* ('the mother is always certain'). From this, it follows that a surrogate mother has the right to keep the child if she wants. In this regard, the drafters of the Russian Family Code were guided by the recommendations made by a group of European experts in biomedical science in 1989.[9]

Thirdly, those few legal rules on surrogate motherhood that existed in Russian law before the new Law on Citizens' Health 2011 was adopted covered different situations, namely, where genetic material came from the prospective parents or commissioning couple (hereafter 'intended parents'), or from one of them, or

---

[6] Nevertheless, it was known to take place in practice. See 'Theme Issue: Surrogate Mothers' (2010) 4(4113) *Ogonyek* 1 February 2010, 30, 33.

[7] The word 'implantation' (*implantatsija*—in Russian) used in the Family Code is not the right one and needs clarification, as actually it means embryo transfer. The Family Code followed the terminology used in the previous Law on Citizens' Health 1993, where it was stated that every adult woman of reproductive age had the right to access 'to artificial fertilisation and embryo implantation' (s 35).

[8] Family Code, s 51, para 4(2).

[9] Council of Europe, *Report on Human Artificial Procreation*, Principles set out in the report of the Ad hoc Committee of Experts in Biomedical Science (CAHBI, 1989), Principle 14. See at <www.coe.int/t/dg3/healthbioethic/texts_and_documents/default_en.asp>.

from neither of the intended parents (ie, from the donors). There was neither prohibition of nor any differentiation between these situations in the law, which meant that an infertile couple could use both donors' oocytes and sperm if there was a medical indication to that effect.

The 2011 Law contains a new rule in this regard, which raises more questions than the answers it provides (section 55). It defines surrogate motherhood as

> gestation of and giving birth to a child (including premature birth) under a contract made between a surrogate mother (a woman who carries a foetus after transfer of a donor's embryo) and potential parents, whose germ cells were used for fertilisation, or a single woman, for whom it is impossible to gestate and give birth to a child due to medical reasons.

A literal interpretation of the wording of this provision suggests that infertility treatment with the use of surrogacy and a donor's genetic material is available for a single women only but not for couples, whether married or not. It is not necessary to be a medical professional in order to say that there is hardly any medical reasoning behind this provision.

The wording of this rule also leaves no doubt that a single man may not be a party to a surrogacy contract.

II. Legal Requirements on a Surrogate Mother and the Intended Parents

The Law on Citizens' Health 2011 fixes three main requirements on a surrogate mother, which were previously stipulated at the governmental level in the Ministry of Health Regulation 2003. Thus, under the new 2011 Law, a woman who has given her written informed consent to medical intervention may serve as a surrogate mother, provided she:

(a) is between 20 and 35 years old;
(b) has at least one healthy child; and
(c) has received a medical statement that she is healthy (in 'satisfactory state of health').[10]

The Law on Citizens' Health 2011 also introduced another provision into Russian law that is principally new and that filled a serious gap in Russian regulation. It is stated in this Law that a married woman can serve as a surrogate only with the consent of her husband.[11] The main reason for this is that a surrogate's husband will become a child's legal father if she decides to keep the child.

---

[10] Section 55(10).
[11] *Ibid.* By 'marriage' the Law means 'a marriage registered in the order stipulated by Russian legislation.

There are no other requirements regarding a surrogate mother stipulated in Russian law.[12]

Concerning the legal requirements imposed on intended parents, the situation is more complicated, and the new Law on Citizens' Health 2011 did not make it any easier.

The provisions of the Family Code 1995 that regulate registration of the intended parents as the legal parents of a child conceived through ART refer to a married couple and not to a single woman or a single man, nor to a cohabiting couple (section 51, (4 part 2)). From this, many registries of civil status concluded (and there were certain reasons for that) that single persons or those who were not married to each other could not, according to the law, be registered as the legal parents of a child born 'for them' by a surrogate mother.

This confusing provision of the Family Code resulted in several disputes in Russian courts, where the applicants were either not married to each other or were single women, or even single men, because civil status registries, with reference to the Family Code, refused to register them as the legal parents of children born 'for them' by surrogate mothers. In many cases the petitioners' claims were satisfied, and the registries were ordered to register the birth of the children.[13] There were even two cases where the petitioners were single 'intended fathers' who won the proceedings and were registered as the legal fathers of the children born for them by surrogate mothers (with the use of donors' oocytes).[14] To decide otherwise would mean leaving children born to surrogates acting for unmarried couples or single persons without legal parents, and placing them for adoption or into foster care, or worse—ie with the State institutions—at the same time as there are people who are eager to become the legal parents of these children and take care of them.

The Law on Citizens' Health 2011 does not regulate the order of registration of birth of a child born through assisted reproduction, but attempts to approach this problem from another angle by regulating who may have access to ART. It is stated in this Law (section 55(3)) that

> a man and a woman, married as well as not married, have the right to have access to assisted reproduction, provided they gave their mutual informed consent to medical interference; a single woman also has the right to have access to assisted reproduction if she gave her informed consent to medical interference.

The previous Law on Citizens' Health 1993 spoke only about the right of 'every adult woman of reproductive age' to benefit from ART (section 35).

In this connection a question arises: Why does neither the new 2011 Law, nor the previous 1993 Law mention a single man? Does it mean that men with fertility

---

[12] Interestingly, with regard to the sperm and oocyte donors, according to the Ministry of Health Order, there is a special question on sexual orientation in the donor's application form that those who would like to act as donors must fill in. But there is nothing of the kind regarding surrogate mothers.

[13] See, eg, RF Supreme Court Ruling on the case No 78-Ф08-1314 of 8 September 2008.

[14] See, eg, at <www.surrogacy.ru/surrogacy_news8.php; www.jurconsult.ru/news/news40.php> and <www.jurconsult.ru/news/news39.php>.

problems may not get access to IVF treatment? Regarding the 1993 Law, the answer most probably will be: 'Certainly not.' We could hardly assume that the drafters of the 1993 Law pursued a goal to restrict the access of men to assisted reproduction; there was no reasonable explanation for this, and moreover, methods of medical treatment of male infertility had already been applied widely in medical practice at the time the 1993 Law was elaborated.[15] It should rather be assumed that, taking into account the time when the draft Law was elaborated— the early 1990s, when extramarital and, moreover, same-sex cohabitation was not as widespread as it is nowadays—the explanation was simply that infertility treatment was conventionally associated with the medical treatment of women. In practice, it was usually married couples who would come to medical clinics, even if male, and not female, infertility was the problem, and actual treatment was often carried out on the woman and not on the man. This explanation, however, does not sound so convincing now.

The new Law on Citizens' Health 2011, having defined who might apply to receive ART as fertility treatment clarified, to a certain extent, the confusion caused by the Family Code regarding unmarried couples.[16] However, it did not solve the uncertainty that existed with regard to single men. If interpreted literally, this provision means that a single man who has infertility problems but does not have a wife or female partner, may not benefit from advances in medicine and cannot gain access to ART. We need time to understand how this Law will work in practice. Currently, we can only speculate as to why the provision of the 2011 Law on access to assisted reproduction did not name single men among those who have this right, and the consequence this might have. On the one hand, we can hardly assume that the 2011 Law intended to deny access to fertility treatment for single men. On the other hand, the opposite conclusion suggests itself from the wording of the Law and, moreover, is supported by another, already-mentioned provision of the same Law that excludes single men from surrogacy contracts. In such a case the question of the constitutionality of this provision arises as it contradicts the principles of the Constitution of the Russian Federation 1993 of equality of rights and freedoms for men and women and equal opportunities for their realisation (Article 19), of the right of all to health care and medical help (Article 41) and the constitutional provision on state support for the family, maternity, paternity and childhood (Article 7), not to mention the contradiction with the social reality of male infertility.

Another angle of the problem arising in connection with surrogate motherhood was demonstrated by one of the recent cases considered by Moscow courts.[17] In this case, a 58-year-old woman, whose son had died from cancer, applied to the medical clinic for IVF with the use of the donor's oocytes and her deceased son's sperm, to

---

[15] The previous Ministry of Health IVF Regulation 1993 stipulated male fertility as a separate ground for IVF treatment.

[16] And it could not, as the spheres of regulation of each of these laws were different.

[17] See <www.rg.ru/2011/06/02/surrogat.html and ria.ru/video/20110609/386133361.html>.

be carried out with the subsequent transfer of embryos to a surrogate mother. To be confident in the success of her undertaking, the woman got two surrogates involved, and each of them delivered two babies. Thus, four children were born. The woman—the 'intended mother' of these four children and their genetic grandmother—claimed to be registered in their birth certificates as the children's legal mother. The civil status registry refused to register her as the legal mother on the ground that the Family Code provided for registration only of a married couple as the legal parents. The 'intended mother' lost the case in both sets of court proceedings (and we can only assume that her age was the main reason). Her lawyers were going to appeal further to the Supreme Court; however, in the meantime, the birth of the children was not officially registered, and this meant that, from a legal point of view, they did not exist, with all the consequences arising therefrom.

Nevertheless, despite all the contradictions, discrepancies and gaps that exist in surrogacy regulation, surrogate motherhood is developing in Russia and the number of surrogate motherhood programmes continues to increase.[18] In the opinion of the President of the Russian Association of Human Reproduction, Vladislav Korsak, it will grow in proportion to demand.[19] Surrogacies are developing not only in number, but also as regards the diversity of situations in which they occur, and consequently the diversity of legal problems arising therefrom. For instance, having arrangements with more than one surrogate may create a problem with registration of the children as having been born on the same day, if they were in fact born on different days (as happened in one case—with a difference of two weeks in what was entered in the medical documents issued by the hospital). It required a court judgment to get the children's births registered as if they had been born on the same day.

III. Enforceability of Surrogacy Arrangements

It is hardly possible to give a precise answer as to whether surrogacy contracts are considered legally binding under Russian law or not. Neither legal nor court guidance has been given in this respect. The only thing that is currently defined is who may be the parties to a surrogacy contract. It may be recalled that under the Law on Protection of Citizens' Health 2011 (see section II. above), the parties to such a contract may be, on the one hand, the woman wishing to serve as a surrogate and, on the other hand, a married or unmarried couple, or a single woman. The rest depends on what is in the contract.

Since under Russian law a surrogate mother has the right to keep a child, this aspect—one of the main aspects of enforceability of surrogate arrangements—is

---

[18] See above n 3.
[19] 'Theme Issue: Surrogate Mothers', above n 6, 32.

not covered by legal regulation of surrogacy in Russia. At the same time, there could be other issues that might be relevant in this regard (for instance, recovery of payments or compensation). In the event of a dispute, whether a surrogacy contract is enforceable depends on the facts of the particular case and the terms of the particular contract. Thus, it may be recognised as void for being against public policy and morality,[20] or because it contains conditions that are extremely unfavourable to the surrogate mother, and the court finds that the surrogate mother's situation was such that she was forced to conclude this transaction in circumstances of which another party took advantage.[21] The surrogate arrangements certainly may not contain provisions prohibiting the surrogate from terminating the pregnancy, as every woman, under Russian law, has the right to decide maternity issues on her own,[22] and such a provision in a contract would interfere with the individual's autonomy.[23] There could be also problems with provisions requiring a surrogate mother, for instance, to live in a particular place and not visiting her home city, as this would interfere with her constitutional right to travel freely and choose a place of temporary or permanent residence.[24] Such provisions may invalidate a surrogacy contract as a whole or in part, and accordingly may make it unenforceable in whole or in part.

IV. Payments in Surrogacy: 'Commercial' v 'Altruistic' Surrogacy

Payments in surrogacy specifically are not regulated in Russian law at all, and that means that the arrangement may be commercial or altruistic. Medical expenses of surrogates are usually compensated; loss of earnings might be compensated as well. However, surrogates often ask for a monthly allowance. As to payment for the service rendered, the parties may try to make it covertly, first, because it is unclear how it might be accepted and interpreted by a court in the event of a dispute and, secondly, because such payment constitutes income for a surrogate mother and she will be expected to pay taxes on it. These two considerations may, to a significant extent, explain why the parties prefer to keep surrogate arrangements private and, if there are any problems, to solve them quietly and not to go to the courts.

---

[20] The Civil Code, s 169.

[21] The Civil Code, s 179.

[22] The Law on Protection of Citizens' Health 2011 (s 56); the Law on Protection of Citizens' Health 1993 (s 36).

[23] Russian Constitution 1993, Art 22(1) states: 'Everyone shall have the right to freedom and personal inviolability.'

[24] Russian Constitution 1993, Art 27(1).

Two years ago, the services of surrogate mothers in Russia might on average cost US \$15,000–20,000.[25] But if the intended parents wanted a surrogate with a higher education, they would have to pay more.[26]

V. Legal Parenthood

Legal relations between parents and children, under Russian law,[27] are based on the children's filiation, established in the order laid down by law, ie on the fact of registration of the child's parents as his or her legal parents in the child's birth certificate and the birth registry book in a civil status registry. As far as filiation of a child born to a surrogate mother is concerned, as mentioned in section I. above, the Russian Family Code stipulates that the intended parents are registered as the child's legal parents, provided the surrogate mother has given her consent to this.

If a surrogate mother does not use her right to keep a child and the intended parents have been registered as the legal parents, the child's status, and accordingly the parents' rights and duties, are precisely the same as in the case of a child conceived in a natural way. The registration procedure is also the same as in the case of ordinary registration of a child's birth, with just one exception. The intended parent shall present, apart from other documents which are required for birth registration, a medical clinic's 'official note' (medical statement) that confirms that the surrogate gave her consent to the intended parents' registration as the legal parents.[28]

If a surrogate mother decides to keep a child and refuses to give her consent to the intended parents' registration as the legal parents, she will be registered as the child's legal mother in the same way as a 'natural' mother is, upon presenting her identification document (passport) and a medical clinic's 'statement' certifying that she delivered the child. If she is married, her husband, due to the presumption of paternity, will become the legal father of the child. As mentioned earlier, the Law on Citizens' Health 2011 closed a serious gap in Russian law having stipulated that a married woman may serve as a surrogate only with the written consent of her husband.

To finalise parental rights before a child is born is not allowed by Russian law; the child's birth certificate can be issued only after the child's birth. Upon registration of a child's birth, the parental rights are considered to be finalised.

In principle, Russian law permits the contestation of paternity or maternity. With regard to assisted reproduction issues, however, there is a special rule in the

---

[25] Theme Issue: Surrogate Mothers', above n 6, 32.
[26] See <http://sptimes.ru/index.php?action_id=100&story_id=36172>.
[27] Family Code, s 47.
[28] Federal Law on Registration of Civil Status 1997, s 16(5).

Family Code, which prohibits subsequent contesting of parentage based on ART grounds. The law says (section 52(3 (2))) that

> a married couple who have agreed to implantation of an embryo into another woman, as well as a surrogate mother … when contesting paternity or maternity, cannot refer to these circumstances after registration of the child's parents in a birth registration book.[29]

If donors' genetic material has been used in the course of infertility treatment, this has no legal consequences for the donors with regard to parentage. The Ministry of Health Regulation stipulates that the donors 'provide their gametes … to other persons to overcome infertility and do not undertake parental obligations towards a future child'.[30]

Regarding legal parenthood issues in the private international law context, Russian law refers to nationality (citizenship) as a connecting factor. It is stated in the Family Code that the establishment and contesting of paternity (maternity) is determined under the law of the State whose citizenship a child has by birth (section 162(1)). Parental rights, however, in accordance with the Code, shall be determined under the law of the State where the parents and children have a common place of residence. The law of the country of the child's nationality (citizenship) in such a case is used as a connecting factor only if there is no common place of residence. With regard to child maintenance issues and other parent–child relations, the law also allows, upon a petitioner's request, application of the law of the country where a child permanently resides (section 163).

If the intended parents of a child born by a surrogate in Russia need to take the child to their home country, getting an entry visa for a child and further legalisation of the child in his or her parents' country may be a problem, particularly given the fact that in many countries, to consider parent—child relations finalised it is necessary to receive a court judgment. For instance, such a requirement exists in Australia.[31] In Russia, on the contrary, these issues, as has been shown, are administratively regulated (by registration of the child's birth in a State body for registration of civil status) and no court is involved.

---

[29] By 'these circumstances' the Code means that the child was conceived through IVF with involvement of a surrogate mother.

[30] Regulation approved by RF Ministry of Health Order No 67 of 26.02.2003, above n 2, para 6.

[31] In my practice, there was a case when I was asked to give a legal opinion to an Australian couple who expected a child to be born in Moscow to a Russian surrogate mother. I explained to the Australian authorities that no mandatory court proceedings were stipulated in Russian law that would be aimed at recognition of the intended couple's parental rights towards the child born for them to a surrogate.

VI. Nationality of the Child

The basic principle of Russian law concerning a child's nationality (citizenship) is that a child shall not be left stateless. The Federal Law on Citizenship of the Russian Federation 2002 states (section 12):

1. A child shall acquire Russian citizenship by birth[32] if as of the date of birth of the child:
   a) both the child's parents or the child's only parent have/has Russian citizenship (irrespective of the child's place of birth);
   b) one of the child's parents has Russian citizenship and the other parent is a stateless person or has been declared missing or if this parent's whereabouts are unknown (irrespective of the child's place of birth);
   c) one of the child's parents has Russian citizenship and the other parent is a foreign citizen, provided that the child has been born in the territory of the Russian Federation or if otherwise the child becomes a stateless person;
   d) both of the child's parents or the child's only parent residing in the territory of the Russian Federation are foreign citizens or stateless persons, on condition that the child has been born in the territory of the Russian Federation, while the State where the child's parents are citizens does not grant its citizenship thereto.
2. A child who stays in the territory of the Russian Federation and whose parents are unknown shall become a Russian citizen if the parents fail to appear within six month after the time the child was found.

Thus, to summarise, with regard to children born on the territory of Russia, whose parents are foreign citizens, the law stipulates that these children acquire Russian citizenship by birth only if their parents (foreign citizens) are permanently residing in the Russian Federation and the country of the parents' citizenship will not provide children born in Russia with the parents' citizenship. Therefore, a child born on the Russian Federation territory acquires citizenship of its parents under the parents' personal law (*lex personalis*). Only where the State whose citizens the child's parents are does not provide citizenship to the child, may the child acquire Russian citizenship.

VII. Advertisement

There are no legal rules that specifically address the advertisement of surrogate motherhood. Strictly speaking, since the law allows surrogate motherhood, it should be legal to advertise surrogacy services, and indeed numerous advertisements may be found on the Internet.

---

[32] It is possible to acquire Russian citizenship: (i) by birth; (ii) as a result of being admitted for Russian citizenship; (iii) as the result of reinstatement of Russian citizenship; and (iv) on other grounds set out by law (Federal Law on Citizenship 2002, s 11).

Obviously, a positive answer also should be given to the question whether it is it legal to broker surrogacy arrangements on a commercial basis, because, technically, there is no prohibition under the law. Lawyers working in this area, however, are more cautious than are potential surrogate mothers, and usually include legal support of surrogacy in a law firm profile that lists it amongst other family law issues. However, all in all, there are not many law firms working in this area so far, and only a few of them openly refer to surrogacy matters on their sites. They do not call it 'brokering' but 'legal services', although the services may include the firm's work on selection of potential surrogate mothers. Therefore, with possible future regulation in this area in mind, it is important to differentiate between providing legal guidance or consultation on assisted reproduction issues, including surrogate motherhood arrangements, and the search for and selection of surrogate mothers.

VIII. Rights of the Child Born Through a Surrogacy Arrangement and Rights of the Surrogate Mother

A child born through assisted reproduction and, specifically, through a surrogacy arrangement, provided that his or her filiation has been properly registered, has the same rights towards his or her legal parents and other family members as a child born through natural conception. Thus, if the intended parents were registered as the child's legal parents in a civil status registry, these rights are in respect of the intended parents and their families. If a surrogate mother refused to give the child to the intended parents, and if she was registered as the child's legal mother, these rights are in respect of the surrogate mother and her family members. The rights of a child also cover the right to inherit from his or her legal parents and other relatives, just as it is stipulated with regard to children conceived in a natural way.

The Russian Family Code, after the UN Convention on the Rights of the Child 1989, states that a child has the right to know, as far as is possible, his or her parents (section 54(2)). This is the only provision in Russian law from which it might be concluded that a child, in principle, has the right to know his or her origins. Nevertheless, as to the child's right to know his or her surrogate mother, currently there are no provisions at all that, even if interpreted in the broadest way, could lead us to a positive answer to this question. On the contrary, there are general medical law rules on the confidentiality (medical secrecy) of medical services, as well as on the confidentiality of assisted reproduction procedures specifically.

As to to the rights of a surrogate mother, the main question that Russian law addresses is her right to keep the child to whom she gave birth. However, as has been said above, if a surrogate mother does not use her right to keep the child, she is, under the law, a stranger to this child and does not have any legal right to apply to maintain contact with him or her at all.

IX. Concluding Remarks

While thinking about any future international regulation that would be a workable instrument and would also ensure flexibility, it seems necessary to make two general, interconnected observations.

First, it is necessary to clear up a confusion that currently exists in the area of surrogate motherhood. In order to do this, we need first of all to differentiate between what is called 'full' (or 'gestational') surrogacy and what is called 'partial' (or 'traditional') surrogacy.

It is important to make it clear that new things require new regulation. Assisted reproduction technology and surrogate motherhood are the achievements of biomedicine; they appeared in the last quarter of the twentieth century, and there should be a special regulatory framework invented for this purpose specifically, with a clear understanding that it is designed to address new medical phenomena and new social problems. In this respect, gestational and so-called 'traditional' surrogacy are different in principle. 'Traditional surrogacy' is not, in fact, surrogacy at all: it is not an IVF treatment, and there is no fertilisation outside the human body and no embryo transfer; at best, it is artificial insemination with a donor's sperm. That is why this term is confusing: the word 'traditional' refers us to the Old Testament;[33] but surrogate motherhood did not exist at that time, and The Holy Book did not use this terminology. To apply biblical stories to contemporary realities is misleading and makes complicated things even more complicated. Therefore, it seems necessary to be clear about the difference between these two 'types' of surrogate motherhood and the need to approach each of them differently.

Secondly, in order to make legal regulation of surrogate motherhood arrangements more clear and straightforward, it seems important to recognise that the adoption mechanism is not an appropriate tool in this regard. Adoption is an old concept intended to be used for another purpose. It is a legal mechanism that allows a child who has been left without parents (for whatever reason) to find a new family and not remain in an orphanage.

In the case of IVF, there is usually a commissioning couple, whom we have called 'intended parents' (or a single person), who have been dreaming about having a child and are eager to become this child's legal parents following his or her

---

[33] Sarah, Abram's wife, had no children, and she asked Abram to go to her slave-girl Hagar with the hope that Sarah would 'obtain children by her'. So, Abram 'went in to Hagar, and she conceived ...' See Genesis: 16. See also similar stories about Rahel and her maid Bilhah and about Leah and her maid Zilpah (Genesis: 30).

birth. Most probably, adoption began to be used to finalise parental rights in the case of ART because there was no other legal mechanism at hand. However, this does not exclude the use of another regulatory framework, which will be specially created for this purpose and would therefore be more appropriate. Besides, the use of an adoption mechanism in the context of international surrogacy arrangements will conflict with the existing regulation of international adoption, which itself is a very controversial and complicated matter.

20

South Africa

MELODIE SLABBERT AND CHRISTA ROODT*

I. Introduction and Background

The social, ethical and religious issues relating to surrogate motherhood are well-documented.[1] Surrogate motherhood is presently comprehensively regulated in South African law following the promulgation of chapter 19 of the Children's Act on 1 April 2010.[2] Prior to this date, altruistic surrogacy was not uncommon, and although not explicitly prohibited (and also not viewed as *contra bonos mores* as was commercial surrogacy),[3] was an uncertain and risky undertaking.

Prior to the present statutory regulation of surrogacy, altruistic surrogacy arrangements were subject to contract law and legislation and regulations pertaining to artificial insemination,[4] with the status of the child born as a result of such an arrangement determined by the Children's Status Act.[5] This Act (now

---

* This chapter is dedicated to the memory of Professor Diederika Pretorius, author of *Surrogate Motherhood: A worldwide view of the issues* (Springer, Charles Thomas, 1994). As the leading expert on the legal aspects of surrogate motherhood in South Africa, Professor Pretorius published widely on the topic, and her research has been extensively cited in the Law Reform reports referred to in this chapter.

[1] See, in general, ML Lupton, 'Surrogate parenting: The advantages and disadvantages' (1986) 11 *Tydskrif vir Regswetenskap/Journal for Juridical Science* 148; D Pretorius, 'A comparative overview and analysis of a proposed surrogate motherhood agreement model' (1987) 20 *Comparative and International Law Journal of Southern Africa* 275; D Pretorius, 'Practical aspects of surrogate motherhood' (1991) *De Jure* 52; D Pretorius, 'Surrogate motherhood: A detailed commentary on the draft bill' (1996) *De Rebus* 114; PL Volpe, 'My mother, my sister' (1989) *De Rebus* 369; Pretorius, above n 1; B Clarke, 'Surrogate motherhood: Comment on the South African Law Reform Commission's Report on Surrogate Motherhood (Project 65)' (1993) 110 *South African Law Journal* 769.

[2] Act 38 of 2005. Chapter 19 came into effect on 1 April 2010.

[3] Both predecessors of the Children's Act, ie the Child Care Act 74 of 1983 (s 24), and the Children's Act (s 249) prohibit the exchange of money/consideration for the adoption of a child. In addition, surrogate motherhood is often viewed as a deviation and departure from what society regards as conventional motherhood and parenthood (see M Lupton, 'The right to be born: Surrogacy and the legal control of fertility' (1988) 21 *De Jure* 36, 45).

[4] Eg the regulations regarding the artificial insemination of persons and related matters, issued in terms of the Human Tissue Act 65 of 1983. (These regulations were published under GN R1182 in *Government Gazette* (hereinafter '*GG*') 10283 of 1986-06-20 and amended by GN R1354 in *GG* 18362 of 1997-10-17.)

[5] Act 82 of 1987.

repealed) gave statutory recognition to the Latin maxims *mater semper certa est* and *pater est quem nuptiae demonstrant*, with the result that the mother who gave birth to a child, and her husband, if she was married, were regarded as the legal parents of the child that was born.[6] The commissioning parents in a surrogate relationship could become the legal parents of such a child only if they followed the legal route of adoption in terms of the (now repealed) Child Care Act.[7] In terms of section 5(1)(b) of the Children's Status Act, it was presumed that if a surrogate mother was married, both she and her husband consented to the artificial fertilisation, and the child born of such fertilisation was therefore deemed to be their legitimate child.

Commissioning parents furthermore faced legal uncertainty when a surrogate mother refused to hand over the child to the commissioning parents for adoption. They had no way of knowing whether a court would order specific performance of the surrogate mother's contractual duties. The contract could be viewed as *contra bonos mores*, based on the notion that the practice, which introduces the surrogate mother as a third party into the family and marriage relationship, 'distorts' the concept of the family and the marriage.[8]

South Africa captured the world's attention in 1987 when a grandmother, Pat Anthony, acted as a surrogate for her daughter, Karen Ferreira-Jorge, and became the first surrogate in the world to give birth to triplets.[9] The unsatisfactory position and uncertainties regarding surrogate motherhood led to the South African Law Reform Commission's investigation into the matter, culminating in two documents, namely, *Working Paper 38: Surrogate Motherhood*[10] and the *Report on Surrogate Motherhood.*[11] Following the *Report of the Ad Hoc Committee on the Report of the SA Law Commission on Surrogate Motherhood*[12] and the SALRC's *Project 110: Review of the Child Care Act*, as well as the *Report: Review of the Child Care Act,*[13] the resolution was adopted to regulate rather than ban or criminalise surrogacy. This culminated in chapter 19 of the Children's Act. Its provisions are to be read against the backdrop of chapter 2 of the Constitution, which inter alia

---

[6] Section 5(1)(a) of the Children's Status Act provided: 'Whenever the gamete or gametes of any person other than a married woman or her husband have been used with the consent of both that woman and her husband for the artificial fertilisation of that woman, any child born of that woman as a result of such artificial fertilisation shall for all purposes be deemed to be the legitimate child of that woman and her husband as if the gamete or gametes of that woman or her husband were used for such artificial fertilisation.'

[7] Section 17(a) of Act 74 of 1983. This provision allows a commissioning couple to adopt a child born as a result of surrogacy, even if both of them are not the child's genetic parents.

[8] Clarke, above n 1, 770.

[9] In February 2011, another grandmother gave birth to a grandchild as the surrogate mother carrying their embryo to term. See <http://abcnews.go.com/Health/WomensHealth/surrogate-grandmother-woman-birth-grandson-61/story?id=12912270> (visited 3 August 2011).

[10] Project 65 (April 1991).

[11] SALRC (1993).

[12] February 1999.

[13] December 2002.

entrenches the right to parental care[14] and declares the best interests of the child to be of paramount importance in any matter relating to a child.[15]

Surrogacy is not an issue that relates to children only but involves a range of other legal considerations (arising from contract, the medico-legal or fundamental rights context). The choice of the Children's Act as the vehicle for the regulation of surrogacy is fraught with problems. The regulation of the artificial insemination of the surrogate mother, for example, falls within the scope of the National Health Act[16] and its relevant regulations. Chapter 8 of this Act regulates artificial insemination, but it has not yet been put into operation. The Human Tissue Act (promulgated almost 30 years ago) and regulations relating to artificial insemination in terms of this Act still apply. The practical effect of this is that more than one statute and different sets of regulations[17] will ultimately have to be read together to appreciate the implications and scope of the regulation of surrogacy.

The practice of surrogacy dates back to biblical times; it is also bound to remain controversial and contested as long as infertility exists. Strauss[18] already pointed out in 1968 that of all legal rules, none provides a more sensitive barometer of the very complex and nuanced meta-juridical, societal, religious and cultural forces than those related to procreation and reproduction. With changing notions of mother-, father- and parenthood and the family, the possibility exists that attitudes regarding surrogacy may also change.

II. Legal Requirements Relating to Surrogate Motherhood

A. Surrogate Mother

Legal requirements relating to the surrogate mother apply in respect of a range of specific issues, starting with the issue of consent to the surrogate motherhood agreement. First, apart from the surrogate mother's consent to the agreement, the husband or partner (including a same-sex partner[19]) of a surrogate mother, in instances where the surrogate mother is not the genetic parent of the child

---

[14] Constitution of the Republic of South Africa, 1996, s 28(1)(a).

[15] *Ibid*, s 28(2).

[16] Act 61 of 2003.

[17] No regulations regarding ch 19 have yet been published.

[18] SA Strauss, 'Therapeutic abortion and South African law' (1968) *South African Medical Journal* 710, 710.

[19] Before the enactment of the Children's Act, the Constitutional Court held in *J v Director-General, Department of Home Affairs* 2003 (5) SA 621(CC), that if the ovum of one woman and a donor's sperm have been used for the artificial insemination of another woman, and the two women are living together in a permanent life partnership, a child born of such insemination is deemed for all purposes to be the legitimate child of the two women.

(in other words, in cases of full surrogacy),[20] must also consent to the surrogate agreement, and must become a party to the agreement.[21] If this person (husband or partner) unreasonably withholds his (or her) consent, the court may confirm the surrogate motherhood agreement without this person's consent.[22]

In addition, a surrogate mother must:

(a) be legally competent to enter into a surrogate motherhood agreement;[23]

(b) in all respects, be a suitable person to act as surrogate mother;[24]

(c) understand and accept the legal consequences of the surrogate motherhood agreement and the relevant provisions of the Children's Act, including her rights and obligations in terms of the agreement and the provisions of the Act;[25]

(d) not be using surrogacy as a source of income;[26]

(e) have entered into the surrogate motherhood agreement for altruistic and not for commercial reasons;[27]

(f) have a documented history of at least one pregnancy and viable delivery;[28]

(g) have a living child of her own;[29] and

(h) hand the child born as a result of a valid surrogate motherhood agreement over to the commissioning parent(s) as soon as reasonably possible after the birth of the child.[30]

Moreover, it should also be noted that:

(a) The court will confirm the surrogate motherhood agreement only if the commissioning parent is or commissioning parents are unable to give birth to a child, and this condition must be permanent and irreversible.[31]

---

[20] Full surrogacy takes place when an embryo is created using the gametes of one or both of the commissioning parents (or donors, or a combination of these persons). The surrogate mother is thus not genetically related to the child that she carries.

[21] Section 293(2) of the Children's Act.

[22] *Ibid*, s 293(3).

[23] *Ibid*, s 295(c)(i).

[24] *Ibid*, s 295(c)(ii).

[25] *Ibid*, s 295(c)(iii).

[26] *Ibid*, s 295(c)(iv).

[27] *Ibid*, s 295(c)(v).

[28] *Ibid*, s 295(c)(vi).

[29] *Ibid*, s 295(c)(vii).

[30] *Ibid*, s 297(1)(b).

[31] *Ibid*, s 295(a). The reference to the permanent and irreversible condition causing the infertility must be distinguished from instances where single men or same-sex commissioning couples are unable to have children as a result of physical reality instead of medical indications. Commissioning parents may include a single person, spouses, same-sex or heterosexual civil union partners, as well as same-sex or heterosexual life/permanent partners, provided that he or she is, or they are permanently and irreversibly unable to give birth: Children's Act, s 295(a), read with the definition of 'commissioning parent' in s 1(1) of the Act, ss 292(1)(c), 293(1) and 294 of the Act, and s 13 of the Civil Union Act 17 of 2006. See J Heaton, unpublished draft report, 'International surrogacy: South Africa', submitted to the Family Law Committee of the International Law Association (1 August 2011) 2.

(b) The surrogate mother, her partner, spouse or relatives, have no right of parenthood or care of the child born as a result of such agreement.[32]

(c) The surrogate mother, her partner, spouse or relatives have no right of contact with the child so born, unless if so indicated in the surrogate motherhood agreement.[33]

A surrogate mother who is also the genetic parent of the child (in other words, in cases of partial surrogacy)[34] has the right to terminate the surrogate motherhood agreement at any time prior to the lapse of 60 days after the birth of the child, by filing notice to the court to this effect.[35] A court will terminate the confirmation of the agreement between the surrogate mother and the commissioning parents only if convinced that the surrogate mother's decision is a voluntary one and that she understands the consequences of the termination, and may issue any other order that it deems fit in the best interests of the child. The surrogate mother will incur no liability if she exercises this right, except to compensate the commissioning parents for the expenses they incurred in terms of the agreement, as provided for in the Act.[36] These provisions clearly distinguish between full and partial surrogacy in the context of acquiring parental rights. In the case of full surrogacy, the surrogate motherhood agreement will confer full parental rights on the commissioning parents from the moment of the child's birth, whereas in the case of partial surrogacy, these are technically suspended for a 'cooling-off' period of 60 days following the birth of the child, during which period the surrogate mother has the right to terminate the contract and keep the child.

It is therefore clear that the surrogate mother, if genetically related to the child, has the right to cancel the agreement and keep the child, whereas this clearly does not apply in the instances where the surrogate mother is only carrying the child for the commissioning parents (eg in the instance of full surrogacy). It is interesting to note in this regard that some scholars argue that compelling the surrogate mother to hand over the child against her will amounts to 'sacrificing a woman's reproductive autonomy to the principle *pacta servanda sunt*',[37] even in cases of full surrogacy. It has also been argued that specific enforcement of a surrogate motherhood agreement against the will of the surrogate mother may potentially violate her rights to dignity, privacy and bodily autonomy, including the child's right to dignity.[38]

---

[32] Children's Act, s 297(1)(c).

[33] *Ibid*, s 297(1)(d).

[34] Partial surrogacy applies in cases where the surrogate mother's ovum or ova is/are fertilised using the sperm of the commissioning man or male donor. The surrogate mother in this instance is both the genetic and gestational mother of the child.

[35] Children's Act, s 298(1).

[36] *Ibid*, s 301.

[37] Clarke, above n 1, 777.

[38] A Cockrell, *Bill of Rights Compendium* (Durban, Butterworths, looseleaf) para 3E28.

i. _Requirements Regarding the Artificial Insemination_
of the Surrogate Mother

The artificial fertilisation of the surrogate mother must also comply with the relevant regulations issued in terms of the Human Tissue Act in cases of full surrogacy.[39] At the time of writing (February 2012), the relevant parts of chapter 8 of the National Health Act and draft regulations that relate to artificial fertilisation had not been put into operation.[40] The 1986 regulations were not intended to include surrogacy within their ambit, but do not preclude the practice.[41]

It is necessary at this point to note briefly the difference between the concepts 'artificial insemination' and 'artificial fertilisation', as the different sets of regulations refer to both terms. Although the 1986 regulations refer to 'artificial insemination' in the description of the title, the Human Tissue Act itself refers to the 'artificial fertilization of a person'.[42] The draft 2011 regulations define 'artificial fertilization' as

> the introduction by other than natural means of a male gamete or gametes into the internal reproductive organs of a female person for the purpose of human reproduction and includes artificial insemination, in vitro fertilisation, gamete intrafallopian tube transfer, embryo intrafallopian transfer or intracytoplasmic sperm injection.

The same regulations refer to 'artificial insemination' as the 'placing of male gametes (sperm) into the female reproductive tract by means other than copulation'.

Briefly, the 1986 regulations provide that artificial fertilisation may only be performed by a medical doctor or a person acting under his supervision,[43] with the written consent of the woman and her husband or partner,[44] after having complied with prescribed formalities relating to patient and donor files, tests, examinations, enquiries, consents, information and so forth.[45] In view of the limitations of the 1986 regulations, reproductive specialists presently follow the draft 2007 and 2011 regulations relating to the artificial fertilisation of persons,

---

[39] Regulations regarding the artificial insemination of persons and related matters, published under Government Notice R1182 in _GG_ 10283 of 20 June 1986, and amended by Government Notice R1354 in _GG_ 18362 of 17 October 1997.

[40] These draft regulations were first published on 5 January 2007 in _GG_ 29527, GN R8. A series of draft regulations issued in terms of ch 8 of the National Health Act, including those relating to artificial fertilisation, were again published for public comment on 1 April 2011 (_GG_ 34159 GN R262). There are slight differences between the two draft sets of 2007 and 2011.

[41] Clarke, above n 1, 769.

[42] The regulations only define 'in vitro fertilization', and describe this as 'the bringing together outside the human body of a male and a female gamete and the placing of the zygote in the womb of a female person'. The description of 'artificial fertilization of a person' is similar to the definitions in the National Health Act and draft regulations (see below).

[43] Regs 3 (a doctor must remove or withdraw the gametes) and 11(1), 12 and 13 (a doctor must effect the artificial fertilisation) of the 1986 Regulations, as amended in 1997. For more detail, see MN Slabbert, 'Medical law' (South Africa) in Blanpain (ed) _International Encyclopaedia of Laws_ (Kluwer, 2011) §§ 226–31.

[44] Regs 5(d) and 8(1).

[45] Regs 4, 5, 6, 9 and 10.

which mirror current international practice standards and requirements.[46] These regulations, inter alia, stipulate that only three zygotes or embryos (or less) may be transferred to the recipient (eg surrogate mother) during an embryo transfer procedure, unless a medical reason requires otherwise.[47]

If the surrogate mother provides her own ova for the creation of the embryo, she must comply with specific requirements (eg relating to age, medical, genetic and psychological history) regarding gamete donors.[48] The regulations stipulate that ova taken from a woman younger than 18 years may not be used in artificial insemination,[49] whereas 2008 Practice Guidelines issued by the Southern African Society of Reproductive Medicine and Endoscopic Surgery (SASREG) regarding Gamete Donation[50] state than donors younger than 21 years should first be evaluated by a psychologist. The preferable age of female donors is between 21 and 34 years. The same Guidelines advise that oocyte donation treatment performed on post-menopausal women, eg women older than 50 years, be considered with caution. This means that if a surrogate mother provides her own eggs (eg partial surrogacy), she should not be younger than 18 years old, but preferably between 21 and 34 years. If she only carries the child for the commissioning parents (full surrogacy), she should preferably not be older than 50 years. The Tzaneen grandmother who made history in 1987 when she gave birth to her own grandchild was the exception, and it is unlikely that a similar situation will arise in South Africa in future.

ii. Enforceability of Surrogacy Arrangements

The Children's Act contains specific requirements relating to the content of surrogate motherhood agreements. First, these agreements must be in writing and confirmed by the High Court.[51] This specific requirement makes it clear that a written contract between a surrogate mother and commissioning parents will be invalid if not confirmed by the High Court.

Moreover, no surrogate motherhood agreement will be valid unless:

(a) the agreement is signed by all the parties thereto (including the partner or spouse of the surrogate mother, if applicable);[52]
(b) the agreement is concluded in the Republic of South Africa;[53]

---

[46] See above n 40.
[47] Reg 12 of the 2001 regulations relating to artificial fertilization of persons, published on 1 April 2011 for public comment.
[48] Reg 5 of the 1986 regulations; reg 7 of the 2011 regulations.
[49] Reg 10(1)(c) of the 2001 regulations.
[50] Guidelines available at < http://www.fertilitysa.org.za/TreatmentGuidelines/Reproductive-Medicine.asp> (visited 10 August 2011).
[51] Children's Act, s 292.
[52] *Ibid*, s 292(1)(a).
[53] *Ibid*, s 292(1)(b).

(c) at least one of the commissioning parents, or in the case of only one commissioning parent, this person, is domiciled in South Africa at the time that the agreement is entered into;[54]

(d) the surrogate mother (and her husband or partner, if relevant) is domiciled in South Africa at the time of concluding the contract;[55] and

(e) the agreement is confirmed by the High Court within whose jurisdiction the commission parent(s) is or are domiciled or habitually resident.[56]

No agreement will be confirmed by the High Court if the partner or spouse of the surrogate mother, as well as the partner or spouse of the commissioning parent, is not a party to the agreement and has not provided his or her consent to the arrangement in writing.[57] If a spouse or partner of a surrogate mother not genetically related to the child to be born unreasonably withholds his or her consent, the court may confirm the agreement.[58]

A surrogate agreement must be confirmed by the court before the surrogate mother is artificially inseminated.[59] Artificial insemination may not be performed on the surrogate mother after the lapse of 18 months after the confirmation of the agreement by the court.[60] The surrogate motherhood agreement may also not be terminated after the artificial insemination of the surrogate mother.[61] The artificial insemination of the surrogate mother must be specifically authorised by the court which validates or confirms the surrogate motherhood agreement.[62]

A court may also not confirm the agreement unless the agreement makes adequate provision for the contact, care, upbringing and general welfare of the child, who is entitled to be born in a stable environment. The child's position in the event of the death of the commissioning parents or one of them, or their divorce or separation before the birth of the child, must be considered.[63] The interests of the child to be born as a result of an agreement are of paramount importance, and regard must be had to the personal circumstances and family situations of all the relevant parties.[64]

Recent cases, however, illustrate that the requirements relating to surrogate motherhood agreements are far from clear. There are presently no regulations promulgated in terms of the Children's Act relating to surrogacy. The Deputy

---

[54] *Ibid*, s 292(1)(c).

[55] *Ibid*, s 292(d). The court may dispose with this requirement on good cause shown (s 292(2)). One such example is where one of the commissioning couple has a foreign relative who is willing to act as a surrogate mother. See Heaton, above n 31, 1.

[56] Children's Act, s 292(e).

[57] *Ibid*, s 292(1) and (2).

[58] *Ibid*, s 292(3).

[59] *Ibid*, s 296(1)(a).

[60] *Ibid*, s 296(1)(b).

[61] *Ibid*, s 297(1)(e), subject to ss 292 and 293.

[62] *Ibid*, s 303(1).

[63] *Ibid*, s 295(d).

[64] *Ibid*, s 295(e).

Judge President of the South Gauteng High Court has, however, issued a Practice Directive dealing with these applications. A portion of this Directive reads as follows:

3. In light of these provisions, prospective applicants have from time to time sought directives from this office as to whether such applications are to be placed for hearing on the ordinary roll, or whether they are to be placed for hearing in chambers.
4. A directive is accordingly issued that;
    4.1 A party who seeks to bring an application in terms of the section must first have the application issued by the Registrar in the ordinary course;
    4.2 The court file with all its contents must however, be brought to this office, immediately after issue;
    4.3 This office will upon receipt of the court file and the application, allocate the matter for hearing to a particular Judge, who shall give further directives as to how the matter is to be heard;
    4.4 The applicant's attorneys must specifically refer this office and the court hearing the application to the provisions of section 295 of the Act when the court file is delivered to this office and when the application is heard.
    4.5 The parties must comply in all respects with such further directives and requirements as may be stipulated by the Judge to whom the file has been allocated.[65]

The first unreported judgment from the South Gauteng High Court, *Ex Parte Applications for the Confirmation of Three Surrogate Motherhood Agreements* (GSJ),[66] emphasises some of the practical problems relating to surrogacy arrangements.[67] In this case Wepener J, with Victor J concurring, postponed the applications *sine die* to give the applicants an opportunity to rectify their applications to enable the court to consider the matters on their merits.

The judgment clearly indicates that court confirmation of the agreement is not a mere 'rubber stamp' and that the court, in considering all the facts on which the application is based, will regard the interests of the child to be born of paramount importance.[68] Expert reports need to be very detailed, comprehensive and provide enough factual exposition to support an expert's recommendation.[69] In this case, a psychologist's on-line evaluation of one of the commissioning fathers[70] was found to be unacceptable, as it reinforced an impression of 'babies for sale on order'.[71]

---

[65] Practice Directive 5 of 2011.

[66] Unreported case no 2011/153, 2011/154, 2011/679, 2011/1314, 2011/1315, 2011/1316, 1-3-2011).

[67] M Carnelley and S Soni, 'Surrogate motherhood agreements' 2008 (2) 36 *Speculum Juris* 36.

[68] See para 12 of the judgment.

[69] *Ex Parte Applications for the Confirmation of Three Surrogate Motherhood Agreements* (GSJ), para 12. See above n 66.

[70] *Ibid*, para 21.

[71] *Ibid*.

A very recent judgment of the North Gauteng High Court[72] in October 2011, following specific instruction by the Deputy Judge President to the judges to develop consistent and uniform standards and guidelines regarding surrogate motherhood agreements, brings more clarity regarding the contents of these agreements.[73] In this judgment, Tolmay J and Kollapen J expressed their concern that no details regarding specific expenses in respect of the surrogate mother were provided, as a danger exists that 'generic payments for expenditure without specificity may well run the risk of disguising the payment of compensation'.[74] A detailed and specific list of surrogacy expenses should be provided to minimise the possibility of abuse. Referring to constitutional jurisprudence affecting same-sex couples[75] and the non-discrimination provision of the Constitution, the Court cautioned against creating 'a utopia' for children born as a result of surrogate motherhood arrangements that does not reflect the social reality of present-day South Africa where many children grow up without a father or a mother.[76] The Court also insisted that full details regarding the agency that facilitates the surrogate motherhood agreement be disclosed.[77] In addition, full details regarding the surrogate mother's financial background and position should also be investigated and explained, as well as a comprehensive psychological report regarding the suitability of the surrogate mother. The last-mentioned must include details regarding how handing the baby over to the commissioning parents will affect her; as well as a full medical profile detailing the possible dangers that the pregnancy may hold for her or the intended child.[78] Any disease that may be transmitted from mother to child, such as HIV, should also be disclosed.[79] The Court ruled

[72] Case number 29936/11, in the *ex parte* matter between *WH, UVS, LG, and BJS*, delivered early in October 2011 (still unreported). In this case, the first and second applicants (the commissioning parents) are two married males, who are Dutch and Danish citizens respectively, domiciled in South Africa. The authors are very grateful to Tolmay J of the North Gauteng High Court, for making the judgment available for the purpose of this chapter.

[73] Para 9 of the judgment. The Court invited the Bar, the Law Society and the Centre for Child Law to make submissions as *amici curiae* to the Court regarding the correct approach in surrogacy agreements, specifically where the genetic material used is not that of the parties; the approach, if any, if same-sex couples apply for a surrogate motherhood agreement to be made an order of court; and the appropriate steps that should be followed and factors that should be considered in the best interests of the child (*ibid*, para 10).

[74] *Ibid*, para 29.

[75] See *Minister of Home Affairs v Fourie and Another* 2006 (1) SA 546 CC; *Du Toit v Minister of Welfare Population Development* 2003 (2) SA 196 CC; *J v Director General Department of Home Affairs* 2002 (5) BCL on 436 CC; *National Coalition for Gay and Lesbian Equality and Others v Minister of Home Affairs* 2002 (6) SA 1 CC; and *Gory v Glover NO and Others* 2007 (4) SA 97 CC.

[76] Case number 29936/11, above n 72, paras 54—55.

[77] *Ibid*, para 66: 'An affidavit by the agency should also be filed containing the following: (a) the business of the agency, (b) whether any form of payment is paid to or by the agency in regard of any aspect of the surrogacy, (c) what exactly the agency's involvement was regarding the (i) introduction of the surrogate mother, (ii) how the information regarding the surrogate mother was obtained by the agency and (d) whether the surrogate mother received any compensation at all from the agency or the commissioning parents.'

[78] *Ibid*, para 67.

[79] *Ibid*.

that the origin of the gametes (not mentioning the identity of the gamete donor) must also be stated.

The determination of the suitability or not of the commissioning parents or the surrogate mother is one that may be subjective. Quite rightly, the Court stated that courts should ensure that when exercising their discretion in this regard, personal perceptions should not influence any decision on the suitability of a person either to accept parenthood or to act as a surrogate mother.[80] However, previous criminal convictions, particularly relating to violent crimes or crimes of a sexual nature, must be disclosed, including the circumstances surrounding these.[81] The judgment in the final instance provides a list of issues that the affidavit should contain.[82]

iii. Payment in Terms of the Surrogate Motherhood Agreement

The statutory provisions relating to surrogacy are clear on payments in respect of surrogacy. The type of expenses that are recognised clearly point to a prohibition of commercial surrogacy. Apart from the fact that no person in relation to a surrogate motherhood agreement may promise or give to another person, or receive from another person, any compensation, money or reward of any kind,[83] no promise or agreement for the payment of any compensation to the surrogate mother or any other person, including for the execution of such an agreement, will be enforceable,[84] except in the case of a claim for:

(a) compensation for expenses directly related to the artificial fertilisation of the surrogate mother, the resulting pregnancy, the birth of the child and the confirmation of the surrogate motherhood agreement by the High Court;[85]

(b) loss of earnings incurred by the surrogate mother as a result of the surrogate motherhood agreement;[86] or

---

[80] *Ibid*, para 69.

[81] *Ibid*.

[82] See *ibid*, para 77. The affidavit should contain the following: all factors set out in the Children's Act, together with documentary proof where relevant; details regarding any previous applications for surrogacy; the division in which the application was brought, whether this was granted and/or refused and, if refused, the reasons for the refusal; a clinical psychologist's report in respect of the commissioning parents, and a separate report relating to the surrogate and her partner; a medical report regarding the surrogate mother, which must include the details referred to above; details of, and proof of payment of, any compensation for services rendered, either to the surrogate herself or to the intermediary, the donor, the clinic or any third party involved in the process; all agreements between the surrogate and any intermediary or any other person involved in the process; full particulars, if any agency was involved, of any payment to such agency, as well as an affidavit by that agency containing the information referred to in n 77 above; details, if any, if the commissioning parents have been charged with or convicted with a violent crime, or a crime of a sexual nature.

[83] Children's Act, s 301(1).

[84] *Ibid*, s 301(2).

[85] *Ibid*, s 301(2)(a).

[86] *Ibid*, s 301(2)(b).

(c) insurance to indemnify the surrogate mother for death or disability that may result from the pregnancy and the birth of the child she agreed to carry.[87]

Medical or legal professionals providing a bona fide professional service relating to the surrogate motherhood agreement (eg, drawing up of the contract) and its execution (eg, the artificial insemination of the surrogate mother) are entitled to reasonable compensation for their services.[88]

Despite these provisions, a commissioning couple launched a court application in January 2011 in the Durban High Court to compel the surrogate mother carrying their child to keep her part of the agreement, as it had transpired that this woman had made a 'wish list', which included a Volkswagen Polo and a sum of R100,000. The surrogate mother, in an agreement following the application, agreed to receiving an amount of R10,000 per month for the period of her pregnancy, as well as R70,000 for her loss of income. The commissioning parents would cover the medical expenses relating to the pregnancy and birth for a period up to three months after the birth.[89]

iv. Advertisements Recruiting Surrogate Mothers or Surrogacy Services

The advertising (for profit or with the view to compensation) of a woman's willingness to enter into a surrogate motherhood agreement is specifically prohibited.[90] This means that it is illegal to broker surrogacy arrangements on a commercial basis. However, a woman is free to offer her services to enter into a surrogate motherhood agreement that complies with the provisions of the Act and in terms of which she will be compensated only for reasonable expenses provided for in the Act. Advertisements for egg donors in South Africa are common and offer to pay between R5,000 and R6,000 per donation.[91] The same agencies recruiting egg donors normally also advertise for surrogate mothers,[92] but refer the process to the relevant artificial insemination clinics and lawyers specialising in surrogacy arrangements.[93]

v. Rights of the Surrogate Mother

The surrogate mother's rights in respect of the child born as a result of the agreement are discussed below. The termination of a surrogate motherhood agreement

---

[87] *Ibid*, s 301(2)(c).

[88] *Ibid*, s 301(3).

[89] Unreported case. See T Broughton, 'Unborn baby a hostage to greed', *The Mercury*, 19 January 2011.

[90] Children's Act, s 303(2).

[91] See,eg,<http://baby2mom.co.za/page/11597/Become-Egg-Donor-#%2FPage%2F11597%2FEgg-Donors> (visited 2 August 2011).

[92] See <http://www.surrogatemom.co.za/#%2FPage%2F11609%2FSurrogacy> (visited 2 August 2011).

[93] It is uncertain whether a referral fee applies in these instances.

has specific implications regarding parental rights.[94] The surrogate mother may decide to terminate the pregnancy in terms of the Choice on the Termination of Pregnancy Act,[95] which provides for abortion on request of the pregnant woman during the first 12 weeks of the pregnancy.[96]

The surrogate mother has to inform the commissioning parents and consult them before the pregnancy is terminated.[97] However, they may not prevent her from terminating the pregnancy in accordance with the provisions of the Choice on the Termination of Pregnancy Act, which clearly provides that it is a criminal offence to prevent the lawful termination of a pregnancy or to obstruct access to a facility for the termination of a pregnancy.[98]

The surrogate mother will not be liable to the commissioning parents for terminating the pregnancy, except to compensate them for expenses provided for in terms of the Act, except if the pregnancy has to be terminated on medical grounds.[99]

The surrogate mother, or her partner, spouse or relatives has or have no right of contact with the child so born, unless so indicated in the surrogate motherhood agreement.[100]

The surrogate mother's identity is protected in terms of the Act, and her identity and that of all the other parties to the surrogate motherhood agreement may not be published without their written consent.[101]

B. The Child

i. Status of the Child

A child's legal ties to parents confer a specific status in society, the latter associated with a specific level of care and support. The child's identity is furthermore vested in the family unit, which endows the child with 'a heritage and a history'.[102]

With the artificial insemination of the surrogate mother in cases of full surrogacy, more than one embryo (but not more than three) may be transferred to the surrogate mother's uterus, which may result in the birth of more than one surrogate child. Whether the birth of surrogate twins or triplets is desirable or in the best interests of these children, is a separate question that must be considered carefully.

---

[94] *Ibid*, s 299.
[95] Act 92 of 1996. See also s 300(1) of the Children's Act.
[96] Act 92 of 1996, s 2.
[97] Children's Act, s 300(2).
[98] Act 92 of 1996, s 10.
[99] Children's Act, s 300(3).
[100] *Ibid*, s 297(1)(d).
[101] *Ibid*, s 302.
[102] M Lupton, 'Artificial reproduction and the family of the future' (1998) 17 *Med Law* 93, 95.

Melodie Slabbert and Christa Roodt

The surrogacy provisions clearly require that a child contemplated in terms of a valid surrogate motherhood agreement will need to be genetically related to both the commissioning parents, or if this is impossible as a result of medical, or biological or other valid reasons, related to at least one of the commissioning parents.[103] This provision is deemed harsh and discriminatory by practising reproductive specialists,[104] as it is possible that both the commissioning parents may suffer from (male or female) infertility. Some legal scholars, however, argue that to allow surrogacy where the commissioning parent is or both commissioning parents are infertile would amount to a 'commissioned adoption' and would hence be unacceptable.[105] It would also encourage the practice of commissioning parents 'shopping around' with the intention to create children with specific characteristics. An ordinary adoption for these persons is not always possible, as Pretorius[106] points out. There may be long waiting lists for newborn white babies, for example, or the person or couple may be too old to qualify as an adoptive parent(s). As will be pointed out in section III. on relevant fundamental rights below, the current provision potentially infringes on an infertile person's right to make decisions regarding reproduction, entrenched in section 12(2)(a) of the South African Constitution, including that person's rights to dignity and privacy.[107]

A valid surrogate motherhood agreement (eg one that has been confirmed by the High court, as explained above), will have the following effect on the status of the child born as a result of such an agreement:

(a) the child born as a result of the agreement is for all purposes regarded as the child of the commissioning parent(s) from the moment of the child's birth,[108] thus reversing the *mater semper certa est* rule; and

(b) the child born as a result of the agreement will have no claim for maintenance or of succession against the surrogate mother, her husband or partner, or any of their relatives.[109]

If the commissioning parents and surrogate entered into an agreement which has not been confirmed by the court as prescribed in terms of this Act, or a contract that does not comply with the requirements regarding the surrogate motherhood agreement as specified in terms of the Act, in other words, an invalid contract, a child born in terms of such an arrangement will be deemed to be the legal child of the person giving birth to him or her, in other words, the surrogate mother.[110]

---

[103] Section 294. The provision refers to the use of the gametes of the commissioning parents(s).

[104] Eg Dr Aldo Esterhuizen, an embryologist from the Medfem Clinic, in an e-mail correspondence to one of the authors during 2010.

[105] See D Meyerson, 'Surrogacy arrangements' in C Murray (ed), *Gender and the new South African constitutional order* (Cape Town, Juta, 1994) 121, 123.

[106] Pretorius, 'Practical aspects of surrogate motherhood', above n 1, 59–61; Pretorius, 'Surrogate motherhood', above n 1, 117–19.

[107] Sections 10 and 14 of the Constitution.

[108] Children's Act, s 297(1)(a).

[109] *Ibid*, s 297(1)(f).

[110] *Ibid*, s 297(2).

The termination of a surrogate motherhood agreement, on the other hand, has the following effect on the status of a child born as a result of such an agreement:

(a) if the agreement is terminated after the birth of the child, all parental rights will vest in the surrogate mother, her husband or partner (if relevant), or, if none, in the commissioning father;[111] and

(b) if the agreement is terminated before the child's birth, parental rights will vest in the surrogate mother, her husband or partner (if relevant), or, if none, in the commissioning father, from the child's birth.[112]

In the event of a termination of the surrogate motherhood agreement, the surrogate mother and her husband or partner, or, if none, the commissioning father, is obliged to accept parenthood of the child born as a result of the agreement,[113] with the commissioning parents having no parental rights in respect of such a child (and which can be obtained only through the legal adoption of the child).[114] The child will accordingly have no claim for maintenance or of succession against the commissioning parents or any of their relatives.[115] In practice, however, this means that a surrogate mother carrying a child in terms of a full surrogacy arrangement (in other words, having no genetic relation to the child) may be compelled to accept parenthood and all its concomitant duties and responsibilities, which is bound to cause her anguish.

It is also very likely that some surrogate mothers, despite the Act limiting payment to reasonable expenses only, may be desperate enough to enter into these contracts for the limited financial benefit that they may receive. This concern has also been expressed in the recent judgment in the North Gauteng High Court. The Court mentioned the deep socio-economic disparities and the prevalence of poverty as factors that may increase the possibility of abuse of underprivileged women who enter into these agreements solely for the financial benefit,[116] however limited this may be. The cost of full surrogacy is high (presently estimated around R200,000),[117] which clearly makes this an option for the affluent only. This illustrates how difficult it is to achieve a nuanced balancing of the rights and interests of all the parties to a surrogate arrangement. The best interests of the child, as mentioned already, are of paramount importance.[118]

---

[111] *Ibid*, s 299.

[112] *Ibid*, s 299(b).

[113] *Ibid*, s 299(c).

[114] *Ibid*, s 299(d).

[115] *Ibid*, s 299(e).

[116] *Ex parte* matter between *WH, UVS, LG, and BJS*, para 64. See above n 72.

[117] According to Jenny Currie, founder of the Baby2mom Egg Donation and Surrogacy Programme. For more detail, see <http://baby2mom.co.za/page/11597/Become-Egg-Donor-#%2FPage%2F11597%2FEgg-Donors> (visited 10 August 2011).

[118] See *Jooste v Botha* 2000 (2) SA 199 (T), where the court states that this standard is a general guideline only, and not a rule of horizontal application. If it is interpreted to override all other legitimate interests of parents, siblings and other parties, this would prevent the imprisonment or dismissal of a parent where this is not in the child's best interests (at 210C-E).

ii. Rights of the Child Born as a Result of a Valid Surrogate Motherhood Agreement

The rights of the child born as a result of a valid and confirmed surrogate motherhood agreement are the following:

(a) The child is for all purposes the legal child of the commissioning parents and has no claim for maintenance or a claim of succession against the surrogate mother, her husband or partner, or relatives.

(b) The child's right of contact with or access to the surrogate mother will depend on the specific provisions of the individual surrogacy arrangement.

The Children's Act contains a specific provision relating to the rights of children born as a result of artificial insemination. Section 40 (resembling the repealed section 5 of the Children's Status Act) provides that

> [w]henever the gamete or gametes of any person other than a married person or his or her spouse have been used with the consent of both such spouses for the artificial fertilisation of one spouse, any child born of that spouse as a result of such artificial fertilisation must for all purposes be regarded to be the child of those spouses as if the gamete or gametes of those spouses had been used for such artificial fertilisation.[119]

Moreover, for the purpose of this provision, it is presumed that both spouses provided consent, until the contrary is proven.[120] Furthermore, confirming the common law presumption of *mater semper certa est*, section 40(2) states that (subject to the provisions relating to the artificial insemination of the surrogate mother elsewhere in the Act), whenever the gamete or gametes of any person has or have been used for the artificial insemination of a woman, any child born to that woman as a result of this insemination must for all purposes be regarded as that woman's child.

These provisions are necessary to provide certainty regarding parenthood for children born as a result of artificial insemination generally, and are distinguished from those pertaining to surrogate motherhood. Section 40(3) makes it clear that no right, responsibility, duty or obligation will exist between a child born from artificial insemination by donor gamete(s) and the said donor.

Children born as a result of artificial insemination and surrogacy, or the guardians of these children, are entitled to have access to medical information concerning the children's genetic parents while still minors, as well as to any other information concerning the children's genetic parents, but in the last instance not before these children reach the age of 18 years.[121]

The identity of the gamete donor providing the gamete(s) for the artificial insemination may not be disclosed under this provision, nor may the identity

---

[119] Children's Act, s 40(1)(a).
[120] *Ibid*, s 40(1)(b).
[121] *Ibid*, s 41(1).

of the surrogate mother.[122] The child's right to his or her genetic identity, eg the right to know one's parentage, has been the focus of international discussion.[123] The recognition in the Children's Act of the right of children born as a result of a surrogacy arrangement to know their biological origins, a central part of knowing their identity, is in line with international developments.[124] For obvious reasons, this right cannot include knowledge regarding the donor's identity.

The identity of a child born following a surrogate motherhood agreement is protected, and no facts that may reveal such child's identity may be published.[125]

III. Fundamental Rights Considerations

The regulation of surrogate motherhood implicates a range of constitutional considerations. The fundamental rights of the surrogate mother and of the child born following a surrogacy arrangement, as well those of the commissioning parent(s), not to mention the partner or spouse of the surrogate mother and the gamete donors, are all intricately interwoven. Relevant rights at stake are the right to make decisions regarding reproduction (as part of the right to freedom and security of the person);[126] the rights to human dignity,[127] privacy[128] and equality;[129] and

---

[122] *Ibid*, s 41(2). Reg 18 of the 2011 draft regulations relating to the artificial fertilisation of persons prohibits the disclosure of the identity of the person who donated a gamete.

[123] See, eg, S Wilson, 'Identity, geneology and the social family: The case of donor insemination' (1997) 11 *International Journal of Law, Policy and the Family* 270.

[124] Art 8 of the UN Convention on the Rights of the Child states that parties must 'undertake to respect the right of the child to preserve his or her identity ... where a child is illegally deprived of some or all of the elements of his or her identity, States Parties shall provide appropriate assistance and protection, with a view to re-establishing speedily his or her identity'. The 'best interests of the child' standard may also be employed to formulate an argument in favour of these children having access to knowledge regarding their genetic heritage.

[125] Children's Act, s 302(2).

[126] Constitution, s 12(2).

[127] *Ibid*, s 10. In this context, surrogacy is seen as analogous to slavery, and hence contrary to human dignity. The idea of the so-called commodification of babies as a result of surrogacy also potentially violates the intrinsic value of human life, and is hence arguably in conflict with human dignity. Producing a child for money itself denigrates human dignity. These arguments, however, have to be balanced against arguments in support of the reproductive rights of infertile persons.

[128] Privacy rights enable individuals to make decisions about their lives (eg those relating to marriage, procreation, contraception, family relationships and child-rearing) without interference by the State. Privacy, in terms of South African law, is protected both by the Constitution and by the common law action for invasion of privacy (as an impairment of the *dignitas*) under the *actio iniuriarum*.

[129] Section 9(1) of the Constitution provides that everyone is equal before the law and has the right to equal protection and benefit of the law, whereas s 9(3) and (4) prohibit direct or indirect discrimination on one or more grounds, some of which are listed (not a closed category). Excluding, eg, certain couples or individuals from the practice of surrogacy or artificial insemination (eg homosexual couples) would violate their rights to equality. In *J v Director-General, Department of Home Affairs* 2003 (5) SA 621(CC), the court held that if the ovum of one woman and a donor's sperm have been used for the artificial insemination of another woman, and the two women are living together in a permanent life partnership, a child born of such insemination is deemed for all purposes to be the legitimate child of the two women. See above n 19.

rights relating to the protection of children.[130] For the purpose of this brief chapter, only a few aspects will be highlighted here.

Section 12(2) of the Constitution provides that

> [e]veryone has the right to bodily and psychological integrity, which includes the right—(a) to make decisions concerning reproduction; (b) to security in and control over their body ...

This right provides the constitutional framework for the regulation of surrogate motherhood. This right is closely related to the right to found (conceive and have) a family, which is entrenched in international human rights law.[131] Infertility is without doubt a serious obstruction to the realisation of the reproductive right of persons.

Preventing an unmarried woman from becoming a surrogate mother (or a childless unmarried or married woman) may be said unjustifiably to limit her constitutional right to reproductive freedom entrenched in the Bill of Rights. The Act does not exclude a single woman from becoming a commissioning parent. Similarly, excluding an infertile commissioning couple (eg where both male–female or male–male and female–female are infertile) from entering into a surrogacy agreement by virtue of the requirement that one or both of the commissioning parents must provide gamete(s) for the artificial insemination of the surrogate mother, constitutes a possible violation of their right to reproductive autonomy. Despite arguments that these persons should follow the route of normal adoption (in order to avoid so-called 'commissioned adoptions'), this is not always a straightforward matter, as present impediments may frustrate such couples' efforts to adopt.

The discussion above alluded to the right of the child to know his or her biological origins, which is recognised in the Children's Act. This right does not extend to knowinf the identity of the gamete donor(s) involved in a surrogacy arrangement, unless they specifically provide their consent that their identities be disclosed. As explained in section II. above, a surrogacy agreement may also provide for contact between a surrogate mother and the child born as a result of a surrogate motherhood agreement.

IV. Applicable Private International Law Rules Relating to Surrogacy

The above discussion dealt with the various aspects of in-country surrogacy, where all the relevant parties are domiciled in South Africa. This section relates to

---

[130] Constitution, s 28.

[131] Art 23(2) of the International Covenant on Civil and Political Rights, for example, recognises the right of men and women of marriageable age to found a family. Art 14(1)(a) and (b) of the African Women's Protocol, oblige States Parties to ensure that the right of women to control their fertility, and their right to decide whether to have children, the number of children and the spacing of children, are respected and promoted.

cross-border surrogacy and sets out the relevant connecting factors, the structure of the conflicts rule found in South African law and the recognition of the consequences of valid surrogacy undertaken in South Africa.

Section 292(1)(b)–(e) of the Children's Act sets out the requirements for validity of a surrogate motherhood agreement in terms of South African law. The validity of a surrogate motherhood agreement is governed by South African law if the agreement was concluded in South Africa and at least one commissioning parent as well as the surrogate mother and her husband or partner are domiciled in South Africa at the time of entering into the agreement. The meaning and interpretation of 'domicile' as a connecting factor in South African law is governed by the Domicile Act.[132] The definition of 'parents' in the Act has yet to be amended to include the commissioning parents of a surrogate child.[133]

Couples who do not have their domicile in South Africa are excluded from commissioning a surrogate child. At least one of the commissioning parents must be domiciled in South Africa to qualify for the legal protection offered by the Act.

The requirement concerning the domicile of the surrogate mother and her partner may be disposed of on good cause shown. The confirmation by the High Court within whose area of jurisdiction the commissioning parent or parents are domiciled or habitually resident[134] is required under subsection (e). This provision displays all the qualities of a unilateral conflicts rule.[135] It indicates *when* South African law applies to a surrogate motherhood agreement, instead of identifying a single connecting factor for the category of validity of a surrogate motherhood agreement that would point in the direction of the applicable law.[136]

The unilateral conflicts rule contained in section 292 of the Children's Act is the first specific private international law rule that exists for surrogacy in South African law. Thus far, it seems to be the only one. A unilateral conflicts rule safeguards the opportunity for the South African judiciary to exercise discretion and control over surrogacy agreements, which a multilateral conflicts rule cannot do. The unilateral structure of the rule also precludes the insertion of any choice of law or choice of court clauses into the agreement. As such, the parties are not at liberty to select the law applicable to their agreement, and the rule itself finds application by virtue of designating the court that is competent to confirm the surrogate motherhood agreement. The law governing the contract is not in issue. The situation is simply that, if a South African court has jurisdiction to confirm, it will apply the *lex fori*. Knowing which court will be confirming their

---

[132] Act 3 of 1992.

[133] Domicile Act, s 2(3).

[134] E Schoeman, and C Roodt, 'South Africa' in R Blanpain (gen ed), *International Encyclopedia of Laws* (2007) (Alphen aan den Rijn, Kluwer) §§ 37–43.

[135] CF Forsyth, *Private International Law*, 4th edn (2003) (Lansdowne, Juta) 8–9.

[136] A formula that identifies which law applies if the surrogate motherhood agreement is concluded in South Africa, and which law applies if it is concluded in another State, would be readily identifiable as a multilateral conflicts rule.

agreement and the law it will apply, lends important predictability and certainty to the situation.

The unilateral conflicts rule also displays a number of potential weaknesses. First, it does not avoid the risk of limping situations that arises when a surrogate motherhood agreement is valid in the country in which it was concluded but is invalid elsewhere. Secondly, if each jurisdiction regulates the issue in its own, uniquely different way, surrogate-born children may continue to be exposed to a number of legal and practical risks.

In the absence of a Convention that regulates the legal consequences of surrogacy agreements, ordinary rules of private international law will apply in a situation where commissioning parents who had had a child by a valid surrogacy agreement in South Africa, settled in a foreign country.[137] These rules will determine the child's status and the legal consequences arising from the relationship between the child and the commissioning parents. The commissioning parents will be the legal parents of the child when South African law is the applicable law, unless that foreign country considers surrogacy to be contrary to its public policy. A situation may arise where the commissioning parents are in a same-sex relationship and their status as legal parents of the child is not recognised in the country in question.[138]

Adoption in terms of the 1993 Hague Convention on Protection of Children and Cooperation in respect of Intercountry Adoption may be an option for foreigners who do not meet the domicile requirement in the Children's Act but who are habitually resident in a State Party. Neither altruistic nor commercial surrogacy would be a legal option for such a couple, even if either or both of them donated gametes for the artificial insemination of the surrogate mother. However, the likelihood of their meeting all the legal requirements set by the Children's Act and the Hague Convention is rather slim.[139]

V. Conclusion

Despite some measure of certainty that chapter 19 of the Children's Act has brought in respect of the legal regulation of surrogate motherhood, some practical problems which were highlighted above, as well as a few omissions, remain.

---

[137] See Heaton, above n 31, 2.

[138] *Ibid.*

[139] Among other requirements are the subsidiarity principle; no contact between prospective adopting parents and the child's biological parents until the subsidiarity principle has been complied with; consent requirements and agreement between the respective central authorities for the intercountry adoption of a child who was conceived as a result of an invalid surrogacy agreement. South African courts are cautious of granting sole guardianship and sole care of South African children to foreigners who intend to adopt. See *AD v DW (Centre for Child Law as Amicus Curiae; Department of Social Development as Intervening Party)* 2008 (3) SA 183 (CC); Heaton, above n 31, 3.

Some of these issues have been clarified in a recent judgment. Only time will tell whether the bold step to regulate surrogate motherhood by means of comprehensive legislation will prove to have been wise. A unilateral conflicts rule exists, but by its very nature it regulates when South African law applies, without setting any requirements for South Africans who conclude surrogacy agreements in a foreign country.

21

Spain

PATRICIA OREJUDO PRIETO DE LOS MOZOS

I. Preliminary Remarks

In the late 1980s the Spanish Parliament adopted an anti-surrogacy approach that is still prevalent, at least as far as domestic surrogacy is concerned. The first Spanish Law on Human ART[1] made it clear that surrogacy cannot result in the legal effects that the participants seek, and the rule has remained unaffected (see section II. below). However, this clear situation has recently become more uncertain, due to the liberal approach the administrative authorities have adopted in relation to the recognition of certain parental relationships created by means of surrogacy in foreign countries (see section III. below). Indeed, such an administrative foreign surrogacy-friendly approach not only justifies the maintenance of the internal veto, but also (and mainly) explains the lack of agreement of the Spanish courts as to the recognition of such foreign surrogacy (see section IV. below).

II. The Legislative Ban

The abovementioned anti-surrogacy approach is set out in Article 10 of the current Spanish Law on Human ART:[2] its first paragraph provides that surrogacy agreements are null and void; the second establishes that the legal mother of children born of a surrogate mother is determined through childbirth; and the third leaves open the determination of the father–child relationship by means of legal action.[3]

---

[1] *Ley* 35/1988 of 22 November, *sobre técnicas de reproducción humana asistida*, Boletín Oficial del Estado (hereinafter 'BOE') no 282, 24 November 1988.

[2] *Ley* 14/2006 of 26 May, *sobre técnicas de reproducción humana asistida*, BOE no 126, 27 May 2006.

[3] Art 10 (*'Gestación por sustitución'*) provides: '1. Será nulo de pleno derecho el contrato por el que se convenga la gestación, con o sin precio, a cargo de una mujer que renuncia a la filiación materna a favor del contratante o de un tercero. 2. La filiación de los hijos nacidos por gestación de sustitución será determinada por el parto. 3. Queda a salvo la posible acción de reclamación de la paternidad respecto del padre biológico, conforme a las reglas generales.'

Thus, even if there is no express bar against the practice,[4] the negative approach of the Law is clear: in fact, the Parliament relied on the Palacios Report, drafted by a special parliamentary commission, which led to the conclusion that the practice could entail the exploitation of women and the commodification of children.[5] The Law sets out an unambiguous denial of the enforceability of surrogacy agreements, irrespective of their altruistic or commercial basis. The parties to such a contract cannot ask for the execution of the usual reciprocal obligations, ie the obligation of the gestational mother to renounce motherhood and give the baby away, and the obligation of the intended parents to pay the surrogate's expenses and, where surrogacy is commercial, economic compensation. The *mater semper certa est* rule is reaffirmed, so that the legal parents of any newborn child are the gestational mother and, if she is married, her husband or her wife[6] notwithstanding the possibility of the biological father[7] pleading before the courts for the determination of his fatherhood. As a logical consequence of this negative approach, there is no regulation either as to the legal requirements on a surrogate mother and on the intended parents, or as to the rights and duties of the persons involved (such as the right of termination of pregnancy, contacts between parents and children or knowledge of biological links, etc).

The lack of a specific prohibition entails that the Spanish Law also lacks administrative sanctions against those persons involved in the practice. It should be noted that Article 26 of Law 14/2006 establishes three kinds of infringements: slight, severe and very severe. Severe and very severe infringements are certain behaviours explicitly included in a list, where no express reference to any action linked to surrogate motherhood can be found. Slight infringements derive from the violation of any prohibition or duty settled by the Law that does not entail a severe or very severe infringement. But, as said before, neither the behaviour of the parents (intended and surrogate), nor the intervention of third persons (such as doctors, brokers or intermediaries, advertisers, lawyers) is directly prohibited. Where surrogacy takes place in Spain, there is no sanction other than the civil denial of the intended effects. There are no consequences from the viewpoint of criminal law, at least if the practice is entered into openly. If, however, a woman pretends that she has given birth, and another woman, who does give birth, hands

---

[4] See M Atienza, *Bioética, Derecho y Argumentación* (Lima/Bogotá, Themis, 2010) 153–54; S Álvarez González, 'Efectos en España de la gestación por sustitución llevada a cabo en el extranjero' (2010) 10 *Anuario Español de Derecho internacional privado* 339, 347.

[5] See M Palacios Alonso, 'Ley sobre técnicas de Reproducción asistida (35/88) de 1988 a 2005' in L Morillas Cuevas, I Benítez Ortuzar and J Peris Riera (eds), *Libro homenaje al Prof Dr Ferrando Mantorani* (Madrid, Dickinson, 2005) 13, 19; B Souto Galván, 'Aproximación al estudio de la gestación de sustitución desde la perspectiva del Bioderecho' (2005) *Foro Nueva época* 275, 280.

[6] See Art 116 Spanish Civil Code (hereinafter 'Cc'); notice that Art 44 Cc asserts that marriage has the same requirements and effects, notwithstanding the sex of the parties, ie, that marriage in Spain is a right recognised also to same-sex partners.

[7] This possibility is not recognised as regards the intended biological mother in a gestational surrogacy, ie in the situation where the eggs belong to the intended mother and not to the surrogate mother.

over the child to the first woman, both of them would commit a criminal offence (see Articles 220 and 221 of the Spanish Criminal Code).

The absence of criminal and/or administrative sanctions against surrogacy would seem to evidence some kind of a quasi-tolerant approach that might be invoked where intended parents resort to surrogacy in Spain and wish their parenthood to be recognised. For it is possible to attain their aim: once the father–child relationship is established by the courts in favour of the genetic father, the gestational mother could renounce motherhood and the children could be adopted by the father's wife or husband.[8] The other possibility consists in resorting to foreign authorities and/or laws, and asking the Spanish authorities to recognise the parental relationship created abroad.

III. The (Administrative) Recognition of Foreign Surrogacy

There is a leading case in Spain concerning foreign surrogacy, which has triggered the current surrogacy-friendly approach of the Spanish administrative authorities. The case concerns two married Spanish men who resorted to surrogacy in California. They attempted to register in the relevant Spanish Consulate two babies who, according to the certificate of the Californian registrar, were the sons of both men, but their request was denied.[9] As the chancellor in charge of the register had noted that the children had been born from a surrogate mother, it was declared, by a decision (*Auto*) of 10 November 2008, that the surrogate was the legal mother. The couple lodged an appeal before the *Dirección General de los Registros y del Notariado* (DGRN), the administrative body entrusted with all issues relating to the Civil Register.[10] This body, which is dependent on the Ministry of Justice, granted the appeal and ordered the registration by means of its *Resolución* of 18 February 2009.[11] But the Court of First Instance no 15 of

---

[8] See MR Díaz Romero, 'La gestación por sustitución en nuestro ordenamiento jurídico' (2010) 7527 *Diario La Ley* 2. Against, Palacios Alonso, above n 5, 20.

[9] See M Requejo Isidro, 'Spanish homosexual couple and surrogate pregnancy', available at <www.conflictoflaws.net/2008/spanish-homosexual-couple-and-surrogate-pregnancy>.

[10] Art 9 of the Law of the Civil Register of 8 June 1957 (*Ley del Registro civil*), BOE no 151, 10 June 1957 (hereinafter 'LCR').

[11] *Westlaw Aranzadi* RJ 2009/1735. Concerning this decision, see Álvarez González, above n 4, 347–54; R Bercovitz Rodríguez-Cano, 'Hijos made in California' (2009) *Actualidad Civil Westlaw Aranzadi*, BIB 2009/411; E Farnós Amorós, 'Inscripción en España de la filiación derivada del acceso a la maternidad subrogada en California. Cuestiones que plantea la Resolución de la DGRN de 18 de febrero de 2009' (2010) 1 *InDret*; JC Fernández Rozas and S Sánchez Lorenzo, *Derecho internacional privado*, 6th edn (Cizur Menor, Civitas, 2011) 434–36; A Quiñones Escámez, 'Doble filiación paterna de gemelos nacidos en el extranjero mediante maternidad subrogada' (2009) 9 *InDret* (fn 2); A Quiñones Escámez, 'Nota a Res DGRN de 18 de febrero de 2009' (2009) *Revista Española de Derecho Internacional* 215–17; P Orejudo Prieto de los Mozos, 'Nota a Res DGRN de 18 de febrero de 2009' (2009) 9 *Anuario Español de Derecho Internacional* 1244–52; P Orejudo Prieto de los Mozos, 'Recognition in Spain of

Valencia annulled this decision, at the request of the Public Prosecutor, by means of its Judgment of 15 September 2010.[12] This Judgment was confirmed by the Court of Appeal of Valencia (Section 10) on 23 November 2011.[13]

Some days after the Judgment of 15 September 2010 was issued, the DGRN published an *Instrucción* (of 5 October 2010)[14] containing certain commands directed to the authorities in charge of the civil status registers (consular, municipal and central) in Spain. Analysis of these commands proves that the DGRN intended to respond to the complaints of gay couples concerning the inequity in the treatment of comparable situations. When a man and a woman of procreative age ask for entry in the Spanish civil status registers of the births of their children born from a surrogate mother, there is no reason for the registrar to suspect that surrogacy is involved, and so registration is granted. But when the intended parents are two men, surrogacy is evident and registration is denied. To solve this factual (rather than legal) discrimination, the DGRN could have asked the civil register authorities to reinforce their verification of the registered facts. However, instead it instructed the authorities in charge of the civil status registers to favour the entry of births upon recognition of the foreign judgment that created the parent–child relationship. Thus, as the civil status registries are the authorities that would usually deal with the recognition of such parenthood,[15] the *Instrucción* would entail that, in the majority of situations, a foreign surrogacy will have effects in Spain.

The *Instrucción* begins by recalling that Article 10.3 of Law 14/2006 enables the recognition of biological fatherhood in favour of the intended father. Therefore it seems that for the DGRN, this provision would principally show that the ban

---

Parentage Created by Surrogate Motherhood' (2011) *Yearbook of Private International Law* 619; M Requejo Isidro, 'Spanish homosexual couple and surrogate pregnancy-II', available at <www.conflict oflaws.net/2009/spanish-homosexual-couple-and-surrogate-pregnancy-ii>.

[12] *La Ley* 152885/2010. See Álvarez González, above n 4, 349–53; M Requejo Isidro, 'Spanish homosexual couple and surrogate pregnancy-III', available at <www.conflictoflaws.net/2010/surrogate-motherhood-and-spanish-homosexual-couple-iii>; Orejudo Prieto de los Mozos (2011), above n 11, 631–32.

[13] *Sentencia de la Audiencia Provincial de Valencia*, no 826/2001, *Westlaw Aranzadi* JUR 2011/420242.

[14] BOE no 243, 7 October 2010. See M Guzmán Zapatero, 'Gestación por sustitución y nacimiento en el extranjero: hacia un modelo de regulación (sobre la Instrucción DGRN de 5 de octubre de 2010' (2010) 10 *Anuario Español de Derecho internacional privado* 731; Álvarez González, above n 4, 356–61; M Requejo Isidro, 'Another twist in surrogacy motherhood saga', available at <www.conflictoflaws .net/2010/another-twist-in-surrogacy-motherhood-saga>.

[15] Spanish nationals generally attempt to have their status as parents of a child born through a surrogate recognised in Spain by resorting to the authorities in charge of the Spanish civil status registers. The purported Spanish parents must obtain some documentation for the children (eg, passports), which depends on the previous entry of their birth. Therefore they demand such entry, and Spanish authorities must determine whether the birth affects a Spanish citizen: otherwise, because the birth took place in a foreign country, it cannot be included in the Spanish civil status register (Art 15 LCR). Because the children will be Spanish, according to Art 17.1 a) Cc, only if they can be considered born out of Spanish, it is necessary to decide if the foreign parent–child relationship can be recognised. See JC Fernández Rozas and P Rodríguez Mateos, 'Atribución de la nacionalidad española' in JC Fernández Rozas *et al*, *Derecho español de la nacionalidad* (Madrid, Tecnos 1987) 133, 142–43.

is not that complete—that some effects can be recognised in those situations where surrogacy has taken place in a foreign country.[16] But the DGRN limits the possibility for recognition by means of deriving from this very same rule (that demands a judgment from the Spanish courts in order to establish fatherhood) a requirement that for a foreign parental relationship to be recognised, it must have been established by means of a ruling. Consequently, the submission of the foreign judgment would be a prerequisite for the registration of any foreign surrogacy,[17] and neither of the two other methods provided in Spanish rules for entering a child in the civil status registers can be employed:[18] both the first directive (first point) and the second directive of the *Instrucción* declare that it is not possible to enter the birth in the civil status register through the most commonly used methods, ie the declaration of the fact of the birth, accompanied by the corresponding medical certification;[19] and the submission of a certificate from the foreign civil register.[20] As a result, no effects can be granted to a surrogacy established according to a foreign law without the intervention of a judicial authority.

The DGRN further instructs (second point of the first directive) that if there is a foreign ruling declaring the parental relationship, the recognition of the ruling, prior to the entering of the birth in the civil status register, is to be accomplished

---

[16] The invocation of this article with a view to recognising a parent–child relationship created by surrogate motherhood abroad seems, at the very least, controversial. This rule, as said in section II. above, stipulates that the father–child relationship may be determined through corresponding legal action, when the mother–child relationship has been settled in accordance with the *mater semper certa est* rule. But the DGRN deliberately ignores Art 10.2 of Law 14/2006. Furthermore, the rule would allow for the recognition only of a *father*–child relationship. See both arguments in P de Miguel Asensio, at <www.pedrodemiguelasensio.blogspot.com/2010/10/la-instruccion-de-la-dgrn-de-5-de .html>.

[17] Indeed, the appeal lodged before the Court of Appeal of Valencia tried to prove that the Californian relationship would be registered under the rules settled by the *Instrucción*, but the Court noted that no ruling was submitted by the appellants.

[18] Álvarez González, above n 4, 358.

[19] See Art 168 of the *Reglamento del Registro Civil* of 14 November 1958, BOE no 396, 11 December 1958, and no 18, 21 January 1959 (hereinafter 'RRC'). For such impossibility, there is a convincing line of reasoning that the DGRN fails to mention: Spanish law rejects the possibility of an anonymous birth. Indeed, the Spanish Tribunal Supremo ruled the practice of registering births without the mother's record unconstitutional by means of its Judgment of 21 September 1999 (*Westlaw Aranzadi RJ* 1999/6944). See M Ballesteros de los Ríos, 'Reclamación de filiación materna frustrada por no ser practicada la prueba biológica esencial y adopción declarada nula por asentimiento prestado con antelación al parto (Comentario a la STS de 21 de septiembre de 1999)' (1999) *Derecho Privado y Constitución* 37; R Durán Rivacoba, 'El anonimato del progenitor' (2004) *Actualidad Civil* 2081; A Nieto Alonso, 'Reproducción asistida y anonimato de los progenitores' (2004) *Actualidad Civil* 2309; F Rivero Hernández, 'La constitucionalidad del anonimato del donante de gametos y el derecho de la persona al conocimiento de su origen biológico (de la STC 116/1999, de 17 de junio, al affaire *Odièvre*)' (2004) *Revista Jurídica de Cataluña* 105. Thus, under Spanish law there must always be a mother, who is always the woman who gives birth (see, again, Art 10.2 of Law 14/2006); it is impossible to enter a birth when the medical certification does not mention the parturient.

[20] Therefore, the DGRN ignores the applicability of Arts 81 and 85 RRC and Art 23 LRC, which are the articles that set the requirements for a registration based upon foreign certification. It is true that it is very unlikely that the requirements are met in surrogacy cases (see JPI no 15 of Valencia, Judgment of 15 September 2010 and the references above, n 12), but there is no reason to close out the possibility a priori, as the DGRN means to do.

(in the majority of cases) by the authorities in charge of the civil status registers. In fact, automatic recognition is feasible as long as the judgment has been issued in a proceeding similar to Spanish *jurisdicción voluntaria*, ie if the proceeding is uncontested,[21] and the majority of rulings in this matter are comparable to *actos de jurisdicción voluntaria*. There is no need to resort to the competent courts and follow the internal (Spanish) *exequatur* procedure, unless there is a convention applicable to the recognition of the decision and it remits the question to the internal procedure of the requested State.[22]

Should the Spanish civil register authorities carry out recognition of the foreign ruling according to the usual rule, they would effect a 'substantial' or 'conflictual' recognition (*reconocimiento material* or *reconocimiento conflictual*). This means that they would give effect to the foreign ruling only if the relationship created is consistent with the law applicable according to the Spanish rules on the conflict of laws.[23] Therefore, recognition would be denied in the vast majority of the cases, since Article 9.4 of the Spanish Civil Code stipulates that for a parent–child relationship, the law applicable is the national law of the child. Hence, Spanish law (Law 14/2006 on Human ART) would apply. In order to avoid such an outcome and favour recognition of the parental relationship, the DGRN gives instructions for 'procedural' recognition, ie recognition based on the assessment of a specific number of requirements (third point of the first directive):

(a) The first condition for recognition is that the judgment, as well as any other public document that might be submitted, complies with all the requirements for public foreign documents to be considered equivalent to a national public document.[24]

(b) The second condition is the assessment of the international jurisdiction of the foreign authority. In words of the DGRN, the foreign court must have founded its jurisdiction on 'criteria equivalent to those prescribed in the Spanish law'. Should this assessment be accomplished by the courts, it would entail both a search for relevant connections between the situation and the foreign court, and the exclusion of fraudulent forum shopping. As

---

[21] There is no general rule in the Spanish legal system prescribing automatic recognition for foreign judgments issued in uncontested proceedings, but there is an habitual practice in this sense. See JC Fernández Rozas and S Sánchez Lorenzo, above n 11, 201.

[22] See P Orejudo Prieto de los Mozos, 'Procedural Treatment of Recognition of Foreign Judgments in the Practice of Spanish Authorities' (2009) XIII *Spanish Yearbook of International Law* 27.

[23] And sometimes subject also to the control of the international jurisdiction of the foreign authority and to its conformity with the Spanish international *ordre public*. See Fernández Rozas and Sánchez Lorenzo above n 11, 202; M Virgós Soriano and FJ Garcimartín Alférez, *Litigación internacional. Derecho Procesal Civil Internacional*, 2nd edn (Cizur Menor, Aranzadi, 2007) 712–14. In relation to this matter, see also S Álvarez González, above n 4, 359.

[24] See Arts 144 and 323.3 of *Ley 1/2000 de Enjuiciamiento Civil* of January 2000 [Law of Civil Procedure], BOE no 7, 8 January 2000; no 90, 14 April 2000; and no 180, 28 July 2001. See also Arts 86–91 RRC. For further information concerning these requirements, see P Jiménez Blanco, 'La eficacia probatoria de los documentos públicos extranjeros' (2000) 0 *Anuario Español de Derecho Internacional Privado* 365.

a result, it is very likely that recognition would be denied. But the DGRN fails to mention fraud, so it is quite likely that the civil register authorities will commit themselves to seeking for reasonable connections between the relationship and the foreign country. And such connections usually occur, as the country of origin is usually the country of nationality and domicile of the surrogate mother, the place where the surrogacy agreement was concluded and the place where the child was born.

(c) According to the third condition, the Spanish authorities must ensure that all the procedural rights of the parties, and particularly those of the surrogate mother, have been guaranteed in the foreign procedure. Fulfilment of this requirement can be mostly taken for granted, since, as stated earlier, if the authorities in charge of the civil status register are competent to recognise the foreign judgment, it is because the judgment was issued in an uncontested proceeding, ie because there was no claimant and defendant but only interested applicants.

(d) The fourth condition involves three different issues. The DGRN asks the authorities in charge of the civil status register to verify that there has been 'no infringement of the best interests of the child and of the rights of the mother', that 'the consent of the latter has been obtained in a free and voluntary way, without error, violence or fraud', and that 'the mother has sufficient natural capacity'. The first assertion is close to the usual public policy control,[25] but public policy is not expressly mentioned. This lack of an express mention of public policy as such is worth noting, as it constitutes clear evidence of the surrogacy-friendly approach of the DGRN. Any mention of the exception is deliberately omitted, probably in order to prevent a civil register authority denying recognition on grounds of public policy.[26] The second and the third statements, though, involve a level of control unusual in regard to the Spanish rules for recognition and enforcement of judgments. When there is a ruling by a public authority, it is habitually supposed that all the requirements set by the law of the country of such authority have been met.[27] And there is no reason to suspect that the foreign legal system would not demand that consent is free and voluntary, and that the surrogate mother is fully capable. Thus, the verification of these conditions entails some kind of review of the merits of the ruling that suggests an unjustified distrust of foreign authorities, and burdens the

---

[25] In this sense, Guzmán Zapatero, above n 14, 734; M Guzmán Zapatero, 'El acceso al registro español de los nacidos en el extranjero mediante gestación por sustitución' (2010) *El Notario del siglo XXI* 51, 52.

[26] See P de Miguel Asensio, at <www.pedrodemiguelasensio.blogspot.com/2010/10/la-instruccion-de-la-dgrn-de-5-de.html>.

[27] In this sense, the doctrine of the DGRN deviates from the general rule prohibiting review of the merits without a convincing explanation for such deviation. Concerning the prohibition, see Fernández Rozas and Sánchez Lorenzo, above n 11, 224; and Virgós Soriano and Garcimartín Alférez, above n 23, 412 and 635–36.

Spanish authorities with the difficult task of assessing the foreign ruling. It remains to be seen how this assessment is to be accomplished.

(e) The fifth and final condition demands that the ruling must be final and the surrogate mother's consent irrevocable.

IV. The (Judicial) Denial of Recognition of Foreign Surrogacy by the Courts

The problem with the doctrine of the DGRN is that Spanish courts have not been able to agree with the administrative authorities on the viability of the recognition of foreign surrogacy. Indeed, as discussed in section III., there have already been two judicial decisions concerning the leading case described above, which demonstrate that it is very probable that the entry in the register of the birth of the children born out of a surrogate mother could be temporary. Both the *Ministerio Fiscal* (Public Prosecutor) and any person showing a legitimate interest might challenge the decision of the authorities in charge of the civil status registers, and the appeal would almost certainly succeed.

There would be two main grounds for Spanish courts to deny recognition of the judgment, in the event that such recognition is required to be fulfilled by means of an *exequatur* procedure or where an appeal is lodged against the registry. The first objection to recognition would derive from an assessment of the international jurisdiction of the foreign authorities, at least if such assessment is done according to the traditional doctrine of the Spanish courts. The Spanish courts usually verify three particulars. First, the matter should not be reserved to Spanish authorities by means of exclusive grounds of jurisdiction. Secondly, there must be a real, effective connection between the State of origin and the situation. And lastly, the parties should not have resorted to foreign authorities in the search for the application of a more favourable law or in order to avoid the application of a given law. Thus, with regard to this third point, Spanish courts must make sure that there has not been forum shopping,[28] and there is little doubt as to the result of the application of such a filter in foreign surrogacy cases, bearing in mind that the reason for Spanish (nationals and residents) intended parents to go abroad is that the practice is banned in Spain.[29]

The second obstacle to recognition could be the public policy exception. If the reason for the Spanish Parliament banning the practice is that it could lead to the commodification of children and the exploitation of women, it is not unlikely that

---

[28] Fernández Rozas and Sánchez Lorenzo, above n 11, 238–39.

[29] It may be noticed that the DGRN denied, in its *Resolución*, that such forum shopping occurred in the leading case, for it focused on the competence of the register authority, and not on the competence of the Californian judicial authorities. But see, in the opposite sense, the Jugdment of the Court of Appeal of Valencia of 23 November 2011.

the Spanish judicial authorities would reject giving effects to any foreign judgment on this issue.[30] Of course, these reasons could be re-evaluated, but so long as the necessary debate does not take place in Spain, recognition ought to be denied, except in two situations. The first is where the situation lacked the corresponding *Inlandsbeziehung* at the moment of its foundation, ie when it was not related to the forum when the surrogacy agreement was celebrated.[31] Secondly, the guarantee of the best interests of the child. In order to satisfy the best interests requirement, a nuanced application of the public policy reservation could be applied, so as to recognise the relationship of the biological father and the child, and to avoid the need to resort to the courts for that purpose. And where neither of the intended parents has a biological link with the child, recognition could be based on the relationship of authority inherent in the parental link (guardianship). In both cases, partial recognition would avoid a child having no legal link with any of the intended parents under the Spanish legal system.[32] Lastly, the situation would no longer be hindered if the other intended parent (mother or father) applied for (and obtained) the adoption of the child.

---

[30] See, in this sense, the Jugdment of the Court of Appeal of Valencia of 23 November 2011.

[31] For instance, if the intended parents used a surrogate while they were US citizens and were domiciled in California, yet acquired the Spanish nationality afterwards.

[32] The avoidance of such a situation was one of the arguments that the DGRN used in its *Resolución* to justify the prevalence of the best interests of the child above any other consideration.

22

Ukraine

GENNADIY DRUZENKO

I. Introduction

The first case of successful surrogacy in Ukraine and in the whole of the Commonwealth of Independent States took place in Kharkiv city in 1995. So far 30 clinics have been licensed in Ukraine to cure infertility by means of assisted reproductive technologies (ART), and at present about 20–22 provide ART services. Six of them are State owned and the rest are private. About 10 per cent of the Ukrainian ART clinics' patients are foreigners.[1]

There are no official statistics as to how many surrogacies are performed in Ukraine. However, it has been reported that in 2006 alone there were 32 cases of successful surrogacy.[2]

II. Legal Framework

Ukraine is a country which espouses one of the most liberal approaches toward surrogacy in Europe. Article 281(7) of the Civil Code of Ukraine declares that

> an adult woman or man has the right to be cured by means of assisted reproductive technologies subject to medical indications and upon terms and according to procedure prescribed by law.[3]

It is worth mentioning that Article 281 of the Civil Code is entitled 'Right to life', and all its provisions obviously pertain to any natural person, regardless of nationality.

---

[1] I Лагутенко, 'За склом вітчизняної репродуктології' (2011) 6 *Медичний світ* 4 (I Lahutenko, 'Beyond domestic reproductology glass' (2011) 6 *Medical World* 4).
[2] С Франчук, 'Юридичні та етичні аспекти репродуктивної медицини' (2007) 50 *Юридична газета* 6 (S Franchuk, 'Legal and ethical aspects of reproductive medicine' (2007) 50 *Legal Gazette* 6).
[3] The Civil Code of Ukraine, sometimes referred to as a 'small constitution', entered into force on 1 January 2004. Since then Art 281 has been amended by Law No 2135-IV of 2 November 2004.

Pursuant to this provision, the Ministry of Health of Ukraine issued the Instruction on the Application of Assisted Reproductive Technologies,[4] which contains a list of such technologies, including surrogate motherhood.

In turn, the Family Code of Ukraine[5] regulates the paternal affiliation of a child carried by a surrogate mother. Article 123(2) of the Family Code provides:

> If the human embryo conceived by the spouses (a man and a woman) by means of assisted reproductive technologies has been transferred to another woman's body, such spouses shall be the parents of the child.[6]

Moreover, another provision of the Code prevents a surrogate mother from claiming maternal affiliation with the child conceived by a 'commissioning couple' (or 'intended parents') and then implanted into a surrogate mother's womb.[7]

However, the Rules of Civil Registration in Ukraine provide that a surrogate mother should give a notarised consent for the intended couple's registration as the child's parents.[8] Theoretically, if a surrogate mother refused to give such consent, a commissioning couple would have no choice but to bring an action and require a court to order an office of civil registration to register them as parents of the child born to a surrogate mother. Since according to Ukrainian legal doctrine the Family Code's (as well as any other Code's) provisions override any administrative regulations, the outcome of such an action would be clearly in favour of the intended parents. Yet there is no reported relevant case law so far.

The Ukrainian legislation is silent concerning commercial surrogacy. However, the Civil Code of Ukraine sets forth the principle of the freedom of contract as one of the general foundations of civil legislation.[9] Article 6(1) of the Civil Code elaborates the aforementioned principle in the following words:

> The parties shall be entitled to enter into a contract not provided for by the civil legislation acts but complying with the general foundations of the civil legislation.[10]

And Article 627(1) of the Code details what freedom of contract means:

> [T]he parties shall be free to conclude a contract, to choose a counterparty and to determine the provisions of the contract taking into consideration the requirements of this Code, other acts of civil legislation, usual business practices, requirements of rationality and justice.

---

[4] The Instruction was approved by the Order of the Ministry of Health of Ukraine No 771 of 23 December 2008 and has the status of a legally binding Act.

[5] The Family Code of Ukraine entered in force on 1 January 2004 simultaneously with the Civil Code of Ukraine.

[6] All acts of Ukrainian legislation are quoted as of 20 January 2013.

[7] Art 139(2) of the Family Code of Ukraine.

[8] Paragraph 11 of Section 1 of Chapter III of the Rules of Civil Registration in Ukraine approved by the Order of the Ministry of Justice of Ukraine of 18 October 2000 No 52/5 as amended.

[9] Art 3(3) of the Civil Code of Ukraine.

[10] Art 6(1) of the Civil Code of Ukraine.

All these provisions lay down foundations for a vibrant commercial surrogacy market in Ukraine, since they determine that commercial surrogacy which is not prohibited by the Ukrainian legislation is thus completely legal.

However, it is worth mentioning that on 22 March 2002, Ukraine signed the Convention of the Council of Europe on Human Rights and Biomedicine (4 April 1997) without any reservations. Article 21 of the Convention provides that 'the human body and its parts shall not, as such, give rise to financial gain'.[11] Therefore, if the Convention were to be ratified by the Ukrainian Parliament and come into force in Ukraine, becoming part of domestic legislation,[12] it would be prohibited to pay to use a surrogate mother's womb for carrying and delivering a child for genetic parents. At the same time, the Convention entering into force will not prevent would-be parents from paying some sort of compensation to a surrogate mother for loss of earnings, medical care, etc.

Therefore, it might be concluded that Ukrainian legislators chose a clear approach in favour of genetic intended parents (perhaps, at a cost to the surrogate mother) and in fact allowed the commercialisation of surrogacy which has made Ukraine one of the global centres of commercial surrogacy. If and when the Parliament of Ukraine ratifies the already signed Convention of the Council of Europe on Human Rights and Biomedicine, things will probably change, reducing the commercial attractiveness of surrogacy in the country.

There are some explicit limits imposed on surrogacy by Ukrainian legislation. First of all, the intended couple should be married, since only spouses enjoy the right to be registered as parents of their genetic child carried and delivered by a surrogate mother.[13] The Rules of Civil Registration in Ukraine specify that:

> In case of a child given birth to by the woman who was implanted with a human embryo conceived by *spouses* by means of assisted reproductive technologies, the State registration of the birth is performed on application of the *spouses* who have given consent for such transplantation.[14]

This provision is based on Article 123(2) of the Family Code of Ukraine cited above, which mentions only spouses and not any other couples who are entitled to be legal parents of their child delivered by a surrogate mother. As only heterosexual marriage is legal in Ukraine,[15] same-sex couples, as well as single persons, are prevented from becoming parents through surrogacy.

---

[11] The text of the Convention, the chart of signatures and ratifications, the list of declarations, reservations and other communications and the explanatory report thereon are accessible on-line at <www.conventions.coe.int/Treaty/Commun/QueVoulezVous.asp?NT=164&CL=ENG>.

[12] Art 9(1) of the Constitution of Ukraine declares that '[i]nternational treaties that are in force, agreed to be binding by the Verkhovna Rada of Ukraine, are part of the national legislation of Ukraine'.

[13] Art 123(2) of the Family Code of Ukraine, cited at n 6 above, envisages only 'spouses' and not any other couple's right to be parents of the child delivered by a surrogate mother.

[14] Paragraph 11 of Section 1 of Chapter III of the Rules of Civil Registration in Ukraine approved by the Order of the Ministry of Justice of Ukraine of 18 October 2000 No 52/5 as amended (emphasis added).

[15] Art 21(1) of the Family Code of Ukraine defines marriage as 'matrimony of a man and woman'.

To avoid any vagueness in the law and to give an unequivocal answer to the question whether a same-sex couple married under a jurisdiction which recognises same-sex marriage could be recognised as intended parents under Ukrainian domestic law, the Parliament of Ukraine recently amended Article 139(2) of the Family Code of Ukraine.[16] The amendment inserted only this short bracketed phrase '(a man and a woman)' after the words 'conceived by spouse'. Therefore, since Law No 3760-VI came into force on 14 October 2011, it is impossible for a same-sex spouse to deliver a child using a surrogate mother in Ukraine.[17]

Secondly, to be registered as the parents of a child born by a surrogate mother, the intended parents should provide a register office with a certificate confirming that the genetic material for the baby comes from at least one of them.[18] However, it remains unclear who is authorised to issue such certificates, their requirements and the issuing procedure. Nevertheless, the use of gametes from both male and female donors does not lead to the intended parents' recognition and registration as the child's parents under Ukrainian law, since genetic kinship between at least one of them and the child is a legal prerequisite for such recognition and registration.[19]

Thirdly, Ukrainian legislation does not envisage the possibility of so-called 'traditional surrogacy', where a surrogate mother is impregnated with the intended father's sperm. In such a case the surrogate and genetic mothers would be the same person, and therefore it would be impossible to register another woman as a mother of the child. Article 123(2) of the Family Code of Ukraine and derived legal acts clearly cover only cases when 'a *human embryo* conceived by the spouses (a man and a woman) by means of assisted reproductive technologies *has been transferred to another woman's body*' (emphasis added).

Another restriction imposed on surrogacy, as well as on other methods of ART, by the Ukrainian legislator is that the would-be parents may have recourse

---

[16] See Law No 3760-VI of 20 September 2011.

[17] *Cf* the well-publicised case of a Belgian gay couple, Peter Meurrens and Laurent Ghilain, whose son, Samuel, was delivered by a Ukrainian surrogate in Ukraine. The child spent more than two years in a Ukrainian orphanage because he was not a citizen of the Ukraine, so that country did not issue legal papers, including a passport; neither was Samuel a citizen of Belgium, because that country, while not having any laws for or against surrogacy, did not issue legal papers. Finally, in February 2011, the Belgian Government issued a passport to Samuel, and thus he arrived in Belgium and was reunited with his intended homosexual parents. Since the last amendments to the Family Code of Ukraine entered into force, such a 'happy ending' for this story would be simply impossible. An outline of Samuel's and his intended parents' ordeal may be found, eg, at <www.msnbc.msn.com/id/41800437/ns/world_news-wonderful_world/t/boy-stuck-years-ukraine-arrives-belgium/No.T0EETPVIyt9> or at <www.pinknews.co.uk/2011/02/23/belgian-gay-couple-to-be-reunited-with-baby-son>.

[18] Paragraph 11 of Section 1 of Chapter III of the Rules of Civil Registration in Ukraine approved by the Order of the Ministry of Justice of Ukraine of 18 October 2000 No 52/5.

[19] Although no Act of the Parliament of Ukraine explicitly requires genetic kinship between the child and at least one of his or her would-be parents (Art 123(2) of the Family Code uses the wording 'human embryo *conceived by the spouses*' (emphasis added), which to the author's mind leaves room for different interpretations), and only an instruction approved by the order of the Ministry of Justice of Ukraine clearly requires confirmation of such genetic kinship, the 'American case' described in section III.B. below confirms that genetic kinship between the child and at least one of his or her would-be parents is crucial for the would-be parents' recognition and registration.

to these techniques only if they are unable to conceive, carry or deliver a child in a natural way. Medical indications for resorting to surrogacy are determined by the Instruction on the Application of Assisted Reproductive Technologies issued by the Ministry of Health of Ukraine.[20] The Instruction provides that surrogacy might be applied for only in cases of spouses' infertility or a high risk to a woman's and/or a would-be child's health, in particular:

— the absence of the uterus (congenital or acquired);
— deformation of the uterine cavity or neck in cases of congenital malformation, or as a result of diseases in the past;
— intrauterine adhesions;
— four and more recurrent unsuccessful IVF attempts with multiple transfers of high-quality embryos not resulting in pregnancy.[21]

The same Instruction imposes certain requirements on a potential surrogate mother, determining that she should be an adult, legally capable woman, who has delivered at least one healthy, living child of her own and does not have any medical contraindications. Further, a would-be surrogate mother should sign a written consent for surrogacy.[22] There is no explicit, legally-binding age limit for potential surrogate mothers. Although most clinics which assist surrogacy recommend choosing as a surrogate mother a woman aged between 18 and 35, cases in which mothers have carried children for their daughters are known and not that rare.[23]

The Instruction on the Application of Assisted Reproductive Technologies also regulates the number of IVF embryos which may be transferred into a woman's womb. It recommends transferring one or two embryos; transfers of three embryos is subject to a patient's assent. Transfers of more than three IVF embryos is not allowed.[24]

III. Relevant Case Law

Although there is a good deal of surrogacy in Ukraine, only a few relevant cases have been reported so far.[25] Therefore it is possible to outline all of them in this chapter.

---

[20] Above n 4.

[21] All medical prescriptions for surrogacy are listed in para 2 of s 7, 'Surrogacy motherhood', of the Instruction.

[22] Para 4 of s 7, 'Surrogacy motherhood', of the Instruction.

[23] The first case of surrogacy in Ukraine was of this sort: in 1995 the mother carried and delivered a child for her daughter who was infertile due to the congenital absence of her uterus.

[24] Para 3.6.(б) of s 3, 'Methods of treatment by ART', of the Instruction.

[25] According to the Law of Ukraine 'On Access to Judicial Decisions' of 22 December 2005 No 3262-IV, all judicial decisions held by Ukrainian courts should be accessible online through the Single State Register of Judicial Decisions, the Government-administered free electronic database.

A. 'Ukrainian' Cases

In 2007, the surrogate mother and at the same time genetic grandmother of the child won a case against the child's genetic father, who was ordered to pay child maintenance. The peculiarity of this case was that the surrogate mother was registered as the baby's legal mother, since her daughter (and the child's genetic mother) was in only a domestic partnership with the child's genetic father and was not married to him.[26]

In October 2009, a district court, at the request of the parents, 'synchronised' the date of birth of their child delivered by the genetic mother with that of two other babies delivered by a surrogate.[27]

B. 'American' Case

Jeanette Runyon and her husband Michael Woolslayer, both US citizens, in 2006 concluded a contract with the Kyiv-based Isida clinic and would-be surrogate mother, Ukrainian citizen Oleksandra O, who in October 2007 delivered a child. The Ukrainian register office issued a birth certificate for the newborn baby, in which Ms Runyon and her husband were indicated as the child's parents, but the US Embassy declined to issue a US passport for the baby.

It turned out that in 2007, the embryo implanted in the surrogate mother's womb had been conceived by fertilisation of a donor's egg with donated sperm, and thus neither Ms Runyon nor Mr Woolslayer was a genetic parent of the baby delivered by Oleksandra O.

The Ukrainian Police accused Ms Runyon of human trafficking and initiated a criminal prosecution against her, which was later dismissed. However, the child was retained in Ukraine. Moreover, in October 2010, a Ukrainian court ordered the register office to amend the child's birth certificate in such a way as to delete from it the names of Ms Runyon and her husband, and to substitute assumed names in line with the procedures applicable to children whose parents are unknown.[28]

C. 'Canadian' Case

In 2009, a Canadian couple of Ukrainian origin conceived an IVF embryo which was transferred into a surrogate mother's womb in Lviv (Ukraine). When the

---

[26] The judgment of the Kyivskiy district court of the Simferopol city of 02.08.2007 on case No 22-ц-6502/2007.

[27] The judgment of the Holosiyivskiy district court of the city of Kyiv of 22.10.2009 on case No 2-5254/09.

[28] The judgment of the Solomyanskiy district court of the city of Kyiv of 6 October 2010 on case No 2-2283-1/10.

baby was born in 2010, the Ukrainian register office registered the spouses as the child's parents.

However, the couple was prevented from leaving Ukraine with the baby, since in the case of surrogacy, Canadian legislation requires judicial recognition of the parental rights of intended parents and judicial permission for the baby to leave the country where he or she was born.

Therefore the spouses asked a Ukrainian court to establish their paternal rights and allow the baby to leave Ukraine. Even though Ukrainian legislation does not set up a procedure for such judicial 'confirmation' of already-established paternal rights, the court applied an analogy with adoption law and satisfied the claim.[29]

D. 'French' Case

A Frenchmen, Patrice Le Roch, and his father, Bernard, were detained in March 2011 for trying to smuggle out Patrice's twin daughters born to a surrogate mother.

They said they acted out of despair after the French Government refused to issue the babies with passports because it does not recognise surrogacy. Finally they faced a €1,500 fine and the confiscation of their van, but were not jailed.[30]

It might be concluded from the cases outlined above that the challenges for non-Ukrainian would-be parents are generated mainly by their own domestic law or authorities, and not by Ukrainian legislation and administrative practices. In most cases, Ukrainian register offices and courts have been rather cooperative towards foreign intended parents.

IV. Draft Law Proposals[31]

This overview of the Ukrainian surrogacy legal framework and practices would be incomplete without mentioning draft laws introduced to the Ukrainian Parliament and awaiting consideration by MPs.

One bill concerning surrogacy has been cosidered by the sixth Parliament of Ukraine,[32] namely: Draft Law No 8282 of 02.11.2011, introduced by MPs Ms Lukyanova and Ms Kovalevska.[33]

---

[29] The judgment of the Shevchenkivskiy district court of Zaporizhzha city of 13 December 2010 on case No 2-0-239/10.

[30] The judgment of the Berehovo district court of 17 May 2011 on case No 1-131/11.

[31] All draft laws officially introduced to the Parliament of Ukraine are accessible free of charge through the official website of Verchovna Rada (the Parliament) of Ukraine at <http://w1.c1.rada.gov .ua/pls/zweb_n/webproc2>.

[32] Sixth convocation of the Parliament of Ukraine lasted form 23 November 2007 to 12 December 2013.

[33] The first edition of the Draft Law was introduced to the Parliament on 23.03.2011 by Ms Lukyanova, MP, alone.

Draft Law No 8282, passed the Parliament on 16 October 2012, but was vetoed by the President.[34] According to the Rules of Procedures of the Verkhovna Rada (the Parliament) of Ukraine, new convocation should consider President's veto and either agree with them and reject the bill or override a veto by two-thirds majority.[35]

Originally, Draft Law No 8282 proposed to amend the Family Code of Ukraine with the introduction of new Article 123-1, which would have limited access to ART exclusively to legally capable Ukrainian citizens who are at least 21 years of age and not being treated at or on the register of a psychiatric or drug abuse clinic. The amended draft, which passed the Parliament on 16 October 2012, does not impose minimum age limits on surrogate mothers, but intends to ban foreigners who are citizens of or reside in a country where surrogate motherhood is prohibited by law, from recognition as parents of the child delivered by a surrogate mother in Ukraine. The Bill also aims to impose a 51 years upper age limit for surrogate mothers (unless an exception would be granted according to the procedure should be set up by the Cabinet of Ministers) and an explicit requirement of genetic kinship between the child and at least one of the would-be parents, as well as absence of such kinship between a surrogate mother and the child delivered by her (unless the surrogate is a relative of one of the would-be parent), as compulsory prerequisites for surrogacy.

It is obvious that if this Draft Law is passed by the Parliament, the Ukrainian surrogacy market will change significantly, particularly if it becomes closed to most European intended parents. However, the cnances that the current Parliament[36] overrides President's veto is next to nothing.

V. Conclusion

As might be seen from the legal frameworks, administrative practices and case law concerning surrogacy in Ukraine outlined above, Ukraine is a favourable country for intended parents. Surrogacy, including commercial surrogacy, is allowed, and the would-be parents' right to a child delivered by a surrogate mother is protected by law.

However, most scholars and practitioners agree that surrogacy currently is under-regulated in Ukraine. Indeed, this seems true, bearing in mind that Ukraine is a civil law country where gaps in legislation will rarely be filled by case law. Recently, Ukrainian legislators introduced into the Parliament some Bills aimed

---

[34] According Art 106(30) of the Constitution of Ukraine the President of Ukraine has a right of limeted (or suspensive) veto which may be override by two-thirds vote of the Parliament (Art 94(4) of the Constitution of Ukraine).

[35] Art 106(2) and 135(1,2) of Law On Rule of Procedure of the Verkhovna Rada of Ukraine No 1861-VI of 10 February 2010.

[36] The Seventh Parliament of Ukraine commenced its work on 12 December 2012.

at making surrogacy regulation more comprehensive. Some of them have already been passed by the Parliament, others have been rejected and one of them has been vetoed by the President and returned to the Parliament. If Draft Law No 8282 becomes the law of the land in Ukraine (which is unlikely), Ukrainian ART clinics will close their doors to foreign intended parents arriving from countries where surrogacy is prohibited, which scenario is in turn fraught with the risk of a black or/and grey surrogacy market being established.

The administrative practices show that regardless of nationality, would-be parents usually do not face legal problems resulting from surrogacy in Ukraine. However, according to Ukrainian law, intended parents should be required to fulfil some preconditions, namely, be a heterosexual married couple and have genetic kinship with the child delivered by a surrogate mother.

Cross-border challenges usually arise when the would-be parents' country does not recognise surrogate motherhood and declines to issue a passport to a child delivered by a surrogate mother.

Therefore, Ukraine, as a country favourable to surrogacy which espouses one of the most permissive approaches to would-be parents, and thus attracts more and more foreign intended parents, should be interested in negotiating and concluding an international convention on cross-borders aspects of surrogacy.

23

United Kingdom

MICHAEL WELLS-GRECO[*]

I. Introduction

Existing UK legislation[1] covering surrogacy arrangements—the Surrogacy Arrangements Act 1985 ('the 1985 Act'), the Adoption and Children Act 2002, the Human Fertilisation and Embryology (Deceased Fathers) Act 2003, the Human Fertilisation and Embryology Act 2008[2] ('HFEA 2008') and a number of statutory instruments including the Human Fertilisation and Embryology (Parental Order) Regulations 2010[3]—is based (in part) on the conclusions of the 1984 Warnock Report.[4] The Warnock Committee took the view that although surrogacy arrangements were to be discouraged because of the potential difficulties, where they did take place, there could be no question of the surrogate mother being forced by any contractual obligation to give up that child. UK law does not recognise surrogacy as a binding agreement on either party. Thus surrogacy is legal in the UK, although it is illegal to advertise[5] for surrogates or commissioning parents. Amongst the guiding principles underpinning the legislation is the rule that no money other than 'reasonable expenses' should be paid to the surrogate; there is no strict definition of what constitutes 'reasonable expenses'.

---

[*] I am grateful to the anonymous reader of this chapter for his or her comments and suggestions.

[1] In the UK there are three separate legal systems: the law of England and Wales, the law of Scotland and the law of Northern Ireland. This is an overview of surrogacy in the UK. While the HFEA 2008 is a UK-wide legislative instrument and it is correct to refer to the UK here, reflecting national autonomy, there are differences in the official registration documents issued in the constituent nations of the UK.

[2] The majority of its provisions came into force in October 2009, with the provisions relating to parenthood in April 2009. The HFEA 2008 is an amending piece of legislation, amending the Human Fertilisation and Embryology Act 1990.

[3] (SI 2010/986.) The 2010 Regulations ensure that the policy in relation to parental orders is closely aligned with up to date adoption legislation by applying the Adoption and Children Act 2002, the Adoption and Children (Scotland) Act 2007 and the Adoption (Northern Ireland) Order 1987, with modifications, to parental orders.

[4] *Report of the Committee of Enquiry into Human Fertilisation and Embryology 1984* (known as the 'Warnock Report'), available at <www.hfea.gov.uk/2068.html>. See also *Surrogacy: Review for health ministers of current arrangements for payments and regulation 1998* (known as the 'Brazier Report'), available at <www.dh.gov.uk/en/Publicationsandstatistics/Publications/PublicationsLegislation/DH_4009697>.

[5] The relevant provisions of the HFEA 2008 are dealt with in this chapter.

Academic and practitioner commentary,[6] together with judicial intervention, have increasingly begun to analyse the effect of the UK's law and approach
to surrogacy. In doing so, it may be observed that UK law supports surrogacy
if it fits a model deemed acceptable: purportedly altruistic,[7] consenting and
privately arranged. In this chapter, by reference to the legislation and case law,
the framework of this model is considered. What appears is the complexity of
domestic and international surrogacy matters, with the cases serving as 'cautionary tales',[8] highlighting the legal, emotional and financial consequences of surrogacy arrangements. The challenges with which national courts have grappled
are plentiful:

(a) how to establish parenthood;
(b) citizenship and immigration;
(c) parental responsibility;
(d) the validity, legality and enforceability of cross-border surrogacy con-
    tracts;
(e) the recognition of foreign birth certificates;
(f) abduction;[9]
(g) the rights of the child to identity/to know his or her origin.

Other challenges not yet addressed but of equal concern are:

(a) the laws of succession and inheritance;
(b) the authenticity/falsification of documents (birth certificates, passports,
    paternity declarations, letters of consent);
(c) maternity, paternity or parental employment rights of the commissioning
    parents;
(d) advertisement;
(e) fertility tourism (with foreign fertility clinics in places such as India,
    Ukraine and the USA now actively promoting their services, and with
    global information at everyone's fingertips, it is not uncommon to regard

---

[6] P Beaumont and K Trimmings, 'International surrogacy arrangements: an urgent need for legal
regulation at the international level' (2011) 7(3) *Journal of Private International Law* 627; J Herring,
'Whose baby is it anyway?' (2011) *New Law Journal* 161, 195; A. Hutchinson, 'International surrogacy arrangements: time for a multi-lateral convention' (2011) *International Family Law*, Nov, 303;
N Gamble and L Ghevaert, 'International surrogacy: payments, public policy and media hype' (2011)
41 (May) *Family Law* 504; J Millbank, 'Unlikely Fissures and Uneasy Resonances: Lesbian Co-mothers,
Surrogate Parenthood and Fathers' Rights' (2008) 16 *Feminist Legal Studies* 141.

[7] To quote the *Impact Assessment of the Human Fertilisation and Embryology (Parental Order)
Regulations 2010* (January 2010; on file with author): 'Surrogacy can provide a vital opportunity, where
a woman is unable to bear a child herself, for a couple to have a child that is genetically related to one
or both of them.'

[8] Quoting McFarlane J, in *Re G (Surrogacy: Foreign Domicile)* [2007] EWHC 2814, para 4.

[9] See *W&W v H (Child Abduction: Surrogacy) No 2* [2002] 2 FLR 252 and *W&W v H (Child
Abduction: Surrogacy) No 1* [2002] 1 FLR 1008.

cross-border surrogacy as 'procreative' or 'fertility tourism' (or, more recently, 'cross-border reproductive care'[10])); and, more broadly,

(f) the balancing of procreative liberty and welfare, and the role of law in such a personal and intimate area of human life.[11]

We now turn to look at the detail of the UK's approach to surrogacy.

II. Legal Parenthood

Under UK law, the woman who carries a child is the legal mother. Unless the child is subsequently adopted or parenthood is transferred by judicial order, the legal mother of a child born through surrogacy is always, at birth, the surrogate mother, whether or not she is also the genetic mother[12] (and irrespective of whether the surrogacy took place in the UK or elsewhere and where the child is born).

In relation to a child conceived as a result of treatment with donor sperm by a married woman, her husband will be treated as the child's father, unless it is shown that he did not consent to his wife's treatment.[13] This provision (and others which operate to determine legal parenthood) is subject to the common law presumption that a child is the legitimate child of a married couple.[14] This means that the commissioning father has no automatic claim to legal parenthood, even if he is the biological father.

If the surrogate is in a civil partnership at the time of treatment then her partner will be treated as a parent of the child, unless it can be shown that she did not consent to the treatment.[15] It is possible, therefore, for two male or female partners to achieve the status of parent with respect to a child born by means of a surrogacy arrangement.[16]

---

[10] F Shenfield, J de Mouzon, G Pennings, AP Ferraretti, A Nyboe Andersen, G de Wert, V Goossens and the ESHRE Taskforce on Cross Border Reproductive Care, 'Cross border reproductive care in six European countries', *Human Reproduction*, first published online 26 March 2010.

[11] UK law must be considered against the backdrop of human rights instruments, in particular the United Nations Convention on the Rights of the Contracting Child 1989; and, whilst not child-specific, the European Convention on Human Rights is relevant, in as much as the UK as a Member State is bound inter alia by Arts 8 and 14 to respect private and family life without discrimination. It is worth noting, then, that public policy is not just a cultural option, or a strategy that States are free to decide whether to implement or not: it rather reflects the increasingly complex perspective from which family law and private international law issues must be viewed in Europe, ie a perspective where the point of view of the forum is no longer a merely 'national' one but embodies that State's international undertakings concerning, inter alia, the protection of human rights.

[12] HFEA 2008, s 33; see also *The Ampthill Peerage* [1977] AC 547.

[13] *Pater est quem nuptiae demonstrant.* HFEA 2008, s 35.

[14] HFEA 2008, ss 35 and 38.

[15] HFEA 2008, s 42.

[16] HFEA 2008, s 54.

If the surrogate is unmarried (or it is proven that her husband or civil partner has not consented to the treatment), the male commissioning parent may be treated as the legal parent if the child is created using his sperm. In contrast, a sperm donor could not be the father, provided sperm is donated to a licensed clinic and his sperm is used in accordance with this consent.[17] Where the female commissioning parent's eggs are used but not the male commissioning parent's gametes, the surrogate will be the child's only legal parent.

It is therefore possible for a child born of surrogacy to have:

(a) only one legal parent, who may or may not be genetically linked;
(b) two legal parents who have no genetic connection to the child;
(c) two legal parents both of whom may be female, neither or one of whom may be genetically linked to the child.

It will be shown below that the parental order is the legal mechanism for transferring the status of a parent from the surrogate (and in some cases her male partner) to the commissioning parents. It should be noted at the outset that there may be added complications with the application of the laws on parenthood and in the granting of a parental order if the commissioning couple have entered into an overseas surrogacy arrangement. In *X and Y (Foreign Surrogacy)*,[18] under English law the Ukrainian surrogate was the legal mother and her husband the legal father. Under Ukrainian law the commissioning parents were the legal parents and were named on the birth certificate. So far as the law in Ukraine was concerned, the gestational surrogate and her husband retained no legal responsibility for the children. The effect was that the children were marooned stateless and parentless, whilst the commissioning parents could neither remain in the Ukraine nor bring the children to the UK. Having satisfied the immigration authorities by DNA tests (which had to be processed in the UK, thus causing further delay) that the male applicant was the biological father of both children, the children were given discretionary leave to enter 'outside the rules' to afford the applicants the opportunity to regularise their status under English law, hence the application for the parental order. Similar issues were faced by the commissioning couple in *Re IJ (A Child) (Foreign Surrogacy Agreement: Parental Order)*.[19] The application of international conflicts of law rules on parentage leave children born abroad through surrogacy extremely vulnerable.

---

[17] HFEA 2008, s 41 provides: 'Persons not to be treated as father: (1) Where the sperm of a man who had given such consent as is required by paragraph 5 of Schedule 3 to the 1990 Act (consent to use of gametes for purposes of treatment services or non-medical fertility services) was used for a purpose for which such consent was required, he is not to be treated as the father of the child. (2) Where the sperm of a man, or an embryo the creation of which was brought about with his sperm, was used after his death, he is not, subject to section 39, to be treated as the father of the child. (3) Subsection (2) applies whether W was in the United Kingdom or elsewhere at the time of the placing in her of the embryo or of the sperm and eggs or of her artificial insemination.'

[18] *X and Y (Foreign Surrogacy)* [2008] EWHC 3030 (Fam).

[19] *Re IJ (A Child) (Foreign Surrogacy Agreement: Parental Order)* [2011] EWHC 921 (Fam).

III. Legal Requirements on a Surrogate Mother and the Commissioning Parents

The 1985 Act (as amended) defines 'surrogate mother' and surrogacy arrangement,[20] and places restrictions on the conduct and arrangement of surrogacy in the UK. The Human Fertilisation and Embryology Acts 1990 and (now) 2008 dictate parenthood in assisted reproduction situations (including surrogacy) and make the rules on parental orders, which were specifically designed for surrogacy.

With the legal parent(s)'s consent, parenthood, since 1994, can be transferred to the commissioning couple by means of a parental order.[21] A parental order has transformative effect and, if granted, is of like effect to an adoption order, with the consequence that the child is for all purposes treated in law as a child of the couple and not of any other person. The provisions apply whether the surrogate is in the UK or elsewhere at the time of the placing in her of the embryo or the sperm and eggs, or of her artificial insemination. Commissioning parents may apply to a civil court for a parental order, provided the specified conditions set out in section 54 of the HFEA 2008 are met (together the 'section 54 conditions'):

(a) both commissioning partners apply;[22]
(b) at least one of the commissioning parents must be a genetic parent of the child;[23]
(c) the commissioning partners must be—
   (i) husband and wife,
   (ii) civil partners of each other, or
   (iii) two persons who are living as partners in an enduring family relationship and are not within prohibited degrees of relationship in relation to each other;[24]
(d) the application is made more than six weeks and less than six months after the birth;[25]

---

[20] The 1985 Act is available at <www.legislation.gov.uk/ukpga/1985/49>. Note that there are two versions of this Act: one version extends to England and Wales and Northern Ireland only; another has been created for Scotland only. With respect to the former, s 1(2) reads: '"surrogate mother" means a woman who carries a child in pursuance of an arrangement—(a) made before she began to carry the child, and (b) made with a view to any child carried in pursuance of it being handed over to, and parental responsibility being met (so far as practicable) by, another person or other persons'; with respect to Scotland, reference is made to 'parental rights being exercised' as opposed to 'parental responsibility'.

[21] HFEA 2008, s 54.

[22] HFEA 2008, s 54(1). An application for a parental order is made by means of Form C51 (in England and Wales) and Form 22 (in Scotland).

[23] HFEA 2008, s 54(1)(a) and (b).

[24] HFEA 2008, s 54(2).

[25] HFEA 2008, s 54(3).

at the time of the application and the making of the order, the child's home is with the commissioning parents;[26]

    (e) at the time of the application and the making of the order, either or both of the applicants must be domiciled in the UK or in the Channel Islands or in the Isle of Man;[27]

    (f) at the time of making the order, both applicants must have attained the age of 18;[28]

    (g) the applicants can satisfy the court that the surrogate mother who carried the child and any other person who is a parent of the child, but is not one of the applicants, has freely and with full understanding of what is involved agreed unconditionally to the making of the parental order. Such consent may be given only once the child has reached six weeks old;[29]

    (h) no money or other benefit (other than for expenses reasonably incurred) has been given or received by either of the applicants for or in consideration of—

        (i) the making of the parental order,

        (ii) any agreement required,

        (iii) the handing over of the child, or

        (iv) the making of any arrangements with a view to the making of the order, unless authorised by the court.

In other words, provided that all these conditions are met, a UK court is enabled to order that the commissioning couple are to be treated in law as the parents. If any of the conditions listed above cannot be satisfied then it will not be possible to obtain a parental order. This might apply, for example, if the commissioning parents have no genetic link with the child or if the commissioning parent is single. Securing the position of the commissioning parents may then be difficult and will involve an application to the court for adoption, special guardianship or a residence order.

While it is beyond the scope of this chapter to delve fully into the history of surrogacy[30] and each of the section 54 conditions, what follows is a brief sketch of a selection of these conditions.

A. Applicants

Whereas the HFEA 1990 only provided for cases in which the commissioning couple were married, the HFEA 2008 is more expansive: since 6 April 2010, civil

---

[26] HFEA 2008, s 54(4)(a).

[27] HFEA 2008, s 54(4)(b).

[28] HFEA 2008, s 54(5).

[29] HFEA 2008, s 54(6). The consent (or opposition) to a parental order is made by means of Form C52 (in England and Wales) and Form 23 (in Scotland).

[30] For a description of the framework within which surrogacy arrangements developed in the UK up to 1998, see the Brazier Report, above n 4.

partners (two people of the same sex registered in a civil partnership) and two persons living as partners in an enduring family relationship are also able to apply for a parental order. A single person remains unable to apply for a parental order.[31]

B. Domicile in the UK

In *Re G (Surrogacy: Foreign Domicile)*,[32] McFarlane J found himself unable to make a parental order as it transpired that neither of the commissioning parents was domiciled anywhere in the UK. A person is generally domiciled in the country in which he is considered to have his permanent home.[33] *Re G* involved a Turkish couple who came to England, where a baby was conceived as a result of a surrogacy arrangement made between the couple and the surrogate mother. It took nine months of litigation to find an alternative solution using international adoption law[34] (which entailed a full local authority assessment of the commissioning parents, and expert evidence confirming that the couple would be permitted to adopt in Turkey). The court warned that if other commissioning parents followed this path, coming to the UK for surrogacy as foreign nationals not domiciled in any part of the UK, the court would impose on them (in addition to their own legal costs) the State's costs for resolving the position. To quote McFarlane J:

> In the event that any agencies involved in facilitating or advising on surrogacy arrangements are approached by a couple who are not domiciled in the UK, or indeed any solicitor who may be approached by such a couple for legal advice, [they] must advise that pursuant to rule 110 of The Family Procedure (Adoption) Rules 2005 the 'court may at any time make such orders as to costs as it thinks just'. Such orders for costs can be made against the commissioning non-domicile couple and can include payment of the legal costs of the proceedings, payment for the costs incurred by CAFCASS. Clearly, whether such costs should be paid will depend upon the circumstances of each case given that this court takes the view that the provision for surrogacy arrangements for non UK domicile couples are to be discouraged, it follows that the legal aspects to such arrangements should not become the financial responsibility of the British taxpayer. Any court faced with an application such as that which has been considered within this Judgment should give active consideration to the making of a costs order. ...[35]

---

[31] However, in the unusual circumstances that prevailed in *A & A v P, P & B* [2011] EWHC 1738 (Fam) (discussed in section VIII. below), Theis J held that the court had jurisdiction to make a parental order in favour of a married couple, after the death of the husband.

[32] *Re G (Surrogacy: Foreign Domicile)* [2007] EWCH 2814 (Fam).

[33] Dicey, Morris and Collins, *The Conflict of Laws*, 14th edn (with 4th supplement) (London, Sweet & Maxwell, 2010) (see, in particular, paras 6-030 to 6-048). It should also be noted that a person is domiciled in a jurisdiction rather than in a country. So, in a non-unified legal system an individual is domiciled in a particular unit (eg in England and Wales or Scotland rather than in the UK). The UK concept is unrelated to nationality, residence or citizenship.

[34] Pursuant to s 84 of the Adoption and Children Act 2002.

[35] Note 18, at para 52(f) of judgment.

The criterion of domicile was considered by the High Court in *Z and another v C and another*.[36] The application for a parental order concerned twins, born in November 2010, who were conceived as a result of a surrogacy agreement between the applicants (a same-sex Israeli couple resident in London) and a clinic in India, arranged through a surrogacy agency in Israel. One of the applicants was the biological father of the twins. The surrogate mother was Indian and played no active part in the proceedings. The preliminary issue for the court to determine was whether one of the applicants was domiciled in England at the time of the application. After a thorough examination, the court was persuaded that the assertion of English domicile was genuine and was not a misuse of proceedings or contrived to secure any immigration benefit.

Non-commercial surrogacy arrangements where neither member of the commissioning couple is domiciled in any part of the UK, whilst not illegal, are to be discouraged on the ground that it will not be open to the commissioning parents to apply for a parental order with respect to the child.

C. Consent

In the case of *X & Y (Foreign Surrogacy)*,[37] a couple had made a surrogacy arrangement with an Ukrainian woman who gave birth to twins using anonymously donated eggs fertilised by the male applicant's sperm. In deciding the application, Hedley J reviewed the issue of consents required by the surrogate and her husband.

The court must be satisfied that both the surrogate and any other person who is a parent of the child, but who is not one of the applicants, have freely, and with full understanding of what is involved, agree unconditionally to the making of a parental order in favour of the commissioning parents. This does not require the agreement of a person who cannot be found or is incapable of giving agreement. It should be noted that, unlike in the case of the adoption legislation, the court has no power to dispense with a required consent, however unreasonable the withholding of that consent may be or however much the welfare of the child is prejudiced by such refusal. No specific reason for that can be ascertained.

D. *Ratione Temporis*

Section 30(2) of the HFEA 2008 provides for a non-extendable time limit of six months from the date of birth for the making of the parental order application. There is no power to extend, for which no specific reason can be ascertained. Where the child is born abroad under a foreign arrangement, immigration

---

[36] *Z and another v C and another* [2011] EWHC 3181 (Fam).
[37] *X & Y (Foreign Surrogacy)* [2008] EWHC 3030 (Fam).

difficulties may arise which prevent and delay the child's home being with the applicants.

E. *Ratione Loci*

An application for a parental order cannot be progressed until the child is habitually resident and within the jurisdiction. In *Re K (Minors) (Foreign Surrogacy)*,[38] the English High Court was asked to indicate whether a parental order was likely to be granted in relation to twins born in India following a foreign commercial surrogacy agreement between the commissioning parents habitually resident in England and a married couple in India. The egg was from an anonymous donor fertilised by the sperm of the male applicant. The children were in India. The court had to consider whether to give an indication that a parental order was likely to be granted in the future, in order to assist the parents seeking entry clearance for the twins into the UK. The matter was listed before Hedley J, but the application could not be progressed as the children were not habitually resident in England and Wales and thus the court lacked jurisdiction. However, Hedley J made the following obiter comments:

> I am not necessarily averse to making obiter comments about this case. It is clear beyond a peradventure that the conditions [for a parental order] are fulfilled in this case. The guardian has intimated that she sees no present warning signs so far as her welfare assessment is concerned; however, it must be (and is) understood that that is a provisional observation and not a conclusion. So far as approval of sums is concerned … it appears that this was a publicly regulated clinic in which the clinic prescribed the sums paid to the surrogate which were non-negotiable. In other cases such arrangements have been approved.[39]

A court considering an application for a parental order will be assisted by a detailed written report from a specialised guardian, known as a Parental Order Reporter (POR). At present the guidance issued to local authorities and health authorities is contained in Circular LAC (94)25.[40] There is not as yet a corresponding LAC in respect of the HFEA 2008. The guidance requires local authority social services to make enquiries when they are aware that a child has been, or is about to be, born as a result of a surrogacy arrangement. The POR's primary areas of investigation appear to be in respect of welfare, consent and commerciality. The POR is required to consider the circumstances in which the consent of the mother (and as appropriate) the father were obtained. The POR guardian must make an enquiry into and assessment of whether the expenses met by the commissioning couple were reasonably incurred, and if unable to do so must explain why.

---

[38] *Re K (Minors) (Foreign Surrogacy)* [2010] EWHC 1180.
[39] *Ibid*, [9].
[40] Available at <www.dh.gov.uk/en/Publicationsandstatistics/Lettersandcirculars/LocalAuthorityCirculars/AllLocalAuthority/DH_4004636>.

Since 1994 the granting of parental orders in appropriate cases has become an accepted and unremarkable aspect of the work of the family court. Parental orders are subject to specific national (ie (1) England and Wales; (2) Northern Ireland; (3) Scotland) legislation because the underlying adoption legislation is itself nation-specific rather than UK-wide.[41] By the end of 2009, Blyth writes that 725 parental orders had been registered in England and Wales, three in Northern Ireland, and 34 in Scotland.[42] The UK Department of Health states that approximately 50–70 parental orders are granted each year.[43] In the UK, a child's birth should be registered with one of the three General Register Offices (GROs) (ie for England and Wales, Northern Ireland, or Scotland) within six weeks of the child's birth. Following the issue of a parental order, the child's name is entered on a Parental Order Register maintained by the relevant GRO, and the child's original birth certificate is replaced with a new certificate that specifies the child's name (which may be different from the name given at birth) and identifies the commissioning parents as the child's legal parents.

IV. Enforceability of Surrogacy Arrangements

Under UK law a surrogacy agreement is not legally binding—it is unenforceable. Section 1A of the 1985 Act provides that 'no surrogacy arrangement is enforceable by or against any of the persons making it', ie surrogacy contracts are unenforceable in the UK courts.[44] Two sets of reasons could be invoked in this regard. First, the surrogate mother cannot be required by the commissioning parents to hand over the child under any contractual provision. Secondly, legal parenthood can be established only by the means set forth in the law but not by agreement. Thus, the commissioning parents cannot be required to hand over any money, or recover any money paid to the surrogate under the terms of such an agreement, or take responsibility for the child without a parental order (or other court order). This means that surrogates can (and do, as discussed further below) change their minds and refuse to surrender the child at birth.

---

[41] Births and Deaths Registration Act 1953 (England and Wales); Births and Deaths Registration (Northern Ireland) Order 1976 (SI 1976/1041 (NI 14)) (Northern Ireland); the Registration of Births, Deaths and Marriages (Scotland) Act 1965 (Scotland).

[42] E Blyth, 'Parental Orders and identity registration: one country three systems' (2010) 32:4 *Journal of Social Welfare and Family Law* 345.

[43] Impact Assessment of the Human Fertilisation and Embryology (Parental Order) Regulations 2010 (January 2010; on file with author).

[44] S1A of the 1985 Act. S1A inserted by HFEA 1990, s 36(1).

V. Payments in Surrogacy: Requirement of No Money or Other Benefit (Other Than for Expenses Reasonably Incurred)

Another issue currently exercising the minds of practitioners and the courts, and one of the most publicised criteria, is the requirement that no money or other benefit, other than for 'reasonable expenses', has been given to the surrogate mother. The courts in the UK do, however, have the discretion retrospectively to authorise payments made to the surrogate mother, and will do so (and have done so) in appropriate circumstances.

The statute affords no guidance as to the basis of any such approval or what 'reasonable expenses' means. It is clearly a policy decision that commercial surrogacy agreements should not be regarded as lawful; equally, there is clearly a recognition that sometimes there may be reasons to do so.

In *Re L (A Minor)*,[45] the High Court considered a US commercial surrogacy agreement. While the surrogacy agreement the applicants entered into in Illinois (USA) was wholly lawful in that jurisdiction, it was unlawful in the UK per se because the payments made by the applicants went beyond reasonable expenses. For the first time the court made it clear that the welfare of any child born by means of a surrogacy arrangement will trump public policy on payments. The Parental Order 2010 Regulations[46] import into parental order applications the welfare test,[47] with the result that welfare is no longer merely the court's first consideration but becomes its paramount consideration. The effect of the change is that it will only be in the clearest case of the abuse of public policy (such as child trafficking) that the court will be able to withhold an order if welfare considerations otherwise support the making of an order.

In *Re S (Parental Order)*,[48] Hedley J dealt with a surrogacy case involving a British married couple who went to California and commissioned a surrogate mother, who was implanted with an anonymously donated egg fertilised with the sperm of the British husband. Twins were born; and prior to their birth the surrogate mother's rights were extinguished according to Californian law and there was a declaration that the British couple would be the lawful parents of the

---

[45] *Re L (A Minor)* [2010] EWHC 3146.

[46] The significant change in HFEA 2008 is the enlargement of the scope of applicants and the welfare test. The effect of 2010 Regulations is to import into s 54 applications the provisions of s 1 of the Adoption and Children Act 2002.

[47] The checklist is similar to that under the Children Act 1989, and includes consideration of the child's ascertainable wishes and feelings regarding the decision (considered in the light of the child's age and understanding), the child's particular needs, the child's age, sex, background and any of the child's characteristics which the court or agency considers relevant, and the relationship which the child has with relatives and with any other person in relation to whom the court or agency considers the relationship to be relevant.

[48] *Re S (Parental Order)* [2010] 1 FLR 1156.

children. The couple applied for a parental order. Significant sums were spent on medical and legal expenses. The outstanding sum paid to the surrogate mother was $23,000. This sum could not be accounted for fully. The court accepted that part of the sum was attributable to the expenses of the surrogate mother incurred by reason of the pregnancy, but a significant portion of the sum did go beyond 'reasonable expenses'. Hedley J considered that when evaluating the merits of a case with an international aspect, the court has to be satisfied that the commercial surrogacy arrangements were not used to circumvent childcare laws, so that arrangements are approved in favour of individuals who would not have been approved as parents in this country. In addition, the court must be alert to any signs that the payment has meant that the child has effectively been bought, or that the payment made, while it may on first appearance seem modest, is not in fact of such substance that it overbore the will of the surrogate.

Once again the court was faced with the issue of commerciality in *A and A v P, P and B*.[49] The total payments made directly to the surrogate mother were £4,500, approximately.[50] That sum was made up of a combination of payments for loss of earnings, an after-delivery charge and other relatively modest payments. In addition, various payments were made to the clinic in accordance with the agreement, which included the cost of accommodation, food and care at the clinic for the surrogate mother who stayed at the clinic during her pregnancy. Theis J held:

> On the information I have it is likely that the payments were more than expenses reasonably incurred. For example, I was told that it was understood the loss of earnings figure was based on two years loss of earnings. There is no evidence in this case of Mr and Mrs A acting in anything other than the utmost good faith, or that the level of payments or the circumstances of the case could be said to have overborne the will of the surrogate mother. In those circumstances I authorise ... the payments that were made to the surrogate mother in accordance with the agreement.[51]

In *Re X and Y (Children)*,[52] the applicants, Mr and Mrs A, entered into surrogacy agreements with two women in India who had been contacted via a company at a fertility clinic in New Delhi (India). The company was responsible for finding surrogates who had already given birth to a child. The applicants were advised to use two surrogate mothers to increase the chance of a successful birth. The applicants did not consult legal advice in the UK before they travelled to India. The women gave birth to X (a boy), and Y (a girl). Mr A was the children's biological father, and the biological mother was an anonymous egg donor.

The surrogacy company drew up agreements, which concerned the surrogacy arrangement and financial terms. The first part provided for the applicants to be the sole carers of the children and for the surrogate mothers to renounce all legal rights with respect to the children. The second part provided for financial arrangements for

---

[49] *A and A v P, P and B* [2011] EWHC 1738 (Fam).
[50] *Ibid*, [32].
[51] *Ibid*, [34].
[52] *Re X and Y (Children)* [2011] EWHC 3147.

the applicants to pay the surrogates 2,000,000 rupees (£27,000 approximately), comprising in part medical expenses and compensation. The clinic was not a party to, nor responsible for, the financial agreement between the surrogates and the applicants.

Following birth, both mothers signed consent forms confirming the birth, receipt of payment and consent to removal from India. Mr and Mrs A then applied for parental orders in the UK. In considering the application, the court considered:

(a) whether the payment was in contravention of 'reasonable expenses';
(b) whether retrospective authorisation of any payment was required; and
(c) whether the paramountcy of the child's welfare is engaged in decisions concerning the retrospective authorisation of payments.

Out of the 2,000,000 rupees paid to the clinic by Mr and Mrs A, 1,400,000 rupees was for medical care and 670,000 rupees was for non-medical expenses such as legal fees and compensation for the surrogates, coordinator and donor, if applicable. The applicants accepted that the payment went beyond reasonable expenses but sought the court's authorisation, relying on the fact that they acted in good faith, with no attempt to defraud, and that the payments were not so disproportionate that the granting of parental orders would be an affront to public policy. On behalf of the children it was also argued that the payments should be authorised retrospectively, and that the children's welfare required the making of parental orders.

While it appears from the case law that 'any payment described as compensation (or some similar word) as prima facie being a payment that goes beyond reasonable expenses',[53] these cases illustrate the opacity of what is and what is not a reasonable expense. The courts have showed themselves to be more concerned to secure the future of a particular child than to maintain strict rules on expenses. In Hedley J's words:

> What the court is required to do is to balance two competing and potentially irreconcilably conflicting concepts. Parliament is clearly entitled to legislate against commercial surrogacy and is clearly entitled to expect that the courts should implement that policy consideration in its decisions. Yet it is also recognised that as the full rigour of that policy consideration will bear on one wholly unequipped to comprehend it let alone deal with its consequences (ie the child concerned) that rigour must be mitigated by an application of a consideration of that child's welfare. That approach is both humane and intellectually coherent. The difficulty is that it is almost impossible to imagine a set of circumstances in which by the time the case comes to court, the welfare of any child (particularly a foreign child) would not be gravely compromised (at the very least) by a refusal to make an order.[54]

If it is desired to control commercial surrogacy arrangements, regulatory involvement and controls need to operate before the court process is initiated, ie at the border, or even before. Although the detail of such controls would clearly need careful thought, tackling the issues at an earlier stage is surely a better approach

---

[53] *Ibid*, note 19, [7].
[54] Note 18, [24].

than leaving breaches of the law to be discovered only after a child is born (and in the case of international surrogacy, awaits travel documentation), by which time welfare considerations are bound to preside and the court will, although possibly at great expense and complexity, be compelled to find some solution.

To avoid the commercialisation of surrogacy and the growth of profit-driven agencies, the 1985 Act prohibits organisations, or people other than commissioning parents or surrogate mothers themselves, from undertaking certain activities relating to surrogacy on a commercial basis. Section 59 of the HFEA 2008 allows bodies that operate on a not-for-profit basis to receive payment for providing some surrogacy services.[55] Not-for-profit bodies are not permitted to receive payment for offering to negotiate a surrogacy arrangement or for taking part in negotiations about a surrogacy arrangement.[56] These activities are not unlawful if there is no charge, however. A non profit-making body might charge, for example, for enabling interested parties to meet each other to discuss the possibility of a surrogacy arrangement between them. A not-for-profit body can also compile information about surrogacy. Not-for-profit organisations are, for example, able to charge for establishing and keeping lists of people willing to be a surrogate mother, or commissioning parents wishing to have discussions with a potential surrogate mother. Section 1 of the 1985 Act (as amended) provides that non profit-making bodies can recoup the costs of doing only the activities for which they are no longer prohibited from charging. It provides that any reference to a 'reasonable payment' is to a payment which does not exceed the body's costs reasonably attributable to the doing of the act.[57]

The role that surrogacy agencies perform in the surrogacy process is an aspect not to be ignored. McFarlane J has been critical of the lack of oversight and regulation of such agencies:

> The court's understanding is that surrogacy agencies … are not covered by any statutory or regulatory umbrella and are therefore not required to perform to any recognised standard of competence. I am sufficiently concerned by the information uncovered in these two cases to question whether some form of inspection or authorisation should be required in order to improve the quality of advice that is given to individuals who seek to achieve the birth of a child through surrogacy. Given the importance of the issues involved when the life of a child is created in this manner, it is questionable whether the role of facilitating surrogacy arrangements should be left to groups of well-meaning amateurs. To this end, a copy of this judgment is being sent to the Minister of State for Children, Young People and Families for her consideration.[58]

The regulation of surrogacy agencies requires attention.

---

[55] One of the better-known organisations, Childlessness Overcome Through Surrogacy (COTS), was set up by a partnership between Kim Cotton, who has herself been a surrogate on two occasions, and Gena Dodd, a commissioning mother.

[56] S2(1) of the 1985 Act prevents a third party (though not a surrogate or commissioning parents) from initiating or taking part in negotiations, offering or agreeing to negotiate, or compiling any information with a view to its use in making, or negotiating the making of, surrogacy arrangements.

[57] See House of Lords Explanatory Note on the HFEA 2008, available at <www.publications.parliament.uk/pa/ld200708/ldbills/006/en/08006x-d.htm>.

[58] *Re G (Surrogacy: Foreign Domicile)* [2007] EWHC 2814 (Fam), note 32, [29].

VI. Nationality of the Child

There are complex rules about bringing a surrogate child into the jurisdiction. To ensure parity with adoption legislation, the Parental Order Regulations 2010 ensure that where a parental order is made in the United Kingdom and one or both of the commissioning couple are British citizens, the child—if not already so—will become a British citizen.[59] In other situations (depending on whose gametes are used, the immigration status of the gamete provider and the marital status of the surrogate mother) entry clearance for immigration purposes will be required.[60]

VII. Advertisement

Under the 1985 Act (as amended by section 59 of the HFEA 2008), it is an offence to publish or distribute an advertisement that someone may be willing to enter into a surrogacy arrangement, or that anyone is looking for a surrogate mother, or that anyone is willing to facilitate or negotiate such an arrangement. This prohibition does not apply to an advertisement placed by, or on behalf of, a non profit-making body, provided that the advertisement refers only to activities which may legally be undertaken on a commercial basis. This would mean that a not-for-profit body could advertise that it held a list of people seeking surrogate mothers and a list of people willing to be involved in surrogacy, and that it could bring them together for discussion. The law covers adverts online worldwide as well as in print, if they are placed by someone in the UK and can be viewed in the UK.[61]

VIII. Rights of the Child Born Through a Surrogacy Arrangement

In this subject, the issue of a child's right to information about his or her parentage—especially genetic parentage—and the role of law (nationally and internationally) in either promoting or securing this matter loom large. An individual who is the subject of a parental order has a legal right to obtain his or her original 'long' birth certificate,

---

[59] British Nationality Act 1981, s 1(5)(a) and (5A)(a).

[60] The UK Border Agency has issued guidance known as 'Inter-Country Surrogacy and the Immigration Rules' (2009), available at <www.ukba.homeoffice.gov.uk/sitecontent/documents/residency/Intercountry-surrogacy-leaflet>.

[61] R Fenton, S Heenan and J Rees, 'Finally fit for purpose? The Human Fertilization and Embryology Act 2008' (2010) 32:3 *Journal of Social Welfare and Family Law* 275.

revealing the identity of his or her birth mother, at the age of 16 in Scotland[62] and at the age of 18 elsewhere in the UK.[63] The Parental Order Regulations 2010 also provide that where the subject of a parental order applies to the court or Registrar General for information about the parental order, he or she must have been informed about the availability of counselling and have been given a suitable opportunity to receive counselling. Section 31 of the HFEA 2008 allows all donor-conceived people whose details are kept on the HFEA Register of Information to have the opportunity to contact genetic siblings in adulthood, thereby extending access to information on the register.

Although the circumstances that have arisen in *A and A v P, P and B*[64] are extremely rare, they bring into sharp focus the difficulties that may arise in surrogacy arrangements in the human rights context. The court had to consider whether it was enabled to make a parental order in favour of a deceased commissioning parent (the applicant husband died after the application for a parental order was issued by the commissioning parents but prior to the making of the order). While this case raises interesting issues about statutory interpretation, the court's consideration of the Human Rights Act 1998 and the United Nations Convention of the Rights of the Child[65] in a surrogacy setting has brought to the fore live questions with respect to the child's right to an identity and to family life.

There is no doubt that the use of assisted reproduction technologies has raised new questions about how the legal relationships that result from their use are to be identified. The law in the UK has always attached a special significance to a person's status. In *The Ampthill Peerage*,[66] Lord Wilberforce said:

> There can hardly be anything of greater concern to a person than his status as the … child of his parents: denial of it, or doubts as to it, may affect his reputation, his standing in the world … It is vitally necessary that the law should provide a means for any doubts which may be raised to be resolved, and resolved at a time when witnesses and records are available.

Lord Wilberforce was describing there the status of legitimacy under the then current law in the context of a disputed peerage claim. But a similar view, with appropriate modifications, may be taken of the significance of the status of parentage in all matters, surrogacy included, in view of the legal consequences that flow from that relationship.

---

[62] The Parental Orders (Human Fertilisation and Embryology) (Scotland) Regulations 1994 (SI 1994/2804); the Registration Services (Prescription of Forms) (Scotland) Regulations 2009 (SI 2009/314).

[63] The Parental Orders (Human Fertilisation and Embryology) Regulations 1994 (SI 1994/2767); the Human Fertilisation and Embryology (Parental Orders) (Consequential, Transitional and Saving Provisions) Order 2010 (SI 2010/986).

[64] Above n 31.

[65] The UK signed the Convention on 19 April 1990, ratified it on 16 December 1991 and it came into force on 15 January 1992.

[66] *The Ampthill Peerage* [1977] AC 547, 568G–H.

Theis J found that *A and A v P, P and B*[67] was fundamentally about identity rights and the recognition of a parent–child relationship which is central to the child. It was held that the effect of not making a parental order would have been an interference with that family life (the child would not have been treated as though born to both applicants). The court's responsibility is to 'guarantee not rights that are theoretical and illusory but rights that are practical and effective'.[68] Although Theis J was able to grant a parental order within the existing law in this case because the father had died after issuing the application, what would have happened if either of the parents had died earlier, perhaps during the pregnancy?

It should be noted, for completeness, that there is no single piece of legislation that covers child protection in the UK, but rather a myriad of laws and guidance. The surrogate child benefits from the same rights and protection in the UK in complete parity with all other children.

IX. Rights of the Surrogate Mother

It has been established that the law in the UK does not recognise surrogacy as a binding agreement on either party. There is very little that the commissioning parents can do to secure their position prior to the birth, even in the case of gestational surrogacy where the baby is genetically related to both commissioning parents and not the surrogate. The law is clear: a commissioning couple cannot apply for a parental order unless the child is already in their care with the consent of the surrogate. Should they apply for a residence order in respect of the child, or try to invoke any other form of legal process to compel the surrogate to hand over the child, they are almost inevitably bound to fail. Surrogacy arrangements will not be enforced by the back door. Unless the surrogate is, quite apart from the surrogacy arrangement, entirely unfit to parent the child,[69] she is unlikely to be ordered to give up the child. In determining disputes between the surrogate and the commissioning parents, the courts will look to the child's welfare needs, the child's interests being paramount.[70] The ensuing court proceedings may be costly, both in terms of legal expenses and emotions. Provided the surrogate has the appropriate parenting skills and that there is a strong and loving attachment between her and the child who is thriving in her care, it will be very difficult for the commissioning parents to displace that attachment and obtain residence of the child in place of the surrogate, although they may otherwise be able to meet

---

[67] Above n 31.

[68] *Ibid*, citing *Marckx v Belgium* [1979] 2 EHRR 330 at paragraph 31.

[69] The court's paramount consideration is a child's welfare, and a court in England and Wales must have regard in particular to the factors listed in s 1(3) of the Children Act 1989—the so-called 'welfare checklist'—as well as the principles of Art 8 of the European Convention for the Protection of Human Rights and Fundamental Freedoms—the right to respect for family life.

[70] Children Act 1989, s 1.

the child's needs. Even where there is alleged deception on the part of the surrogate in entering into the surrogacy arrangement (eg that she never intended to go through with it, or otherwise deceived them or the court), reprehensible as her conduct may be, the crucial question for the court is what is in the child's best interests. Thus in *Re TT*,[71] the court ordered that the child should remain with the surrogate mother in whose care she had been since her birth five months before and who was thriving, although the court was concerned about aspects of the surrogate mother's character that might be flawed and might impact upon her parenting; whereas in *Re P (Surrogacy: Residence)*,[72] residence of a child was granted to the biological father where a surrogate lied to two sets of commissioning parents in surrogacy arrangements under which she bore two children using the sperm of the commissioning fathers. During the pregnancies she told each couple that she had miscarried, but then went on to care for the children with her husband, her deceit coming to light only when her eldest child left home and contacted the surrogacy agency. The eldest of the two children was six years old by the time the case was heard, and remained with the surrogate and her husband, but the court decided that it was in the best interests of the younger child, then 18 months, that he should reside with his biological father.

In *Re MB*,[73] the principle was established of a competent woman's right to refuse any medical or surgical treatment needed by a foetus, even if the consequence may be the death or serious handicap of the child she bears. To the author's knowledge, there has been no explicit UK case law considering this principle in the context of surrogacy.[74]

The surrogate mother also enjoys maternity rights extending after the birth (these rights do not extend to the commissioning mother). The commissioning parents may qualify for statutory adoption leave or parental leave.[75] The entitlement of an employee on maternity leave to pay and other benefits is governed by a number of different pieces of legislation.[76]

---

[71] *Re TT* [2011] EWHC 33 (Fam). I am grateful to Barbara Connolly QC for bringing this judgment to my attention and her comments on surrogacy presented at the International Bar Association's conference in Dubai (30 October to 4 November 2011).

[72] *Re P (Surrogacy: Residence)* [2008] 1 FLR 177, upheld on appeal, *Re P (Residence: Appeal)* [2007] EWCA Civ 1053.

[73] *Re MB (Caesarean Section)* [1997] 2 FLR 426—whether phobia of needles rendered a pregnant woman temporarily incompetent, allowing the court to order a forced Caesarean.

[74] For completeness, reference (with acknowledgement to the anonymous reader of this chapter) should be made to *St George's Healthcare NHS Trust v S* [1998] 3 WLR 936, in which the Court of Appeal found that a competent adult woman was entitled to refuse a Caesarean section even if her decision would lead to the death of a 36-week-old foetus. Judge LJ said: 'The autonomy of each individual requires continuing protection, particularly when the motive for interfering is as readily understandable, and indeed to many would appear commendable.' He also suggested that '[p]regnancy does not diminish a woman's entitlement to decide whether or not to undergo medical treatment. Her right is not reduced or diminished merely because her decision to exercise her right may appear morally repugnant.'

[75] I am grateful to the anonymous reader of this chapter for this comment.

[76] The Equality Act 2010; the Employment Rights Act 1996; the Maternity and Parental Leave etc Regulations 1999 (SI 1999/3312); the Social Security Contributions and Benefits Act 1992; the Statutory Maternity Pay (General) Regulations 1986 (SI 1986/1960).

X. The Way Forward

Surrogacy can never be risk-free and it cannot be ignored. Every attempt should be made to minimise the risks of surrogacy. There are many questions in this field, and in addition to the difficulties considered in this chapter, a number of other legal hurdles and sociological considerations require attention. For example, what happens if the surrogate mother decides to terminate the pregnancy, or if the child is born with serious disabilities? What happens in the case of miscarriage or multiple births? Should counselling, support and advice services available to adopted children and their families be made available to children born as a result of surrogacy? Do those agencies involved in surrogacy arrangements have the requisite expertise to assist in setting up surrogacy arrangements, and are their activities sufficiently monitored? What will the surrogacy arrangement mean to these children as they grow up and try to unravel and come to terms with their origins? Added to such complications are the difficulties of procuring the necessary immigration papers for foreign-born infants. Reliable data on complication rates during pregnancy and pregnancy outcomes may not be available. The quality of medical treatment may be substandard. Often more embryos are transferred than the home country would permit, risking higher rates of multiple pregnancy which endanger both woman and foetus, requiring very costly pre-natal and post-natal care—which must then be borne by the parents or the healthcare system of the home country after the parents return there.

It is clear from this brief overview of the case law and the legislation in this area that the UK approach is consistent in all cases: the court applies *lex fori*. We have seen the courts retrospectively approving surrogacy payments made overseas which go beyond reasonable expenses, thus demonstrating the creativity of the UK courts in finding alternative solutions where a surrogacy arrangement does not fit the UK's acceptable model (purportedly altruistic, consenting and privately arranged). The questions now for the UK[77] are:

(a) how to regulate the impact of the perceived increase of cross-border surrogacy arrangements on its substantive law; and

(b) whether existing law and practice adequately safeguard the welfare of the child, the surrogate, her family and the commissioning couple.[78]

---

[77] A review of the HFEA 2008 and the Parental Order 2010 Regulations is due in November 2012.

[78] This is based on the premise that as the number of international surrogacy agreements rapidly rises, there is an increasingly urgent need for international regulation of this pressing socio-legal problem. To ensure protection of the various vulnerable parties, some form of regulation is required. But first a further objection has to be considered: even if regulation appears to be necessary, it may be undesirable, because its effect would be to make the current situation worse. Some of those who are opposed to surrogacy in principle wish to avoid regulation, arguing that it will legitimise rather than discourage the practice. This was the majority view of the Warnock Report. Others, who accept surrogacy as a valid practice, fear that a stringent regulatory framework could result in driving many arrangements underground, so depriving surrogates and commissioning couples of whatever guidance

Because of the variety of domestic responses to surrogacy—from complete ban to a very liberal approach—any action at supranational level should consider the setting of common standards both for substantive and private international law on legal parenthood after surrogacy, whilst providing protection to the surrogate and her family. A comprehensive multilateral instrument specifically aimed at resolving the challenges of cross-border surrogacy has various advantages: it is accessible; it facilitates certainty by permitting States to agree upfront about the form and content of the legal consequences; and it usually saves time. These are all characteristics that stakeholders, such as the judiciary, the legislator, the executive, academia and the children themselves, require.

As lawyers, we tend to think of the law in terms of discrete subjects: family law, the law of trusts, the law of torts, medical ethics and so on. This can make the law more readily navigable, but can mean that issues arise with legal relationships that straddle a number of different subjects. Reaching an understanding of surrogacy takes more than one disciplinary approach. In fact, it takes a constellation of multi-disciplinary conversations, in places big and small, in order to achieve a coherent and fully-considered response to surrogacy. The ultimate goal of this commendable book's project is to prepare a document that would serve as a basis for a future international Convention on aspects of surrogacy arrangements. It is the author's hope that in conducting the review, there is consultation as widely as possible with individuals and organisations with interests in the practice of surrogacy. Consultation with, for example, the UN High Commissioner for Refugees, UN Children's Fund (UNICEF), the European Committee on Legal Cooperation and the Hague Conference on Private International Law would be invaluable (it is also sensible, from a practical point of view, that the stakeholders should not duplicate work done by others). Along with the commissioning parents and the clinics that serve them, the donors, surrogates and children are the major players in this unfolding history, and their insight and experience are crucial to an understanding of the scope and extent of the problem areas and how these can—and should—be addressed.

is currently offered by clinics and voluntary agencies in the field. The author has concluded that the risks of not having a regulatory framework are greater than any entailed by introducing one.

24

United States of America

STEVEN H SNYDER

I. Introduction

The problems presented by cross-border surrogacy programmes generally revolve around establishment of parentage and citizenship of the resulting children when they return to their intended parents' home country. Countries that have adopted an express political policy rejecting surrogacy may refuse to allow the intended parents to register their children as full citizens of their native country. Some insist that the surrogate who gave birth to the child is the child's legal mother (and, often, her husband the father), without taking any notice of or giving effect to express court orders to the contrary in the country where the surrogacy occurred that effectively terminate those rights. This creates parentage, citizenship, residence and social benefit issues that adversely impact the child and the child's family when they return home.

A simple solution to some of the problems and issues cited above, particularly with regard to surrogacy programmes completed in the US, is for the countries-of-origin of the intended parents to give full force and effect to the US court orders and judgments establishing the parentage of the intended parents and terminating the parental rights of the surrogate (and her husband, if any). This would be done under the principle of international comity.[1]

---

[1] 'Comity' is defined as 'a willingness to grant a privilege, not as a matter of right, but one of deference and good will' (*Black's Law Dictionary*, 6th edn (St Paul, MN, West Publishing Co, 1990) 267). Under principles of international comity, courts of one country or jurisdiction will give effect to the laws and judicial decisions of another, not as a matter of obligation but out of deference and respect. *Hilton v Guyot* is a landmark US Supreme Court opinion, which based recognition of foreign judgments on 'the comity of nations' and formally established the rules of international comity and reciprocity in the US judicial system: *Hilton v Guyot*, 159 US 113 (1895). *Hilton* established a generous federal court recognition policy that is basically followed today: '[W]e are satisfied that, where there has been opportunity for a full and fair trial abroad before a court of competent jurisdiction, conduct in a trial upon regular proceedings, after due citation or voluntary appearance of the defendant, and under a system of jurisprudence likely to secure an impartial administration of justice between the citizens of its own country and those of other countries, and there is nothing to show either prejudice in the court, or in the system of laws under which it is sitting, or fraud in procuring the judgment, or any other special reason why the comity of this nation should not allow it full effect, the merits

Unfortunately, there seems to be resistance to this solution based, most notably, on the substantially varying political views and policies regarding surrogacy as a morally acceptable and permissible family-building option from country to country. Refusal to recognise foreign court orders and judgments may, in part, be rooted in the home country's effort to enforce its internal policy on surrogacy outside its borders by refusing to recognise court orders and judgments from more permissive countries, and denying establishment of the intended parentage, nationality and citizenship of the resulting children. This effectively has a chilling effect on the home country's citizens' desire to participate in surrogacy in another country where it is, indeed, permitted. Unfortunately, this ongoing refusal readily and efficiently to establish parentage and citizenship in international surrogacy cases is certainly not rooted in deference to the best interests of the resulting children, since those interests are not well served under the current international system, or lack thereof.

II. General US Federal and State Law Regarding Surrogacy

The Tenth Amendment to the United States Constitution states:

> The powers not delegated to the United States by the Constitution, nor prohibited by it to the States, are reserved to the States respectively, or to the people.

Under this provision and the concept of 'state sovereignty' that it creates, the power to establish and regulate parentage has always been historically a state, not a federal, function. Thus, there is no federal statute or regulation that affects surrogacy and the parentage of the resulting children either positively or negatively. It is up to each state individually to determine whether and how its respective laws will treat surrogacy arrangements and the parentage of the resulting children.

The social and legal reaction to and perception of surrogacy in the US have evolved significantly over the last 30 years. In the early 1980s, there was no established law of any kind in the US that governed surrogacy, and in vitro fertilisation (IVF)[2] was a new medical procedure that was relatively unreliable. Therefore, the vast majority of surrogacy arrangements during this time were traditional surrogacies, meaning that the surrogate was artificially inseminated with the sperm of the intended father (or sperm donor), and then gestated and subsequently

---

of the case should not, in an action brought in this country upon the judgment, be tried afresh, on a new trial or appeal, upon the mere assertion of the party that the judgment was erroneous in law or in fact.' American courts will accord considerable deference to foreign adjudications as a matter of comity. Courts of other countries typically do the same.

[2] Removal of an egg from a woman's ovary and fertilisation of the egg outside the womb in a petri dish.

delivered to the intended parent(s) a child that was her own genetic offspring. This was an unprecedented and ethically uncertain concept for many, and public attention across the US was irresistibly focused on the issue when the first dispute over custody between a surrogate and the intended parents was litigated and decided in New Jersey in *Matter of Baby M*.[3]

The New Jersey Supreme Court in *Baby M* publicly wrestled with the social ramifications of surrogacy as a new family-building procedure, the dearth of any previous legal context for determining parentage in surrogacies and the inadequacy of existing law to resolve the ethical quandary of intent versus genetic relationship in determining such parentage. The court's dilemma was highly publicised and sensationalised by every newspaper and in every state in the US. Ultimately, the Court in *Baby M* decided that existing parentage law could not be used to deprive a genetically-related birth mother of parental rights to her child without her consent. In the five years following *Baby M*, there was clear legislative response to surrogacy as it was presented in that case. Approximately 10 states passed prohibitive or restrictive legislation regarding surrogacy, most of which did not distinguish between traditional surrogacy and gestational surrogacy.[4]

While various state legislatures were passing this restrictive legislation, surrogacy evolved with the advent of more reliable and successful IVF procedures. By the early 1990s, the majority of surrogacies were gestational surrogacies. This eased the ethical dilemma for many, and surrogacy became more common and socially accepted. In 1993, the California Supreme Court decided *Johnson v Calvert*,[5] adopted the first phase of California's intent analysis (stating that the person(s) who initiate a surrogate pregnancy with the intent of becoming the resulting child's legal parents are entitled to become the child's legal parents as against the rights of the gestational mother and the genetic contributors) and judicially ratified the enforceability of gestational surrogacy arrangements in California. In 1998, the California courts extended the intent test in *Buzzanca v Buzzanca*,[6] and thereafter approximately 10 other states passed permissive or facilitative legislation regarding surrogacy. The tide has turned, and the strong trend in US state surrogacy legislation is now to permit and effectively regulate surrogacy, not prohibit it.

State law concerning surrogacy varies widely and generally falls into one of three categories. The first category includes states whose legislatures have been proactive in passing specific legislation, whether permissive or prohibitory, that specifically applies to and/or governs surrogacy (see statutes of Texas[7]). The second category includes states that have no statutes that apply to surrogacy but whose

---

[3] *Matter of Baby M*, 109 NJ 396, 537 A2d 1227 (NJ 1988).
[4] Surrogacy via *in vitro* fertilization in which the egg of the intended mother or an egg donor is fertilized outside the womb in a petri dish with the surrogate gestating the resulting embryo so that the surrogate delivers a child of whom she is not the genetic mother.
[5] *Johnson v Calvert*, 5 Cal 4th 84, 19 Cal Rptr 2d 494, 851 P 2d 776 (cert denied 510 US 874, 114 S Ct 206, 126 L Ed 2d 163) (Cal 1993).
[6] *Buzzanca v Buzzanca*, 61 Cal App 4th 1410, 72 Cal Rptr 2d 280 (Cal Ct App 1998).
[7] Vernon's Texas Code Annotated, Family Code, § 160.750 *et seq*.

appellate courts have affirmatively decided contested and litigated surrogacy cases to create case law precedent that applies to and/or governs surrogacy (see statutes and case law of California[8]). The third category includes those states that have neither statutes nor case law that apply to and/or govern surrogacy (see statutes of Minnesota[9]). In states that fall into this last category, surrogacy rises or falls on the application of and options available under existing parentage, termination of parental rights and adoption law as it existed before surrogacy became a viable family-building option. The pre-existing laws of parentage, termination of parental rights and adoption are applied to create the parental relationships originally intended by the parties to a surrogacy arrangement.

In all states that fall into each of these three categories (including those with prohibitory legislation), surrogacy is being successfully carried on and concluded with the blessing of the relevant courts of law in *uncontested* cases in which parentage orders can be entered with the cooperation and approval of all the parties. This is the case in virtually all surrogacies in the US.[10] Even in New York and Michigan, where compensated surrogacy is criminalised, there are existing court orders affirming the parentage of intended parents under existing law as long as the parties are all in agreement.[11]

III. Effect of Court-ordered Parentage in Surrogacy Proceedings

A. What is Different Among the Various States?

The primary difference among the states is the procedure by which parentage is finally established following the birth of a child under a surrogacy agreement. As discussed above, there are numerous states that allow surrogacy by statute and establish clear procedures as to how parentage of the child is established. Examples are: Texas and Utah, which have adopted the surrogacy provisions of

---

[8] California Family Code, § 7570 *et seq*; *Johnson v Calvert*, above n 5; *Buzzanca v Buzzanca*, above n 6.

[9] Minnesota Statutes Annotated Chapter 257.

[10] Based on an anecdotal study of surrogacies as referenced in 2002, of an estimated 14,000–16,000 reported surrogate births through that date, only 88 had resulted in any dispute between the surrogate and the intended parents, most of which never reached the courts: D Morgenstern Katz, 'Why More and More Infertile Women Are Turning to Others to Bear Their Babies' (December/January 2002) *Parenting Magazine* 88. Of those 88, only 23 were surrogates who threatened to keep the baby (usually to leverage some contractual benefit to themselves, not because they really wanted the child), and 65 were parents who did not want the resulting children (because of divorce, bankruptcy, health condition, number, etc). If true, this evidences an uncontested success rate of greater than 99.5%. The cases that are contested in court get the most publicity, but they are definitely in a tiny minority. This conforms to the author's professional experience as well.

[11] See *Arredondo v Nodelman*, 622 NYS 2d 181 (1994).

the Uniform Parentage Act of 2000, as amended in 2002, and which require court pre-approval of a written surrogacy agreement in order to establish the intended parent(s)' legal parentage and notification to the court following the child's birth to amend the birth certificate; Virginia, in which a similar procedure is used under the Uniform Status of Children of Assisted Conception Act (1988); Florida, in which a similar procedure is used under Florida's independent surrogacy laws; and Illinois, in which parentage is automatically administratively established without court involvement prior to birth by attorney 'letters of compliance' with all of the provisions of the governing surrogacy law.

There are other states in which parentage following surrogacy is established pursuant to appellate law developed by decisions in litigated court cases. Examples are: Massachusetts, in which pre-birth establishment of parentage in surrogacies has been formally ratified by its Supreme Court in *Culliton v Beth Israel Deaconess Medical Center*[12] and *Hodas v Morin*[13]; California, in which pre-birth orders are also permitted in surrogacies pursuant to *Johnson v Calvert*[14] and *Buzzanca v Buzzanca*[15]; and Ohio, in which intended parents may establish parentage post-birth pursuant to *Belsito v Clark*[16] and *JF v DB*.[17]

Lastly, there are some states with statutes that expressly limit or prohibit surrogacy, and a much larger majority of states with no legislation or case law that either affirms or prohibits surrogacy. In states like Michigan and New York, where surrogacy is purportedly illegal, as previously stated above, there are still numerous examples of cases in which the courts have signed and entered court orders establishing the intended parentage of children born to surrogate mothers pursuant to written surrogacy agreements.[18] In the larger majority of states with no statutes or case law regarding surrogacy, parentage is established according to pre-existing statutes regarding paternity, maternity, termination of parental rights and adoption.

In both of the immediately foregoing categories of states, surrogacy can still be accomplished; however, the exact nature and procedure of the parentage proceedings vary depending on the genetic make-up of the child in gestation and the specific laws of each state. If the child is the genetic product of both of two opposite-sex intended parents (intended mother's egg, intended father's sperm) who both want parental rights, a simple paternity/maternity establishment proceeding may be all that is necessary to establish parentage based on genetic relationship alone. This results in a single judgment for paternity/maternity and a birth certificate with both intended parents' names on it.

If there is a sperm or egg donor with only one genetic intended legal parent (male or female) then a paternity or maternity proceeding to establish the genetic

---

[12] *Culliton v Beth Israel Deaconess Medical Center*, 435 Mass 285 (2001).
[13] *Hodas v Morin*, 442 Mass 544 (2004).
[14] Above n 5.
[15] Above n 6.
[16] *Belsito v Clark* 644 NE 2d 760 (1994).
[17] *JF v DB*, 879 NE 2d 740 (2007).
[18] See *Arredondo v Nodelman*, above n 11.

parent's parentage is followed by a termination of the parental rights of the surrogate (and/or egg donor, if known). This results in a judgment for paternity (usually) followed by a judgment terminating the surrogate's parental rights, and a birth certificate with just the single intended genetic parent's name on it.

If there is a sperm or egg donor with only one genetic intended parent and a second non genetically-related intended parent (whether opposite sex or same-sex partners), both of whom desire legal parental rights, the genetic parent's paternity (or maternity) is established through a paternity or maternity proceeding and, only in those states in which a simple parentage order establishing the parentage of both intended parents is unavailable, a second-parent adoption may be performed to create the legal relationship with the second, non genetically-related intended parent. This results in a judgment for paternity or maternity that may also be followed by a judgment for adoption and a birth certificate with both intended parents' names on it.

Thus, depending on the law of each particular state and the manner in which it addresses (or does not address) surrogacy, surrogacy may still be accomplished, but the procedure in each such state will vary.

B. What is the Same Among the Various States?

What is identical from state to state is that once a court does approve and ratify the intended parentage in a surrogacy matter, the intended parent(s) obtain a judgment of the court that confirms their parentage and establishes their right(s) to be named on the child's birth certificate. It does not matter whether the state in which such a judgment is obtained is one with positive law supporting surrogacy, negative law restricting or prohibiting surrogacy, or no law. If, in the circumstances of the particular case, a court has considered the parties' request for a parentage order and determined that it is in the child's best interests that the intended parent(s) receive legal parentage, a judgment is entered, and it is enforceable against all necessary parties who received notice of and participated in the proceeding. This is true in any state in the US for all purposes once the judgment becomes final.

Essentially, a judgment becomes final when it is no longer appealable. If a judgment is rendered in a federal court (which would not be the case in a surrogacy proceeding since these are governed by state law), a party who disagrees with or contests the judgment must appeal it within 30 days of the date the judgment was entered.[19] This period of time may vary for judgments entered in state courts. In Minnesota, the time to effect an appeal from a judgment is 60 days from the date the judgment was entered.[20] This period of time will generally be between 30 and 60 days in virtually every state. If the judgment is not appealed, it becomes

---

[19] Federal Rule of Appellate Procedure 4 (2010).
[20] Minnesota Rule of Appellate Procedure 104 (2010).

final for all purposes subject to very narrow provisions that grant relief on other, specified grounds.

In cases in which all parties agree and mutually consent in adequate court pleadings and/or testimony to the entry of judgment (as in virtually all surrogacy proceedings), it would be virtually impossible to appeal successfully or overturn such a judgment. This is the reason why all US courts of which the author is personally aware ignore this theoretical appeal period and allow the amendment of the relevant birth certificates, obtaining of passports and departure from the US to foreign jurisdictions in the case of all international intended parents before the appeal period has actually expired. The US courts seem to accept the practical reality that all such surrogacy parentage determinations are final and effective as against all parties for all purposes, in spite of the appeal period. The fact that virtually all surrogacy parentage determinations in the US are stipulated to with the collective consent of all parties makes them essentially impervious to any such appeal. This appeal period should not be the basis for any delay in recognising the intended parents as the child's parents immediately upon their return to their home country.

If a judgment is not timely appealed and becomes final, a party can seek additional relief from the judgment for only a few, very narrow reasons. If a party alleges that there has been fraud or mistake, or that there is newly-discovered evidence that was not previously available, or certain other limited grounds, the party may make a motion asking for relief from the judgment. Such a motion must be made within a 'reasonable time' and no later, in most cases, than one year after the date the judgment was entered.[21] To the author's knowledge, this ground for appealing a surrogacy judgment has never been asserted in the US, and it is not expected to be relevant to any past, current or future surrogacy parentage determinations in the US.

It is important to emphasise that a judgment is effective only against necessary parties who receive notice of and participate in the proceeding. In a surrogacy case, this would obviously include the surrogate, her spouse, if any, and the intended parent(s). These parties always appear in surrogacy parentage cases, either by actual appearance or through signed pleadings.

However, such cases often involve either sperm or egg donors. If that is the case, the donors also have presumptive parental rights by virtue of their genetic relationship to the child, under virtually all state parentage statutes, that can be terminated only by judicial order, and, at least according to the courts in Ohio, they are entitled to notice of and participation in the parentage proceedings.[22]

---

[21] See Federal Rule of Civil Procedure 60 (2010) and Minnesota Rule of Civil Procedure 60 (2010).

[22] See *Dantzig v Biron*, 2008 WL 187532 (Ohio App 4 Dist 2008) (Appeal denied) and *Rice v O'Flynn*, 2005 WL 2140576 (Ohio App 9 Dist 2005), each stating that an egg donor (originally anonymous in those cases) is a 'necessary party' entitled to notice of and participation in legal proceedings to determine the parentage of a resulting child through surrogacy.

The practical problem in surrogacy parentage proceedings in the US is that the vast majority of them that involve donors involve *anonymous donors*. By definition and express agreement, such donors cannot be identified and cannot be given notice of or participate in the parentage court proceedings. As a result, most such donors are never aware of the parentage proceedings, and the effectiveness of the *de facto* 'termination' of their legal rights usually relies solely on their continuing anonymity. This author has no reason to believe that this insulating anonymity will be changed, voluntarily by the parties or legislatively by the federal or state governments, any time in the near future.

On the other hand, if a donor is known then he or she can be given notice of the parentage proceeding at the conclusion of the surrogacy, and make an appearance by signing the pleadings and requesting the termination of any presumptive legal parentage he or she may retain by virtue of his or her genetic link to the child. As to donors who are so joined, the termination of their parental rights also becomes final once the judgment becomes final.

Therefore, subject to the foregoing discussion, an intended parent will obtain a judgment evidencing his or her parentage of the child following a surrogate birth, whether that judgment is for parentage, termination of parental rights or second-parent adoption. The same judgment will issue in any state where parentage proceedings are initiated. Once an intended parent obtains such a judgment, that judgment will generally become final, subject to only rare and limited exceptions not usually present in surrogacy cases, within a period from 30 to 60 days following the date on which it is entered. It would be a very rare occasion on which a judgment entered based on the mutual consent of all parties, as in a surrogacy proceeding, would ever be appealed, and it is highly unlikely that any such appeal would succeed. The judgment will become final to the same degree in all cases, whether the surrogate appeared personally at a court hearing or appeared only through her signed consents or other pleadings.

Once the judgment becomes final, it goes without saying that all of the surrogate's actual or presumptive parental rights disappear, and the surrogate no longer has any legal standing or basis to claim any legal relationship to or authority over the resulting child. The surrogate has absolutely no further legal rights to exert any control over the child or the child's subsequent parentage. As a result, it is unnecessary to have the surrogate appear in any subsequent step/second-parent adoption or other proceeding, and her legal consent thereto is no longer necessary. Asking the surrogate for any consent after such a judgment in order to establish legal parentage in either the US or in the child's home country would be contrary to logic and the established legal relationships at that point in time.

C. Why are such State Judgments Effective in all US States?

The basis for this author's stating that a judgment of parentage/termination of parental rights/adoption in any US state is effective in all US states, lies in the Full

Faith and Credit Clause. The Full Faith and Credit Clause—Article IV, Section 1, of the US Constitution—provides:

> Full Faith and Credit shall be given in each State to the public Acts, Records, and judicial Proceedings of every other State.

The statute that implements the clause[23] further specifies that 'a state's preclusion rules should control matters originally litigated in that state'. The Full Faith and Credit Clause ensures that judicial decisions rendered by the courts in one state are recognised and honoured in every other state. In drafting the Full Faith and Credit Clause, the Framers of the Constitution were motivated by a desire to unify their new country while preserving the autonomy of the states. To that end, they sought to guarantee that judgments rendered by the courts of one state would not be ignored by the courts of other states. The Supreme Court reiterated the Framers' intent when it held that the Full Faith and Credit Clause precluded any further litigation of a question previously decided by an Illinois court in *Milwaukee County v ME White Co*.[24] The Court held that by including the clause in the Constitution, the Framers intended to make the states

> integral parts of a single nation throughout which a remedy upon a just obligation might be demanded as of right, irrespective of the state of its origin.

The Full Faith and Credit Clause is invoked primarily to enforce judgments. When a valid judgment is rendered by a court that has jurisdiction over the parties, and the parties receive proper notice of the action and a reasonable opportunity to be heard, the Full Faith and Credit Clause requires that the judgment receive the same effect in other states as in the state where it is entered. A party who obtains a judgment in one state may petition the court in another state to enforce the judgment. When this is done, the parties do not relitigate the issues, and the court in the second state is obliged to recognise and honour the judgment of the first court in full in determining the enforceability of the judgment and the procedure for its execution. This principle has even recently been invoked to establish the recognition of a pre-birth order establishing parentage in a surrogate birth in California (a state which formally recognises surrogacy via appellate court authority) for the intended parents who reside in New York (a state which criminalises compensated surrogacy arrangements).[25]

---

[23] 28 USCA § 1738.

[24] *Milwaukee County v ME White Co*, 296 US 268, 56 S Ct 229, 80 L Ed 220 (1935).

[25] See *DP v TR*, F-04079-10 (2010). Brady Klein Weissman won a significant ruling in this 'Full Faith and Credit' case. In *DP v TR*, a New York State court upheld a California *pre-birth order* and judgment of paternity for twins conceived through gestational surrogacy. The court ruled that the US Constitution's Full Faith and Credit Clause trumps New York's public policy barring surrogacy. In fact, the court stated that both federal and state law hold that a state's policy is not a valid basis to deny Full Faith and Credit to another state's properly adjudicated judgment. In the case at hand, a gay couple had twins through gestational surrogacy in California, and obtained a pre-birth order of dual paternity in 2001. In 2010, the couple became involved in a child support proceeding where one of the men sought to escape support obligations by challenging the validity of the California parentage ruling in light of the New York state anti-surrogacy policy. As noted by attorney Steven J Weissman: 'This decision gives a good deal of surety, especially to the non-biological father, that his parentage cannot later be challenged because of New York's public policy against surrogacy.'

D. What is the US Department of State's Position Regarding the Adoptions often Required in Surrogacy Matters?

The US State Department representative who has dealt with many international inquiries as to whether US second-parent adoptions in surrogacy matters are subject to the Hague Adopted Convention, has consistently answered in the negative. As a result, whether any particular surrogacy parentage proceeding requires a second-parent adoption has no effect on the fact that, once the US court judgment becomes final, the US State Department policy to date is that no additional action is necessary in any other home country to finalise the parentage of the resulting child. The child is, for all purposes in all US states, fully and finally the child of the intended parents as declared by any US state court in such a proceeding.

E. What is the Citizenship Status of Children born in the US to Parents from Other Countries?

The 14th Amendment to the United States Constitution states:

> All persons born or naturalized in the United States, and subject to the jurisdiction thereof, are citizens of the United States and of the State wherein they reside. No State shall make or enforce any law which shall abridge the privileges or immunities of citizens of the United States; nor shall any State deprive any person of life, liberty, or property, without due process of law; nor deny to any person within its jurisdiction the equal protection of the laws.

Since the children born as the result of surrogate arrangements between US-resident surrogates and intended parents from countries outside the US are eventually born in the US, each of these children is a citizen of the United States without further legal action under the 14th Amendment. Each such child is entitled to a US passport. The issuance of such passports and the child's citizenship status are in keeping with applicable US federal immigration and constitutional law.

25

Venezuela

ELEONORA LAMM[*]

I. Legal Framework

In Venezuela there is no domestic law on surrogacy nor a general law on assisted reproductive techniques (ART), except for Article 204 of the Civil Code (CCiv) which regulates filiation in cases of artificial insemination.[1]

Moreover, the general principle is that the mother is the woman who gives birth to the child, according to Article 197 of the Civil Code.

II. Jurisdiction

Although there is no law on ART in Venezuela, the right to procreation using these techniques has been recognised by the *Tribunal Superior de Justicia* (Supreme Tribunal of Justice) (TSJ).

In Venezuela, *la Sala Constitucional del Tribunal Superior de Justicia* (the Constitutional Chamber (SC) of the Supreme Tribunal of Justice) is empowered to make mandatory interpretations of the Constitution, as provided in Article 335 of the *Constitución de la República Bolivariana de Venezuela* (Constitution of the Bolivarian Republic of Venezuela) (CRBV).[2]

---

[*] I should like to thank Dr Gladys Rodríguez, Dr Mirian Rodriguez and Dr Haydee Barrios for their contributions.

[1] Art 204 CCiv: 'The husband cannot disown a child pleading his impotence, unless it is manifest and permanent. The disownment is not admissible, even in that case, when conception has taken place through artificial insemination of the wife with the consent of her husband.'

[2] Art 335 CRBV: 'The Supreme Tribunal of Justice shall guarantee the supremacy and efficacy of constitutional rules and principles; it shall be the supreme and ultimate interpreter of the Constitution and shall see to the uniform interpretation and application of the same. Interpretations established by the Constitutional Division concerning the contents or scope of constitutional rules and principles are binding on the other division of the Supreme Tribunal of Justice and on all of the other courts of the Republic.'

Thus, the Constitutional Chamber of the Supreme Tribunal of Justice (TSJ SC sentence no 1456, 27 July 2006) ruled on the remedy of *Amparo*[3] submitted by a woman who requested a clinical centre to give her a sample of her dead husband's sperm in order to carry out a process of in vitro fertilisation (IVF). The clinical centre, where the sample was conserved, refused to give it to the woman because there was no approval (there was no express consent) from the deceased husband. The Supreme Tribunal of Justice granted the remedy and, as noted above, also recognised the right to procreation (regulated under Article 76 CRBV[4]) by ART. It argued that the

> right to bear children is inherent to the human person, thus those who decide to pro-
> create have the right to do so without further limitations than those established by the
> Constitution and laws. Today, methods have been attempted to make possible that those
> who naturally cannot do so, have the real and effective possibility of having children, in
> favour of the consolidation and welfare of the family.

Furthermore, regarding surrogacy and filiation, the Chamber stated that

> until the law that regulates the bioethical principles laid down in Article 127 of the
> Constitution[5] is issued, before the reality and the constitutional coverage that in this
> matter must exist, this Chamber does not want to overlook the fact that in the practice
> of ART using sperm, egg and/or womb donors, the important thing is that in terms of
> filiation, maternity and paternity be granted to those who have expressed and really had
> the procreational will, ie the will and desire to have children, and not to those who have
> rendered a service for the success of the assisted reproductive technique.[6]

According to this interpretation of the Constitutional Chamber of the Supreme Tribunal of Justice, the principle established by Article 197 of the Civil Code— '*Mater in sures semper certa est*'—can change. In cases of ART using a womb donor, ie surrogacy cases, the mother would no longer be the woman who gives birth to the child but the one who has the procreational will. Thus filiation would be established by a new element or requisite called 'procreational will', ie the will and desire to have children, and no relationship would be created with those who have rendered a service aimed at the success of the assisted reproductive technique.

The Supreme Tribunal of Justice does not directly rule on the legitimacy of sur-rogacy agreements,[7] but it does seem to lean toward their recognition. However,

---

[3] *Amparo Constitucional* for violation of the right to procreate (Art 76 CRBV and Art 16(e) of the Convention on the Elimination of All Forms of Discrimination against Women (CEDAW)), the right to free development of personality (Art 20 CRBV), and the right to maternity with no discrimination (Arts 56, 76 and 21 CRBV).

[4] Art 76 CRBV: 'Motherhood and fatherhood are fully protected, whatever the marital status of the mother or father. Couples have the right to decide freely and responsibly how many children they wish to conceive, and are entitled to access to the information and means necessary to guarantee the exercise of this right....'

[5] Art 127 states: 'The genome of a living being shall not be patentable, and the field shall be regu-lated by the law relating to the principles of bioethics.'

[6] For the dissenting opinion, this was going beyond the *thema decidendum*.

[7] The Chamber clarifies that will not rule on the subject of surrogate motherhood, because although it is related to ART, it has not been regulated yet. Thus, until the enactment of a law, the issues related to surrogacy will be treated only when the Chamber is asked to resolve a specific conflict on the subject.

the Tribunal stated that in such a case, the mother would be the intending mother (procreational will) and not the person who gives birth to the child.

A. The Biological Link

Notwithstanding the provision of the Civil Code which states that the mother is the person who gives birth to the child (Article 197 CCiv), or what was established by the Supreme Tribunal of Justice, which in a surrogacy case seemed to grant filiation in favour of the intending parents because they would have the procreational will (sentence no 1456 of 2006, above), it is important to stress that in surrogacy cases some scholars[8] would establish filiation on the basis of the biological link, according to the biological trend of Venezuelan law.

This position is based on a joint interpretation of constitutional and special civil provisions[9]. Article 56 CRBV[10] establishes the rights of everyone to know the identity of their parents[11] and to obtain public documents that prove their biological identity, in accordance with the law; in the same vein, Article 75[12] establishes the right of children and adolescents to be raised in their family of origin.[13] Furthermore, Article 76 CRBV protects motherhood, in general, from the moment of conception.[14]

To this, it is necessary to add the ruling of the Constitutional Chamber of Supreme Tribunal of Justice of 14 August 2008 (TSJ SC Decision No 1443, 14 August 2008). In this case a married woman asked for the constitutional right to register her child, conceived with a father who was someone other than the legal father, ie her husband, which compromised the principle of legal paternity (Articles 201 to 212 CCiv). The Tribunal considered that

> when there is a contradiction between the biological and legal identity, and certain knowledge of the biological identity is possible, this must prevail over the legal identity,

---

[8] G Rodríguez R de Bello, *Trabajo de investigación jurídica en el área de Bioética Jurídica*, forthcoming.

[9] Ley Orgánica para la Protección del Niño y Adolescente [Law for the Protection of Children and Adolescents] (LOPNA), *Official Gazette* No 5.266 of 2 October 1998. Modified on 10 December 2007, *Official Gazette* No 5.859 of 10 December 2007.

[10] Art 56 CRBV: 'Every person has the right to his own name ... and to know the identity of his father and mother. The State guarantees the right to investigates maternity and paternity. All persons have the right to be registered free of charge with the Civil Registry Office after birth, and to obtain public documents constituting evidence of their biological identity, in accordance with law. Such documents shall not contain any mention classifying the parental relationship.'

[11] See also Art 25 LOPNA.

[12] Art 75 CRBV: '... Children and adolescents have the right to live, be raised and develop in the bosom of their original family. ...'

[13] See Art 26 LOPNA. See also Art 17 LOPNA—right to identification; Art 18 LOPNA—right to be registered in the Civil Registry; Art 22 LOPNA—right to public ID.

[14] Art 76 CRBV: '... The State guarantees overall assistance and protection for motherhood, in general, from the moment of conception, throughout pregnancy, delivery and the puerperal period, and guarantees full family planning services based on ethical and scientific values. ...'

because the biological identity gives the child his genetic identity and the knowledge to be the child of his biological ancestors.

Thus, it asserts the primacy of the biological identity over the legal identity based on Articles 56[15] and 76 CRBV,[16] according to the provisions of Article 7 CRBV[17] and the interests of the child (Article 78 CRBV[18] and Article 8 LOPNA[19]).

According to the Supreme Tribunal of Justice, the presumption of paternity (legal paternity) may be overridden in support of a full and effective constitutional right, such as the right to know the biological (genetic) identity.

Thus, if this interpretation is applied to a surrogacy case, it means that, according to the interpretive arguments established in sentence no 1443 of 2008, which is more recent than sentence no 1456 of 2006, the biological link—biological/genetical mother—would prevail over the 'procreational will'—intending mother—(as established by sentence no 1456 of 2006).[20] Also, the biological link—biological mother—would prevail over the gestational mother (legal mother according to Article 197 CCiv).

According to this interpretation, the origin of the genetic material is not irrelevant and could have some importance in a surrogacy case.

The argument of judgment no 1443 of 2008 would benefit—unless there is a future different interpretation by the Supreme Tribunal of Justice—the woman who provides her eggs (the biological/genetic mother), not the woman who gestates the baby (legal and gestational mother). It would be an exception to Article 197 of the Civil Code. Thus, although it does not legitimise surrogacy, it could be used to determine the maternity of the intending and genetic mother (when the intending mother also provides her eggs) in cases of gestational surrogacy.

To sum up, the Supreme Tribunal of Justice turns away from the principle stated under Article 197 of the Civil Code. According to judgment no 1456 of 2006, the mother would be the one who has the 'procreational will'—the intending mother; while according to the biological criteria and the interpretation given by sentence no 1443 of 2008, the mother could be she who provided the genetic material. While

---

[15] See above n 10.

[16] Above n 4.

[17] Art 7 CRBV: 'The Constitution is the supreme law and foundation of the legal order. All persons and organs exercising Public Power are subject to this Constitution.'

[18] Art 78 CRBV: 'Children and adolescents are full legal persons and shall be protected by specialized courts, organs and legislation, which shall respect, guarantee and develop the contents of this Constitution, the law, the Convention on Children's Rights and any other international treaty that may have been executed and ratified by the Republic in this field. The State, families and society shall guarantee full protection as an absolute priority, taking into account their best interests in actions and decisions concerning them. The State shall promote their progressive incorporation into active citizenship, and shall create a national guidance system for the overall protection of children and adolescents.'

[19] This article considers the best interests of the child as a paramount principle to interpret and apply the law.

[20] This procreational will can match with the will of the biological (genetic) or the legal mother (gestational) or none of them. According to judgment no 1443 of 2008, when the gestational mother, the intending mother and the biological mother are not all the same person, the last one should prevail.

the first judgment refers to surrogacy and seems to lean towards its recognition in the future, the second judgment does not refer to that procedure.

Now, without prejudice of all that has been said, it is important to stress that the Supreme Tribunal of Justice has not yet deliberated on the subject of surrogacy. So far there has been no new pronouncement by the Tribunal, and the truth is that we shall have to wait to see what happens or what the Tribunal decides in a specific surrogacy case.

Thus, although what was stated by both rulings may help, today in Venezuela, in order to inscribe a child as the child of the intending mother—not as the child of the woman who gave birth to him or her—a judicial authorisation would be necessary.[21]

III. The Reality in Venezuela Given the Lack of Legal Regulation

As there is no law on surrogacy in Venezuela, the principle seems to be that it is not allowed but neither is it forbidden. Most scholars,[22] though, consider that surrogacy agreements should be null and void because of the lack of object and cause.[23] According to Venezuelan law, a contract must meet the requirements under Articles 1141, 1155 and 1157 of the Civil Code in order to be valid and effective. The first provision establishes the requirements for the existence of the contract (valid consent, legal object, legal cause). It is understood that neither the human body nor parts of humans can be traded; it is contrary to the general principles of law and to public policy. Without prejudice to this, the reality is that although surrogacy is not forbidden, currently in Venezuela a surrogacy agreement does not have juridical validity.

According to the Civil Code, the legal mother is the person who gives birth to the child; and if she is married, her husband would be the father because the paternity of the mother's husband is presumed (Article 201 CCiv). Thus, according to the Civil Code, the legal parent(s) of the child will be the surrogate mother (and her husband), not the intending parents. Consequently in Venezuela,

---

[21] See Art 84 of the Ley Orgánica del Registro Civil [Civil Registration Act] (LORC), *Official Gazette* No 39.264 of 15 September 2009. Among other things, this Law regulates the registration of birth and has no rules on surrogacy. Thus, the need for a judicial authorisation is also based on this gap.

[22] See, among others, R Bernad Mainar, *Efectos Jurídicos de las Nuevas Técnicas de Reproducción Humana* (Venezuela, Universidad Catolica Andres Bello, 2000) 107; G Guerrero Quintero, 'Genética y filiación en el derecho venezolano' (1997) 134 *Boletin de la Academia de Ciencias Políticas y Sociales* 467.

[23] Lopez Herrera considers that surrogacy is immoral and against public policy: F López Herrera, 'Consideraciones sobre las nuevas formas de originar la vida humana a la luz del Código Civil de Venezuela' in *Estudios sobre Derecho de Familia* (Caracas, Universidad Católica Andrés Bello, 2001) 117.

adoption[24] is used to establish the filiation in favour of the intending parents, with all its inconveniences and disadvantages.[25]

In particular spousal adoption will be used. According to this, after the birth of the child, the intending father recognises the child as his if the surrogate mother is single (Article 209 CCiv). If she is married, the child is presumed to be the child of the surrogate mother's husband. Thus, the surrogate mother's husband should contest his paternity based on the lack of biological link (the genetic material is not his; Article 201 CCiv) or on the fact that he did not authorise (consent) the insemination of his wife (Article 204 CCiv). Once paternity is contested, the intending father my recognise[26] the child.

In both cases, after the recognition by the intending father, if he is married, his wife (the intending mother) may adopt the baby (spouse adoption). There would, however, be an 'infringement' of the adoption rules if the surrogate mother was implanted with an embryo composed of the intending parents' genetic material. In this case the intending mother would be expected to adopt her own biological child, with the disadvantages and differences in treatment between men and women that this situation generates.

Another mechanism that is used in Venezuela to determine parentage in favour of the intending parents is to certify the intending mother as the one who gave birth to the child.[27] In Venezuela, this behaviour constitutes a crime.[28] Also, if the intending parents register as their own a child who was given to them by the biological mother—and her husband—in order to avoid a legal adoption, the practice is condemned and the Penal Code considers it a crime.[29]

To date, there has been no official notice of any case on surrogacy in Venezuela. It is being carried out in secret and clandestinely, although it is not considered to be a frequent practice.

---

[24] Regulated under Arts 406–429 LOPNA.

[25] Among others, as there is no law, and Art 197 CCiv states that the woman who gives birth to the child is considered to be the legal mother, the surrogate mother may always decide to keep the baby. In that case, the intending parents would have no action and no right or claim.

[26] See Arts 217–225 CCiv and Arts 95, 96, 97 and 98 LORC.

[27] The Civil Registration Act (LORC) establishes, among other things, that births will be registered under: Arts 84 and 86 LORC (birth statement before the Civil Registry Unit of the private or public establishment of health); Art 86.2 LORC (those health centres that do not have a Civil Registry Unit, or in cases of births other than in hospital, the birth statement shall be made before the corresponding Civil Registry Unit up to 90 days after birth); Art 89 LORC (those born abroad, who are the sons/daughters of a Venezuelan father or mother, and who have not been registered before the relevant diplomatic or consular representation, may make the declaration before the local registrar in Venezuela, who will verify the authenticity of the foreign document).

[28] This false declaration constitutes the crime of 'false testimony before a public official' under Art 320 of the Venezuelan Penal Code. (See also Arts 157.1, 157.3 and 161 LORC and Arts 17, 18, 19, 20, 21, 22, 224 and 225 LOPNA.)

[29] See Art 405 of the Penal Code, which punishes by imprisonment a person for hiding or changing a child in order to remove or alter his civil status, and who registers a child that does not exist. This behaviour may also constitute the crimes of trafficking, false testimony and misappropriation of identity, among others.

IV. Private International Law Considerations on Surrogacy

A. International Jurisdiction

The autonomous Venezuelan legislation on private international law, ie Law on Private International Law (LDIP),[30] contains a number of criteria conferring jurisdiction on the Venezuelan judges, on the basis of which they could come in contact with legal cases involving foreign law. Thus, in connection with a surrogacy entered into abroad or situations arising from it, including the establishment of parentage, or any other situation involving relevant foreign elements, a Venezuelan judge may intervene on the basis of such criteria.

The principal criterion conferring international jurisdiction is the domicile of the defendant (Article 39 LDIP).[31] It is important to note that the Venezuelan judges would have jurisdiction not only when the defendant has his or her domicile in Venezuela, but also when the defendant has his or her domicile abroad in the cases contemplated in Articles 40, 41 and 42 LDIP.

Article 42 LDIP[32] lists special criteria that confer jurisdiction on actions concerning the status of persons or family relationships, such as parallelism (according to which the Venezuelan judges would have jurisdiction if the applicable law is Venezuelan law), or when the parties expressly or tacitly submit to their jurisdiction, provided the cause has some effective link to the forum (whether objective or subjective), eg that one of the intending parents is Venezuelan or resident in Venezuela.

Another important criterion is the *forum necessitatis*, which allows the Venezuelan judges to issue provisional measures for the protection of persons (eg children) who are in Venezuela (it does not require habitual residence) although they do not have jurisdiction over the case.[33]

B. Applicable Law

In Venezuela, any resolution of cases containing foreign elements is based on the order of precedence of sources established under Article 1 of the Inter-American

---

[30] As published in the *Official Gazette* (Venezuela) No 36.511 of 6 August 1998.

[31] Art 39 LDIP. 'In addition to the jurisdiction being vested by law on the Venezuelan courts in actions filed against persons with a domicile in the national territory, the Courts of the Republic shall have jurisdiction in actions filed against persons having their domicile abroad in cases contemplated in Articles 40, 41 and 42.'

[32] Art 42 LDIP: 'Venezuelan courts shall have jurisdiction to hear cases resulting from the filing of actions on the status of persons or on family relationships: 1) when Venezuelan Law is competent, under the provisions hereof, to govern the substance of the litigation; 2) when the parties expressly or tacitly submit to their jurisdiction, provided the cause of action has some effective link with the forum.'

[33] Art 43 LDIP: 'Venezuelan courts shall have jurisdiction to adopt provisional measures to protect persons being in the territory of the Republic, even when lacking jurisdiction to hear the substance of the litigation.'

Convention on General Rules of Private International Law (CIDIP II)[34], which applies only if the States connected to the particular case have ratified that instrument, as Venezuela has.

If the Convention is not applicable, the order of precedence of sources is enshrined under Article 1 LDIP, which provides:

> Issues of fact related to foreign legal systems shall be governed by the rules of Public International Law on the issue, in particular those established in international treaties in force in Venezuela; in lack thereof, Venezuelan rules of Private International Law shall be applied; in lack thereof, use shall be made of analogy and, finally, generally accepted principles of Private International Law shall govern.[35]

Regarding surrogacy, in Venezuela there is no autonomous or conventional rule governing this specific matter. In other words, there is no specific rule in Venezuelan private international law for international surrogacy cases in Venezuela.

If the case refers to the establishment of filiation or relations between parents and children, according to Article 24 LDIP, the applicable law would be the law of the child's domicile[36] (meaning habitual residence according to Article 13 LDIP[37]).[38] The domicile or habitual residence of the intending parents is not relevant. The child's nationality is not relevant either.

It is important to emphasise that habitual residence is a factual concept (not a temporal one, as the law does not request a term), and its determination is governed by the particular circumstances of each case.[39]

Thus, if the child's domicile is in a country where surrogacy is legally accepted, in principle surrogacy would also be valid in Venezuela. This would only be in principle though. If the intending parent(s) ask for its recognition in Venezuela, any Venezuelan judge (or other competent Venezuelan authorities, if that is the case) may consider invoking the public policy exception, if he or she considers that surrogacy violates the essential principles of Venezuelan public policy, according to Article 8 LDIP.[40] Public policy plays an exceptional role in preventing the application of foreign law.

---

[34] Art 1 CIDIP II: 'Choice of the applicable law governing facts connected with foreign law shall be subject to the provisions of this Convention and other bilateral or multilateral conventions that have been signed or may be signed in the future by the States Parties./In the absence of an international rule, the States Parties shall apply the conflict rules of their domestic law.'

[35] The last source could be very useful for cases in which there is no regulation on the matter.

[36] Art 24 LDIP: 'The establishment of filiation, as well as the relations between parents and their children, are governed by the law of the child's domicile.'

[37] Art 13 LDIP: 'The domicile of a child and incompetent persons being subject to parental power, to guardianship or curatorship, is found in the territory of the State where they have their regular residence.'

[38] If applicable, see also Arts 59–61, 63, 66, 69 and 72 of the Bustamante Code.

[39] According to this criterion, the habitual residence of the child could be in the foreign country where the child is born as a consequence of the surrogacy agreement, even in the cases where the intending parents are permanent residents of Venezuela and have travelled to another country to enter into a surrogacy agreement.

[40] Art 8 LDIP: 'Provisions of foreign law to be applied in accordance with this statute, shall only be excluded when their application would produce results being clearly incompatible with the essential principles of Venezuelan public policy.'

With more reason, and because of the absence of a law that legalises/authorises surrogacy in Venezuela, the Venezuelan authorities could also invoke the public policy exception if the child's domicile is in Venezuela, so that the applicable law is Venezuelan law, and it is asked to accord recognition to the surrogacy agreement or the effects of the surrogacy agreement entered into abroad. In these situations Article 5 LDIP might also be applicable. This states:

> Issues of law having been created in accordance with a foreign law in a foreign jurisdiction exercising an internationally acceptable ground of jurisdiction shall have effect in the Republic, provided they are not in contradiction to Venezuelan rules of conflict, that the Venezuelan law claims exclusive competence over the matter, or that they are not clearly incompatible with general principles of Venezuelan public policy.

Any attempt by the intending parents to register the child born as a consequence of a surrogacy agreement[41]—in Venezuela or overseas[42]—in principle would be subject to consultation with the National Electoral Council,[43] which now has jurisdiction over the Civil Registry. It is considered that even if this body could be persuaded not to deny the child's registration in its pronouncement, it would wait for the court ruling on filiation for the purpose of identifying the parents in the birth certificate.

In any case, filiation should be established by the courts, and it is important to take into account that in Venezuela[44] the principle of the best interests of the child is invoked strongly in the decisions of the Supreme Court and lower courts.[45] It is also important to stress that it too has been considered as a criterion for conferring jurisdiction, although it is not expressly stated as a criterion for conferring jurisdiction of Venezuelan judges.[46]

In addition, although judges may consider surrogacy as against public policy, the doctrine of private international law in general is widely inclined to accept an attenuated public policy exception,[47] under which, taking into account the principle of the best interests of the child, it would be possible to accept the effects of a surrogacy agreement that could benefit the child (food, clothing, identification, etc), even though surrogacy itself may be rejected.

---

[41] Ie to ask for the recognition of the birth certificate granted in the foreign State recognising the intending parents as legal parents, or the foreign judgment recognising the intending parents as legal parents.

[42] See Art 89 LORC, above n 26.

[43] See <www.cne.gov.ve/registrocivil/index.php/concepto_registro_civil>.

[44] See Art 78 CRBV and Art 7 LOPNA previously cited.

[45] Among others, TSJ SCC, Exp No 2009-000464, 18 February 2011. Sentence of the Juzgado Superior en lo Civil, Mercantil, Tránsito y del Protección del Niño y del Adolescente de la Circunscripción Judicial del Estado Anzoátegui, 21/07/2010.

[46] See TSJ/SPA, Exp No 2009-1005, 13 January 2010; TSJ/SPA, Exp No 2011-0071, 28 April 2011. Available at <www.tsj.gov.ve>.

[47] Such attenuated public policy has no specific regulation, but it is widely recognised by the Venezuelan doctrine of PIL.

Thus, notwithstanding the provisions of Article 8 LDIP, this public policy reservation may not be applicable because of the interests of the child and, in particular, his or her right to identity (Article 56 CRBV).

If the situation were handled through an adoption, according to Article 25 LDIP, the law of their domicile will apply to the adopting parent and the adopted child, as to all substantive requirements necessary for the adoption's validity.

C. Recognition and Enforcement of Foreign Judgments

On this matter, the sources in Venezuela are:

(a) the Inter-American Convention on Extraterritorial Validity of Judgments and Arbitral Awards;
(b) Article 53 LDIP.

The Inter-American Convention stipulates public policy as a condition for the *exequatur* of foreign judgments (Article 2(h)[48]). Thus, in principle, a Venezuelan judge could rely on this article if the intending parents seek to recognise or enforce a foreign decision that recognises the parentage of a child born as a consequence of a surrogacy agreement. Consequently, among ratifying States, there is a possibility that Venezuela might not recognise the foreign judgment granting the intending parents' legal parentage on public policy grounds.

The Law on Private International Law, on the other hand, eliminated public policy as a condition for *exequatur*.[49] (In contrast to the article of the Code of

---

[48] Art 2 of the Inter-American Convention on Extraterritorial Validity of Judgments and Arbitral Awards provides that the foreign judgments, awards and decisions referred to in Art 1 shall have extraterritorial validity in the States Parties if they meet the following conditions: (a) they fulfil all the formal requirements necessary for them to be deemed authentic in the State of origin; (b) the judgment, award or decision and the documents attached thereto that are required under the Convention are duly translated into the official language of the State where they are to take effect; (c) they are presented duly legalised in accordance with the law of the State in which they are to take effect; (d) the judge or tribunal rendering the judgment is competent in the international sphere to try the matter and to pass judgment on it in accordance with the law of the State in which the judgment, award or decision is to take effect; (e) the claimant has been summoned or subpoened in due legal form substantially equivalent to that accepted by the law of the State where the judgment, award or decision is to take effect; (f) the parties had an opportunity to present their defence; (g) they are final or, where appropriate, have the force of res judicata in the State in which they were rendered; (h) they are not manifestly contrary to the principles and laws of the public policy (order public) of the State in which recognition or execution is sought.

[49] Art 53 LDIP: 'Foreign judgments shall be effective in Venezuela provided they meet the following requirements: 1) That they should have been issued in civil or commercial matters, or, generally, in matters related to private juridical relationships; 2) That they should have force of res judicata under the law of the State where they were pronounced; 3) That they should not relate to in rem rights on real property situated in the Republic or that exclusive jurisdiction to deal with the case should not have been taken away from Venezuela; 4) That the court of origin should have had jurisdiction to hear the cause, under the general principles on jurisdiction established by Chapter IX hereof; 5) That the defendant should have been duly served, with sufficient time to appear, and that, generally, procedural guarantees should have been afforded to ensure a reasonable possibility of defence; 6) That they should not be incompatible with a previous judgment having authority of res judicata; and that there

Civil Procedure that was the source applied prior to the enactment of the Act.) It is estimated that when the legislator removed the requirement of public policy, he intended to banish it for the *exequatur*, but there are opposing views about this. In this sense, some judicial pronouncements ignore the law and demand this requirement.[50] However, in general, it is understood that Law does not require public policy as a condition for *exequatur*, so under this Law it could be easier to recognise or enforce a foreign judgment that recognises the parentage of a child born as a consequence of a surrogacy agreement.

To date, there has been no official notice of any international surrogacy case. It is unofficially known, though, that couples have gone to countries where surrogacy is practised, especially to the United States, and entered into surrogacy agreements.

should not be pending, before Venezuelan Courts, a trial with the same object and between the same parties having commenced before the foreign judgment had been issued.'

[50] Among others, TSJ/SCC, Exp 2005-000700, 26 June 2007; TSJ/SCC, Exp 2009-000464, 14 April 2011.

Part Two

Cross-border Surrogacy:
International Perspectives

26

A Possible Future Instrument on International Surrogacy Arrangements: Are There 'Lessons' to be Learnt from the 1993 Hague Intercountry Adoption Convention?

HANNAH BAKER[1]

I. Introduction

The Hague Conference on Private International Law was delighted to have been asked to participate in the seminal workshop on international surrogacy arrangements organised by Professor Beaumont and Dr Trimmings. It was an informative experience to attend the workshop and to listen to the interventions concerning the various national approaches to surrogacy, and the multitude of State responses which have been adopted regarding this legal, social and ethical dilemma.

This chapter starts by providing a brief overview of how the Hague Conference on Private International Law came to be involved in the area of international surrogacy arrangements. It sets out the current mandate for the Hague Conference's work in this field before turning to look at some of the possible 'lessons' which may be drawn from, first, the drafting and, secondly, the implementation and practical operation of the 1993 Hague Intercountry Adoption Convention,[2] for any possible future instrument on international surrogacy arrangements. However, it should be noted that this chapter contains tentative, preliminary thoughts only. As is set out in section II. below, the mandate to intensify the Hague Conference's work in the field of international surrogacy was given only in April 2011 and research into this subject is consequently still in its infancy. This chapter, written in August 2011,

---

[1] The views expressed in this chapter are personal in nature and not those of the Hague Conference on Private International Law.
[2] Full title: The Hague Convention of 29 May 1993 on Protection of Children and Cooperation in Respect of Intercountry Adoption (hereinafter, the '1993 Convention', or simply 'the Convention').

therefore offers no more than 'starting thoughts' for what will be an extremely interesting research journey over the course of the next year, and possibly beyond.

II. The Hague Conference on Private International Law and International Surrogacy: A Brief Background

To understand how the Hague Conference on Private International Law became involved in the area of international surrogacy arrangements, it is necessary to look back to 2001 and the informal consultations which took place regarding the future work programme of the Hague Conference. During these consultations, the topic of the 'private international law issues surrounding the status of children and, in particular, the recognition of parent–child relationships' ('filiation'), was suggested as a possible future area of work for the Conference.[3] However, at that time, and for a number of years beyond, no Members showed any keen interest in taking up the topic as an area of work.

However, in 2009/2010, a number of events occurred which were to change this. First, New Zealand wrote to the Secretary General of the Hague Conference expressing concern about the increasing number of international surrogacy arrangements with which its State authorities were having to deal, and the legal complexities these cases involved. In particular, New Zealand was concerned at the possible use of the 1993 Convention in such cases, and asked for advice from the Permanent Bureau as to whether the Convention could be applied appropriately as a 'solution' to the difficulties the cases posed. More informally, another State also indicated its concern to the Permanent Bureau regarding the growth of cases involving legal complexities as a result of international surrogacy arrangements.

At the Council on General Affairs and Policy of the Hague Conference in April 2010, the letter from New Zealand and the Permanent Bureau's response were shared with delegates. In addition, Israel produced a Working Document[4] stressing that multilateral action needed to be taken in the sphere of international surrogacy arrangements. Other States also spoke in support of the Permanent Bureau undertaking further research in this area, as well as in relation to the broader question of the private international law issues surrounding the status of children,

---

[3] 'Observations concerning the Strategy of the Hague Conference—Observations made by other international organisations and observations made in a personal capacity in response to the Secretary General's letter of 30/31 July 2001', Preliminary Document [hereinafter 'Prel Doc'] No 20 for the attention of the Nineteenth Session.

[4] Working Document No 3 for the attention of the Council on General Affairs and Policy of the Hague Conference, 7–9 April 2010.

particularly the recognition of parent–child relationships.[5] As a result of these discussions, the Permanent Bureau was invited to take up the topic informally suggested nine years prior, and

> to provide a brief preliminary note to the Council of 2011 on the private international law issues surrounding the status of children (excluding adoption) and, in particular, on the issue of recognition of parent–child relationships (filiation).[6]

Further, in relation specifically to international surrogacy, the Council, 'acknowledged the complex issues of private international law and child protection arising from the growth in cross-border surrogacy arrangements'.[7] It also noted that the impact of international surrogacy cases on the practical operation of the 1993 Convention would be placed on the draft agenda of the Special Commission meeting on the practical operation of the 1993 Convention which was to take place in June 2010.[8] The Council further agreed that private international law questions relating to international surrogacy arrangements should be kept under review by the Permanent Bureau.

In June 2010, at the Special Commission meeting, the interplay between international surrogacy cases and the 1993 Convention was discussed. The Conclusions of the Special Commission noted that the number of international surrogacy arrangements was increasing rapidly, and expressed concern over the uncertainty surrounding the status of children born as a result of the arrangements. Importantly, the Special Commission concluded that the use of the 1993 Convention in cases of international surrogacy was inappropriate,[9] and recommended that the Hague Conference should carry out further study of the legal, especially private international law, issues surrounding international surrogacy.[10]

Pursuant to its 2010 mandate, the Permanent Bureau prepared a briefing note on the private international law issues surrounding the status of children for the Council on General Affairs and Policy of 2011.[11] In light of developments, and in particular the conclusions of the 2010 Special Commission meeting, the note necessarily focused on the very real practical problems that were occurring in States

---

[5] Report of Meeting No 3 of the Council on General Affairs and Policy of the Hague Conference, 7–9 April 2010.

[6] Conclusions and Recommendations of the Council on General Affairs and Policy of the Hague Conference, 3–5 April 2010, p 3.

[7] *Ibid.*

[8] The Special Commission of June 2010 on the practical operation of the Hague Convention of 29 May 1993 on Protection of Children and Cooperation in Respect of Intercountry Adoption (17–25 June 2010). Hereinafter 'the Special Commission'.

[9] For a brief summary regarding some of the reasons why use of the 1993 Convention is inappropriate in this context, see para 43 of Prel Doc No 11, below n 11.

[10] See the Conclusions and Recommendations of the Special Commission of June 2010 on the practical operation of the Hague Convention of 29 May 1993 on Protection of Children and Cooperation in Respect of Intercountry Adoption (17–25 June 2010), paras 25–26.

[11] Prel Doc No 11 of March 2011, 'Private international law issues surrounding the status of children, including issues arising from international surrogacy arrangements', available at <www.hcch.net/upload/wop/genaff2011pd11e.pdf>.

as a result of international surrogacy arrangements. Preliminary Document No 11 received a very supportive response from Members and led to the Conference's most recent mandate, which is

> to intensify ... work in the area [of private international law issues surrounding the status of children, including issues arising from international surrogacy arrangements] with emphasis on the broad range of issues arising from international surrogacy arrangements. The Permanent Bureau should during the next year continue gathering information on the practical needs in the area, comparative developments in domestic and private international law, and the prospects of achieving consensus on a global approach.

> The Permanent Bureau should also consult with the legal profession as well as with health and other relevant professionals concerning the nature and incidence of the problems occurring in this area.[12]

The Permanent Bureau is to provide a preliminary report on progress to the Council in 2012.

This recent mandate, whilst asking for an emphasis to be placed on the difficulties arising from international surrogacy arrangements, is still broad in its overall remit. This was a deliberate decision by Members of the Hague Conference. The conclusion of Preliminary Document No 11 stated that either the issues arising in international surrogacy cases could, for the purposes of considering possible future international regulation, be considered as part of the broader framework of private international law issues surrounding the status of children (ie, as part of the difficulties arising in cross-border cases as a result of conflicts of law issues in relation to legal parentage), or international surrogacy could be looked at as a 'burning issue' on its own. The Council determined that further research should be undertaken to determine the desirability and feasibility of working on the challenges posed by international surrogacy within a broader context. Some questions central to this research will be:

(a) how far States are experiencing practical difficulties relating to legal parentage in cross-border cases which fall outside the surrogacy context (two examples of possible cases were given within Preliminary Document No 11, but research is necessary to determine how far such cases are occurring in practice);

(b) how far a broad approach is feasible, bearing in mind the apparent diversity of private international law rules relating to the establishment and contestation of legal parentage; and

(c) how far the difficulties experienced in international surrogacy cases demand a specific focus which can be achieved only by a single-issue instrument.

---

[12] Conclusions and Recommendations of the Council on General Affairs and Policy (5–7 April 2011), paras 17 to 20, available at <www.hcch.net/upload/wop/genaff_concl2011e.pdf>.

III. Are there 'Lessons' to be Learnt from the 1993 Convention for Any Future Instrument on International Surrogacy?

A. A Preliminary Thought: How Ready a Comparison Should Be Drawn Between Intercountry Adoption and International Surrogacy?

In 1993, Hans van Loon said of intercountry adoption:

> It manifests our shrinking world, in which human lives, activities and interests become more and more interwoven, and over ever larger distances. At the same time, since to a large extent it is in fact a movement of children from economically developing countries to industrialized countries, it is also a symptom of the demographic, economic, social and political differences, as well as the gross inequalities of living conditions which continue to exist on our planet.[13]

The similarities between intercountry adoption and international surrogacy are apparent. Whilst international surrogacy arrangements do not always involve a movement of children from 'economically developing' to 'industrialised' countries (although this often may indeed be the case), such arrangements certainly represent a practice which 'manifests our shrinking world' and one which is a clear 'symptom' of the 'economic, social and political' differences between countries. However, that said, how readily should we assume that there are transferable 'lessons' which can be taken from the approach agreed upon by the international community in relation to intercountry adoption and used in the context of international surrogacy? How similar a position are we really in to that which faced the international community in 1987 when the issue of intercountry adoption was being (re)considered?[14]

When one considers the impetus behind the desire for multilateral regulation of both intercountry adoption and international surrogacy, important similarities are apparent both as regards the way the practices came to the attention of the international community and the issues which were/are of concern. This suggests that the resulting 1993 Convention, which aims, after all, to address some of

---

[13] See JHA Van Loon, 'International Co-operation and Protection of Children with regard to Intercountry Adoption' (1993-VII) 244 *Recueil des cours* 195, para 1. This publication was based on, and an extension of, the *Report on Intercountry Adoption*, which the author wrote in preparation for the negotiations on what became the 1993 Convention, referred to in n 16 below.

[14] This was, in fact, the second time intercountry adoption had been considered by the Hague Conference, there having been an instrument dealing with intercountry adoption concluded in 1965, ie the Hague Convention of 15 November 1965 on Jurisdiction, Applicable Law and Recognition of Decrees Relating to Adoptions. See 'Note on the desirability of preparing a new convention on international co-operation in respect of intercountry adoption', drawn up by Hans Van Loon, Secretary (Prel Doc No 9 of December 1987—Proceedings of the 16th Session, Tome I, pp 165–85), regarding the reasons why it was considered that a new Convention might be appropriate.

these concerns, may contain transferable 'lessons' for international surrogacy. For example, in relation to both intercountry adoption and international surrogacy, a convergence of social and demographic factors appears to have resulted in a large increase in the incidence of cases globally, which, in turn, seems to have focused international attention on the issue, prompted international concern and led to a desire to explore international regulation.[15] Further, as a result of the growth in cases, awareness regarding abuses of the practices has also contributed to a desire to see international regulation. In relation to intercountry adoption, it is clear from the 1990 Van Loon Report[16] that the sale and trafficking of children in the context of intercountry adoption was a major concern and impetus behind the exploration of new international legislation. Indeed, by 1989, the United Nations Convention on the Rights of the Child had already explicitly addressed such concerns and openly encouraged States to explore multilateral agreements to combat such practices.[17] In relation to international surrogacy, concern has been expressed in the media and in academic writing about the vulnerability of the parties involved in such arrangements. Further, a number of cases have already been reported involving the sale and trafficking of both women and children.[18] Another concern which has clearly prompted the exploration of international regulation for both intercountry adoption and international surrogacy is the difficulty of the 'limping' legal status of the child as a result of the practices and the negative legal consequences flowing from this for the child. In intercountry

---

[15] In relation to intercountry adoption, the practice started turning into a 'world-scale trend' in the late 1960s /early 1970s. At this time, in many industrial countries adoption was becoming more widely accepted as an institution, but the number of children 'available' for adoption was declining sharply as a result of social and demographic changes. At the same time a general change of consciousness in industrialised countries was arousing a greater interest in and engagement with developing countries, including with the fate of the children in these countries. From this time, the incidence of cases continued to grow: data from 1993 showed an increase in international adoption in the previous decade of 62%. Whilst the numbers were increasing, the social and demographic nature of the phenomenon caused unease amongst the international community. As Hans van Loon has stated (above n 13): 'As long as only the existence of children deprived of their families had a structural character, the problem of intercountry adoption could be phrased, in a relatively straightforward fashion, as: how to find a family for this child? The question became ambiguous when, as a result of declining fertility, birth control and changed attitudes, the impetus and motivation for intercountry adoption arising from the industrialised countries also acquired a structural character. At this point a structural "supply" of children "available" for adoption abroad in economically developing countries met with a structural "demand" for such children in economically advanced countries. The language of economics made its appearance and intercountry adoption became a more complex and controversial social phenomenon.' In relation to international surrogacy arrangements, factors including the advance in reproductive science, the advent of the Internet, and the continuing decrease in children (particularly healthy babies) 'available' for domestic and intercountry adoption have converged to create a significant growth in cases of international surrogacy. Combined with this growth in cases, the same structural dynamics as described above have attracted international concern.

[16] *Report on Intercountry Adoption*, drawn up by JHA Van Loon (Prel Doc No 1 of April 1990— Proceedings of the Seventeenth Session, Tome II, pp 11–119). Hereinafter, the '1990 Van Loon Report'.

[17] Adopted and opened for signature, ratification and accession by General Assembly Resolution 44 /25 of 20 November 1989, entry into force 2 September 1990. Hereinafter, the 'UNCRC'. See Art 21, in particular Art 21(c)–(e).

[18] Eg, see Prel Doc No 11, above n 11, at Ch VI. See another more recent example, reported at <http://allthingssurrogacy.com/articles/2/18/attorney-admits-guilt-in-baby-selling-ring>.

adoption, there was concern that adoptions granted in one State were not always recognised in another, and that often a child validly adopted in one State had to undergo a second adoption in the State to which he or she was moved.[19] In international surrogacy cases, the most obvious legal problem resulting from the arrangements is the frequent inability of the 'receiving State' to recognise the legal parentage of the intending parent(s), and the consequent perilous position of the child.[20] Lastly, in relation to both, there has been an apparent recognition by States that the practice is causing *global* problems to which unilateral solutions were (in the case of intercountry adoption) and are (in the case of international surrogacy) not sufficient.[21]

However, whilst there are real similarities in terms of the reasons behind the call for international regulation of intercountry adoption and international surrogacy, we should not lose sight of certain fundamental differences between the institutions. This is because these fundamental differences may have an impact on how far it is *desirable* to regulate international surrogacy in a similar way to intercountry adoption and also how far it is *feasible* to do so. For example, one obvious distinction between intercountry adoption and international surrogacy is that, in the case of adoption, the focus is on finding a family for a child in need, whilst in the case of surrogacy a child is (pro-)created to satisfy the desire of the adult(s) for a child. Whilst intercountry adoption may not be so ideologically 'pure' as this distinction assumes,[22] the regulation of intercountry adoption was based upon the international consensus, expressed in the Preamble to the 1993 Convention, and originating from the UNCRC and the UN Declaration of 1986,[23] that

> the child, for the full and harmonious development of his or her personality, should grow up in a family environment ... [and] that intercountry adoption may offer the advantage of a permanent family to a child for whom a suitable family cannot be found in his or her State of origin ....[24]

---

[19] See, eg, the discussion above n 13, paras 108–12.

[20] See the many examples given in Prel Doc No 11, above n 11, at Ch IV, 'Case Examples'.

[21] In relation to intercountry adoption, see above n 13, at para 168.

[22] Since the 'structural demand' is such (see the quote at n 15 above) that intercountry adoption may sometimes be as much about satisfying the desire of the prospective adoptive parents for a child as it is providing a family for a needy child. See also, in this respect, the Draft 'Accreditation and Adoption Accredited Bodies: General Principles and Guide to Good Practice', Guide No 2 under the 1993 Convention, drawn up by the Permanent Bureau (Prel Doc No 2 of May 2010), at para 7: 'As intercountry adoption is too often considered by prospective adoptive parents as a right to have a child, the Central Authorities, the competent authorities and the accredited bodies are faced with the ethical need continually to refocus the meaning of their statements and their actions on the real reason for the existence of intercountry adoption, which is to seek a family for a child.'

[23] The United Nations Declaration on Social and Legal Principles relating to the Protection and Welfare of Children, with Special Reference to Foster Placement and Adoption Nationally and Internationally (General Assembly Resolution 41/85, of 3 December 1986).

[24] See the Preamble of the 1993 Convention, at paras 2 and 4. See also, eg, the Conclusions of the Special Commission of June 1990 on intercountry adoption, Prel Doc No 3 of August 1990, at 129, para. 4: 'The starting point for the Convention should be the United Nations Convention on the Rights of the Child ... which calls for the conclusion of multilateral agreements to promote the standards set by its Article 21'.

Moreover, this *legal* consensus was itself based perhaps on a quasi-universal *cultural* consensus concerning the institution of adoption. As the 1990 Van Loon Report makes clear, aside from certain States with a Sharia law-based legal system, there was general global agreement that adoption was an acceptable option for the alternative care of children in certain specific situations.[25] It could therefore be argued that it was this legal and cultural consensus which enabled negotiations on intercountry adoption to move beyond a debate regarding the practice itself, and to focus instead on the necessary safeguards and cooperation to ensure inter-country adoptions only ever occurred 'in the best interests of the child and with respect for his or her fundamental rights'.[26]

In relation to international surrogacy, there is currently no such broad legal or cultural consensus concerning the practice itself. In fact, as the country reports at the Aberdeen Workshop demonstrated, there is a spectrum of cultural and legal responses to the institution: from complete prohibition of any form of surrogacy, through to complete liberality, including acceptance of commercial surrogacy. Indeed, this raises another thorny issue regarding which there is an absence of consensus: the approach to the economic aspects of surrogacy. Monetary issues were incredibly difficult to agree upon and regulate in relation to intercountry adoption (see below); however, Article 21(d) of the UNCRC at least provided negotiators with a legal 'baseline' (although whether 'proper' financial gain can ever be justified in the intercountry adoption process remains a highly contentious issue).[27] Such issues are arguably even more challenging in the context of interna-tional surrogacy. With international surrogacy arrangements, initial impressions suggest that many of the cases involve *commercial*, for-profit, arrangements. Not surprisingly, therefore, this has led to the emergence of intermediaries with a clear financial interest.

This chapter does not intend to say that there must necessarily be interna-tional consensus on all these issues for regulation of international surrogacy arrangements to succeed. After all, the 1993 Convention does not mandate that all Contracting States engage in intercountry adoption; it simply puts in place safeguards and procedures *if* they do so. Further, whilst there is no specific legal principle in the UNCRC on international surrogacy comparable to Article 21 on intercountry adoption, there are arguably different, equally relevant, international legal principles which could, and should, form the legal 'baseline' for States to move forward together in considering regulation of international surrogacy, eg Articles 3 and 7 of the UNCRC. However, the differences between the institutions of adoption and surrogacy do mean that careful consideration must be given to drawing too ready a conclusion that the 1993 Convention may be adapted wholesale, as it were, to create a new convention for international surrogacy.

---

[25] See the 1990 Van Loon Report, above n 16, at Ch II(A).

[26] Preamble to the 1993 Convention.

[27] See section III.B. below, for a limited discussion of how this issue was dealt with in the context of the 1993 Convention.

That said, there is no doubt that there are some important experiences under the 1993 Convention from which lessons may be learned when thinking about taking any steps towards international regulation (in whatever form) of international surrogacy.

B. Some Tentative 'Lessons'

i. The Importance of an Inclusive Approach to the Formation of any Multilateral Instrument

In the first document submitted to Members of the Hague Conference regarding the possible development of a new instrument on international cooperation in respect of intercountry adoption, it was recognised that

> if the Conference were to decide also to establish a system of mutual information and co-operation between sending and receiving countries, such a decision would, by its very nature require the Conference to open its doors for non-Member, sending countries, to participate on an equal footing with Member States.[28]

It was noted that, in relation to the 1965 Hague Convention on Adoption, amongst many other difficulties the Convention faced 20 years on, one major obstacle to the Convention's success was that many 'sending countries' had not acceded and would not accede to the 1965 Convention, 'if only because they have had no possibility to participate in its elaboration'.[29] Members of the Conference agreed with this statement, and the Secretary General was invited to obtain assurances from non-Member States involved in intercountry adoption that they would be willing to cooperate with the Conference in future work on the topic. Such assurances having been obtained,[30] the Sixteenth Session of the Hague Conference on Private International Law[31] mandated the preparation of a convention, but re-emphasised that it considered 'to be indispensable the participation in this Special Commission of non-Member States from which many of these children come'.[32] It was also important to the success of this work that other international organisations interested in intercountry adoption appeared willing to cooperate with the Hague Conference in this regard.[33]

The success of the 1993 Hague Intercountry Adoption Convention is undoubtedly founded on this early insight shown by the drafters. The Convention now has 89 Contracting States[34] (it is one of the most widely-ratified private

---

[28] See above n 14, at para 58.
[29] *Ibid*, at para 40.
[30] After an extensive networking campaign by the Permanent Bureau of the Hague Conference.
[31] Which met at The Hague from 3–20 October 1988.
[32] Hague Conference on Private International Law, Sixteenth Session, Final Act (The Hague, 20 October 1988), under B, para 1.
[33] See above n 13, at para 169.
[34] As of 5 March 2013.

international law treaties) and has attracted broadly equal support from States of origin and receiving States. This balance is of fundamental importance for the success of the Convention. Moreover, the international intergovernmental and non-governmental organisations which were so cooperative in the drafting of the 1993 Convention have been, and continue to be, a crucial support, both in terms of assisting with the promotion of the Convention[35] and in helping to ensure its effective practical operation.[36]

Whilst any future drafting of an instrument on international surrogacy arrangements may not face the same difficulty concerning non-Members of the Hague Conference (the Conference's membership has increased from 34 in 1987 to 72 in 2013[37]), it remains as important today as it was in 1987 to ensure that all States affected by the difficulties surrounding international surrogacy cases[38] are actively engaged in the elaboration of any possible future instrument. It may be trite to state, but an international instrument, however beautifully crafted, will serve no useful purpose if a certain sector of the States involved in the area is not willing to ratify it. Further, as with the 1993 Convention, cooperation with other international organisations will be vitally important to ensure that international action regarding this subject is as coordinated and coherent as possible, and that post-Convention work (including promotion and support with implementation/ operation) is as effective as possible.

ii. The 'Nature' of a Possible Multilateral Instrument

The 1993 Convention was a novel international instrument in many ways. As Hans Van Loon has described, it is a 'multi-dimensional instrument', at one and the same time a human rights instrument, an instrument for judicial and administrative cooperation and a private international law instrument.[39]

— It is a human rights instrument because the 1993 Convention seeks to define, reinforce and add to the principles and norms laid down in the UNCRC by introducing substantive safeguards and procedures. However, unlike most international human rights instruments, which aim to enhance the protection of rights in the context of single domestic legal order, the 1993 Convention focuses on a transnational phenomenon and seeks to protect the rights of children and of all others involved in at least two domestic legal orders.

---

[35] Eg, the UN Committee on the Rights of the Child often encourages States to ratify/accede to the 1993 Convention as a way of implementing Art 21 of the UNCRC.

[36] Eg, the ISS, UNICEF and many other international organisations provide vital support and assistance in this regard.

[37] Comprising 71 States and one Regional Economic Integration Organisation, the European Union (as of 5 March 2013).

[38] And, indeed, all States, since States that are currently not affected by international surrogacy may well be in future.

[39] Please note, this paragraph is a summary of paras 182 to 184 of the work cited above at n 13, at paras 182–84.

— It is an instrument for judicial and administrative cooperation, much like the 1980 Hague Child Abduction Convention, or indeed the Hague Conventions on legal cooperation. However, its scope is considerably broader than these other Conventions, and hence one would detract from its full meaning to describe it only in this way.

— Lastly, it is comparable to a traditional private international law instrument in that it provides for the recognition in all Contracting States of an adoption made in conformity with the Convention, and in this way contributes to banning the curse of 'limping adoptions'. However, it does so not by vesting jurisdiction in the authorities of either the State of origin or the receiving State and by designating the applicable law, but rather by assigning to each State duties for which it has primary responsibility and by requiring the two States to take *joint* overall responsibility for each adoption made under the Convention. It does not therefore directly solve conflicts of jurisdiction or applicable law, but does help indirectly to avoid and reduce such conflicts.

As Hans van Loon stated:

[P]rivate international law is becoming increasingly permeated by elements of judicial and administrative co-operation and likewise, the fields of human rights and private international law are touching more and more frequently. The convention is the fruit of this new development and, in order to be well understood, it should be looked at with a mind aware of the increasing significance of international co-operation for the unification of private international law and the growing interaction between human rights law and private international law.[40]

It is not difficult to see how such visionary and ambitious thinking may be appropriate in the sphere of international surrogacy arrangements. If there is to be a future international instrument, it will, of course, need to protect the human rights of all those involved in such arrangements by complying with existing international human rights norms, but also, quite possibly, it will need to set down further standards and safeguards in the transnational context of this unique phenomenon. It is easy to see then how effective judicial and administrative cooperation will be necessary to help ensure compliance with any such new standards and safeguards. Further, a key aspect of any future instrument will also surely be ensuring that any children born as a result of an arrangement made in compliance with the instrument have their legal status secured in all relevant jurisdictions (which, of course, is in accordance with the obligations of States under the UNCRC, eg Article 7). It is, in this context, not hard to see how the method of an 'allocation of responsibilities' between the States involved may be of interest.

---

[40] Above n 13, at para 185.

iii. *Safeguarding Against Abuses by Regulating Intermediaries*

The 1993 Convention was based upon the premise that combating international child trafficking[41] in the context of intercountry adoption required 'above all, strict control over the activities of intermediaries, which should meet the criteria defined for them'.[42] Pre-Convention intercountry adoption practice, described as 'chaotic, contradictory and unsatisfactory, and which often relied on profiteering intermediaries of dubious motivations',[43] was to be replaced with an ordered and regulated intercountry adoption system in which each significant actor was either the government or a non-profit entity accredited by the government. 'Independent adoptions',[44] with their inherent susceptibility to child trafficking, were to be discouraged or prevented. In fact, in the subsequent Convention negotiations it became clear that a number of delegates wanted to go further than this original vision and wanted private intermediaries to be *excluded* from the intercountry adoption process altogether, leaving the process to State actors only.[45] However, other delegates strongly disagreed, insisting that each Contracting State should determine the manner in which to perform the Convention's duties.

The final text of the 1993 Convention reflects a compromise between these positions. The Convention allows for the designation of so-called 'accredited bodies'.[46] Such bodies are able to perform some of the (delegable) functions of the State Central Authority, but the bodies are ultimately accountable to a supervising or accrediting authority (Articles 6–13). Basic standards are imposed by the

---

[41] It should be noted that the concept of 'trafficking' in this chapter is taken broadly as the procurement of children through illegal or unethical means. The definition of trafficking as 'the sale of children for purposes of exploitation' is not intended here (see, above n 22, at fn 8).

[42] 1990 Van Loon Report, above n 16, at para 95.

[43] *Ibid*, at para 101.

[44] For a definition of the term 'independent adoption', see 'The Implementation and Operation of the 1993 Intercountry Adoption Convention: Guide to Good Practice', *Guide No 1* (published by The Hague Conference in 2008), at p 16 and Ch 8.6.6., available at <www.hcch.net/index_en .php?act=publications.details&pid=4388>.

[45] As the Explanatory Report on the Adoption Convention, drawn up by G Parra-Aranguren, makes clear, at paras 242–43: 'The question as to whether the responsibilities assigned to Central Authorities by the Convention may be discharged by individuals or private organisations, is a very sensitive issue because, according to experience, most of the abuses in intercountry adoptions arise because of the intervention of such "intermediaries" in the various stages of the adoption proceedings. For this very reason, some participants to the Special Commission did not want to accept that Central Authorities may delegate their responsibilities on accredited bodies, but others insisted on leaving to each Contracting State the determination of the manner in which to perform the Convention's duties. The solution accepted by the draft (article 11) represented a compromise, permitting delegation only to public authorities and to private bodies duly accredited ...'

[46] And, in some cases, approved (non-accredited) persons—see Art 22, which permits the possibility, by way of an option, under certain conditions, requiring a special declaration by a State that persons or bodies not accredited may perform certain functions assigned to the Central Authority by Ch IV of the Convention. Importantly, such persons or bodies are not bound by Art 11(a) and can therefore operate on a 'for-profit' basis (although they are still bound by the general prohibition in Art 32 regarding deriving improper financial or other gain from an activity related to an intercountry adoption). This issue will not be dealt with in this limited chapter.

Convention to guide the accreditation process. These include that an 'accredited body' must pursue only 'non-profit objectives', must be directed and staffed by persons qualified by their ethical standards, and must be subject to supervision by competent authorities of the State as to its composition, operation and financial situation (Article 11). The decision whether to allow accredited bodies to perform child protection or adoption functions in a Contracting State is a policy matter for each individual State (ie, it is not mandatory for States to use accredited bodies). In addition, bodies accredited in one State and wishing to operate in another State must be specifically authorised to do so by the competent authority of *both* States (see Article 12).

Whilst accredited bodies are recognised today as fundamentally important to the intercountry adoption process, the accreditation of these private agencies and their operation within the intercountry process are not without their challenges. This is perhaps best illustrated by the fact that one of the documents under consideration at the 2010 Special Commission meeting was a 166-page document, entitled 'General Principles and Guide to Good Practice on Accreditation and Adoption Accredited Bodies'. This Guide was developed as a result of the fact that

> the divergent practices on accreditation and supervision of accredited bodies are not conducive to the proper implementation of the Convention and do not always serve the best interests of the child.[47]

Examples of current challenges regarding the accreditation and operation of accredited bodies in the intercountry adoption process are as follows:

(a) The diverging practices across States Parties in terms of the criteria used to grant accreditation and the monitoring and supervision of accredited bodies.[48]

(b) The responsibility or accountability of some accredited bodies in receiving States, in particular bodies that are authorised to operate in States of origin (Article 12) and use foreign partners or independent facilitators to act for them in this State. In this regard, there have been reported difficulties where such 'representatives' have not been regulated or supervised appropriately, where their functions have been ambiguous and/or where the nature and amount of

---

[47] See Prel Doc No 4 of March 2011—Conclusions and Recommendations and Report of the Special Commission on the practical operation of the 1993 Hague Intercountry Adoption Convention (17–25 June 2010) para 16.

[48] The Draft Guide to Good Practice on Accreditation, above n 22, draws upon existing good practice and provides States with some basic standards for accreditation, a basic procedure for the development of an accreditation procedure, and criteria and conditions for the supervision of accredited bodies and renewal of their accreditation.

their remuneration has been unclear.[49] In certain cases this has led to instances of child laundering entering into the intercountry adoption process.[50]

(c) Lastly, one of the most controversial issues has been the costs of intercountry adoptions, and the transparency and accountability of accredited bodies in this regard. Article 11(a) of the Convention is clear that accredited bodies must 'pursue only non-profit objectives', and by Article 11(c) an accredited body must 'be subject to supervision by competent authorities of that State as to its ... financial situation'. Further, accredited bodies are bound by the general Convention obligation in Article 32 that '[n]o one shall derive improper financial or other gain from an activity related to an intercountry adoption,' although 'costs and expenses, including reasonable professional fees of persons involved in the adoption, may be charged or paid'.[51] As the 'The Implementation and Operation of the 1993 Intercountry Adoption Convention: Guide to Good Practice'[52] makes clear, whilst the Convention is concerned with achieving transparency in costs and fees as a means of preventing improper financial gain,[53] problems with the costs of intercountry adoption persist. In some States 'unofficial' fees may be demanded to move the required paperwork through the adoption process, or accredited bodies may find that their clients do not receive child assignments without paying incentives to officials or orphanage directors who make the placement decisions. Such problems are exacerbated by the fact that some accredited bodies will offer such incentives willingly to increase their own placement rate. Once a system of such abuses develops, it can be very difficult to stop. It has been stated generally that '[t]he question of money and its influence on intercountry adoption remains one of the most challenging issues of our times'.[54]

---

[49] *Ibid*, at para 286.

[50] One commentator has stated that receiving States must be more alive to these concerns and should: (1) legislate to ensure that accredited agencies in this situation are legally responsible for the child laundering activities of their foreign representatives; (2) as a matter of accreditation, hold the agency to account for partnering with such representatives who participate in such corrupt practices; and (3) generally prohibit agencies from shifting the risks of the intercountry adoption process in this regard to adoptive parents/birth families through contract clauses which identify risks and then disclaim responsibility. This commentator has concluded that, without such rules in place, 'there will be no incentive for such receiving nation entities to act to prevent such wrongdoing'. See, DM Smolin, 'Abduction, Sale and Traffic in Children in the context of Intercountry Adoption', *Info Doc No 1 of June 2010*, 21. See also the guidance provided at Ch 7.4 of the Draft Guide to Good Practice on Accreditation, above n 22, which supports the responsibility of the accredited body for the actions of its representatives.

[51] But '[t]he directors, administrators and employees of bodies involved in an adoption shall not receive remuneration which is unreasonably high in relation to services rendered' (Art 12(3) of the 1993 Convention).

[52] Above n 44.

[53] Eg through accreditation, regulation and supervision of bodies or persons involved in intercountry adoption.

[54] See Prel. Doc. No 2 of May 2010, n 22, at Ch 9. There are also other difficulties concerning the role of money in the intercountry adoption process more broadly which space prohibits a detailed

Is it the case, therefore, that the delegates who argued for the exclusion of private bodies from the intercountry adoption process have been proven right? This may not necessarily be so. According to Professor Smolin:

> The example of China teaches that a virtual government monopoly of a nation's child welfare and intercountry adoption practice does not eliminate the risks of corruption and child laundering/trafficking.[55]

Despite the fact that China has relied entirely on governmental actors, including a central authority and governmental human welfare institutions/orphanages in the intercountry adoption process,

> [u]nfortunately, recent evidence indicates that once China ceased to have overwhelming numbers of abandoned babies in its institutions, some institutions which had become dependent on intercountry adoption donations/fees began offering money for babies. Government orphanages, in short, are also subject to monetary incentives and corruption.[56]

So, what 'lessons', if any, should we draw from the above when considering the possible regulation of international surrogacy arrangements? First, in relation to the regulation of intermediaries, since unregulated, private international surrogacy arrangements raise concerns similar to those expressed in relation to private/ independent intercountry adoptions, consideration must be given to State regulation or supervision of private bodies/individuals acting as intermediaries in such arrangements. However, bearing in mind the practical insight obtained as a result of the 1993 Convention, if there is to be an attempt at regulation of private intermediaries, consideration might be given as to whether more detailed requirements for their regulation and supervision might be formulated than those contained within the 1993 Convention. Further, there must be an open and frank debate regarding the role of money in international surrogacy arrangements. If it is accepted that intercountry adoption services are remunerated, albeit not without limit, is it analogous to state that a surrogate mother is providing a service which should be remunerated? Should there be a provision similar to Article 32 of the 1993 Convention? How would 'proper' and 'improper' gains be delineated? Importantly, how would 'market' forces be controlled?

At this stage, therefore, the experiences briefly outlined above in the context of the 1993 Convention only raise a host of questions when considering the regulation of international surrogacy which demand further research, thought and reflection.

---

discussion of here, *eg*, the issue of contributions to authorities in States of origin intended to support the development of child protection or adoption services.

[55] Smolin, above n 50, 20–21.

[56] *Ibid*.

IV. A Concluding Thought

As the above analysis has shown, conventions are always imperfect instruments reflecting necessary compromises. They are also, by their nature and of necessity, open-textured and broadly expressed. Nevertheless, they can represent the best opportunity available to us for developing orderly and ethical intercountry operational systems: systems which are particularly important where vulnerable parties such as children are concerned. However, as has been observed in relation to intercountry adoption:

> [T]he mere creation of the Convention ... cannot in itself create an orderly and ethical intercountry adoption. As a practical matter, the success of the Convention is dependent on the actions of national governments in effectively implementing its norms, ideals, procedures, and safeguards.[57]

The implementation of the modern Hague Children's Conventions has been described as a continuing, progressive or incremental process of improvement. Undoubtedly the same will be true if there ever is an instrument on international surrogacy, and this must be kept at the forefront of our minds: the mere creation of a convention would be only the first step (albeit, perhaps, a 'giant leap').

Postscript

Since this article was written in August 2011, the Permanent Bureau of the Hague Conference on Private International Law has published, 'A preliminary report on the issues arising from international surrogacy arrangements', Preliminary Document No 10 of March 2012 (available on the website of the Hague Conference: www.hcch.net, under 'Work in Progress', then 'General Affairs'). This preliminary report was welcomed by the Council on General Affairs and Policy of the Hague Conference which met from 17 to 20 April 2012. The 2012 Council requested that the Permanent Bureau continue the current work under the 2011 Council mandate and further prepare and distribute a Questionnaire in order to obtain more detailed information regarding the extent and nature of the private international law issues being encountered in relation to international surrogacy arrangements, as well as in relation to legal parentage or 'filiation' more broadly. The Questionnaire is to seek views on the needs to be addressed and approaches to be taken. The 2012 Council invited the Permanent Bureau to present its final Report to the Council in 2014.[58]

---

[57] *Ibid*, at 4.
[58] Conclusions and Recommendations of the Council on General Affairs and Policy of the Hague Conference, 17–20 April 2012, para 21.

27

Thinking 'Through' Human Rights: The Need for a Human Rights Perspective With Respect to the Regulation of Cross-border Reproductive Surrogacy

YASMINE ERGAS

I. Introduction

Can and, more to the point, should international human rights law (IHRL) inform the regulation of international reproductive surrogacy? This chapter addresses the question in reference to international commercial surrogacy rather than domestic gratuitous gifting. While there may be instances of trans-border donations of gametes and gestational services, the transnational market in baby-making generally implicates unrelated individuals connected for the specific purpose of the relevant transactions, often by third party intermediaries, in exchange for agreed-upon payment. Whether the goods and services provided are merely remunerated so as to cover living expenses and out-of-pocket costs or allow for higher levels of compensation is immaterial to their definition as commercial exchanges: buyers provide 'good and valid' consideration for the benefits purchased.

International human rights law sets parameters within which any international agreement will have to be situated and by which it will ultimately be evaluated. But *how* IHRL comes into play will depend on the ways in which reproductive surrogacy is characterised, as well as on the mechanisms provided for its regulation and the likely regulatory outcomes. Three questions must be asked:

(a) Are the object and purpose of proposed regulation compatible with human rights law?
(b) Are the mechanisms by which it seeks to ensure those aims acceptable under human rights law?
(c) Are the reasonably predictable outcomes of the proposed regulation such as to raise concerns about the legality of the regulation itself?

After a brief analysis of the claim that IHRL has attained a supra-ordinate status in relation to other bodies of international law, and hence sets the parameters for international agreements, I note that on the most fundamental question—whether the 'best interests of the child' principle *requires* a permissive stance towards the regulation of surrogacy—IHRL does not provide a univocal answer. I proceed to argue that the most significant test of the validity of any agreement is as regards its compatibility with the norms regarding *ius cogens* that are encoded in the Vienna Convention on the Law of Treaties. I then apply this test to problems relating to the object and purpose of any treaty on surrogacy, the means by which it is likely to operate and its potential consequences.

II. The Human Rights Implications of Surrogacy Arrangements

That the current regime of incompatible national legislations creates crises with important human rights implications is evident in dramas such as those of the Balaz[1] and Mennesson[2] twins that have concerned not only Germany and France but also countries from Iceland to Israel, India to Japan, Australia to Italy. In human rights terms, the issues raised resonate, inter alia, with norms regarding the commercialisation of human bodily products and services[3]; the sale of children[4]; the rights of women to employment[5] and to 'liberty and security of person'[6]; the rights of children to grow up in a 'family environment' and to see decisions concerning them guided by their 'best interests'[7]; the rights of adults to form a family, protected from unjustified State interference in their privacy and their homes[8]; the protection of maternity, including the promotion of its 'proper understanding'[9]; and individual rights to the highest attainable standards

---

[1] See *Jan Balaz v Anand Municipality*, LPA 2151/2009, 17 [2009] (*Balaz v Anand*).

[2] See Arrêt no 370 du 6 avril 2011 (10-19.053), Cour de cassation Première chambre civile (*Arret Mennesson*).

[3] Convention for the Protection of Human Rights and Dignity of the Human Being with Regard to Biology and Medicine (Oviedo, 1997) ('Oviedo Convention'), Art 21.

[4] Optional Protocol to the Convention on the Rights of the Child on the Sale of Children, Child Prostitution and Child Pornography (25 May 2000, entered into force 18 January 2002), 2171 UNTS 227 ('CRC Optional Protocol'). Art 2(a) of the Protocol reads: 'Sale of children means any act or transaction whereby a child is transferred by any person or group of persons to another for remuneration or any other consideration.'

[5] Convention on the Elimination of All Forms of Discrimination Against Women (18 December 1979, entered into force 3 September 1981), 1249 UNTS 13 ('CEDAW'), Art 11.

[6] International Covenant on Civil and Political Rights (16 December 1966, entered into force 23 March 1976), 999 UNTS171 and 1057 UNTS 407 ('ICCPR'), Art 9.

[7] Convention on the Rights of the Child (20 November 1989, entered into force 2 September 1990), 1577 UNTS 3 ('CRC'), Preamble.

[8] ICCPR, Art 17.

[9] CEDAW, Art 4(b).

of health.[10] Moreover, at each step along the path of reproductive surrogacy, risks of abuse—and of human rights violations—loom large: when young women are enticed to 'donate' ova without being fully aware of the risks that may accompany the relevant operations; when women are engaged as gestators, sometimes because they have been trafficked or pressured by relatives, or simply by the crushing forces of unemployment and poverty to accept comparatively lucrative contracts that promise to yield many multiples of normal household income; when commissioning parties are 'held up' because gestational carriers or brokers exact higher prices to 'deliver' children, or border guards and consular authorities demand prices either for performing legal duties or for ignoring unspoken but acknowledged illegalities.

III. International Human Rights Law and Surrogacy Regulation

The need to consider human rights law is not only a reflection of the particular crises that have been generated, nor is it only an issue that national legislators and policy-makers need to consider in an individualised and discrete manner, each within the confines of a particular jurisdiction. Rather, human rights bodies, courts and commentators have advanced authoritative claims regarding the special status of IHRL, suggesting that it acts as a *limiting force* that sets the parameters for other international agreements. The Human Rights Committee (HRC), for instance, sharply distinguished between human rights treaties and other inter-State agreements: whereas the former are established for the benefit of those within the jurisdiction of a given State, the latter constitute 'webs of inter-state exchange', such that each State has an interest in the other States' compliance.[11] That reciprocity of interest is lacking, however, where the beneficiaries of an agreement are not other States but individuals within each State's jurisdictional arena. The HRC therefore concluded that the provisions of the Vienna Convention on the Law of Treaties assigning the evaluation of the compatibility of any particular reservation with the treaty at issue to each Contracting State was 'inappropriate' for human rights treaties: that evaluation was best performed by

[10] International Covenant on Social, Economic and Cultural Rights (16 December 1966, entered into force 3 January 1976), 993 UNTS 3, Art 12.

[11] The HRC noted that it 'necessarily falls to the Committee to determine whether a specific reservation is compatible with the object and purpose of the Covenant,' as the 'principle of inter-State reciprocity has no place' in respect to treaties that are not a 'web of inter-state exchanges of mutual obligations' but 'concern the endowment of individuals with rights'. Human Rights Committee, *General Comment 24 (52), General comment on issues relating to reservations made upon ratification or accession to the Covenant or the Optional Protocols thereto, or in relation to declarations under article 41 of the Covenant*, UN Doc CCPR/C/21/Rev1/Add6 (1994).

the Committee itself.[12] The specific nature of IHRL, in other words, entails special effects, such that particular aspects of the normal operation of international law may be suspended. Moreover, the European Court of Justice has held that human rights law delimits not only Member States' domestic conduct but also the scope of their international agreements. Thus, for example, compliance with binding Security Council Resolutions, in accordance with the UN Charter, may be subject to scrutiny with respect to European human rights norms.[13] And the International Court of Justice has found that even where a particular *lex specialis* applies—as, for example, in the context of armed conflict—its provisions are to be interpreted in view of international human rights law.[14] The Court has further held that human rights norms continue to apply unless they have been specifically suspended.[15] International human rights law, these authorities suggest, must frame the regulation of international reproductive surrogacy as that of any other international agreement.

IV. Does IHRL Require a Particular Type of Regulation? Surrogacy and the Best Interests of the Child

But does IHRL require a particular kind of regulation? As a preliminary matter, does IHRL mandate either the legality or the prohibition of international commercial surrogacy per se? One way to answer this question is by asking whether the principle of the 'best interests' of the child, the primacy of which is prescribed by the Convention on the Rights of the Child, entails either a permissive or a prohibitionist stance towards surrogacy.[16] Numerous cases have arisen involving children conceived through surrogacy in jurisdictions in which surrogacy is legal, on the basis of a locally valid contract, whose intended parents are, however, from States in which either surrogacy in general, or commercial surrogacy in particular, is prohibited.[17] Because of the latter States' stance, the commissioning parties' parentage cannot be recognised, leaving the children at risk of being both 'stateless

---

[12] *Ibid.* And, regarding the normal procedures for the evaluation of reservations, see Vienna Convention on the Law of Treaties (23 May 1969, entered into force 27 January 1980), 1155 UNTS 331, Art 20.

[13] See Joined Cases C-402/05 P & C-415/05 P, *Yassin Abdullah Kadi & Al Barakaat International Foundation v Council of the European Union and EC Commission* [2008] ECR I-6351.

[14] *Legality of the Threat or Use of Nuclear Weapons*, 1996 ICJ 226.

[15] *Legal Consequences of the Construction of a Wall in the Occupied Palestinian Territory*, 2004 ICJ 131.

[16] Art 3 of the CRC specifies: 'In all actions concerning children, whether undertaken by public or private social welfare institutions, courts of law, administrative authorities or legislative bodies, the best interests of the child shall be a primary consideration.'

[17] See, eg *Balaz v Anand*, above n 1; *Re X and Y (Foreign Surrogacy)* [2008] EWHC 3030 (Fam), 2008 WL 5326758 (*Re X and Y*).

and parentless'.[18] Faced with such situations, courts have sometimes considered that the welfare of the children trumped restrictive surrogacy regulation. Rather than de facto consigning children to becoming wards of the States in which they were born,[19] or stripping them of the parental relations that they had hitherto enjoyed,[20] courts (and policy-makers) have frequently chosen to legalise filiations that might otherwise have been considered prohibited.

But not all courts have agreed. Faced with a case regarding twins born in California to French parents, the transcription of whose birth certificates had initially been allowed and subsequently annulled, the French *Cour de Cassation* concluded that such an annulment was compatible with the children's human rights. Specifically, because the French provision neither cancelled California's recognition of the children's filiation nor prohibited them from living with the 'spouses X' (ie the commissioning parents), it also did not violate either their right to respect for their family and private life under the European Convention on Human Rights, or their best interests as guaranteed by the Convention on the Rights of the Child.[21] The *Cour de Cassation*, in other words, set its own judgment in the broader international context of the case: by noting that the French annulment did not invalidate California's recognition of the twins' filiation, it drew on US law to uphold French norms that might otherwise have been deemed contrary to IHRL. Whether this decision will withstand review in the European Court of Human Rights remains to be determined. But taken on its own terms, it suggests that when the alternative is not between creating 'stateless and parentless' children on one side or the post facto legalisation of proscribed reproductive arrangements on the other, but between filiation and nationality under one set of rules rather than another, IHRL may be interpreted to allow both permissive and prohibition-ist national approaches to the regulation of international surrogacy. It seems likely that no one position regarding surrogacy will garner universal acceptance: States adopting permissive and prohibitionist national stances will continue to coexist, the former servicing a demand that the latter will continue to generate (while deciding which instances to tolerate and which to prosecute). Together, then, as the *Cour de Cassation* implicitly recognised, prohibitionist and permissive States constitute one over-arching legal regime, such that even a prohibitionist posture may be considered compatible with the 'best interests of the child' principle and other norms of IHRL.

---

[18] *Re X and Y*, above n 17.

[19] *Ibid.*

[20] Corte d'Appello di Bari, causa in unico grado iscritta nel registro generale dell'anno 2008 con il numero d'ordine 175 (*Corte d'Appello di Bari*).

[21] '[U]une telle annulation, qui ne prive pas les enfants de la filiation maternelle et paternelle que le droit californien leur reconnait ni ne les empêche de vivre avec les époux X ... en France, ne porte pas atteinte au droit au respect de la vie privée et familiale de ces enfant au sens de l'article 8 de la Convention européenne des droits de l'homme non plus qu'a leur intérêt superior garanti par ... la Convention internationale des droits de l'enfant ...': *Arret Mennesson*, above n 2.

V. Can a Surrogacy Treaty Survive
Ius Cogens Scrutiny?

But even the compatibility of a permissive treaty that explicitly seeks to promote respect for the best interests of the children born of surrogacy arrangements cannot be evaluated solely with respect to this principle. Rather, such a treaty must also not run counter to *ius cogens* norms. In the terms of the Vienna Convention on the Law of Treaties, a treaty 'is void if, at the time of its conclusion, it conflicts with a peremptory norm of general international law'.[22] Whether a peremptory norm is violated will depend, however, on the nature of the convention itself—in the first instance, on its object and purpose. Is commercial surrogacy compatible with *ius cogens* norms? Specifically, if a permissive convention were to posit—whether explicitly or implicitly—that surrogacy entails the transfer of children for compensation (as appears ineluctable in commercial surrogacy[23]), would this constitute a 'sale' proscribed by current understandings of *ius cogens*?[24] Sales of human beings have been discussed in various legal contexts, in particular in reference to slavery and human trafficking, but also with reference to adoption. In both slavery and human trafficking, the relevant commercial exchanges have clearly been viewed as prohibited.[25] Moreover, while the catalogue of *ius cogens* norms is undefined, there is consensus that such norms proscribe slavery.[26] Some may, however, question the analogy between slavery or human trafficking and the kinds of transactions involved in adoption and, by extension, surrogacy. In particular with respect to slavery, the commercial exchanges can be understood as but one aspect of a more generally proscribed reification and commodification of human beings. Slavery is, as the 1926 Convention specified and the subsequent Supplementary Slavery Convention reiterated, 'the status or condition of a person over whom *any or all* of the powers attaching to the right of ownership are exercised, and "slave" means a person in

---

[22] Vienna Convention on the Law of Treaties, above n 12, Art 53.

[23] If, as has sometimes been suggested, gestational surrogacy ought to be viewed from the perspective of a service contract, such that the carrier is engaged to perform the service of gestation, then, presumably, the relevant transactions would not be predicated on the ultimate transfer of the child to the commissioning parties (ie, the intended parents.) Rather, the carrier's contractual obligations would be deemed performed at the birth of the child.

[24] Under the Vienna Convention on the Law of Treaties, it is also possible for *ius cogens* norms to evolve. See Vienna Convention on the Law of Treaties, above n 12, Art 64.

[25] See Slavery Convention (25 September 1926, entered into force 9 March 1927), 212 UNTS 17, amended by the Protocol amending the slavery convention (7 December 1953, entered into force 7 December 1953), 182 UNTS 51 (together, 'the Slavery Convention'); Supplementary Convention on the Abolition of Slavery, the Slave Trade, and Institutions and Practices Similar to Slavery (7 September 1956, entered into force April 30, 1957), 226 UNTS 3 ('Supplementary Slavery Convention').

[26] See CM Bassiouni, 'International Crimes: Jus Cogens and Obligatio Erga Omnes' (1996) 59 *Law and Contemporary Problems* 63, 68 (inter alia noting that the 'legal literature discloses that the following international crimes are *jus cogens*: aggression, genocide, crimes against humanity, war crimes, piracy, slavery and slave-related practices, and torture').

such condition or status'.[27] The powers referred to here presumably include those regarding the ability to treat a person as an alienable commodity rather than as a subject of rights, that is, as a being endowed with agency. Thus, what characterises the slave is his or her inability to negotiate the conditions of the exchange by which he or she changes hands: the Supplementary Slavery Convention explicitly prohibits, as a practice analogous to slavery, the giving (or promise thereto) of a woman 'without the right to refuse' in marriage in exchange for payment 'of a consideration in money or in kind'.[28] But the conditions into which a human being is transferred, and not only the modality of the transfer, can denote an exchange as pertaining to slavery. The Supplementary Slavery Convention also proscribes.

> [a]ny institution or practice whereby a child or young person under the age of 18 years, is delivered by either or both of his natural parents or by his guardian to another person, whether for reward or not, with a view to the exploitation of the child or young person or of his labour.[29]

Here it is the end-goal of the transfer, the 'exploitation of the child', that leads to the prohibition, rather than the monetary exchange. How, then, does surrogacy fit within these parameters?

There can be little doubt that the commodification of human beings runs counter to the primary thrust of contemporary international human rights law: the transfer of persons in exchange for consideration presumptively entails a reduction of the person to a chattel, such that rights of possession are (at least implicitly) recognised and conveyed. At issue, here, is the status of human beings as beings to whom property rights are per se inapplicable. More specifically, the Convention on the Rights of the Child explicitly bans all sales of children[30]; the reduction of sales of children

---

[27] Supplementary Slavery Convention, Art 26 (emphasis added).

[28] *Ibid*, Art 1(c)(i).

[29] *Ibid*, Art 1(d).

[30] CRC, Art 35 (emphasis added): 'States Parties shall take all appropriate national, bilateral and multilateral measures to prevent the abduction of, the sale of or traffic in children for any purpose or in any form.' See also CRC Optional Protocol. The Preamble of the Optional Protocol expresses the Parties' 'grave' concern 'at the significant and increasing international traffic in children for the purpose of the sale of children, child prostitution and child pornography'. This tripartite enumeration—sale, prostitution and pornography—indicates a distinct preoccupation with the sale of children in general and not only with sales for the particular purposes of prostitution or pornography. 'Sale' is further defined in the Optional Protocol as 'any act or transaction whereby a child is transferred by any person or group of persons to another for remuneration or any other compensation': CRC Optional Protocol, Art 2(a). National legislation on adoption has reiterated the prohibition against any form of compensation, also incorporating a similar definition of 'sale'. Thus, in 2001, the French Civil Code was amended to provide that the consent of the legal representative of the child to an adoption must be given freely, and obtained without any consideration ('Le consentement doit etre libre, obtenu sans aucune contrepartie, après la naissance de l'enfant …'): France, Loi no 2001-111 du 6 février 2001 relative à l'adoption internationale, Code civil, Art 370-3. And the Penal Code of Morocco was amended in 2003 to criminalise all sales of children, the sale of a child being defined as 'any act or transaction that produces the transfer of a child from any person or group of persons to another person or group of persons against remuneration or any other advantage' ('tout acte ou toute transaction faisant intervenir le transfert d'un enfant de toute personne ou de tout groupe de personne a' une autre personne ou a' un autre groupe de personne contre remuneration ou tout autre avantage'): Morocco Penal Code, Art 467-1, as amended by Act No 24-03 of 11 November 2003.

figures prominently among the motivations of the Adoption Convention[31]; and human trafficking is subject to international criminal sanction.[32] And yet the Adoption Convention, reflecting language already inscribed in the Convention on the Rights of the Child, proscribes '*improper* gain', thereby recognising that some forms of payment will be legitimate.[33] Moreover, attentive observers of adoption markets have remarked on the failure of strategies designed to eradicate commercialisation, and indeed have argued for its open recognition.[34] And a recent proposal for the regulation of surrogacy by the editors of this volume contains clear indications regarding the parameters for determining allowable payments.[35] Moreover, in other contexts, payments for human beings would arguably not be seen as either analogous to slavery or as violating *ius cogens* proscriptions. While kidnapping (as an aspect of piracy) constitutes such a violation, the payment of a ransom to free hostages is distinguishable from the crime itself. Less dramatically, but of greater statistical significance, the exaction of a bride-price or a dowry, although potentially prohibited under other provisions of IHRL, has also not been taken to rise to level of violating *ius cogens*, and the widespread use of such practices (with at least implicit State consent) suggests that it would be difficult to find a proscription in customary international law. While it may be desirable to eliminate the payment-for-people aspect of international commercial surrogacy, that element frankly seems to inhere in the market itself. Whether a treaty that can pass the *ius cogens* test is adopted will depend not simply on the characterisation of surrogacy, but also on legislative and judicial understandings of the general prohibition against the sale of human beings.

Even if the object and purpose of a permissive surrogacy treaty were to be considered compatible with IHRL, however, the mechanisms set in place to

---

[31] Convention On Protection Of Children And Co-Operation In Respect Of Intercountry Adoption (29 May 1993, entered into force 1 May 1995). See, generally, G Parra-Aranguren, *Explanatory Report on the Convention on Protection of Children and Co-operation in Respect of Intercountry Adoption*, available at <hcch.net/upload/expl33e.pdf> (citing a Memorandum prepared by the Permanent Bureau of the Hague Conference on Private International Law in the drafting stages of the Adoption Convention that included among the requirements the new convention should be designed to meet, 'a need for a system of supervision in order to ensure that these standards are observed (what can be done to prevent intercountry adoptions from occurring which are not in the interest of the child; how can children be protected from being adopted through fraud, duress *or for monetary reward*)' (emphasis added)). For a discussion of the Adoption Convention in the context of norms regarding the prohibition of sales of children, see HC Kennard, 'Curtailing the Sale and Trafficking of Children: A Discussion of the Hague Conference Convention in Respect of Intercountry Adoptions' (1993–1994)14 *University of Pennsylvania Journal of International Business Law* 632.

[32] Protocol to Prevent, Suppress and Punish Trafficking in Persons, Especially Women and Children, Supplementing the United Nations Convention Against Transnational Organized Crime (15 November 2000, entered into force 25 December 2003).

[33] Adoption Convention, Art 8 (emphasis added).

[34] 'The connection between money and intercountry adoption is a fact of life and it is better to acknowledge that and try to regulate it,' comments the Secretary of the Hague Conference on Private International Law. J Degeling, *The Intercountry Adoption Guide to Good Practice Revisited: Good practice and real practice*, Hague Conference on Private International Law, Nordic Adoption Council Meeting, 2009, 4–5 November, 2009, Rejkavik, Iceland. See also D Spar, *The Baby Business: How Money, Science, and Politics Drive the Commerce of Conception* (Boston, Mass, Harvard Business School Press, 2006).

[35] K Trimmings and P Beaumont, 'International Surrogacy Arrangements: An Urgent Need for Legal Regulation at the International Level' (2011) 7 *Journal of Private International Law* 627.

regulate the actual transactions might not survive scrutiny. If a contract were to be considered enforceable, thereby imposing on the gestational carrier an obligation to surrender to the commissioning parties the child she had borne, it could arguably be considered violative of prohibitions against indentured servitude, cruel and unusual punishment, and general habeas corpus norms. Moreover, the sale of reproductive services per se could be seen as contravening prohibitions against utilising 'the human body and its parts ... as such ... [for] financial gain'.[36]

But prohibitive treaties may also run counter to significant IHRL proscriptions, in particular if such treaties de facto entail a substantial risk that children would be stateless. As has been noted, the risk of statelessness has permeated international surrogacy cases.[37] International human rights law has long both enjoined States from arbitrary deprivations of nationality and detailed specific obligations to prevent it. Referring specifically to children, the International Covenant on Civil and Political Rights establishes that 'Every child has a right to acquire a nationality,'[38] a requirement that is reiterated in the Convention on the Rights of the Child.[39] More generally, both the European Convention on Nationality and the American Convention on Human Rights establish every person's right to a nationality.[40] If, as has so often seemed the case in recent dramas, a State's unwillingness to recognise the filiation of children born of surrogacy arrangements translates into such children's statelessness, a de facto violation of *ius cogens* norms may be found.

In this context, it is difficult to envisage an effective treaty that does not require careful examination of the fundamental issues raised by IHRL. Given the urgency of the need for regulation, however, and the compelling obligation to avoid placing ever more children in the cross-fire of conflicting national legislation because their parentage (and hence citizenship) cannot be securely established, the best approach is to find convergence where possible—around a methodological framework designed to reduce risks to the children as well as to the adults involved. The answer to the more substantive questions that involve the characterisation of surrogacy will necessarily emerge from the work of national legislatures and courts, operating within domestic legal frameworks that both reflect and refract pressures from domestic constituencies, but also in relation to continuing international dialogue.

---

[36] Oviedo Convention, Art 21. See also Charter of Fundamental Rights of the European Union [2010] OJ C83/389.

[37] For a careful discussion of this issue, see C Achmad, *International Commercial Surrogacy: A 21st Century International Human Rights Challenge to Children and Women Requiring Enhanced Protection* (unpublished LLM thesis in Public International Law), University of Leiden, 2011 (on file with the author).

[38] ICCPR, Art 24(3).

[39] CRC, Art 7: 'The child shall ... have ... the right to acquire a nationality.' Specific protections regarding the child's right to his or her identity, including nationality, are in Art 8.

[40] See European Convention on Nationality (6 November 1997), ETS 166, Art 4 ('everyone has the right to a nationality'); American Convention on Human Rights (22 November 1969, entered into force 18 July 1978), OAS Treaty Series No 36, 1144 UNTS 123, Art 20(1) ('every person has the right to a nationality').

Part Three

General Report on Surrogacy

28

General Report on Surrogacy

KATARINA TRIMMINGS AND PAUL BEAUMONT

I. Introduction

Recent developments and research in the area of reproductive medicine have resulted in various treatment options becoming available to infertile couples.[1] One of the oldest methods of assisted reproduction is artificial insemination. This procedure involves the fertilisation of a woman's ovum by the artificial delivery of a sperm in her vagina or uterus. A more recent and increasingly common reproductive technique is in vitro fertilisation (IVF). During IVF, an ovum is fertilised by a sperm in a test tube or a petri dish. The embryo is then transferred to a woman's womb, or is frozen in liquid nitrogen and stored to be implanted later. In vitro fertilisation is often a complementary element of another method of assisted reproduction known as surrogate motherhood. Surrogate motherhood is

---

[1] Generally on assisted reproductive technologies and associated problems, including legal and some ethical issues, see eg M Kokiasmenos and L Mihalich, 'Assisted Reproductive Technology' (2004) 5 *The Georgetown Journal of Gender and the Law* 619; S Bychkov Green, 'Interstate Intercourse: How Modern Assisted Reproductive Technologies Challenge the Traditional Realm of Conflicts of Law' (2009) 24 *Wisconsin Journal of Law, Gender and Society* 25; B Knoppers and S LeBris, 'Recent Advances in Medically Assisted Conception: Legal, Ethical and Social Issues' (1991) 17 *American Journal of Law and Medicine* 329; M Abdul-Kareem and A Killian (eds), 'Assisted Reproductive Technologies' (2010) 11 *Georgetown Journal of Gender and the Law* 411; A Grammaticaki-Alexiou, 'Artificial Reproduction Technologies and Conflict of Laws: An Initial Approach' (1999-2000) 60 *Louisiana Law Review* 1113; N Cameron, 'Pandora's Progeny: Ethical Issues in Assisted Human Reproduction' (2005-2006) 39 *Family Law Quarterly* 745; L Hogue, 'Avoiding Parentlessness by Assisted Reproductive Technology (ART): A Proposal for Enforcing Contracts and Avoiding the Public Policy Doctrine in Interstate Cases' (2004-2005) 4 *Whittier Journal of Child and Family Advocacy* 269; G Bernstein, 'The Socio-Legal Acceptance of New Technologies: A Close Look at Artificial Insemination' (2002) 77 *Washington Law Review* 1035; J Rosato, 'The Children of ART (Assisted Reproductive Technology): Should the Law Protect Them From Harm?' [2004] *Utah Law Review* 57; J Daar, 'Accessing Reproductive Technologies: Invisible Barriers, Indelible Harms' (2008) 23 *Berkeley Journal of Gender, Law & Justice* 18; E Waldman, 'Cultural Priorities Revealed: The Development and Regulation of Assisted Reproduction in the United States and Israel' (2006) 16 *Health Matrix* 65; 'Developments in the Law: Medical Technology and the Law' (1989-1990) 103 *Harvard Law Review* 1519; and J Robertson, 'Procreative Liberty and Harm to Offspring in Assisted Reproduction' (2004) 30 *American Journal of Law & Medicine* 7.

a technique used normally in cases where the female partner of a couple is unable to carry a child.[2]

A surrogate mother may be defined as a woman who carries a child pursuant to an arrangement made before she became pregnant, and made with the sole intention of the resulting child being handed over to another person or other persons and the surrogate mother relinquishing all rights to the child. There are two types of surrogacy: traditional surrogacy and gestational surrogacy.[3] In traditional surrogacy, the surrogate mother becomes pregnant with the sperm of the intended father (usually by insemination, and seldom through sexual intercourse) or is inseminated with donor sperm. The surrogate mother is genetically related to the child. In traditional surrogacy arrangements the parties may act with or without the assistance of an intermediary (ie a broker and/or a fertility clinic). In gestational surrogacy, an embryo is created by IVF, using the egg of the intended mother (or a donor egg) and the sperm of the intended father (or a donor sperm). As a result, the surrogate mother has no genetic relationship with the child. In the context of gestational surrogacy, the surrogate mother is sometimes referred to as a 'gestational carrier' or 'gestational host'.[4] Gestational surrogacy arrangements always involve at least one intermediary (ie a fertility clinic/physician). Differences between the traditional and gestational surrogacy imply important legal and moral questions. Most important is the question whether traditional surrogacy should be treated differently from gestational surrogacy, given the existence of a genetic link between the surrogate mother and the child in the former case.[5]

Surrogacy attained public visibility over two decades ago, in the mid-1980s,[6] through the notorious cases of *Baby Cotton*[7] in the United Kingdom and *Baby M*[8]

---

[2] Additionally, surrogacy as a method of procreation is utilised by single parents and gay couples. See Rosato, above n 1, 59.

[3] See eg J Zuckerman, 'Extreme Makeover—Surrogacy Edition: Reassessing the Marriage Requirement in Gestational Surrogacy Contracts and the Right to Revoke Consent in Traditional Surrogacy Agreements' (2007-2008) 32 *Nova Law Review* 661, 662–65.

[4] V Browne-Barbour, 'Bartering for Babies: Are Preconception Agreements in the Best Interest of Children?' (2004) 26 *Whittier Law Review* 429, 436.

[5] See M Field, 'Reproductive Technologies and Surrogacy: Legal Issues' (1991–1992) 25 *Creighton Law Review* 1589, 1595.

[6] S Markens, *Surrogate Motherhood and the Politics of Reproduction* (Berkeley, University of California Press, 2007) 9.

[7] *Re C (A Minor) (wardship: surrogacy)* [1985] FLR 846 (Latey, J). A surrogate mother in England was artificially inseminated with the sperm of an American intended father, to carry a baby for him and his infertile wife. The surrogate mother delivered the child without ever having met the couple. The intended parents applied for custody of the child in the UK. Following an investigation into the welfare of the child, the intended parents were awarded custody and permitted to remove the child to the United States. The surrogate mother did not raise any objections.

[8] *Matter of Baby M* (1988, NJ) 537 A2d 1227. The parties, Ms Whitehead as the surrogate mother and Sterns as the intended parents, entered into a surrogacy agreement. Ms Whitehead conceived by IVF and delivered a baby girl. The baby was thereupon taken by the Sterns. The next day, however, Ms Whitehead said that she could not live without the baby and removed her from the Sterns. The father obtained a court decision ordering enforcement of the contract and return of the child. Upon learning of it, Ms Whitehead fled with the baby to Florida. There she was apprehended, the baby removed by force and returned to the Sterns. Ms Whitehead was awarded visitation rights. For analysis of the case, see eg

in the United States. Since then, despite controversies over ethical aspects of surrogate motherhood,[9] surrogacy has become an increasingly popular method of reproductive technology.[10] Surrogacy targets the same clientele as its counterpart, adoption.[11] It follows that with an increasingly limited global market for adoption,[12] surrogacy will continue expanding.[13] It is no exaggeration to say that the modern world has already witnessed the development of an extensive international surrogacy market.[14] This market, although initially largely unnoticed, has recently attracted a great deal of interest from the media.[15] Undoubtedly, one of the key factors that have enabled the current expansion of the cross-border surrogacy market is the ever-increasing ease of access to information via the Internet.[16]

L Behm, 'Legal, Moral and International Perspectives on Surrogate Motherhood: The Call for a Uniform Regulatory Scheme in the United States' (1999) 2 *DePaul Journal of Health Care Law* 557, 568–57; A Wolfson Latourette, 'The Surrogate Mother Contract: In the Best Interests of Society?' (1990-1991) 25 *University of Richmond Law Review* 53; E Scott, 'Surrogacy and the Politics of Commodification' (2009) 72 *Law and Contemporary Problems* 109, 112–17; C Spivack, 'The Law of Surrogate Motherhood in the United States' (2010) 58 *American Journal of Comparative Law* 97, 98–101.

[9] See eg M Freeman, 'Is Surrogacy Exploitative?' in S McLean (ed), *Legal Issues in Human Reproduction* (Dartmouth, Dartmouth Publishing Company Limited, 1989) 164–84; K Rothenberg, 'Gestational Surrogacy and the Health Care Provider: Put Part of the "IVF Genie" Back Into the Bottle' (1990) 18 *Medicine and Health Care* 345; W Wagner, 'The Ethical and Legal Implications of Hired Maternity' (1990) 35 *American Journal of Jurisprudence* 187; B Knoppers and S LeBris, 'Recent Advances in Medically Assisted Conception: Legal, Ethical and Social Issues' (1991) 17 *American Journal of Law and Medicine* 329; and Cameron, above n 1.

[10] LA Brill, 'When Will the Law Catch Up With Technology? Jaycee B v Superior Court of Orange County: An Urgent Cry for Legislation on Gestational Surrogacy' (1999-2000) 39 *Catholic Lawyer* 241, 241.

[11] I Lebowitz-Dori, 'Womb for Rent: The Future of International Trade in Surrogacy' (1997) 6 *Minnesota Journal of Global Trade* 329, 329.

[12] International Social Service (ISS), 'Evaluation of the Practical Operation of the Hague Convention of 29 May 1993 on Protection of Children and Co-operation in Respect of Inter-country Adoption', 3. Also N Cantwell, UNICEF Innocenti Research Centre, 'Intercountry Adoption—A Comment on the Number of "Adoptable" Children and the Number of Persons Seeking to Adopt Internationally' (2003) V *The Judge's Newsletter* 69, 72, available at <www.hcch.net/upload/spring2003.pdf>.

[13] *X & Y (Foreign Surrogacy)* [2008] EWHC 3030 (Fam), [26]. Hedley J cautions that 'as babies become less available for adoption … more and more couples are likely to be tempted to follow the applicants' path to commercial surrogacy in those places where it is lawful'.

[14] Permanent Bureau of the Hague Conference, 'Private International Law Issues Surrounding the Status of Children, Including Issues Arising From International Surrogacy Arrangements', Preliminary Document [hereinafter 'Prel Doc'] No 11, March 2011, para 11, available at <www.hcch.net/upload/wop/genaff2011pd11e.pdf> ('2011 Hague Report'). See also T Krim, 'Beyond Baby M: International Perspectives on Gestational Surrogacy and the Demise of the Unitary Biological Mother' (1996) 5 *Annals of Health Law* 193, 225 (noting that 'the global surrogacy market is quickly emerging'); and U Smerdon, 'Crossing Bodies, Crossing Borders: International Surrogacy Between the United States and India' (2008-2009) 39 *Cumberland Law Review* 15, 15 (acknowledging 'an increasingly global expansion of surrogacy programs').

[15] Eg S Thakur, 'Mother for Only Nine Months', *BBC News*, 21 March 2008; S Nolen, 'Desperate Mothers Fuel India's "Baby Factories"', *ScrippsNews*, 13 February 2009; R Mendick and S Bhatia, 'Couple Buy Child From India "Baby Factory"', *London Evening Standard*, 6 May 2009; J McBrearty, 'Sarah Jessica Parker: Surrogacy on the Rise After Celeb Success', *Sky News*, 11 December 2009; P Datta, 'Surrogacy Goes Into Labour', *The Times of India*, 15 May 2010; and F Elliott, 'Wombs for Hire: Shame of the Women Who Must Fill West's Demand for Babies', *The Times*, 10 April 2012.

[16] See J Reich and D Swink, 'Outsourcing Human Reproduction: Embryos & Surrogacy Services in the Cyberprocreation Era' (2011) 14 *Journal of Health Care Law & Policy* 241 (cyberprocreation = 'using the Internet to create human life').

Despite its expanding nature, the global surrogacy market remains completely unregulated, leaving parties to cross-border surrogacy arrangements at a serious risk of exploitation and resulting in complex legal problems in individual cases of cross-border surrogacy arrangements. It is believed, therefore, that there is an urgent need for regulation of cross-border surrogacy arrangements at the international level.

Some commentators have questioned whether, given ethical questions surrounding surrogacy, regulation is the right way forward, as it might have the unintended consequence of encouraging more international surrogacy arrangements.[17] It is believed here, however, that in an increasingly globalised world, all attempts to impose a complete prohibition on cross-border surrogacy arrangements are doomed to failure. A global ban on surrogacy would simply move surrogacy arrangements to the black market, thereby exposing the parties to a greater risk of exploitation.[18] It is also very difficult to believe that all States would ratify a Treaty that imposed a global ban, and therefore intending parents would continue to go to States where the ban was not accepted. Therefore, the only way forward is regulated international surrogacy arrangements; especially for the sake of children born through these arrangements, as their best interests must be the primary concern.

The pro-regulation stand is thus not to approve of the practice but to choose the 'lesser of the two evils'—a regulated global surrogacy market over an unregulated one.[19]Anyhow, the form of Convention that is proposed in this chapter does not envisage an increase in international surrogacy cases. In contrast, it is hoped that the Convention will act as a deterrent to those who would like to take advantage of individuals involved in international surrogacy arrangements, ie vulnerable surrogate mothers as well as intended parents. It will do this by creating minimum standards in relation, inter alia, to health issues, informed consent, and checks on the suitability of the intended parents and of the surrogate mother. It is hoped that even States that allow commercial surrogacy would ratify the Convention and thereby accept these minimum standards. The Convention must be designed in a way that makes this possible, or the minimum standards will be in vain.

---

[17] See eg V Browne-Barbour, 'Bartering for Babies: Are Preconception Agreements in the Best Interest of Children?' (2004) 26 *Whittier Law Review* 429, 467. According to Barbour, surrogacy arrangements should uniformly be regarded as void and unenforceable.

[18] This view is shared by other commentators, eg A Hatzis, '"Just the Oven": A Law & Economics Approach to Gestational Surrogacy Contracts' in K Boele-Woelki (ed), *Perspectives for the Unification and Harmonisation of Family Law in Europe* (Antwerp, Intersentia, 2003) 428; AG McEwen, 'So You Are Having Another Woman's Baby: Economics and Exploitation in Gestational Surrogacy' (1999) 32 *Vanderbilt Journal of Transnational Law* 271; and E Anderson, *Value in Ethics and Economics* (Cambridge, Mass, Harvard University Press, 1993) 176–79. At a national level, evidence may be drawn from China where, following a complete ban on surrogacy arrangements, the 'surrogacy market' moved underground. See Browne-Barbour, above n 17, 462.

[19] The Permanent Bureau of the Hague Conference has rightly noted that 'creating safeguards around a system and finding solutions for the challenges it poses, does not necessarily entail facilitating and promoting such a system': Permanent Bureau of the Hague Conference, 'A Preliminary Report on the Issues Arising from International Surrogacy Arrangements', Prel Doc No 10, 10 March 2012 ('2012 Hague Report'), para 59, available at <www.hcch.net/upload/wop/gap2012pd10en.pdf>.

II. Domestic Legal Approaches to Surrogacy

Domestic legal responses to surrogacy differ widely between jurisdictions. Generally speaking, some countries decided to regulate surrogacy (eg the United Kingdom and Israel), some to prohibit it (eg France and Germany) and some to ignore it (eg Belgium and Finland). Jurisdictions that chose to regulate surrogacy further differ on, for example, whether surrogate mothers should be allowed to receive payments beyond reasonable pregnancy-related expenses (so called 'commercial surrogacy'), or whether surrogacy agreements should be legally enforceable.

In a more specific way, according to their domestic approaches to surrogacy, countries may be grouped into the following categories: 'surrogacy-friendly' jurisdictions, anti-surrogacy jurisdictions and jurisdictions with a relatively neutral approach to surrogacy.[20] 'Surrogacy-friendly' countries have become 'hubs' of the international commercial surrogacy market, attracting intended parents both from anti-surrogacy jurisdictions as well as jurisdictions with a relatively neutral approach to surrogacy.

A. 'Surrogacy-Friendly' Jurisdictions

The term 'surrogacy-friendly' jurisdictions refers to countries where commercial surrogacy is legal and, as a result, these jurisdictions attract substantial numbers of intended parents from abroad. Countries that fall within this category are characterised by the following features:[21]

— Commercial surrogacy is legal.
— Commercial surrogacy is performed on a relatively large scale.
— There are legal measures which allow the intended parents (or at least one of them) to obtain legal parentage.
— There is no nationality, domicile or habitual residence prerequisite for the intended parents.

Of the States that participated in our project, the following jurisdictions may be classified as 'surrogacy-friendly': India, Uganda, Ukraine, the US states of Alabama, Arkansas, California, Connecticut, Illinois, Iowa, Maryland, Massachusetts, Minnesota, Nevada, North Dakota, Ohio, Oregon, Pennsylvania, South Carolina, Tennessee, Texas, Utah, West Virginia and Wisconsin, Russia and the Mexican State of Tabasco.[22] On the grounds of the existing legal basis for the practice of

---

[20] The analysis below is a synthesis of information contained in the National Reports on Surrogacy (Part One of this book) and additional resources as referred to throughout the analysis.

[21] See also 2012 Hague Report, above n 19, para 28.

[22] Additionally, countries which did not participate in our project but have been reported as States that do not prevent commercial surrogacy include Thailand, Georgia, Armenia, Moldova (*ibid*, fn 93) and Belarus, Kazakhstan and Kyrgyzstan (K Svitnev, 'Legal Control of Surrogacy—International

commercial surrogacy in these jurisdictions, three sub-categories of countries have been identified within this group. First, countries where commercial surrogacy is practised on an unregulated basis; secondly, countries where commercial surrogacy is allowed by judicial precedent; and thirdly, countries where commercial surrogacy is allowed by statute. The following section will analyse each of the above categories separately.

i. *Commercial Surrogacy is Practised on an Unregulated Basis*

a. India

The most notable example of a jurisdiction where commercial surrogacy is practised on an unregulated basis is India.[23] India has steadily emerged as one of the most popular destinations for cross-border surrogacy arrangements and is now considered as the 'hub' of the international commercial surrogacy market. The exact extent of the Indian surrogacy market is not known, but it is estimated that the practice has doubled in the last few years.[24] Our empirical research has revealed that between 2006 and 2009, the numbers of cross-border surrogacy arrangements handled by participating surrogacy agencies operating in India increased sharply—from 2 in 2006 to 16 in 2009 and from 0 in 2006 to 20 in 2009 respectively.[25] Moreover, the second agency recorded that, compared with the year 2009, the figures for 2010 would have presumably tripled by the end of that year, with 40 arrangements being handled between 1 January and 31 August.[26] Both agencies reported that the largest proportions of intended parents came from the USA and the UK.[27]

Despite the fact that cross-border surrogacy in India has reached 'industry proportions',[28] commercial surrogacy operates on an unregulated basis in this jurisdiction.[29] Although no Indian law expressly permits commercial surrogacy, it is

---

Perspectives' in JG Schenker (ed), *Ethical Dilemmas in Assisted Reproductive Technologies* (Berlin, Walter de Gruyter GmbH & Co KG, 2011) 149, 159.

[23] Other developing countries where cross-border commercial surrogacy operates without regulation, although at a considerably smaller scale than in India, include eg Thailand and Uganda. Nevertheless, it has been reported that in Thailand, a draft Bill to regulate cross-border surrogacy is currently under consideration: 2012 Hague Report, above n 19, fn 97. The market in Uganda appears to be of a rather regional character. The majority of intended parents reportedly come to Uganda from other African countries, in particular Kenya, Burundi, Rwanda, Congo and Southern Sudan. Nevertheless, there are reports of some intended parents also coming from Europe and Asia. See B Isoto, 'National Report on Surrogacy: Uganda', unpublished (on file with the authors).

[24] Centre for Social Research, 'Surrogate Motherhood—Ethical or Commercial', available at <www.womenleadership.in/Csr/SurrogacyReport.pdf>.

[25] See section III. below.

[26] *Ibid.*

[27] *Ibid.*

[28] *Yamada v Union of India*, 2008 INDLAW SC 1554 (29 September 2008) para 9. Indeed, an estimated 200,000 clinics across India offer fertility treatment including surrogacy. A Malhotra, 'Commercial Surrogacy in India' [2009] *International Family Law Journal* 9.

[29] The legal vacuum appears to be one of the major incentives for the flourishing surrogacy market: Malhotra, above n 28. Other factors include the ready availability of surrogate mothers, a wide choice of egg and sperm donors, and relatively low costs of the service: *ibid.* See also Law Commission of

considered legal as no law prohibits it either.[30] Currently, surrogacy is governed in India by non-binding National Guidelines for Accreditation, Supervision and Regulation of ART Clinics in India, promulgated by the Ministry of Health and Family Welfare, the Government of India, and the Indian Council of Medical Research and the National Academy of Medical Sciences in 2005 ('the Guidelines').[31]

Eligibility Criteria

The Guidelines set out relatively detailed eligibility criteria for a surrogate mother.[32] On the side of the intended parents, there is only one eligibility requirement, a medical need for surrogacy.[33] Nevertheless, given the non-binding character of the Guidelines, medical facilities commonly impose further conditions on the intended parents, for example by restricting their services to heterosexual couples (married or non-married) only.

Types of Surrogacy

The Guidelines seek to discourage traditional surrogacy, stating that 'an oocyte donor cannot act as a surrogate mother for the couple to whom the oocyte is being donated'.[34] No more than three embryos should be transferred to a surrogate mother during any one treatment cycle.[35]

Intermediaries (eg Lawyers, Medical Institutions)

The Guidelines are largely silent on the issue of intermediaries in surrogacy arrangements. The sole recommendation made in this respect in the document is that ART clinics should not advertise their surrogacy programmes.[36]

Legal Parenthood

According to the Guidelines, the surrogate mother is not regarded as the legal mother of the child.[37] The child is presumed to be 'the legitimate child of the

---

India, *Need for Legislation to Regulate Assisted Reproductive Technology Clinics as Well as Rights and Obligations of Parties to a Surrogacy*, Report No 228, 5 August 2009, para 1.7 ('Law Commission of India Report'). The standard fee is between $25,000 and $30,000, which is one-third of the price in developed countries (eg USA): *ibid*.

[30] Law Commission of India Report, above n 29, para 3.5(a). See also ch 12 of this book.

[31] National Guidelines for Accreditation, Supervision and Regulation of ART Clinics in India, 2005 ('the Guidelines'), in ch 12 of this book.

[32] In particular, a surrogate mother should not be over 45 years of age, must have been tested for HIV and, in case she is a relative of the intended parents, should belong to the same generation as the intended mother. Additionally, a woman cannot act as a surrogate mother more than three times in her life: *ibid*, para 3.10.

[33] Surrogacy is to be made available only to persons for whom it would be 'physically or medically impossible/undesirable to carry a baby to term': *ibid*, para 3.10.2.

[34] *Ibid*, para 3.5.4.

[35] *Ibid*, para 3.5.12.

[36] *Ibid*, para 3.10.4.

[37] See Law Commission of India Report, above n 29, para 1.14.

couple, born within wedlock, with consent of both spouses, and with all the attendant rights of parentage, support and inheritance'.[38] Sperm/egg donors have no parental rights in relation to the child.[39] The birth certificate is issued in the name of the genetic parents.[40] The intended parent(s) are required to prove their genetic link to the child through DNA evidence.[41] Practical implications of these provisions appear to be as follows:

(a) Where both the intended mother and the intended father are genetically related to the child, they will both appear on the birth certificate as the legal parents (see Figure 1).

Figure 1: Intended Father + Intended Mother

(b) Where only the intended father is genetically related to the child and an egg donor is used, the intended father and the surrogate mother will be stated on the birth certificate as the legal parents (see Figure 2). Nevertheless, reported case law suggests that in some cases, in particular where the arrangement has been commissioned by a single intended father, only the intended father's name will appear on the birth certificate and no mother will be stated there (see Figure 3).[42]

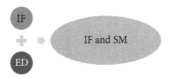

Figure 2: Intended Father + Egg Donor (1)

---

[38] Guidelines, above n 31, para 3.16.1.

[39] *Ibid.*

[40] *Ibid*, para 3.5.4.

[41] *Ibid*, para 3.10.1. The paragraph further states that if the intended parents are genetically related to the child and they establish it through DNA tests, they do not need to adopt the child to establish legal parenthood. Otherwise, a child born through surrogacy must be adopted by the genetic (biological) parents. Concerns have, however, been expressed in relation to this provision, as the Hindu Adoption and Maintenance Act 1956 does not allow non-Hindus to adopt a Hindu child. It has been suggested that, alternatively, the intended parents could petition for guardianship under the Guardians and Wards Act 1890. See A Malhotra, 'All Aboard the Fertility Express', unpublished (on file with authors).

[42] See eg Belgian cases of *C*, Court of First Instance Brussels 6 April 2010, and *AM & ND*, Court of First Instance Nivelles 6 April 2010. As discussed in ch 3 of this book.

Figure 3: Intended Father + Egg Donor (2)

(c) Where only the intended father is genetically related to the child and the ovum is provided by the surrogate mother (traditional surrogacy), the intended father and the surrogate mother will be listed on the birth certificate as the legal parents (see Figure 4).

Figure 4: Intended Father + Surrogate Mother

Legend:
IF = intended father
IM = intended mother
SM = surrogate mother
ED = egg donor

The above examples represent the most common scenarios that occur in cross-border surrogacy cases. Other scenarios, such as cases where only the intended mother or neither of the intended parents is genetically related to the child, occur with a lower frequency; however, available case law does not indicate how civil registrars in India proceed in such cases.

Nationality

As a rule, children born through surrogacy to foreign intended parents do not become Indian nationals within the meaning of section 3 of the Citizenship Act 1955, even though they are born in India.[43]

Payments

The Guidelines expressly entitle the surrogate mother to financial compensation beyond expenses incurred during her pregnancy and post-natal care relating to

---

[43] This was confirmed by the Indian Government in the cross-border surrogacy case of *Jan Balaz*. See section IV. below. See also ch 12 of this book.

pregnancy. The precise sum should be determined after a discussion between the intended parents and the intended surrogate mother.[44]

Enforceability

The issue of enforceability of surrogacy arrangements is not dealt with specifically in the Guidelines; nevertheless, commentators believe that surrogacy arrangements are enforceable in India. As surrogacy contracts are treated as commercial contracts in India, their enforceability would be governed by the Indian Contract Act 1872.[45] Under section 10 of this Act, all agreements are contracts if they are made by the free consent of parties competent to a contract, for a lawful consideration and with a lawful object, and are not expressly declared void.[46] The actual enforcement of a surrogacy arrangement in India would fall within the scope of section 9 of the Indian Code of Civil Procedure.[47]

Future Prospects

The Guidelines, being of a non-statutory and non-binding nature, have been criticised for 'lacking teeth and [being] often violated'.[48] In the absence of statutory regulation, the questions of legal parenthood and nationality in cross-border surrogacy cases have in the past few years puzzled Indian courts, including the Supreme Court of India.[49] The courts have in response highlighted the need urgently to remedy the unsatisfactory status quo.[50] It has therefore been decided that the inadequate regulation should in the near future be replaced by federal statutory provisions. At the federal level, the Assisted Reproductive Technologies (Regulation) Bill 2010 (the 'Draft Bill') is currently pending with the Parliament of India.[51] The federal Government has also drafted the Assisted Reproductive

---

[44] See Guidelines, above n 31, para 3.5.4, which states: 'All the expenses of the surrogate mother during the period of pregnancy and post-natal care relating to pregnancy should be borne by the couple seeking surrogacy. The surrogate mother would also be entitled to a monetary compensation from the couple for agreeing to act as a surrogate; the exact value of this compensation should be decided by discussion between the couple and the proposed surrogate mother.'

[45] See ch 12 of this book.

[46] *Ibid.*

[47] Malhotra, above n 41.

[48] Malhotra, above n 28.

[49] Eg *Balaz v Anand Municipality*, No 3020, Special Civil Application (Gujarat High Court, 2008); *Union of India & ANR v Jan Balaz and others*, Special Leave to Appeal (Civil) No 31639, Supreme Court of India, 2009; and *Baby Manji Yamada v Union of India & Anr*, Writ Petition No 369 of 2008, Supreme Court of India. For a detailed analysis of both cases, see ch 12 of this book.

[50] Eg the High Court of Gujarat in *Balaz v Anand Municipality*, No 3020, Special Civil Application (Gujarat High Court, 2008) stating at para 21 that 'there is extreme urgency to push through the legislation answering all these issues'.

[51] See ch 12 of this book for a detailed analysis of the Draft Bill. The Draft Bill has been discussed by a number of commentators, eg A Sharma, 'The Draft ART (Regulation) Bill: In Whose Interest?' (2009) VI *Indian Journal of Medical Ethics* 36; Malhotra, above n 28; and Dr Justice Lakshmanan, 'Legalise Altruistic Surrogacy, Prohibit Commercial Ones', *The Hindu*, 15 August 2010, available at <www.thehindu.com/opinion/open-page/article570924.ece>.

Technologies (Regulation) Rules 2010.[52] Additionally, at the state level, the Maharashtra Assisted Reproductive Technology (Regulation) Act 2011 is currently pending in the State of Maharashtra.[53]

If the Draft Bill is adopted in its current form, commercial surrogacy will remain legal in India. This fact has attracted substantial criticism by commentators, in particular on the grounds that rather than thoroughly regulating the industry and protecting the interests of surrogate mothers, the Draft Bill promotes the interests of fertility clinics and actively encourages procreative tourism in India.[54]

ii. Commercial Surrogacy is Allowed by Judicial Precedent

The most prominent example of a jurisdiction where commercial surrogacy operates on the basis of a judicial precedent is the US state of California.[55] As early as in 1993, the California Supreme Court, in the case of *Johnson v Calvert*,[56] developed the 'intent-based' approach to the establishment of legal parenthood in surrogacy cases, and judicially confirmed the enforceability of surrogacy arrangements.[57] According to the intent approach, the intent of the parties as expressed in the surrogacy agreement controls the determination of the legal motherhood. *Johnson v Calvert* involved a gestational surrogacy agreement between Mark and Crispina Calvert (the intended parents) and Anna Johnston (the surrogate mother). An embryo created from the Calverts' genetic material was implanted into Anna's uterus. In return for three payments totalling $10,000 and a life insurance policy, Anna agreed to relinquish all parental rights to the child. During the pregnancy, however, the relationship between the parties deteriorated. This prompted the intended parents to seek a court declaration that they were the parents of the child. In response, Anna filed a petition to be declared the mother. The two petitions were consolidated and the trial court ruled that the Calverts were the

---

[52] See ch 12 of this book.

[53] *Ibid.*

[54] Sharma, above n 51.

[55] Other examples are Massachusetts (*Culliton v Beth Israel Deaconess Medical Center*, 435 Mass 285 (2001), and *Hodas v Morin*, 442 Mass 544 (2004)) and Ohio (*Belsito v Clark*, 644 NE2d 760 (1994), and *JF v DB*, 879 NE2d 740 (2007)). In Massachusetts, a pre-birth establishment of legal parenthood is possible in accordance with the above precedents, whereas in Ohio the intended parents may establish parentage post-birth following the decision in *Belsito*. See ch 24 of this book. See also F Berys, 'Interpreting a Rent-A-Womb Contract: How California Courts Should Proceed When Gestational Surrogacy Arrangements Go Sour' (2005-2006) 42 *California Western Law Review* 321.

[56] *Johnson v Calvert* 5 Cal 4th 84, 19 Cal Rptr 2d 494, 851 P2d 776 (cert denied 510 US 874, 114 S Ct 206, 126 L Ed 2d 163) (Cal 1993). For analysis of the case, see eg D Morgan, 'A Surrogacy Issue: Who is the Other Mother?' (1994) 8 *International Journal of Law and the Family* 386; A Vorzimer, 'The Egg Donor and Surrogacy Controversy: Legal Issues Surrounding Representation of Parties to an Egg Donor and Surrogacy Contract' (1999-2000) 21 *Whittier Law Review* 415, 415–17; L Behm, 'Legal, Moral and International Perspectives on Surrogate Motherhood: The Call for a Uniform Regulatory Scheme in the United States' (1999) 2 *DePaul Journal of Health Care Law* 557, 572–77; K Rothenberg, 'Gestational Surrogacy and the Health Care Provider: Put Part of the "IVF Genie" Back Into the Bottle' (1990) 18 *Law, Medicine & Health Care* 345, 345–46.

[57] See ch 24 of this book.

'genetic, biological and natural father and mother', found the contract enforceable and denied Anna's claim to maternity. The Court held:

> Anna Johnston is the gestational carrier of the child, a host in a sense ... [She] and the child are genetic hereditary strangers. ... Anna's relationship to the child is analogous to that of a foster parent providing care, protection, and nurture during the period of time that the natural mother, Crispina Calvert, was unable to care for the child.

Anna appealed. The Supreme Court of California affirmed the first instance decision and resolved the issue by looking to the intent of the parties in signing the contract. The Court held that under the Federal Uniform Parentage Act 1973 (which, however, was not specifically designed for surrogacy), both gestation and genetic ties can give rise to a presumption of motherhood. As both Anna and Crispina presented evidence of motherhood,[58] and the Court could find no clear preference in the Uniform Parentage Act as between the fact of physical gestation and birth and blood test evidence in determining motherhood, the Court decided to look at the intentions of the parties involved. The Court held that when gestation and genetics

> do not coincide in one woman, the woman who intended to bring about the birth of a child that she intended to raise as her own is the natural and legal mother of the child in California.[59]

In practice, the intent of the parties is often formalised through a 'pre-birth parentage order' which declares the intended parents as the legal parents before the child is born.[60] Once the 'pre-birth parentage order' has become final, it is

---

[58] Anna through gestation and birth, and Crispina through her genetic link to the child.

[59] The application of the intent in California was subsequently widened by the California Court of Appeal decision in the case of *Buzzanca v Buzzanca*, 61 Cal App 4th 1410, 72 Cal Rptr 2d 280 (Cal Ct App 1998). In this case, the intended parents, Luanne and John Buzzanca, decided to have an embryo genetically unrelated to either of them implanted in a surrogate mother, who would carry and give birth to the child for them. After the pregnancy, the intended parents split up, and the question arose as to who were the child's legal parents. The trial court concluded that the child had no legal parents. On appeal, this decision was reversed and the Court of Appeal held that even though neither of the intended parents was genetically related to the child, they were still her legal parents given their initiating role as the intended parents in her conception and birth. Nevertheless, in the 1994 case of *In re Marriage of Moschetta*, 30 Cal Rptr 2d 893 (Ct App 1994), the California Court of Appeals made a finding that in a traditional surrogacy case, the intended mother could not rely on her intent to establish legal motherhood. The case concerned a dispute between the divorcing intended parents and the traditional surrogate as to who was the legal mother. As in *Johnson v Calvert*, the Court applied the provisions of the Uniform Parentage Act. The Court concluded that, unlike in *Johnson*, there were no competing motherhood presumptions between the intended and the surrogate mother as the intended mother had no genetic ties with the child. Consequently, there was no dispute as to maternity to decide. The Court concluded that the intended mother would have to adopt the child as a surrogacy agreement could not constitute an agreement on adoption as it violated statutory requirements regarding consent in adoption. For analysis, see eg Vorzimer, above n 56, 420–26.

[60] S Snyder and M Byrn, 'The Use of Prebirth Parentage Orders on Surrogacy Proceedings' (2005-06) 39 *Family Law Quarterly* 633, 634 (the article may be accessed online at <www.//open.wmitchell.edu/cgi/viewcontent.cgi?article=1231&context=facsch>). The authors, however, explain that pre-birth parentage orders are not appropriate in all surrogacy scenarios. In the light of the decision in *Moschetta*, a successful outcome is likely to depend on the genetic make-up of the child: *ibid*. (For an extracted version of the article, see S Snyder and M Bryn, 'The Use of Prebirth Parentage Orders in Surrogacy Proceedings' (2006) 23 *GPSolo (ABA General Practice, Solo & Small Firm Division)* 14.)

enforceable against all parties who participated in the proceedings (including the surrogate mother).[61]

iii. *Commercial Surrogacy is Allowed by Statute*[62]

The most popular destination of intended parents in cross-border commercial surrogacy cases with a statutory regulation is Ukraine. Another Eastern European jurisdiction that appears to be an increasingly common destination of intended parents in cross-border surrogacy cases is Russia.[63] Although the Russian regulation of surrogacy is less comprehensive than the Ukrainian one, the two regulatory systems share important common features:

(a) the issue of payments in surrogacy is not addressed by the legislator so commercial surrogacy is presumed to be legal;

(b) there is no nationality/residency/domicile requirement for the intended parents; and

(c) the transfer of legal parenthood to the intended parents is carried out through an administrative procedure, and the consent of the surrogate mother is needed for the intended parents to be registered as the legal parents.

Given the frequency of cross-border surrogacy arrangements involving Ukraine, the focus of the analysis below is on this jurisdiction. A detailed analysis of surrogacy regulation in Russia may be found in chapter nineteen of this book.

a. Ukraine

Relevant statutory instruments that regulate surrogacy in Ukraine include the Family Code of Ukraine 2004 and the Instruction of the Order of the Ministry of Health of Ukraine No 771 of 23 December 2009[64] (the 'Instruction').

Eligibility Criteria

The Instruction imposes a number of requirements on a surrogate mother, for example medical fitness and a prior live birth. No upper age limit is stipulated. On the side of the intended parents, only heterosexual couples are eligible to commission surrogacy in Ukraine,[65] and there must be a medical need for surrogacy.[66]

---

[61] See ch 24 of this book.

[62] Eg Ukraine, Russia, Mexico (the State of Tabasco) and the US (Illinois, Florida, Arkansas and Texas).

[63] Svitnev, above n 22, at 155.

[64] The Instruction is a legally binding act and was issued by the Ministry of Health pursuant to Art 281 of the Ukrainian Civil Code ('Right to Life').

[65] Only heterosexual marriage is legal in Ukraine so surrogacy is not available to either same-sex couples or single persons. See Art 21 of the Family Code, which defines marriage as 'matrimony of a man and woman'. See also ch 22 of this book.

[66] Instruction, s 7, para 2.

Types of Surrogacy

At least one of the intended parents must be genetically related to the child;[67] however, traditional surrogacy is not envisaged by Ukrainian legislation.[68] The number of embryos that can be transferred to a surrogate mother is limited to three, although a transfer of only one or two embryos is recommended.[69]

Legal Parenthood

Article 123(2) of the Family Code states that the intended parents are to be regarded as the legal parents of a child born as a result of a surrogacy arrangement. This rule is reaffirmed by Article 139(2) of the Family Code, which explicitly prevents a surrogate mother from claiming maternal affiliation to the child. Nevertheless, the Rules of Civil Registration require that a surrogate mother gives a notarised consent for the intended parents to register as the legal parents of the child.[70] However, commentators believe that as the consent is only an administrative act, in the case of a refusal by the surrogate mother to consent to the registration, Ukrainian courts would look favourably on the intended parents.[71]

Once consent has been granted by the surrogate mother, the intended parents will be listed on the child's birth certificate in any scenario that falls within the scope of Ukrainian legislation (see section II.A.i.a. above, 'Types of Surrogacy', and the figures below), that is:

(a) where both intended parents are genetically related to the child (see Figure 5);

Figure 5: Intended Father + Intended Mother

(b) where only the intended father is genetically related to the child (ovum provided by a donor) (see Figure 6);

---

[67] It is a prerequisite for the registration of the intended parents as the legal parents of the child, according to para 11 of section 1 of Chapter III of the Rules of Civil Registration in Ukraine, approved by the Order of the Ministry of Justice of Ukraine of 18 October 2000 No 52/5.

[68] The Family Code (Art 123(2)) makes it clear that only cases where 'a human embryo conceived by the spouses (a man and a woman) by means of assisted reproductive technologies has been transferred to another woman's body' fall within the scope of surrogacy legislation.

[69] Instruction, s 3, para 3.6. (6).

[70] Rules of Civil Registration, approved by the Order of the Ministry of Justice of Ukraine of 18 October 2000 No 52/5 as amended, Ch III, s 1, para 11.

[71] See ch 22 of this book.

Figure 6: Intended Father + Egg Donor

(c) where only the intended mother is genetically related to the child (sperm provided by a donor) (see Figure 7).

Figure 7: Sperm Donor + Intended Mother

Legend:
IF = intended father
IM = intended mother
SM = surrogate mother
ED = egg donor
SD = sperm donor

Nationality

As a rule, children born through surrogacy to foreign intended parents in Ukraine do not qualify for Ukrainian citizenship by birth under Article 7 of the Ukrainian Citizenship Act.[72]

Payments

There is no express provision on payments in surrogacy in Ukrainian legislation. The basis for the practice of commercial surrogacy therefore derives from the assumption that what is not prohibited is legal. This is used in combination with the principle of the freedom of contract enshrined in the Ukrainian Civil Code.[73]

Enforceability

Enforceability of surrogacy arrangements is not regulated in Ukraine and the issue has not yet been tested by Ukrainian courts. Nevertheless, commentators

---

[72] The Article states that '[a] person, whose parents or one of the parents were citizens of Ukraine at the time of his/her birth is a citizen of Ukraine'. As explained in 'Legal Parenthood' above, the surrogate mother is not viewed by Ukrainian legislation as the legal parent.
[73] Civil Code, Arts 6(1) and 627.

have suggested that, as far as the principal obligation of the surrogate mother to relinquish the child is concerned, courts are likely to favour the intended parents over the surrogate mother.[74]

Future Prospects

The future of commercial surrogacy in Ukraine is uncertain, with two Bills to amend surrogacy regulation currently pending before the Ukrainian Parliament. Interestingly, one of the Bills seeks to discourage procreative tourism in Ukraine, proposing that citizens of countries where legal parenthood acquired in Ukraine in surrogacy cases cannot be recognised, should be banned from using surrogacy services in Ukraine.[75] Evidently, if this Bill is passed by the Parliament, the cross-border surrogacy market in Ukraine will be significantly restricted.

B. Jurisdictions with a Relatively Neutral Approach to Surrogacy

The category of jurisdictions with a relatively neutral approach to surrogacy comprises two alternative approaches. First, the term refers to countries where surrogacy is regulated whilst only an altruistic form of surrogacy is permitted; and, secondly, the expression covers jurisdictions where both forms of surrogacy (ie altruistic or commercial) remain unregulated.

i. Surrogacy is Regulated Whilst only Altruistic Surrogacy is Permitted

Altruistic surrogacy is allowed and regulated by statute in two European Union (EU) Member States: the United Kingdom and Greece. Outside the EU, relevant statutes have been passed, for example, in Israel, South Africa, New Zealand, Australia (five Australian states and one Australian territory[76]) and several US states.[77] The underlying policy aim in these jurisdictions is to prohibit commercial surrogacy arrangements and to limit surrogacy to a relatively small number of altruistic arrangements. These countries commonly impose stringent require-ments on the domicile/habitual residence/residence of the intended parents and/ or the surrogate mother.[78] As a result, these jurisdictions generally do not attract

---

[74] See ch 22 of this book.

[75] Draft Law No 8282 to amend the Family Code of Ukraine. See ch 22 of this book.

[76] New South Wales, Queensland, South Australia, Victoria and Western Australia, and the Australian Capital Territory. See ch 2 of this book.

[77] Eg Washington, Nevada, Virginia and New Hampshire.

[78] Eg the intended parents must be resident in the jurisdiction in Australia—the Australian Capital Territory, New South Wales, Queensland and Western Australia. In South Australia the requirement is of domicile. Similarly, in the UK, the intended parents must be domiciled in the country. This require-ment appears to be strictly enforced in the UK. In particular, in *Re G (Surrogacy: Foreign Domicile)* [2007] EWHC 2814, the court refused to grant a parental order as neither of the intended parents was domiciled in the UK. The case involved an altruistic surrogacy arrangement between a Turkish couple and an English surrogate. Following the court's refusal to grant a parental order, the couple waged a nine-month long legal battle to find an alternative solution. Finally, international adoption law was applied to enable the couple to take the child out of the UK and bring it to Turkey. For a more detailed

potential intended parents from abroad.[79] On the contrary, intended parents from some of these jurisdictions account for a large number of persons commissioning cross-border surrogacy arrangements in the 'surrogacy-friendly' jurisdictions.[80]

Altruistic surrogacy is available in these jurisdictions to specific qualified persons, with the eligibility criteria normally being set out in relevant statutory instruments. In some of these jurisdictions, intended parents automatically gain legal parenthood upon the birth of the child;[81] in others, a mechanism for the transfer of legal parentage from the surrogate mother to the intended parents is provided for by the relevant legislation.[82] The meaning of 'altruistic' varies among the jurisdictions. In most countries, the intended parents are allowed to pay reasonable pregnancy-related expenses to the surrogate mother. The term 'reasonable expenses' may either be undefined,[83] or specified as including medical expenses and/or legal expenses, and/or travel costs associated with the pregnancy, and/or accommodation expenses associated with the pregnancy, and/or counselling expenses and/or insurance premiums.[84] Additionally, in some jurisdictions, the surrogate mother is allowed to receive reimbursement for lost income.[85] Lastly, in Israel, additional monthly compensation payments for pain and suffering are possible.[86]

Two distinct regulatory approaches may be identified among these countries: statutes which require court/special committee pre-approval of the surrogacy arrangement; and statutes which do not require such pre-approval.

a. No Pre-Approval Required

Typical examples of the approach where no pre-approval of the surrogacy arrangement is required are the United Kingdom and Australia (New South Wales, Queensland, South Australia and the Australian Capital Territory).[87]

---

analysis of this case, see ch 23 of this book. See also D Howe, 'International Surrogacy—A Cautionary Tale' [2009] *Family Law* 61. In Greece, both the intending mother and the surrogate mother must be domiciled in Greece. In Israel, both the surrogate mother and the intended parents must be habitually resident in the country; and in South Africa, at least one of the intended parents and the surrogate mother (and her husband/partner if applicable) must be domiciled in South Africa.

[79] See eg, ch 9 of this book. An additional deterrent is the ban on commercial surrogacy in these countries, as finding an altruistic surrogate is more difficult than finding a commercial one.

[80] Eg UK. See section III. below.

[81] Eg South Africa and Greece.

[82] Eg UK, Australia and New Zealand.

[83] Eg UK.

[84] Eg Australia (New South Wales, Queensland, South Australia, Western Australia, Victoria); New Zealand; Greece; South Africa; US (Virginia, Nevada and Washington).

[85] Eg Australia (New South Wales, Queensland and Western Australia); Greece; South Africa; Israel; and US (New Hampshire).

[86] See ch 14 of this book.

[87] The key pieces of legislation through which surrogacy is regulated in these jurisdictions are the Surrogacy Arrangements Act 1985, the Human Fertilisation and Embryology Act 1990 ('HFEA 1990') and the Human Fertilisation and Embryology Act 2008 ('HFEA 2008') in the UK; the Surrogacy Act 2010 in Australia (New South Wales); the Surrogacy Act 2010 in Australia (Queensland); the Family Relationship Act 1975 in Australia (South Australia); and the Parentage Act 2004 in the

Legal Parenthood at Birth

Upon the birth of the child, legal motherhood is established in these jurisdictions on the basis of the birth rule, with legal paternity depending upon the marital status of the surrogate mother. The surrogate mother is regarded as the legal mother of the child (whether or not she is also the genetic mother) and her husband/partner (if applicable) is presumed to be the legal father of the child.[88]

Transfer of Legal Parenthood

To extinguish the legal status of the surrogate mother (and her husband/partner as applicable) and reassign legal parenthood to the intended parents, the intended parents have to go through a post-birth legal process. In the UK, this process is known as the 'parental order application'. An equivalent of the 'parental order application' in Australia is the 'parentage order application'. A parental order in the UK/a parentage order in Australia will be issued if:

  (a) the surrogacy arrangement is not commercial;[89]
  (b) the intended parents are domiciled/resident in the jurisdiction;[90]
  (c) the surrogate mother and her husband/partner (if applicable) have consented to the transfer of parentage;[91] and

---

Australian Capital Territory. See chs 2 and 23 of this book. For further reading, see eg J McCandless and S Sheldon, 'The Human Fertilisation and Embryology Act (2008) and the Tenacity of the Sexual Family Form' (2010) 73 *MLR* 175; P Anderson, 'An Evaluation of Surrogacy Law and Its Potential Development in the UK; Is There a Clear Way Forward?' (2010) 2 *King's Student Law Review* 37; M Brazier, 'Regulating the Reproduction Business?' (1999) 7 *Medical Law Review* 166; N Gamble and L Ghevaert, 'The Chosen Middle Ground: England, Surrogacy Law and the International Arena' [2009] *International Family Law Journal* 22; N Gamble and L Ghevaert, 'In Practice: The Human Fertilisation and Embryology Act 2008: Revolution or Evolution?' [2009] *Family Law* 730; J Millbank, 'The New Surrogacy Parentage Laws in Australia: Cautious Regulation or "25 Brick Walls"?' (2011) 35 *Melbourne University Law Review* 165; and M Keyes, 'Cross-Border Surrogacy Agreements' (2012) 26 *Australian Journal of Family Law* 28.

[88] The UK HFEA 2008, s 33(1), which sets rules for the establishment of parenthood in cases of assisted reproduction, states: 'The woman who is carrying or has carried a child as a result of the placing in her of an embryo or of sperm and eggs, and no other woman, is to be treated as the mother of the child.' Section 35(1) of the same Act further states that if, at the time of the procedure, the woman 'was a party to marriage' and the embryo was not created with the sperm of 'the other party to the marriage', then 'the other party to the marriage' is to be treated as the father of the child unless it is shown that he did not consent to the procedure. Similarly, in Australia the federal Family Law Act 1975, referring to the prescribed laws of the states and territories as to parental status, sets out the rule that the surrogate mother is regarded as the legal mother of a child born as a result of a pregnancy achieved by means of a fertility procedure, and her consenting partner/spouse is viewed as the legal father (see ch 2 of this book).

[89] UK HFEA 2008, s 54(8). For Australia, see ch 2 of this book, fn 24.

[90] The requirement of domicile may be found in the UK and South Australian legislation (HFEA 2008, s 54(4)(b); and Family Relationships Act 1975 (SA), s 10HA(2)(b)(iv), respectively). In the remaining Australian jurisdictions, the requirement is of residence. See ch 2 of this book, fn 27. In the UK, the question of domicile surfaced in the case of *Re G (Surrogacy: Foreign Domicile)* [2007] EWHC 2814 (in the context of the HFEA 1990), and in the case of *Z and another v C and another* [2011] EWHC 3181 (Fam) (in the context of the HFEA 2008).

[91] UK HFEA 2008, s 54(6). For Australia, see ch 2 of this book, fn 25.

(d) the application is made less than six months after the birth of the child.[92]

Additional requirements, not common to or identical in all jurisdictions, relate to:

(a) a genetic link between the applicants and the child;[93]
(b) the age of the applicants;[94]
(c) the marital status of the applicants;[95] and
(d) physical care of the child.[96]

Lastly, a number of additional requirements that differ largely between the various jurisdictions may be found in Australia.[97]

Discretion

Generally, the courts have no discretion to grant a parental order/parentage order if the statutory requirements are not met. Nevertheless, in New South Wales and Queensland, the statutory acts allow the judges to dispense with some of the requirements in exceptional cases, provided that this is in accordance with the child's best interests.[98] It must be noted, however, that in both of these Australian jurisdictions the requirement that the arrangement is altruistic is a mandatory requirement which cannot be waived by the court.[99] The position is completely different in the UK, where the courts have no discretion in relation to matters other than the payments made by the intended parents to the surrogate mother. In particular, under section 54(8) of the Human Fertilisation and Embryology Act

---

[92] HFEA 2008, s 54(3). For Australia, see ch 2 of this book, fn 28. In the UK and the Australian Capital Territory, the child must be at least six weeks old at the time of the application (HFEA 2008, s 54(3) and Parentage Act 2004 (ACT), s 25(3), respectively). In Queensland and South Australia, the child must be at least four weeks old at the time the application is made, and in New South Wales the Child must be at least 30 days old (Surrogacy Act 2010 (Qld), s 21(1)(a); Family Relationships Act 1975 (SA), s 10HB(5); and Surrogacy Act 2010 (NSW), s 16(1)). See ch 2 of this book, fn 28.

[93] The UK legislation requires that at least one of the intended parents is genetically related to the child. The same prerequisite may be found in the Australian Capital Territory and South Australia (HFEA 2008, s 54(1)(a) and (b); Parentage Act 2004 (ACT), s 24(d); and Family Relationships Act 1975 (SA), s 10HA(2)(b)(viii)(B), respectively). See ch 2 of this book, fn 40.

[94] In the UK, the Australian Capital Territory, South Australia and New South Wales, the intended parents must have attained the age of 18. In Queensland, the minimum age requirement for the intended parents is 25. See HFEA 2008, s 54(5); and ch 2 of this book, fns 35–37.

[95] The UK HFEA 2008 excludes single people from applications for a parental order. Nevertheless, couples, regardless of whether they are married or not, or in a civil partnership, are eligible to apply. The situation is largely different in Australia, where in all jurisdictions except South Australia, single people can apply for a parentage order. No Australian jurisdiction differentiates between de facto and married couples, although same-sex couples are excluded in South Australia and Western Australia. See HFEA 2008, s 54(2); and ch 2 of this book, fns 43, 44 and 46.

[96] In the UK, New South Wales and Queensland, the child must be living with the intended parents at the time of the application. In the Australian Capital Territory and South Australia, the judge must 'take into account whether the child is living with the intended parents at the time of application'. See HFEA 2008, s 54(4)(a); and ch 2 of this book, fns 53–54.

[97] For details see ch 2 of this book.

[98] See *ibid*, fn 58.

[99] Surrogacy Act 2010 (NSW), ss 23(2) and 18(2)(a); and Surrogacy Act 2010 (Qld), ss 22(2)(e)(vi) and 23(1).

2008, UK courts are entitled to authorise retrospectively payments exceeding reasonably incurred expenses. It is to be noted that, surprisingly, this provision has been relied on successfully in all parental order applications involving commercial cross-border surrogacy arrangements.[100]

Alternative Solutions

In the UK, there are limited options for the intended parents if any of the statutory requirements for a parental order are not met. In particular, the intended parents might need to apply for adoption, special guardianship or a residence order.[101]

In Australia, the intended parents can apply for a parenting order under the federal Family Law Act 1975. The effect of parenting orders is fundamentally different from the effect of parentage orders, as parenting orders in Australia do not create legal parenthood but only determine parental responsibility.[102] Alternatively, in some cases the intended parents may be able to adopt the child under state and territory adoption legislation.[103] The legislation on parenting orders and adoption operates separately from the state surrogacy laws and is governed by the principle of the best interests of the child. It appears from published case law that in cross-border cases involving Australian intended parents, the provisions of the federal Family Law Act 1975 on parenting orders are relied upon far more frequently than state legislation on parentage orders or state/territorial adoption legislation.

Enforceability of the Surrogacy Arrangement

The principal clause of the surrogacy arrangement, ie the obligation of the surrogate mother to hand the child over to the intended parents, is unenforceable in the UK and all Australian jurisdictions. The obligation of the intended parents to hand over any payment to the surrogate cannot be enforced in the UK; however, it is enforceable in most Australian jurisdictions.[104]

b. Pre-Approval Required

The category of countries operating the pre-approval system includes Greece, Israel, South Africa, Australia (Western Australia and Victoria), New Zealand and some US states (eg Virginia and New Hampshire).[105] In these jurisdictions, a

---

[100] See section IV. below.
[101] See ch 23 of this book.
[102] See ch 2 of this book.
[103] *Ibid.*
[104] *Ibid.*
[105] The key pieces of legislation through which surrogacy is regulated in these jurisdictions are: Act no 3089/2002 on Medically Assisted Reproduction, and Act no 3305/2005 on Application of Medically Assisted Reproduction in Greece; the Embryo Carrying Agreement Act (Agreement Authorization & Status of the Newborn Child) 5756-1996 in Israel; Ch 19 of the Children's Act 38 of 2005, with effect from 1 April 2010, in South Africa; the Surrogacy Act 2008 (WA) in Western Australia; the Assisted

surrogacy arrangement must be approved by a court or a committee prior to the fertility procedure, to confirm compliance with the requirements of the legislation.[106] If the approval is granted, the parties are authorised to proceed with the arrangement.

Legal Parenthood

Save for New Zealand and the two Australian jurisdictions, the rules regarding legal parenthood in surrogacy cases are strikingly different from the rules in the countries which do not require a pre-approval of a surrogacy arrangement.[107] Generally, the official approval of the surrogacy arrangement will result in an automatic acquisition of legal parenthood by the intended parents from the moment of the birth of the child.[108] The situation is slightly different in Israel, where a child born as a result of a surrogacy arrangement does not have a legal parent upon birth but only an appointed guardian (a welfare officer). The intended parents have to initiate proceedings for a parenting decree within seven days following the birth. The parenting decree will normally be granted (unless the child's best interests justify a different decision).[109]

In the two Australian states that fall within the 'pre-approval' category (ie Western Australia and Victoria), the rules on legal parenthood are the same as they are in those Australian jurisdictions where no pre-approval of a surrogacy arrangement is required (see above). In summary, the legal mother of a child born through surrogacy in Western Australia or Victoria is always, at birth, the surrogate mother, whether or not she is also the genetic mother. Nevertheless, the legislation provides for a procedure for a transfer of legal parenthood to the intended parents. This procedure is called the 'parentage order application'. An alternative method through which legal parenthood may be transferred in these jurisdictions is adoption. Another choice for the intended parents is to apply for

---

Reproductive Treatment Act 2008 (Vic) in Australia (Victoria); the Human Assisted Reproductive Technology Act 2004 in New Zealand; RSA §§ 168-B:1 to -B:32 (2007) in the US state of New Hampshire; and Va Code Ann §§ 20-156 to -165 (2007) in the US state of Virginia. For further reading, see eg C Shalev, 'Halakha and Patriarchal Motherhood—An Anatomy of the New Israeli Surrogacy Law' (1998) 32 *Israeli Law Review* 51; J Carbone, 'Law, Politics, Religion and the Creation of Norms for Market Transactions: A Review of the Birth of Surrogacy in Israel by D Kelly Weisberg' (2005-2006) 39 *Family Law Quarterly* 789; D Papadopoulou-Klamaris, 'Medically-Assisted Reproduction in Greek Law' (2008) 61 *Revue hellénique de droit international* 521.

[106] Judicial approval is required, eg, in Greece, South Africa, the US (Virginia and New Hampshire). In Israel, the surrogacy arrangement must be approved by a State-appointed seven-member committee composed of medical specialists, a psychologist, a social worker, a legal specialist and a clergy representative of the parties' religion. In Australia, the surrogacy arrangement must be authorised by the Western Australian Reproductive Treatment Council in Western Australia and the Victorian Patient Review Panel in Victoria. In New Zealand, a prior ethics approval of a surrogacy arrangement by the Ethics Committee on Assisted Reproductive Technology is required.

[107] In particular, Greece, South Africa, Israel and US (Virginia).

[108] Eg Greece, South Africa and US (Virginia) (nevertheless, in cases of traditional surrogacy, the surrogate mother can terminate the contract within the first six months of pregnancy).

[109] See ch 14 of this book.

a 'parental order', the effect of which, however, is not the transfer of legal parent-hood but only a determination of parental responsibility.

In New Zealand, the rule on legal parenthood at birth is the same as in the Australian jurisdictions, ie the surrogate mother is regarded as the legal mother. The only method to create full legal parenthood in a surrogacy case in New Zealand is through adoption. Alternatively, the intended parents can seek a guardianship or a parenting order to obtain parental responsibility in relation to the child.

ii. All Forms of Surrogacy Remain Unregulated (neither Expressly Banned nor Expressly Permitted)

Countries where surrogacy remains unregulated include, for example, Belgium, Hungary, the Czech Republic, The Netherlands, Ireland, Japan, Brazil, Argentina, Venezuela, Mexico (States of Coahuila, Mexico City), Guatemala, Spain, Australia (Northern Territory) and some US states (eg Minnesota and Wisconsin). These countries neither expressly ban nor allow surrogacy; nevertheless, any surrogacy arrangement (commercial or altruistic) would be considered void and unenforceable.[110]

a. Commercial Surrogacy

Some of these jurisdictions criminalise commercial surrogacy arrangements.[111] In Ireland, for example, commercial surrogacy would violate section 2(2) of the Criminal Law (Human Trafficking Act 2008), which criminalises the selling of a child, or offering or exposing the child for sale, or inviting the making of an offer to purchase a child.[112] Human trafficking laws would be violated by commercial surrogacy in The Netherlands too.[113] In the Czech Republic, commercial surrogacy would amount not only to child trafficking under section 168 of the Criminal

---

[110] Either by an express provision (eg arts 489 and 491 of the Civil Code of the Mexican State of Coahuilla; art 338 of the Civil Code of the Mexico City; and art 10 of the Spanish Act on ART—Ley 14/2006, sobre técnicas de reproducción humana asistida, BOE no 126, 27 May 2007), or under general principles of law (Ireland, the Czech Republic, Argentina, Brazil, Hungary, Venezuela, Belgium, The Netherlands). See chs 16, 13, 6, 1, 4, 11, 25, 15 and 3 of this book, respectively. For further reading on Japan and the US, see Y Semba *et al*, 'Surrogacy: Donor Conception Regulation in Japan' (2010) 24 *Bioethics* 348; and R Rao, 'Surrogacy Law in the United States: The Outcome of Ambivalence' in R Cook and others (eds), *Surrogate Motherhood: International Perspectives* (Oxford, Hart Publishing, 2003) 23, at 26–28.

[111] In contrast, in other countries where surrogacy remains unregulated, it is unclear whether surrogacy would amount to a criminal act. This is the case, eg, in Japan, where commercial surrogacy would 'probably be considered a criminal offence', or in Hungary, where even altruistic surrogacy could potentially amount to a criminal act of an 'Illegal Use of Human Body' or of the 'Change of the Family Status'; however, the relevant provisions of the Criminal Code have not yet been tested in the context of surrogacy. See chs 15 and 11 of this book, respectively.

[112] See ch 13 of this book.

[113] See ch 17 of this book.

Code, but also to the crime of 'entrusting of a child into the care of another for the purposes of paid adoption' under section 169 of the Criminal Code.[114]

b. Altruistic Surrogacy and Legal Parenthood

A few of the countries falling within this category have recorded isolated occurrences of altruistic surrogacy carried out by specialised medical facilities.[115] In the absence of regulation of altruistic surrogacy by legislation, internal guidelines of these clinics[116] or other relevant guidelines[117] normally apply to regulate the procedure. Legal parenthood in these altruistic surrogacy cases is established through the application of general parentage rules. This means that the woman who gives birth to the child is regarded as the legal mother of the child.[118] If the surrogate mother is married, her husband is viewed as the legal father of the child.[119] Some countries have a specific provision for pregnancies achieved with the use of ART, ie the husband of the surrogate mother is regarded as the legal father if he consented to the fertility procedure.[120] If the intended father is genetically related to the child, the intended parents might under certain conditions be able to obtain legal parenthood using provisions on determination of paternity (intended father) and adoption legislation (intended mother).[121] In particular, if the surrogate mother is

---

[114] See ch 6 of this book.

[115] Eg the Czech Republic and Japan. It is estimated that annually approximately 15 surrogate pregnancies are facilitated by IVF clinics in the Czech Republic; nevertheless, only one clinic openly admits to offering surrogacy services. The clinic requires that the intended mother provide her own genetic material (see ch 6 of this book). In Japan, only one doctor openly admits to offering surrogacy services (see ch 15 of this book).

[116] Eg the Czech Republic, Japan and Belgium. See chs 6, 15 and 3 of this book, respectively.

[117] Eg in Ireland, clinics operate under the guidelines of the Medical Council of Ireland. In Brazil, surrogacy is regulated by the Federal Medical Board Resolution on Assisted Reproductive Technology. The Resolution contains a detailed regulation of surrogacy, including, eg, requirements that the intended mother is the egg donor, that there is a medical need for surrogacy, and that the surrogate and the intended mother are close relatives (although regional authorities have discretion to relax this requirement). In The Netherlands, only one medical centre offers surrogacy, and the procedure is carried out in accordance with relevant ministerial guidelines and the Guidelines on IVF-surrogacy issued by the Dutch Society for Obstetrics and Gynaecology. See chs 13, 4 and 17 of this book, respectively.

[118] Eg Argentina (Art 242 of the Civil Code), Brazil (Art 1597 of the Civil Code), the Czech Republic (s 50a of the Family Act), Venezuela (Art 201 of the Civil Code), Guatemala (Art 199 of the Civil Code), the Civil Code of Japan, Spain (Art 10 of the Act on ART—Ley 14/2006, sobre técnicas de reproducción humana asistida, BOE no 126, 27 May 2007, and Art 116 of the Civil Code), Belgium (Art 312 para 1 of the Civil Code), The Netherlands (Art 1:198 of the Civil Code) and Mexico (Mexico City) (Art 340 of the Civil Code). Current Hungarian legislation is not clear on the issue of legal motherhood; nevertheless, a new Hungarian Civil Code (not in force yet) expressly provides that the woman who bore the child is to be treated as the legal mother (see ch 11 of this book).

[119] Eg Argentina (Art 243 of the Civil Code), Brazil (Art 1597 of the Civil Code), the Czech Republic (s 51 of the Family Act), Venezuela (Art 201 of the Civil Code), Guatemala (Art 199 of the Civil Code), Spain (Art 116 of the Civil Code), Belgium (Art 315 of the Civil Code), The Netherlands (Art 1:199(a) of the Civil Code), Mexico (Mexico City) (Arts 324ff of the Civil Code).

[120] Eg Brazil (Art 1597 of the Civil Code).

[121] This appears to be possible, eg, in Brazil, the Czech Republic, Argentina, Venezuela, Japan, Spain and Mexico (Mexico City).

married, her husband may be able to surrender or contest his paternity.[122] If the surrogate mother is not married, or her husband has surrendered or contested his paternity, the paternity of the intended father may be established.[123] The intended mother may then be able to adopt the child through spousal adoption.[124]

Nevertheless, alternative avenues to achieve the transfer of legal parenthood may be available in some jurisdictions.[125]

c. Trend Towards Regulation

In some of these jurisdictions, legal regulation of surrogacy is currently being considered.[126] In Belgium, for example, a number of alternative legislative proposals on surrogacy have been introduced since early 2012, including a proposal to criminalise commercial surrogacy, a proposal to modify the existing law on affiliation, or a proposal to modify both affiliation and adoption laws to accommodate legal parentage arising from surrogacy. In the Czech Republic, the new Draft Civil Code contains some provisions to accommodate altruistic surrogacy arrangements; however, no specific rules on affiliation are contemplated.[127] In Argentina, there are currently four Bills specifically on surrogacy pending at the national level. Of these, three take a favourable stand on altruistic surrogacy, whilst the fourth Bill expressly prohibits the practice.[128]

---

[122] In the Czech Republic, eg, the husband of the surrogate mother may surrender his paternity by declaration. In Brazil, he can prove in a court procedure that he is not the genetic father and the birth certificate will be amended to reflect that fact. In Argentina, the surrogate mother's husband can 'contest his paternal affiliation based on the lack of biological link. The same applies to Venezuela where there is also an additional ground for the contestation of paternity—ie the lack of consent to the fertility procedure on the side of the surrogate's husband.

[123] In the Czech Republic, for example, the intended father can become the legal father of the child through a consenting declaration of paternity made together with the surrogate mother. In Brazil, the intended father can declare his paternity at the Registry, or initiate a paternity investigation before a court (to be established by means of DNA). In Argentina, courts have interpreted provisions granting the surrogate mother's husband the right to contest paternity (Arts 250 and 259 of the Civil Code) as implicitly acknowledging the right of the genetic intended father to recognise the child as his own.

[124] Eg the Czech Republic (certain restrictions apply, however; in particular, the surrogate mother must not be a relative of the intended mother and the intended parents must be a married heterosexual couple); Brazil; Argentina; Venezuela; and Spain. It has been suggested that as a matter of practice domestic surrogacy arrangements are also implemented 'beneath the veil of adoption' in Hungary (see ch 11 of this book).

[125] Eg a divestment of parental responsibility of the surrogate mother and her husband, and a subsequent joint adoption of the child by the intended parents (The Netherlands—see ch 17 of this book); and a voluntary recognition of maternity by the intended mother/a judicial establishment of maternity initiated by the intended mother (both possible only if there is no mother listed on the birth certificate) (Belgium—ch 3 of this book).

[126] This is often in response to growing practical problems domestic authorities have to face in cross-border surrogacy cases in the absence of effective regulation. Eg in Ireland, it has been reported that there are currently at least 15 children, born through surrogacy abroad, stranded in their country of birth. C O'Brien, 'Surrogacy Guidelines to be Issued Next Month' *The Irish Times*, 11 November 2011, available at <www.irishtimes.com/newspaper/ireland/2011/1123/1224308000862.html>.

[127] See ch 6 of this book, noting that the birth rule will remain the sole principle of the determination of maternity even after the adoption of the new Civil Code.

[128] See ch 1 of this book.

C. Anti-Surrogacy Jurisdictions

The term 'anti-surrogacy jurisdictions' refers to countries where surrogacy in both its forms (ie altruistic and commercial) is outlawed.[129] This category of jurisdictions includes, for example, Germany, France, China, Australia (Tasmania), certain US states (eg Michigan, New York and the District of Columbia) and to some extent the Mexican State of Queretaro.[130]

The policy approach behind the ban on all forms of surrogacy includes arguments such as:

(a) surrogacy violates the child's and the surrogate mother's human dignity, reducing them to a mere object of a contract;[131]
(b) surrogacy leads to an undesirable situation of 'split motherhood';[132]
(c) surrogacy is contrary to the interests of children;[133]
(d) neither the human body nor the civil status of persons may be subject to private arrangements;[134] and
(e) if allowed, surrogacy would result in legal, social and ethical chaos.[135]

i. Enforceability

Surrogacy arrangements (both altruistic and commercial) are void and unenforceable in these jurisdictions as they violate the statutory prohibition of surrogacy.[136] Commercial surrogacy arrangements are void also on the ground that they offend public policy.[137]

---

[129] In Germany, eg, surrogacy is expressly prohibited by the Embryo Protection Act 1990, which bans medical interventions used for reproduction regarded as 'abusive' or leading to 'split' motherhood. Certain prohibitive provisions related to surrogacy may be found also in the Adoption Placement Act 2001. In China, surrogacy is outlawed by the Administrative Measures for Assisted Human Reproductive Technology 2001 and the Ethical Principles of Assisted Human Reproductive Technology and Human Sperm Bank 2003. In the Mexican State of Queretaro, surrogacy is prohibited by Art 400 of the Civil Code. In France, surrogacy is banned under the Bioethics Act 1994 (Loi no 94-653 du juillet 1994 relative au respect du corps humain). See chs 8, 5 and 16 of this book, respectively.

[130] It appears that in Queretaro (Mexico) only surrogacy arrangements where there is no genetic link between the child and the intended parents are outlawed (see ch 16 of this book). See also B McMahon, 'The Science Behind Surrogacy: Why New York Should Rethink Its Surrogacy Contract Laws' (2011) 21 *Albany Law Journal of Science and Technology* 359; and Rao, above n 110, at 24–26.

[131] Eg Germany.

[132] *Ibid.*

[133] China. It is believed that the interests of children as the weaker party should be of paramount concern and should far outweigh the interests of any adult party. See ch 5 of this book.

[134] France (see ch 7 of this book).

[135] China (see ch 5 of this book).

[136] See eg, chs 8 and 5 of this book. Art 16-7 of the French Civil Code expressly provides: 'Any agreements relating to procreation or gestation for a third party are void.' See ch 7 of this book.

[137] *Ibid.*

ii. Legal Parenthood

If, despite the ban, a surrogacy arrangement is entered into, general rules on legal parenthood will apply. This will mean that the surrogate mother will be regarded as the legal mother and her husband (if married) will be viewed as the legal father of the child.[138] It might, nevertheless, be possible for the surrogate's husband to contest paternity and for the intended father subsequently to acknowledge his paternity[139] (or have his paternity established by a court[140]). The intended father would also be able to acknowledge his paternity/have his paternity judicially established if the surrogate mother was unmarried. The intended mother might then be able to adopt the child. This can, however, prove problematic, as adoption legislation might be ineffective in cases where 'the adoptive parents took part in a procurement which is unlawful or contrary to public policy'.[141]

Interestingly, in the Australian state of Tasmania, the ban on surrogacy does not affect the operability of adoption legislation in (at least altruistic) surrogacy cases. Quite the contrary, the Surrogacy Contracts Act 1993 (Tas), which prohibits all forms of surrogacy, expressly states that it 'does not affect the operation of any law relating to the adoption or guardianship of children'.[142] Although the issue has not been tested before a court, it seems to be possible for the court to 'make an adoption order in favour of the intended parents on the basis of a family relationship'.[143]

iii. Criminalisation

In most of the anti-surrogacy jurisdictions, it is a criminal offence to act as an intermediary in a surrogacy arrangement and/or medically to facilitate surrogacy arrangements (altruistic or commercial).[144]

III. Statistical Survey of Cross-border Surrogacy Arrangements: Anecdotal Evidence

Statistical data on cross-border surrogacy arrangements are scarce at best. The obvious reason is that this information is extremely difficult to obtain, in particular

---

[138] Eg Germany (ss 1591 and 1592(1) of the Civil Code respectively).

[139] Eg Germany (s 1592(2) of the Civil Code). An acknowledgement of paternity appears to be the only avenue to 'circumvent' the ban on surrogacy in France (see ch 7 of this book).

[140] Eg Germany (s 1592(3) of the Civil Code).

[141] See ch 8 of this book. German courts have applied a strict standard based on the view that where the intended father is recognised as the legal parent, adoption by the intended mother is not indispensable. Adoption would be granted only if absolutely necessary for the child's well-being (*ibid*).

[142] Surrogacy Contracts Act 1993 (Tas), s 8. See ch 2 of this book.

[143] See ch 2 of this book. Only one case involving Tasmanian intended parents has been reported thus far (*Lowe & Barry* [2001] FamCA 625). In this case the intended parents did not apply for adoption but opted for an application for a parenting order before the Family Court under the Federal Family Law Act 1975. For analysis of the effect of a parenting order, see section II.B.i.a., 'Alternative Solutions', above. See also ch 2 of this book.

[144] Eg France, China and Germany.

due to the illicit nature of these arrangements in many jurisdictions, the lack of a central 'registry' of such arrangements at national levels and the unwillingness of private intermediaries to share information for research purposes. All of these problems were experienced by the authors of the present study. As a result, data obtained through the present statistical survey have to be considered as anecdotal evidence only and no general conclusions can be derived from them.

A. Methodology

The aim of the survey was to map the magnitude of the problem and current patterns in international surrogacy. The survey was not intended to be exhaustive; rather, it was aimed at demonstrating the seriousness of the problem and the pressing need for a legislative response to international surrogacy. Given the total lack of statistical data on international surrogacy, it is hoped that the survey will, nevertheless, push the level of knowledge forward.

A detailed questionnaire was drafted and sent out via e-mail to approximately 80 surrogacy agencies, fertility clinics and legal practitioners from a variety of 'surrogacy-friendly' jurisdictions, in particular the United States, India and Ukraine. Contact e-mail addresses and the information that the particular agency/clinic/legal practitioner (hereafter 'the intermediary') offered services in the area of cross-border surrogacy were obtained from their respective websites. The questionnaire sought to obtain information on the numbers of cross-border surrogacy cases handled by the intermediary between 1 January 2006 and 31 August 2011; information on the profile of the intended parent(s) (ie country of residence, nationality, age, sexual orientation and marital status); information on the profile of the surrogate mother (ie country of residence, nationality, age, marital status and information on whether she has children of her own); and information about the surrogacy arrangement itself (ie date of the receipt of the application, the type of surrogacy and the number of children born as a result of the arrangement). The final part of the questionnaire asked for information on legal problems that arose in relation to the respective arrangements. These were divided into 'enforcement problems' and 'other legal problems'. The 'enforcement problems' sub-section was broken down into 'enforcement problems on the side of the intended parents' and 'enforcement problems on the side of the surrogate mother'. This section of the questionnaire also sought the outcome of the respective enforcement problem and was split into 'procedural aspects' and 'substantive aspects'. The 'other legal problems' sub-section was divided into 'legal problems arising from the conflict of laws' and 'other legal problems arising at a later stage'. The former comprised 'immigration problems', 'legal parenthood' and 'other'; and the latter included 'custody dispute between the parties', 'access dispute between the parties' and 'other'. To eliminate potential personal data protection concerns, the intermediaries were asked to ensure that information provided in response to the questionnaire was anonymised. The questionnaire was designed in English.

The questionnaire consisted of five main questions. The first two questions contained five sub-questions each; the third question contained three sub-questions; the fourth question contained four sub-questions; and the last question contained six sub-questions. Nine of the sub-questions were a simple tick box; the remaining 14 sub-questions needed specific information in response.

The survey included all cross-border surrogacy applications dealt with by the intermediary between 1 January 2006 and 31 August 2011, irrespective of when the case was closed.

Only 10 intermediaries responded positively to the request to participate in the research. Of these, however, nine were unable to complete the questionnaire due to incomplete records and/or a lack of financial/personal resources. Consequently, only one legal practitioner, based in the United States, kindly completed the questionnaire. He is referred to below as 'Participant 1' and his responses are analysed in section III.B.i., 'Long questionnaire results'. To complement the data obtained from Participant 1 through the questionnaire, a personal interview was later conducted with this participant. Information obtained during this interview has been incorporated into the 'Long questionnaire results' analysis.

Of the nine intermediaries who reacted positively to the research study but were unable to complete the original questionnaire, four agreed to provide at least some brief information on numbers of cross-border surrogacy arrangements handled by them within a specified period of time, and on the countries of residence of intended parents involved in these cases. A new questionnaire was therefore drafted for this purpose, consisting of two questions only, each of which required specific information in response. This questionnaire is referred to as the 'short questionnaire', and responses to this questionnaire are analysed below in section III.B.ii., 'Short questionnaire results'. Like the 'long questionnaire', the 'short questionnaire' was also designed in English. The cut-off period for this survey, however, varied from 31 August 2010, through 31 December 2010 to 31 August 2011, depending on when the questionnaire was completed by the particular intermediary. The survey included all cross-border surrogacy applications dealt with by the intermediary between 1 January 2006 and 31 August 2010/31 December 2010/31 August 2011 (as applicable), irrespective of when the case was closed. The intermediaries that participated in this survey may be described as follows:

(a) Participant 1—a US-based surrogacy agency (cut-off date: 31 August 2011);

(b) Participant 2—a US-based surrogacy agency (cut-off date: 31 December 2010);

(c) Participant 3—a US-based surrogacy agency operating in India (cut-off date: 31 August 2010);

(d) Participant 4—an India-based surrogacy agency (cut-off date: 31 August 2010).

During the course of the research study, the authors were approached by a French non-profit organisation which seeks to promote legalisation of gestational surrogacy in France, with a kind offer of assistance in the empirical part of the research study. The membership of this organisation includes in particular persons who have become parents through cross-border surrogacy. A new questionnaire was therefore drafted to be circulated among the members of this organisation. The questionnaire was modelled on the 'long questionnaire' but was slightly more detailed than its predecessor. In particular, two new questions were added: a question on a family relationship between the surrogate mother and the intended parents; and a question on payments to the surrogate mother. The organisation then kindly translated the questionnaire into French and distributed it among its members. Altogether, 13 responses were received. These responses are analysed below in section III.B.iii, 'Individual intended parents' responses'.

B. Findings of the Survey

i. Long Questionnaire Results

a. Number of Applications

As Table 1 below shows, between 2006 and 31 August 2010, Participant 1 handled 31 cross-border surrogacy cases. A steady increase of an average proportion of

Table 1: Number of Applications

Number of Applications		
	Number	Per cent
2006	3	10%
2007	6	19%
2008	9	29%
2009	11	35%
2010 (until 31 August)	2	6%
Total	**31**	**100%**

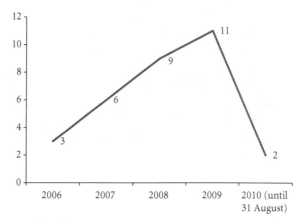

Figure 8: Number of Applications

8 per cent was recorded between 2006 and 2009.[145] Accordingly, the numbers of applications rose from three in 2006 to 11 in 2009. (See Figure 8.)

b. Country of Residence of the Intended Parents

The majority of intended parents (60 per cent) came from Europe, in particular Germany (26 per cent), Italy (16 per cent), France and Spain (6 per cent each) and the UK and Norway (3 per cent each). At 19 per cent and 16 per cent respectively, residents of Israel and Canada also accounted for large proportions of intended parents. (See Table 2 and Figure 9.)

Table 2: Intended Parents' Country of Residence

IPs' Country of Residence		
	Number	**Per cent**
Germany	8	26%
Israel	6	19%
Canada	5	16%
Italy	5	16%
France	2	6%
Spain	2	6%
United Kingdom	1	3%
Peru	1	3%
Norway	1	3%
Total	**31**	**~100%**

[145] Unexpectedly, figures for the first part of the year 2010 appear to be showing a decreasing trend. Nevertheless, it is suggested that not much weight is attached to this fact as comprehensive data are not available for 2010.

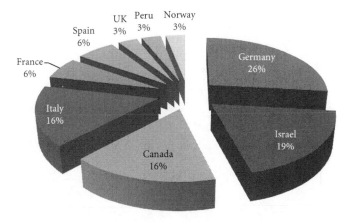

Figure 9: Intended Parents' Country of Residence

c. Nationality of the Intended Parents

In all but one of the cases, the nationality of the intended parents corresponded to their respective countries of residence. The exception was a Canadian couple who, although resident in Canada, were not Canadian citizens. Their nationality was, however, not known. This finding suggests that intended parents do not tend to seek a more favourable forum through a change of their country of residence prior to commissioning a surrogacy arrangement abroad. (See Table 3 and Figure 10.)

Table 3: Nationality of the Intended Parents

Nationality of the IPs[*]		
	Number	Per cent
German	8	27%
Israeli	6	20%
Italian	5	17%
Canadian	4	13%
French	2	7%
Spanish	2	7%
British	1	3%
Norwegian	1	3%
Peruvian	1	3%
Total	**30**	**100%**

[*] In one case the nationality of the intended parents was not available.

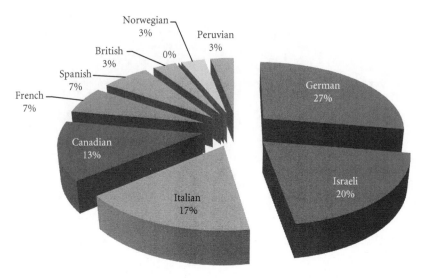

Figure 10: Nationality of the Intended Parents

d. Intended Parents' Age Range

At 35 per cent and 26 per cent respectively, the majority of the intended parents were in their early 40s and late 30s. This finding is consistent with a generally accepted assumption that most intended parents would have struggled with infertility for many years and would have chosen surrogacy only after all other alternatives have failed. Intended parents in their late 40s accounted for 6 per cent of all intended parents. Interestingly, 10 per cent of intended parents were over 50, and the same proportion was below 30. Nevertheless, there were no intended parents aged below 25. (See Table 4 and Figure 11.)

Table 4: Intended Parents' Age Range

IPs' Age Range		
	Number	**Per cent**
Below 25	0	0%
25–30	3	10%
31–35	4	13%
36–40	8	26%
41–45	11	35%
46–50	2	6%
Over 50	3	10%
Total	**31**	**100%**

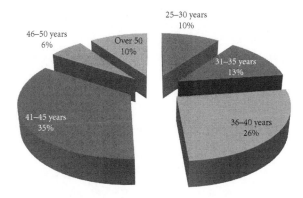

Figure 11: Intended Parents' Age Range

e. Intended Parents' Sexual Orientation

The vast majority of intended parents (68 per cent) were heterosexual couples. These were followed by homosexual gay couples, who accounted for 16 per cent of all intended parents. In four cases (13 per cent), the intended parent was a heterosexual single person. Lastly, in one case (3 per cent) a surrogacy arrangement was commissioned by a bisexual single parent. (See Table 5 and Figure 12.)

Table 5: Intended Parents' Sexual Orientation

IPs' Sexual Orientation		
	Number	Per cent
Heterosexual couple	21	68%
Homosexual gay couple	5	16%
Heterosexual single parent	4	13%
Bisexual single parent	1	3%
Total	**31**	**100%**

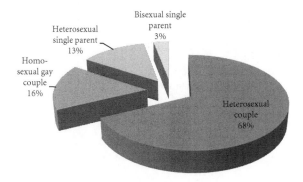

Figure 12: Intended Parents' Sexual Orientation

f. Intended Parents' Country of Residence and Sexual Orientation

Of the five homosexual gay couples, four were Israeli residents. The remaining gay couple were Italian residents. There was one heterosexual and one bisexual single parent from Italy. Lastly, one heterosexual single parent each came from Israel, France and Peru. (See Table 6.)

Table 6: Intended Parents' Country of Residence and Sexual Orientation

Count	IPs' Country of Residence and IPs' Sexual Orientation				
	IPs' Sexual Orientation				
	Heterosexual couple	Homosexual gay couple	Heterosexual single parent	Bisexual single parent	Total
Italy	2	1	1	1	5
Germany	8	0	0	0	8
Canada	5	0	0	0	5
Israel	1	4	1	0	6
Spain	2	0	0	0	2
France	1	0	1	0	2
United Kingdom	1	0	0	0	1
Peru	0	0	1	0	1
Norway	1	0	0	0	1
Total	21	5	4	1	31

g. Intended Parents' Marital Status

The majority of intended parents were married couples (65 per cent). Cohabitating couples accounted for 19 per cent of all intended parents. Marital status was not applicable in relation to five cases (16 per cent) as these concerned single intended parents. (See Table 7 and Figure 13.)

Table 7: Intended Parents' Marital Status

IPs' Marital Status		
	Number	Per cent
Married	20	65%
Cohabitation	6	19%
N/A	5	16%
Total	31	100%

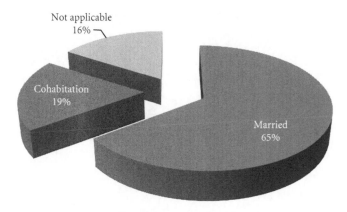

Figure 13: Intended Parents' Marital Status

h. Surrogate Mother's Country of Residence and Nationality

In all cases, the surrogate mother was a US national with US residency status. (See Tables 8 and 9.)

Table 8: Surrogate Mother's Country of Residence

SM Country of Residence		
	Number	Per cent
USA	31	100%
Total	**31**	**100%**

Table 9: Nationality of the Surrogate Mother

Nationality of the SM		
	Number	Per cent
American	31	100%
Total	**31**	**100%**

i. Surrogate Mother's Age Range

Interestingly, the highest proportion of surrogate mothers (42 per cent) were aged between 36 and 40. This appears to be above the ideal childbearing age for a traditional surrogate, but possibly is reasonable for a gestational surrogate.[146] The

---

[146] See section III.B.i.l. below.

Table 10: Surrogate Mother's Age Range

SM Age Range		
	Number	Per cent
Below 25	0	0%
25–30	9	29%
31–35	9	29%
36–40	13	42%
Over 40	0	0%
Total	**31**	**100%**

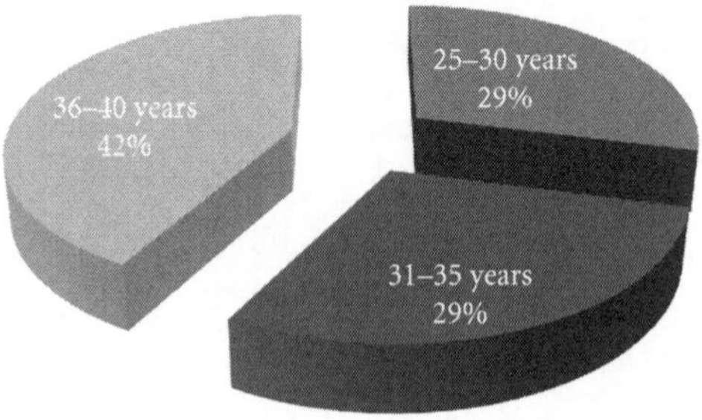

Figure 14: Surrogate Mother's Age Range

remaining 58 per cent were split evenly between the age categories of '25–30' and '31–35' (29 per cent each). No surrogate mothers were younger than 25 years or older than 40 years. (See Table 10 and Figure 14.)

j. Surrogate Mother's Marital Status

The vast majority of surrogate mothers (23, 74 per cent) were married. Only one surrogate mother (3 per cent) was divorced. The remaining 23 per cent of surrogate mothers were single. (See Table 11 and Figure 15.)

Table 11: Surrogate Mother's Marital Status

SM Marital Status		
	Number	Per cent
Married	23	74%
Single	7	23%
Divorced	1	3%
Widowed	0	0%
Total	**31**	**100%**

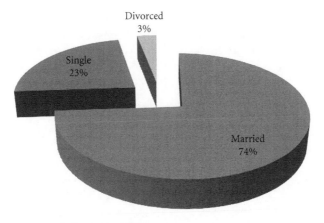

Figure 15: Surrogate Mother's Marital Status

k. Surrogate Mother: Children of Her Own

In all cases, the surrogate had had a child of her own before she became a surrogate mother. (See Table 12.)

Table 12: Surrogate Mother: Children of Her Own

	SM Children of Her Own	
	Number	Per cent
Yes	31	100%
No	0	0%
Total	**31**	**100%**

l. Type of Surrogacy

All arrangements were gestational, meaning that the surrogate mother was not genetically related to the child in any of the cases. In 13 cases (42 per cent), the ovum was supplied by the intended mother. In all of these cases, the sperm was provided by the intended father. Consequently, there was a full genetic link between the child and both intended parents in 42 per cent of the cases. Nevertheless, the highest proportion of applications involved a donor egg fertilised by the intended father's sperm (15, 48 per cent). In one of these cases (3 per cent), the egg donor was non-anonymous, whereas in the remaining 14

Katarina Trimmings and Paul Beaumont

cases (45 per cent) the ovum was donated by an anonymous donor. In one case (3 per cent) both donated egg and donated sperm were used for fertilisation. The remaining two cases (6 per cent) concerned gay intended parents, and in both cases an anonymous donor egg was fertilised by both intended fathers' sperm. (See Table 13 and Figure 16.)

Table 13: Type of Surrogacy

Type of Surrogacy		
	Number	Per cent
IF sperm + donated egg (anonymous)	14	45%
IF sperm + IM egg	13	42%
Other*	2	6%
IF sperm + donated egg (non-anonymous)	1	3%
Donated sperm + donated egg (anonymous)	1	3%
IM egg + donated sperm (anonymous)	0	0%
IM egg + donated sperm (non-anonymous)	0	0%
Donated sperm + donated egg (non-anonymous)	0	0%
IF sperm + SM egg	0	0%
Total	**31**	**~100%**

* Both intended fathers' sperm + donor egg (anonymous).

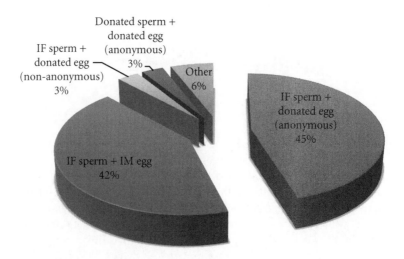

Figure 16: Type of Surrogacy

m. Intended Parents' Sexual Orientation and Type of Surrogacy

As Table 14 below indicates, all five single intended parents (heterosexual and bisexual) were male, and all of them supplied their own sperm for fertilisation of an anonymously donated ovum. The same scenario applied to all five homosexual gay couples. Of these, in three cases sperm was provided by one of the intended fathers, and in two cases both intended fathers' sperm was used. In relation to heterosexual couples, 13 out of 21 supplied their own sperm and ovum. In seven cases, the intended father's sperm and a donor ovum were used for fertilisation (in six cases the ovum was donated anonymously and in one case the ovum donor was known to the intended parents). Lastly, one heterosexual couple used both donor egg and donor sperm for fertilisation.

Table 14: Intended Parents' Sexual Orientation and Type of Surrogacy

Count		IPs' Sexual Orientation and Type of Surrogacy				
		IPs' Sexual Orientation				
		Heterosexual couple	Homosexual couple-gay	Heterosexual single parent	Bisexual single parent	Total
Type of surrogacy	IF sperm + IM egg	13	0	0	0	**13**
	IF sperm + donated egg (anonymous)	6	3	4	1	**14**
	IF sperm + donated egg (non-anonymous)	1	0	0	0	**1**
	Donated sperm + donated egg (anonymous)	1	0	0	0	**1**
	Other[*]	0	2	0	0	**2**
Total		**21**	**5**	**4**	**1**	**31**

[*] Both intended fathers' sperm + donor egg (anonymous).

n. Children Born as a Result of the Arrangement

At 32 per cent, the highest proportion of cases involved a single child. In 23 per cent of cases, twins were born as a result of the arrangement. The remaining 10 per cent concerned miscarriages or cases where the child was still to be born

(23 per cent) or embryos were just to be transferred to the surrogate mother (13 per cent). (See Table 15 and Figure 17.)

Table 15: Children Born as a Result of the Arrangement

Children Born as a Result of the Arrangement		
	Number	Per cent
One	10	32%
Two	7	23%
Miscarried	3	10%
To be born	7	23%
Embryos to be transferred	4	13%
Total	**31**	**~100%**

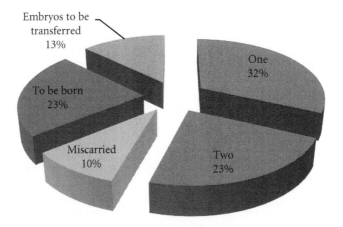

Figure 17: Children Born as a Result of the Arrangement

o. Surrogate Mother's age Range and Children Born as a Result of the Arrangement

Although there does not appear to be a correlation between the age of the surrogate mother and multiple pregnancies, there is some indication that surrogate mothers in their late 30s were more likely to miscarry than their younger counterparts. It must, however, be pointed out that the evidence is purely anecdotal and much weight cannot therefore be placed on it. (See Table 16.)

Table 16: Surrogate Mother's Age Range and Children Born as a Result of the Arrangement

SM Age Range and Children Born as a Result of the Arrangement					
Count			SM Age Range		Total
		25–30	31–35	36–40	
Children Born as a Result of the Arrangement	1	4	2	4	10
	2	1	3	3	7
	Miscarried	1	0	2	3
	To be born	3	3	1	7
	Embryos to be transferred	0	1	3	4
Total		9	9	13	31

p. Legal Aspects

Enforcement Problems

As Table 17 shows, no enforcement problems were reported by Participant 1.

The following information was provided by Participant 1 as complementary material during a personal interview with one of the authors:

(a) *Change of mind of the SM.* During a personal interview, Participant 1 expressed the view that enforcement problems due to a change of mind of the surrogate mother were very rare and that it was only because of publicity by the media that the public perceived these cases as a common result.[147]

(b) *Miscarriage.* Participant 1 noted that miscarriages occurred with some frequency, but in his practice had never resulted in legal problems. According to most surrogacy contracts in the US,[148] following a miscarriage the surrogate mother is free to withdraw or the intended parents are allowed to choose another surrogate. Normally, the surrogate mother would have received an embryo transfer fee (approximately $500) as a compensation for going through the embryo transfer. She would have also been reimbursed

---

[147] Interview with Participant 1, 1 September 2011.

[148] It must, however, be pointed out that there is no uniformity among the contracts in the US as there is no governmentally approved or other standard form. The quality of the contract depends on the experience and professional knowledge of the practitioner who drafts it. *Ibid.*

for any expenses incurred in travel, lost wages or day care for medical appointments.[149]

(c) *Abortion.* The question of abortion is dealt with specifically within a surrogacy contract, but as a practical matter had never occurred in any cross-border surrogacy cases handled by Participant 1. Participant 1 further stated that he had 'never had a surrogate [who] terminated pregnancy against the wishes of the intended parents, and [he had] to date never had a set of intended parents that have asked the carrier to terminate or selectively reduce a pregnancy'.[150]

(d) *Child born with birth defects.* In one case, a child was born with 'an apparent hearing loss'. The intended parents, a French couple, were 'nervous about receiving the child' as they perceived that 'there was not great support for deaf children in France'. Nevertheless, after being advised by Participant 1, who explained the details of their obligations under the surrogacy contract and the responsibility as the legal parents in the eyes of the relevant US law, they willingly took the child home and are currently raising it.

(e) *Multiple birth.* Participant 1 said that, in his practice, he had never encountered a cross-border case where more than a set of twins had been born. None of these multiple births had caused problems between the parties.[151]

(f) *Breakdown of the intended parents' relationship.* Participant 1 stated that he had 'never had a set of intended parents in a cross-border case that would have dissolved their relationship whilst surrogacy was pending'. Similarly, to his knowledge, 'none of them have done so afterwards'.[152]

(g) *Non-compliance with the financial aspects of the surrogacy arrangement by the intended parents.* Participant 1 had never encountered a case where the intended parents had not paid all of the bills and expenses that they were obligated to pay.

---

[149] The surrogate mother would, however, commonly not be entitled to any part of her fee until 56 days after the date of the embryo transfer. (The period of 56 days is the common period for miscarriage as established by medical statistics.) From that point forward, if the surrogate mother miscarries, she is entitled to a pro rated amount of her fee based on a number of days that she was pregnant to the total normal gestation. Accordingly, '[i]f she miscarries at for example nine weeks after 56 days then it's actually 63 days, she'll get 63 days percentage of the fee that she had negotiated because she has performed that much of her service'. Participant 1 pointed out that '[t]here is never any conflict over it, it is just calculated and agreed upon in the contract between the parties and it is very simple'. *Ibid.*

[150] *Ibid.*

[151] The number of embryos implanted to the surrogate mother is dealt with within the contract, which generally states that the number is to 'comply with the general practice of fertility physicians in the US'. This means that the average standard number of embryos is two in normal circumstances. In more specific terms, the contract states that 'for the protection of both sides of the contract, the surrogate agrees to receive a transfer of two embryos unless the attending physician recommends a different number' (this could be one, three or four). Nevertheless, in the latter case, the surrogate mother and the intended parents have to agree to that different number. Consequently, if the physician recommends three or four, and the surrogate is not comfortable with that, she cannot be coerced into receiving more embryos than she has agreed to in the contract. *Ibid.*

[152] *Ibid.*

(h) *Becoming aware of the legal problems they would face trying to bring the child to their country of residence and/or to acquire legal parenthood there.* In all cross-border cases dealt with by Participant 1, the intended parents had successfully returned to their home countries.[153] It appears that the intended parents were unaware of the legal problems they were likely to face when trying to get legal parenthood established in the country of birth recognised in their home country. Consequently, in none of the cases were these problems used by the intended parents as a basis not to receive the child and take it to their country.

Table 17: Enforcement Problems

Reason(s) for Enforcement Problems		Final Outcome	
On the Side of the Intended Parents	**On the Side of the Surrogate Mother**	**Procedural Aspect**	**Substantive Aspect**
a. Child born with birth defects **b.** Multiple birth **c.** Breakdown of the intended parents' relationship **d.** Non-compliance with the financial aspects of the surrogacy arrangement **e.** Becoming aware of the legal problems they would face trying to bring the child to their country of residence and/or to acquire legal parenthood there **f.** Other	**a.** Simply changed her mind as to handing the child over to the intended parents **b.** Miscarriage **c.** Abortion **d.** Other	**a.** Voluntary Settlement **b.** First instance court decision **c.** Second instance court decision **d.** Third instance court decision **e.** Other	**a.** Child to be looked after by the intended parents **b.** Child to be looked after by the surrogate mother **c.** Other arrangement
None	None	N/A	N/A

Other Legal Problems

The other legal problems that might have affected Participant 1 are set out below and in Table 18.

(a) *Immigration problems.* No immigration problems arose in any of the cross-border surrogacy cases dealt with by Participant 1. During the interview, Participant 1 expressed the view that this could be attributed to the US

---

[153] See 'Other legal problems' below.

Table 18: Other Legal Problems

Legal Problems Arising from the Conflict of Laws			Other Legal Problems Arising at a Later Stage		
Immigration Problems	Legal Parenthood	Other	Custody Dispute between the Parties	Access Dispute between the Parties	Other
None	See comment in (b) Legal parenthood	None	None	None	None

citizenship rules which enable the intended parents to obtain an American passport for the child. Participant 1 summed up the issue as follows:

> In none of the cases I have handled have the parents been unable to return to their home country, get through customs and return to their home. ... So there have never been any cases where the children would have been stuck in the US and unable to return to their country of origin.

Nevertheless, Participant 1 pointed out that there is a potential for immigration problems on the side of the intended parents if the child is born prematurely or with a health condition which requires a prolonged hospitalisation. The intended parents might then be at risk of expiry of their visas, which are usually visitor visas with the maximum duration of nine weeks. Participant 1 noted that it is the responsibility of the intended parents 'to plan the type of entry into the country to receive their child in a way that is as flexible as possible to accommodate for those possible unexpected outcomes'.

(b) *Legal parenthood.* Participant 1 has encountered no legal problems obtaining parentage orders reflecting the desired intended parentage in the US. The problems that have occurred related to parents who returned to their home country and sought to register their child, particularly in France and Germany. Participant 1 envisages that these problems will become more common 'now that the issue is being consciously registered by more and more national governments'.[154]

ii. Short Questionnaire Results

a. Number of Applications

As the tables and figures below show, generally, the Participants recorded a steady increase in the numbers of cross-border surrogacy arrangements dealt with over the period from 2006 to 2011 (as applicable).[155]

---

[154] Interview with Participant 1, 1 September 2011.

[155] An exception was Participant 1, year 2009, where a temporary decrease in the number of surrogacy arrangements from 26 in 2008 to 20 in 2009 was recorded. See Table 19 and Figure 18. Also,

Participants 1 and 2 (ie US-based agencies) both reported a sharp rise, from 4 in 2006 to 30 in 2010, and from 10 in 2006 to 68 in 2010 respectively, an increase of 7.5 and 6.8 times respectively. Similarly, the numbers of arrangements handled by Participants 3 and 4 (ie agencies operating in India) between 2006 and 2009 rose sharply from 0 in 2006 to 20 in 2009, and from 2 in 2006 to 16 in 2009 respectively. Moreover, in relation to Participant 3, compared with the year 2009, the figures for 2010 would have probably tripled by the end of that year, with 40 arrangements having been handled between 1 January and 31 August 2010.

Participant 1 (US-Based Agency)

Table 19: Number of Applications

Number of Applications		Number
Application Year	2006	4
	2007	7
	2008	26
	2009	20
	2010	30
	2011 (before 31 August)	48
	Total	**135**

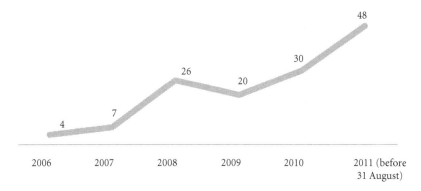

Figure 18: Number of Applications

with respect to Participant 4 there was no increase in 2007 as the number of cross-border cases dealt with within that year stayed the same as in 2006 (2 cases each). See Table 22 and Figure 21.

Participant 2 (US-Based Agency)

Table 20: Number of Applications

Number of Applications		
		Number
Receipt of the application	2006	10
	2007	12
	2008	36
	2009	58
	2010	68
	Total	**184**

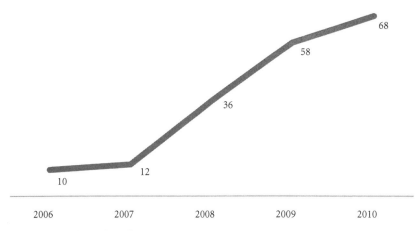

Figure 19: Number of Applications

Participant 3 (US-Based Agency Operating in India)

Table 21: Number of Applications

Number of Applications		
		Number
Receipt of the application	2006	0
	2007	0
	2008	7

(Continued)

Table 21: (*Continued*)

Number of Applications	
	Number
2009	20
2010 (before 31 August)	40
Total	**67**

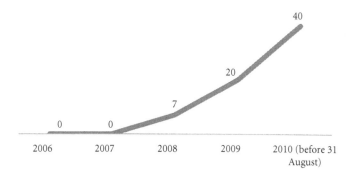

Figure 20: Number of Applications

Participant 4 (India-Based Agency)

Table 22: Number of Applications

Number of Applications		
		Number
Receipt of the application	2006	2
	2007	2
	2008	10
	2009	16
	2010 (before 31 August)	11
	Total	**41**

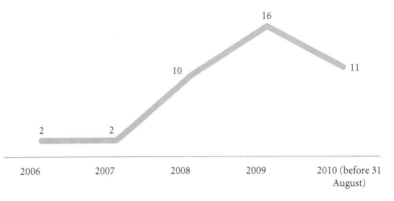

Figure 21: Number of Applications

b. Country of Residence of the Intended Parents

As the tables and figures below show, the countries of residence of the intended parents cover a wide variety of jurisdictions from different continents, including Europe, North America, Australasia and Africa.

According to the records of both Participant 1 and Participant 2, the United Kingdom and France ranked among the most common countries of residence of intended parents commissioning surrogacy in the US. In particular, the United Kingdom accounted for 89 per cent and 9 per cent respectively, and France accounted for 5 per cent and 20 per cent respectively. Participant 2 also recorded a significant volume of intended parents from Israel (20 per cent) and Sweden (13 per cent).

In relation to Participant 1, the remaining 6 per cent were spread among three other European countries—Ireland (3 per cent), Germany (2 per cent) and Spain (1 per cent). Participant 2 also recorded some applications from these countries—4 per cent, 3 per cent and 6 per cent respectively. Proportions of 4 per cent and 3 per cent were recorded by Participant 2 also in relation to The Netherlands and Switzerland (4 per cent each) and Belgium (3 per cent). Intended parents from Australia, Norway, Italy and Canada accounted for 2 per cent each. At 1 per cent each, the remaining 9 per cent was spread evenly among a variety of countries from across the globe, ie Europe (Slovakia, the Czech Republic, Iceland, Portugal and Denmark), Asia (Singapore and Korea), North America (Mexico) and South America (Chile).

Records of Participants 3 and 4 show the prevalence of US intended parents commissioning surrogacy arrangements in India (96 per cent and 32 per cent respectively).[156] For both agencies, the second most common category of intended

---

[156] It must be noted, however, that in relation to Participant 3 the prevalence of US intended parents is likely to be associated with the fact that the agency, although operating in India, is based in

parents was 'UK residents' (4 per cent and 16 per cent respectively). Interestingly, at 13 per cent, the 'number three' jurisdiction recorded by Participant 4 was Nigeria. A significant number of applications were also received by Participant 4 from Australia, France and Sri Lanka (8 per cent each), and Canada and Israel (5 per cent each). Lastly, The Netherlands and Mauritius accounted for 3 per cent each.

To sum up, given the fact that the sample evidence is purely anecdotal, it is impossible to make sweeping conclusions drawn from the outcomes. Nevertheless, some trends can be observed, and these may be summarised as follows:

(a) Residents of countries from across the globe travel to the US or India with the intention of commissioning a surrogacy arrangement there.

(b) Residents of European countries, headed by the UK and France, appear to be the two most common categories of intended parents commissioning surrogacy in the US. Apart from the UK and France, the following European States are represented in particular: Spain, Germany, Ireland, Belgium, The Netherlands and Switzerland.

(c) Israeli residents also account for a large number of intended parents commissioning surrogacy in the US.

(d) US residents appear to be the most common category of intended parents commissioning surrogacy in India. They are followed by UK residents.

Participant 1 (US-Based Agency)

Table 23: Intended Parents' Country of Residence

IPs' Country of Residence		
	Number	Per cent
United Kingdom	137	89%
France	8	5%
Ireland	4	3%
Germany	3	2%
Spain	2	1%
Total	**154**	**100%**

the US. Presumably, the 'recruitment' of intended parents is directed primarily towards a domestic, ie US, audience.

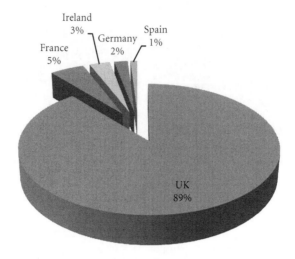

Figure 22: Intended Parents' Country of Residence

Participant 2 (US-Based Agency)

Table 24: Intended Parents' Country of Residence

IPs' Country of Residence		
	Number	**Per cent**
France	37	20%
Israel	36	20%
Sweden	23	13%
United Kingdom	17	9%
Spain	11	6%
Netherlands	8	4%
Switzerland	7	4%
Ireland	7	4%
Belgium	5	3%
Germany	5	3%
Australia	4	2%
Norway	4	2%
Italy	4	2%
Canada	3	2%
Mexico	2	1%
Slovakia	2	1%
Iceland	2	1%
Portugal	2	1%

(Continued)

Table 24: (*Continued*)

IPs' Country of Residence		
	Number	Per cent
Czech Republic	1	1%
Chile	1	1%
Singapore	1	1%
Denmark	1	1%
Korea	1	1%
Total	**184**	**100%**

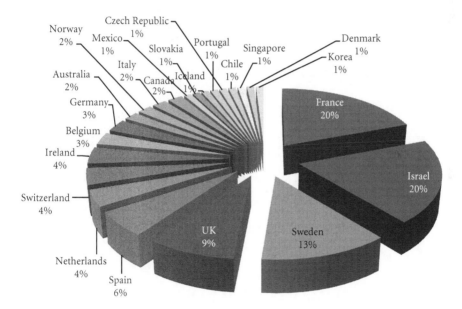

Figure 23: Intended Parents' Country of Residence

Participant 3 (US-Based Agency Operating in India)

Table 25: Intended Parents' Country of Residence

IPs' Country of Residence		
	Number	Per cent
USA	64	96%
United Kingdom	3	4%
Total	**67**	**100%**

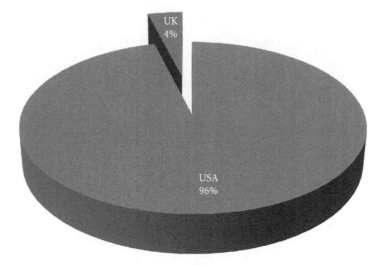

Figure 24: Intended Parents' Country of Residence

Participant 4 (India-Based Agency)

Table 26: Intended Parents' Country of Residence

IPs' Country of Residence		
	Number	Per cent
USA	12	32%
United Kingdom	6	16%
Nigeria	5	13%
Australia	3	8%
France	3	8%
Sri Lanka	3	8%
Canada	2	5%
Israel	2	5%
Netherlands	1	3%
Mauritius	1	3%
Total	**38**	**~100%**

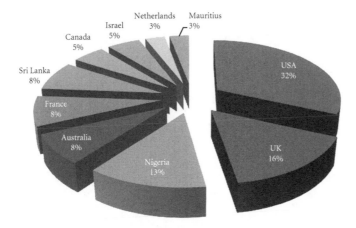

Figure 25: Intended Parents' Country of Residence

iii. *Individual Intended Parents' Responses*

a. Country of Residence of the Intended Parents

The vast majority of the participating intended parents (11, 85 per cent) were resident in France. In one case each (8 per cent), the intended parents were resident in Belgium and Luxembourg respectively. (See Table 27 and Figure 26.)

Table 27: Intended Parents' Country of Residence

IPs' Country of Residence		
	Number	Per cent
France	11	85%
Luxembourg	1	8%
Belgium	1	8%
Total	**13**	**~100%**

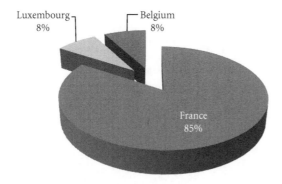

Figure 26: Intended Parents' Country of Residence

b. Nationality of the Intended Parents

In 11 cases (85 per cent) the intended parents were French nationals, and in two cases (15 per cent) the intended parents were citizens of Belgium. (See Table 28 and Figure 27.)

Table 28: Nationality of the Intended Parents

Nationality of the IPs		
	Number	Per cent
French	11	85%
Belgian	2	15%
Total	**13**	**100%**

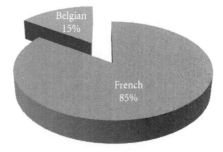

Figure 27: Nationality of the Intended Parents

c. Intended Parents' Age Range

At 42 per cent each, the intended parent(s) were most commonly in their early and late 30s. In one case (8 per cent), the intended parent(s) were in their late 20s, and in another one case (8 per cent), the intended parents were in their late 40s. (See Table 29 and Figure 28.)

Table 29: Intended Parents' Age Range

IPs' Age Range		
	Number	Per cent
Below 25	0	0%
25–30	1	8%
31–35	5	42%
36–40	5	42%
41–45	0	0%
46–50	1	8%
Over 50	0	0%
Total	**12**	**100%**

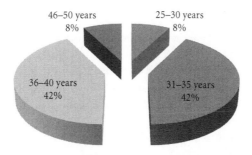

Figure 28: Intended Parents' Age Range

d. Intended Parents' Sexual Orientation

The vast majority of intended parents (10, 77 per cent) were heterosexual couples. The remaining 24 per cent were spread evenly among homosexual single parents, heterosexual single parents and homosexual gay couples (one, 8 per cent each). (See Table 30 and Figure 29.)

Table 30: Intended Parents' Sexual Orientation

IPs' Sexual Orientation		
	Number	Per cent
Heterosexual couple	10	77%
Homosexual single parent	1	8%
Heterosexual single parent	1	8%
Homosexual couple-gay	1	8%
Total	**13**	**~100%**

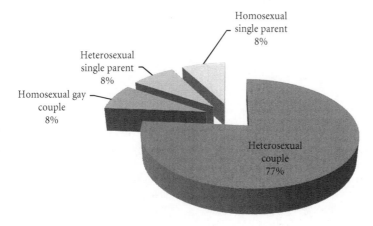

Figure 29: Intended Parents' Sexual Orientation

e. Intended Parents' Marital Status

The majority of intended parents were married couples (54 per cent). Cohabitating couples accounted for 23 per cent of all intended parents. One couple (8 per cent) were living in a civil partnership. Lastly, marital status was not applicable in relation to two cases (15 per cent) as these concerned single intended parents. (See Table 31 and Figure 30.)

Table 31: Intended Parents' Marital Status

IPs' Marital Status		
	Number	Per cent
Married	7	54%
Cohabitation	3	23%
Civil partnership	1	8%
Not applicable	2	15%
Total	**13**	**100%**

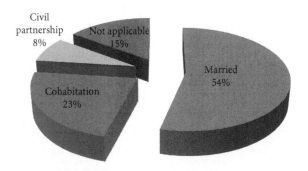

Figure 30: Intended Parents' Marital Status

f. Surrogate Mother's Country of Residence and Nationality

At 38 per cent, most intended parents commissioned surrogacy in the USA (California) (five cases). Interestingly, in four cases (31 per cent) the surrogate mother was resident in Canada. In two cases (15 per cent), the intended parents travelled to Russia. Lastly, in one case (8 per cent) each, the country of residence of the surrogate mother was Ukraine and India respectively.

In all 13 cases, the nationality of the surrogate mother matched her country of residence. (See Tables 32 and 33, and Figure 31.)

Table 32: Surrogate Mother's Country of Residence

SM Country of Residence		
	Number	Per cent
USA (California)	5	38%
Canada	4	31%
Russia	2	15%
Ukraine	1	8%
India	1	8%
Total	**13**	**100%**

Table 33: Nationality of the Surrogate Mother

Nationality of the SM		
	Number	Per cent
American	5	38%
Canadian	4	31%
Ukrainian	2	15%
Russian	1	8%
Indian	1	8%
Total	**13**	**100%**

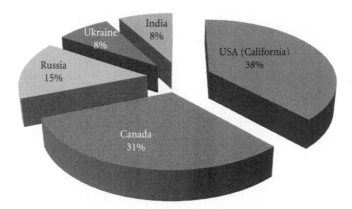

Figure 31: Country of Residence and Nationality of the Surrogate Mother

g. Surrogate Mother's Marital Status

The vast majority of surrogate mothers (12, 92 per cent) were married. Only one surrogate mother (8 per cent) was single. (See Table 34 and Figure 32.)

Table 34: Surrogate Mother's Marital Status

SM Marital Status		
	Number	Per cent
Married	12	92%
Single	1	8%
Total	**13**	**100%**

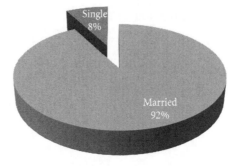

Figure 32: Surrogate Mother's Marital Status

h. Surrogate Mother: Children of Her Own

In all 13 cases, the surrogate had had a child of her own before she became a surrogate mother. (See Table 35.)

Table 35: Surrogate Mother: Children of Her Own

SM Children of Her Own		
	Number	Per cent
Yes	13	100%
Total	**13**	**100%**

i. Type of Surrogacy

One of the 13 cases (8 per cent) involved traditional surrogacy where the surrogate's ovum was fertilised by the intended father's sperm.[157] In almost half of the

---

[157] This case involved a surrogate mother resident in Russia who was in a family relationship with the intended parents. Interestingly, the arrangement was not altruistic and the surrogate mother was reimbursed for her pregnancy-related expenses and paid an additional fee.

cases (six, 46 per cent) genetic material was supplied by both intended parents. In the same number of cases (six, 46 per cent) an egg donor was used. In four of these cases, the donor was anonymous, and in two cases the donor was known to the intended parent(s). (See Table 36 and Figure 33.)

Table 36: Type of Surrogacy

Type of Surrogacy		
	Number	**Per cent**
IF sperm + IM egg	6	46%
IF sperm + donated egg (anonymous)	4	31%
IF sperm + donated egg (non-anonymous)	2	15%
IF sperm + SM egg	1	8%
Donated sperm + donated egg (non-anonymous)	0	0%
Donated sperm + donated egg (anonymous)	0	0%
IM egg + donated sperm (non-anonymous)	0	0%
IM egg + donated sperm (anonymous)	0	0%
Total	**13**	**100%**

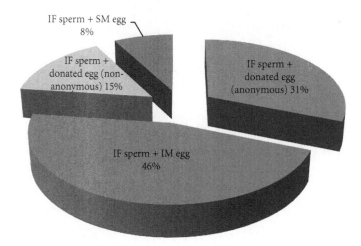

Figure 33: Type of Surrogacy

j. Children Born as a Result of the Arrangement

At 54 per cent, the highest proportion of cases involved twins. In four cases (31 per cent) a single child was born as a result of the arrangement. In one case (8 per cent) the surrogate mother miscarried. Lastly, in one case (8 per cent) the baby was not born as it had been aborted. (See Table 37 and Figure 34.)

Table 37: Children Born as a Result of the Arrangement

Children Born as a Result of the Arrangement		
	Number	Per cent
One	4	31%
Two	7	54%
Miscarried	1	8%
Aborted	1	8%
Total	**13**	**~100%**

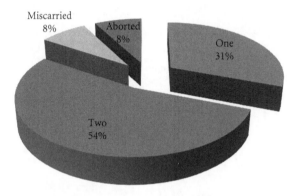

Figure 34: Children Born as a Result of the Arrangement

k. Intended Parents and Surrogate Mother in a Family Relationship

In 11 out of the 13 cases (85 per cent) there was no family relationship between the intended parents and the surrogate mother. In the remaining two cases (15 per cent) the intended parents were in a family relationship with the surrogate mother. (See Table 38 and Figure 35.)

Table 38: Intended Parents and Surrogate Mother in a Family Relationship

IPs and SM in a Family Relationship		
	Number	Percent
No	11	85%
Yes	2	15%
Total	**13**	**100%**

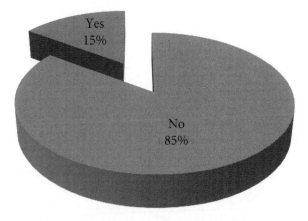

Figure 35: Intended Parents' and Surrogate Mother in a Family Relationship

l. Payments to the Surrogate Mother

The vast majority of cases (10, 77 per cent) involved a commercial surrogacy arrangement where the surrogate mother received an extra fee in addition to her pregnancy-related expenses. In two cases (15 per cent) the arrangement was altruistic in nature, as the surrogate was reimbursed only for her pregnancy-related expenses. The participants further reported that both of these cases involved a gestational surrogacy arrangement commissioned in Canada. In one of these cases, there was a family relationship between the surrogate mother and the intended parents. (See Table 39 and Figure 36.)

Table 39: Payments to the Surrogate Mother

Payments to the SM		
	Number	Per cent
SM reimbursed for expenses that occurred due to her pregnancy + paid an additional fee	10	77%
SM reimbursed only for expenses that occurred due to her pregnancy (eg lost wages, medical expenses, etc)	2	15%
Not known	1	8%
Total	**13**	**100%**

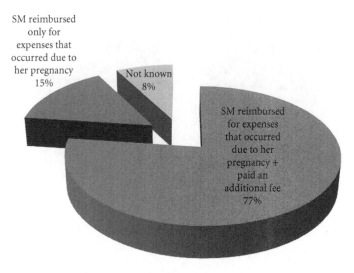

Figure 36: Payments to the Surrogate Mother

m. Legal Aspects

Enforcement Problems

In one case, enforcement problems were reported by the intended parents. In this case, a Ukrainian surrogate mother decided to undergo abortion, allegedly after having received information about potential legal problems the intended parents could face when trying to establish their legal parentage in France. The baby was aborted despite the strong opposition of the intended parents who were also the genetic parents of the child. The intended parents reported that the experience had caused them an extreme emotional trauma.

Other Legal Problems

Not all intended parents provided sufficiently clear and/or detailed information on the legal problems they had encountered in relation to the arrangement. A brief summary analysis of the data that were considered comprehensible enough to be included in the study may be found below:

(a) *Immigration problems.* Immigration problems were reported in one case which involved a surrogacy arrangement commissioned by a single Belgian gay man in India. As Indian citizenship rules are not based on the *ius soli* principle, the child was unable to acquire Indian citizenship.[158] Similarly, the child could not at that point become a Belgian citizen as the legal parentage of the intended father had not been established yet (relevant

---

[158] For background information on the problem of nationality in the context of cross-border surrogacy arrangements, see section IV.B.ii. below.

proceedings were still pending before a Belgian court).[159] To enable the intended father to bring the child 'home', the child was issued emergency travel documents by the Belgian Government.

(b) *Legal parenthood.* In six cases, the intended parents reported that they had sought the registration of a foreign birth certificate/foreign judgment that accorded them parentage in the French civil status records.[160] Of these, three cases involved Canada, two involved California and one involved India. In all six cases, the registration was refused. In a further three cases (two involving California and one Canada), the intended parents, being aware of the commonly adverse outcome, did not even apply for the registration.

It appeared from the responses that, in some cases, the intended father was able to establish his legal parenthood using the avenue of the 'acknowledgement of paternity'.[161] Nevertheless, in none of these cases was the intended mother (even if genetically related to the child) able to regularise her relationship with the child. As a result, the intended mother was placed in a very vulnerable position, especially in the event of a custody dispute or a paternal death.

IV. Cross-border Surrogacy

A. Dual pattern: Legal Reasons and Economic Reasons

The variety of domestic responses to surrogacy has led to widespread *forum shopping*, where infertile couples seeking to have a child through surrogacy travel from one country to another, purposely choosing 'surrogacy-friendly' jurisdictions as their destinations. Cross-border travel for the purpose of hiring a surrogate mother has been termed 'procreative tourism'.[162] By and large, the majority of 'procreative tourists' are childless Western couples attracted by 'low-cost' surrogacy services and a 'ready availability of poor surrogates'[163] in places like India, Eastern Europe and South America.[164]

---

[159] *Ibid.*

[160] For more information, see section IV.B.iii.a. below.

[161] *Ibid.*

[162] R Deech 'Clones, Ethics and Infertility or Sex, Sheep and Statutes' (1998-1999) 2 *Quinnipiac Health Law Journal* 133, 133. See also R Storrow, 'Quests for Conception: Fertility Tourists, Globalisation and Feminist Legal Theory' (2005-2006) 57 *Hastings Law Journal* 295; and A Donchin, 'Reproductive Tourism and the Quest for Global Gender Justice' (2010) 24 *Bioethics* 323. For a discourse on the future of procreative tourism, see R Storrow, 'Travel into the Future of Reproductive Technology' (2010-2011) 79 *UMKC Law Review* 295.

[163] *Yamada v Union of India*, 2008 IND LAW SC 1554, 9 (29 September 2008) (known as '*The Baby Manji*' case).

[164] K Farmer, 'International Surrogacy Choices', 29 June 2009, *Ezine @rticles*, available at <www.// ezinearticles.com/?International-Surrogacy-Choices&id=2538590>. In the US, eg, the total costs of a sur-

It is usually the case that the law lags behind medical advances and corresponding social developments.[165] Unfortunately, international surrogacy is not an exception. There is a complete void in the international regulation of surrogacy arrangements, as none of the existing international instruments contains specific provisions designed to regulate this emerging area of international family law.

In the absence of a global legislative response, highly complex legal problems arise from international surrogacy arrangements.[166] Among these problems, the most prevalent are the questions of legal parenthood and the nationality of the child.[167] In addition, a number of other legal hurdles can easily be envisaged. For example, what happens if the intended parents refuse to accept the child because it suffers from a serious disability[168] or because their relationship breaks down before the child is born?[169] What happens if the surrogate mother changes her mind and

rogacy arrangement fall between $59,000 and $80,000. This contrasts sharply with India, where the costs of a surrogacy arrangement normally range from $10,000 to $35,000. See Smerdon, above n 14, 32.

[165] For a relevant theoretical discourse, see M Shapiro, 'Is Bioethics Broke? On the Idea of Ethics and Law "Catching Up" With Technology' (1999-2000) 33 *Indiana Law Review* 17. See also A Hecht, 'The Wild Wild West: Inadequate Regulation of Assisted Reproductive Technology' (2001) 1 *Houston Journal of Health Law and Policy* 227, 229–34.

[166] *X & Y (Foreign Surrogacy)* [2008] EWHC 3030, [8]. Hedley J warned that 'many pitfalls confront the couple who consider commissioning foreign surrogacy,' and that 'potentially difficult conflict of law issues arise which may have wholly unintended and unforeseen consequences'. See also L Theis *et al*, 'Re X and Y (Foreign Surrogacy)*: "A Trek Through a Thorn Forest"' (2009) 39 *Family Law Journal* 239.

[167] Courts and legislators in different jurisdictions have developed several approaches to legal parenthood in surrogacy cases. The most common of these approaches are the gestational test (ie the birth test), the genetics test, the intent test and the 'best interests of the child' test. According to the birth test, the woman who gives birth to a child is viewed as the legal mother of the child, even if she is biologically unrelated to the child. (See, eg, the UK HFEA 2008, s 33(1), which states: 'The woman who is carrying or has carried a child as a result of the placing in her of an embryo or of sperm and eggs, and no other woman, is to be treated as the mother of the child.') In accordance with the genetics test, the child's legal parents are determined on the basis of genetics. Where the intent test is applied, the intent of the parties as expressed in the surrogacy agreement controls the determination of the legal parenthood. (See eg *Johnson v Calvert*, 5 Cal 4th 84, 19 Cal Rptr 2d 494, 851 P 2d 776 (Cal 1993); section II.A. above.) Lastly, according to the 'best interests of the child' test, the determination of legal parenthood is guided by the welfare of the child. See, eg, P Laufer-Ukeles, 'Gestation: Work for Hire or the Essence of Motherhood? A Comparative Legal Analysis' (2002) 9 *Duke Journal of Gender Law & Policy* 91; C Spivack, 'The Law of Surrogate Motherhood in the United States' (2010) 58 *American Journal of Comparative Law* 97, 101–09; C Kindregan, 'Considering Mom: Maternity and the Model Act Governing Assisted Reproductive Technology' (2009) 17 *Journal of Gender, Social Policy & the Law* 601, 611–14 (analysing the 'birth mother test' and the 'genetic connection test for maternity' in surrogacy cases in the US context); D Wald, 'The Parentage Puzzle,: The Interplay Between Genetics, Procreative Intent, and Parental Conduct in Determining Legal Parentage' (2006-2007) 15 *Journal of Gender, Social Policy & the Law* 379; A Larkey, 'Redefining Motherhood: Determining Legal Maternity in Gestational Surrogacy Arrangements (2003) 51 *Drake Law Review* 605, 621–27; E Hisano, 'Gestational Surrogacy Maternity Disputes: Refocusing on the Child' (2011) 15 *Lewis & Clark Law Review* 517, 543–52; and B Lewis, 'Three Lies and a Truth: Adjudicating Maternity in Surrogacy Disputes' (2010-2011) 49 *University of Louisville Law Review* 371.

[168] See eg N Hyder, 'Couple Request Surrogate Mum to Abort over Disability', *BioNews*, 11 October 2010, available at <www.bionews.org.uk/page_71982.asp>.

[169] See eg 'Surrogate Mum of Twins Unfazed After Baby Deal Fall Apart', *CBC News*, New Brunswick, 13 September 2011, available at <http://www.cbc.ca/news/canada/new-brunswick/story/2011/09/13/nb-bathurst-surrogate-parent-1245.html>.

decides to keep the child?[170] At a later stage, other complications may arise, such as a cross-border custody and access dispute between the intended parents residing in one country and the surrogate mother in another, a dispute over maintenance and financial support, or a dispute over international child abduction.[171]

Legal problems arising from the lack of international regulation of surrogacy arrangements are, however, not the only cause for concern in this respect. Another great worry springing from the unregulated character of 'procreative tourism' is the potential for a 'black market' preying on peoples' emotional or economic needs.[172] This concern is particularly legitimate in cases of surrogacy for profit, where the commercial nature of these arrangements renders them often akin to child trafficking or trafficking in women.[173]

The following section will examine in detail the issues of nationality and legal parenthood in cross-border surrogacy cases as they arise and are dealt with in different jurisdictions. Thereafter a separate section will concisely address the ethical concerns that surround commercial cross-border surrogacy.

B. Nationality and Legal Parenthood

i. *Acquisition of Legal Parenthood in the State of Birth*

Following the birth of a child through surrogacy in a surrogacy-friendly jurisdiction, the child is normally transferred into the physical care of the intended parents. The intended parents may be able to have their names placed on the birth certificate immediately upon the birth of the child. This is possible, for example,

---

[170] Eg recent UK domestic case *CW v NT & Anor* [2011] EWHC 33.

[171] The problem of child abduction in the context of an international surrogacy arrangement surfaced in the case of *W and B v H (Child Abduction: Surrogacy)* [2002] 1 FLR 1008. This case involved a surrogacy agreement made in California between a Californian couple and an English surrogate. It was agreed that during the pregnancy the surrogate mother would stay in England and only return to California for the birth. A dispute arose, however, between the parties after it was discovered that the surrogate mother was carrying twins. The surrogate decided to give birth to the children in England. The couple sought an order under the inherent jurisdiction of the High Court for the summary return of the children to California under the 1980 Hague Convention on Civil Aspects of International Child Abduction. The central issue was whether, at the time immediately before the retention, the twins were habitually resident in California or in England. It is a prerequisite for the operation of the Convention that the child concerned has a habitual residence. In the instant case, however, the Court held that the children were neither habitually resident in California nor habitually resident in England. It was concluded that infants born through surrogacy have no habitual residence for the purposes of the Hague Abduction Convention. As a result, the Convention was found inapplicable to cases of international surrogacy.

[172] T Krim, 'Beyond Baby M: International Perspectives on Gestational Surrogacy and the Demise of the Unitary Biological Mother' (1996) 5 *Annals of Health Law* 193, 195. See also Hedley J in *X & Y (Foreign Surrogacy)* [2008] EWHC 3030, [29]: '[T]he present law might encourage the less scrupulous to take advantage of the more vulnerable, unmarried surrogate mothers and to be less than frank in the arrangements that surround foreign surrogacy.'

[173] J Chernick, 'Memorandum: Is There a Need to Regulate Intercountry Surrogate-Pregnancy Agreements in Private International Law?' (on file with the authors).

in California, where the intended parents may apply for a so called pre-birth court order declaring them the legal parents of the child at birth.[174] In other countries, for example Ukraine and Russia, the intended parents may be immediately placed on the birth certificate if certain conditions are met, including the requirement that the surrogate mother consents.[175] In some jurisdictions, such as India, only the intended parent who has a genetic link with the child can be listed on the birth certificate. The existence of the genetic link must first be proved through a DNA test.[176] If the requirements of the State of birth do not allow the names of the intended parents to be placed on the birth certificate immediately upon the birth of the child, the intended parent(s) will seek a court order permitting the amendment of the birth certificate to reflect this fact following, for example, an acknowledgement of paternity by the intended father, or adoption by the intended mother or by both intended parents (in particular where neither of the intended parents is genetically related to the child). As a result, formal evidence of the acquisition of legal parenthood in the country of birth by the intended parent(s) can take various forms, including an original birth certificate, an amended birth certificate, a judicial decision, an administration decree or an adoption order. Nevertheless, acquisition of legal parenthood in the country of birth through adoption is far less common than the acquisition of legal parenthood through the application of parentage rules.[177]

ii. Entry into the Intended Parents' Home Country

Following the acquisition of legal parenthood in the State of birth, the intended parents will seek to take the child out of that State of birth and bring him or her to their 'home' State. For this purpose, they will need to secure passport or travel documentation for the child, so the question of nationality comes into play. Here two alternative scenarios may arise: first, the child acquires citizenship of the State of birth via the *ius soli* principle; secondly, the citizenship rules of the State of birth will not allow the child to acquire the nationality of this State.

a. Scenario 1: Child Obtains Citizenship at Birth via the *ius soli* Principle

This scenario occurs in surrogacy arrangements involving the United States as the State of birth. Pursuant to the 14th Amendment to the US Constitution, 'all persons born ... in the United States ... are citizens of the United States'. Consequently, a child born in the United States as a result of a surrogacy arrangement is automatically a US citizen and is therefore entitled to a US passport.[178] Due to the US citizenship rules, there have been no recorded cases of intended

---

[174] See section II.A. above.
[175] *Ibid.*
[176] *Ibid.*
[177] See also section IV.B.iii. below.
[178] See ch 24 of this book.

parents being stranded in the US with their children.[179] Generally, the intended parents are able to obtain a birth certificate and a passport within approximately two weeks of the birth of the child, and can then return with the child to their home country.[180]

b. Scenario 2: Child does not Obtain Citizenship via the *ius soli* Principle

This scenario occurs in surrogacy arrangements involving other frequented 'surrogacy-friendly' jurisdictions, including Ukraine, India and Thailand, where the child does not obtain citizenship via the *ius soli* principle and the intended parents often encounter serious difficulties in obtaining travel documents for the child.

Nationality by Descent

The intended parents normally apply to the local consulate of their home country for a passport for the child, to allow them to leave the country of birth and to bring the child to their home State. Nationality rules of different States vary significantly and are commonly very complex. Generally, such laws provide for the possibility of nationality by descent, ie the child has an automatic right to citizenship if at least one of his or her legal parents is a national of the given State.[181] This implies that in order to determine the issue of nationality by descent, legal parenthood must first be established. The question of legal parenthood will be handled differently in civil law and common law countries.[182] Most civil law countries will apply their private international law rules on recognition, whereas countries of the common law tradition (including some mixed legal system countries, in particular Israel) will normally apply their internal law (*lex fori*).[183]

Some of the jurisdictions falling within the latter category formally take a more liberal approach and, for nationality purposes, require only a proof of a genetic link rather than a proof of the legal parenthood under internal law. For example, Israeli citizenship may be conferred on a child born as a result of a cross-border surrogacy arrangement if at least one of the intended parents is an Israeli citizen and if this

---

[179] Interview with Participant 1, section III.A. above.

[180] *Ibid*. Nevertheless, in cases involving the UK, an application for an entry clearance must be made by the intended parents to bring the child to the country. This requirement applies regardless of the fact that the child has obtained a US passport, as 'every child who is not a British citizen and is coming to live in the United Kingdom permanently, must obtain entry clearance before travelling to [that] country': Home Office, UK Border Agency, 'Inter-country Surrogacy and the Immigration Rules', para 58, available at <www.ukba.homeoffice.gov.uk/sitecontent/documents/residency/Intercountry-surrogacy-leaflet> ('UK Border Agency Rules').

[181] Eg Germany (the German Nationality Act, s 3), Belgium (the Belgian Nationality Act, Art 8), Hungary (the Hungarian Nationality Act, s 3(1)–(2)), the Czech Republic (the Czech Nationality Act, s 4), Brazil (the Brazilian Constitution, Art 12, I, C), The Netherlands (The Netherlands Nationality Act, Art 3), UK (the UK Nationality Act 1981, s 2), Ireland (Irish Nationality and Citizenship Acts 1956 to 2004) and Israel.

[182] See section IV.B.iii. below.

[183] For a detailed analysis of the two differing approaches to legal parenthood in cross-border surrogacy cases, see section IV.B.iii. below.

person is genetically related to the child.[184] According to Irish citizenship rules, a child born outside Ireland is automatically an Irish citizen by descent if the intended father can prove a genetic link to the child by a DNA test.[185] It appears that in both Israel and Ireland, however, the provisions on nationality by descent have not been applied automatically in cross-border surrogacy cases. In particular, it has been reported that in several cases of gay intended parents, the family court in Israel denied the men's petition to proceed with paternity tests at the Israeli Consulate in India.[186] Similarly, the Irish Department of Foreign Affairs has reputedly refused to issue passports for children born through surrogacy arrangements in the Ukraine, even though DNA tests have shown the Irish intended father to be the genetic parent.[187]

In the UK, acquisition of citizenship by descent solely on the basis of a genetic link between the child and the intended father is possible only in cases where the surrogate mother is not married. Guidance issued by the UK Border Agency for international surrogacy cases in this respect states:

> [Where] the male of the commissioning couple provides the sperm … and the surrogate mother is unmarried, the male who provides the sperm will be considered for immigration and nationality purposes, as the resultant child's father, so long as he is so identified on official documentation and can prove his connection by way of accredited DNA evidence.[188]

Where the child acquires nationality by descent, the intended parents will be able to obtain a passport for the child.

Discretionary Grant of Nationality

If the child does not obtain citizenship of the intended parents' country at birth, a discretionary grant of citizenship might be possible. The outcome will often depend on the genetic make-up of the child.

Neither Nationality by Descent nor Discretionary Grant of Nationality Possible

Where an application for a discretionary grant of citizenship is not successful[189] or not possible at all,[190] the child becomes stateless and without a universally recognised legal parentage. The intended parents are left stranded in the State of birth, with a potential additional complication that, due to immigration rules,

---

[184] To prove the existence of the genetic link, a DNA test is required. The test must be carried out in Israel (although the sample may be retrieved abroad) and is possible only with the permission of an Israeli court. Nevertheless, once a genetic link is confirmed through the DNA test, the genetic intended parent is automatically regarded as the legal parent. See ch 14 of this book.

[185] See ch 13 of this book.

[186] See ch 12 of this book. See also ch 14.

[187] See ch 13 of this book.

[188] UK Border Agency Rules, above n 180, para 25. See *Re X (Children)* [2011] EWHC 3147 (Fam), [21]. Also *Re IJ (A Child)* [2011] EWHC 921 (Fam), [11].

[189] This is usually on the ground that due to differing approaches to legal parenthood, the intended parents are not regarded by the home State as the legal parents of the child.

[190] Eg because of the lack of a genetic connection between the child and the intended parents.

they might not be able to remain in the State of birth indefinitely.[191] It is often only at this stage that the intended parents realise that the legal parentage they have obtained in the State of birth is not universally recognised as, contrary to their belief, their home country views the surrogate mother (and her husband, if married) as the legal parent(s) of the child.

A classic practical example of such a situation is the English case of *X & Y (Foreign Surrogacy)*.[192] A married British couple entered into a surrogacy agreement with a married Ukrainian surrogate. The surrogate mother was implanted with embryos created using donor eggs fertilised by the intended father's sperm. The surrogate mother gave birth to a set of twins. Under Ukrainian law, the British couple were considered the legal parents of the children and were registered as such on the birth certificates. Under English law, however, the legal parents of the twins were the surrogate mother and her husband.[193] The conflict between English and Ukrainian law resulted in parental status being lost for both couples. This left the children without legal parents and without rights to either British or Ukrainian citizenship. As a result, the children were, in the words of Mr Justice Hedley, 'marooned, stateless and parentless, whilst the couple could neither remain in the Ukraine nor bring the children to the UK'. In the end, following a long delay due to DNA tests, the children were granted discretionary leave to enter the UK outside the Immigration Rules,[194] to make it possible for the couple to apply for a parental order under section 30 of the Human Fertilisation and Embryology Act 1990. The decision was based on the principle of the paramountcy of the welfare of the child.

Different countries have created varying ad hoc temporary solutions to enable the intended parents eventually to bring their children, born as a result of a surrogacy arrangement abroad, to their home State. It must be pointed out, however, that in the current regulatory vacuum, many cross-border surrogacy cases have turned out to be very problematic, with solutions having to be sought through

---

[191] Eg the *Baby Manji* case, above n 163, where the child's Japanese grandmother had to travel to India to care for her granddaughter, as the intended father had to return to Japan upon the expiration of his visa.

[192] *X & Y (Foreign Surrogacy)* [2008] EWHC 3030. Hedley J took this case into open court precisely in order to 'illustrate the sort of difficulties that currently can and do appear'. For analysis of the case, see Theis *et al*, above n 166.

[193] Under s 27 of the HFEA 1990, the woman who carries the child, regardless of genetics, is treated as the legal mother, even if the surrogacy takes place outside of the UK. In addition, despite the fact that the intended father was biologically related to the twins, because the surrogate mother was married, UK law presumed her husband to be the twins' father (s 28). The HFEA 1990, s 27(3) states that it will remain the case that the woman who carries a child following assisted reproduction (anywhere in the world) is the child's mother, unless the child is subsequently adopted or parenthood is transferred through a parental order. (References are to the 1990 Act as the case had been decided before the HFEA 2008 entered into force.)

[194] An application for entry clearance had to be made by the intended parents. Entry clearance will only be granted if one of the intended parents is genetically related to the child and on condition that the intended parents will apply for a parental order under s 30 of the HFEA 2008, and where evidence suggests that it is likely that such an order will be granted. UK Border Agency Rules, above n 180, paras 41–42 and 26–28.

diplomatic channels. As a result, these cases have often taken an extended period of time to resolve.[195] Examples of remedies, other than the one adopted in *X & Y (Foreign Surrogacy)*,[196] that have been indentified in available case law and news reports from a variety of jurisdictions include:

(a) *Child is issued an identity certificate and travel documents by the birth country 'outside the rules' and a visa (on humanitarian grounds/as a one-time exception) by the intended parents' home country.* This solution was adopted after a long legal battle by the intended father to bring his genetically-related baby daughter to his home country in the Japanese–Indian case known as the *Baby Manji* case.[197] The application concerned a surrogacy arrangement between Japanese intended parents and an Indian surrogate mother. Before the child was born, the intended parents had divorced and the intended mother then refused to participate further in the arrangement. This caused the intended father immense difficulties in obtaining travel documents for the child. It took over three months to resolve the issue temporarily, with the child being eventually issued an Indian identity certificate and travel documents 'outside the rules'. The Japanese Embassy in New Delhi then granted the child a one-year visa on humanitarian grounds.[198]

A similar outcome to that in the *Baby Manji* case, although after a substantially longer period of litigation, was achieved in the German–Indian case of *Jan Balaz*.[199] The *Balaz* case concerned twin boys born as a result of a commercial surrogacy arrangement between a German married couple and an Indian surrogate. The children were conceived with the intended father's sperm and an egg from an Indian egg donor. On the birth certificate, the intended father's name was shown as the father and the surrogate mother's name was shown as the mother. The intended

[195] Eg the case of Jan Balaz, where German intended parents Jan Balaz and Susanne Lohle were left stranded with their twin boys in India for over two years. See '*(a) Child is issued an identity certificate and travel documents by the birth country "outside the rules" and a visa (on humanitarian grounds/as a one-time exception) by the intended parents' home country*', below. For a detailed analysis of the case, see ch 12 of this book. Another example is the case of Belgian gay intended parents Peter Meurrens and Laurent Ghilain, who commissioned surrogacy in Ukraine. Due to immigration problems they were unable to remove the child from Ukraine, and the boy spent over two years in a Ukrainian orphanage. Eventually, the Belgian Government issued a Belgian passport for the boy, using this opportunity to highlight the need for regulation of surrogacy: *MSN News*, 26 February 2011, available at <www.msnbc.msn.com/id/41800437/ns/world_news-wonderful_world/t/boy-stuck-years-ukraine-arrives-belgium/ .T0EETPVIyt9>.
[196] *X & Y (Foreign Surrogacy)* [2008] EWHC 3030.
[197] *Baby Manji Yamada v Union of India et al*, Writ Petition No 369 of 2008, Supreme Court of India.
[198] For a detailed analysis of the case, see ch 12 of this book. Also K Points, Commercial Surrogacy and Fertility Tourism in India: The Case of Baby Manji', available at <www.caseplace.org/pdfs/BabyManjiTN.pdf>.
[199] *Union of India & ANR v Jan Balaz and others*, Civil Appeal No 8714 of 2010 Supreme Court of India; see ch 12 of this book.

parents were unable to secure German passports or a visa for the children, so they attempted to seek Indian passports. The Gujarat High Court ruled that since the surrogate mother was an Indian national, the children could also be considered as Indian citizens and would be entitled to Indian passports. This decision was challenged, however, by the Government of India, which insisted that as the children were born to a surrogate mother, they were not entitled to Indian citizenship. Eventually, and rather unexpectedly, after a litigation period of over two years, the children were issued Indian identity documents and exit permits by the Indian Government. Despite its prolonged refusal to grant a visa, the German Government eventually relented and made a one-time exception by issuing visas for the children.[200]

(b) *Child is allowed to enter the intended parents' home country through a visitor/tourist visa.* Published case law in New Zealand indicates that intended parents have regularly been able to bring their children born as a result of international surrogacy to New Zealand through a 12-month visitor visa.[201] Although New Zealand law and policy generally do not permit children born overseas as a result of a cross-border surrogacy arrangement to be brought into New Zealand,[202] relevant ministers have discretion to grant a visa to allow entry to New Zealand on a case-by-case basis.[203] Given its discretionary nature, however, the media have reported cases where this process was far from straightforward.[204]

In a 2004 altruistic surrogacy case involving British intended parents and an Indian surrogate mother, children born as a result of the arrangement were initially denied passports by the British High Commission but were eventually granted a one-year visitor visa by the UK. The twins were conceived with the gametes of the intended parents, and the surrogate mother was the children's genetic grandmother.[205]

---

[200] See ch 12 of this book.

[201] See *Re an application by KR and DGR to adopt a female child* [2011] New Zealand Family Law Reports 429, and *Re an application by BWS to adopt a child* [2011] New Zealand Family Law Reports 621.

[202] See Guidelines on International Surrogacy issued by the Ministry of Social Development of New Zealand, stating that a child born as a result of a surrogacy arrangement abroad 'will not meet immigration policy requirements for a New Zealand residence visa or permit': Ministry of Social Development, 'International Surrogacy', available at <www.cyf.govt.nz/documents/adoption/international-surrogacy-information-sheet.pdf> ('NZ Ministry Guidelines').

[203] See ch 18 of this book.

[204] See, eg, a story of a New Zealand couple stranded in Thailand with their genetically-related baby daughter as New Zealand authorities refused to grant a visa to the baby: 'Parents of Surrogate Born Daughter Battle to Bring Her Home', 3 *News*, 28 August 2009, available at <www.3news.co.nz/Parents-of-surrogate-born-daughter-battle-to-bring-her home/tabid/817/articleID/118792/Default.aspx>.

[205] See ch 12 of this book.

It also appears to be an option for Dutch intended parents to apply for a short-stay (ie tourist) visa for their child to enter The Netherlands before the issue of legal parenthood can be assessed by Dutch authorities.[206]

(c) *Child is granted a residence permit by the intended parents' home country.* This solution was arrived at after months of negotiations in a Norwegian case, where a Norwegian single intended mother commissioned surrogacy in India with the use of an Indian egg donor and a Scandinavian sperm donor.[207]

iii. Transfer of Legal Parenthood to the Intended Parents in their Home State

Once the intended parents have brought the child to their home State, they will seek to confirm the child's status through the recognition of the legal parenthood established in the country of birth in their 'home' country. Generally, the problem of transfer of legal parenthood is treated differently in civil law countries and in common law jurisdictions. In most civil law countries, the issue of the legal parenthood of a child born abroad will be approached through the application of relevant private international law rules on recognition of foreign judgments, legal facts or juridical acts (the 'conflict of laws' or the 'recognition' method). In contrast, in most common law countries, internal law (*lex fori*) will be applied to the establishment of legal parenthood where a child is born outside the jurisdiction.[208]

a. Civil Law Countries

Traditional Approach

As mentioned above, in civil law countries, the issue of legal parenthood in cross-border surrogacy cases is usually approached from the private international law perspective, through the method of recognition.[209] Depending on

---

[206] See ch 17 of this book.

[207] See ch 12 of this book.

[208] These two distinct methodological approaches were identified also in the 2012 Hague Report, paras 35–41, above n 19.

[209] Nevertheless, this does not appear to be always the case, as in at least one reported application, Japanese authorities opted for the '*lex fori*' approach ('the Yoko Kondo case'). The Yoko Kondo case concerned a Japanese couple in their 50s who commissioned a gestational surrogacy arrangement in California, using a donated egg and the intended father's sperm. The surrogate mother gave birth to a set of twins in 2002. The intended parents' application to the consulate for registration of US birth certificates was rejected by the Japanese Government. The couple then initiated legal proceedings in Japan. The court upheld the decision of the Government, reasoning that according to Japanese law, the woman who gave birth to the children is their legal mother. The decision was affirmed by the Osaka High Court and the Japanese Supreme Court. See ch 15 of this book. Although in some civil law countries there is no relevant case law to date, it is assumed that this would be the most likely avenue to be opted for by intended parents in a cross-border surrogacy scenario, eg Venezuela, Argentina and Mexico. See chs 25, 1 and 16 of this book, respectively.

the availability of legal remedies in the country of birth (often conditioned upon the genetic make-up of the child), the intended parents will normally seek recognition of a birth certificate, an acknowledgement of paternity or a judgment issued in the country of birth that accorded them legal parenthood in their home country.[210] This application may be made during the immigration process (where legal parenthood must be established as a preliminary question to the determination of nationality),[211] or once the intended parents are back in their home country with the child (seeking to regularise the child's legal status).[212] To dispose of the intended parents' application, authorities of their home State will usually apply relevant private international law rules on recognition of foreign judgments, legal facts or juridical acts. However, recognition will often be refused on the grounds of public policy, placing the intended parents in a precarious situation. Examples include cases from a variety of jurisdictions.

(1) Japan

In the Japanese case of *Aki Mukai*[213] an embryo was created using the couple's genetic material at a clinic in Nevada, and twin boys were born as a result of the arrangement in 2003. The children were brought to Japan on US passports, but the Japanese Government refused the couple's application for registration of US birth certificates in Japan. The couple then initiated recognition proceedings before a Japanese court. The court held:

> [A] judicial decision rendered by a foreign court acknowledging the establishment of a natural parent–child relationship between persons who are not eligible for such a relationship under the Civil Code is contrary to public policy as prescribed in Article 118, item 3 of the Code of Civil Procedure and therefore not effective in Japan.

Another reported case where Japanese authorities refused to recognise a birth certificate issued in India was the *Baby Manji* case.[214] An added complication in this instance was that the intended parents had divorced before the child was born, and the intended mother then decided not to make any claim to the child. The relevant civil registrar in India issued a birth certificate with only the father's name on it, without making any reference to the mother. The Japanese authorities, however, refused to recognise the birth certificate and instructed the intended

---

[210] In cases where legal parenthood was acquired in the country of birth through adoption, recognition of a foreign adoption order will be sought instead. It appears, however, that this scenario occurs in a small minority of cross-border surrogacy cases, so the analysis will focus on the alternative, more common situations as listed above. See also ch 17 of this book, noting that the vast majority of Dutch intended parents in cross-border surrogacy cases seek recognition of their legal parentage established in the country of birth on the basis of 'the alleged creation of legal familial ties, ie parentage'.

[211] See 'Nationality by descent' in section IV.B.ii.b. above.

[212] Eg, this would normally be the case where the child obtained citizenship of the country of birth via the *ius soli* principle. See section IV.B.ii. above.

[213] *Aki Mukai*, Supreme Court, Second Petty Bench, 23 March 2007, 61.2 Minshū 619. See ch 15 of this book.

[214] See section IV.B.ii. above. See also ch 12 of this book.

father (who was also the genetic father) to adopt the child instead, pursuant to Indian and Japanese laws.[215]

(2) Spain

In one Spanish case, a Spanish gay couple entered into a gestational surrogacy arrangement with a surrogate mother in California. Twins were born as a result of the arrangement, and the intended fathers sought the registration of the births at the Spanish consulate in Los Angeles. The request was denied on the grounds that the applicable law was Spanish law and that surrogacy was prohibited in Spain. Interestingly, the consulate took the 'applicable law' approach rather than the 'recognition' approach. The couple appealed to the Ministry of Justice. The Ministry disagreed that the issue was a matter of applicable law and insisted that the 'recognition' method be applied. The Ministry overturned the first instance administrative decision, recommending that the births of the twins be registered in Spain.[216] The prosecutor launched an appeal. The first instance court agreed with the Ministry that the matter was a question of recognition, however it argued that the recognition would be against public policy and ordered that the decision of the Ministry to register the intended fathers as the legal parents pursuant to the Californian birth certificates be annulled.[217]

(3) The Netherlands

In The Netherlands, courts have consistently refused to recognise birth certificates where there was no mother stated in the document. In one case, a Dutch surrogate mother decided to take advantage of the possibility of an anonymous birth in France in order to avoid being listed on the child's birth certificate as the mother of the child she was carrying for a gay Dutch couple. Upon the birth of the child, the intended fathers returned to The Netherlands with a French birth certificate on which only one parent, ie the biological father, was listed. The Dutch authorities refused to register the birth certificate on the grounds of public policy. The District Court of The Hague concurred with the registrar's view, opining that to recognise a birth certificate where no details about the mother were available would violate the child's right to know his or her parents, guaranteed by Article 7 of the United Nations Convention on the Rights of the Child.[218]

A different line of reasoning was used by the same court in another case which concerned a 'typical' cross-border commercial surrogacy arrangement commissioned by a Dutch gay couple in California. In this case a pre-birth order was issued by the Superior Court of California, which ordered that, upon the birth

---

[215] See ch 12 of this book.

[216] Decision of the Ministry of Justice, Madrid, 18 February 2009, No 2575/2008.

[217] Decision of the Tribunal de Primera Instancia No 15 of Valencia, 15 September 2010, No 193/2010. The decision was upheld on appeal: Audiencia Provincial de Valencia (Seccion 10a), 23 November 2011, No 826/2011.

[218] See ch 17 of this book.

of the child, the intended fathers be placed on the child's birth certificate as the legal parents. Once back in The Netherlands, the men sought recognition of the birth certificate. Their application was refused by the court with the following reasoning:

> The judicial decision from the Superior Court of California of 15th August 2008 cannot be recognised since it is contrary to Dutch public policy, bearing in mind the afore-mentioned fundamental rule of family law (*mater certa semper est*) and the fact that the judicial decision was ordered without the legal mother first being determined.[219]

(4) France

Normally, the first step for French intended parents involved in cross-border surrogacy arrangements is to apply to the French consulate for the registration of a foreign birth certificate or the foreign judgment that accorded them parentage in the French civil status records.[220] If the application is successful, the intended parents will obtain 'a French public document of the highest standard of proof that firmly establishes parentage according to French law'.[221] A decision of the consulate to register the birth may, however, be questioned by the *Ministère public*, who can request the registration to be annulled on the grounds of public policy. The ultimate decision is then to be taken by the *Cour de cassation*.

Such a situation arose in two recent cases, each of which involved a surrogacy arrangement commissioned in the US (California and Minnesota respectively) by a French married couple. In both cases, legal parenthood was established in the US by a judgment.[222] The *Cour de cassation* accepted the request of the *Ministère public* and held that a registration of the judgments would violate public policy as

> according to current law, it is contrary to the principle that the status of persons may not be a subject of private agreements ... to give effect, in relation to parentage, to an agreement on surrogacy.[223]

Towards a more Liberal Trend

Consistent with the general trend towards an increased focus on the 'best interests' of the child, more liberal developments have emerged recently in some civil law jurisdictions. Judicial/administrative authorities in these countries 'invented' various

---

[219] The District Court of The Hague, 23 November 2009, Case no 328511 / FA RK 09-317 (unpublished).

[220] French intended parents may also apply for recognition of a foreign birth certificate before the *Conseil d'Etat*. See 'Towards a More Liberal Approach', below.

[221] See ch 7 of this book.

[222] Cour de Cassation, Chambre Civile 1, 6 avril 2011, 09-66.486, Publié au bulletin, and Cour de cassation, civile, Chambre civile 1, 6 avril 2011, 10-19.053, Publié au bulletin. See ch 7 of this book.

[223] Cour de Cassation, Chambre Civile 1, 6 avril 2011, 09-66.486, Publié au bulletin, per ch 7 of this book.

ad hoc partial solutions, eventually leading to (at least) partial recognition of the
legal parenthood established in the country of birth.

(1) Full Recognition of a Foreign Birth Certificate

In two recent French cases, each of which concerned a child born to a gay couple
through surrogacy in India, the court held that if a DNA test proves a genetic
link between the child and the intended father, a foreign birth certificate must
be treated as 'any foreign civil status record and thus be given effect, even in
surrogacy cases'.[224] The fact that surrogacy arrangements are contrary to French
public policy does not affect the obligation of the authorities to give primary
consideration to the best interests of the child in all actions concerning children,
in accordance with Article 3(1) of the United Nations Convention on the Rights
of the Child.[225]

A similar approach was taken in a series of court decisions in Belgium:
Samuel,[226] *AM&ND*[227] and *C*.[228] The case of *Samuel* involved a traditional surrogacy arrangement in Ukraine, with the intended father being genetically related
to the child. A Ukrainian birth certificate listed the surrogate mother and the
intended father as the legal parents of the child. Recognition of the Ukrainian
birth certificate in Belgium was then sought by the intended parents. The court
granted the request, pointing out that the decision was not meant to give effect
to the surrogacy arrangement (which was contrary to public policy) but only
concerned the establishment of the intended and genetic father's paternity. The
recognition was seen as desirable in the light of the child's interests.

Both *AM&ND* and *C* concerned a surrogacy arrangement commissioned in
India by a Belgian single man as the intended parent. In both cases an egg donor
was used and sperm was provided by the intended fathers. In each case, an Indian
birth certificate listed the intended father as the legal parent, but there was no
mention of a mother on the birth certificate. In both cases, the Indian birth
certificate was recognised in Belgium on the grounds of the best interests of the
child. In the latter case, human rights arguments were used to justify the decision.
In particular, it was held that a refusal to recognise the birth certificate would
infringe the child's and the intended father's right to family life, guaranteed by
Article 8 of the European Convention on Human Rights.

Lastly, it appears that full recognition of a foreign birth certificate in a cross-
border surrogacy case is possible in Hungary too. In particular, it has been
reported that 'case-law suggests that Hungarian courts may recognise the for-

---

[224] Cour de Cassation, Chambre Civile 1, 6 avril 2011, 09-66.486, Publié au bulletin, ch 7 of this
book, section B.

[225] *Ibid.*

[226] *Samuel*, Court of First Instance Brussels, 15 February 2011; see ch 3 of this book.

[227] *AM & ND*, Court of First Instance Nivelles, 6 April 2011; *ibid.*

[228] *C*, Court of First Instance Brussels, 6 April 2010; *ibid.*

eign birth certificate … without *ex officio* investigating the circumstances of the conception and the birth'.[229]

(2) Partial Recognition of a Foreign Birth Certificate

In several recent cases in Belgium, the courts have recognised a foreign birth certificate as a valid authentic instrument in so far as it established the legal parentage of the intended father. This outcome was first arrived at in the case of *H & E*.[230] This involved a surrogacy arrangement between a Belgian married couple and a Ukrainian surrogate mother. Embryos were created using the intended parents' gametes, and the surrogate mother gave birth to a set of twins. Birth certificates were issued in Ukraine, listing the intended parents as the legal parents of the children. The couple then sought recognition of the birth certificates in Belgium. The court held that it could not recognise the intended mother as the legal mother of the child as such recognition would undermine the Belgian domestic rule on legal motherhood (ie the rule that the woman who gives birth to a child is to be regarded as the legal mother). The court opined, however, that there was nothing wrong with recognising the legal parenthood of the intended father. This resulted in a partial recognition of the birth certificates, ie the documents were recognised in so far as they established the legal parentage of the intended father.

Belgian courts have applied the 'partial recognition' approach analogously to cases involving gay couples as intended parents, with the outcome that only the man who was genetically related to the child was recognised as the legal father. An example is the case of *M & M*,[231] which involved a surrogacy arrangement commissioned by a Belgian gay couple in California. Donor eggs and the intended fathers' genetic material were used to create embryos. The arrangements resulted in the birth of a set of twins. Before the birth of the children, the Californian Supreme Court declared both men to be the genetic and legal parents, and ordered that their names be placed on the birth certificates once the children were born. The children were brought to Belgium on US passports. Once in Belgium the couple sought registration of the birth certificates in the civil register. The registration was opposed by the public prosecutor, however, so the men decided to initiate legal proceedings for recognition of the Californian birth certificates. Although the first instance court refused the recognition on the grounds of public policy, this decision was overturned on appeal. The appellate court acknowledged that surrogacy contracts were void under public policy principles, but held that the illicit nature of such contracts could not infringe on the superior interests of the child. Refusal to recognise the Californian birth certificates would deprive the children of any parentage link with their genetic father, and this would discriminate against them harshly. Consequently, the court recognised the legal parenthood of the genetic father, thus partially recognising the Californian birth certificates.

---

[229] See ch 11 of this book.
[230] *H & E*, Court of First Instance Antwerp, 19 December 2008; see ch 3 of this book.
[231] *M & M*, Court of Appeal Liège, 6 September 2010; *ibid*.

(3) Recognition of a Judgment on Parenthood Issued in the Country of Birth

In December 2011, the Austrian Constitutional Court was called upon to decide a case involving a cross-border surrogacy arrangement between an American surrogate mother (resident in the US state of Georgia) and Austrian/Italian intended parents.[232] The couple were Austrian residents, although only the intended mother was an Austrian citizen. As surrogacy is prohibited in Austria, the couple decided to explore the option of cross-border surrogacy. Consequently, two surrogacy arrangements were commissioned by the couple in the US (in 2006 and in 2009 respectively), with the same surrogate mother and in both cases the couple using their own genetic material. Two children were born as a result of these arrangements. The children became US citizens by birth, and later also obtained Austrian citizenship. However, when the intended mother claimed child benefits, the Austrian Ministry of Interior requested that the Austrian nationality be withdrawn on the basis that surrogacy was illegal in Austria, that under Austrian law the surrogate mother remained the children's legal mother and that the US court's decision establishing legal parenthood of the intended mother could therefore not be recognised in Austria. These arguments were, however, rejected by the Austrian Constitutional Court on the following grounds, among others:

(a) The US judgment determining legal parenthood of the intended mother was taken without reference to Austrian law and was therefore valid under norms of private international law.

(b) The Austrian law prohibiting surrogacy was not a part of Austrian public policy (*ordre publique*) so public policy could not override the recognition of the US judgment.

(c) The surrogate mother could not be forced by Austrian law into the position of the legal mother against her will.

(d) When determining the issue of nationality, the Ministry of Interior had acted arbitrarily by ignoring scholarly views and case law on public policy, and by failing to consider the welfare of the children.

(4) Administrative Initiatives

In Spain, a more lenient approach has recently been taken at the administrative level. In October 2010, the *Dirección General de los Registros y del Notariado*, which is an administrative body in charge of the Civil Register, issued a Resolution to instruct civil registrars how to proceed in cases involving cross-border surrogacy.[233] Normally, civil registrars in Spain register legal parenthood established by a foreign

---

[232] Decision of the Constitutional Court (*Verfassungsgerichtshof*) No B 13/11-10, 14 December 2011, full text in German is available at <www.//eudo-citizenship.eu/caselawDB/docs/AT%20VfGH%20 B1311_10.pdf, and a summary of the decision in English can be found at www://eudo-citizenship.eu/ citizenship-case-law/?search=1&name=&year=&country=Austria&national=1>.

[233] Instrucción de 5 de octubre de 2010, de la Dirección General de los Registros y del Notariado, sobre regimen registral de la filiación de los nacidos mediante gestación por sustitución; see ch 21 of this book.

judgment only if the judgment has first been formally recognised by a Spanish court. The Resolution, however, instructs the registrars that in cross-border surrogacy cases, the prior recognition of the foreign judgment by the court is not necessary. Instead, if certain conditions are met, the civil registry is competent to pronounce the authenticity of the foreign judgment and to register the birth in Spain without recognition of the foreign judgment by a court. The Resolution requires, for example, that:

(a) the foreign judgment was issued in uncontested proceedings;
(b) procedural rights of the parties, in particular the surrogate mother, were guaranteed in the foreign proceedings;
(c) there was no infringement of the best interests of the child and the surrogate mother; and
(d) the surrogate mother gave her consent freely and voluntarily, without error, violence or fraud.[234]

Importantly, the Resolution does not require that the foreign judgment is not contrary to Spanish public policy.[235]

Administrative initiatives in The Netherlands indicate that in due course the country might also move towards a more permissive approach to cross-border surrogacy. In particular, in a letter from the Secretary of State for Safety and Justice (F Teeven) addressed to the Chairman of the House of Representatives dated 16 December 2011,[236] the Secretary summarised the problems that arise from cross-border surrogacy arrangements in The Netherlands and proposed, amongst others, the following measures:

(a) cross-border surrogacy arrangements should be accepted in The Netherlands where at least one of the intended parents shares a genetic link with the child; and
(b) no judgment should be passed on the expenses paid to the surrogate mother in cross-border scenarios.

Undoubtedly, the proposed approach goes against the current Dutch policy on surrogacy,[237] and it is unclear whether the proposed regulation would extend to domestic surrogacy cases too.

---

[234] *Ibid.*
[235] *Ibid.*
[236] F Teeven (Ministry of Justice), 'Onderwerp Draagmoederschap', 16 December 2011, available at <www.google.co.uk/url?sa=t&rct=j&q=&esrc=s&frm=1&source=web&cd=1&ved=0CE0QFjAA& url=http%3A%2F%2Fwww.rijksoverheid.nl%2Fbestanden%2Fdocumenten-en-publicaties%2Fkame rstukken%2F2011%2F12%2F16%2Fbrief-tweede-kamer-draagmoederschap%2Fdraagmoederschap. pdf&ei=8agGUMCvAoTPhAeR8ZHYBw&usg=AFQjCNE3nkzqBGfBJYlliGSBP10Y8aihiw&sig2=j49 4p4s9wS8hlDU06i7U_A>.
[237] Currently, surrogacy is not regulated in The Netherlands; nevertheless, commercial surrogacy is criminalised under Dutch law. For a detailed overview of the Dutch domestic approach to surrogacy, see ch 17 of this book.

(5) Acknowledgement of Paternity

In some countries a more liberal approach has been taken in relation to acknowledgement of paternity by intended fathers in cross-border surrogacy cases. It has been reported that in Germany, for example, 'the public policy exception seems to be handled less strictly [in cases of acknowledgement of paternity] than in questions of motherhood as a whole'.[238] In at least one reported German cross-border surrogacy case, German authorities applied foreign (Russian) law to decide whether the intended father had undertaken a valid acknowledgement of paternity in Russia. This resulted in the acknowledgement undertaken by the intended father in Russia being held valid in Germany.[239]

In two cases in Switzerland, intended fathers successfully acknowledged the child before a Swiss court, following a refusal by a Swiss consulate to recognise the foreign birth certificate.[240] In one of these cases, the acknowledgement of paternity was possible even though the intended father was not the genetic father of the child.[241]

Lastly, according to French law, it is open to French intended fathers in cross-border surrogacy cases to acknowledge paternity to establish their legal parenthood.[242] This avenue was advocated by the *Conseil d'Etat* during the review of the French Bioethics Act 1994 in July 2011. In particular, the *Conseil d'Etat* suggested that 'the prohibition of the establishment of maternity between the intending mother and the child should be maintained'; however, 'acknowledgement of paternity should become the main alternative to the prohibition of surrogacy'.[243]

b. Common Law Countries

As mentioned above, in most common law jurisdictions, the law of the forum, ie the *lex fori*, will be used to determine legal parenthood of a child born as a result of a cross-border surrogacy arrangement. In some of these jurisdictions, domestic law on parenthood expressly states that it has an extraterritorial effect, ie it applies regardless of whether the child was born in the State concerned or abroad.[244] Available case law confirms that a foreign birth certificate cannot suffice as a proof of legal parenthood; instead, parenthood is to be decided in accordance with the *lex fori*.[245] In a number of common law jurisdictions, this approach has been

---

[238] See ch 8 of this book. For a comprehensive analysis of the German approach to paternity see S Kamei, 'Partitioning Paternity: The German Approach to a Disjuncture Between Genetic and Legal Paternity With Implications for American Courts' (2009-2010) 11 *San Diego International Law Journal* 509.

[239] AG Nürnberg, UR III 0264/09, 14 December 2009; see ch 8 of this book.

[240] 2012 Hague Report, above n 19, para 37.

[241] *Ibid.*

[242] See ch 7 of this book.

[243] 'La Révision Des Lois de Bioéthique', étude du Conseil d'État parue à la Documentation française, in particular pp 47–54; see ch 7 of this book.

[244] Eg the UK (HFEA 2008, s 33(3)) and New Zealand (the Status of Children Act 1969, s 5(3)).

[245] In the UK, for example, the issue was first tested before the High Court in *X & Y (Foreign Surrogacy)* [2008] EWHC 3030 (Fam). The court made it clear that English law on parenthood applied to the determination of legal parenthood in a cross-border surrogacy case.

reaffirmed through guidance issued by the State authorities for intended parents in cross-border surrogacy cases. For example, guidance issued by the UK Border Agency states that

> anyone considering entering into an inter-country surrogacy arrangement must remember that if they reside in the United Kingdom, they are subject to United Kingdom law and the definitions which underlie it.[246]

Similarly, a guidance document published by the Irish Ministry of Justice and Equality provides that in considering the issue of legal parenthood in relation to children born as a result of a surrogacy arrangement outside Ireland, 'the Irish authorities are required to apply Irish law'.[247] The document further notes that 'foreign birth certificates or court orders are not necessarily binding in Irish law or upon Irish authorities'.[248] In the same way, the guidance produced by the Ministry of Social Development of New Zealand makes it plain to the intended parents that:

> In all cases of international surrogacy, where you arrange for a child to be born to a surrogate mother overseas, and you intend to bring the child back to live with you in New Zealand, New Zealand Law will apply. In particular, you should be aware that the legal relationship between you (as the commissioning parents) and a child born as a result of a surrogacy arrangement taking place overseas, will be governed by New Zealand Law.[249]

Despite the fact that commercial surrogacy is illegal/against public policy in these countries, it appears that there are two possible avenues through which intended parents in commercial cross-border surrogacy cases, who are living in common law jurisdictions, may be able to achieve a full transfer of legal parenthood. It must, however, be noted that these avenues are rather uncertain as they have been used by courts solely as ad hoc remedies, with no guarantee that they will be granted to all intended parents. A successful outcome is sometimes dependent on the existence of a genetic link between the child and at least one of the intended parents.

Application of Legislation on Altruistic Surrogacy

In those common law countries where surrogacy is regulated and the legislation provides for a mechanism for the transfer of legal parenthood, the intended parents might be able to utilise these provisions, if relevant statutory requirements can be satisfied. However, given the fact that the transfer procedure was designed by the legislator exclusively for altruistic surrogacy cases, the analogous use of

---

[246] UK Border Agency Rules, above n 180, para 10.

[247] Ministry of Justice and Equality, 'Citizenship, Parentage, Guardianship and Travel Document Issues in Relation to Children Born as a Result of Surrogacy Arrangements Entered into Outside the State' section 1, available at <www.inis.gov.ie/en/JELR/20120221%20Guidance%20Document.pdf/Files/20120221%20Guidance%20Document.pdf>.

[248] *Ibid.*

[249] NZ Ministry Guidelines, above n 202.

these provisions in cross-border commercial surrogacy cases is possible only where the courts have discretion to relax the statutory limit on the payment to the surrogate mother. Currently, this is possible only in the UK,[250] where, under section 54(8) of the Human Fertilisation and Embryology Act 2008, the courts are entitled retrospectively to authorise payments made to the surrogate mother exceeding reasonable pregnancy-related expenses in parental order applications.[251] The landmark decision was the case in *Re L (a minor)*,[252] where legal parenthood was awarded to a British couple who had entered into a surrogacy arrangement in Illinois, USA. The court held that, despite the fact that payments to the surrogate mother had exceeded reasonable expenses, the child's welfare dictated that the parental order be made. The court concluded that one of the effects of the Human Fertilisation and Embryology Act 2008 was that the child's welfare should not only be taken into consideration but should be the court's paramount consideration in parental order proceedings involving international surrogacy arrangements.[253] The court held:

> The effect of that must be to weight the balance between public policy considerations and welfare ... decisively in favour of welfare. It must follow that it will only be in the clearest case of the abuse of public policy that the court will be able to withhold an order if otherwise welfare considerations support its making.[254]

The court nevertheless acknowledged the tension between the public policy against commercial surrogacy and the paramountcy of the welfare principle, and

---

[250] Other common law jurisdictions where domestic legislation provides for a mechanism for the transfer of legal parenthood in altruistic surrogacy cases are the Australian states of New South Wales, Queensland, South Australia, Western Australia, Victoria and the Australian Capital Territory. In these jurisdictions, intended parents in altruistic surrogacy cases may apply for a parentage order the effect of which is a full transfer of legal parenthood from the surrogate mother (and her husband if applicable) to the intended parents. The procedure is not applicable, however, in commercial surrogacy cases. For more information, see section II.B. above.

[251] Section 54 of the HFEA 2008 replaced s 30 of the HFEA 1990 and permitted civil partners and couples in an enduring family relationship to apply for a parental order, in addition to married couples. Applications for a parental order under s 30 of the HFEA1990 in the cross-border context included *Re X & Y (Foreign Surrogacy)* [2008] EWHC 3030 (Fam); *Re S (Parental Order)* [2009] EWHC 2977 (Fam); and *Re G (Surrogacy: Foreign Domicile)* [2007] EWHC 2814.

[252] *Re L (a minor)* [2010] EWHC 3146 (Fam).

[253] *Ibid*, [9]. Justice Hedley explained that the Human Fertilisation and Embryology (Parental Orders) Regulations 2010 apply certain provisions of current adoption legislation (ie the Adoption and Children Act 2002) to applications for parental orders under s 54 of the HFEA 2008. In particular, the application of s 1 of the Adoption and Children Act 2002 to parental order applications means that the child's welfare is the court's paramount consideration when deciding whether or not to make a parental order. See also *Re X Children* [2011] EWHC 3147 (Fam), [30]. The Human Fertilisation and Embryology (Parental Orders) Regulations 2010 give effect to s 54 of the HFEA 2008 and replace the Parental Orders (Human Fertilisation and Embryology) Regulations 1994 and the Parental Orders (Human Fertilisation and Embryology) (Scotland) Regulations 1994. For more information, see 'Explanatory Memorandum to the Human Fertilisation and Embryology (Parental Orders) Regulations 2010', No 985/2010, available at <www.legislation.gov.uk/uksi/2010/985/pdfs/uksiem_20100985_en.pdf> ('Explanatory Memorandum').

[254] *Re L (a minor)* [2010] EWHC 3146 (Fam), [10].

expressed the view that applications for authorisation under section 54(8) of the 2008 Act should continue to be scrutinised carefully on a case-by-case basis.[255]

The line of reasoning established in *Re L (a minor)* was followed in 2011 cases: *Re X (Children)*,[256] *A and A v P, P and B*[257] and *Re IJ (A Child)*.[258] *Re X (Children)* involved two separate commercial surrogacy arrangements between one British couple and two Indian surrogate mothers. One child was born as a result of each of these arrangements, and parental orders were awarded to the British couple. In the case of *A and A v P, P and B*, a British couple entered into a surrogacy arrangement in India. Sadly, the intended father, who was also the genetic father, died unexpectedly during the parental order proceedings. Although it was not clear whether the intended mother was genetically related to the child,[259] the court concluded that the paramountcy of the welfare principle required that a parental order be made.[260] Lastly, the case *of IJ (A Child)*[261] concerned a surrogacy arrangement which was entered into between a British couple and a married Ukrainian surrogate. The child was conceived as a result of the fertilisation of an egg from an anonymous egg donor by sperm from the intended father. The intended parents experienced difficulties in obtaining immigration clearance for the entry of the child to the UK[262]; however, once in the country, they were able to apply successfully for a parental order.

To sum up, reported case law shows that despite the underlying public policy against commercial surrogacy in the UK, the courts have generally been sympathetic to the situation of the intended parents, using their discretion to authorise payments exceeding reasonable expenses under section 54 of the Human Fertilisation and Embryology Act 2008. It appears that a parental order would indeed be denied only in the case of 'a clear abuse of public policy'.[263] The test

---

[255] *Ibid*, [12].

[256] *Re X (Children)* [2011] EWHC 3147 (Fam).

[257] *A and A v P, P and B* [2011] EWHC 1738 (Fam).

[258] *Re IJ (A Child)* [2011] EWHC 921 (Fam).

[259] The uncertainty was due to the fact that five embryos were transferred to the surrogate mother's womb, two of which were formed from the intended mother's eggs and three from donor eggs. All eggs were fertilised with the intended father's sperm: *A and A v P, P and B* [2011] EWHC 1738 (Fam), [4].

[260] Consideration was given also to the United Nations Convention on the Rights of the Child, in particular Art 8 of that Convention, which requires Contracting States to protect the child's right to identity. The court held that the concept of identity included the legal recognition of a relationship between a child and his or her parents. If the application for a parental order was rejected, it would seriously impact the child's right to have his identity protected. In particular, the consequences of not making an order in this case would be as follows: '(i) There is no legal relationship between the child and his biological father; (ii) The child is denied the social and emotional benefits of recognition of that relationship; (iii) The child may be financially disadvantaged if he is not recognised legally as the child of his father (in terms of inheritance); (iv) The child does not have a legal reality which matches the day to day reality; (v) The child is further disadvantaged by the death of his biological father.' *Ibid*, [26].

[261] *Re IJ (A Child)* [2011] EWHC 921 (Fam).

[262] *Ibid*, [3].

[263] *Re L (a minor)* [2010] EWHC 3146 (Fam), [10].

to determine the issue of public policy involves an assessment of several separate questions:

(a) Was the payment disproportionate to reasonable expenses? Can it be classified as 'a payment effectively buying children overseas'?
(b) Were the intended parents acting in good faith and without 'moral taint'? Was the sum paid such as to 'overbear the will' of the surrogate mother?
(c) Were the intended parents acting in an attempt to defraud the authorities? Were the arrangements used to 'circumvent the childcare laws' in the UK?[264]

In compliance with the test, evidence that public policy had not been 'clearly abused' was drawn in the litigated cases from facts such as:

(a) the applicants were genuine, acting in good faith and without any intention to defraud the authorities;[265]
(b) the applicants acted on the basis of erroneous/incomplete legal advice received from a foreign surrogacy agency;[266]
(c) the payments to the surrogate mother were in the view of the court not disproportionate;[267] or
(d) the level of payments could not have overborne the will of the surrogate mother.[268]

This is not to suggest, however, that the courts have found the process of authorisation comfortable. In the words of Hedley J:

> The difficulty is that it is almost impossible to imagine a set of circumstances in which by the time the case comes to court, the welfare of any child (particularly a foreign child) would not be gravely compromised (at the very least) by a refusal to make an order. ... If public policy is truly to be upheld, it would need to be enforced at a much earlier stage than the final hearing of a section 30 application.[269]

(1) Effect of a Parental Order: Transfer of Legal Parenthood

The effect of a parental order is that it provides for a child to be treated as the legitimate child of the intended parents, with, inter alia, the attendant rights of inheritance from the intended parents and the right to be registered as a British citizen.[270] A parental order confers parental responsibility for

---

[264] *X & Y (Foreign Surrogacy)* [2008] EWHC 3030 Fam, [21]; and *Re S (Parental Order)* [2009] EWHC 2977 (Fam).
[265] *Re X (Children)* [2011] EWHC 3147 (Fam), [32] and [41]. Also *X & Y (Foreign Surrogacy)* [2008] EWHC 3030 (Fam), [21].
[266] *Re L (a minor)* [2010] EWHC 3146 (Fam), [8].
[267] *Re X (Children)* [2011] EWHC 3147 (Fam), [41].
[268] *A and A v P, P and B* [2011] EWHC 1738 (Fam), [33].
[269] *X & Y (Foreign Surrogacy)* [2008] EWHC 3030 Fam, [24]. The reference to 'section 30' is to HFEA 1990.
[270] Explanatory Memorandum, above n 253, para 2.1. See also UK Border Agency Rules, above n 180, para 37 (the child can be registered as a British citizen under s 3(1) of the British Nationality Act 1981, ie acquisition of British citizenship 'other than by descent').

the child exclusively on the intended parents, and extinguishes the parental responsibility of anyone else.[271]

However, where the intended parents do not meet the statutory requirements for application for a parental order,[272] alternative solutions have to be resorted to. In particular, the intended parents might need to apply for adoption, special guardianship or a residence order.[273] A full transfer of legal parentage in a surrogacy situation can, nevertheless, be achieved only through a parental order under the Human Fertilisation and Embryology Act 2008 as described above, or through adoption.[274] Although an adoption order produces the same effects as a parental order, a successful application of adoption legislation to surrogacy cases in the UK (in particular cases involving commercial surrogacy) is rather uncertain.

(2) Parental Responsibility v Legal Parenthood

Special guardianship and a residence order can be considered only as 'second best' options in the UK, as neither of them confers full legal parenthood on the intended parents; the intended parents acquire only parental responsibility.[275] It should be pointed out that legal parenthood and parental responsibility, although interrelated, are not identical concepts. Parental responsibility, as understood in English law, may be characterised as follows:

(a) Parental responsibility is subsumed within the concept of legal parenthood (ie a parental/adoption order confers parental responsibility on the intended parents). Legal parenthood is 'a matter of responsibility rather than of rights'.[276] Parental responsibility is defined as 'all the rights, duties, powers, responsibility and authority which by law a parent of a child has in relation to the child and his property',[277] and comprises at least the following:[278]

  (i) bringing up the child;
  (ii) having contact with the child;
  (iii) protecting and maintaining the child;
  (iv) disciplining the child;

---

[271] N Lowe and G Douglas, *Bromley's Family Law*, 10th edn (Oxford, Oxford University Press, 2007) 317.

[272] The most common reasons could be that neither of the intended parents is genetically related to the child, that the six-month time limit for the application for a parental order has passed, that neither of the intended parents is domiciled in the UK, or that the surrogate mother refused to give her consent to the transfer of legal parenthood. For a detailed analysis of the UK legislation, see section II. above.

[273] See ch 23 of this book. See also section II. above.

[274] Lowe and Douglas, above n 271, 305, stating that generally legal parentage can be achieved in three ways: (i) it can be assigned automatically (not applicable to surrogacy); (ii) it can be acquired through the making of a parental order under the HFEA 2008; or (iii) it can be acquired through adoption.

[275] *Ibid*, 419 and 436.

[276] *Ibid*, 369.

[277] *Ibid*, 374.

[278] *Ibid*, 377.

524 Katarina Trimmings and Paul Beaumont

(v) determining and providing for the child's education;

(vi) determining the child's religion;

(vii) consenting to the child's medical treatment;

(viii) consenting to the child's marriage;

(ix) consenting to the child's adoption;

(x) vetoing the issue of the child's passport;

(xi) taking the child outside the UK and consenting to the child's emigration;

(xii) administering the child's property;

(xiii) naming the child;

(xiv) representing the child in legal proceedings;

(xv) disposing of the child's corpse; and

(xvi) appointing a guardian for the child.

(b) Parental responsibility is a narrower concept than legal parenthood as it does not include, for example, the rights of inheritance from the intended parents or the right to be registered as a British citizen. Similarly, the child does not fall within the meaning of 'children' in formal documents, including 'family trusts, grandparents' wills and pension policies'.[279]

(c) Parental responsibility ends upon the child attaining his majority. In contrast, legal parenthood is an enduring status; it does not end with the child's majority but applies throughout the child's lifetime. Legal parenthood can be extinguished only by the court granting an adoption or parental order.[280]

(d) At birth, parental responsibility is automatically assigned to each of the married parents (ie surrogate mother and her husband, if married) or to the unmarried mother (ie unmarried surrogate mother). Where the surrogate mother is unmarried, the intended father can acquire parental responsibility after the child's birth, inter alia, by being registered as the father on the child's birth certificate, by making a parental responsibility agreement with the surrogate mother, by obtaining a parental responsibility order, by obtaining a residence order (in this case a separate parental responsibility order must be made) or upon being formally appointed as the guardian of the child.[281] Where the intended parents are married or in a civil partnership, the intended mother can subsequently acquire parental responsibility as a step-parent.[282]

(e) Parental responsibility is not lost merely because someone else acquires it.[283] This implies that a surrogate mother (and her husband if applicable) does not cease to have parental responsibility over a child solely because it is subsequently acquired by the intended parents. Parental responsibility can be transferred from the surrogate mother (and her husband if applicable) to the intended parents only through a parental/adoption order.[284]

---

[279] N Gamble and Associates, 'Legal Status: Legal Parenthood and Adoption', available at <www.nataliegambleassociates.co.uk/page/parenthood/57/>.

[280] Lowe and Douglas, above n 271, 377.

[281] Ibid, 409–10.

[282] For more information see ibid, 422–23.

[283] Ibid, 430.

[284] Ibid, 431.

Although applications for special guardianship or a residence order are not commonly opted for by intended parents in cross-border commercial surrogacy cases in the UK, the avenue of parental responsibility appears to be frequently used by intended parents in cross-border commercial surrogacy cases in Australia.[285] In Australia, the intended parents can apply for a parenting order under the federal Family Law Act 1975, the effect of which is that it determines parental responsibility without transferring legal parenthood to the intended parents.[286] Reported case law indicates that the majority of applications in cross-border surrogacy cases are for parenting orders.[287]

Application of Adoption Legislation

Where legislation on altruistic surrogacy cannot be applied,[288] intended parents in cross-border surrogacy cases might be able to achieve a full transfer of legal parenthood through adoption. Available case law indicates that this has been the trend in cross-border surrogacy cases in New Zealand and to some extent in Australia.[289] In New Zealand, where the welfare test points to the outcome that the child's best interests will be best served by the child remaining in the care of the intended parents, it appears that a domestic adoption order under the New Zealand Adoption Act 1955 will be granted.[290] This seems to be the case in altruistic as well as commercial cross-border surrogacy cases.[291]

New Zealand judges have, nevertheless, voiced concerns over the application of adoption legislation to cross-border surrogacy cases, in particular the fact that the contemporary nature of cross-border surrogacy arrangements made the adoption

---

[285] See above n 250, explaining why a full transfer of legal parenthood through a parentage order is not possible in cross-border commercial surrogacy cases in Australia. See also n 289 below on the application of domestic adoption legislation in cross-border surrogacy cases in Australia.

[286] See section II.B. above.

[287] See ch 2 of this book, fn 73, noting that out of 29 published surrogacy cases, 19 were applications for parenting orders.

[288] Eg because the scope of the legislation is limited to domestic surrogacy arrangements (either by express provisions or implicitly) and no discretion is afforded to courts regarding the payments to the surrogate mother (eg Australia, see ch 2 of this book), or because the legislation on altruistic surrogacy does not contain specific provisions on the transfer of legal parenthood in surrogacy cases (eg New Zealand, see ch 18 of this book).

[289] See ch 18 of this book; and ch 2, fn 151, noting that of the 17 published international surrogacy cases, one was an adoption application and one for leave to adopt.

[290] See ch 18 of this book. Although in all published cross-border surrogacy cases in New Zealand the child was genetically related to at least one of the intended parents, there is no indication in the case law that a different approach would be taken by the courts in the absence of the genetic link. See, eg, *Re an application by BWS to adopt a child* [2011] New Zealand Family Law Reports 621, where the relevant issues to be considered by the court in making an adoption order were summarised as follows: (i) whether the adoption needed to be effected as an intercountry adoption; (ii) whether the egg donor's consent to adoption was required; (iii) if the intended parents were fit and proper to parent the children; (iv) whether the payment made to the surrogate mother was in breach of s 25 of the Adoption Act 1995; and (v) if the child's best interests and welfare would be promoted by the making of an adoption order.

[291] Altruistic: *Re KJB and LRB (Adoption)* [2010] New Zealand Family Law Reports 97; commercial: *Re an application by KR and DGR to adopt a female child* [2011] New Zealand Family Law Reports 429; and *Re an application by BWS to adopt a child* [2011] New Zealand Family Law Reports 621.

legislation inappropriate to deal with the issue.[292] It was also recommended that adoption applications in cross-border surrogacy cases be scrutinised carefully on a case-by-case basis.[293] Not surprisingly, judges have raised policy considerations with respect to payments to surrogate mothers, noting that such payments did not 'sit well with New Zealand's efforts to prohibit certain commercial transactions relating to human reproduction,'[294] but concluded that it was not the role of the court to impose those policy considerations. Instead, it was the task of the legislator to 'put in place rules and protocols surrounding IVF procedures undertaken in foreign countries by New Zealanders'.[295]

It ought to be noted that, initially, there was some confusion in New Zealand as to whether cross-border surrogacy cases should be treated as cases of intercountry adoption, and therefore dealt with under the 1993 Hague Adoption Convention. Guidelines on International Surrogacy issued by the Ministry of Social Development of New Zealand advised intended parents that

> [a]n intercountry adoption is the only way [intended parents] can create a legal parental relationship with a child born as a result of a surrogacy arrangement in a country that is a signatory to the Convention, eg India, USA.[296]

This (clearly incorrect) approach was, however, rejected by New Zealand courts.[297]

c. Mixed Legal Systems

Two countries with mixed legal systems involved in our research study were South Africa and Israel.[298] The South African national report (chapter twenty) does not discuss the possibility of South African intended parents travelling to a 'surrogacy-friendly' jurisdiction with the view to commissioning a surrogacy arrangement there and then seeking recognition of their parental status in South Africa. Presumably, the issue has not yet been tested before South African courts, or relevant judicial decisions have not been reported. In any case, it appears that there is not a tendency among South African nationals/residents

---

[292] *Re KJB and LRB (Adoption)* [2010] New Zealand Family Law Reports 97, para 39; see ch 18 of this book, fn 90.

[293] *Ibid,* para 37; see ch 18 of this book, fn 91.

[294] *Re an application by BWS to adopt a child* [2011] New Zealand Family Law Reports 621, para 83; see ch 18 of this book, fn 109.

[295] *Re an application by KR and DGR to adopt a female child* [2011] New Zealand Family Law Reports 429, para 20; see ch 18 of this book, fn 99.

[296] See NZ Ministry Guidelines, above n 202.

[297] See *Re application by L* [2003] New Zealand Family Law Reports 529, para 19; *Re an application by KR and DGR to adopt a female child* [2011] New Zealand Family Law Reports 429, para 14; and *Re an application by BWS to adopt a child* [2011] New Zealand Family Law Reports 621. On the inapplicability of the 1993 Hague Adoption Convention to cross-border surrogacy cases, see section V. below.

[298] Both South Africa and Israel combine three legal traditions. In South Africa, it is a civil law system inherited from the Dutch, a common law system inherited from the British and a customary law system inherited from indigenous Africans. Israel's legal system is a combination of common law, civil law and Jewish law.

to commission surrogacy arrangements abroad.[299] The situation is, however, diametrically opposed in Israel, as Israeli nationals/residents, in particular Israeli male same-sex couples, account for a large number of intended parents commissioning surrogacy abroad.[300]

Where at least one of the intended parents is genetically related to the child, the transfer of legal parenthood in cross-border surrogacy cases appears to be relatively straightforward in Israel. Once a genetic link is confirmed through a DNA test, the genetic intended parent is regarded as the legal parent and is registered as such, without any reference being made to the involvement of the surrogacy procedure in the official records.[301] The Israeli Ministry of Interior has confirmed that, like in common law jurisdictions, foreign birth certificates cannot suffice as a proof of parenthood in Israel.[302] The only avenue for the non-genetic intended parent to regularise his or her relationship with the child is through adoption.[303]

iv. Conclusion

For a number of reasons, the above examples of solutions 'invented' by judicial and administrative authorities of different countries to fill in the existing legal vacuum on surrogacy are, unfortunately, far from adequate. First, in many jurisdictions, procedures used to achieve these solutions were originally not designed for surrogacy situations and are therefore not suitable for application to surrogacy cases. As a result, the procedures are often very complex and lengthy, adding additional stress and costs for the intended parents, who might be forced to stay in the country of birth for an extended period of time. Secondly, in addition to their ad hoc nature, in relation to legal parenthood these remedies normally offer partial solutions only, whereby merely the position of the intended father is regularised. The position of the intended mother (or the other intended father in the case of gay intended parents) remains uncertain, with often no or only limited options of acquiring legal parenthood.[304] This is particularly true in relation to some civil law countries. In other jurisdictions, the situation appears to be even more alarming, as often no remedies at all are available to either of the intended parents. In Australia, for example, many intended parents cannot acquire legal parenthood but only parental responsibility through a parental order under the

---

[299] No South African intended parents were recorded in our statistical survey. See section III. above.

[300] Our statistical survey has revealed that in cross-border surrogacy arrangements facilitated by two US agencies between 2006 and 2010, 19% of each involved Israeli intended parents. More detailed data were provided by one of the agencies, and these showed that 67% of the Israeli intended parents were gay couples. See section III. above.

[301] See ch 14 of this book.

[302] *Ibid*. This approach has been questioned in the case of HCJ 566/11 *DM-M et al v The Ministry of Interior* (currently pending before the Israeli High Court of Justice).

[303] See ch 14 of this book.

[304] One of the options might be adoption; however, in some countries the adoption process might be far from straightforward where the child was born as a result of a commercial cross-border surrogacy arrangement.

federal Family Law Act 1975. Although this enables them to care for the child on a day-to-day basis, it does not acknowledge them as the child's legal parents.[305] Lastly, it has rightly been pointed out that many cross-border surrogacy cases are further complicated by a 'catch 22' dimension, meaning that the intended parents must return from the country of birth in order to establish legal parentage in their home country, but often find it difficult to bring a child into their home country before first establishing legal parentage.[306]

In jurisdictions where the ad hoc, partial remedies have been crafted, there is a clear trend to focus primarily on the best interests of the child, with the result that the welfare principle trumps the public policy concerns that surround cross-border (in particular commercial) surrogacy. Despite the obvious tension between the two policy goals, the inclination to favour the best interests of the child is based on the objective to lessen the detrimental impact of the legal limbo for children born as a result of a cross-border surrogacy arrangement. Given the absence of a regulatory framework, this line of reasoning is considered reasonable. Indeed, courts in cross-border surrogacy cases are faced with a *fait accompli* where the welfare of a very young child is at stake, and it would therefore be unrealistic to expect them to implement the policy considerations against commercial surrogacy strictly at this late stage. This is not to say, however, that the current situation is desirable or satisfactory. Indeed, the present status quo clearly points to the need for a global regulatory mechanism of cross-border surrogacy to ensure that the legal status of children born through cross-border surrogacy is 'remedied by a more direct, transparent and inclusive legislative response'.[307]

C. Summary of Ethical Concerns

A number of commentators have expressed objections against commercialisation of surrogacy.[308] These objections may be summarised as follows:

— Commercialisation of conception, reduction of women to their child-bearing capacity and commodification of women's bodies and children.[309]

---

[305] For more information, including analysis of the difference between legal parenthood and parental responsibility, see section IV.B.iii.a. above.

[306] See Millbank, above n 87, 198.

[307] *Ibid*, 203.

[308] Eg RL Lee, 'New Trends in Global Outsourcing of Commercial Surrogacy: A Call for Regulation' (2009) 20 *Hastings Women's Law Journal* 275.

[309] Eg D Spar, *The Baby Business: How Money, Science and Politics Drive the Commerce of Conception* (Harvard, Mass, Harvard Business School Press, 2006) (the book has been reviewed by J Robertson in 'Commerce and Regulation in the Assisted Reproduction Industry' (2006-2007) 85 *Texas Law Review* 665); C Kerian, 'Surrogacy: A Last Resort Alternative for Infertile Women or Commodification on Women's Bodies and Children' (1997) 12 *Wisconsin Women's Law Journal* 113; R McCormick, 'Surrogacy: A Catholic Perspective' (1991–1992) 25 *Creighton Law Review* 1617; W Wagner, 'The Ethical and Legal Implications of Hired Maternity' (1990) 35 *The American Journal of Jurisprudence* 187; Lee, above n 308. The view that surrogacy commodifies women's bodies is opposed by some commentators on the grounds of the 'freedom of choice' and/or the 'party autonomy' arguments. See, eg,

— Exploitation of women in developing countries due to a disparity of status between surrogate mothers and intended parents.[310]
— Concerns over the physical well-being of surrogate mothers.[311]
— Displacement of resources from adoption to surrogacy.[312] When millions of orphaned or abandoned children in the developing world are in need of families, there is no need to produce more children. Intercountry adoption should instead be encouraged as an alternative to surrogacy.[313]
— Risk of 'commissioning' children for sinister purposes, including paedophilia, or other forms of physical or psychological abuse.[314]
— Concerns over trafficking in women and children.[315]

C Kerian, 'Surrogacy: A Last Resort Alternative for Infertile Women or a Commodification of Women's Bodies and Children?' (1997) 12 *Wisconsin Women's Law Journal* 113; J Grant, 'Intimate Work: The Regulation of Female Sexuality and Reproduction' (1992) 1 *Review of Law and Women's Studies* 225; M Neal, 'Protecting Women: Preserving Autonomy in the Commodification of Motherhood' (2010-2011) 17 *William & Mary Journal of Women and the Law* 611 (suggesting that 'decision-making autonomy' of women should be preserved but assisted reproductive technologies need to be regulated); M Holcomb and M Byrn, 'When Your Body is Your Business' (2010) 85 *Washington Law Review* 647; K Krawiec, 'Altruism and Intermediation in the Market for Babies' (2009) 66 *Washington and Lee Law Review* 203 (arguing that the 'baby trade' should 'be recognised for what it is—a market with similarities to and differences from other markets'); K Swift, 'Parenting Agreements, the Potential Power of Contract, and the Limits of Family Law (2006-2007) 34 *Florida State University Law Review* 913; B Bix, 'Private Ordering and Family Law' (2010) 23 *Journal of the American Academy of Matrimonial Lawyers* 249; M Schultz, 'Reproductive Technology and Intent-Based Parenthood: An Opportunity for Gender Neutrality' [1990] *Wisconsin Law Review* 297; G Cohen, 'The Right Not To Be a Genetic Parent?' (2007–2008) 81 *Southern California Law Review* 1115; M Garrison, 'Law Making for Baby Making: An Interpretive Approach to the Determination of Legal Parentage' (1999-2000) 113 *Harvard Law Review* 835; and E Jackson, *Regulating Reproduction, Law, Technology and Autonomy* (Oxford, Hart Publishing, 2001).

[310] Eg, the story of a 22-year-old, Kavita Rakesh, who, due to pressing financial problems her family was facing, took a heartbreaking decision to abort her own baby to become a surrogate mother: F Elliot, 'Only Baby the Couple Can Afford Is a Stranger's', *The Times*, 10 April 2012. Concerns over exploitation of women in developing countries due to a disparity of status have also been expressed in the context of international adoption: see, eg, T Perry, 'Transracial and International Adoption: Mothers, Hierarchy, Race and Feminist Legal Theory' (1998) 10 *Yale Journal of Law and Feminism* 101; and D Smolin, 'Intercountry Adoption and Poverty: A Human Rights Analysis' (2007) 36 *Capital University Law Review* 413 (analysing in depth 'the hard choices involved at the intersection of poverty and adoption').

[311] Eg, the story of a 30-year-old surrogate mother, Pamela Vaghela, who died in an Ahmedabad hospital in May 2012 during a routine check-up after delivering a baby for American intended parents: *The New Indian Time Express*, 14 June 2012, available at <www.newindianexpress.com/editorials/article542128.ece>. Also concerns over placements of multiple embryos into surrogate mothers: eg, *A and A v P, P and B* [2011] EWHC 1738 (Fam), where five embryos were placed in the surrogate mother's womb.

[312] M Ryznar, 'International Commercial Surrogacy and Its Parties' (2010) 43 *John Marshall Law Review* 1009.

[313] E Bartholet, 'International Adoption: Propriety, Prospects and Pragmatics' (1995-1996) 13 *Journal of the American Academy of Matrimonial Lawyers* 181.

[314] An example in a domestic context is the *Huddleston* case, *Huddleston v Infertility Clinic of America Inc* (20 August 1997) (Superior Court of Pennsylvania), where a single man 'commissioned' a genetically-related child through a traditional surrogacy agreement in Pennsylvania. The baby, however, died six weeks after the birth as a result of physical abuse. See 2011 Hague Report, above n 14, para 31.

[315] Eg the Belgian case of *Baby D*, Court of Appeal, Ghent, 5 September 2005, where a Belgian surrogate entered into a surrogacy arrangement with a Belgian couple. The surrogate later informed the couple that she had miscarried, whilst 'selling' the baby to a Dutch couple she had met online (see

— Potential for abuses related to sex selection, pre-implantation diagnosis and selection of physical characteristics where donor gametes are used (commissioning 'designer babies').[316]

Fierce criticism has been directed in particular at the Indian commercial surrogacy market. One Indian commentator has expressed the view that commercial surrogacy in India 'mirrors the plight of the poor of an underdeveloped country who are willing to sell something as sacrosanct as their women's motherhood'.[317] The dark sides of the Indian surrogacy market were described as follows:

> Exploitation, extortion and ethical abuses in surrogacy trafficking are rampant, go undeterred and surrogate mothers are misused with impunity. … It is a free trading market, flourishing and thriving in the business of babies.[318]

Alarmingly, concerns related to commercial surrogacy in India are not purely theoretical but are substantiated by empirical findings. In particular, a research study entitled 'Surrogate Motherhood—Ethical or Commercial', carried out by the Indian Centre for Social Research, has revealed a number of areas of concern, including:

— *Delay in signing contracts.* Contracts were often not signed until the fourth month of a pregnancy, when the risk of miscarriage was lower than in the early stages of pregnancy.

---

ch 17 of this book). Also the case of a well-known California surrogacy lawyer, Theresa Erickson, who was jailed recently for involvement in a 'baby-selling scheme' where surrogate mothers were promised up to $45,000 to travel to Ukraine to be implanted with embryos that would then 'be offered for sale during the third trimester': N Dillon, 'Surrogacy Lawyer Jailed for Baby-Selling Scheme' *NY Daily News*, 24 February 2012, <available at www.articles.nydailynews.com/2012-02-24/news/31097238_1_hilary-neiman-surrogate-mothers-surrogate-mom>.

[316] J Zehr, 'Using Gestational Surrogacy and Pre-Implantation Diagnosis: Are Intended Parents Now Manufacturing the Idyllic Infant?'(2008) 20 *Loyola Consumer Law Review* 294; K Plummer, 'Ending Parents' Unlimited Power to Choose: Legislation is Necessary to Prohibit Parents' Selection of their Children's Sex and Characteristics' (2003) 47 *Saint Louis University Law Journal* 517; K Karsjens, 'Boutique Egg Donations: A New Form of Racism and Patriarchy' (2002) 5 *DePaul Journal of Health Care Law* 5; A Vorzimer, 'The Egg Donor and Surrogacy Controversy: Legal Issues Surrounding Representation of Parties to an Egg Donor and Surrogacy Contract (1999–2000) 21 *Whittier Law Review* 415, 427 (noting a case where a single intended father sought to achieve that six embryos were inserted into the surrogate mother's womb with the goal of a triplet pregnancy; the man was then planning to 'pick the best' of the three children for himself and place the other two for adoption). Also M Darnovsky, '"Moral Questions of an Altogether Different Kind": Progressive Politics in the Biotech Age' (2010) 4 *Harvard Law & Policy Review* 99 (raising the concern over 'consumer-based eugenics' in the context of assisted reproduction generally).

[317] Malhotra, above n 41. Other critics of the Indian commercial surrogacy market include, eg, Lee, above n 308; Ryznar, above n 312; and Smerdon, above n 14. One commentator, although being critical of the Indian surrogacy market in its current unregulated form, argues that 'India's decision to permit commercial surrogacy is a defensible one' and calls for 'application of a labour rights framework to help reconcile the competing values of contractual autonomy and protection from exploitation': J Rimm, 'Booming Baby Business: Regulating Commerical Surrogacy in India' (2008–2009) 30 *University of Pennsylvania Journal of International Law* 1429.

[318] A Malhotra, 'Commercial Surrogacy in India' [2009] *International Family Law Journal* 9.

— *Motivation for becoming a surrogate mother.* Most surrogate mothers listed poverty as the sole reason for their decision to carry a child for someone else.
— *Lack of independent advice.* Many surrogate mothers were illiterate and their only source of information was the infertility clinic facilitating the arrangement.
— *Lack of transparency in relation to the payments.* The study revealed that fees were in all cases determined arbitrarily by the infertility clinic.
— *Lack of free will when taking a decision to become a surrogate mother.* There were concerns about pressure from families and infertility clinics to become a surrogate.[319]

The above legitimate concerns about a completely free market in cross-border surrogacy point towards the need to protect the vulnerable (surrogate mothers, childless couples who are desperate to have children, and embryos which will, it is hoped, become children) by creating minimum standards for any cross-border surrogacy arrangement through international regulation.

V. A Convention on Surrogacy

A. Need for Regulation

It has been widely recognised that there is an urgent need for a multilateral, legally-binding instrument that would establish a global, coherent and ethical practice of international surrogacy.[320] In 2010, the problem of international surrogacy arrangements was identified as an emerging international family law issue that required further study and discussion by the Special Commission on the practical operation of the Hague Convention of 29 May 1993 on Protection of Children and Cooperation in Respect of Intercountry Adoption. The Commission noted that the number of international surrogacy arrangements was rising rapidly, and voiced concern 'over the uncertainty surrounding the status of many of the children who are born as

---

[319] Centre for Social Research, 'Surrogate Motherhood—Ethical or Commercial', available at <www.womenleadership.in/Csr/SurrogacyReport.pdf>. The study was based on interviews with 100 surrogate mothers, 50 intended parents and infertility clinics.

[320] Eg T Krim, 'Beyond Baby M: International Perspectives on Gestational Surrogacy and the Demise of the Unitary Biological Mother' (1996) 5 *Annals of Health Law* 193; I Lebowitz-Dori 'Womb for Rent: The Future of International Trade in Surrogacy' (1997) 6 *Minnesota Journal of Global Trade* 329; S Fiandaca, 'In Vitro Fertilization and Embryos: The Need for International Guidelines' (1997–1998) 8 *Albany Law Journal of Science and Technology* 337; W Davis and J Dalessio, 'Reproductive Surrogacy at the Millennium: Proposed Model Legislation Regulating "Non-Traditional" Gestational Surrogacy Contracts' (1999-2000) 31 *McGeorge Law Review* 673; Spar, above n 309; and Lee, above n 308. See also *X & Y (Foreign Surrogacy)* [2008] EWHC 3030 (Fam), [29].

a result of these arrangements'.[321] The Commission also noted that the use of the Adoption Convention in cases of international surrogacy was inappropriate.[322]

The issue was also raised at the Hague Conference General Affairs Meeting in April 2010 (by Israel),[323] as well as at the International Family Justice Judicial Conference for Common Law and Commonwealth Jurisdictions in Cumberland Lodge, England, in August 2009.[324] Even more importantly, the problem of cross-border surrogacy arrangements was discussed in depth at the Hague Conference Council on General Affairs and Policy meeting in April 2011.[325] It was proposed at the meeting that if there was sufficient interest among Member States of the Hague Conference, the Conference should engage in further work in the area of international surrogacy. In particular, it was suggested that the Permanent Bureau

> intensifies its work on the private international law aspects of the establishment and contestation of legal parentage, in particular on the broader range of private international law issues arising from international surrogacy arrangements.[326]

The Permanent Bureau proposed that it continue to gather information on 'the practical needs in the area, comparative developments in domestic and private international law, and the prospects of achieving consensus on a global approach'.[327] It also proposed to carry out consultations with legal, health and other relevant professionals.[328] The Hague Conference Council on General Affairs and Policy in April 2011 reached the following conclusions:

> *Private international law issues surrounding the status of children, including issues arising from international surrogacy arrangements*

---

[321] Hague Conference on Private International Law, 'Conclusions and Recommendations Adopted by the Special Commission on the Practical Operation of the Hague Convention of 29 May 1993 on Protection of Children and Cooperation in Respect of Intercountry Adoption', para 25, available at <www.hcch.net/upload/wop/adop2010concl_e.pdf> ('Conclusions and Recommendations of the 2010 Special Commission'). The Special Commission also recommended that the Hague Conference carry out further study of the legal, especially private international law, issues surrounding international surrogacy: *ibid*, para 26.

[322] *Ibid.* The Hague Adoption Convention itself is not an appropriate instrument to resolve problems arising from international surrogacy arrangements as some of the key requirements of the Convention cannot be met in international surrogacy cases: (i) *consent*—the Adoption Convention requires that the consent of the birth mother must be given *after* the birth of the child; (ii) *subsidiarity*—the Adoption Convention is based on the principle that due consideration is given to the possibility of the child being placed in his/her State of origin; (iii) *procedural safeguards*—under the Adoption Convention a child can be entrusted to the adoptive parents only if both States have agreed that the adoption may proceed; and (iv) *prohibition on contact*—the Adoption Convention lays down the rule that there should be no contact between the adopters and the child's birth family. See 2011 Hague Report, above n 14, para 43.

[323] Hague Conference on Private International Law, 'Council on General Affairs: Conclusions and Recommendations', 7–9 April 2010, available at <www.hcch.net/upload/wop/genaff2010concl_e.pdf>.

[324] See 'Conclusions and Resolutions from the Cumberland Lodge Conference', 4, available at <www.hcch.net/upload/resolutions_famlawconf09.pdf>. The Conference was attended by 42 judges from 23 jurisdictions.

[325] 2011 Hague Report, above n 14.

[326] *Ibid*, para 54.

[327] *Ibid.*

[328] *Ibid.*

17. The Council welcomed the Report prepared by the Permanent Bureau on the above subject.

18. The Council invited the Permanent Bureau to intensify its work in the area with emphasis on the broad range of issues arising from international surrogacy arrangements. The Permanent Bureau should during the next year continue gathering information on the practical needs in the area, comparative developments in domestic and private international law, and the prospects of achieving consensus on a global approach.

19. The Permanent Bureau should also consult with the legal profession as well as with health and other relevant professionals concerning the nature and incidence of the problems occurring in this area.

20. The Permanent Bureau should provide a preliminary report on progress to the Council in 2012.[329]

In accordance with the above authorisation, the Permanent Bureau presented a preliminary report to the Council at the 2012 meeting on General Affairs and Policy.[330] The Council requested the Permanent Bureau to continue the current work under the 2011 mandate by preparing and distributing a Questionnaire in order to acquire

more detailed information regarding the extent and nature of the private international law issues being encountered in relation to international surrogacy arrangements.[331]

A final report is to be presented by the Permanent Bureau to the Council in 2014.[332]

B. Legislative Approach[333]

Given the extremely wide variety of domestic responses to surrogacy observed elsewhere in this book, a Convention on surrogacy should not aim at unification of the conflict rules. Rather than focusing on traditional rules on jurisdiction and applicable law, the Convention should establish a framework for international cooperation, with emphasis on the need for substantive safeguards and on procedures for courts, administrative authorities and private intermediaries. There should be an agreed division of functions between the countries involved, and

---

[329] Hague Conference on Private International Law, 'Council on General Affairs and Policy of the Conference (5–7 April 2011): Conclusions and Recommendations Adopted by the Council', available at <www.hcch.net/upload/wop/genaff_concl2011e.pdf>.

[330] Hague Conference on Private International Law, 'Council on General Affairs and Policy of the Conference (17–20 April 2012): Conclusions and Recommendations Adopted by the Council', para 21, available at <www.hcch.net/upload/wop/gap2012concl_en.pdf>.

[331] *Ibid*.

[332] *Ibid*.

[333] For 'some initial thoughts' on possible legislative approaches to an instrument on international surrogacy by the Hague Conference, see 2012 Hague Report, above n 19, paras 44–63, available at <www.hcch.net/upload/wop/gap2012pd10en.pdf>.

the countries dealing with the different functions will apply their own laws to those functions. Lastly, a generous approach should be taken with respect to the recognition of cross-border surrogacy arrangements made under the Convention framework and their effects under that framework, subject to a public policy exception.

Within this multilateral framework, detailed regulation should be left to bilateral agreements between Member States. The Convention would give Member States maximum flexibility to agree on details of international surrogacy arrangements, including issues such as suitability of intended parents, suitability of a surrogate mother and payments in surrogacy arrangements. The Convention would set only minimum standards and would not prevent State Parties from setting higher standards for international surrogacy arrangements.[334]

C. Objectives of the Convention

Applying a functional approach based on the division of responsibilities—as set out above—the primary goals of the Convention should be:

(a) to develop a system of legally-binding standards that should be observed in connection with international surrogacy arrangements;

(b) to develop a system of supervision to ensure that these standards are observed; and

(c) to establish a framework of cooperation and channels of communication between the jurisdictions involved.

D. Effects of the Convention

The establishment of a framework of cooperation amongst Contracting States will achieve a triple effect. First, it will promote the exchange of information and the transmission of documents between the countries concerned, with the aim of facilitating practical solutions. Secondly, it will reduce 'limping' or unrecognised surrogacy arrangements. Thirdly, it will help to combat trafficking in women and children, and other comparable abuses such as the abduction and sale of women

---

[334] The same approach is taken by the Adoption Convention. It sets out only minimum standards that must be observed within the intercountry adoption process, and Contracting States are encouraged to establish higher standards. Permanent Bureau of the Hague Conference on Private International Law, 'Report and Conclusions of the Second Special Commission on the Practical Operation of the Hague Convention of 29 May 1993 on Protection of Children and Cooperation in Respect of Intercountry Adoption (17–23 September 2005)', para 42, available at <www.hcch.net/upload/wop/adop2005_rpt-e.pdf> ('Report and Conclusions of the Second Special Commission'). See also G Parra-Aranguren, 'Explanatory Report on the Convention on Protection of Children and Co-operation in Respect of Intercountry Adoption', available at <www.hcch.net/upload/expl33e.pdf;> ('Explanatory Report'), esp paras 108–09, 113, 126, 175, 254, 259, 373, 383 and 388; and W Duncan, 'The Protection of Children's Rights in Inter-Country Adoption' in L Heffernan (ed), *Human Rights—A European Perspective* (Dublin, The Round Hall Press, 1994) 338.

and children.[335] It is to be noted, however, that, like the Adoption Convention, the Surrogacy Convention would not aspire to combat these abuses directly. The Convention would tackle the abuses only indirectly, as 'it is expected that the observance of the Convention's rules will bring about the avoidance of such abuses'.[336]

E. Template

It is suggested that the cooperative framework on cross-border surrogacy be based on the template of the highly successful 1993 Hague Convention on Protection of Children and Cooperation in Respect of Intercountry Adoption ('the Adoption Convention').[337] The Adoption Convention appears to be the most suitable model for a number of reasons.[338]

First, having attracted 89 Contracting States[339] from around the globe, the Adoption Convention has been one of the most effective instruments in the area of international protection of children.[340] This success is particularly due to the fact that from the formal introduction of the subject at the Hague Conference in 1988,[341] the work on the Convention attracted equally countries of origin and receiving countries.[342] Indeed, the Contracting States to the Adoption Convention include such important countries of origin as India[343] and China,[344] and almost all of South America (including those South American countries that are not

---

[335] See Hague Conference on Private International Law, 'Conclusions of the Special Commission of June 1990 on Intercountry Adoption', Prel Doc No 3, August 1990, *Actes et Documents de la Dix-Septième Session 10–29 May 1993*, para 12.

[336] 'Explanatory Report', above n 334, para 52.

[337] The Hague Convention on Protection of Children and Cooperation in Respect of Intercountry Adoption, 29 May 1993. For a careful and thoughtful analysis of the lessons that can be learned from the Adoption Convention for a possible Surrogacy Convention, see ch 26 of this book by Hannah Baker.

[338] For discussion of the interface between adoption and assisted reproductive technologies generally, see eg E Bartholet, 'Beyond Biology: The Politics of Adoption & Reproduction' (1995) 2 *Duke Journal of Gender Law & Policy* 5; N Cahn, 'Old Lessons for a New World: Applying Adoption Research and Experience to ART' (2011) 24 *Journal of American Academy of Matrimonial Lawyers* 1; and S Appleton, 'Adoption in the Age of Reproductive Technology' [2004] *The University of Chicago Legal Forum* 393.

[339] As of 1 March 2013. See Hague Conference on Private International Law, 'Convention of 29 May 1993 on Protection of Children and Cooperation in Respect of Intercountry Adoption: Status Table', available at <www.hcch.net/index_en.php?act=conventions.statusprint&cid=69> ('Status Table').

[340] 'Report and Conclusions of the Second Special Commission', above n 334, para 8.

[341] On 19 January 1988, the Permanent Bureau of the Hague Conference submitted the subject of international cooperation in the area of intercountry adoption to the Special Commission on general affairs and policy of the Conference. See 'Explanatory Report', above n 334, para 1.

[342] It is to be noted that the Contracting States currently include the US and many other receiving countries, as well as a large number of sending countries. See 'Status Table', above n 339.

[343] India ratified the Convention on 6 June 2003. The Convention entered into force for India on 1 October 2003. See 'Status Table', above n 339.

[344] China ratified the Convention on 16 September 2005 and it has been in force for China since 1 January 2006. See 'Status Table', above n 339.

Member States of the Hague Conference).[345] It has rightly been pointed out that the wide spectrum of participating countries

> is a convincing indication that the Convention has managed to strike the right balance between the concerns of the States of origin and the receiving States—a prerequisite for the confidence needed for its successful operation.[346]

Accordingly, in order to produce a document that will effectively tackle the problem of cross-border surrogacy, it is imperative to ensure that both the 'supply countries' and the 'demand countries' are actively involved.[347]

Secondly, it is important to note that like surrogacy today, in the 1980s, international adoption was a morally sensitive issue. The Adoption Convention, having been drafted in a very flexible and morally neutral way, has dealt with these objections very successfully. It is envisaged that the Convention on surrogacy would adopt a similar approach.

Thirdly, the Adoption Convention provides a valuable set of safeguards for children, birth parents and prospective adoptive parents in adoptions carried out under it. In addition, it is hoped that the Convention will have an impact beyond the scope of Convention adoptions, so that children involved in non-Convention adoptions will also be able to benefit from the Convention safety mechanism. In order to attain this objective, Contracting States are strongly recommended to apply 'the standards and safeguards of the Convention to the arrangements for intercountry adoption which they make in respect of non-Contracting States'.[348] In a similar way, it is hoped that the standards set by the Convention on surrogacy will encourage good practice in non-Convention cases too. This is particularly important given the fact that, at the onset, the ethical controversy over surrogacy might make some countries reluctant to participate formally.

Last but not least, adoption and surrogacy have a number of features in common. As institutions of family law[349]—adoption and surrogacy may be viewed as 'two possibilities on a menu of choices to pursue in [infertile couples'] quest for children'.[350] It has been suggested that cases of traditional surrogacy (ie where the surrogate mother is also the genetic mother of the child) are ordinary adoption cases, as due to the very strong bond the surrogate mother has the right to

---

[345] In particular, Brazil, Chile, Costa Rica, Ecuador, Panama, Paraguay, Peru, Uruguay and Venezuela (Member States of the Hague Conference); and Belize, Bolivia, Colombia, El Salvador, Guatemala (Non-Member States of the Hague Conference). See 'Status Table', above n 339.

[346] 'Report and Conclusions of the Second Special Commission', above n 334, para 8.

[347] See section II. above.

[348] Hague Conference on Private International Law, 'Report and Conclusions of the Special Commission on the Practical Operation of the Hague Convention of 29 May 1993 on Protection of Children and Cooperation in Respect of Intercountry Adoption, 28 November–1 December 2000', para 56, available at <www.hcch.net/upload/scrpt33e2000.pdf>. This recommendation was reaffirmed by the 2010 Special Commission. See 'Conclusions and Recommendations of the 2010 Special Commission', above n 321, para 36.

[349] An alternative view is that surrogacy (or more generally assisted reproduction) is an aspect of reproductive autonomy, and should be treated as a matter of contract law: Appleton, above n 338, 393.

[350] *Ibid*, 394.

regard the child as her own.[351] This approach was taken by courts in a number of traditional surrogacy cases, including the famous US case *In re Baby M*,[352] which involved a traditional surrogacy agreement where, following the birth of the child, the surrogate mother changed her mind and decided to keep the baby. The court, having considered the case against the background of adoption law, refused to enforce the surrogacy agreement between the surrogate mother and the intended father, who was also the genetic father of the child.

Despite the above commonalities, it may be argued that there is a fundamental difference between adoption and surrogacy; in particular, that the former institution is a more or less altruistic act that serves primarily the needs of a child in need of a family, whereas the latter represents a means of meeting the private needs of a childless couple (adoption as a 'child focused service' versus assisted reproduction in general as an 'adult-focused service').[353] Unfortunately, however, this distinction has become increasingly blurred in the past few decades. Nowadays, it is no longer true that the sole objective of adoption is to find nurturing families for orphaned or abandoned children. If the claim about the exclusively child-centred focus of adoption reflected the reality, there would not be so many adoptable children with special needs (ie older children, handicapped children, or children in sibling groups) waiting for a family.[354] Very often adoption, like surrogacy, serves primarily the needs of childless adults.[355]

F. Scope of the Convention

The Convention should be applicable to all cases where intended parent(s) and the surrogate mother are habitually resident in different Contracting States,

---

[351] A Struycken, 'Surrogacy, A New Way to Become a Mother? A New PIL Issue' in K Boele-Woelki *et al* (eds), *Convergence and Divergence in Private International Law* (The Hague, Eleven International Publishing, 2010) 357; A Miller, 'Baseline, Bright-line, Best Interests: A Pragmatic Approach for California to Provide Certainty in Determining Parentage' (2002-2003) 34 *McGeorge Law Review* 637, 699; and Garrison, above n 309, 898. Also B Atwell, 'Surrogacy and Adoption: A Case of Incompatibility' (1988) 20 *Columbia Human Rights Law Review* 1, 15 (arguing that the ultimate objective of a surrogacy arrangement is to 'make the contracting couple legal parents of the child through adoption').

[352] *Matter of Baby M* (1988, NJ) 537 A 2d 1227. For more details on the case, see above n 8. Another similar example is the case of *Adoption of Matthew B*, 232 Cal App 3d 1239, 284 Cal Rptr 18 (1991).

[353] R Storrow, 'Marginalising Adoption Through the Regulation of Assisted Reproduction' (2006) 35 *Capital University Law Review* 479, 483.

[354] The problem of large numbers of 'children with special needs' who are waiting for families has been acknowledged on a number of occasions. See, eg, International Social Service (ISS), 'Evaluation of the Practical Operation of the Hague Convention of 29 May 1993 on Protection of Children and Cooperation in Respect of Intercountry Adoption', 7–9; and 'Report and Conclusions of the Second Special Commission', above n 334, paras 116–19.

[355] See Appleton, above n 338, at 403, who suggests that adoption, which traditionally represented a 'public face' of family law, has nowadays acquired a 'private face' (a means of meeting private needs of childless adults). See also K Ja Sook Bergquist, 'International Asian Adoption: In the Best Interests of the Child? (2004) *Texas Wesleyan Law Review* 343, 346: 'Motivation for adoption ha[d] shifted from the altruistic, finding a home for a parentless child, to the supply and demand economics of finding children for childless couples.'

regardless of whether the arrangement is commissioned in the surrogate mother's country, in the intended parents' country or in a third country.[356] The terminology used in the Adoption Convention to describe the countries involved in an intercountry adoption case should be modified for surrogacy from 'the country of origin' (of the child) to 'the country of birth' (of the child) and from 'the receiving country' (of the child) to the 'home country of the intended parents'.

Habitual residence should be chosen over nationality or residence. This is, first, to ensure that the authorities of the intended parents' home State and the State of birth respectively have sufficient information to assess accurately the suitability of the prospective parents and the surrogate mother. No less importantly, the preference for habitual residence points to the importance of some form of permanency in the surrogate mother's residence in the jurisdiction. This is to prevent cases where a woman is brought to a 'surrogacy-friendly' jurisdiction solely for the purpose of serving as a surrogate mother there.[357] There is an inherent danger of human rights abuses in such a practice, as the move might be involuntary and thus clearly amount to trafficking in women.

Nevertheless, it is recognised that, given the varying interpretations of the concept of habitual residence,[358] a stable connection between the surrogate mother/the intended parents and the country in question will not automatically be guaranteed

---

[356] Situations where the embryo transfer is carried out at by a medical facility based in a non-Convention country would also fall within the scope of the Convention as long as the requirement that the intended parent(s) and the surrogate mother are habitually resident in different Contracting States is fulfilled.

[357] In 1995, Dutch police uncovered a criminal gang responsible for luring young Polish women to act as surrogate mothers for infertile couples in The Netherlands, Belgium and Germany. The women were recruited through advertisements in Polish newspapers which promised 'discretion' and 'good fees' in return for their services as surrogate mothers. In the course of the investigation, the identity of a number of couples involved was established, although it was unlikely that the babies would be taken away from them. The criminals faced custodial sentences for organising surrogate motherhood for commercial gain and/or for trafficking in women. Abi Daruvala, 'Poles Hired as Surrogate Mums in Illegal Trade', *Independent*, 4 June 1995, available at <www.independent.co.uk/news/world/poles-hired-as-surrogate-mums-in-illegal-trade-1584960.html>.

[358] Where there is clear evidence of an intention to commence a new life in another State then the existing habitual residence will be lost and a new one acquired. Courts have accepted that acquisition of a new habitual residence may occur within a short period of time (eg, *Re J (A Minor) (Abduction: Custody Rights)* [1990] 2 AC 562; *Re F (A Minor) (Child Abduction)* [1992] 1 FLR 548; and *DeHaan v Gracia* [2004] AJ No 94 (QL), [2004] ABQD 4) or even immediately (eg, Bundesgericht, II. Zivilabteilung (Tribunal Fédéral, 2ème Chambre Civile) Décision du 15 novembre 2005, 5P.367/2005 /ast—Switzerland). Nevertheless, recent judicial developments in Europe indicate that 'some degree of integration', determined among other factors by the duration of a person's stay on the territory of an EU Member State, should be required before habitual residence may be established: Case C-523/07 *A* [2009] ECR I-2805 (Third Chamber). In this case, the ECJ concluded that 'habitual residence' corresponded to the place which reflected some degree of integration by the child into a social and family environment. In particular, the following facts should be taken into consideration: the duration, regularity, conditions and reasons for the stay on the territory of a Member State and the family's move to that State; the child's nationality; the place and conditions of attendance at school; linguistic knowledge; and the family and social relationships of the child in that State (*ibid*). Even more recently, in the case of *Mercredi*, the ECJ concluded that in ascertaining the habitual residence of a very young child, the focus should be on the place of the centre of interests of the child ascertained by the habitual residence of the custodial parent: Case C-497/10 PPU *Mercredi v Chaffe* [2010] ECR I-14309, judgment of 22 December 2010, esp paras 51–56 (First Chamber). See the lengthy analysis of habitual residence,

if habitual residence is used as an unconstrained connecting factor. It is therefore suggested that the Convention specifies a minimum period of residence that would be required in order for the habitual residence to be enough for the Convention to apply. This period will be a matter for the negotiators of the Convention, but it could be one or two years, and it is envisaged that this additional requirement would apply only to cases involving non-nationals of the relevant country.

A similar approach is taken by the Convention of 1 August 1989 on the Law Applicable to Succession to the Estates of Deceased Persons ('the Hague Succession Convention 1989'). According to Article 3(1), 'succession is governed by the law of the State in which the deceased at the time of his death was habitually resident, if he was then a national of that State'. If the deceased was not a national of the given State, the law of this State governs succession only if the deceased 'had been resident there for a period of no less than five years immediately preceding his death'.[359]

G. Fundamental Principles

The Convention should be based on two fundamental principles: the principle of the best interests of the child; and the principle of genetic connection.

i. Best Interests of the Child

The Convention should ensure that the best interests of the (putative) child shall be the paramount consideration in intercountry surrogacy arrangements.[360] Although the child is not yet born when a surrogacy arrangement is put in place, it is necessary at that stage to anticipate whether it will be in the best interests of any child that emerges from the womb of the surrogate mother to be handed over to the intended parents to be brought up as their child. Such a best interests analysis is relevant in determining many questions in the surrogacy process, eg: How many embryos should be implanted in the surrogate mother? Is the surrogate mother healthy enough to enable the embryo to become a healthy child? Are the intended parents suitable to look after the child or children that emerge from the surrogate mother's womb? This requirement is in accordance with Article 3(1) of the UN Convention on the Rights of the Child ('UNCRC'), which requires that the child's best interests be a primary consideration in all actions concerning children.[361] Pursuant to Article 3(2) of the UNCRC, account must

highlighting its very varied interpretation, in PR Beaumont and PE McEleavy, *Private International Law, Anton*, 3rd edn (Edinburgh, W Green, 2011) 175–209.

[359] Hague Succession Convention 1989, Art 3(2).

[360] This requirement reflects the over-arching principle of intercountry adoption. In particular, Art 1 of the Adoption Convention requires that intercountry adoptions 'take place in the best interests of the child and with respect for his or her fundamental rights'. Similarly, the Preamble to the Convention highlights the importance of intercountry adoptions being carried out 'in the best interests of the child and with respect for his or her fundamental rights'.

[361] United Nations Convention on the Rights of the Child, adopted by General Assembly Resolution 44/25 of 20 November 1989, Art 3(1).

also be taken of the rights and duties of other persons concerned, in this case the surrogate mother and the intended parents. As their interests are also entitled to legal protection, a balance must be achieved among the interests of all parties to a surrogacy arrangement.[362]

Practical measures that would support the best interests principle would include:

(a) ensuring the intended parents are suitable; and
(b) preserving information about the identity of the surrogate mother (and an egg/sperm donor if involved).[363]

Although there has been some controversy over whether it is justified to deny intended parents the presumption of parental fitness,[364] it is suggested here that the best interests principle demands that suitability checks are indeed carried out. This is consistent with Article 19(1) of the United Nations Convention on the Rights of the Child, which imposes on the States Parties an obligation to

> take all appropriate legislative, administrative, social and educational measures to protect the child from all forms of physical or mental violence, injury or abuse, neglect or negligent treatment, maltreatment or exploitation, including sexual abuse, while in the care of parent(s), legal guardian(s) or any other person who has the care of the child.

Such protective measures include preventative measures.[365]

ii. Genetic Connection[366]

Not only should surrogacy be seen as the last resort, but it should be restricted to instances where at least one of the intended parents is genetically related to the child. It has rightly been pointed out that there is no need to create more children, as there are millions of children around the world who are in need of adoption, waiting for a loving home. The Convention must ensure that cross-border surrogacy is not perceived as a possible 'shortcut' to obtaining a genetically non-related child from abroad. It must give a clear message that the proper route to obtaining a genetically non-related child is through adoption. The requirement of a genetic connection between the child and at least one of the intended parents will reaffirm the relevance of the Adoption Convention and ensure that the value of that Convention is not undermined.

---

[362] 'Explanatory Report', above n 334, para 49.

[363] In the context of intercountry adoption, practical measures to reinforce the best interests principle include: (i) ensuring the adoptability of the child (Art 4(a)); (ii) storing information on the child and his/her biological family (Art 30); and (iii) matching the child with suitable adoptive parents (Art 16(d)). See 'Report and Conclusions of the Second Special Commission', above n 334, para 29.

[364] Eg Vorzimer, above n 316, 426 (writing in the US context, bases his argument against the screening of the intended parents on the 'constitutional right to procreate').

[365] UNCRC, Art 19(2).

[366] At a domestic level, the requirement of a genetic connection between the child and at least one of the intended parents can be found in surrogacy legislation of several countries, eg the UK, Ukraine, Australia (ACT and South Australia).

H. Framework of Cooperation

i. Central Authority

The Convention would require each Contracting State to constitute a Central Authority, charged with cooperation with its counterparts and with the supervision of private agencies operating within its jurisdiction. To save costs associated with the implementation of the Convention, States that are Parties to the Adoption Convention could entrust the Central Authorities for intercountry adoption with the duties under the surrogacy Convention too. As an additional avenue to recover some of the costs, the Convention could authorise the Central Authorities to charge the intended parents an administrative fee.

ii. Delegation of Duties

Like the Adoption Convention, the Convention on surrogacy could allow for the delegation of the functions of the Central Authority to other public bodies[367] or to officially approved (ie accredited) private agencies[368] (such as fertility clinics or surrogacy brokers).[369] The process of accreditation would serve as one of the key safeguards in intercountry surrogacy cases. The Convention might offer suggestions as to the requirements for such approval (eg that the organisation is based in the given country, that the organisation pursues non-profit objectives, that its staff members are properly trained, etc). Matters such as the number of accredited bodies, the extent of an accredited body's functions, accreditation procedure, the criteria for accreditation and its renewal, and the supervision of accredited bodies would be left to the policy-makers of individual Contracting States.[370] Nevertheless, it is preferable that accredited bodies be accountable to the Central (or other government) Authority.

Article 22(2) of the Adoption Convention implicitly allows non-accredited bodies or persons that 'meet the requirements of integrity, professional competence, experience and accountability of that State' and 'are qualified by their ethical standards and by training or experience' to work in the area of intercountry adoption.[371] States are, however, not obliged to accept the involvement of non-accredited bodies or persons, by making an express declaration to this

---

[367] See Adoption Convention, Arts 8 and 22.

[368] See Adoption Convention, Arts 9 and 22.

[369] Certain functions would not be delegable and will have to be performed exclusively by Central Authorities. Non-delegable functions in the context of intercountry adoptions are set out in Art 7(2) of the Adoption Convention.

[370] 'Report and Conclusions of the Second Special Commission', above n 334, para 48.

[371] Art 22(2) allows Contracting States to make a declaration to that effect. As at 21 January 2013, only four out of 89 Contracting States have made such a declaration: Canada (for New Brunswick, Newfoundland & Labrador, Nova Scotia, Nunavut, Ontario, Prince Edward Island, Saskatchewan and the Yukon), Italy, USA and Colombia.

effect.[372] The Explanatory Report to the Convention clarifies that this solution was adopted as a 'reasonable compromise between antagonistic positions'.[373] The result is that non-accredited bodies in some provinces in Canada, in Italy, in Colombia and in the United States can arrange for adoptions to those countries under the Hague Adoption Convention of children habitually resident in 60 of the 89 Contracting States plus mainland China and most of the provinces in Canada. Contrary to the position adopted by the Adoption Convention, in order to minimise the potential for abuses by intermediaries, it is not envisaged that a Convention on surrogacy would allow participation of non-accredited persons or bodies. Given that the Hague Conference operates by consensus, it may be that a Convention will ultimately be adopted only if private agencies that meet certain minimum standards can carry out the surrogacy arrangements between countries that positively opt into this system. A properly regulated approach to cross-border surrogacy is essential, but it will work only if the quality and integrity of the people carrying out the work is high.[374]

iii. Division of Responsibilities

Within the framework of cooperation based on the division of responsibilities between countries of birth and home countries of the intended parents, the law of the intended parents' country of habitual residence will govern the conditions relating to the suitability of the intended parents and the consequential effects of the surrogacy arrangements. The law of the country of the surrogate mother will govern all matters relating to the surrogate mother.

The primary responsibilities of the authorities in the country of birth should include:

(a) establishing conditions under which its residents may serve as surrogate mothers (the Convention might provide some guidance as to, for example, age, marital status, requirement of a prior live birth, adequate preparation, etc);[375]

---

[372] Art 22(4) allows any Contracting State to declare that adoptions of children habitually resident in its territory may take place only if the functions of the Central Authorities are performed by Central Authorities or accredited bodies. As at 21 January 2013 the following 29 States had made such a declaration: Andorra, Armenia, Australia, Austria, Azerbaijan, Belarus, Belgium, Brazil, Bulgaria, Canada (for British Columbia and Quebec), China (for Hong Kong and Macao), Colombia, Denmark, El Salvador, France, Germany, Greece, Hungary, Liechtenstein, Luxembourg, Montenegro, Norway, Panama, Poland, Portugal, Spain, Sweden, Switzerland, Venezuela. The very real difficulties associated with money corrupting governmental bodies and accredited not-for-profit agencies, as seen in the operation of the Hague Adoption Convention, are highlighted by Hannah Baker, in ch 26 of this book, at text accompanying fns 51–56.

[373] Adoption Convention, Art 22(2). See also Explanatory Report, above n 334, para 373.

[374] See ch 26 of this book by Hannah Baker, text accompanying n 57.

[375] As a useful template, relevant provisions of the Virginia statutory law might be used. According to this statute, a surrogate mother must be married, must have had at least one live birth, and giving birth to another child will not pose an unreasonable risk to her physical or mental health or to the health of the child produced through the surrogacy arrangement: Va Code Ann, paras 20-160(B)6 (2004).

(b) ensuring that persons required to give consent to the surrogacy arrangement (ie the surrogate mothers) have been fully informed about the legal aspects of the surrogacy arrangement and the consequences of their decision;

(c) ensuring that the surrogate mother is adequately reimbursed, ie that she has been paid at least a year's living expenses.

(d) ensuring the legal departure of the child from that State to the intended parents' home country.

Correspondingly, authorities in the intended parents' home country would be responsible for:

(a) establishing the conditions regarding the parental fitness of the intended parents (this should be equivalent to requirements on adoptive parents under the law of the country, ie the intended parents must meet the standards of fitness applicable to adoptive parents). The Convention might provide some guidance as to, for example, age limits, the existence of valid marriage, a stable family environment, adequate preparation. As a minimum, married couples would be allowed to use the Convention; nevertheless, Contracting States would be able to extend the application of the Convention to other categories of intended parents on a bilateral basis;[376]

(b) informing intended parents about the legal aspects and consequences of the surrogacy arrangement;[377]

(c) preparing a file on the intended parents (containing information about their identity and background, family and medical history, motivation for surrogacy, relevant social considerations, etc);

(d) authorising and facilitating the child's legal entry into and right to remain in the intended parents' home country;

(e) where required, supervising and protecting the child, and making arrangements for the intended parents to have parental responsibility for the child.

iv. Effective Domestic Implementation and Intra-State Cooperation

In addition to a well-organised cooperative framework between different Contracting States, effective intra-State cooperation will also need to be guaranteed.[378] This can be achieved, however, only if thorough implementation of the Convention is carried out at a domestic level in each particular Contracting State.

---

[376] It is a matter of public policy of individual States to decide whether registered partners (heterosexual or homosexual), unregistered partners (heterosexual or homosexual), single women or single men have the same rights as a married couple.

[377] This process of 'counselling' would be comparable to adoption preparation in the context of intercountry adoption. The need for proper preparation of the prospective adoptive parents was highlighted at the Second Special Commission to review the operation of the Adoption Convention. See 'Report and Conclusions of the Second Special Commission', above n 334, para 90.

[378] *Ibid*, para 42.

Effective intra-State cooperation will in turn help to prevent the occurrence of malpractice and help to combat potential abuses of women and children through avoidance of the Convention.[379]

I. Illicit Activities

Cross-border surrogacy arrangements should be channelled exclusively through State licensed agencies, both in the country of birth and in the home country of the intended parents. Recognition of cross-border surrogacy agreements commissioned either privately or through unauthorised intermediaries should be strictly opposed (outlawed).[380] This will send a clear message to potential intended parents and encourage surrogacy arrangements only through authorised agencies.

J. Other Matters that Require Further Examination

i. Compensation in Surrogacy

In relation to payments in surrogacy, the Convention would establish a 'generous altruistic surrogacy' model, the aim of which would be to strike a balance between concerns over the exploitation of surrogate mothers on the one hand and

---

[379] *Ibid*, para 33. A lesson should be taken from the Adoption Convention, where an inadequate implementation of the Convention in a number of countries of origin in particular has led to widespread abuses such as the sale and abduction of children. Indeed, commentators have reported on documented cases where children (in particular babies) were bought or abducted from their parents and then sold into adoption. The problem of 'abduction, sale and traffic in children and their illicit procurement in the context of intercountry adoption' was acknowledged by the 2010 Special Commission on the Operation of the Adoption Convention: Hague Conference on Private International Law, 'Conclusions and Recommendations and Report on the Special Commission on the Practical Operation of the 1993 Hague Intercountry Adoption Convention (17–25 June 2010', paras 1–2, available at <www.hcch.net/upload/wop/adop2010_rpt_en.pdf>. See also H Kennard, 'Curtailing the Sale and Trafficking of Children: A Discussion of the Hague Conference Convention in Respect of Intercountry Adoptions' (1993-1994) 14 *University of Pennsylvania Journal of International Business Law* 623; D Smolin, 'Intercountry Adoption as Child Trafficking' (2004-2005) 39 *Valparaiso University Law Review* 281; D Smolin, 'Child Laundering As Exploitation: Applying Anti-Trafficking Norms to Intercountry Adoption Under the Coming Hague Regime' (2007-2008) 32 *Vermont Law Review* 1; D Smolin, 'Child Laundering and the Hague Convention on Intercountry Adoption: The Future and the Past of Intercountry Adoption' (2010) 48 *University of Louisville Law Review* 441; P Meier, 'Small Commodities: How Child Traffickers Exploit Children and Families in Intercountry Adoption and What the United States Must Do to Stop Them' (2008) 12 *Journal of Gender, Race & Justice* 185; P Goodman, 'Stealing Babies for Adoption; With US Couples Eager to Adopt, Some Infants Are Abducted and Sold in China', *Washington Post*, 12 March 2006; and A Dohle, 'Inside Story of an Adoption Scandal' (2008-2009) 39 *Cumberland Law Review* 131.

[380] A similar approach is taken by the Adoption Convention. In line with this approach, 'private' or 'direct' adoptions (ie adoptions arranged directly between birth parents and adoptive parents) and 'independent' adoptions (ie adoptions where adoptive parents are approved to adopt in the receiving State and, in the State of origin, locate a child without the involvement of a Central Authority or accredited body in the State of origin) are considered as being incompatible with the Convention. See Adoption Convention, Art 29 and 'Conclusions and Recommendations of the 2010 Special Commission', above n 321, paras 22 and 23.

the commodification of children on the other. The model would seek to ensure that women do not become surrogate mothers because they are enticed with the expectation of high earnings; but if they nonetheless decide to enter into a surrogacy arrangement, they will be adequately compensated. Accordingly, it is considered reasonable that the surrogate mother be compensated, at the minimum, for her lost wages (or reasonable living expenses, if not employed prior to the pregnancy) and medical and other pregnancy-related expenses.[381] The reasonable living expenses could be calculated through a reimbursement entitlement formula set by the Convention, for example three times the minimum salary in the surrogate mother's country of habitual residence. It appears reasonable that the surrogate mother be compensated for at least 12 months' worth of lost wages/living expenses (nine months' pregnancy plus three months' post-birth recovery).[382]

Surrogacy agreements in which an amount paid to the surrogate mother would exceed the acceptable expenses would not fall within the scope of the Convention, and therefore not benefit from the Convention provisions on the recognition and effects of surrogacy arrangements (see section V.J.iv. below) Such arrangements would be classified as constituting child trafficking.

ii. Lawyers' and Intermediaries' Fees

In order to prevent improper financial gain from surrogacy arrangements by fertility clinics and other intermediaries (eg surrogacy agencies and legal practitioners), transparency in costs and fees is necessary. It is suggested that the Convention sets some limits on possible fees and costs, but it is recognised that this cannot be expressed in absolute figures due to widespread variations in incomes and costs in possible Contracting States. The details of financial accountability of accredited bodies should be left to domestic regulation.

iii. Actual Enforcement of Surrogacy Arrangements[383]

Enforcement of surrogacy arrangements, as opposed to the enforceability of foreign orders relating to surrogacy, should be a matter of national law, although

---

[381] As a useful model, relevant provisions of the US Uniform Adoption Act might be used. The Act sets forth the following permissible categories for which payments may be made: payments for all related medical, hospital and pharmaceutical costs; travelling expenses; legal fees; counselling fees for a reasonable time before and after the birth; and also for the birth mother's living expenses for up to six weeks after the birth. The Act further provides that the adoptive parents are not liable for payments if the adoption does not occur.

[382] However, in order to avoid over-compensation, account will have to be taken, where relevant, of the surrogate mother's entitlement to a maternity pay/allowance under the law of the State of her habitual residence.

[383] For background reading on the problem of enforcement of surrogacy arrangements, see eg R Epstein, 'Surrogacy: The Case for Full Contractual Enforcement' (1995) 81 *Virginia Law Review* 2305; D Lascarides, 'A Plea for the Enforceability of Gestational Surrogacy Contracts' (1996-1997) 25 *Hofstra Law Review* 1221; and K Swift, 'Parenting Agreements, the Potential Power of Contract, and the Limits of Family Law' (2006-2007) 34 *Florida State University Law Review* 913 (all arguing for enforceability of surrogacy arrangements). See also ch 27 in this book by Yasmine Ergas, where she argues that

some minimum rules on actual enforcement should be set in the Convention. The same approach was adopted by the drafters of the Hague Convention of 23 November 2007 on the International Recovery of Child Support and Other Forms of Family Maintenance ('the 2007 Hague Maintenance Convention'). Article 32(1) states that 'enforcement shall take place in accordance with the law of the State addressed' subject to the relevant provisions of the Convention. These provisions include, for example, Article 32(2), which imposes the requirement of prompt enforcement; Article 33, which embodies the principle of non-discrimination;[384] and Article 34, which contains the obligation to make available in internal law 'effective measures to enforce decisions under this Convention' and gives an illustrative list of enforcement measures.[385]

iv. Recognition and Effects of Surrogacy Arrangements

A legal parent–child status acquired between the intended parents and the child through the Convention process should be automatically recognised in all Contracting States to the Convention. This might be achieved through adaptation of Article 26 of the Adoption Convention, which specifies that the recognition of the adoption includes recognition of 'the legal parent–child relationship between the child and his/her adoptive parents'.[386] From the procedural perspective, recognition could be achieved, as in adoption, through the use of a 'certificate of conformity' like the one introduced by Article 23 of the Adoption Convention. Article 23 provides:

> An adoption certified by the competent authority of the State of adoption as having been made in accordance with the Convention shall be recognised by operation of law in other Contracting States.

making a surrogacy arrangement enforceable against the surrogate mother could be a breach of the latter's human rights under international law. On this point, however, Ergas's analysis lacks reference to widely-ratified international human rights treaties and is not convincing. The basis for the surrogate mother being required to hand over the child to the intended parents after the birth of the child will not be enforcement of a private contract between the parties, but rather would be the State-regulated agreement that has established the suitability of the intended parents and the surrogate mother to provide a child for the intended parents in what the authorities of the two States concerned believe to be in the best interests of the child, and not exploitative of the surrogate mother.

[384] Art 33 states: 'The State addressed shall provide at least the same range of enforcement methods for cases under the Convention as are available in domestic cases.'

[385] Art 34 states: '(1) Contracting States shall make available in internal law effective measures to enforce decisions under this Convention. (2) Such measures may include: (a) wage withholding; (b) garnishment from bank accounts and other sources; (c) deductions from social security payments; (d) lien on or forced social security payments; (e) tax refund withholding; (f) withholding or attachment of pension benefits; (g) credit bureau reporting; (h) denial, suspension or revocation of various licenses (for example, driving license); (i) the use of mediation, conciliation or similar processes to bring about voluntary compliance.'

[386] Adoption Convention, Art 26(1)(a).

The certificate of conformity serves as 'evidence of a *prima facie* conformity of the adoption with the Convention's system'[387] and for practical purposes, as 'a passport' which suffices as 'evidence of the child's status'.[388] It gives instant 'certainty to the status of the child and eliminate[s] the need for a procedure for recognition of orders, or re-adoption, in the receiving country'.[389] The same results could be achieved for surrogacy.

v. Access to Birth Records by Children Born through Surrogacy Arrangements[390]

The right of the child to obtain information about his or her origin is guaranteed by Article 7(1) of the UN Convention on the Rights of the Child. A balance must, however, be found between the right of the child to know his or her origin and the genetic parent's right to privacy.[391] In the context of intercountry adoption, the right of the child to discover his or her origins is acknowledged by Article 30 of the Adoption Convention. The right is guaranteed, though, only 'in so far as is permitted by the law of that State' (the State of origin). This is to acknowledge the fact that in certain circumstances an unlimited right to information might cause gross inconvenience to the surrogate mother or egg donor.[392]

In traditional surrogacy arrangements the genetic parent is the surrogate mother. In gestational surrogacy arrangements, where only one of the intended parents is genetically related to the child, the term 'genetic parent' refers to either an egg donor or a sperm donor, depending on the circumstances of the particular case. In this case, the right of the child to information on his or her background might prove particularly difficult to enforce, as egg/sperm donor programmes are often anonymous. Additionally, a question to be addressed is whether a child born through a surrogacy arrangement, having attained majority, should have the right to obtain identifying information on the surrogate mother, even if she is not the child's genetic mother.

---

[387] Hague Conference on Private International Law, 'Report of the Special Commission of October 1994', available at <www.hcch.net/index_en.php?act=publications.details&pid=933&dtid=2>.

[388] *Ibid.*

[389] Hague Conference on Private International Law, 'Outline: Hague Intercountry Adoption Convention', available at <www.hcch.net/upload/outline33e.pdf>.

[390] For some background reading, see eg J Sauer, 'Competing Interests and Gamete Donation: The Case for Anonymity' (2009) 39 *Seton Hall Law Review* 919; A Shelf, 'A Need to Know Basis: Record Keeping, Information Access and the Uniform Status of Children of Assisted Conception Act' (1999–2000) 51 *Hastings Law Journal* 1047; C Breen, 'Poles Apart? The Best Interests of the Child and Assisted Reproduction in the Antipodes and Europe' (2001) 9 *The International Journal of Children's Rights* 157, 163–67; and J Carbone and P Gottheim, 'Markets, Subsidies, Regulation, and Trust: Building Ethical Understandings into the Market for Fertility Services' (2005-2006) 9 *The Journal of Gender, Race & Justice* 509.

[391] The right to respect for one's private life is guaranteed by the European Convention on Human Rights, Art 8(1).

[392] 'Explanatory Report', above n 334, para 512. Additionally, Art 16(2) of the Adoption Convention allows for the possibility of not disclosing the identity of the child's biological parents by the State of origin if, 'in the State of origin, these identities may not be disclosed'.

vi. Nationality

Preferably, a child born as a result of a surrogacy arrangement should automatically acquire the nationality of the intended parents' home State (or of one of the intended parents, if they are not nationals of that State). If this is not possible, the Central Authority of the intended parents' home State should be obliged to provide necessary assistance to the intended parents in obtaining the nationality. The recommendation in the context of the Adoption Convention should be followed: '[T]he policy of Contracting States regarding the nationality of the child should be guided by the overriding importance of avoiding a situation in which an adopted child is stateless.'[393]

K. Conclusion

The current unregulated system of cross-border surrogacy is highly unsatisfactory, in particular given the complexity of the legal problems it raises and the risk of exploitation inherent in it. It is therefore essential that this system be replaced by a regulated mechanism. An ex post facto private international law solution is not likely to solve the challenges posed by the global cross-border surrogacy market. Instead, a regulatory framework based on the template of the 1993 Hague Adoption Convention is proposed. Based on this model, a Convention on surrogacy would ensure that controls operate before a surrogacy arrangement is commissioned and that arrangements carried out in compliance with the Convention benefit from automatic recognition of their legal effects in the intended parents' home country. In terms of payments, in order to remain pragmatic, the framework provides for a relatively generous altruistic surrogacy model. The pre-approval system on which the framework is based will allow the countries concerned to agree in each individual case whether an arrangement can proceed and under what conditions. In its essence, the system resembles domestic legal regulation of surrogacy in countries such as Israel, Greece or South Africa. The regulatory framework can therefore be described as a sophisticated domestic approach taken to the international level. It is expected that the framework will tackle successfully the challenges posed by the global cross-border surrogacy market. In particular, it is hoped that the regulation will eliminate the current status quo where, in the absence of a proper alternative regulatory solution, intended parents commission surrogacy abroad and then present a court of their

---

[393] See Conclusions of the 2005 Special Commission ('Report and Conclusions of the Second Special Commission', above n 334, para 17), reaffirmed by the 2010 Special Commission ('Conclusions and Recommendations of the 2010 Special Commission', above n 321, para 19). Yasmine Ergas, in ch 27 in this book. argues that States have an obligation under international human rights law to avoid the statelessness of a child born through a surrogacy arrangement (see text accompanying fns 37–40). Nevertheless, the Convention should enable Contracting States to draw a line on the numbers of cross-border surrogacy arrangements that would be allowed, in case States are not prepared to grant many citizenships to children born as a result of cross-border surrogacy arrangements.

home country with a *fait accompli*, leaving the court no other realistic option than to reach a decision that undermines the country's public policy. It is suggested that once the framework of regulation is functioning, no exceptions should be allowed, and intended parents involved in arrangements that do not comply with the Convention should be denied any remedies.

INDEX